SHAKESPEARE SURVEY
70

Creating Shakespeare

SHAKESPEARE SURVEY
ADVISORY BOARD

Jonathan Bate	Claudia Olk
Margreta de Grazia	Lena Cowen Orlin
Michael Dobson	Reiko Oya
Ton Hoenselaars	Simon Palfrey
Russell Jackson	Richard Proudfoot
John Jowett	Emma Smith
Kathleen E. McLuskie	Ann Thompson
Lucy Munro	Stanley Wells

Assistants to the Editor Mimi Ensley, Richard Fahey, Michael Vaclav and Sara Marie Westh

(1) Shakespeare and his Stage
(2) Shakespearian Production
(3) The Man and the Writer
(4) Interpretation
(5) Textual Criticism
(6) The Histories
(7) Style and Language
(8) The Comedies
(9) *Hamlet*
(10) The Roman Plays
(11) The Last Plays (with an index to *Surveys 1–10*)
(12) The Elizabethan Theatre
(13) *King Lear*
(14) Shakespeare and his Contemporaries
(15) The Poems and Music
(16) Shakespeare in the Modern World
(17) Shakespeare in his Own Age
(18) Shakespeare Then Till Now
(19) *Macbeth*
(20) Shakespearian and Other Tragedy
(21) *Othello* (with an index to *Surveys 11–20*)
(22) Aspects of Shakespearian Comedy
(23) Shakespeare's Language
(24) Shakespeare: Theatre Poet
(25) Shakespeare's Problem Plays
(26) Shakespeare's Jacobean Tragedies
(27) Shakespeare's Early Tragedies
(28) Shakespeare and the Ideas of his Time
(29) Shakespeare's Last Plays
(30) *Henry IV* to *Hamlet*
(31) Shakespeare and the Classical World (with an index to *Surveys 21–30*)
(32) The Middle Comedies
(33) *King Lear*
(34) Characterization in Shakespeare
(35) Shakespeare in the Nineteenth Century
(36) Shakespeare in the Twentieth Century
(37) Shakespeare's Earlier Comedies
(38) Shakespeare and History
(39) Shakespeare on Film and Television
(40) Current Approaches to Shakespeare through Language, Text and Theatre
(41) Shakespearian Stages and Staging (with an index to *Surveys 31–40*)
(42) Shakespeare and the Elizabethans
(43) *The Tempest* and After
(44) Shakespeare and Politics
(45) *Hamlet* and its Afterlife
(46) Shakespeare and Sexuality
(47) Playing Places for Shakespeare
(48) Shakespeare and Cultural Exchange
(49) *Romeo and Juliet* and its Afterlife
(50) Shakespeare and Language
(51) Shakespeare in the Eighteenth Century (with an index to *Surveys 41–50*)
(52) Shakespeare and the Globe
(53) Shakespeare and Narrative
(54) Shakespeare and Religions
(55) *King Lear* and its Afterlife
(56) Shakespeare and Comedy
(57) *Macbeth* and its Afterlife
(58) Writing About Shakespeare
(59) Editing Shakespeare
(60) Theatres for Shakespeare
(61) Shakespeare, Sound and Screen
(62) Close Encounters with Shakespeare's Text
(63) Shakespeare's English Histories and their Afterlives
(64) Shakespeare as Cultural Catalyst
(65) *A Midsummer Night's Dream*
(66) Working with Shakespeare
(67) Shakespeare's Collaborative Work
(68) Shakespeare, Origins and Originality
(69) Shakespeare and Rome
(70) Creating Shakespeare

Shakespeare Survey: A Sixty-Year Cumulative Index
Aspects of *Macbeth*
Aspects of *Othello*
Aspects of *Hamlet*
Aspects of *King Lear*
Aspects of Shakespeare's 'Problem Plays'

SHAKESPEARE SURVEY

70

Creating Shakespeare

Articles from the World Shakespeare Congress, 2016

EDITED BY

PETER HOLLAND

CAMBRIDGE
UNIVERSITY PRESS

University Printing House, Cambridge CB2 8BS, United Kingdom

One Liberty Plaza, 20th Floor, New York, NY 10006, USA

477 Williamstown Road, Port Melbourne, VIC 3207, Australia

314–321, 3rd Floor, Plot 3, Splendor Forum, Jasola District Centre, New Delhi – 110025, India

79 Anson Road, #06-04/06, Singapore 079906

Cambridge University Press is part of the University of Cambridge.

It furthers the University's mission by disseminating knowledge in the pursuit of education, learning and research at the highest international levels of excellence.

www.cambridge.org
Information on this title: www.cambridge.org/9781108417440
DOI: 10.1017/9781108277648

© Cambridge University Press 2017

This publication is in copyright. Subject to statutory exception and to the provisions of relevant collective licensing agreements, no reproduction of any part may take place without the written permission of Cambridge University Press.

First published 2017

Printed in the United Kingdom by TJ International Ltd, Padstow, Cornwall

A catalogue record for this publication is available from the British Library

ISBN 978-1-108-41744-0 Hardback
ISSN 0080-9152

Cambridge University Press has no responsibility for the persistence or accuracy of URLs for external or third-party internet websites referred to in this publication and does not guarantee that any content on such websites is, or will remain, accurate or appropriate.

EDITOR'S NOTE

This volume of *Shakespeare Survey* is made up, almost entirely and apart from the annual reviews, of articles derived from papers given at the World Shakespeare Congress, held in Stratford-upon-Avon and London in August 2016. So many excellent papers were given at the Congress that the next volume of *Survey*, volume 71, will also be devoted to articles emerging from the Congress. We have divided the materials according to the two topics of the Congress's title, 'Creating and Re-Creating Shakespeare', with 70 on 'Creating' and 71 on 'Re-Creating', though it might be arguable whether some pieces might belong in either volume. The first four articles in this volume represent the plenary sessions. The rest have been arranged in three somewhat arbitrary sections. I am grateful to Peter Holbrook, Chair of the International Shakespeare Association, and Nick Walton, its Executive Director, together with all the members of the team, for their tireless labours in organizing the Congress.

Unless otherwise indicated, Shakespeare quotations and references are keyed to *The Complete Works*, ed. Stanley Wells, Gary Taylor, John Jowett and William Montgomery, second edition (Oxford, 2005).

Volume 71 will be at press by the time this volume appears. The theme of Volume 72 will be 'Shakespeare and War'. Submissions should be addressed to the Editor at The Shakespeare Institute, Church Street, Stratford-upon-Avon, Warwickshire CV37 6HP, to arrive at the latest by 1 September 2018 for volume 72. The theme of Volume 73 will be 'Shakespeare and the city' with a deadline for submissions of 1 September 2019. Pressures on space are heavy and priority is given to articles related to the theme of a particular volume. Please send a copy you do not wish to be returned. Submissions may also be made as attachments to email to pholland@nd.edu. All articles submitted are read by the Editor and at least one member of the Advisory Board, whose indispensable assistance the Editor gratefully acknowledges.

Review copies should be addressed to the Editor as above. In attempting to survey the ever-increasing bulk of Shakespeare publications, our reviewers inevitably have to exercise some selection. We are pleased to receive offprints of articles which help to draw our reviewers' attention to relevant material.

CONTRIBUTORS

MEGAN ELIZABETH ALLEN, *Washington University in St Louis*
NAOMI BAKER, *University of Manchester*
SHAUL BASSI, *Università Ca' Foscari Venezia*
PAMELA ALLEN BROWN, *University of Connecticut*
HELEN COOPER, *Magdalene College, Cambridge*
KEEGAN COOPER, *Indiana University/Purdue University Indianapolis*
HUGH CRAIG, *University of Newcastle, Australia*
JOSÉ A. PÉREZ DÍEZ, *University of Leeds*
MICHAEL DOBSON, *The Shakespeare Institute, University of Birmingham*
GREGORY DORAN, *Royal Shakespeare Company*
PAUL EDMONDSON, *Shakespeare Birthplace Trust*
RUSSELL JACKSON, *University of Birmingham*
HOWARD JACOBSON, *Novelist*
JOHN JOWETT, *The Shakespeare Institute, University of Birmingham*
PETER KIRWAN, *University of Nottingham*
HESTER LEES-JEFFRIES, *St Catharine's College, Cambridge*
ADRIAN LESTER, *Actor and Director*
JULIA REINHARD LUPTON, *University of California, Irvine*
ELISABETH LUTTEMAN, *Uppsala University*
GORDON McMULLAN, *King's College London*
KATHARINE EISAMAN MAUS, *University of Virginia*
RUTH MORSE, *Université-Paris-Diderot*
LUCY MUNRO, *King's College London*
JOHN V. NANCE, *Florida State University*
NATÁLIA PIKLI, *Eötvös Loránd University, Budapest*
ADRIAN POOLE, *Trinity College, Cambridge*
STEPHEN PURCELL, *University of Warwick*
CAROL CHILLINGTON RUTTER, *University of Warwick*
CHARLOTTE SCOTT, *Goldsmiths College, University of London*
LAURIE SHANNON, *Northwestern University*
JAMES SHAW, *University of Oxford*
SIMON SMITH, *The Shakespeare Institute, University of Birmingham*
GARY TAYLOR, *Florida State University*

LIST OF CONTRIBUTORS

AYANNA THOMPSON, *George Washington University*
JESÚS TRONCH, *Universitat de València*
MARGARET TUDEAU-CLAYTON, *University of Neuchâtel*
CLAIRE VAN KAMPEN, *Composer*
ADAM ZUCKER, *University of Massachusetts Amherst*

CONTENTS

List of Illustrations		page xi
GREGORY DORAN	'Think when we talk of horses . . .'	1
ADRIAN LESTER	In Dialogue with Ayanna Thompson	10
HOWARD JACOBSON AND ADRIAN POOLE	Shakespeare and the Novel: A Conversation	19
CLAIRE VAN KAMPEN	*Music Still*: Understanding and Reconstructing Shakespeare's Use of Musical Underscore	30
GORDON MCMULLAN	Remembering and Forgetting in 1916: Israel Gollancz, the Shakespeare Tercentenary and the National Theatre	40
MICHAEL DOBSON	Four Centuries of Centenaries: Stratford-upon-Avon	50
PAUL EDMONDSON	Writing and Re-writing Shakespeare's Life: A Roundtable Discussion with Margreta de Grazia, Katherine Scheil, James Shapiro and Stanley Wells	58
SHAUL BASSI	The Merchant *in* Venice: Re-creating Shakespeare in the Ghetto	67
CAROL CHILLINGTON RUTTER	Shakespeare's *The Merchant of Venice* in and beyond the Ghetto	79
JOSÉ A. PÉREZ DÍEZ	What the Quills Can Tell: The Case of John Fletcher and Philip Massinger's *Love's Cure*	89
JESÚS TRONCH	What if Greg and Werstine Had Examined Early Modern Spanish Dramatic Manuscripts?	99
JOHN JOWETT	Exit Manuscripts: The Archive of Theatre and the Archive of Print	113
LUCY MUNRO	''Sblood!': Hamlet's Oaths and the Editing of Shakespeare's Plays	123
ADAM ZUCKER	Antihonorificabilitudinitatibus: *Love's Labour's Lost* and Unteachable Words	135
GARY TAYLOR, JOHN V. NANCE, AND KEEGAN COOPER	Shakespeare and Who? Aeschylus, *Edward III* and Thomas Kyd	146
HUGH CRAIG	Authorial Attribution and Shakespearean Variety: Genre, Form and Chronology	154
HESTER LEES-JEFFRIES	'My mother's maids, when they did sew and spin': Staging Sewing, Telling Tales	165
HELEN COOPER	Why Prospero Drowned His Books, and Other Catholic Folklore	174
PAMELA ALLEN BROWN	Why Did the English Stage Take Boys for Actresses?	182

CONTENTS

SIMON SMITH	Acting Amiss: Towards a History of Actorly Craft and Playhouse Judgement	188
ELISABETH LUTTEMAN	'What imports this song?': Spontaneous Singers and Spaces of Meaning in Shakespeare	200
RUTH MORSE	Shakespeare's Depriving Particles	207
LAURIE SHANNON	Shakespeare's Comedy of Upright Status: Standing Bears and Fallen Humans	213
MARGARET TUDEAU-CLAYTON	'Worth the name of a Christian'?: The Parabolic Economy of *The Two Gentlemen of Verona*	219
MEGAN ELIZABETH ALLEN	'Titus, unkind': Shakespeare's Revision of Virgil's Aeneas in *Titus Andronicus*	228
JULIA REINHARD LUPTON	'Cut him out in little stars': Juliet's Cute Classicism	240
KATHARINE EISAMAN MAUS	The Will of Caesar: Choice-making, the Death of the Roman Republic and the Development of Shakespearean Character	249
NATÁLIA PIKLI	'As for that light hobby-horse, my sister': Shakespearean Influences and Popular Discourses in *Blurt Master Constable*	259
NAOMI BAKER	Messianic Ugliness in *A Midsummer Night's Dream* and *The Winter's Tale*	272
STEPHEN PURCELL	Shakespeare Performances in England, 2016	287
JAMES SHAW	Professional Shakespeare Productions in the British Isles, January–December 2015	326

The Year's Contribution to Shakespeare Studies 340
  1. Critical Studies *reviewed by* CHARLOTTE SCOTT 340
  2. The Cambridge Guide to the Worlds of Shakespeare *reviewed by* RUSSELL JACKSON 356
  3. Shakespeare in Performance *reviewed by* RUSSELL JACKSON 361
  4. Editions and Textual Studies *reviewed by* PETER KIRWAN 371

Abstracts of Articles in Shakespeare Survey 70   385
Shakespeare Survey 70 Index   390

ILLUSTRATIONS

1. Bird's-eye view of Stratford-upon-Avon, by J. Ross Brown, 1908. Shakespeare Birthplace Trust. Public domain. *page* 54
2. Samuel West as David Garrick, preparing to recite the Jubilee Ode, Holy Trinity Church, Stratford-upon-Avon, 22 April 2016. Photograph by the author. 56
3. *The Merchant in Venice*, final scene. On location in the Jewish Ghetto, Venice, directed by Karin Coonrod. Photograph by Andrea Messana. 68
4. *The Merchant in Venice*, 4.1. On location in the Jewish Ghetto, Venice, directed by Karin Coonrod. Graziano (Sorab Wadia) berating Shylock (Ned Eisenberg) in the trial scene. Photograph by Andrea Messana. 74
5. *The Merchant of Venice*, Prologue. On location in the Jewish Ghetto, Venice, directed by Karin Coonrod. Francesca Sarah Toich as Lancillotto and full company. Photograph by Andrea Messana. 81
6. *The Merchant of Venice*, 3.1. On location in the Jewish Ghetto, Venice, directed by Karin Coonrod. Five Shylocks (Sorab Wadia, Adriano Iurissevich, Andrea Brugnera, Ned Eisenberg, Jenni Lea-Jones) wail the loss of Jessica. Photograph by Andrea Messana. 86
7. Claramonte's autograph of *El valiente negro en Flandes*, BNE 15690 (fol. 10r). © Biblioteca Nacional de España. 107
8. Pedro Calderón de la Barca's *El galán fantasma*, BNE 15672 (fol. 71v). © Biblioteca Nacional de España. 109
9. *El valiente negro en Flandes* by Andrés de Claramonte, BNE 15690 (fol. 1r). © Biblioteca Nacional de España. 110
10. Sir Edward Durning-Lawrence, Bt, *Bacon is Shake-Speare* (London, 1910), p. 102. 139
11. Number of function words used differently in a set of Shakespeare comedies compared to five other play sets. Eight plays in each set; 100 very common function words tested; threshold for a significant difference, Welch's *t*-test p <.01. 157
12. Number of function words used differently in a set of Shakespeare comedy characters and in five other sets of characters. Eight characters in each set; 100 very common function words tested; threshold for a significant difference, Welch's *t*-test p <.01. 158
13. Number of function words used differently in pairs of genre play sets. Fourteen plays in each set; 100 very common function words tested; threshold for a significant difference, Welch's *t*-test p <.01. 159
14. Number of function words used differently in pairs of genre and author play sets. Fourteen plays in each set; 100 very common function words tested; threshold for a significant difference, Welch's *t*-test p <.01. 160

LIST OF ILLUSTRATIONS

15. Number of function words used differently in various pairs of genre and author play sets, including Shakespeare and non-Shakespeare comedy-tragicomedy sets. Fourteen plays in each set; 100 very common function words tested; threshold for a significant difference, Welch's *t*-test p <.01. — 160
16. Number of function words used differently in pairs of play sets, including pairs of sets by decade. Fourteen plays in each set; 100 very common function words tested; threshold for a significant difference, Welch's *t*-test p <.01. — 161
17. Number of function words used differently in pairs of various play sets, including verse and prose plays and verse and prose play parts. Fourteen plays in each set; 100 very common function words tested; threshold for a significant difference, Welch's *t*-test p <.01. — 162
18. Pyramus and Thisbe, mother of pearl and marble inlaid into Lydian stone, Dirck van Rijswijck, Amsterdam, 1659, Rijksmuseum. Public domain (www.rijksmuseum.nl/en/collection/BK-16468). — 245
19. *The Winter's Tale*, 2.2, Sam Wanamaker Playhouse, directed by Michael Longhurst. Niamh Cusack as Paulina. Photograph by Marc Brenner. — 290
20. *A Midsummer Night's Dream*, 2.2, Shakespeare's Globe, directed by Emma Rice. Zubin Varla as Oberon and Meow Meow as Titania. Photograph by Steve Tanner. — 293
21. *The Taming of the Shrew*, 3.2, Shakespeare's Globe, directed by Caroline Byrne. Amy Conroy and Imogen Doel as servants, Aoife Duffin as Katherine and Genevieve Hulme-Beaman as Bianca. Photograph by Marc Brenner. — 295
22. *A Midsummer Night's Dream: A Play for the Nation*, 2.1, RSC, touring, directed by Erica Whyman. Lucy Ellinson as Puck and Chu Omambala as Oberon. Photograph by Topher McGrillis. — 300
23. *Hamlet*, 3.1, RSC, Royal Shakespeare Theatre, directed by Simon Godwin. Paapa Essiedu as Hamlet. Photograph by Manuel Harlan. — 303
24. *The Tempest*, 1.2, RSC, Royal Shakespeare Theatre, directed by Gregory Doran. Mark Quartley as Ariel and Simon Russell Beale as Prospero. Photograph by Topher McGrillis. — 306
25. *Henry V*, 3.6, Regent's Park Open Air Theatre, directed by Robert Hastie. Jessica Regan as Montjoy and Michelle Terry as Henry V. Photograph by Johan Persson. — 308
26. *The Tempest*, 3.1, Donmar at King's Cross, King's Cross Theatre, directed by Phyllida Lloyd. Harriet Walter as Prospero. Photograph by Helen Maybanks. — 310
27. *As You Like It*, 2.4, National Theatre, Olivier Theatre, directed by Polly Findlay. Rosalie Craig as Rosalind. Photograph by Johan Persson. — 315
28. *King Lear*, 1.1, Talawa Theatre Company, Royal Exchange Theatre, Manchester, directed by Michael Buffong. Don Warrington as Lear. Photograph by Jonathan Keenan. — 318
29. *The Shadow King*, Malthouse Theatre, Barbican Theatre, directed by Michael Kantor. Kamahi Djordon King as the Fool and Damion Hunter as Edgar. Photograph by Jeff Busby. — 320
30. *The Complete Deaths*, Spymonkey, touring, directed by Tim Crouch. Aitor Basauri as himself/Shakespeare. Photograph by Ludovic des Cognets, courtesy of Spymonkey (www.spymonkey.co.uk). — 324

'THINK WHEN WE TALK OF HORSES...'

GREGORY DORAN

I sometimes think Shakespeare's favourite word is '*Now*'!

It creates excitement and tension and insists on the vivid present; it demands the immediate.

'**Now** all the youth of England are on fire' says the Chorus of *Henry V* and 'For **now** sits Expectation in the air'.

'**Now**' takes you right into the moment and coincides our experience of the present with the action on stage.

'**Now** is the winter of our discontent' announces the soon-to-be King Richard III as he launches himself into the chaos of his rise to power.

'**Now** I am alone' says Hamlet.

'**Now** might I do it, pat, **now** while he is a praying'.

'**Now**, Gods stand up for bastards' says Edmund in *King Lear*, the play I am rehearsing at the moment.

'**Now** the hungry lion roars' whispers Puck.

'I feel **now** the future in the instant' urges Lady Macbeth.

And Iago wakes up Desdemona's father yelling 'Even **now, now,** very **now,** an old black ram / Is tupping your white ewe'.

With that potent short monosyllable '**Now**', Shakespeare pulls his audience into an act of complicity with the performers, a magical, alchemical reaction, a charm which happens even now, now, very now, and lasts for the two hours' traffic of the stage.

Shakespeare's theatre, any theatre, is surely the home of 'now'.

That ephemerality is part of its charm. The baseless fabric of a vision which melts into air, into thin air – an insubstantial pageant, which like the great Globe itself will dissolve, and leave not a wrack behind.

It is transitory: 'a dream, a breath, a froth of fleeting joy'; 'as brief as the lightning in the collied night', as brief as Macbeth's candle which reminds him that life's but a walking shadow, a poor player that struts and frets his hour upon the stage and then is heard no more.

Until now.

When I was appointed as artistic director, we started a journey through the entire canon of Shakespeare's plays in this space, the Royal Shakespeare Theatre, beginning with *Richard II* in October 2013, and we have filmed each one of them, broadcasting them live into cinemas around the country and indeed around the world. We also stream the productions for free into schools, providing teachers with a toolkit to help them introduce the plays to their pupils.

And what we are striving to achieve is perhaps the hardest thing to capture – Shakespeare's 'now, now, very now-ness' on screen.

We are currently a third of the way through the canon (with *King Lear* next on the slate) and I am very proud of our back catalogue of productions (which are all available on DVD).

This is the text of the first plenary session of the 2016 World Shakespeare Congress in Stratford-upon-Avon, delivered on Monday 1 August

GREGORY DORAN

I have spent the last twenty years of my career, on and off, exploring how to capture stage productions on screen, either as a good archive recording or as something else, as something re-conceived for the small screen, which can preserve the text and still grip the viewer.

I am not the first director at Stratford to want to record productions for posterity, and I'd like to consider some of those widely differing instincts, and perhaps try to analyse what they tell us.

[EXTRACT ONE: *Henry V*, opening Chorus. The first extract shown during the plenary session was of Oliver Ford Davies as the Chorus in my own recent production of *Henry V*.]

The Chorus begins by admitting the inadequacy of the resources at the theatre's disposal to create the events leading up to the Battle of Agincourt. He begs our indulgence, and our complicity, if we will allow the actors to work on our 'imaginary forces'. It won't work without that, 'for 'tis your thoughts which now must deck our kings' he says, and then he gets down to specifics:

> Think when we talk of horses that you see them,
> Printing their proud hooves i' th' receiving earth

And here's the challenge that confronts anyone attempting to translate Shakespeare onto the screen. Essentially, on film, we expect to see horses, and are reluctant to accept anything less or to fill in the gaps with our own imagination, and certainly not to 'work, work [our] thoughts' to create them. For the image not the word is the medium of film.

So if you have horses, you don't need any of the words Shakespeare uses to describe them. But what words! Here is the observant French Lord Grandpre describing the ragged English cavalry drawn up for battle. Listen to how he closes in on the scene, from the horses' eyes to the tackle in their mouths – a final devastating detail:

> The horsemen sit like fixèd candlesticks,
> With torch-staves in their hand, and their poor jades
> Lob down their heads, dropping the hides and hips,
> The gum down-roping from their pale dead eyes
> And in their palled dull mouths the gimmaled bit
> Lies foul with chewed grass, still and motionless.

Indeed, often in rehearsal we talk about how Shakespeare's speeches act like a camera script. Listen to the Chorus calling the shots as the fleet sets sail from Hampton Pier. He focuses on the silken banners, a close-up of the ship boys clambering up the hempen tackle, the shipmaster's whistle, then the wide shot as the sails fill and the huge ships pull out to sea. Cut to the view from the cliff top of the whole fleet like a 'city on the inconstant billows dancing'.

And Shakespeare uses this technique again in *King Lear*. Edgar, describing the imaginary cliff at Dover, moves from 'the crows and choughs that wing the midway air' to the samphire gatherer (dreadful trade) half way down, to the fishermen way below on the beach.

Shakespeare pre-dates film. He works in images which he gets you, his audience, to supply, to imagine in your heads. And that is an active live interaction, or what we call a play.

Shouldn't we leave plays then to be a memory in the minds of our audiences?

Well, I can only tell you, this is nothing new. It stretches back over a century here in Stratford. The first attempt to capture Shakespeare productions goes back to 1911. It starts with the indomitable actor-manager Frank Benson. Benson signed a contract with the Co-operative Cinematograph Company to film a series of four of his productions: *Julius Caesar*, *Macbeth*, *Taming of the Shrew* and *Richard III*.

Veteran actress Eleanor Elder described the filming of *Julius Caesar* in her diary. Her account gives some insight into the performances captured in those short reels, and indicates that the emphatic acting style may not precisely represent the way it was in the theatre itself.

Benson, known affectionately as 'Pa' by the company, was directing the proceedings from the stalls.

Of course everything has to be changed: business quickened and a lot of talk left out altogether. Our instructions are to put plenty of movement into it – to keep within certain lines drawn on the stage; and to do as we are told, and to obey orders shouted at us without being disturbed, or letting it affect our acting. We shall be muddled when we go back to the play proper.

'THINK WHEN WE TALK OF HORSES...'

We have done Caesar, a most trying performance. We rehearse everything before we play it. Weird sights we are too – eyelashes and lips made up, and a little rouge. Awful blinding mauve light flickers at us all the time. The flying, hurried way we got through it was quite funny; and the language too ('Give your cue and get off'). Cassius exclaimed 'Good gracious, Hullo!'

When egged on to murder Caesar, Brutus made his exit saying: 'I can't do it. You beasts!'

Pa was yelling 'Good!' or 'Buck up! do this!'.[1]

Sadly only *Richard III* survives. It reveals Benson's flamboyant performance as Richard, a part he had played regularly since 1886. It was recorded in the original 1879 Memorial Theatre, which burnt down in 1926. The Swan Theatre now stands in the shell of that original building.

[EXTRACT TWO: the second extract shown was of Frank Benson as Richard III.]

After Benson's *Richard III*, we have a very large gap in any recorded productions from Stratford. The next foray into the filming of Shakespeare performance came in the star-studded Stratford of the 1950s when the new medium of television decided it needed a bit of culture direct from Stratford and arranged to live broadcast a production of *The Merry Wives of Windsor*. It does not appear to have been recorded, so the earliest surviving version was sourced from a relay of the second half. It was screened on 2 October 1955.

[EXTRACT THREE: *Merry Wives of Windsor*. A very rare clip from Glen Byam Shaw's famous Stratford production, with his wife Angela Baddeley as Mistress Page, Joyce Redman as Mistress Ford and Anthony Quayle (who was running the company at the time) as Sir John Falstaff.]

That, as far as we know, is the only other filmed recording of a Stratford production before 1959. There were of course sound recordings made for archive purposes only, which recently came to light, and which I collected together in two double CD sets called *Essential Shakespeare*. If you haven't heard these British Library sound Archive recordings, I urge you to do so, for you hear Laurence Olivier viperous as Coriolanus and a sonorous Paul Robeson as Othello.

Then in 1959 came a production of *A Midsummer Night's Dream*, which was filmed on three cameras for American television in the theatre in Stratford-upon-Avon. It starred Charles Laughton (in one of his final stage performances) as Nick Bottom, and he introduces the film by taking his viewers around Stratford (which looks remarkably similar to today) and even goes for a row on the Avon before heading into his dressing room and handing over to the director, a young Peter Hall, at the back of the stalls to introduce the production, as if it is about to happen live right before you. Watching it over five decades later, I still found myself excited by the sense of occasion, of something special about to happen, and it's something I have tried to capture in the presentation of our *Live from* productions today.

In fact, the production was not live, but filmed on stage over several days, and interwoven with audience reaction shots.

But by the time the company gained its royal charter in 1961 and became the Royal Shakespeare Company, with Peter Hall as its director, there was renewed interest in filming productions, and a new relationship with the BBC.

Hall obviously caught the filming bug, because when he and John Barton mounted *The Wars of the Roses* (the *Henry VI* plays and *Richard III* shaped into three parts), he committed them to film. It was a project of massive ambition. Even though the BBC had filmed their own version of the Histories in fifteen episodes in 1960, screened as *An Age of Kings*, they committed to this new cycle. The BBC's Michael Bakewell wrote: 'what was intended was to recreate a theatre production in television terms – not merely to observe it but to get to the heart of it'.

The productions again were filmed in this very theatre, but the stalls were boarded over to create a 360-degree studio space. They were landmark productions that defined the company's renewed emphasis on verse speaking and an unsentimental performance style.

---

[1] J. C. Trewin, *Benson and the Bensonious* (London, 1960), p. 176.

GREGORY DORAN

[EXTRACT FOUR: from *The Wars of the Roses: Richard III*, recorded in SMT in 1964. A clip from the wooing scene from *Richard III*, with Ian Holm, and Janet Suzman as Anne.]

We are fortunate that both *An Age of Kings* and *The Wars of the Roses* has been made available on DVD by John Wyver and his company Illuminations, of which more later.

Peter Hall then made another film (a 'proper' film) of *A Midsummer Night's Dream* (in 1968) in the grounds of nearby Compton Verney, with Judi Dench as Titania, naked but for a few ivy leaves and some green paint. The film may never have achieved classic status, but it does start with a good joke. The opening shot shows a pleasant English landscape and over this the caption 'Athens' appears, neatly underlining the essential artificiality of Shakespeare's world and the challenge of recreating it in literal terms.

Two other productions from Hall's era were filmed: *As You Like It* (in 1963) directed by Michael Elliot, and Clifford Williams's production of *The Comedy of Errors*. *As You Like It* reproduces the stage set in a studio, while the stripped back *Comedy of Errors* is filmed in front of a live audience at the Aldwych.

[EXTRACT FIVE: *As You Like It*. Vanessa Redgrave's startlingly fresh performance as Rosalind, breathless with love.]

Hall's successor Trevor Nunn was an avid advocate of filmed versions of his Shakespeare productions. He began with *Antony and Cleopatra*, one of the plays from the 1972 Roman season, with his then wife Janet Suzman as Cleopatra and Richard Johnson as Mark Antony. The design is clearly influenced by the extraordinary excitement around the blockbuster exhibition at the British Museum of the Egyptian boy-king Tutankhamun, which opened that year.

In 1976 Nunn had explored Shakespeare in the new studio environment of The Other Place in Stratford, which had opened in an old tin shed (once part of the costume store), and already seen some revelatory productions by Buzz Goodbody of *Hamlet* with Ben Kingsley and *King Lear*. Ian McKellen and Judi Dench wanted to do *Macbeth* in this exciting new space, and what resulted was a now legendary stripped-down production of that play which explored its claustrophobic intimacy as never before. The production was subsequently filmed in studio, exploiting techniques impossible to employ in the theatre, with much use of close-up and whispering to the camera.

Another show which became a box office smash was Trevor's production of Guy Woolfenden's musical version of *The Comedy of Errors*, with Judi Dench, Michael Williams and Roger Rees. And again, that was filmed on stage by ATV.

Trevor was asked to return to direct the final performance in TOP in 1989, before its redevelopment. The production was *Othello* with Willard White as the Moor and Ian McKellen again as Iago. Trevor's own personal style, which inclined to the naturalistic with realistic settings and detailed props, lent itself to this method of filming.

Meanwhile McKellen's success at the National Theatre with *Richard III* had inspired him to lead the drive towards making a film of that play in 1995, having learnt greatly from the experience of playing it. Just as Kenneth Branagh had learnt about the play *Henry V* from playing the lead role in Adrian Noble's 1984 brilliant production of the play, an experience he put to good, if uncredited, use in his own film of the play five years later in 1989.

McKellen and Nunn were reunited in 2006 to create a *King Lear* for the RSC's Complete Works Festival. The production was filmed for TV and stands as a good archive recording of the production.

TERRY HANDS

It was perhaps Trevor Nunn's growing preference for realism that prompted his successor as artistic director, Terry Hands, to explore a more abstract, less literal, more European style with his designer Abdel Farrah and regular leading actor Alan Howard. And this may account for their apparent lack of interest in committing their many great productions to film.

When I asked Terry Hands himself about this, he said with his typical cryptic wit: 'At the time we did talk of Michelangelo's greatest statue being the one he carved in ice.'

Vasari mentions the story of how one day in January 1494 it snowed heavily in Florence and Piero de Medici asked the eighteen-year-old Michelangelo to carve a statue in the snow, in the courtyard of his Palazzo. The reputation for the ice statue's brilliance was only enhanced by its evanescence.

Perhaps the real reason that so few of Terry's productions were filmed was that RSC leading actors such as Ian Richardson, Helen Mirren and Alan Howard were not thought to have the commercial clout then, and the BBC were engaged in their own filming of the canon, which Terry admits he and his colleagues at Stratford regarded with some disdain. Whatever the reason, as Terry himself mourns, 'we lost Mark Rylance's Hamlet, Ian Richardson's Ford, Helen Mirren's Queen Margaret, and David Suchet's Iago'.

The production most frequently requested and most disappointingly not available from Terry's regime is Bill Alexander's 1984 production of *Richard III* with Antony Sher. I know. I never saw it myself. I wish I had, as I am now married to him!

It is worth noting that Terry did achieve a wonderful TV version of *Cyrano de Bergerac* with Derek Jacobi. But, personally, I regret the lack of a record of his Shakespeare productions. As a teenager, I watched their entire History cycle, in which Alan Howard played all the major kings bar Henry IV, and an acclaimed Coriolanus. We have sound recordings of all these productions, lodged (and available to listen to) at the British Library, but I wish I were able to see some of those memorable moments to refresh my memory of them: Falstaff greeting and being rejected by an almost automaton, robotic, gilded, armour-clad King Henry in the snow at the end of *Henry IV Part Two*; or Caius Martius suspended over the gates of Corioles.

I don't believe these productions were just ice statues that my teenage memory has crystalized into great ones.

BROOK'S DREAM

Alan Howard appeared as Oberon in perhaps the most famous RSC production of the twentieth century: Peter Brook's *A Midsummer Night's Dream*, in 1970. Brook, it seems, never allowed this production to be filmed, so for those of us not lucky enough to see this historic, game-changing production, we can only read the reviews, and many accounts of those that did, or pore over photographs and the extended promptbook which was produced, and wonder what it was like. I have talked to a lot of the actors in that production, and worked with many of them: Alan Howard himself, Patrick Stewart, Sarah Kestelman, John Kane and Barry Stanton. And I know how extraordinary the rehearsals were too. But does the lack of filmed evidence of the production diminish or indeed enhance its reputation?

In fact, there are a few minutes of film available which give a taste of the production, but in the mythology that surrounds Brook's *Dream* there is also tell of a film of the entire production, and tantalizing clues to its whereabouts. Apparently filmed while the production was in Japan, no doubt it will turn up someday.

But why did Brook not allow the production to be filmed? I suspect the answer is simple and celebrates the uniqueness and specialness of the production as a theatre event that exists only when it is alive and happens only between the live audience and the moment of the words creating that particular magic. And to render it in film would be to kill it. It's a production whose revolutionary boldness and its influence may perhaps be inflated by its disappearance into air, into thin air, but it was certainly a production which re-defined now-ness.

Peter Brook was of course not averse to filming Shakespeare productions. After the stage success of *Dream*, he filmed his famous 1962 production of *Lear* at Stratford, a decade later, on location in the desolate, frozen landscapes of Jutland in Denmark. And of course he cut the play quite ruthlessly, for which he received a deal of criticism.

But Brook put his finger on the challenges of transferring Shakespeare onto film. 'The problem of filming Shakespeare', he said, 'is one of finding ways of shifting gears, styles and conventions lightly and deftly on the screen as within the mental processes' inside a person, which can be reflected by blank verse but not by the screen's 'consistency within each single image.'[2]

So film is too literal: or Shakespeare is too abstract for film. He suits the bare stage where the mind contributes what is missing, enhancing the words and limited only by the capacity of the audience's imaginations.

ADRIAN NOBLE

If Terry Hands seemed not to be interested in the potential of filming the productions from his regime, his successor Adrian Noble was, although he made only one film, and again it was *A Midsummer Night's Dream*, the third Stratford *Dream* to be committed to celluloid. Adrian attempted to realize the success of his own 1994 stage production and re-conceived the play for film, rather than merely recording his production.

Adrian himself distinguished the central challenge of the exercise: that on stage you have to appeal to the ear, but on film the principal sense you are appealing to is the eye.

He suggested that people love words less these days, that they don't have the love and relish of language that they used to have, and he said 'If you lose words you lose a lot in life.' Nevertheless, and perhaps inevitably, the text of this *Dream* was radically cut, in particular the lovers' scenes.

Adrian also made the point that on stage the narrative works in a linear fashion, whereas on film it works more vertically like airplanes stacking up waiting to land at Heathrow, each of the plots needs to be kept alive by more regularly revisiting them, which meant that in the edit suite he had to chop and cut back between scenes much more frequently than Shakespeare does or than we need to on stage.

He also found certain scenes that he had already shot in the film studio were redundant by the time he came to the edit suite.

MY OWN JOURNEY

My own journey in exploring how to transfer stage productions onto the small screen began in 1995 when I directed my partner, Antony Sher, in *Titus Andronicus* at the Market Theatre in Johannesburg, in just post-apartheid South Africa. The production was an event, as it marked Tony's first ever return to the country of his birth, and so like Titus, he came 'bound with laurel boughs to re-salute his country'.

We filmed the production for the South African Broadcasting Corporation (SABC) with six cameras over three performances and a day of pick-ups in the theatre. The result is, again, a good archive of the production.

The same could be said of an RSC production of *The Winter's Tale* that we did in 1999 with Heritage Theatre filmed at the Barbican. It is a worthy archive of the experience of watching the production in the theatre, but somehow a second-hand one. It somehow remains inert.

What do I mean by that? Well, by capturing the wide picture of the event it somehow failed to allow you to participate. You somehow felt outside looking in. And it did not solve the problem of scale. When the camera went in on a close-up of Tony Sher as Leontes delivering one of his blistering rages and projecting to the back row (Row T) of the Barbican Theatre, it felt uncannily like that dizzying dolly zoom shot in *Jaws* where the camera simultaneously zooms in and pans out on Roy Scheider seeing the shark for the first time.

We wanted to capture the live-ness of the event but somehow only caught its past-ness. So in our next venture we tried something different. In 1999 we did a production of *Macbeth* in the Swan Theatre, which subsequently toured to Japan and the United States. *Macbeth* is said to be a cursed play. It isn't: it's just that it's very hard to do, to manage to reach the audience's own imaginative experience of the play. But we were

---

[2] Peter Brook, 'Finding Shakespeare on Film', TDR 11 (1966), 117–21; 120.

lucky and the production was lauded in the press as the best since Trevor Nunn's a quarter of a century before.

During our final performances at the Young Vic in London, the then Culture Secretary Chris Smith came to see the production, and in an unprecedented move, phoned Michael Jackson, chief executive of Channel 4, suggesting that it was vital that they found a way of producing a film of this particular production. I guess perhaps because it caught something of the 'now now very nowness' of the moment.

John Wyver, director of a media company called Illuminations, came on board. They had filmed Deborah Warner's *Richard II* with Fiona Shaw in 1997, and had just produced a BBC film of Phyllida Lloyd's production of the Benjamin Britten opera *Gloriana* for Opera North with Josephine Barstow as Queen Elizabeth. John and I discussed how to capture the excitement of watching that *Macbeth* in the theatre, the relentless hold it has upon you, the sense of being trapped in the same room with a couple planning murder, the spontaneity, the feeling you have that it is unfolding in real time before your eyes, and you could stop it if you wanted. Your presence in the same space is crucial and, without you, the play would not happen. With film, it's different. If you watch it or not, it has no impact on the action. It continues if you leave the room. A play you feel does not. The question is simple: how can you begin to reproduce that sheer immediacy in a medium as fixed as film?

I also wanted to let the words do it. Most film adaptations of Shakespeare inevitably cut large portions of the text. They have horses, if you like, and therefore don't need to describe them. I wanted to keep a larger portion of the text, and lessen the irrelevant detail of the play's setting, to find a vivid neutrality that would not draw attention to itself.

Eventually we decided upon the Round House in Chalk Farm to film the production. The venue, built in 1846, had once been a railway engine shed. It housed a turntable for manually turning round the trains, and the undercroft, a series of brick wall spokes on a supporting wheel underpinning that turntable, provided wonderful film locations, with rooms whose walls apparently receded into nothing.

Macbeth is, in many ways, the most filmic of Shakespeare's plays with its short, quick-fire scenes and its hurtling, dynamic momentum. In the film I tried to capture its raw energy and dangerous intimacy. I wanted a technique that would echo the jerky attempts of a film cameraman in a war zone trying to capture events as they unfolded. Our director of photography, and cameraman, Ernie Vincze, chose to film virtually the entire play on a single handheld camera, giving the action a sense of giddy immediacy and edgy unpredictability, borrowing techniques of fly-on-the-wall documentaries, which I felt echoed the experience of watching the play in the theatre.

[EXTRACT SIX: *Macbeth* 1999.]

Our last day of filming coincided with the anniversary of our first day of rehearsal. Harriet Walter, playing Lady Macbeth, said to me that, if I had asked her to play Lady M for a whole year, she would probably have declined the offer, but because it grew organically from the production, to the world tour, to the filming, it had flown by.

My own feeling was that the whole year's acquaintance with the play had allowed the performances to reach a sort of depth and visceral comprehension of the play, which is rare in other filming situations, where the actors are lucky if they get a few days' rehearsal to acquaint them with the extremity of feeling which Shakespeare requires of his characters. The actors could breathe the language and could reproduce it wherever I asked them to play the scene, which in one case meant Harriet playing part of the letter scene submerged in a bath.

That production had a modest budget. In fact we joked at the time that we had less time and less money to make our film of *Macbeth* than Orson Welles had when he filmed his *Macbeth* in 1947 (he had twenty-three days to shoot, and $700,000) — our Channel 4 budget was £450,000 and we shot it in twelve days. That's a pretty staggering ten minutes of screen time per day!

GREGORY DORAN

HAMLET

In 2008 the RSC, now under Michael Boyd's artistic directorship, was approached (via John Wyver) to do the first-ever live broadcast of a theatre production to cinemas across the globe with my production of *Hamlet* with David Tennant and Patrick Stewart. The Met in New York had pioneered this idea with their opera productions but nobody had by then tried to capture and simultaneously broadcast a theatre production.

For a variety of reasons, including nervousness on the part of some of the actors (it's fine fluffing the odd line in front of a thousand people one night, but in front of the whole world?), we did not go ahead with that proposal, and indeed the National Theatre successfully ran with the proposal and have been doing so since *Phedre* with Helen Mirren in 2009. In fact I am glad we did not do a live relay of that particular production, as we then got the chance to film it for BBC2. Again we chose to film it in a single location and wanted to find a venue which captured the vivid neutrality of the Roundhouse. Eventually we alighted on a derelict Jesuit Seminary in Mill Hill, North London.

I am very proud of our film of *Hamlet*, but here's an interesting thought. When listening to the archive sound recording of the stage production, recorded during the run in Stratford, I was reminded just how many laughs there were. David Tennant (playing Hamlet) and I had both noticed the line when the young prince says 'I have of late, but wherefore I know not, lost all my mirth.' Might not the line imply that, at one time, Hamlet was indeed a funny guy? And David's performance elicited wonderful sardonic humour from the prince. The scene where Hamlet mercilessly teases Polonius or his banter with that callow pair Rosencrantz and Guildenstern set the audience on a roar in the theatre. But of course, because the film has no live dimension, this humour is not immediately evident in the film version of the same production. The wit in David's performance as Richard II, the first of our *Live from Stratford-upon-Avon* broadcasts, gives ample testimony to the humour in the role, and in the play, because it is amplified by having a live audience share the humour, which is shared in turn with the cinema audience.

JULIUS CAESAR

Our next foray into capturing stage productions on film was a mixture both of re-conceiving the play for a different medium (filming it in a different location) and of recording performance live in this theatre. In 2012, to coincide with the London Olympics, I did a production of *Julius Caesar* for the Olympic Shakespeare Festival. The BBC were keen to film the production but wanted it ready before we had completed its run in Stratford. So we hit upon a novel solution. The play is divided between the public and the private scenes, the backstage plotting and the presentational forum scenes. So we would film the private scenes first, in a London location, and edit it together with the public forum scenes once the production was in preview in Stratford.

Therefore, we brought the rehearsal period forward and, after a very few weeks in our Clapham rehearsal room, we filmed the play in the very vivid neutrality of Oriental City, a disused Chinese Hypermarket in Colindale, just off the North Circular. The production was in fact set in an anonymous contemporary African State, and somehow the rather anonymous modernity of the shopping centre provided a good fit. We assassinated Julius Caesar on the escalator. Then we filmed the public scenes, principally the central forum scene, on stage in Stratford during a live preview performance, using handheld cameras among the crowd. The two matched seamlessly together.

Julius Caesar is in some senses a hybrid, both of live capture and of a production re-conceived for the small screen. It is not a film, like Brook's *Lear*, Branagh's *Henry V*, McKellen's *Richard III* or Noble's *Dream*, but something in between.

My predecessor Michael Boyd generously allowed his chief associate to pursue these film projects, but never developed the idea of film capture himself. Although I regret that he was never able to film his crowning achievement in producing his entire History Cycle in 2007–8.

The *Live from*s which we are now engaged in, here in Stratford-upon-Avon, are a midway point between film and recording stage performance. They celebrate the 'now now very now-ness' of the live experience. They capture an immediacy, a danger if you like. But they also share the experience, by being a communal one. I remember being thrilled that my twin sister would be sitting down in her local cinema to watch it in Denver, Colorado, while my brother did so in North Wales, and my in-laws in South Africa did the same.

You share the actual performance as you sit down in real time with the audience in Stratford to watch the production: you laugh, gasp and cry with them, and applaud together at the end (a novel experience in the cinema!) and, even if you are watching an encore screening, the effect is curiously the same. You enjoy the 'now, now very now-ness' which is Shakespeare's appeal.

So what now? What next? I guess as technology moves on, so will we. We are already. This autumn, I am directing a production of *The Tempest* here in this theatre. We have conceived it with Intel and The Imaginarium Studios. It will involve cutting-edge technology. Ariel will be an onstage presence, but he will also have an avatar digitally projected in real time, a revolutionary new technique never seen on stage before. The ship will sink, and Juno will arrive on her chariot drawn by gilded peacocks, all created by the amazing new technology being developed by companies such as Intel. We will do our *Live from*, but we will need to explore new ways of achieving that.

So watch this space. But always at the centre of our work will be the words Shakespeare wrote, delivered live by actors in this space, inspiring your imagination, in the quick forge and working-house of thought. How we share that more widely with a world that is hungry for new experience remains to be seen.

My suspicion is that the next step in our wider engagement with audiences will involve new modes of virtual reality to allow you to take part, or to participate in the action as it takes place, that we will forge new ways of acknowledging the audience and allowing them the experience of being in that room, and immersing themselves in the terror or the joy that Shakespeare makes his audiences feel.

Can you carry on watching as Gloucester is blinded, as the Macbeths decide to murder Duncan, as Iago deludes Othello? Can you imagine the thrill of being in that crowd as Mark Antony turns the mob from mourners to murderers, or the breathless intimacy of being in the moonlit garden as Juliet whispers her love to Romeo, or the joy of sitting in that virtual deck chair in that sunny forest of Arden as Rosalind and Orlando play endless variations in the game of love?

What I am sure of is that Shakespeare himself would have been at the forefront of that technology, and I am sure too that he is sitting on his digital cloud somewhere applauding our efforts, but encouraging us to be bolder yet.

'**Now**, entertain conjecture of **that** time!'

[EXTRACT SEVEN: Two Hamlets. I concluded the plenary session with a double clip from the filmed production of *Hamlet* we did in 2008 and, to bring us right up to date, one from the *Live from* of Paapa Essiedu, then playing the role in the Royal Shakespeare Theatre.]

IN DIALOGUE WITH AYANNA THOMPSON

ADRIAN LESTER

AYANNA THOMPSON (AT): Adrian will start by speaking for a few minutes about performing Shakespeare and then we'll begin the dialogue.

ADRIAN LESTER (AL): Good morning ladies and gentlemen. It's so nice to be on this stage. When I got asked to do this I thought, 'you better say something knowledgeable, or at least say something that's half-decent.' And so there's a couple of thoughts I wanted to share with you.

During my performance as Rosalind in Cheek By Jowl's *As You Like It*, as we travelled to Germany, Japan, Vienna, Seattle, and then to BAM in New York and, similarly, when Peter Brook's *Hamlet* went around the world, I wrote notes about the reaction of the audience to some of the soliloquies.

I'm going to look at those notes because, well… I'm an actor. And I'm on stage. With an audience. And no script. If I don't look at this, you'll be here for hours. Actors are funny creatures. We are odd. We spend our professional lives pretending to be someone else. We try to see through their eyes and speak their words. I think nowhere in the English language are the characters and the words used to express those characters as complex or as multilayered as in Shakespeare's plays. He was an actor himself. Therefore the use of language on stage had a twofold power. It has an effect on the actor as they speak the lines, while at the same moment it has an effect on the audience as they hear those lines spoken. Performing one of Shakespeare's great soliloquies really pushes the actor to develop distinct and conflicting points of view. It's a great help when you're playing these lines over and over again, performance after performance, matinee and evening in different continents around the world. It's a great help because the interplay between these separate points of view creates conflict and from that conflict comes drama. The kind of drama that can play itself out even when there is only one person on stage talking to himself. What I've found to be true with Shakespeare is that these separate points of view can at times be hidden from each other and only revealed to the character and the audience at a certain moment in the play.

Now I should explain. Let's take Angelo in *Measure for Measure*. He meets Isabella, a nun who's trying to advocate for her brother's life, trying to save her brother by talking to Angelo. He falls completely in love, or in lust, with her when he sees her. A feeling that is unknown to him before that point. And as she leaves, she says to him, 'Save your honor' (2.2.163), a form of goodbye that means 'God save your honor.' And he replies, 'From thee; even from thy virtue. / What's this? What's this? Is this her fault? Or mine? / The tempter or the tempted, who sins most, ha?' (2.2.164–7). The question he asks, 'what's this?', has to be asked by someone, or something, and it has to be directed at someone or something. Yes, in a soliloquy we speak to the audience, but that's too

---

Tuesday 2 August 2016, The Royal Shakespeare Theatre, World Shakespeare Congress, Stratford-upon-Avon.

Ayanna Thompson would like to thank Farah Karim-Cooper, Ann Thompson and Peter Holbrook for coming up with the idea for this plenary dialogue at the WSC, and Jonathan Hope for the invaluable preparation time.

simplistic. It's more than that. We, all of us humans, we speak to change – either to the character opposite us, to the other characters in the room with us, or to some aspect of the world around us. Indeed, if we actors open our mouths and the words we say don't have a target, something to aim at, then what we say becomes unfocused, becomes undetailed, and it turns into empty words. 'I had as lief the town crier spoke my lines' (*Hamlet*, 3.2.3–4).

Angelo continues, 'Not she, nor doth she tempt. But it is I' (2.3.170). And further on in the speech, 'What dost thou, or what art thou, Angelo? / Dost thou desire her foully for those things / That make her good?' (2.3.178–80). Angelo's sense of himself is disturbed. He asks himself questions, and as he does so another element of his personality is revealed, both to himself in that moment and to us, the audience. His mask slips and we watch him change. But what's more … we watch his reaction to the discovery of that change. Like Othello in the very powerful Act 3, scene 3, the so-called 'Temptation Scene,' when he declares:

> Why, why is this?
> Think'st thou I'd make a life of jealousy,
> To follow still the changes of the moon
> With fresh suspicions? No, to be once in doubt
> Is once to be resolved. Exchange me for a goat
> When I shall turn the business of my soul
> To such exsufflicate and blowed surmises
> (*Othello*, 3.3.180–6)

But then minutes later, in the same scene, Othello says, 'I'll tear her all to pieces!' (3.3.437) and 'Oh, blood, blood, blood!' (3.3.455); all in the same scene. Pushed by Iago, Othello changes. An aspect of his nature that has been hidden within himself, or is completely unknown to him, suddenly reveals itself in front of the audience, and at that moment he completely changes.

Here's another example, Henry V, during what we call the dark night of the soul, wanders through the field on the eve before Agincourt, and says:

> Upon the King.
> 'Let us our lives, our souls, our debts, our care-full wives,
> Our children, and our sins, lay on the King!'
> We must bear all. (*Henry V*, 4.1.227–30)

Henry V goes on to question the idea of ceremony and the pomp and circumstance that are given to a king, all of which completely destroy his peace of mind and his ability to sleep. His courage, in that moment, is put to the test. And under that pressure he changes. He finishes that scene on his knees, terrified, begging God for forgiveness.

So many characters are created in this way in Shakespeare's plays: they shift. Like diamonds, if you like, they are multifaceted and they shift and change in front of us, showing us the different colours to their characters as they go along. Richard II, in that incredible scene where he comes back to England and is given bad news, takes resolve. And then he is given more bad news, and he takes resolve. You watch the character oscillate between despair and status. The actors that can pull that off are few and far between, as far as I'm concerned. One of them did it recently for the BBC and he was amazing. Again, changing, shifting, twisting in front of us and all the while the character reacts to these elements as they are revealed.

To me, these shifting points of view exist because the way we see ourselves changes day to day. In a soliloquy it's as if the person you fear you might be is in conversation with the person everyone else expects you to be. Watching a character we care about discover something that forces him to change before our eyes is great, but I think that watching that discovery, that internal discovery, using Shakespeare's language can be brilliant. That kind of moment, a moment of self-discovery, is what makes us human. Because, and here's my thing, ladies and gentlemen, we don't really know who we are. We don't. We don't know why we're here. And, given the right circumstances, none of us really knows what we're capable of. We find out who we are day to day as we interact with one another. We deal with our agreements, our disagreements. And under those pressures, we deal with those conflicts, trying to move forward, to find a resolution. From what I've experienced so far on stage, Shakespeare is the only writer who consistently captures that understanding. Thank you very much.

AT: Adrian was really kind to send me his remarks yesterday, so I had time to think about them. Adrian, I'm really interested in your comments about relationality and the way that identity is determined for you in terms of relationality, and the tension that you describe about how people see one versus how one sees oneself. I was wondering if you wanted to talk that through for a character, a Shakespearean character, and then maybe even for yourself. I am interested in the way you think people see you and the expectations they have about you as an actor or, you know, human being.

AL: I think that a lot of Shakespeare's characters have that conflict. The greatest ones do, I think. The greatest roles, whose lines we quote time and time again, seem to exist with a sense of duality. And if you write about them or try to study them, you think, well this person is this, but they're also this, but then later on they become this, but then they also have this. And those conflicts, those separate masks that people wear, can confuse one. Hamlet, of course, has that, and Mac ... [*Adrian stops suddenly, voice trailing off*], that leading character in that Scottish play, has that as well.

Well, who has on occasion talked to themselves? I have. Sometimes you'll write something and think, 'oh I don't know if it's right,' and you'll speak it out, won't you? You'll sound it out – I think the Americans call it sounding it out. But who are you sounding it out to? Who's listening? If I was to stand on stage with all of Hamlet's soliloquies and think, 'oh I'm speaking to the audience,' that would reduce what's going on: 'O, what a rogue and peasant and slave am I! / Is it not monstrous that this player here' (*Hamlet*, 2.2.552–3). Let me paraphrase the rest: in a fit, a dream of passion, could bring himself to tears about the subject of Hecuba, when Hecuba means nothing to him. And yet here I sit, unpregnant of my cause, and if I were to consider what I had to do with my father, and my uncle, and my mother, I would drown the stage with tears ... Hamlet ends up shouting and then laughs at himself for doing nothing but shouting. There has to be, I think, in any actor worth his salt, there has to be an awareness, or self-awareness, of the character. You have to be able to look at the character, shake the character, give them a little push, a shove, and not just recite the words, but reinvent a relationship that gives you the ability to look at yourself, laugh at yourself, push yourself, poke yourself, comment on yourself every night with an audience watching. If we can do that, something takes place that is live and not recited. That's why I think theatre will never go away. Watching something live and in the moment with the right actors and the right directors, that's amazing and I'm sure we've all had experiences like that, be it Shakespeare or not.

I think trying to push yourself to see how other people see you in life can be worrisome if pushed too far. It can be worrisome. Everything we do is a slight manipulation of the outside world. Yes, we dress for the cold, but actually on some level we dress to manipulate what we think the outside world's opinion of us is. Especially when we're dressing up to go somewhere. Can you see how the thread in my shoes matches my trousers? I'll say no more. But to be honest we all engage in that act; we are all aware on some level. When we write something, we are acutely aware that somebody else could misunderstand it. When we speak in public, we are acutely aware that somebody else could misinterpret our words and spin them and tie them into a different argument. And this awareness pushes us. We oscillate between comfort, security, and a slight sense of insecurity, a healthy insecurity. We agree to meet and discuss and talk in forms, in polite forms. We have a template for conversation, 'Good morning, how are you? I'm fine, how are you?' We join in to that template before we move on to reveal more about ourselves. If you meet someone who straightaway reveals things about themselves, they're kind of weird. You've got to go through the template, you've got to go through the form.

Anyway, I digress, but in Hamlet's case, he spends the whole play acutely aware of his limitations: 'O that this too too sullied flesh would melt, / Thaw, and resolve itself into a dew, / Or that the Everlasting had not fixed / His canon 'gainst self-slaughter' (1.2.129–32). Hamlet wants a sense of purification because he thinks he's too dirty, sullied and soiled to be part of this lineage – what his mother has done, what his uncle has done. And that sense of betrayal destroys his belief in his relationship to God, to love, to his mother, to his father, to duty, and to the country. And he constantly asks himself and the audience questions, all the way through the play. And that's the reason why *Hamlet* has become or is one of Shakespeare's greatest plays. Does that kind of answer the question?

AT: That was amazing, yes. The next question I want to pose to you actually comes from Pascal Aebischer, who is a wonderful performance scholar, and who is interested in different performance practices for different media. In looking over your body of work, I see that you have worked in various very different performance media. For those who don't know, Adrian starts on a soap opera show on television, then is in Cheek by Jowl's stage production of *As You Like It*, then is in the Stephen Sondheim musical *Company*, then does the blockbuster film *Primary Colours*, then does Kenneth Branagh's filmed version of *Love's Labour's Lost*, then stars in Peter Brook's *Hamlet* both on stage and on film, then stars in *Henry V* at the National, then stars in the television show *Hustle*, then stars in *Red Velvet*, an original play about Ira Aldridge written by his brilliant wife Lolita Chakrabarti, then stars in *Othello* at the National, and then stars in the television show *Undercover*. You are all over the place in terms of the media that you work in: you've done television, film, live theatre, and you've also done filmed live theatre. So the question is, how do you change your skills for the different media that you are acting in, especially for Shakespeare productions in different media?

AL: I choose each job as it comes along, or the job chooses me. As an actor you don't really have the power to say, 'I want that.' You can only really say no to the things you don't want, that's your only real power. But I grab hold of the things that I think are going to make me a better actor. Whatever they may be. And I get restless easily. Once I'd had success doing one thing, in one medium, some people couldn't understand why I didn't just keep doing that. 'Just do that, people know you for that'. Just do that.'

AT: How are you not in musicals constantly? Right? Have you seen this man dance and sing? It's unreal.

AL: Thank you, I owe you a fiver. I, actually, I'd love to do another musical. That's something I really want to do, but it's just that once I've done a piece of work I do want to move on and do something else. I'll never leave the stage alone because I find that when you're acting on stage your intellectual capacity as an actor – your muscles, your vocal capacity, your physicality – they all get a workout when you're working on stage. And on screen that isn't quite so true. So I know I'll never leave the stage alone. I keep saying that what you do with a cannon on stage, you do with a laser on camera.

AT: Do you feel like you could do an example of the laser acting versus the cannon? I'm putting you on the spot. Even if it's just a gesture.

AL: I hadn't prepared anything but um ... In this space if you're moving while you're in this space the audience has to watch your whole body. Also, I have to be aware on this thrust stage that if I do this, someone's getting my back. I can't settle there for too long. I have to do this [*moving his whole body*], which means they [*a section of the audience*] get a ninety-degree angle while they [*another section of the audience*] get three-quarters. So you have to be aware of that, of what people see.

On screen the audience is here. A three-quarter on screen is that [*moving his head a little*]. And then if I want to go to a ninety-degree focus on screen it's that [*same move*]. Then because the camera's so close, let's say the camera is you [*Adrian points to a member of the audience sitting directly in front of him*]. Because the camera's so close, you never bring your eyes to the area around the lens because your eye is drawn to the lens itself. Also if your eyeline goes that close you could "bottle it" as they call it. You look down it. And the people watching on screen feel as though you are looking at them directly and breaking their belief in the narrative. So it's always good to glance past it and allow the camera to be at a very slight angle to your face. Unless, as in *Hustle*, you're talking directly to the camera and need the audience at home to feel as though you can enter the story on screen at will.

On stage, if I move, [*Adrian walks around a little*] you are aware of the whole body, you are aware of my gestures. You're aware of the whole body. If I stop moving, [*Adrian stands still*] and use my hands while I'm speaking, then, in your mind's eye you shrink your area of perception to just here [*Adrian indicates an area from his hips to just above the top of his head*]. You do a three-quarters shot, a half shot. If my hands stop moving and look as though they have no purpose in this conversation, then what I'm doing with my voice and my face is bringing you all into a close-up. Because your area of perception shrinks to from just above my shoulders to the top of my head. I can be still, but not for too long because these people here are at a ninety-degree angle, while these folks are kind of at one hundred and twenty degrees. So the whole experience of my stillness will be different for them. So that's kind of a difference I think between camera work and stage work.

AT: That's an exciting demonstration. So Pascal Aebischer is in a seminar about filmed versions of live productions – like NT Live, in which you participated for *Othello*. Did you feel that you altered your body, performance, or anything when you were being filmed during the NT Live night?

AL: Yes, I did, definitely.

AT: We knew that. Now you must elaborate. And if you can demonstrate that would be even better too. I owe you a fiver.

AL: At the NT Live, the cameras were placed at this level. There were six of them. Static, static, static, one on a track going around the side, and two in the back that could take close-ups. So for action that took place where Othello was listening to the action but he wasn't part of the scene, I would stand somewhere here in this space in the Olivier Theatre. But I couldn't when we were doing NT Live. I had to stand here because the camera couldn't focus on me where I normally stood. When performing in the Olivier Theatre to reach the top, the gods, I would lift my eyes to play this angle so that the audience up there felt connected to the story and the character [*Adrian looks up at the top row of seats in the theatre*]. But when doing the NT Live, I completely ignored them. Sorry! I had to. I completely ignored them because on camera, let's say the camera is directly in front of me again, if I do that on camera [*Adrian looks up*], it looks like I'm doing this [*Adrian tilts his head far back*]. The camera accentuates the angle so I couldn't afford to keep doing this in the theatre [*Adrian looks up at the seats again*] because it looked on camera like I was doing that [*throws head back*]. I'd be going through a soliloquy then suddenly, you'd have my chin. 'Look at my very meaningful chin.' And that wouldn't really work. So I tried not to do it. The angle difference for a camera can be quite quite small.

Also, I allowed myself not to project when I was in the theatre for NT Live. We were miced, which felt really odd. It's such a physical show and we had to be careful of, cover your ears [*Adrian taps on the mic*], careful of all of that. When I grabbed Iago and he grabbed me, we had to be very careful of that kind of bang. So there you are being completely free in a moment you've done fifty times before, and then you suddenly have to go, 'Oh no, watch my mic!' It's just really annoying. It's like being in the middle of a fight or something, and then going, 'Not the hair, not the hair!' We all know that feeling, right? [*huge laugh from the audience*]. That got a louder laugh than the other one. There's a lot of vain people out there. So you had to be constantly aware, technically of what was required by camera.

Also, some of the ways you can act on stage, some of the ways we were taught in drama school – concentration on voice production, diction, clarity, the belly full of sound, and the support, and the diaphragm, and so on and so forth – employing those techniques on camera, in the same ways you would to speak to the 1,100 people in the Olivier Theatre, looks like you're acting. It does, it looks like you're pretending. On camera, it is better for some things to be so quiet that you make the audience in the cinema lean in: 'Wait, what was that?' Or in a moment of passion, like the scene with Desdemona, it is better not to always think 'They must have my face.' Because we instinctively, subconsciously, recognize that as false. If we don't see the person's face, if we don't catch the actor's movements completely, we're thinking 'What is going on?', and that's actually good because that's just like life. But without the cameras, in a big house, you really can't afford to do that. Because whatever you're feeling, you need to give it that lift, that weight, and then kick it right up to the gods, which on camera would look false.

AT: So now I want to ask you about a topic you don't like to talk about, but we've talked about it a lot because we've had conversations over the years. Let's start by talking about your actor training in terms of interpretation, pronunciation, physicality and race. So start with training and then we'll go from there.

AL: I trained at RADA for three years, and they train everything really. Voice, production, all the usual techniques, I won't go into them. The Alexander technique, which I suppose, to simplify it, would be the optimal way to use and move within your skeletal system with your muscles free of tension, finding perfect balance as you sit, stand, crawl and speak in front of an audience. Because the tensions you feel as an actor once you get on stage in front of people can start to find a home in certain parts of your body. And once it finds a home, it can destroy the very act of being free and open and expressive, which is what you want. And this goes for singers, dancers, you name it. We learned a Stanislavski system of acting and method to break down human behaviour into its component parts and then to put it back together again slowly. Class by class, month by month, and week by week, over a two-year period we did this before we stepped on stage and started to perform for the public. We studied text, we looked at lots of different plays. For me I had never looked at Shakespeare before then, and so it was a real eye opener for me to study in that way. And we slowly put all of those things together, and then we got to perform for our peers, for our teachers, and then for the public. As for race ...

AT: Was it mentioned at all during your training? Was there ever a conversation about it?

AL: No. Dr. Oliver Neville, who was the principal at RADA at the time, was very passionate about the art of acting and said 'You will start to be an actor ten years after leaving this place.' At that time there was no kind of fast route to 'Oh, I got picked up by a TV show' or 'Oh, I made it, I'm in a film six months after leaving.' He didn't believe in that. He said, 'You know, that might happen, and that will be great. But if you rest on the things that made your first quick and easy success, you'll find yourself trapped three years afterwards. You will be an actor ten years after leaving this building.' And ten years after leaving RADA I kind of knew what he meant.

Race was never discussed. While rehearsing with Peter Brook for *Hamlet*, I mistakenly was trying to link one scene with another with another with another, and make a conscious sense of what Hamlet goes through by understanding it as an actor and trying to tie the scenes together. And I found a great release when Peter and I were talking about that, and he kind of came to the conclusion that actually character is something that takes place in the eye of the audience. And what I had to do was to be true and specific in every scene, separate from the others. If we agree that Hamlet is under great pressure, if we agree that he is asking himself questions, if we agree that he's at sea and worried and unsure, then making a conscious decision to play certain things when you go through the text means that you consciously narrow the bandwidth of human behaviour and all that is unconscious in our behaviour. You squeeze it down because you're making a logical sense of it as you play it, rather than play that scene to the hilt, play this scene to the hilt, play this other scene to the hilt. If it's love and worry and concern and dutiful son, play it, play it. Two scenes later if it's despair and anger and wanting to kill your mother, play it. Don't let one inform the other. Let the audience do that. Because then you have the greatest chance of taking that audience on that journey, rather than making it narrow and something that they can understand consciously by the time they stand up and are about to exit the theatre. If you play a moment scene by scene by scene, on its own, disconnected, then hopefully it's something that's going to stay with people as they're on the way to their car, as they're talking to their friends the next day, or whatever.

And that to me is the best way of getting Shakespeare's works to live, and the same therefore with race. I will do what I will do with a complete disregard for what anyone wishes to think of me with regard to my colour. I will do what I do. I've been in situations where I've said, 'Oh, I'm taking my kids to school', and they've made some comment on colour. They've made some comments on colour and I think, 'When I take my kids to school in the morning, I don't do it as a black man.' However you wish to see it, when you see the image, let it speak unto you what it will, but I don't do it as a black man. I don't even do it as a man. I do it as a parent. Or not even that, I do it as a caretaker, as a guardian for the young people I love, that's how I do it. So entering into that simple act, some observation, some external observation of colour, race, age, sexuality, gender, I can't walk into the bounds of your limited conversation and then sit down and discuss with you what ignorances you have and how valid you feel they may or may not be.

AT: Alright, *Othello* ...

AL: Yeah ... so scratch everything I just said!

AT: So with that idea, then how did you work through *Othello*?

AL: It's hard. One of the very early conversations I had with Nick [Hytner], I said let's help the audience not focus on race; this was my reaction to everyone talking about race in the play. Let's see if we can, in this day in age, with a National Theatre audience, help them not to focus on race. Let's see if we can encourage the audience to see character before colour. Let's see. And we did that in a very simple way, by having other black actors on stage, which I know is becoming quite common now. But when Othello strikes Desdemona, having a couple of other black actors in uniform react in shock at how disgusting and terrible it is, for some people who wish to have the play support certain beliefs they have, the reactions of disgust by the other black actors helps to rock them. It helps us to try to see the man more than the shape of him, the colour of him.

It's hard in a play where the character is racially abused. And then, because of the poison that's dripped into his ear, his own points of view about himself become tainted by the very things Iago has said. So you watch that poison sink in, take shape, and take root until he says: "This fellow's of exceeding honesty" (3.3.256). And then the speech:

> Haply for I am black,
> And have not those soft parts of conversation
> That chamberers have; or for I am declined
> Into the vale of years—yet that's not much—
> She's gone. I am abused, and my relief
> Must be to loathe her. (3.3.267–72)

I think that is the real power of abuse. It's much more than simply insulting someone. Abuse, real abuse, to an individual or a group affects how those people see themselves and, for them, that changes everything. So it's quite hard in that play to get the audience to see character and not colour. I discussed it with Hugh Quarshie recently, who went further with their production by having a black actor play Iago. Hugh and I agreed that a strange thing has happened in the way Act 3, scene 3, where Othello shifts, is being played. Before, when the character was played by white actors, the speed of that shift, which is almost impossible to act believably, was given an excuse of 'Well, he returns to his barbaric state' or, a hundred years ago, 'It is the native heat of Africa coming through him.'

AT: It was only fifty years ago!

AL: I was being kind. All these judgements about why the jealousy happened so quickly and took root so swiftly were made on the basis of 'Well, he's black isn't he?' Basically, that's how it went. It's insulting and quite stupid really. And now, you have huge waves of black actors taking over the role. And when they come to that point in the play, they always, always think something's missing. It's as if a scene has gone, or a speech has gone, or a couple of beats are missing because it's too quick. It's just too quick and doesn't quite make sense. Everything else around it is disgusting and powerful and supports the play as a complete tragedy; it's upsetting. But that moment really has to work, otherwise you kind of don't have the play really. And so these actors have struggled with that one particular moment, night after night, performance after performance, and are still struggling with it.

I don't like the play. I do think it's brilliant, but I don't like it. And if I see it and it's fantastic, I hate it. It makes me feel uncomfortable. I worry for Desdemona. I'm disgusted at that kind of behaviour. I'm disgusted by the fact that Iago makes people laugh. It's as if Shakespeare has carved right into something in our human nature and we haven't grown in that area in 400 years because it still works, it still gets us. And then if I go to see the play and it's terrible – bad direction, bad acting – well, then I'm angry for all sorts of different reasons. And I hate it. So, I'm kind of stuck.

AT: That was such a good and honest answer. And I remember when we talked during your run in the National production, that it was the moment that you said 'Othello's occupation's gone' (3.3.362). Was that the moment that Othello changed or switched from the Othello of old to the one that's poisoned?

AL: Yeah, that is the switch. And when he leaves right after that moment and comes back and says, 'Thou hast set me upon the rack' (3.3.340). Doubt can't really be resolved. You can't resolve yourself back to innocence because you will always have doubts. As soon as you fully accept doubt, you're done. Othello accepts doubt about his wife and can never be resolved because he will always doubt. In performance we have to find some way around the dream that Iago comes up with. Such a flimsy bit of proof, and it is on that that Othello says, 'Now do I see 'tis true' (3.3.449). The guy was in bed with another guy. They got close, and then he said he was thinking of your wife when he got close to me, and Othello goes, 'That's it, it's true.' It's really hard to make that work in front of an audience. And sometimes the incredulity of that, even if the actors work well and make you believe it, you kind of start thinking, 'Othello must be stupid', which I really didn't want to happen.

AT: Your performance was brilliant. But my reaction was precisely the one you described about seeing a good *Othello*. I thought everything about this production was amazing, but I hated it, and I hated the white audience around me.

AL: Nick Hytner was the same. He would watch the performance and when Rory [Kinnear] did a certain moment and just turned and spoke to the audience, people laughed. We had rehearsal the next day and Nick would come in and would be angry that they laughed and would watch us do it again, looking for the thing that made them laugh. And when he couldn't find it, he shifted us around a little bit and said, ok try that. The next night, the audience laughed again. Nick came in again and said, 'We haven't got it yet. We've got it when they shut up and don't laugh at it.' And we worked and worked and worked. I don't think we ever got rid of all of the laughs, but we reduced them.

I met someone in the bar afterwards the show and I went, 'The audience laughs, they laugh at it. And the character's being racially abused and then when you look out you see mainly white faces, some laughing, and it makes me feel uncomfortable.' You know, then here's me projecting a racial thing onto it: 'They're all racists and they hate me', – which isn't the case. So, the person at the bar, who had just watched the show said, 'You're only response is to laugh.' And I said, 'Yeah, but it says something about the audience', and I got quite heated about it. And then this person calms me down and says, 'When else do they laugh? Do they laugh when you kill Desdemona?' And I said, 'Yeah, there are some laughs.' And he said, 'Do you think they find that funny? Do you think they're all murderers?' And I said, 'No.' He said, 'They laugh because it's painful. It's shocking, and it's almost unbelievable.' And those are almost the same moments for Iago – they are almost unbelievable. Which goes back to the point which you made in the Arden edition about the play's comical structure. Performing *Othello*, it's a tricky beast. A tricky beast.

AT: So, what would your ideal next Shakespearean role be? Is there something you definitely want to do?

AL: I don't know really. I was thinking the other day that as I've gotten older, I've gotten better. I just have. I've had more practice. I'm not so self-aware, so self-conscious. I'm more intelligent. And I'm a parent and that kind of opens up your heart in a way that you can't really explain. Anyway, so now I'm better so I'd love the chance to go back and play some of the juvenile leads. And I won't do this! I'm not going to be one of those actors who turns fifty and is giving you his Romeo. Colouring in the grey in the mirror: 'I've still got it!' That's not going to happen. But I do feel that I have a greater understanding now of what it would take to play those roles. But in all seriousness, now I suppose I look around at Richard III and at King Lear, and I'm happy to wait a bit.

AT: You know who I think you should do? Cleopatra!

AL: My wife [Lolita Chakrabarti] would kill me.

AT: You would be fantastic.

AL: Yeah, Cleopatra's one. I did a scene from Cleopatra in school where I was Cleopatra and . . .

AT: Do you remember any of it?

AL: No. I'm trying to be butch, and you're destroying that. I'm trying to be really manly. No, I don't remember any of it but I remember I played Jocasta in an all-male version of *Oedipus* that we did at RADA. We split the year into two groups, and the girls did one Greek play and we did another. And I remember working on all of the things I needed to get hold of to play her, and it wasn't to make myself a woman. In many ways, it was to make myself more androgynous. So not to take on board any received ideas of femininity but to try and lose the male ones. So once you're in the middle . . .

AT: Alright, you've got to demonstrate again.

AL: No!

AT: Oh, come on.

AL: Once you're in the middle and you tell the audience that you're Jocasta, and the mother of Oedipus, the audience projects the rest on to you. So, there is nothing false. You just try to trim down everything that goes against their projection.

I will show you one thing but I'll stay in the chair. When I was doing Rosalind [in Cheek by Jowl's *As You Like It*], I remember I walked in heels for a bit at home. But it was to emasculate myself, to understand how to move in the court shoes I would be given. I didn't want to clunk around like I was only used to wearing trainers, which I am. So, I did that for a bit, and I found that raising the heel takes away the movement from your ankle. It kind of locks your ankle, and you can't use your ankle to cushion your walk. It's locked into this position. So you have to use your knees. And as soon as you use your knees, it rocks your hips. I had to learn to do that without going thump, thump, thump. So I had to practice that.

Another thing I did was to grow my nails long, which meant that whenever I was picking something up I couldn't do that [Adrian clutches the notepad in front of him]. I had to lay the pads of my hands onto my object because my nails would get in the way. So everything changed. I would handle that by reaching for an object like this, which immediately softens the wrist because the wrist isn't in the angle above the object, it suddenly goes underneath. Or you have to do this, and use the pads of your fingers.

Another thing I had to do was to take the elbow in. Because once you do that, you soften the line of the body. So even handling this book and opening it and finding the right chapter was all pads of the fingers with the elbows in. In that action you can see it immediately softens the expression and makes it less male. And I pushed my Adam's apple back up so that the resonance of my voice became less chest and less stomach and became more head as it does now. So I did all that and at the same time they stick me in a dress and call me Rosalind.

AT: Adrian, thank you so much. Shakespeareans love you; you should probably stand up and bow.

SHAKESPEARE AND THE NOVEL: A CONVERSATION

HOWARD JACOBSON AND ADRIAN POOLE

ADRIAN POOLE (AP): So let's put ourselves at ease by beginning in the graveyard – the graveyard with which Howard's novel *Shylock is My Name* begins. Just in case any of you haven't read it yet, Howard might like to describe the meeting between two men in this graveyard, the relationship that will be at the core of the novel, and why he put them together in this way. Howard.

HOWARD JACOBSON (HJ): Just a word about graveyards. I do seem to have reached that stage of life where I have to begin every novel in a graveyard and end every novel in a graveyard, and just in case anybody's interested in what my next novel might be – it's all in a graveyard. I've always thought when Prospero says 'Every third thought shall be my grave', why only one in three? What else is he thinking about? So it came naturally to me.

That's not a serious way of answering your question. When I started the equivalence business, a modern version of something else, I went very literal-minded and thought 'I have to find an equivalence for everything.' Then you start, and they shed themselves. But to begin with, I wanted an equivalent to Shylock and that was going to be a man I called Simon Strulovitch, who is an art collector, something of a Shakespearean, a philanthropist, the father of a daughter going off the rails and, to all intents and purposes, a widower (his wife is just not available to him and very ill and not there to talk to). And in that way, he met most of the things that interested me in Shylock, the being a widower, the bringing up of a daughter, a father bringing up a daughter all on his own. I very quickly discovered that he was no adequate equivalent to Shylock because there isn't an equivalent to Shylock. Shylock is too towering a figure. So I had to do Shylock. How do you bring back Shylock? I didn't want to do anything fancy, I don't do magic realism, I just wanted him to be there – no questions asked. He's just there. And the place where it seemed to me he would most appropriately appear, to my imagination anyway, was a cemetery. So the novel begins with Strulovitch attending a grave, his mother's grave, which he hasn't attended very conscientiously, and seeing somebody else talking to a grave. He knows at once that the person he is talking to is Shylock. And why wouldn't he be there? Well, he's always been there.

AP: You could perhaps have called the novel *Shylock's Ghost*, had you not decided to use it as the title for a BBC documentary instead. Let's try and keep *Hamlet* at bay for the moment. There is more than a touch of *Hamlet* floating around in the novel. At one point Strulovitch hears, who knows from where, the word 'Swear', over his daughter's birth, an echo of Hamlet hearing the ghost of his father, and that's not the only such thing. So, *Shylock's Ghost* – did you consider other possible titles?

HJ: My first title was *A Wilderness of Monkeys*, which as you remember is from Shylock's comments when he discovers that Jessica has run off, stolen his ducats, even gone back to get some more. And

---

Wednesday 3 August 2016, The Royal Shakespeare Theatre, World Shakespeare Congress, Stratford-upon-Avon.

a turquoise ring. Now he hears that she's sold the ring to buy a monkey. And he says 'I would not have given it for a wilderness of monkeys.' I wanted *A Wilderness of Monkeys*, but my publishers would not have it, I think because they thought it would end up in the natural history section of a bookshop, along with *Zoo Time*, my earlier novel. So, I wanted something that Shylock had said, and Shylock does say, 'Shylock is my name.' When Portia asks 'Which is the merchant here, and which the Jew?' he responds: 'Shylock is my name.' It's an assertion of his name; he isn't just a Jew.

As for 'Swear', I'm glad you mentioned that because I've been thinking about what that 'swear' is doing. This book is very much about the obligations that parents and children bear to one another, and the 'swear' thing is that sacred obligation to avenge your father. Shylock and Hamlet are both avengers: Hamlet is a reluctant avenger, Shylock is a failed avenger. Shylock wants to avenge and doesn't succeed; Hamlet doesn't want to avenge and succeeds.

AP: And yet in your novel the 'old mole', to which you also allude at one point, is in fact Leah, the dead wife and mother rather than the father figure.

HJ: Yes. I think the minute I knew Shylock had to be there, it suddenly became a subterranean novel. There's much of the past, there's much to excavate. So I came up with the idea that Shylock would talk to his wife and that his wife would be forever. That's how he's seen in the opening of the novel: the person in the grave he's addressing is Leah. She's mentioned only once in Shakespeare's play, but mentioned with such force, it seems to me, that I felt entitled to suppose that he adored his wife and misses her, and would want to talk to her. He's a very lonely man in the play, and I wanted to make more of his loneliness. As for her being underneath the ground, I felt many Wordsworthian impulses when writing this, as well as Shakespearean. And I like the idea of Leah being there, rolled round in Earth's diurnal course with rocks and stones and trees. So when he's asked 'Well where is Leah?', she's everywhere. And he talks to her throughout the novel, reads to her – even reads *Portnoy's Complaint* to her.

AP: And surprisingly they chuckle together.

HJ: Yes, they laugh together. I wanted to restore Shylock's sense of humour. It is there in the play, but it's often missed in productions. I would like *more* of it in the play. I'm not such a fool as to suppose I can improve on Shakespeare, but I know a little bit more than Shakespeare did about Jews. It's the only thing I've got over Shakespeare: Jews. And he seems to think that Jews talk about the Old Testament all the time. They do some of the time but not *all* the time.

AP: We'll come back to daughters in due course and in a moment or two I'm going to ask you to read a passage from the novel in which we will hear the Wordsworthian echo you've mentioned. But before we do that, a moment longer on the basic moves you've made here. Would you accept the suggestion that one of the things that attracts novelists to Shakespeare is the sense of inadequate justice having been done to minor characters, to women, to scapegoats? And that one of the opportunities and provocations for a novelist is precisely to do more justice to characters who have been given no voice or not enough voice or actually the wrong words? I'm thinking of a critical moment both in the play and in your novel when a very famous speech is taken away from Shakespeare's character. You see how I'm concealing exactly whom.

HJ: They're guessing, they're very smart.

AP: Yes, and anyway they've read it already. But back to the question: would that be a fair description of what you thought of yourself and other novelists doing, in the cause of redistributing justice?

HJ: I'm not sure that I would have the nerve to think that I could add to Shakespeare in any way or do justice to anything that I feel that Shakespeare has not done justice to.

AP: Is that a kind of diffidence trope you're wheeling out?

HJ: No, it's a natural, it's a true born diffidence. I am diffident. And certainly I'm diffident when it comes to Shakespeare; if you can't be diffident when it comes to Shakespeare, you're in trouble. What I feel, rather, is that the play continues in one's imagination, that the people are so intensely there for you when you're watching the play or when you're reading it, or even more than that for me, long, long afterwards when you're thinking about things. And once you've read Shakespeare, he's in your mind all the time. I'm not saying you think Shakespeareanly, but the world is another world because he wrote of it, so you want to go on peopling your world with his characters.

For example, I always fancied doing Malvolio's revenge. It's the only time I thought of doing a novel about Shakespeare – it wasn't *my* idea to do this one. There's something about Malvolio going offstage saying 'I'll be revenged on the whole pack of you' that really got me going. I never did it because I thought it would be the most acrid, bitter, savage novel that anybody's ever written and that I was altogether too wedded personally to the idea of revenge. I have so many people on whom to avenge myself. I have so many causes that I thought I'd better stay away from it. But, of course, I do give Shylock the opportunity in this novel to wish he'd said that.

AP: But you also give Malvolio's line to your Jessica figure, Strulovitch's daughter Beatrice, at the end of the novel, the very last line. Or to be more exact you get Strulovitch to imagine or anticipate her saying this. He sees or thinks he sees the resemblance between her and Shylock, 'her stony unforgivingness'. It's as if he wants to attribute to her his own thwarted rage, wants her to take it on for him. Let me read the two final lines. The punctuation seems important: the paragraph break, the absence of speech marks.

> Were he to ask her what she was thinking he had little doubt how she would answer.
> I will be revenged on the whole pack of you.

HJ: Yes, I cannot tell you why I did that. I had no intention of doing that. These things just happen; the novel was ending, and I suddenly heard Jessica, my Jessica, say that. She is actually a much more admirable figure than Shakespeare's Jessica. I'm not improving on Shakespeare's Jessica. I just think Shakespeare's done so well at creating an ingrate of a daughter that why bother to do another one? So I thought it would be interesting to see that relationship, to re-imagine it intensely on the father's behalf, but also on the daughter's. I cannot bear Shakespeare's Jessica saying 'this house is hell'. I cannot bear Jessica, Shakespeare does not allow me to bear Jessica, she is one of the most horrible characters he ever created. I don't normally like talking about whether people are nice or horrible, but it just happens that she is a particularly horrible girl. And I did want to write about a girl who would have a father like that, who would drive her father around the bend with her waywardness.

I've never brought a daughter up. I've never had a daughter. But I watched my father having trouble with my sister, and the whole family shuddered for a few years because it was so intense. And I bled for them both. I know how awful it is. And I wanted to write about this, how awful it is. A child is born to you, and it's a precious thing, and you love it, and you imagine what its future might be, and if it's a girl, you'll hope that she'll be intelligent and bright and indomitable and fierce and lovely to your eye, and one day she walks in with Lorenzo. The agony of that. You have to do justice to the agony of that. But on the other hand, you have to imagine what it's like to be the girl who brings someone who doesn't look like Lorenzo to her; he looks like Hamlet, Coriolanus even. And how painful it is to her to have a father who won't leave her alone. I have brought comedy into this novel because Strulovitch chases his daughter Beatrice – my Jessica – all over England. He chases after her, beats up the lovers she's with, and gives her a hard time of it. She's had a hard time. It's not just Jews, of course; it's the children of any minority, they are hard-pressed because their parents are so anxious about their defections.

AP: Let's hear from the novel itself now. A passage which, by pre-agreement – let us not conceal the artifice – we have chosen. One that

I think is particularly interesting. It makes me think of that great phrase of Shakespeare's (from *Romeo and Juliet*) 'ancient grudge', though I'm not sure if it actually features in this . . .

HJ: No, you've certainly got me worried, but put it in.

AP: No matter. I've found it on an earlier page (p. 124). But over to you for this passage (it begins on p. 194). Perhaps you'd like to set it up by explaining a bit more about the relations between Strulovitch and Shylock – and Leah.

HJ: Strulovitch and Shylock talk and talk and talk. That's the centre of the novel and readers seem to think these are the best parts, when Shylock and Strulovitch are just talking – about everything: being men, being Jewish, everything. But Shylock also talks to Leah, his wife. He is anxious about the fact that his presence is prompting Strulovitch to have vengeful thoughts and he isn't sure whether to encourage these or not. Look at him now, Shylock says to Leah, as Strulovitch paces the floor plotting the revenge he won't in the end have the courage to carry out.

'The man lacks resolution, Leah. Tell me what I should do – spur him on or let him be?'

He waited for her to tell him what she thought. They spoke so often for so long when she was alive. They spoke and spoke. When she was no longer there to speak to him, it was as though a cord connecting him to life was severed. He would go to the synagogue to speak to other men but their company could not replace hers. Theirs had not been a synagogue marriage. They spoke ideas, not faith. Leah had never been circumscribed by convention or tradition. She was like a fountain of clear, fresh thought. So when she went, his throat dried and his mind atrophied. He didn't want to see anything, because where was the value of sight if what he saw he could not share with her? He closed his ears to music. He stopped reading until he began to read to her again at her graveside. He saw no point in activity, and would sit for hours, thinking nothing, in a vacancy that was nearer to non-existence than sorrow. What had his life been to him before Leah? He couldn't remember. There was no before Leah. That his house became a hell for his daughter, who couldn't rouse him or interest him in her life, he accepted. Leah's death made him a bad father. Or, if he'd been a bad father before – a man who lived only for the love he bore his wife – the death of that too-loved wife made him a worse one. Poor, poor Jessica then, doubly deprived. No wonder. No excuse, but no wonder. And when he did rediscover some of his old energy it hadn't been out of any renewed concern for her well-being. He wished he could have lied to himself. And to her. *I lived again for you, Jessica, I remembered what I owed you.* But the truth of it was different. It had been the Gentiles who had pricked him back into animation. In their contempt he found the twisted stimulus to live again.

It is rage not love that propels a man to action.

When he looked up he saw Strulovitch occupying his own patch of garden, walking to and fro, a man without a wife to talk to, lost in reflection, moving his lips soundlessly.

He had no trouble reading what Strulovitch was saying. 'I will do such things . . .'

He was sympathetic to the frustration. He too would once have done *such things*.

What they are, yet I know not . . .

But at least Strulovitch had what was still to come to look forward to. What things they were, yet he knew not. Whereas Shylock was busted. What he'd done he'd done, and what he had yet to do, he never would do now.

I miss the future, Shylock thought.

'So tell me,' he again asked Leah. 'Do I restrain him or whip him up into the vengeful rage he's been longing for all his life?'

The cold earth in which Leah was rolled around gave its deepest moan.

'Very well then,' Shylock said. 'In this, as in everything else, I will be guided by you.'

AP: It is a wonderfully rich passage, Howard. I don't know if this is an important thing or important to you, but I can't help hearing in that penultimate sentence, not only Wordsworth but Emily Brontë – 'cold in the earth' – and with 'rolled around' and 'deepest moan' – this has a distinctly literary feel to it. I wondered why literariness or the conscious invocation of literariness at this particular moment?

HJ: It's not conscious; it's just what's in my head. Those are the things in my head. I was a morbid boy. The books that I read when I was a teenager, I liked it if there was death in them. The operas I liked going to particularly were operas in which

SHAKESPEARE AND THE NOVEL: A CONVERSATION

a woman had died and a man wept – Puccini. I played Puccini in my room when I was thirteen years old, played records of men sobbing. I would sob along with them. I grieved over all these courtesans and prostitutes before I knew what courtesans and prostitutes were. I was missing women; I read novels by women, so I read *Jane Eyre*, I read the Brontës, I read *The Mill on the Floss*. I was sorry for myself, sorry for all these lonely girls I read about. Jane Eyre made a big impression on me, more than Oliver Twist. I can't explain that. I was morbid. My parents were very anxious about this and my father felt that I should have been taken to a psychologist or something because I wasn't listening to Bill Haley or anything. You want to stop me, you want to hear more about my morbidity. I'm in flow.

AP: You warned me about the flow. So I want to pick you up on the pity and self-pity which you've just alluded to. That's actually a very important theme in this novel, particularly in the part of it you've described as broad comedy, yet the equivalent of Shakespeare's Antonio, your character D'Anton, you seem to take more seriously than most of the other occupants of that world. And actually to be rather interested in what makes this melancholy in Shakespeare or the equivalent in your novel. Why? Why does Antonio interest you?

HJ: Why does Antonio interest me? Because of his aesthetic distaste for the Jew. And that interests me because I felt rightly or wrongly that I was the object of such aesthetic distaste when I was a young man at Cambridge. I felt that I was taught by quite a lot of D'Antons. They were usually – my apologies if any of you taught me, no you're too young, but your grandparents might have – but particularly medievalists. They did look at me in a particular way. Now you never know about this, do you. Is it your own paranoia? Every Jew will come to wonder at some point whether the anti-semitism of which he feels he is the object is his own. And I don't know whether this monstrous person that I saw reflected back to me in the eyes of these medievalists was a real picture of me or what I fear I might have looked like. So I've written about this before and Antonio was a good opportunity for it. It is interesting to me that he's almost attractive at the beginning of the play when he talks about his weariness. 'I'm so sad, it wearies me', and then there's that nice, 'It wearies me; I see it wearies you', and then they all indulge in what we used to call 'over-collaboration'. They over-collaborate, it seems to me, Antonio's friends, in his sadness. But it denotes a degree of refined feelings. This is a bunch of people who at times would offer themselves as refined: they speak poetically to one another, about love and so on, until they see Shylock. Then the minute they see Shylock they just become thugs – this finely attuned Antonio, so exquisitely in love with Bassanio, can think of nothing to do when he sees Shylock except spit on him.

AP: I'm tempted to ask if you think that Leavisites ever 'over-collaborated', but I won't. Instead, I want to quote something from near the end of James Shapiro's book, *Shakespeare and the Jews*, about *The Merchant of Venice*. A passage which raises a number of issues with which your novel engages. Shapiro is reflecting here on the tenacity of 'irrational and exclusionary attitudes'. He suggests that:

much of the play's vitality can be attributed to the ways in which it scrapes against a bedrock of beliefs about the racial, national, sexual and religious differences of others ... these darker impulses remain so elusive, so hard to identify in the normal course of things, that only in instances like productions of this play do we get to glimpse these cultural fault-lines. This is why censoring the play is *always* more dangerous than staging it.

This seems to me wonderfully rich and suggestive.

HJ: I'm going to steal one of Shapiro's jokes. He once told me that he had a Jewish uncle in New York who said 'I'm really proud of you for writing *Shakespeare and the Jews*, but couldn't you have called it *The Jews and Shakespeare*?' Such a good joke he won't mind my stealing it. Sorry, we're on more serious business.

AP: I shall be undeflected. I want to ask you two questions. One is whether you agree that censoring the play is always more dangerous than staging it. I'm partially asking that to press you once more when you say you're not improving on Shakespeare, you're not competing with him. What do you feel about censoring the play? Let me ask you that first.

HJ: Well, I don't approve of censoring anything. I think 'anything' has to be out there and we have to deal with it. I'm against all shrinking from anything really, so the whole business of 'that's hurting somebody's feelings' or 'that's dangerous' or so on — we must have trigger warnings and safe spaces — that's all the biggest load of nonsense. Let the world be. I love reading Céline, Louis-Ferdinand Céline: a Nazi, a Fascist, a misogynist, a swine, a complete swine. That doesn't stop him from being a great writer, and often you are not aware of those things within the writer, they are outside. But even if you were aware of those things within the writer, you deal with it. That's part of the challenge. So I agree with what he says and the challenge is good for you. It is good as a reader to be offended. You don't just want to read to recognize yourself, that can be a nice thing, or to encounter sentiments with which you feel sympathy, which is also a nice thing. It is very good for a reader to encounter sentiments with which you feel no sympathy whatsoever. That is part of the reading or the watching experience, that's good.

The problem I have when it's applied to this play is that I wouldn't know what you would want to censor. I do not think *The Merchant of Venice* is an anti-Semitic play. I think James Shapiro thinks the play is more anti-semitically problematic than I do. To me, it's inconceivable that Shakespeare would be an anti-Semite. It's just not possible. Shakespeare could not entertain any prejudice of that kind because of the size of his mind, the natural impulse of his mind. He is drawn towards those who fill others with horror and create bigotry and antagonism in others — he always is. And he goes to find the human in the object of other's people's disdain. And he does that with Shylock; he doesn't save Shylock from the anti-Semitism of others by giving us a philo-Semitic discourse. He might not have a philo-Semitic discourse. He might not have anything nice to say about Jews as a people or Judaism as a religion. He might not know very much or care very much. There aren't any signs he knows very much about it, actually, but what he does do, is he finds the man. This is the man and he renders him as a man capable of the deepest feelings in a play in which people treat rings as though they are just trivial objects to toss around. Who cares about the ring? Shylock. 'It was my turquoise. I had it of Leah when I was a bachelor. I would not have given it for a wilderness of monkeys.' This is somebody with whom these things count, so we feel the man, we feel the weight of the man, and once you feel the weight of a person, you cannot feel any kind of bigotry towards them, it's impossible. You cannot feel anti-Semitic towards a man or woman once you feel the man-ness and woman-ness of them.

AP: So what you have just done is centred the play not just around Shylock but around that moment. That's not a complaint, it's an observation that leads me on to my next question, which is this. When James Shapiro says 'Only in instances, like productions of this play, do we get to glimpse these cultural fault-lines', it seems to me that this is what the novelist can do, and that you have done it. It's not just a *glimpse* of cultural fault-lines but actually a matter of exposing them, of bringing into view things that a drama — the two hours' passage of the stage — cannot do as fully as the novel can. So let's hear it for the novel, I'm encouraging you to say.

HJ: Let's hear it for the novel, sir? Do I get an A+? At last a Cambridge academic not looking at me in that way.

AP: Oh, compliments will get you nowhere.

HJ: Yes, let's hear it for the novel, of course. At no point did I suppose that I could add to Shakespeare's play. But what the novel does — I mean, this novel — has to take into account the passage of time between the writing of that drama and now. And the passage of time is also a history of Shylock, a history of our Shylock, of how Shylock has been conceived. And somehow or other I had to find a way in which Shylock is dealing with the way in which he's been conceived without turning this into an essay. There's an impulse in me, as a novelist, to be an essayist. I quite like discourse in a novel. We're always told in creative writing classes 'show don't tell', very good, very true, but telling can be fantastic. George Eliot wants to tell me: she can tell me, and I will sit and listen. She can sermonize for hours on end, I will listen. A good teller is worth reading and I like to think that I can be a good teller. I certainly aspire to be a good teller. So I wasn't too frightened of that. But I also wanted to keep the thing itself. This is a play, a flesh-and-blood play, and this had to be flesh and blood. But the story of Shylock as a flesh-and-blood figure is the story of how Shylock has been read, understood, misunderstood, misconceived over 400 years, and somehow or other, the words he says have to deal with that. And so far as my novel is an angry novel, and it is at times an angry novel, it is certainly never, ever angry with Shakespeare. It is angry with the way this play has been read. I mean, the way this play has been read is shameful. It's been read so badly.

AP: So you have chosen an interesting variation on two more traditional strategies for re-writing Shakespeare. One involves a complete transposition of the core Shakespearean narrative into the present – the strategy adopted by Jane Smiley with *King Lear* in *A Thousand Acres*, or indeed your companions in this new Hogarth venture, Jeanette Winterson's cover version of *The Winter's Tale* in *The Gap of Time*, and Anne Tyler's of *The Taming of the Shrew* in *Vinegar Girl*. Another is to create a prequel or backstory, as Mary Cowden Clarke did in Victorian times with *The Girlhood of Shakespeare's Heroines*, or more recently, and brilliantly, John Updike with *Gertrude and Claudius*. We can't or at least we shouldn't speak of comparison with the Shakespearean 'original' because of course Shakespeare himself was re-writing all kinds of previous tellings, of the *Romeo and Juliet* story, of *Julius Caesar* and so on. It's just that his are the versions 'everyone knows', no matter how hard historians try to set the record straight about poor Richard III or fortunate Henry V. My point is that the comparisons that novelists invite with their Shakespearean source tend to remain implicit, whereas you have made yours absolutely explicit. This confrontation between the here and now and the there and then is your novel's very subject. And I wonder if there isn't something about *The Merchant of Venice* that may require this in a way that other Shakespearean core narratives don't.

HJ: I don't know whether that's true of this play but I can't imagine ever doing it any other way. I do play the 'equivalence' game, and I grew tired of it. Lots of them slipped away in the novel and there are a few things I regret a bit – they are the equivalences still hanging on. I didn't find that a very challenging exercise, a truly challenging exercise. You think a lot 'oh what am I gonna do', you know, 'I'll set it in Little Venice in London', ain't that smart for God's sake. And then I came up with an idea. Sometimes when I read it out people laugh, but in my heart I'm not sure. It's the casket scene. I've always thought it tedious nonsense since any man with a brain in his head would know that if this is a test of your mettle then of course you choose the lead! Only a schmuck would choose the gold. So I transposed that. My Portia goes to a wife-swapping club and throws three keys onto the carpet. She has three cars outside, one of the keys being hers – a Porsche. I felt like I owed it to the idea of having fun doing it.

But that was not where the life of writing this book was for me. I'm not even sure that the life of writing this book for me was in making it now. I'm not sure that I'm not just as happy imagining the mind of Shylock. Then or now. The Shylock in my novel, is it the Shylock then or is it the Shylock now? I don't think I know the difference. It might be Shylock then. I mean, out of space, out of time, just the man – I know you can't do that – but nonetheless the joy of writing it for me was just getting the man who speaks those words, re-thinking those words, those questions that Strulovitch asks him. Because here was the joy of keeping Strulovitch and other equivalents that I didn't get rid of. Strulovitch can ask Shylock some of those questions you want to ask him. Did you mean it? This merry jest? Did you mean it? How merry was it? Where you really joking? How disappointed were you or rather how pleased were you when the opportunity came for you to claim this pound of flesh? How did it get from being whatever part of your fair person that pleases me (which is a very flirtatious thing he says to Antonio), how did it get to be the heart? Would you have killed him? We often see the knife touching the flesh in the theatre – I saw it the other day. But would you have done it? Central to the Jewish imagination is the story of Abraham and Isaac. When God tells Abraham he has to sacrifice his beloved son to show how much he loves God, and he's ready to do it. And God stays his hand at the final hour. Terrific. He's let off. He pleases God and the son is spared. But would he have done it? And there are pages in this novel in which Shylock thinks whether he would have done it, wishes he could have done it.

AP: Can we just pick out the merriment and the merry jest? Perhaps this is the point to bring Hamlet in, the Hamlet who has been lurking in the background. *Hamlet* would have been your first choice, had you had a free hand?

HJ: Well, it's always been my favourite play of Shakespeare, my favourite work of literature, yes.

AP: And you're not alone in that Hamlet is *the* Shakespearean character above all that novelists have been most inspired by and taken most from. So would you like to say a bit more about that and perhaps tie in the merriment. An interesting word, 'merry', isn't it?

HJ: Yes, he uses it twice. 'Merry bond', 'merry jest'.

AP: And 'I am never merry when I hear sweet music', says Jessica.

HJ: Chip off the old block after all.

AP: Is that what that's all about?

HJ: I don't know, I never know quite how to read that.

AP: And that whole passage in Act 5, between Jessica and Lorenzo, in Belmont – can we just pause for a moment on it? I'm interested in the things you lose from the play, more or less willingly, the more tedious bits with Lancelot Gobbo and so on. But there is also the poetry, some of it really memorable, as in this passage about moonlight and music and myth. Were you ever troubled by that, the difficulty or the challenge of ignoring that?

HJ: No, I like it when I'm at the theatre and they have that interval after Shylock's gone and I can leave. I don't see the point in staying for Act V. I think it was Mercutio of whom it's been said that Shakespeare needed to get rid of him or he'd take over the play. I think this play is about Shylock. It's called *The Merchant of Venice* but Antonio is of slender interest compared to Shylock. Shylock is not in danger of taking over the play; Shylock *has* taken over the play. By the time Shylock's gone, there is no play. And so why hang around? It looks as though Shakespeare wrote it in about three minutes. I know our default position is that Shakespeare is never wrong and I hold to that. Everything that Shakespeare did, he knew what he was doing in the way that an artist does, not that he knew in advance. He created with an assurance and a certainty that seems incomparable in art. So he's never wrong.

AP: Let's come back to *Hamlet*. There's something that Henry James says, in one of his prefaces, when he thinks of 'the prodigious consciousness of Hamlet, the most capacious and most crowded, the moral presence the most asserted, in the whole range of fiction'. James is meditating on the difference between the drama and the novel, and the fact that Hamlet doesn't have the play to himself. No play can have 'a *usurping* consciousness', says James, in the way that a novel can. In a drama it's guaranteed that even Hamlet doesn't have the play to himself. Would you agree with that?

HJ: Yes, he does have a lot of the play, but I love the moment where Hamlet thinks he should kill Claudius and yet Claudius is in prayer, so he decides not. Then he makes that speech that appals Dr Johnson because he says he wants to kill Claudius when he is full of sin so he will go to hell, which seems to me like a fair thing to feel. But what's wonderful to me at that moment is that it's Claudius who is theologically subtle. Claudius knows he can't pray because he is enjoying too much the fruits of his sin. He can't pray and still want to keep his wife, the crown, and so on. And Hamlet hasn't got a clue that that is what's going on. He thinks he's praying and so that is one–nil to Claudius. And then there's Horatio. Often one feels that Horatio is the more distinguished of the two. Hamlet can patronize him appallingly, like when he describes Horatio 'as one in suffering all that suffers nothing', which is really like saying I wish I wasn't as sensitive as I am. And in my favourite graveyard scene, the greatest scene in all literature, you have to take Horatio on board when he says ''Twere to consider too *curiously*, to consider so.' Although, you know, all sympathies in the end are with Hamlet.

AP: All of them?

HJ: All of my sympathies with Hamlet, but I'm listening to Horatio. I'm wondering whether I ought not listen to Horatio more.

AP: This might be the moment for us to pause and throw things open. We have time for some questions.

QUESTIONER 1: I loved your novel very much; it spoke to me in many ways, particularly Strulovitch and his struggle with his faith or religion or whatever you want to call it. I noticed you used the word 'covenant' about three times. It was always sort of at the end of passages, and it is the word Strulovitch struggles to remember. It remains quite a mystery. I was wondering whether you thought about that word in relation to the play?

HJ: Yes, I thought about that word; it is one of those words that crop up when you are thinking about fathers and their parents and their children. It crops up in this novel when Strulovitch, to his own astonishment, is deeply moved by the sight of the newborn baby, and feels that she is born for some reason. He feels that his daughter . . . It's one of those Lawrencian themes now – we are out of Shakespeare at this point. He looks to his daughter and feels she does not belong to herself; that doesn't mean that she belongs to him, but that she is born for some reason. And he finds himself thinking 'Is it some Jewish thing?' And this becomes important when later on he is to worry that she is going out with boys who aren't Jewish. And this is important because there is a lot of stuff . . . we haven't talked about circumcision in this novel but we won't get on to that.

AP: Oh, what a shame.

HJ: There you go again. But you can't deal with the pound of flesh without somewhere or other putting your mind to the medieval fear of Jews wanting to kill Gentiles and Gentiles' children for their blood because they had lost blood themselves. They had done this thing called circumcision, which the medieval imagination did not properly understand and thought was a sort of castration. I'm not saying that is in the play, but it is the baggage behind the play. Circumcision is of course the covenant that every Jewish boy has with God and that is how the covenant is sealed. So I was thinking about how Strulovitch feels it in relation to his daughter. It's an interesting word, 'covenant', a way of thinking about an obligation, an obligation beyond yourself to something bigger than yourself that is part religious and part not – and is mysterious, really.

AP: It is a problem though, isn't it, that 'covenant' is not a word that his daughter will understand?

HJ: Why is that a problem?

AP: Well it's a problem for him and between them. Again this is not a complaint, I think this is one of the best things in the novel, precisely these obstacles between the father and the daughter and the language which they don't share. He is very scornful of her performance art degree at some nowhere college. He's very scornful of a lot of things about her. You are much more generous to her than you are to Shakespeare's Jessica. But it still is a difficulty, an interesting difficulty for the reader as well. That covenant is, as you say, Lawrencian. But young readers of Lawrence, if there are any these days, won't understand the meaning of the word easily.

HJ: I wouldn't have understood the word 'covenant', or the meaning of covenant, when I was a teenager. But then you don't understand anything at that point. You don't understand the word or the concept when you most need them. Here is the tragedy of being young.

AP: And is that why you give Beatrice – your Jessica – the line from Shakespeare at the end? You say you don't know why you give it to her, but isn't it because she hasn't actually got a language of her own yet?

HJ: Well that is a fantastic way of putting it. I mean I can't claim it but I like that idea. And it might be because I feel a kind of guilt, actually, that I too have been involved in punishing her, the young girl. I mean it's not just that the young don't understand covenant, but it's such a burden – the idea that at fourteen or fifteen you're carrying some responsibility for the concept of a covenant that's understood by your parents. As if it's not hard enough already being fourteen.

QUESTIONER 2: I was wondering, did you learn anything about Shakespeare, or otherwise, from Wilbur Sanders?

HJ: An immense amount. Wilbur Sanders was a fellow at Selwyn College and a Cambridge lecturer, he was a New Zealander, he was somebody I met when I had my first job at Sydney University. He was there and we talked together and we brawled together, and then we talked together at Selwyn College some years later. Yes, probably everything. I think maybe he even taught me how to read Shakespeare, but we discussed everything together. Don't ask me to enumerate things because I wouldn't know. I dedicated my novel to Wilbur, who is no longer alive, and I miss him, and I would have loved to be able to talk to him about this play. But as I say in the dedication, the mystery is we never, ever, ever talked about this play together. We talked about *Hamlet* and *Macbeth*. We liked talking together about soliloquies, and I realized that we liked those plays which had soliloquies in them. And if only Shylock had entered Shakespeare's mind five or six years later, he'd have had soliloquies. It was Shylock's bad luck to have entered Shakespeare's mind too early.

QUESTIONER 3: What was the fundamental difference for you between consciously adapting something for this series, and the unconscious appropriation of Shakespeare in your other work, by way of allusion and reference and echo?

HJ: That's a very searching question, and it's hard to answer anything that involves the idea of consciousness. For obvious reasons. I don't know. I think I probably enjoyed writing *Shylock* more than I've enjoyed writing anything. But I enjoyed it most once I decided my responsibility to update something had gone. I enjoyed it when I suddenly could feel, well, I've taken in as much as my limited abilities enable me to take in of this character, of what Shakespeare is doing here, and now I can think it through. So it was like an escape from it. But I can't make that comparison, it's just too difficult. Certainly I would say if you are offered the opportunity to write a novel or some other form of Shakespeare work, take it, because it's so fantastic having that beneath you, such riches beneath you, because every time you're a bit stuck in a novel – you can spend weeks wondering 'where am I going to go now?' – all you do when you're writing a book that's based on Shakespeare's play is reach down and there's a phrase, a line, a speech, a thought, and you're off again. You can't actually go wrong.

AP: A footnote to that might be that every time Shakespeare is invoked by a novelist, there is some kind of rub, or scrape, to use a metaphor suggested by the passage I quoted from Shapiro, a friction between the here and now of writing and the past, even if it's just in the most casual or unconscious word. And of course Shakespeare has infiltrated the collective unconscious of the English language in the sense that we don't always know when we're using, re-using words and phrases on which Shakespeare once put his stamp, or may even have coined.

HJ: Yes, and could I just say one other thing? That if you've got Shakespeare working away, wherever – underneath, or around, or on top of you – you are as close to the source of whatever we mean by creativity as you can be, because it's so much the quality of Shakespeare's plays that, when those characters speak, they are inventing themselves. When the best of Shakespeare's characters speak, they are inventing the language in which

SHAKESPEARE AND THE NOVEL: A CONVERSATION

they are thinking. When Macbeth speaks about pity or something like that, it's not like when Portia speaks. When Portia speaks about pity and mercy, you just feel that it's a sermon – she is giving a Sunday school sermon. And that is how you know that she is not one of Shakespeare's interesting characters. When Macbeth talks about pity, you feel he has to find the language again. I have to find the language again for what it is that I mean – there's no meaning outside that I can find the right word for. Until you create the language, you don't know what you mean and when you're in touch with that, you just feel you're in touch with – it's a grand way of putting it – but kind of chthonic forces of thought and language themselves. I love the word 'chthonic'. But only because I don't know how to say it.

AP: There's a slightly obscene phrase in the novel. Let's share it with you all now: 'chthonic arsehole'.

HJ: Yes, that's one of Strulovitch's phrases for one of his daughter's boyfriends.

AP: Yes, and it's a very good touch that she admires her father for it. She says, 'I don't know any other dad who could come up with a phrase like that.'

HJ: Even if your father is beating up your boyfriend, the fact that he calls him a 'chthonic arsehole' – if you're any kind of daughter at all, you'll have a kind of daughterly pride.

AP: A great moment to close on. Thank you so much.

'MUSIC STILL': UNDERSTANDING AND RECONSTRUCTING SHAKESPEARE'S USE OF MUSICAL UNDERSCORE

CLAIRE VAN KAMPEN

'**music**, *n.* and *adj.* . . . ancient Greek μουσική art presided over by the Muses' *(OED)*

'**still**, *adv.* 3.a Without change, interruption, or cessation; continually, constantly' *(OED)*

Underscoring Shakespeare's text with music and sound (soundscape, sound effects, recordings of wind and rain, etc.) is a natural and accepted convention of our age, a kind of hybrid form, a mix of film and theatre, where lighting, too, can enhance and describe 'mood' and both sound and theatrical lighting vocabulary can direct the focus and emotional journey of the audience. Contemporary theatres are built without a 'pit' or a music gallery where a band would play, and where music would be visible, in sharp contrast to an Elizabethan Playhouse, where music was placed centrally, often visually and always acoustically, over or on the stage.

There are exceptions to our modern rule: the National Theatre sometimes employs the use of the 'ashtrays', the stepped balconies on the side of the Olivier auditorium, where small groups of musicians can be seen to play – though they are always playing through microphones – and in 1987 I conducted a small group of players in the NT's proscenium theatre, the Lyttleton, where we played in front of the stage, in a hydraulically raised pit. This feature of the Lyttleton Theatre is rarely used.

The Royal Shakespeare Company played at the Barbican Theatre (part of the Barbican Centre, opened in 1982) until 2001. This purpose-built theatre for Shakespeare has all the hallmarks of a modern theatre: car parks, accessibility, comfortable, wide auditorium, good seats with plenty of leg room. The auditorium is controlled: as the play is to start, a door at the end of each aisle closes automatically. House lights dim. Lights come up on stage. There is no visible band but music is heard through speakers. There is actually a live band playing some floors further down; the musical director in the studio is watching the stage action through a monitor, and music is cued by the deputy stage manager (DSM) via a headset. Effectively the DSM controls the show, and often cues actors' entrances too, using red and green lights positioned at the stage entrances from the wings or from other positions backstage.

When I took up residence as composer and director of theatre music at Shakespeare's Globe in 1997, it was not the scholarship of how Shakespeare may have used music or what he may have seen and heard which so entirely changed my approach to composing and arranging music for Shakespeare productions. It was, in fact, working within the unique architecture of Shakespeare's Globe theatre, the Wooden O, which demanded further inquiry – and understanding – of the function of music within the plays.

In Shakespeare's outdoor playhouses, the music as an entity carries a strong iconographic statement. Played from the music gallery, it is architecturally balanced between heavenly and earthly worlds and it expresses the influence of the Muses, therefore consolidating the 'great Globe itself' as a stylized and microcosmic representation of the Elizabethan

SHAKESPEARE'S USE OF MUSICAL UNDERSCORE

worldview. By this practical and incontrovertible fact of the placement of 'the music' in the playhouse, Shakespeare as a writer is always responding to music not as a subservient texture but as a potent force, an entity for change, an etheric protagonist in his drama.

Music therefore can operate with different functions: it can serve to re-locate characters; it can also 'change gears' textually – a technique found more often now in the stage musical than in new theatre writing; music can warn as with the placement of the 'music of the hautboys ... under the stage', the famous stage direction in *Antony and Cleopatra* (4.3.10), by using a loud instrument (the shawm, ancestor of the modern oboe) placed in the 'infernal' world, that is, the 'hidden' world of the understage. (Interestingly, this 'infernal' world is at the level of the groundlings, who, standing in the pit, look upwards at the painted 'heavens', and thus, in the Elizabethan worldview, are aspiring to betterment by the grace of the heavenly world). Occasionally, music is used, generally as a song, from the 'earthly' world, which of course, is the stage, on which the characters tread their journey through the play. Music played and sung from this world might have the power to summon spirits whose continuing purpose is to haunt their murderer, and who then appear on stage, such as the ghost in *Julius Caesar*:

[*Music, and a song*]
BRUTUS.   This is a sleepy tune. O murd'rous slumber,
    Lay'st thou thy leaden mace upon my boy
    That plays thee music? – Gentle knave, good night.
    I will not do thee so much wrong to wake thee.
    If thou dost nod, thou break'st thy instrument;
    I'll take it from thee, and, good boy, good night.
    Let me see, let me see, is not the leaf turned down
    Where I left reading? Here it is, I think.
[*Enter the Ghost of Caesar*]   (4.2.318–25)

This is in contrast with the 'heavenly music' asked for by Prospero in *The Tempest* (5.1.52), which plays untroubled by earthly cares, and is pure in its melancholy or solemnity as befits the visitation of the Muse:

           ... And when I have required
Some heavenly music – which even now I do –
To work mine end upon their senses that
This airy charm is for, I'll break my staff,
Bury it certain fathoms in the earth,
And deeper than did ever plummet sound
I'll drown my book.
Solemn music.   (5.1.51–7)

Such music is played (usually unseen) from the realm of the music 'room' – on the gallery itself or hidden (certainly in *The Tempest*) by a curtain at that level. In the reconstructed Globe, from proposals by Professor John Orrell and period references, this level is signified by two representations of the nine muses: Melpomene and Thalia, who are placed as 'figureheads' on either side of the music gallery.

The musicians in the Shakespearean Playhouse share this central gallery above the stage with actors, though generally not at the same time. The exception to this is the appearance of kings and princes who might appear with musical or iconographic support. It is, I would conjecture, positive evidence to say that, after hearing the trumpet calls as the First Folio directions specify in *Richard II* – '*Parle without, and answer within: then a flourish. Enter on the walls, Richard, Carlisle, Aumerle, Scroop, Salisbury*' (3.3.60 s.d.) – the king's trumpeter(s) would have appeared on the 'walls', that is, the gallery above the 'base court' of the stage to give full weight to the rightful – and hereditary – power of the king and court. This is 'music' used not in the etheric sense but as the narrative of power and the conduit of the vocabulary of war. For that reason alone, I conjecture that it would have been *seen* as well as *unseen*, that is, '*Parle without*', played outside – on the earthly and 'base' stage by the trumpeter from Bolingbroke's contingent, and '*answer within*' from Richard's trumpeter, hidden behind the *frons scenae* and probably from backstage behind the music gallery, thus still sounding from the 'higher' level of the muses, which is of course iconographically where a king would sit, placed on a level above his earthly subjects.

The reconstruction of Shakespeare's Globe theatre on Bankside has created an approximate rubric that enables us to experiment, endorse, support and discredit academic theory on many playing practices hitherto assumed and built by academia on sources and references. Amongst considerations of staging, clothing, properties and scenery, the practice of period music reconstruction on copies of period instruments and the use of this music in conjunction with Shakespeare's own stage directions has perhaps given us the greatest understanding of the conventions of seventeenth-century playing practices.

In 1997, under the artistic direction of Mark Rylance, we developed a playing style and experiment that he termed 'Original Practices' – now known in common parlance more often as simply 'OP' work. The principles of 'OP' are to mount productions on the Globe stage using clothing, properties, music and musical instruments which would have been known and available to Shakespeare's company in the 1600s.[1] It is also, and perhaps most importantly, founded on playing Shakespeare in 'shared light' (i.e. without the vocabulary of theatrical lighting onstage, dividing the audience from the actors) and 'shared sound', that is, acoustic sound without electronic enhancement for either actors or music. Simple as this may seem, in 1997 such an approach was both a bemusing and a radical one with regards to current professional playing practices of Shakespeare. The Royal Shakespeare Company had made it their signature to present productions, for the most part, which did the exact opposite: modern dress, contemporary and electronically enhanced music and, often, large sets built with a variety of textures – mixtures of wood, metal, etc., depending on the design decisions of director and designer. Above all, conventional stage performances of Shakespeare prior to the Globe reconstruction were theatrically lit, the lighting choices playing a very important part in focusing the narrative of the story of the play, and making fundamental decisions for the audience in terms of which actor or stage area was to be given priority in any given moment.

The Globe reconstruction which Sam Wanamaker championed and eventually built, has, in spite of being an open-air theatre, near-perfect acoustics which are satisfying for both voice and music. Intriguingly, over the twenty years of the building's life, the 'thousand oak trees' from which it is fashioned have seasoned; and the acoustics have changed accordingly – for the better. It leaves one to wonder whether, in fact, the Burbage brothers went to considerable trouble to transport the timbers from The Theater across the river to their Bankside site not only through financial expediency but also because, as violin makers and luthiers know, seasoned wood creates purer and more focused patterns in sound than green wood. For an open air theatre in 1599, set in the middle of the noisy ambient environment of Bankside, with its street cries, herds of cattle on their way to slaughter and the calls of the 'wherrymen', this would have been a primary concern.

The Globe is built as a cylinder or drum lined with lime plaster, its galleries are vertiginous, and the box-like gallery together with the roof over the stage facilitate a focused resonance for the sounds made by both voice-boxes and soundposts. Bruce Smith in his excellent book *The Acoustic World of Early Modern England* (Chicago, 1999) describes the Globe amphitheatre as having more cubic space per capita than any other theatre in England. I would argue that this fact accounts for the success of the specificity and clarity of acoustic work – both vocal and musical – to be experienced uniquely from the Globe stage. This acoustic precision encourages us to believe that Shakespeare's musical stage directions are not general but specific to a point; whereas the stage pillars can

---

[1] See three articles in Christie Carson and Farah Karim-Cooper, eds., *Shakespeare's Globe: A Theatrical Experiment* (Cambridge, 2008): Mark Rylance, 'Research, Materials, Craft: Principles of Performance at Shakespeare's Globe', pp. 103–14; Jenny Tiramani, 'Exploring Early Modern Stage and Costume Design', pp. 57–65; and Claire van Kampen, 'Music and Aural Texture at Shakespeare's Globe', pp. 79–89.

compromise sightlines, the Globe theatre is a perfect environment for listening.

Professor David Lindley makes a very apposite comment about Shakespeare's own dramaturgical convention with regards to the use of music: 'Instrumental music – whatever symbolic weight it might carry – is almost always assumed to be audible to the characters on stage',[2] that is, that the playwright intended such music always to be 'part of the world of the play'. Late twentieth-century playing conventions have created a world in which the audience have become 'emotional voyeurs', party to an emotional discourse beyond the hearing and experience of the narrative according to the actor onstage – or, at least, the actor as storyteller in the world of the play. Sound scores are often cued with lighting changes which decree and decide visual focus, meaning that the audience is on a different journey from the actor in the play, for the audience is being given both an external commentary and an emotional and visual direction by the director. We are made aware of impending dangers, tragedies, ghosts, murderers, not by characters on stage telling us of them but because the musical underscore has told us of their approach. I propose that by giving the audience such a narrative advantage over the actor we are destroying the very relationships for which Shakespeare was writing: the relationship of actor, audience and architecture which, at the Globe, we call 'the three A's'.

'Original Practice' work is fundamentally involved with the interface of these relationships. Without the use of theatre lighting, with no ability to electronically control underscore to levels where we are able to balance voice with sound under speech, we enable an audience to experience the emotional nature of the story as it unfolds to the characters onstage, and we are also free to look at whatever might draw our focus – whether it is the actor speaking or the actor listening.

Furthermore, and this is the crucial realization that the reconstruction of the Globe has given us, the embrace of the amphitheatre, with 850 seated in galleries all around the auditorium and 700 standing in the yard, means that the audience is not only in very close contact with the actor, but they are also visible to the actor and, furthermore, the audience is very aware that not only can they see the actor onstage in shared light but also, crucially, the actor *can see them*. Now, with one man standing on a summer's afternoon, surrounded by a silent crowd, with groundlings hanging at his feet, looking up to the people in the top galleries against a background of clouds and crying 'O, what a rogue and peasant slave am I', now do we understand why the absence of musical underscore and comment is so important: together, we are all underscore, together, we all comment; and this Hamlet soliloquy is frozen music waiting for the hearts of the audience to melt him into action. Instead of staring into a darkened auditorium, blinded by lights and pretending he can see us, the Hamlet on the Globe stage appeals to a thousand faces all looking back at him. Put a device between this actor, Shakespeare's words and the audience and you fracture the relationship as surely as if you had cut it into tiny pieces.

Shakespeare nurtures this relationship. Not only do we empathize with heroes – if you can call Hamlet one – he does it with villains too, so that it is impossible to write off Richard III for example: with his opening monologue he creates a bond with the audience by sharing with them directly the dreadful nature of his physical self, dealt a bad hand at birth. Shakespeare the dramatist knew that in order to take the audience on a journey, they must first enter into a bond of confederacy.

Early modern instruments are limited in their ability to underscore the spoken word, due to the general lack of dynamic range: most period instruments fall into the category of 'loud' or 'soft'. This can be deceptive: one might think that, as recorders, for example, fall into the category of 'soft' instruments, it is possible to speak over them. In fact, this is difficult, for recorders have almost no dynamic range and their sound is gloriously penetrating, even when the instrument has a low tessitura such as the bass recorder, for instance. Two Elizabethan instruments which do have dynamic range are the cornet and the sackbut (the

---

[2] David Lindley, *Shakespeare and Music* (London, 2006), p. 112.

ancestor of the modern trombone). It is indeed *possible* to underscore the human voice with these, as their tone and dynamic range can be modulated. It is interesting, however, that Shakespeare does not specify these instruments to do so, and, what is more, he specifies, in stage directions, cornet 'flourishes', loud fanfare announcements, in *All's Well that Ends Well* (1.2.0, 2.1.0), *Coriolanus* (1.10.0, 1.11.0, 2.1.201, 2.2.155, 3.1.0) and *Merchant of Venice* (2.1.0, 2.1.46, 2.7.0, 2.9.3). Sometimes cornets are linked with trumpets, as in *Henry VIII*: '*Trumpets, sennet, and cornets*' (2.4.0). Once they are mentioned within the text, when Richard, Duke of York, wishes 'O God, that Somerset, who in proud heart / Doth stop my cornets, were in Talbot's place!' (*Henry VI Part 1*, 4.3.24–5).

It is a widely held belief that cornets replaced trumpets as an 'announcing' instrument (for surgés, sennets, tuckets and fanfares) in the indoor playhouses, as trumpets were deemed to be too loud. *Henry VIII* might indeed be the exception to that rule, but it is an interesting one, for cornets (the shortened form of the instrument's full name: 'cornetto') notably made their way to England in the hands of the Bassano family, at the invitation of King Henry VIII, and were a powerful ingredient not only of his courtly music but also of religious and secular music elsewhere in England during the sixteenth century, including the playhouses at the latter end of Elizabeth's reign.

Here is an instrument of which Shakespeare would have been very aware, for the instrument was played by many across the social strata: at court, by noble and religious consorts together with sackbuts, by the City Waits, and even on street corners and in taverns. Though it is an instrument capable of quiet underscore, the cornet, even played quietly, is so interesting a sound that it is difficult not to listen to its tune at the expense of missing the vocal text it may be supporting. Shakespeare was careful to ensure that the audience's ears are drawn first to the text and not to the music; there is thus no stage direction specifying cornets under text.

He frequently uses music to support the 'real' world of the play, be it a procession, song or dance: in *Antony and Cleopatra*, '*Music plays. Enter two or three Servants with a banquet*' (2.7.0), or in *Coriolanus*, '*Music plays. Enter a Servingman*' (4.5.0). But then there is the knotty problem of music playing under dance, especially where there is text which must be heard over it. In the following passage from *Love's Labour's Lost*, there is no stage direction indicating the start of the music but we know it is playing because the King refers to it:

ROSALINE. Play, music, then. Nay, you must do it soon.
  Not yet? – no dance! Thus change I like the moon.
KING. Will you not dance? How come you thus estranged?
ROSALINE. You took the moon at full, but now she's changed.
KING. Yet still she is the moon, and I the man.
  The music plays, vouchsafe some motion to it.
  (5.2.210–16)

In order for us to be able to hear the dialogue, the underscoring instrument would have to be, I surmise, a lute. This is supported by the stage directions earlier heralding the arrival of 'the music' (i.e. the musician(s) by whom we will hear music) in the form of a stage direction: '*Enter Blackamoors with music; the boy Moth with a speech; the Kings and his lords, disguised as Russians*' (5.2.156). The likeliest scenario is that Moth, the boy page, would have brought his lute with him and would have been prepared to entertain with music and song if need be. The Lords of course, though masked, have come to dance with the ladies and not to act as musicians. This is a happy concordance with the need for some music in the play, but made in a home-spun fashion (though 'noble' of course, as all the characters in the scene – except for Moth who is a page – are aristocrats).

Here is an example, in a very early play, of one of the acting company – who has some very difficult acting challenges in the play – being able to sing and accompany himself on the lute. In terms of OP work, unlike Shakespeare's company, we rarely – if at all – have an actor able enough to act at the standard required to negotiate the text *and* be able to play period instruments. An exception to this was the Globe's *Twelfth Night* which began its life commemorating the 400th anniversary of the first recorded performance in Middle Temple Hall with a production using period clothing and instruments in that same Hall on 2 February 2002. Peter Hamilton Dyer, who played Feste in this production, taught himself to play the pipe and tabor, instruments associated with Shakespeare's original Feste, Robert Armin. The pipe and tabor are not easy instruments to play but the lute and early modern wind and string instruments take many years of study and practice – more than a modern actor would be able or willing to give. The Chamberlain's Men especially engaged trumpeters, of which there were many hanging around London, waiting to be summoned to war. One trumpeter, Tawyer, is mentioned in the stage directions of *A Midsummer Night's Dream* in the First Folio: '*Tawyer with a Trumpet before them*' (5.1.125).

The following excerpt from *Coriolanus* is intriguing because of the stage direction '*Sound still with the shouts*' in the First Folio:

Trumpets, hautboys, drums beat, all together
SECOND MESSENGER.   The trumpets, sackbuts, psalteries, and fifes,
   Tabors and cymbals and the shouting Romans
   Make the sun dance. [*A shout within*] Hark you!

MENENIUS.   This is good news:
   I will go meet the ladies. This Volumnia
   Is worth of consuls, senators, patricians,
   A city full; of tribunes such as you,
   A sea and land full. You have prayed well today.
   This morning for ten thousand of your throats
   I'd not have given a doit. [*Sound still with the shouts.*] Hark, how they joy!   (5.4.49–58)

There is clearly more than one trumpet, more than one hautboy (shawm) and several drums. The stage directions do not specify that they are played unseen or 'within' but the direction of the text makes it clear that these sounds are offstage. They would have to be, because these are absolutely the loudest instruments possible that Shakespeare could have called for. Even so, I have found, when placing 'loud instruments' such as trumpets, drums and shawms as far away as the stairwell literally adjacent to the *outer* skin of the present Globe, that the actors would have to shout their lines to be heard. Thus the Folio SD '*Sound still with the Shouts*' is an example of dramaturgical precision: Shakespeare intends the bursts of sounds from the loud instruments not to exceed the length of the shouts. Note '*shouts*' and not '*shouting*'. A stage direction '*music still*', implies a piece of music, which, in the 1600s, had a particular structure or at least a recognizable melody. '*Sound*' is not '*music*'; '*Sound*' is punctuation. Bear in mind that trumpet calls were very specific and well known to much of the audience, many of them men who had fought in a war. Each call sounded a command: 'parley' or 'attack' or retreat' or 'victory', etc. Drum-calls sounded an energetic and rhythmic support to the cavalry trumpets and also commands to the infantry. Hoboys, whilst not being voices of war, were processional instruments, as well as being in the driving seat of 'loud music' in the Globe theatre's musical arsenal. This is a playwright who knew the acoustic properties of his theatre well and had an expert knowledge of how sound behaved in the amphitheatre. The Globe experience means that we have a physical way to discover and understand these stage directions that is beyond academic surmise and logic.

The stage directions reference only *Trumpets, hoboys* (shawms) and *drums* '*beating all together*', but the text, whist missing out hoboys altogether, mentions sackbuts (the ancestor of the trombone), fifes (like a piccolo) which were instruments of war, tabors (small drums), cymbals and psalteries. These last two instruments are an interesting textual inclusion, because, though known and extant in England, their association was at that time both historical (medieval) and also appertaining to 'the East', that is, a 'foreign' reference. They could of course have been found and included in the grouping of instruments playing offstage but the sound of the psaltery, a delicate and plucked instrument, would have been drowned by the loud instruments of the City Waits, whom the company had possibly hired for their production of *Coriolanus*, a play being performed after the indoor theatres had stamped their musical culture upon London's theatre-going public. Could Shakespeare's references to the psaltery and cymbals be the playwright's gesturing towards an English idea of Rome and an historical musical world? Was the psaltery ever used in early productions of the play? It is entirely possible but, given the composition of theatre bands in 1608, which were being drawn from professional wind-based players in London, it is unlikely. There is no stage direction elsewhere mentioning it or anyone playing it onstage.

Contrast this with a much earlier play, where the stage direction '*music still*' (in the First Folio) appears. The historiography of Shakespeare's '*A Midsummer Night's Dream*' is arguably the most thoroughly documented of all the canon. Usually absent from most of the lists and sources quoted in academe – and in the play's performance history – is a description of the environment in which these productions were performed. Our first piece of evidence is on the frontispiece of the first quarto of '*A Midsommer nights dreame*', the quarto published in 1600, where it states that the play 'hath beene sundry times publickely acted' by the Lord Chamberlain's Men. It is possible that the play was written to celebrate a marriage in 1595, between Elizabeth Vere and William, Earl of Derby at Greenwich palace or the February 1596 wedding between Elizabeth Carey and Sir Thomas Berkeley at the Blackfriars residence of the bride's father, Sir George Carey. Elizabeth Carey was the granddaughter of the Lord Chamberlain to Queen Elizabeth, Lord Hunsdon. Lord Hunsdon was the patron of the Lord Chamberlain's Men, which was Shakespeare's acting company.[3] Here, therefore, are examples of playing spaces that were most definitely not open to the general public but were the noble houses of the elite.

The diversity of performances of this most popular of Shakespeare's plays continues as the seventeenth century unfolds: the public playhouses, first the Globe and, from 1604, the Blackfriars, and touring outside the capital where the company played in civic halls, wool exchanges and market squares. Continuing performance practices of *The Dream* include many additions to the stage directions past the 1623 First Folio text of the play. By the restoration of the theatres in 1660, with a licence granted to Sir William Davenant (the manager of the Duke's Company at Lincoln's Inn Fields) by King Charles II, the development of Shakespeare's plays – including even *King Lear* – included extended songs and dances proclaiming a new form of musical theatre where women played the stage.

I argue that, during Shakespeare's lifetime, the performance practices of the music within *A Midsummer Night's Dream*, consisting, according to the playtext, of songs, dances and trumpet fanfares, varied considerably, depending upon both the environment in which the play was performed and the musical resources available to the Lord Chamberlain's/King's Men. These resources were not always governed by financial exigencies or restrictions but also by social and playing conventions.

If we take a snapshot of an ampitheatre performance of *Dream* in the 1600s, we would probably find that much, if not all, of the music within it was played by members of the company. Looking at the famous 'musicians' scene in *Romeo and Juliet* (4.4), even the quarto edition of 1597 carries the verbal sparring between a servingman and two musicians who have come to play for the wedding of Juliet and Paris. These two may or may not carry instruments and are named as Simon Sound Pot and Matthew Minnikin.[4] There is no music cue in the stage directions to tell us Paris has brought his 'music' with him. In the 1623 Folio, this scene has been enhanced; there is now, as in Q2 (1599), a stage direction to enable us to hear the music offstage, to support the fact that Paris is arriving: '*Play Musicke*' (4.4.22). When we see the musicians, it is likely that they are holding their instruments, which are all stringed ones, judging by their players' names: Simon Catling (a lutenist, as Catling is a term for the gut string for the lute),

---

[3] See Harold F. Brooks, 'Introduction', in *A Midsummer Night's Dream* (London, 1979), pp. xxxiv–lvii.
[4] *Romeo and Juliet* (1597), sig. I2v.

SHAKESPEARE'S USE OF MUSICAL UNDERSCORE

Hugh Rebicke (a rebec player; a rebec was a small wooden three-string fiddle and his first name, Hugh, puns on 'Yew') and James Sound-Post, probably a tenor or bass viol player. It is likely that these three were the following members of the King's Men: Augustine Phillips, a shareholder, and his apprentices Samuel Gilborne and James Sands to whom he bequeathed 'my bass viol ... a cithern, a bandore and a lute'.[5] The reference to 'pipes' in the scene, 'Faith, we may put up our pipes and be gone' (4.4.124), is musically misleading: though it is possible that they all may have carried a set of small bagpipes and/or shawms ready to ceremoniously 'parade' the couple to church, Peter makes no reference to the pipes being the only or leading instrument of each musician. It is very likely indeed that a string player would have 'doubled' on one or several other instruments not related to the family of his main instrument: at Shakespeare's Globe, there are several early music multi-instrumentalists, some of whom play as many as ten different instruments ranging from wind and brass to keyboard and percussion. Some of the players fresh out of early music conservatoire and joining the Globe in 1997 made a conscious decision to acquire a good facility on a number of instruments specifically because it would enable them to offer more musical variety and thus be engaged for more work. Could there be a more 'original practice'? Not much has changed in musicians' lives in the theatre during the last 400 years!

As underscore instruments, Shakespeare's company would have known that the lute, rebec and viol provided a lively and folk-based ensemble that, placed offstage, would be low in tessitura enough for speech from the stage to be heard under the passage in the scene preceding that in which we actually see the makers of the sound we just heard:

CAPULET.   Mass, and well said! A merry whoreson, ha!
    Thou shalt be loggerhead. Good faith, 'tis day.
    The County will be here with music straight,
    For so he said he would. I hear him near.
        [*Play musicke*]
    Nurse! Wife! What, ho, what, Nurse, I say!
        [*Re-enter Nurse*]
    Go waken Juliet. Go and trim her up.
    I'll go and chat with Paris. Hie, make haste,
    Make haste, the bridegroom he is come already.
    Make haste, I say.   (4.4.19–27)

Shakespeare does not specify that the music underscores the scene but it is short enough to read as if it might; what is more, there is the sensation of a procession arriving. The stage direction, however, does not say '*Musicke still*' as we would expect if Shakespeare had wanted it to carry on until the entry of the musicians in the next scene. There is no real break in the scene, as the Nurse immediately turns to her task, as she has been bid, of waking Juliet. An Elizabethan audience would expect the 'processional music' for the Countie Paris to comprise bagpipes, shawm and drum. However, as we have learned, in the Globe it would be impossible to 'cheat' the dynamic level of these instruments down low enough for speech to be heard. Thus, Shakespeare gives us the best of both worlds: we hear lute, rebec and viol, because such a grouping will not aurally interfere with text, but we *see* the musicians we have just heard playing carrying both sets of instruments – pipes and strings. One cannot discount the fact that these same musicians might have played earlier for the dance in 1.5, where the F1 stage direction reads 'Musicke plaies: and the dance' (at 1.5.25). In a contemporary stage or film version of this point in the play, we would not expect to watch actors dancing a whole dance together without text. We would feel that the play had somehow 'stopped'. The convention now, for good reason, is to keep the text moving and to play the ensuing scene over the dance music, which continues at low level. It is possible, if one considers that Capulet's speech that 'the room has grown too hot' (28) refers both to the nature of the dance as well as the temperature of the room (as a result of a 'hot' dance), then the dance itself has to that point been an energetic one. What is more, it has been complete. The Chamberlain's Men were clearly

---

[5] See E. A. J. Honigmann and Susan Brock, *Playhouse Wills, 1558–1642* (Manchester, 1993), p. 73.

a group of multi-talented performers whose dancing was worth watching for its physical feats.

Watching and listening was for an Elizabethan audience who had no easy access to spectacle all part of the show. Music was not 'soundtrack' in 1600; it was a social convention in which many took part. Songs were topical, popular; they had beginnings, middles and ends and were listened to and remembered, for there was little notation. Such a musical moment in this play would have been as precious as the text. The lack of the stage direction '*music still*' under Capulet's text following the dance I would consider to be more evidence for Shakespeare's and his editor's precision in their appointment of musical stage direction to his playtexts.

All of which brings me to my conclusion with a stage direction in the Folio text of Act 4 of *A Midsummer Night's Dream*. Oberon has bid Titania call for music and she does so: 'Musicke, ho musicke, such as charmeth sleepe'. Then there is a stage direction: '*Musick still*' (4.1.82). It is interesting that Oberon, though king of the fairies, and therefore presumably with superior power to rule, asks for music but bids Titania summon it, as if only through the (ethereal) feminine can music sound. The Muses are of course female. Here, the music, which must consist of instruments capable of 'charming sleepe' and therefore must be 'soft' instruments, runs as underscore throughout the rest of the scene. When, at the Globe in 2015, I arranged the music for this point in the play, basing it on Thomas Morley's 'Join hands',[6] the quietest I could achieve under text was a lute, underscored by a bass recorder, played unseen behind the music gallery. It would have been possible for one of Titania's fairies to have played the lute and/or flute but she has dismissed them at the top of the scene. When she calls for 'a roundel and a fairy song' (2.2.1), this is undoubtedly played by those playing fairies, presumably talented boy performers who both sing and play the lute exceptionally. (Any singing, of course, would have to have been performed in this context by boys with unbroken voices in order to preserve the illusion of 'fairies', etheric creatures.) With '*Musick still*' in 4.1 there is, again, no 'outpoint' for the music to stop. There is one place where it naturally would do so on a practical level and that is with the exits of Titania and Oberon and the stage direction '*Winde Hornes*' (F1 at 4.1.102) with the entry of Theseus and Hippolyta. Here is no indication that the horns are played 'within' and so it would seem that they announce the entry of the earthly king and consort. Close attention to the text reveals that there is a physical problem here, if Titania and Oberon are played by the same actors as Theseus and Hippolyta, as they indeed usually are in most modern productions. Here, '*Musicke still*' might provide a clue to how the Elizabethan stage may have solved this problem, one that nowadays we solve with elaborate stage 'business' and physical invention. There is no reason that an Elizabethan audience might have panicked at being asked to listen to a piece of music with no action happening on stage, even if that piece of music, as mine was, was being played 'unseen'. The non-visible nature of music playing would have underlined the 'magic' of the fairy kingdom's continuing presence, even though their 'spirits' had vanished 'into air', as Prospero puts it (*The Tempest*, 4.1.149–50). '*Musicke still*' therefore becomes powerfully significant if it represents the change from the realms of 'fairie' or the supernatural to the 'earthly' one of King, Queen and the mechanicals. Music, the bearer of the inspiration and power of the muses to affect the spirits potentially, has been thus given its own dramatic place in the story. The playwright is clearly aware of the etheric nature in all things: the 'parent and original' brought to earthly life by music. This early musical statement completes its journey in *The Winter's Tale* where Paulina's command 'Music, awake her; strike!' (5.3.98) is written with the playwright's full consciousness that the sweet concord of sounds in the open air had the greatest power to suspend the disbelief of the audience at the Globe and were understood as the intercession of the angels between God and Man.

---

[6] Thomas Morley, *The first booke of consort lessons* (1599), sig. C3a for cittern and B3a for bass viol.

SHAKESPEARE'S USE OF MUSICAL UNDERSCORE

Unlike our own time, where the richness and power of music is constantly dissipated in supermarkets, elevators, shopping malls and restaurants, where we have no choice but to 'tune' out our ears, the theatre Shakespeare knew encouraged the opposite. It was a culture of listening, from the daily news from the steps of St Paul's to the amphitheatres across the river. The concept of 'subservient' underscore was thus unknown, for music had power to charm, to put to sleep, to wake, to elevate the soul. Who better to express Shakespeare's own view than Lorenzo in the *Merchant of Venice*?

> The man that hath no music in himself,
> Nor is not moved with concord of sweet sounds,
> Is fit for treasons, stratagems, and spoils.
> The motions of his spirit are dull as night,
> And his affections dark as Erebus.
> Let no such man be trusted. Mark the music. (5.1.83–8)

REMEMBERING AND FORGETTING IN 1916: ISRAEL GOLLANCZ, THE SHAKESPEARE TERCENTENARY AND THE NATIONAL THEATRE

GORDON MCMULLAN

At the rear of the foyer of the National Theatre in London is the building's foundation stone, which begins with the words 'In Memory of William Shakespeare'. This might strike casual theatregoers, if they notice it at all, as curious. Surely this expression of commemoration would be more logically located half a mile east at Shakespeare's Globe or a hundred miles northwest in the Royal Shakespeare Theatre at Stratford, since these are the two UK theatres that can be guaranteed to offer at least one production of a Shakespeare play at any given moment, whereas the National Theatre's repertoire is, as befits a consciously 'national' theatre, far broader in scope. In 2016, the apparent incongruity of the foundation stone's commemorative function was all the more apparent, since the National, curiously, opened no Shakespeare production during the quatercentenary year (an *As You Like It* was in repertory early in the year, but it opened the previous autumn). Yet the history of the National Theatre was closely tied right from the start to the commemoration of Shakespeare, and there has been a production of at least one Shakespeare play at the National virtually every year since its very first season. Furthermore, its origins and those of both the Royal Shakespeare Company and Shakespeare's Globe are arguably bound up – more than each organization tends to acknowledge – with the prolonged and often tortuous process of commemoration that began with the build-up to the Shakespeare tercentenary of 1916.[1] There are obvious enough reasons why these theatres might not wish to overemphasize their origins in the tercentenary, not least the RSC and the Globe, neither of which especially wishes to be seen as in some way a product of the history of a competitor theatre. Nevertheless, it is a story that can valuably be told, both so as to demonstrate the extent of the interweaving of Shakespearean performance and commemoration across the twentieth century and as a case study in the selective rememberings and, above all, forgettings that constitute the processes of memorialization.

As a point of comparison with the NT's perhaps surprisingly Shakespearean foundation stone, I will turn briefly to another, more modest commemorative marker – a memorial plaque located in the

---

This chapter is an abbreviated version of my chapter in Gordon McMullan and Philip Mead, with Kate Flaherty, Ailsa Grant Ferguson and Mark Houlahan, *Antipodal Shakespeare: Remembering and Forgetting in Britain, Australia and New Zealand, 1916–2016* (London, forthcoming). I am grateful to Philip Mead and to Margaret Bartley, publisher of the Arden Shakespeare series, for agreeing to let me use the material in this chapter.

[1] One index of the long-drawn-out nature of the process is that the foundation stone was laid by the Queen Mother in 1951 on a site near the Royal Festival Hall, yet work on Denys Lasdun's National Theatre – on a site east, not west, of Waterloo Bridge – did not begin until 1969 and the theatre was finally opened in 1976.

Department of English at King's College London. Its wording is simple:

> IN MEMORY OF
> ISRAEL GOLLANCZ KT. LITTD.
> FOR TWENTY-SEVEN YEARS
> PROFESSOR OF ENGLISH LANGUAGE
> AND LITERATURE
> THIS TABLET HAS BEEN PLACED IN
> THE SKEAT AND FURNIVALL LIBRARY
> ITSELF AN EXAMPLE OF HIS
> DEVOTION TO THE
> COLLEGE

Sir Israel Gollancz – medievalist, Shakespearean, cultural entrepreneur – was Professor of English at King's from 1903 until his death in 1930.[2] He had studied under the philologist and medievalist Walter William Skeat (1835–1912) at Christ's College, Cambridge, and he later persuaded Skeat's widow to donate her husband's library to King's; he was instrumental also in King's' acquisition of the library of F. J. Furnivall, founder of the Early English Text Society. The key detail, however, is not the referencing of the means by which these collections came to the college but rather the date the plaque gives for Gollancz's birth: 1864. This is in fact incorrect – Gollancz was born in 1863 – but the mistake is telling because it serves, consciously or otherwise, to align Gollancz with Shakespeare, the tercentenary of whose birth fell in 1864 – which was also the year that initiated the ongoing, unresolved struggle between Stratford-upon-Avon and London for 'ownership' of the Shakespeare industry in Britain. On that occasion, Stratford won resoundingly, hosting a two-week Shakespeare festival and setting in train the process that led to the building of the Shakespeare Memorial Theatre, which later became the Royal Shakespeare Theatre. In 1916, Gollancz sought in effect to reverse that victory and instead focus commemorative activity on London – not simply for its own sake but as a springboard for a vision of Shakespeare that would, he hoped, transcend both the local and the national and acquire a global identity.

That Gollancz should be linked with Shakespeare by way of the plaque at King's is not so surprising both because Gollancz was a consistent presence in the planning for the 1916 tercentenary commemorations and because it appears to be the fate of Shakespeare's commemorators to blur themselves, or to be blurred by others, with the writer in whose memory they are ostensibly operating. Without the assiduous work of Gollancz on behalf of the various memorial committees of which he was 'Hon. Sec.' in the build-up to the 1916 tercentenary, the histories of the National Theatre, the Royal Shakespeare Company and even Shakespeare's Globe would surely have been very different. In and of itself, a counterfactual claim of this kind may or may not have value, of course, so in this article I will offer a brief history of Gollancz's involvement in the 1916 tercentenary in order to do two things: to reflect on the blend of remembering and forgetting that seems to constitute commemoration and to consider the intersection of the Shakespeare tercentenary and the First World War. Gollancz's leading role in the tercentenary – as opposed, say, to his role as a founder of the British Academy – was quite rapidly forgotten in the period between the wars, and this attack of amnesia in respect of an individual seems to me to be synecdochic of the larger forgetting of the impact of the tercentenary on the creation of certain contemporary UK cultural institutions.

To reassemble this history, it is necessary to go back to the time immediately before Gollancz was appointed to his chair at King's. In his preface to the *Book of Homage*, the sumptuous commemorative volume he edited in 1916, he noted the history of planning that had gone into the tercentenary. 'For years past', he wrote, '– as far back as 1904 – many of us had been looking forward to the Shakespeare Tercentenary as the occasion for some fitting memorial to symbolize the intellectual fraternity of mankind in the universal homage

---

[2] On Gollancz as cultural entrepreneur, see Gordon McMullan, 'Goblin's market: Commemoration, anti-semitism and the invention of "global Shakespeare" in 1916', in *Celebrating Shakespeare: Commemoration and Cultural Memory*, ed. Clara Calvo and Coppélia Kahn (Cambridge, 2015), pp. 182–201.

accorded to the genius of the greatest Englishman.'[3] Those plans had, however, been curtailed by the war – 'the dream of the world's brotherhood to be demonstrated by its common and united commemoration of Shakespeare, with many another fond illusion, was rudely shattered',[4] Gollancz notes, sadly – and they had, in any case, already been subject to a good deal of struggle and underachievement before war broke out. The original plan, prompted by a letter to *The Times* in 1903 from a brewer called Richard Badger, had been to erect a statue of Shakespeare in London, but there had been fierce resistance to this mode of commemoration from supporters of the long-established plan to build a state-subsidized National Theatre, led by theatre practitioner Harley Granville Barker and journalist William Archer, whose *Scheme & Estimates for a National Theatre* provided a financial blueprint for the projected building and theatre company.[5] In 1908 the Shakespeare Memorial National Theatre (SMNT) committee was formed from a merger of the Shakespeare Memorial Committee, of which Gollancz had been honorary secretary, and the National Theatre committee – with the ubiquitous Gollancz once more as honorary secretary – and the focus was now on the building of a Shakespeare Memorial National Theatre to be opened in time for the 1916 tercentenary.

Two major fundraising events took place – the Shakespeare Memorial Ball of 1911 and the 'Shakespeare's England' exhibition of 1912 – which promised well but did not, in the end, provide much in the way of funds for the project. The second of these – the 'Shakespeare's England' exhibition at Earl's Court – featured a series of architectural reconstructions designed to give the public the chance to 'walk straight into the sixteenth century and visualize the environment and atmosphere' of the period.[6] The most popular of these buildings was a working replica of the Globe theatre offering excerpts from plays by Shakespeare and his contemporaries. The design derived from a William Poel drawing from 1897, though Poel – long-standing champion of the reconstruction of Elizabethan performance spaces and practices – considered the Earl's Court Globe a travesty of his proposals. Thus even before the onset of the First World War the project was dogged by an ongoing financial shortfall, and it became all too apparent that the imagined theatre would not be built in time for the tercentenary, an unavoidable fact that Gollancz lamented:

We had hoped that, on a site that has already been acquired, a stately building, to be associated with that august name, equipped and adequately endowed for the furtherance of Shakespearian drama and dramatic art generally, would have made the year 1916 memorable in the annals of the English stage.[7]

The committee had not, however, given up hope: in 1914 they had spent £50,000 – over half of the funds they had acquired – on a plot of land in Bloomsbury on which they hoped eventually to build the theatre.

The tercentenary was, because of the war, marked in relatively subdued fashion. It had been agreed long before war broke out that the Shakespeare commemoration would be postponed until the May Day weekend, with the earnest explanation that the change of calendar from Julian to Gregorian in the late sixteenth century meant that 1 May 1916 was in fact four hundred years to the day from 23 April 1616: this decision facilitated the avoidance of any uncomfortable conflation of Shakespeare and Christ and underlines, even as it seeks to elide, the quasi-religious place of Shakespeare in British culture at this time.[8]

---

[3] Israel Gollancz, ed., *A Book of Homage to Shakespeare* (Oxford, 1916), p. vii.
[4] Gollancz, *Homage*, p. vii.
[5] Richard Badger, letter, *The Times*, 28 May 1903; William Archer and H. Granville Barker, *A National Theatre: Scheme & Estimates* (London, 1907).
[6] *The Graphic*, 11 May 1912, pp. 674–5. See Marion F. O'Connor, 'Theatre of the Empire: "Shakespeare's England" at Earl's Court, 1912', in *Shakespeare Reproduced: The Text in History and Ideology*, ed. Jean E. Howard and Marion F. O'Connor (New York, 1987), pp. 68–98; p. 79.
[7] Gollancz, *Homage*, p. vii.
[8] On this, and for a comparative analysis of Shakespearean commemoration in Britain and Germany, see Balz Engler, 'Shakespeare and the Trenches', in *Shakespeare Survey 44* (Cambridge, 1992), pp. 105–12. The *Sydney Morning Herald*,

REMEMBERING AND FORGETTING IN 1916

The tercentenary was marked officially over four days in early May, beginning with a political commemoration at the Mansion House which included the reading out of messages from the King and Queen and from US President Woodrow Wilson and speeches by the Lord Mayor, the US ambassador and the High Commissioners of Australia and South Africa.[9] The message from the King and Queen with which the event opened acknowledged receipt of their copy of an imposing collection of essays, poems and other contributions called *A Book of Homage to Shakespeare*, edited by Israel Gollancz, which *The Times* described as a 'sumptuous volume' which 'may be said to record, in a peculiarly catholic way, what after 300 years the best literary representatives of British and allied culture are saying about Shakespeare'.[10] Certainly the *Book of Homage* – a large, elegantly produced book with a consciously global reach – not only underlines the hegemonic status of Shakespeare in the early twentieth century as an icon of Englishness and Empire but also, as the journalist's phrase 'in a peculiarly catholic way' suggests, serves as a precursor of the future role of Shakespeare as a figure of a global culture not restricted to Empire.

The *Book of Homage* has an astonishingly ambitious sweep, with a hundred and sixty-six contributions in verse and prose in languages from Sanskrit to Setswana celebrating a broad range of versions of, and meanings for, 'Shakespeare' – though with the omission, for obvious enough reasons, of representation from Germany, Austria-Hungary and Turkey. Contributors range from novelists John Galsworthy and Edmund Gosse to poets Wilfred Campbell and René de Clercq, from Nobel Laureate Rabindranath Tagore to the Nobel Prize-winning human biologist Sir Ronald Ross. Each offers a perspective appropriate to their context – 'Dante e Shakespeare' by Italian senator Isidoro del Lungo, say, or 'An Eddic Homage to William Shakespeare' by Icelandic scholar Jón Stefánsson – and most either praise Shakespeare's genius or choose a particular element in Shakespeare's *oeuvre* on which to focus their brief contribution. Many of the contributions are distinctly conservative, expressive of Edwardian patriotism and the colonial mindset – very visibly so in a contribution such as the New Zealander William Pember Reeves's poem 'The Dream Imperial'. Yet there are also contributions that – as Coppélia Kahn and others have demonstrated – complicate our understanding of the work the *Book* was doing, most notably, as David Schalkwyk and others have pointed out, 'A South African's Homage', the only anonymous item in the volume, written in Setswana by Solomon Plaatje, an early ANC activist whom Gollancz met when he was part of a pre-war political delegation to London, and that of future president of the Irish Republic Douglas Hyde, a poem in Gaelic that even in the censored translation which appeared in the printed volume, had potential, as Andrew Murphy has shown, to upset patriotic readers of the *Book of Homage* at the moment of Easter 1916.[11]

The *Book of Homage* is thus unexpectedly inclusive and far-reaching. It performs a cultural moment with brio, enabling the reader to find within its pages the Shakespeare with which he or

---

reporting from London, is a little coy about 23 April being Easter that year, noting simply that '[t]he Shakespeare Tercentenary committee has fixed May 3 as Shakespeare Day, as April 23 falls on a Sunday' (1 March 1916).

[9] See Richard Foulkes, 'The theatre of war: The 1916 tercentenary', in *Performing Shakespeare in the Age of Empire* (Cambridge, 2002), pp. 180–204; p. 199.

[10] *The Times*, 2 May 1916.

[11] For more on these fascinating contributions to the *Book of Homage*, see Coppélia Kahn, 'Remembering Shakespeare imperially: The 1916 tercentenary', *Shakespeare Quarterly* 52 (2001), 456–78; David Schalkwyk and Lerothodi Lapula, 'Sol Plaatje, William Shakespeare and the translation of culture', *Pretexts: Literary and Cultural Studies* 9 (2000), 10–26; Deborah Seddon, 'Shakespeare's orality: Solomon Plaatje's Setswana translations', *English Studies in Africa* 2 (2004), 77–95; Natasha Distiller, *South Africa, Shakespeare and Post-Colonial Culture* (Lewiston, 2005); Andrew Murphy, '"Bhíos ag Stratford ar an abhainn": Shakespeare, Douglas Hyde, 1916', in *Shakespeare and the Irish Writer*, ed. Janet Clare and Stephen O'Neill (Dublin, 2010), pp. 51–63. For further detail, see Gordon McMullan, 'Introduction' to reissue of *A Book of Homage to Shakespeare, 1916*, ed. Israel Gollancz (Oxford, 2016), pp. v–xxxiii.

she is most comfortable. Enthusiasts for nation and empire could read it untroubled, by and large – though they might have baulked a little not only at Plaatje's and Hyde's contributions but also at C. H. Herford's unexpectedly generous and, in context, brave essay, 'The German Contribution to Shakespeare Criticism' – yet the incipient globalist could also find within its pages expressions of hope in a changing world. Its apparent arbitrariness turns out often to be quite precise grouping and, at times, humorous juxtaposition. As an expression of the condition of Shakespeare studies in its moment, the *Book of Homage* is unparalleled but it is far more than that. It makes very apparent how pivotal was the year 1916 in the negotiation between the fading Shakespeare of empire and the emerging global Shakespeare, and it invites the reader to absorb a range of perspectives, by no means all compatible, upon the National Poet. It is, in other words, a *performative* memorial, and it underlines both the complexity and the globalism of Gollancz's outlook.

The second of Gollancz's two main contributions to the tercentenary – clearly the less likely of the two – is the Shakespeare Hut, which also had a tangible global dimension. As I have noted, in 1914, the Shakespeare Memorial National Theatre committee, recognizing the need for action, acquired, at substantial cost, a plot of land at the corner of Keppel and Gower Streets, where the London School of Hygiene and Tropical Medicine now stands, just across from Senate House. Almost immediately, however, war broke out, and the committee had to decide what should be done with the empty site in wartime. Attempts to raise money for the building of a theatre with a war on would be considered insensitive, to say the least, and it was Gollancz who proposed a solution: that he broker an arrangement with the YMCA for the creation of temporary accommodation for overseas troops on the site of the theatre, a series of interconnected buildings to be known as the 'Shakespeare Hut'.

The word 'hut', the standard term at the time for the YMCA's temporary buildings on both the war and the home fronts, does not adequately evoke a sense of the building that was erected on the site. Temporary it may have been, but the Shakespeare Hut included substantial accommodation (scores of thousands of beds were let to Anzac troops between 1916 and the war's end), recreation space, dining facilities, a shop and a concert hall in which Shakespearean performances took place – strictly for the resident soldiers – featuring some of the finest actors of the day, among them Ellen Terry and Johnston Forbes-Robertson, whose American wife Gertrude Elliott combined management of the Hut's theatrical programme with women's suffrage activism.[12] It was hardly the stage the SMNT committee had expected or intended to create, but its existence means nevertheless that Shakespearean performances of a certain kind took place between 1916 and 1919 in a commemorative space on the chosen memorial site – a fact that until recently has simply been forgotten.[13]

The Hut, as Ailsa Grant Ferguson has shown, is a curious, multifaceted space, with resonances that both outweigh and are, in a certain sense, the direct result of its status as a temporary building, a space created in large part with the premise of keeping young soldiers away from the temptations – sex and alcohol, principally – of the wartime cityscape (the same premise applied to the Aldwych Hut for Australian soldiers and the later Eagle Hut, also at Aldwych, for Americans). That the Hut housed Anzac soldiers (mostly, but not entirely, New Zealanders) was, in the SMNT's terms, incidental. What seems to have mattered more to Gollancz than the identity or nationality of the soldiers occupying the Hut – though their overseas origins unquestionably chimed with his global vision for Shakespeare – was the intention that the space

---

[12] See Ailsa Grant Ferguson, 'Lady Forbes-Robertson's war work: Gertrude Elliott and the Shakespeare Hut performances, 1916–1919', in *Woman Making Shakespeare: Text, Reception, Performance*, ed. Gordon McMullan, Lena Cowen Orlin and Virginia Mason Vaughan (London, 2014), pp. 233–42.

[13] See Ailsa Grant Ferguson, '"When wasteful war shall statues overturn": Forgetting the Shakespeare Hut', *Shakespeare* 10 (2014), 276–92.

should house Shakespearean performance and related educational activities, as YMCA secretary Basil Yeaxlee makes clear when he observes to Gollancz in a letter that the Hut will enable 'the purpose of the Shakespeare memorial [to be] fulfilled as far as possible during war time by the arrangement of lectures and rendering of plays'.[14] In the same letter Yeaxlee also notes that the nature of the Hut meant that it could be assembled block by block and thus 'the Concert and Lecture Hall could be put up first', thereby implying his recognition that for his interlocutor the educational and theatrical possibilities of the Hut were paramount. It is the nature of the Hut as a temporary space for soldiers that facilitated the performance on its tiny, setless stage of scenes from Shakespeare by some of the most prominent actors of the day, who would not normally, it can be assumed, have chosen to act in such constricted conditions. This appears to have been the value to Gollancz of the Hut stage – that it enabled the performance of a virtual Memorial Theatre, one that in time provoked a layering of memorial functions as the originary logic of the site – a theatre in memory of Shakespeare – meshed with the accumulating logic of commemoration produced by the Hut's primary function as military accommodation for wartime and thus the deaths, inevitably, of a proportion of those who passed through its doors. Ailsa Grant Ferguson notes that the original funding for the Hut's lounge had come from the mother of a fallen soldier, Lieutenant Leslie Tweedie, who had been killed in 1915, making immediate from the outset the multiply commemorative function of the building and even leading in due course to a counternarrative of the Hut's creation, as the dead soldier's mother later claimed to have created the entire Hut in memory of her son.[15] Such reallocation of memorial function serves as a version of forgetting – forgetting, that is, the impersonal logic of the Hut's memorial status in the natural death of a playwright three hundred years earlier and replacing it with a personal and more immediate commemoration of wartime death by violence.

Theatre history – particularly the internal mythology of a given theatre or company – is constituted by such patchworks of remembering and forgetting, as the presentation of institutional history is adapted to suit subsequent formations and missions are adjusted to map more effectively onto funding regimes. The tension present in the National Theatre project from the beginning – its function, as outlined by Barker and Archer, both to sustain Shakespearean performance and to champion new playwriting – necessarily finds its counterpart in histories of the organization. Daniel Rosenthal's recent history of the National Theatre differs markedly from earlier accounts in this regard, understandably foregrounding Barker and Archer's status as 'founding fathers' but offering generous recognition of the place of the SMNT in the National Theatre's origins.[16] This has not always been the case, as Geoffrey Whitworth's attitude to Gollancz in his earlier history of the NT suggests:

[B]ehind [the] kaleidoscopic maze of committees, flitting to and fro, one glimpses the mercurial figure of Israel Gollancz [...] benign, discreet, master of innocent intrigue [...] with every thread in his hands, and alone capable of unravelling the tangled skein when the right moment came.[17]

Perhaps this gentle caricaturing of Gollancz is simply a function of time passing. As founder, immediately after the war, of the British Drama League, which sought to reinvigorate the National Theatre project in the face of what it saw as the SMNT's sluggishness, Whitworth arguably had an interest in downplaying what Gollancz and the SMNT had achieved, though his final description of Gollancz is affectionate, noting his importance to the Shakespeare National Theatre idea, 'with which

---

[14] Letter from Basil Yeaxlee to Israel Gollancz, National Theatre Archive SMNT2/1/12.
[15] See Ailsa Grant Ferguson, 'The Shakespeare Hut for Anzacs: Building commemoration, performing memory, 1916–19', in *Antipodal Shakespeare*, ed. Gordon McMullan *et al.* (London, forthcoming).
[16] Daniel Rosenthal, *The National Theatre Story* (London, 2013).
[17] Geoffrey Whitworth, *The Making of a National Theatre* (London, 1951), p. 44.

he had been associated from the very beginning, loyal to it through every chance of fortune, and though criticized by some, the axle round which the whole wheel turned'.[18] Others have subsequently tended to be dismissive towards the SMNT committee and towards Gollancz in particular.[19] Sally Beauman, in her history of the RSC, describes Gollancz as 'haughty' and misreads the materials in the NT Archive to the extent of suggesting that the plan and elevation of the Shakespeare Hut that forms part of the collection is of the proposed theatre itself, which she describes sarcastically as 'a long, low structure, resembling a conglomeration of Stratford tea-shops' – as if everyone involved in Shakespearean theatre would eventually defer to Stratford for their design aesthetic – adding that during the war the SMNT did 'nothing [...] except to lease the Bloomsbury site to the YMCA, who built on it a small wooden hut in which to entertain British troops' – an assessment which, as I have shown, is misleading.[20]

I have written elsewhere about the reasons for the resistance to Gollancz, which date right back to the build-up to 1916 and are not always edifying – in brief, the anti-Semitism that pervaded the British establishment in the period – and I will not repeat these arguments here.[21] There may also be an element of the perennial reluctance of theatre practitioners to acknowledge the relevance of academic intervention in their professional zone, particularly when the academic in question adopts the role of cultural entrepreneur, as Gollancz did. Whatever the reason, one effect of the downplaying of the achievements of Gollancz and, along with him, the SMNT is to suppress the significance of the impact of the tercentenary on the shape of British Shakespearean theatre today. It is entirely right and proper that the National Theatre sees Barker and Archer as founding fathers in a way Gollancz is not, and there is no question that the establishment of the National Theatre was the result above all of the sheer doggedness shown by theatre practitioners. Yet without the work of the SMNT, and without Gollancz's commemorative persistence in the shape particularly of the Shakespeare Hut – a creation that helped sustain the SMNT's existence throughout the war and, most importantly, enabled the first performances of Shakespeare on what might be called a memorial stage – it is arguable that the National Theatre project might well have faded away entirely.

It is clear, then, that key elements of the origins of the National Theatre lie in the 1916 tercentenary. What is less well known – though it may account in part for the dismissiveness of Beauman – is that the Royal Shakespeare Company too owes an element of its history to the tercentenary and specifically to Gollancz's entrepreneurship, though the timeline on the RSC's website simply skips the period from 1913 to 1925. In the course of 1918, the young director William Bridges-Adams had a series of conversations with William Archer in which he argued that the best way to proceed with the aim of creating a National Theatre was to found a company *first* and build a theatre *later* – an argument that would haunt the NT for decades. At this point, the pre-histories of the NT and the RSC briefly overlap. In 1919, Bridges-Adams took over from Frank Benson as director of the Stratford-upon-Avon Festival, and Archibald Flower, chairman of the Festival, encouraged the SMNT to support the launching of a new company that – by contrast with Benson, who had done a great deal of cutting – would perform Shakespeare's plays largely uncut (Bridges-Adams acquired the nickname 'Un-a-Bridges-Adams') and would, though based for part of the year in Stratford, have a commitment both to playing in London and to touring. The SMNT chose to support this project, and a joint committee was created between the governors of the Stratford Memorial Theatre and members of the SMNT committee, including Archer,

---

[18] Whitworth, *The Making of a National Theatre*, p. 179.
[19] See, for instance, Jonathan Bate, 'Shakespeare nationalised, Shakespeare privatised', *English* 42 (1993), 1–18.
[20] Sally Beauman, *The Royal Shakespeare Company: A History of Ten Decades* (Oxford, 1982), pp. 96, 69. This misreading of the plans is repeated by Peter Whitebrook in his biography of William Archer (1993), p. 348.
[21] See McMullan, 'Goblin's market', pp. 192ff.

Lyttelton and Gollancz – a rare instance of Shakespearean collaboration between London and Stratford.

The New Shakespeare Company did not directly *become* the Royal Shakespeare Company – it was in fact viewed by influential members of the SMNT, not least George Bernard Shaw, as potentially the basis for a National Theatre company – but it embodied what was to become the RSC blueprint: a Shakespeare-centred repertory company with a base in Stratford, a London programme and a commitment to national touring. And it was funded by SMNT money – or, more precisely, by the income the SMNT committee was currently receiving from the Shakespeare Hut. Between 1919 and its demolition in 1923, the Hut became the temporary home of the Indian YMCA, an arrangement which provided £3,000 a year in rent. It was this exact sum that the SMNT committee used to fund the New Shakespeare Company between 1919 and 1923, only reducing the amount once the Indian YMCA rent was no longer available (i.e., for the 1923 season). Thus, briefly, the Shakespeare Hut, the product of Gollancz's entrepreneurship, underpinned an early phase of the history of the RSC, sustaining Shakespeare performance at Stratford during a difficult period.

It can further be argued that, in a certain way, the third and most recent of Britain's primary Shakespeare-producing theatre companies, Shakespeare's Globe, had its seeds in the 1916 tercentenary. The official history of the reconstructed Globe naturally offers a rather different story of origins, one that lies firmly in the extraordinary inspiration and persistence of Sam Wanamaker – and rightly so, for many reasons. Without Wanamaker's indefatigable energy and extraordinary persuasive powers, the project would never have got off the ground. As Paul Prescott notes, 'few theatrical spaces in the world owe so much to the vision, vitality and perseverance of one person'.[22] Yet, in celebrating Wanamaker's remarkable achievement, the Globe tends understandably to downplay Wanamaker's predecessors in the long-standing project to create a reconstructed Elizabethan theatre in London, above all William Poel, lifelong evangelist for the recreation of early modern conditions of performance, whose 1897 plans for a small-scale replica of the Globe were, to his distaste, the basis for the 'Elizabethan theatre' that had formed the centrepiece of the 'Shakespeare's England' exhibition of 1912, which, as we have seen, was created as a fundraising event for the SMNT.[23] Poel's vision – one that, as it happens, overlapped in key ways with that of Gollancz, though by and large they clashed more than they agreed – was not solely theatrical: it was to create a Shakespeare Memorial that would combine an 'Elizabethan theatre' with 'a Shakespearian Library and Museum' – in other words, an establishment that would be in roughly equal measure theatrical and educational.[24]

The extent to which Wanamaker's project has a direct link with that of Poel depends on which myth of origin you choose. Prescott reports that in a file Wanamaker sent to the Gotlieb Archive at Boston University towards the end of his life he included a programme from the Cleveland Great Lakes Festival of 1936 to which he 'attached a Post-it note with the handwritten exclamation "The Beginning!"', and he notes that Wanamaker had spent the summer of that year playing bit parts on a replica Elizabethan stage at the Festival.[25] 'But', Prescott adds, '"The Beginning" was a movable moment and would depend on which

---

[22] Paul Prescott, 'Sam Wanamaker', in *Poel, Granville Barker, Guthrie, Wanamaker: Great Shakespeareans*, vol. XV, ed. Cary M. Mazer (London, 2013), p. 151.

[23] One connection between Poel and Gollancz is patronage. Poel built a model Globe on the basis of his 1897 plans which was displayed at the inaugural meeting of the London Shakespeare League in 1902: it was funded by Frida Mond, long-term friend of Gollancz and funder of several of his projects and also, later, of the annual Gollancz Memorial lecture at the British Academy.

[24] See Marion O'Connor, 'William Poel', in *Poel, Granville Barker, Guthrie, Wanamaker*, ed. Holland, p. 37. O'Connor cites documents in the Poel Collection in the Theatre department of the Victoria and Albert Museum.

[25] Prescott, 'Sam Wanamaker', p. 151.

version of the genesis story Wanamaker happened to be telling', one of which was that 'the idea of rebuilding the Globe first occur[red] to the fifteen-year-old working-class Chicago boy [when he was] taken by his father to ... [the] World's Fair in 1934, where ... he was struck by the beauty of a reconstructed Globe, one of a dozen or so ersatz landmarks comprising the English Village'.[26] If this sounds very much like the 1912 'Shakespeare's England' exhibition and its replica Globe, that is because the design of the 1934 theatre was in fact based on that of 1912, thus creating a direct causal link between Wanamaker's project, one of the SMNT committee's fundraising events and Poel's original Globe design of 1897.

The point is that it does not especially matter which of these stories, if any, is the correct one. Each underlines the fact that Wanamaker's Globe is the fulfilment of the project that Poel and others had championed since the end of the nineteenth century to build a theatre that would allow Shakespeare performance, to use Poel's own words, 'upon a stage surrounded on three sides by the audience, the only kind of stage where the actor moves and speaks in the Shakespearian focus, [and] only under its conditions [can] the correct interpretation [be] given to his work on the stage'.[27] Prescott is right to note that 'there is a world – or perhaps an ocean – of difference between Poel's antiquarianism and Wanamaker's idea that Shakespeare might serve as the locus and alibi for a joyous civic and communal experience',[28] but he is right too when he acknowledges the 'ancestral link between' Poel and Wanamaker, 'between the neo-Elizabethan movement of the late nineteenth century and the logical, if delayed, fruition of that movement a century later: the opening of the third Globe Theatre'.[29] Shakespeare's Globe has, in the two decades of its existence, become the de facto 'Memorial Theatre' in London, frequently mistaken by tourists for an actual site of Shakespearean memory: Shakespeare's 'own', 'original' Globe refurbished. The challenges over the claims to 'authenticity' that have been made on behalf of the Globe (though rarely by actual Globe employees) are well documented and need not be repeated here, but the point is to acknowledge that the history of the SMNT suggests a mild elision in the Globe's prevailing origin story.[30] In a certain way, this is an instance of the return of the repressed: after all, the new Globe, with its extraordinarily active and engaged education programme, most fully expresses – more so than the educational programmes of its competitors – the dual vision of theatre and education that Poel had consistently championed and that Gollancz sought to develop in the unlikeliest of ways through the creation of the Shakespeare Hut.[31]

The reconstructed Globe is not a direct product of the tercentenary – less so even than is the RSC. Yet its story nonetheless intersects intriguingly with that of Gollancz and the SMNT, and its current status as London's primary producer of Shakespeare means that it, more than the RSC and the National Theatre, occupies for the

---

[26] Prescott, 'Sam Wanamaker', p. 152.
[27] S. R. Littlewood, *The London Shakespeare Commemoration League: Its Purposes and its Story* (London, 1928), p. 5.
[28] Prescott, 'Sam Wanamaker', p. 161.
[29] Prescott, 'Sam Wanamaker', p. 160.
[30] See, for instance, the discussions in the various chapters in Christie Carson and Farah Karim-Cooper, eds., *Shakespeare's Globe: A Theatrical Experiment* (Cambridge, 2008), including Franklin J. Hildy's discussion of Poel in his chapter, 'The "essence of Globeness": Authenticity, and the search for Shakespeare's stagecraft', pp. 13–25.
[31] Poel's evangelism eventually led to a split with Gollancz, with whom he had for a time established a working partnership in the London Shakespeare League. Poel 'challenged Professor Israel Gollancz's assertion that it was not the business of the League to attack the public theatres for their misrepresentations of Shakespeare's plays on the London stage. The matter was brought to the vote, and Sir Israel Gollancz's party was defeated. He and his supporters all resigned, and ... formed the English Shakespeare Association, which holds its meetings at King's College' (see O'Connor, 'Theatre of the Empire', p. 40, citing a letter of Poel's in the London Shakespeare League Journal 10 (Feb 1925), 73). There is a certain irony in the fact that the setless stage in the Shakespeare Hut had offered a context for the presentation of Shakespeare's plays 'independent of scenic effects' *à la* Poel, though of course it was a far cry from the thrust-stage theatre Poel had in mind.

moment the role of London's Shakespeare memorial theatre. This has come about for contingent reasons: in hindsight, the RSC's departure in 2001 from its longstanding base at the Barbican ceded key territory just as the Globe was beginning to establish a bridgehead on the Bankside, whilst the artistic directorship of the National Theatre does not at present appear to view Shakespearean preservation or innovation as a priority. This state of play – the predominance of a reconstructed early modern playhouse in the postmodern theatrical scene – would presumably please Poel, but it would surely baffle the majority of members of the SMNT committee, who would never have foreseen such an outcome. That said, Gollancz himself would in all likelihood cast a benign eye over it all: experience surely taught him that it is the vision, far more than the detail, that matters in the end, and the single most obvious conclusion from the history of the SMNT is that stasis is never achieved.

You build a statue, you build a memorial theatre, you think that by definition commemoration will continue on those sites indefinitely, but it does not: it disappears and then reappears elsewhere in unpredicted locales. The forgetting – perhaps 'suppression' is not too strong a word – of the achievements of Israel Gollancz is synecdochic of the deletion of the memory of the tercentenary as a key impetus in the creation of London's major theatres for the production of Shakespeare – by which I mean both theatrical and cultural production. Commemoration is a looking back, a remembering, but it also, as we have seen, involves a good deal of forgetting. Cultural organizations tend to look back only selectively as the current incumbents seek to avoid being tied to earlier visions of the institution's mission; new myths of origin are established as interest groups compete for foundational recognition. In the case of Shakespeare, the memorial and the national are closely bound, and Gollancz's insistent belief in the inter- or supra-national significance of Shakespeare does not fit comfortably with the overarching narrative of a *national* Shakespeare theatre to which the tercentenary became subsumed. The awkward negotiation between Shakespeare the English national poet and what we now call 'global Shakespeare' arguably began with Gollancz's contribution to the tercentenary, above all the *Book of Homage* with its extraordinary global reach at the time of a world war, but the tensions of Shakespearean commemoration and the ongoing struggle for 'ownership' of Shakespeare have led to a sustained distortion of his role in the establishment of the primary players in the Shakespeare industry in Britain today and it has cost him his place in public memory.

FOUR CENTURIES OF CENTENARIES: STRATFORD-UPON-AVON

MICHAEL DOBSON

When Gordon McMullan and I were first discussing the possibility of there being a joint Stratford and London World Congress in the great Shakespearean anniversary year of 2016, we thought it would be appropriate to remind delegates at the outset of the long history of Shakespearean commemorations in Stratford and London of which that congress would be the latest expression. I say 'in Stratford and London', but of course I really mean 'in Stratford and London respectively', since the history of celebrating Shakespeare in Britain has so often been a history of deplorable, foolish, petty-minded rivalries between the place where Shakespeare really belonged and the place to which he was sometimes reluctantly forced to travel to work. So Gordon and I agreed, with surprisingly little difficulty, that the first Stratford plenary should be prefaced by a few words about the continuing story of Shakespearean anniversary events in Stratford; and that the first London plenary, similarly, should be prefaced by a few words about the continuing story of Shakespearean anniversary events in London. This short conspectus of the history of Shakespearean centenaries in Stratford – which draws on a considerable and still growing body of recent academic work on Shakespearean commemorations and festivities – is one result, and a version of Professor McMullan's corresponding London pre-plenary can be found elsewhere in this volume of *Survey*. Diplomatically, I should stress, the most important thing about these two articles, one about Stratford, one about London, is not their content but the fact that they should be of exactly equal prominence, status and length.

1616

As far as the main business of commemorating Shakespeare is concerned, you might think that most of it had been covered once and for all by the end of 1616, or at the very least by mid-1623. In the immediate aftermath of the playwright's death there was still a theatre company, performing such of the plays as were still in demand, in London; while in Stratford there was soon a suitable monument to the plays' author, complete with an English epitaph, and also with one in Latin.[1] The Latin one likened him to wise Nestor, deep Socrates and poetic Virgil, and stated that, covered by the earth and mourned by the public, Shakespeare now dwelt – perhaps surprisingly – not on Mount Parnassus, among the Muses, as one might expect, but on Olympus:

IVDICIO PYLIVM, GENIO SOCRATEM, ARTE MARONEM,
TERRA TEGIT, POPVLVS MÆRET, OLYMPVS HABET.

Within seven years of Shakespeare's death, furthermore, there would be a conveniently portable book, the First Folio, which spoke both of the Stratford monument and of the London theatre,

---

[1] On the monument, see Samuel Schoenbaum, *William Shakespeare: A Compact Documentary Life* (Oxford, 1987), p. 308; Brian Kemp, *English Church Monuments* (London, 1980), p. 77; Peter Sherlock, *Monuments and Memory in Early Modern England* (Aldershot, 2008), p. 150; Park Honan, *Shakespeare: A Life* (Oxford, 1998), pp. 402–3.

purporting to give author and plays alike a renewed life in print. In some respects the story which Gordon and I each have to tell is the story of how that book's continuing afterlife has complicated the original binary pattern by which Shakespeare had a monument in Stratford and a theatre in London, since its contents have inspired generations of fans to try to complete the respective ends of Shakespeare's earthly commute by putting up monuments in London and theatres in Stratford. These edifices have in turn inspired competing monuments in Stratford and competing theatres in London, apparently ad infinitum.

1764

As far as we know, the 1664 centenary of Shakespeare's birth and the 1716 centenary of his death went completely unmarked in either London or Stratford (the publishers of the Third Folio in 1664 and of Richard Leveridge's *The Comick Masque of Pyramus and Thisbe* in 1716 both missed what their modern counterparts would certainly have seized as opportunities to market them as anniversary publications), but the 1764 bicentenary was a different matter. Admittedly it took the Stratford-upon-Avon town council and the actor, writer and cultural entrepreneur David Garrick five years between them to organize the event by which that anniversary would be commemorated. But to judge from the lasting influence of the stunt which Garrick finally staged in Stratford in 1769, it was worth waiting for.[2]

So many subsequent Shakespearean commemorative events have recapitulated elements of the Stratford Jubilee that it is hard to realize now what a bizarrely original statement it made in 1769.[3] No mere creative artist before Shakespeare had been hailed as a national icon through a combination of music, occasional poetry, visual art, popular song, processions, souvenirs, fancy dress and fireworks, let alone in that artist's provincial home town. Donating a statue of Shakespeare to the new town hall, Garrick helped rebrand Stratford as Shakespeare's; but he also rebranded Shakespeare as Stratford's. Inverting earlier reservations about the playwright's lack of classical learning and metropolitan polish into nationalistic boasts, Garrick declared the upstart crow to have indeed been a Warwickshire Will, miraculously superior as such to all classical and continental rivals ('Our Shakespeare compared to is no man, / No Frenchman, nor Grecian, nor Roman', as one of the songs he composed for the event, 'Warwickshire Will', declared).[4] There were no theatrical performances per se at the Jubilee (since at the time Stratford lacked a sufficiently genteel or capacious playhouse), but Garrick co-opted Holy Trinity Church for a rendition of Thomas Arne's oratorio *Judith*, and put up a special temporary thousand-seat ballroom-cum-temple, the Jubilee Rotunda, for the festival's centrepiece. That was, of course, the recitation of his own *An ode upon dedicating a building, and erecting a statue, to Shakespeare, at Stratford upon Avon*, with music by Arne.[5] It is a fitting tribute to this event's enduring influence

---

[2] The two founding modern studies of Garrick's Jubilee were themselves published in the anniversary year of 1964: Christian Deelman, *The Great Shakespeare Jubilee* (London, 1964); Martha W. England, *Garrick's Jubilee* (Columbus, OH, 1964). See also Michael Dobson, *The Making of the National Poet: Shakespeare, Adaptation, and Authorship, 1660–1769* (Oxford, 1992), ch. 5. For Garrick's own slightly disingenuous account of the event, see his play *The Jubilee* (1769), in Harry William Pedicord and Fredrick Louis Bergmann, eds., *The Plays of David Garrick*, 6 vols. (Carbondale, IL, 1980), vol. 2, pp. 97–125.

[3] On the originality and even profanity of the Jubilee, see Peter Holland, 'David Garrick: Saints, temples and jubilees', *Actes des congrès de la Société française Shakespeare* 33 (2015), http://shakespeare.revues.org/3020 (accessed 7 July 2016); reprinted in Clara Calvo and Coppelia Kahn, eds., *Celebrating Shakespeare: Commemoration and Cultural Memory* (Cambridge, 2015), pp. 15–37. Holland's essay began life as part of the anniversary phenomenon it investigates, as a plenary at the 'Shakespeare 450' conference in Paris in 2014.

[4] The song, including Dibdin's original music, was published in *Shakespeare's Garland, or the Warwickshire Jubilee* (London, 1770), p. 7. Garrick cut the verse about Shakespeare's superiority to the classics when he incorporated this song in *The Jubilee* (see Pedicord and Bergmann, *Plays*, pp. 108–9).

[5] David Garrick, *An ode upon dedicating a building, and erecting a statue, to Shakespeare, at Stratford upon Avon* (London, 1769).

that the Royal Shakespeare Theatre now stands on the site of that rotunda.

Obviously Garrick, an actor-manager from Lichfield, had a vested interest in asserting that a mere theatre professional from the Midlands could speak for his nation's heartland and for its heart alike. But whether or not we view the Ode primarily as a masterpiece of self-promotion, it would be central to the emergence of European romanticism. Like Thomas Jones's 1772 painting 'The Bard' (an illustration of Thomas Gray's 1757 poem of the same name),[6] the Ode presents the artist as the inspired voice of his native landscape and the voice of his freeborn people. There are reasons why it is from this period onwards that Shakespeare too gets irritatingly nicknamed 'The Bard': and there are also reasons why the cult which Garrick inaugurated beside the Avon should so soon have begun to spread around Europe. Goethe would declare 'Shakespeare-Tag' in Frankfurt only two years later, in 1771: from then onwards the establishment both of his nation and of the first fully national Shakespearean society, the Deutsche-Shakespeare Gesellschaft, were matters of historical inevitability. The idea of declaring Shakespeare distinctively vernacular and intensely local proved, perversely, to have enormous international potential.[7] The Jubilee, then, initiated a process by which Stratford-upon-Avon became one of the whole planet's favourite specimens of world-class parochialism.

1816

For the 200th anniversary of Shakespeare's death, one of London's Theatres Royal revived Garrick's play about the Jubilee and the other staged his Jubilee Ode.[8] In Stratford, though, the public had to be content with a revival of the Jubilee itself – or at least with a repetition of some of its central elements, in particular a public feast, a ball and a firework display. It is sometimes said that Stratford had no playhouse before the first Memorial Theatre opened in 1879, but this is not quite true. In the 1760s and early 1770s, Roger Kemble's company, for instance, had visited both the Town Hall and a theatre fitted up in the barn of the Unicorn Hotel just north of the Clopton Bridge (now the Pen and Parchment) – so that in fact John Philip Kemble and Sarah Siddons both acted in Stratford before they did in London.[9] One after-effect of the 1816 festivities, however, was the beginning of simultaneous agitation for an annual Shakespeare event in Stratford, and for a Shakespearean theatre, and both came together in 1827.

I admit that 1827 – the year of Shakespeare's 263rd birthday – doesn't sound like an obvious milestone in the story of Shakespearean centenaries, but the trouble with narrating the development of Shakespearean festivals from here onwards is that ever since the foundation of the mighty Shakespeare Club in 1824, every year in Stratford has been a Shakespearean anniversary year.[10] Let us be honest, in London every 23 April there are other things to do; but ever since the 1820s, Stratford has

---

[6] 'Poised on the edge of cliff clutching a harp, the last surviving bard places a curse on the English invaders before leaping to his death. This dramatic history painting has become iconic for Wales. Based on Thomas Gray's poem *The Bard*, it recounts the tale of Edward I's legendary massacre of the Welsh bards.' Amgueddfa Cymru – National Museum Wales – Art Collections Online https://museum.wales/art/online/?action=show_item&item=1154 (accessed 8 July 2016). Gray's poem includes a prophecy, complete with cryptic allusion to Shakespeare, to the effect that the Anglo-Welsh nation will have no poetry worthy of the bardic tradition until it is ruled by a Welsh dynasty, the Tudors.

[7] See Johann Wolfgang von Goethe, 'Speech on the Shakespeare Day', *Comparative Criticism* 7 (1985), 177–81. On the international spread of the Shakespeare cult after Garrick, see especially Péter Dávidházi, *The Romantic Cult of Shakespeare* (Houndmills, UK, 1998).

[8] See Adrian Poole, 'Relic, pageant, sunken wrack: Shakespeare in 1816', in Calvo and Kahn, *Celebrating Shakespeare*, pp. 57–77; pp. 60–3, pp. 66–8.

[9] See 'The borough of Stratford-upon-Avon: Shakespearean festivals and theatres', in *A History of the County of Warwick: Volume 3, Barlichway Hundred*, ed. Philip Styles (London, 1945), pp. 244–7.

[10] See Susan Brock and Sylvia Morris, *The Story of the Shakespeare Club of Stratford-upon-Avon: 'Long life to the Club call'd Shaksperean'* (Stratford, 2016).

been living out an annual psychic calendar according to which Shakespeare is passionately remembered every spring so that he can be just as passionately forgotten over most of the rest of the year. Staging the procession of Shakespearean characters cancelled at the original Jubilee due to torrential rain, the 1827 birthday celebrations had as their focus the dedication of Stratford's first designated Shakespearean playhouse, the Shakespeare Rooms on Chapel Lane.[11] Among many others, the former child star Henry Betty performed here, during one of his many farewell tours, and the building was only demolished in the early 1870s by James Halliwell-Phillipps, as part of his scheme to give the site of Shakespeare's house at New Place a larger garden. A more lasting union in Stratford of the ideas of Shakespearean memorialization and of Shakespearean performance would have to wait a little longer.

1864

Nationally, the tale of the 1864 tercentenary, sadly, is one of disappointed good intentions, interminable committee meetings, funding shortfalls, personal irritation between representatives of different institutions in London and in Stratford with different cultures and different agendas, and all sorts of other things which it is now completely impossible to imagine.[12] Locally, though, it was not all bad. J. Ross Brown's map (Illustration 1) admittedly dates from later than 1864 (it was published in 1908),[13] but it does show clearly two of the things which made Stratford's celebrations of Shakespeare's 300th birthday so different from preceding festivities. One of them can be seen puffing its way up the centre of the map from left to right. In 1859 Stratford had acquired a railway station, though admittedly the town has never psychologically got used to the idea, and it nowadays manages by a combination of perpetual engineering work and malicious timetabling to have the rail service used as little as possible. But in 1864, Shakespeare's birthday could be celebrated by larger crowds than ever before, with some 30,000 visitors, many on day trips from Birmingham, swelling the population.[14] The other involves the most important local attraction singled out for special illustration in the right-hand margin of Ross's map. In 1847 Shakespeare's birthplace had been acquired for the nation through the establishment of the Shakespeare Birthplace Trust, and this event had given further expression to something implicit in the Jubilee, the idea of Shakespeare as the common property of the people. By 1864 this had developed into a national campaign for the building of a publically funded Shakespearean national theatre (the first articulation of which, an 1848 pamphlet by Effingham Wilson, seeks deliberately to follow up the successful establishment of the Birthplace Trust by adopting the title *A House for Shakespeare*), a campaign which sadly failed for the time being, partly as a result of disagreements as to where it should be sited,

---

[11] A woodcut of the procession adorns the first page of *The Mirror of Literature, Amusement and Instruction* for 5 May 1827: this is now reproduced on a wall in the Great Garden of New Place in Stratford, not only the former site of the Shakespeare Rooms but for many years the mustering-place for the Birthday procession. The *Mirror* woodcut can be consulted digitally via the Folger website: see http://luna.folger.edu/luna/servlet/detail/FOLGERCM1~6~6~334643~144330:Shakspearian-Jubilee-Procession,-18 (accessed 7 July 2016).

[12] The whole story is recounted in Richard Foulkes, *The Shakespeare Tercentenary of 1864* (London, 1984). See also Andrew Dickson, '"The wrong thing in the right place": Britain's tercentenary of 1864' and John Cunningham, '"Solemn and appropriate Shakespearean music": The Stratford tercentenary of 1864', in *Shakespeare Jubilees, 1864–2014*, ed. Christa Jansohn and Dieter Mehl (Zurich, 2015), pp. 13–30, 57–78. On the Working Men's Shakespeare Committee and the (unsuccessful) campaign to raise money for a national theatre and/or a Shakespearean monument via amateur dramatics, see also Michael Dobson, *Shakespeare and Amateur Performance: A Cultural History* (Cambridge, 2011), pp. 89–92.

[13] https://commons.wikimedia.org/wiki/File:Stratford_On_Avon_historic_map_1902.jpg.

[14] On the coming of the railway and the expansion of visitor numbers, see Nicola J. Watson, 'Shakespeare on the tourist trail', in *The Cambridge Companion to Shakespeare and Popular Culture*, ed. Robert Shaughnessy (Cambridge, 2007), pp. 199–226; p. 213.

1. Bird's-eye view of Stratford-upon-Avon, by J. Ross Brown, 1908. Shakespeare Birthplace Trust.

whether in Stratford, or in that bigger settlement inconveniently off to the south-east.[15] Instead Stratford managed a Shakespearean art exhibition in the Town Hall, and a temporary structure, a 'Grand National Pavilion', erected for three weeks near that Unicorn Hotel barn.[16] During the week of the birthday proper, this housed the now-customary dinner and the mandatory fancy dress ball, but these expensively ticketed, exclusive affairs provoked considerable popular resentment. More widely praised were performances of *Othello* and *Much Ado About Nothing*, staged later on in the same building to 4,000-strong audiences, productions which were locally regarded as much more impressive than anything organized in London. In due course, Stratford's new accessibility by rail and, later, by horseless carriage enabled the growing internationalism of the annual birthday festivities to receive official sanction, as the rainbow-coloured ribbons of the original Jubilee were replaced by flags of all nations, now unfurled by ambassadors and other representatives of the civilized world.

---

[15] On this difficulty, see also Michael Dobson, 'Shakespeare and the idea of national theatres', *Shakespeare Survey* 57 (2015), pp. 221–33.

[16] On the art exhibition, the Pavilion, their contents and the accompanying statues, transparencies and fireworks, see Alan Young, 'Art and English commemorations of Shakespeare 1769–1964', in Jansohn and Mehl, *Shakespeare Jubilees, 1864–2014*, pp. 79–98; pp. 87–92.

FOUR CENTURIES OF CENTENARIES: STRATFORD-UPON-AVON

1916

By the time of the tercentenary of Shakespeare's death in 1916, Stratford at last had a permanent Shakespeare Memorial Theatre, opened in 1879 at the expense of the Flower brewing dynasty, but the year's celebrations of the 300th anniversary of Shakespeare's death were all overshadowed by world war. Reporting on the birthday celebrations, the *Coventry Graphic* for 5 May 1916 reproduced a photograph of two soldiers in wheelchairs on Henley Street, with the caption 'A historic picture showing wounded soldiers at the Shakespeare Tercentenary celebrations at Stratford-upon-Avon, delivering wreaths at the immortal bard's birthplace, an eloquent tribute to his memory.'[17] The Birthplace Trust, however, did mount a large and scholarly exhibition of all the key early documents relating to Shakespeare's life in Stratford. This was seen in some quarters as a possessive gesture on the part of Sir Sidney Lee, an assertion of Stratford's claims to Shakespeare made in response to developments in the capital. London, after all, now boasted a university, full of active, professional, academic Shakespeareans such as Sir Israel Gollancz (on whom see Gordon McMullan, elsewhere in this volume).[18]

1964

Stratford's crippling lack of its own team of world-leading Shakespearean academics had of course been decisively remedied by the time of Shakespeare's 400th birthday. The University of Birmingham had established the Shakespeare Institute in 1951, and in the summer of 1964, it being an even-numbered year, it was holding its biennial international conference, the programme from which is preserved in the Shakespeare Institute library.[19] The topic, proving that the problem of coming up with sufficiently vague and inclusive conference themes is not a new one, was 'Shakespeare – Then Till Now'. The conference secretary, incidentally, was a promising recent PhD called Stanley Wells. (Sometimes I wonder what happens to these people.) Of about a hundred attendees, nine were women, and this was still the historical era when all-male advisory boards appeared to reproduce by parthenogenesis. The plenaries in 1964 included the late John Russell Brown on Shakespearean production, and Harold Jenkins on *Hamlet* – a nice unfussy lecture title, just '*Hamlet*'. In between the lectures and panels, delegates got to see the newly rebranded Royal Shakespeare Company performing the whole of both tetralogies of history plays, as directed by Peter Hall and John Barton.

The year's obligatory temporary building, which started life just over the Avon and then toured to Edinburgh and London, was the 300' x 100' 'Shakespeare Pavilion', containing the successor to Sidney Lee's 1916 display of documents, a show, designed by the art and dance critic Richard Buckle, called 'The Shakespeare Exhibition'.[20] Its publicists made some pretty rash claims: a pamphlet also preserved in the Institute library, for instance, promises potential visitors that they will be transported 'bodily' 'to Shakespeare's England, with its pomp and its bathos, its buccaneering and its bawdiness'. Whether on the grounds of the Trades Descriptions Act or those of health and safety, I am sure this would not be legal nowadays. Reviewers had some fairly mixed responses. The same pamphlet quotes the *Sunday Times*:

Whatever picture the words 'Shakespeare Exhibition' conjure up in the mind's eye, the astounding phantasmagoria

---

[17] This and other striking images are reproduced in the Shakespeare Birthplace Trust's online exhibition 'Let Slip the Dogs of War: World War One, Stratford, and Shakespeare,' hosted on historypin: www.historypin.org/en/first-world-war-centenary/let-slip-the-dogs-of-war-world-war-one-stratford-a/geo/52.194072,-1.708552,17/bounds/52.192217,-1.710864,52.195927,-1.70624/pin/262606 (accessed 4 July 2016).

[18] See also Gordon McMullan's excellent 'Goblin's Market: Commemoration, anti-semitism and the invention of "global Shakespeare" in 1916', in Calvo and Kahn, *Celebrating Shakespeare*, pp. 182–201.

[19] See p. PR 2888.

[20] See also Young, 'Art and English Commemorations', p. 97.

which has flowered on the Stratford-on-Avon water-meadows will utterly disrupt it. Indeed, this is no exhibition: it is a dream (edging now and again towards nightmare). Amazed and bemused by turns we float through an ever-changing hallucination; and perhaps will never be quite the same again.

For once, though, Stratford also managed a permanent building, and on time at that. Princess Alexandra of Kent had laid the foundation stone of the sensationally modern new headquarters of the Shakespeare Birthplace Trust on Henley Street, designed by Laurence Williams, only two years earlier, and on Shakespeare's birthday in 1964 the finished Shakespeare Centre was opened by the Duke of Edinburgh. The Centre too has always inspired mixed feelings, but in some quarters it is regarded as a classic of post-war New Elizabethan utopian architecture, and it was legally made a Grade II listed building in 2010.[21] After fifty-two years, then, there is not all that much that the Shakespeare Birthplace Trust can do about it.

2016

Let me close by simply recording some of what happened in Stratford to mark the 400th anniversary of Shakespeare's death. Perhaps we have a less confident attitude to the future nowadays than did the architects of the Shakespeare Centre in 1964: in any event, Stratford in 2016 has gone emphatically back to the roots of Shakespearean commemoration. Illustration 2 is one of my favourite pictures from 2016, taken on 22 April during the dress rehearsal for, of all things, Garrick's Jubilee Ode. Samuel West had just uttered the words 'What the hell have you got me into this time?'

What the hell it was a full-scale revival of the Ode, this time not in a temporary temple of Bardolatry but in Holy Trinity itself. It featured as much of Arne's rather good music as survives and some new passages by Sally Beamish, with the Birmingham-based Ex Cathedra, conducted by Jeffrey Skidmore, filling in for Garrick's original Drury Lane band and singers. The second half of the programme was a new commission,

2. Samuel West as David Garrick, preparing to recite the Jubilee Ode, Holy Trinity Church, Stratford-upon-Avon, 22 April 2016. Photograph by the author.

intended as a contemporary successor to the Ode, 'A Shakespeare Masque', with music by Beamish and libretto by the Poet Laureate, Carol Ann Duffy.[22] The whole thing was commissioned by the Shakespeare Birthplace Trust and the Shakespeare Institute, and produced with help from the RSC: it was broadcast live on BBC Radio 3 and could for some weeks after the

---

[21] See its entry on the Historic England website, https://historicengland.org.uk/listing/the-list/list-entry/1395091 (accessed 5 July 2016).

[22] At the time of writing, Duffy's libretto can still be found at www.bbc.co.uk/programmes/articles/gfBfyH0PzsMbTlrl7Dxyof/a-shakespeare-masque (accessed 20 December 2016).

event even be watched online via the BBC iPlayer. We shall not look upon its like again.[23]

Other elements of the 1769 Jubilee were revisited too. The year's local exhibition, a successor to Garrick's display of allegorical Shakespearean transparencies, was a highly theatrical show at the Compton Verney art gallery nine miles to the south, 'Shakespeare in Art: Tempests, Tyrants, and Tragedies', co-designed by the RSC's Stephen Brimson-Lewis.[24] The Birthplace Trust, meanwhile, were putting the final touches to the stunning redisplay of the site of Shakespeare's house, New Place, as designed by another RSC visionary, Tim O'Brien – a veteran of sufficient years to have worked in his youth on that dreamlike exhibition in 1964. In the best Stratford tradition, the full opening had to be postponed into the early autumn due to torrential rain over the summer, but, again in the best Stratford tradition, the souvenir shop was already up and running in time for the World Shakespeare Congress in the first week of August.

Shakespeare's status as poet of the people, and the RSC's ambition to be a Stratford-based but genuinely national theatre company, were reaffirmed by the epic *Dream 16* project, also known as *A Midsummer Night's Dream: A Play for the Nation*, by which an RSC *Dream* (directed by Erica Whyman) toured the UK using different amateur groups as mechanicals and fairies wherever it went (see the performance review elsewhere in this volume). The BBC jumped on the semi-pro bandwagon too, broadcasting a live radio show from Stratford during the birthday weekend in which all the passages from Shakespeare were performed by Shakespeare Institute PhD students.

The mandatory temporary Stratford building of 2016, then, was the BBC's pop-up studio, which appeared in the lobby of what used to be the Courtyard theatre on Waterside. Much more momentously, in 2016 the RSC finally opened a new auditorium actually in a centenary year, turning part of the shell of the Courtyard into the third Other Place studio theatre. And of course, in the best tradition of 1769, there were fireworks, set off from the roof of the Royal Shakespeare Theatre at the end of the birthday itself, at the close of the RSC's 'Shakespeare Live' variety gala, itself transmitted worldwide by the BBC – a facility sadly unavailable to Garrick, but which you just know he would have used if he had been able to.

One last thing about 2016: the fancy dress element. This year, instead of being corralled into a ball, it invaded the birthday procession, in a fairly disconcerting way. On the stroke of 11am, everyone in the procession and in the vast crowds donned a paper Shakespeare mask. I have been pondering what this meant ever since, often when waking from nightmares, but I now have a provisional theory. At the climax of an ecstatic massed public ceremony of Bardolatry, we were all assuming a little of the godhead.

Which takes me back to 1616 or shortly thereafter, and to that Latin epitaph. Perhaps it was a mistake back then, and whoever the local Latin scholar was should have said that Shakespeare was on Parnassus rather than on Olympus. But after four centuries of organized and sometimes disorganized civic veneration, it surely is not a mistake any more. Not in Stratford-upon-Avon, at least, where Shakespeare is quite definitely a god.

---

[23] On this project, see Paul Edmondson and Ewan Fernie, eds., *New Places: Shakespeare and Civic Creativity* (London, forthcoming, 2017). This was the first time Garrick's Ode had been performed for a Shakespeare anniversary since it was dusted off at Drury Lane in 1816, though it did get revived (albeit a long way from Stratford or London), at the Dartington Hall summer school in Devon in the millennium year of 2000, with Clive Francis as Garrick. I am grateful to Iain Mackintosh for a vivid eyewitness account.

[24] On this show, which included a reunion of the surviving pieces of Romney's enormous painting of the opening storm from *The Tempest*, several Fuselis and a striking new 3D installation by Kristy and Davy McGuire called 'Ophelia's Ghost,' see for example, www.comptonverney.org.uk/shakespeare-art-tempests-tyrants-tragedy/ (accessed 4 July 2016).

WRITING AND RE-WRITING SHAKESPEARE'S LIFE: A ROUNDTABLE DISCUSSION WITH MARGRETA DE GRAZIA, KATHERINE SCHEIL, JAMES SHAPIRO AND STANLEY WELLS

PAUL EDMONDSON

Shakespearian biography is constantly being created and recreated as new directions, themes, methodologies and areas of interest spring up and long-established tropes are recycled and given fresh life. The quatercentenary of Shakespeare's death was commemorated by several major, biographically focused projects and events. There was the launch of the Folger Shakespeare Library's online *Shakespeare Documented*; there was the British Library's exhibition, *Shakespeare in Ten Acts*; the National Archives presented its findings following the new research on Shakespeare's will; the remains of the Curtain Theatre were excavated in Shoreditch; and the Shakespeare Birthplace Trust re-opened the site of New Place, freshly curated and re-presented, following five years of intermittent archaeology.

The anniversary year presented an especially appropriate opportunity to reflect on how and why we write about Shakespeare's life. This article is a digest of a roundtable discussion with some of the leading voices in Shakespearian biography that took place at King's College, London, on Saturday 6 August 2016. In convening the panel, I wanted to bring together two biographers (James Shapiro and Stanley Wells) and two historiographers of biography (Margreta de Grazia and Katherine Scheil). Their contributions as they appear here are extrapolated from a transcript of the discussion and modified by the authors themselves (or by me, with their consent). The occasional overlaps have been left to remain since these help to evoke the emphases and engagements of the live discussion.

HOW DOES BIOGRAPHY DIFFER FROM HISTORY?

Stanley Wells

I would say that biography is a subdivision of history, that the biographer is dealing with historical facts and is trying to create a narrative out of those historical facts. There are many different ways of doing that. Like the historian, the biographer has to rely on documentary evidence. Indeed, the most elementary form of biography, I suppose, is a chronological list of the principal events in the life of the subject.

Biography – more fashionably known now as life-writing – is distinguished by its concentration on a single individual, or occasionally on more than one, as in Michael Holroyd's admirable *A Strange Eventful History* of 2008, subtitled *The Dramatic Lives of Ellen Terry, Henry Irving, and Their Remarkable Families*, which draws attention to the fact that anybody's life is bound up with other people's lives. Holroyd takes three members of the same family and writes in detail about them. If you're writing about Shakespeare you are, inevitably, writing about the people whom Shakespeare knew. Like historians, biographers of persons long dead – such as Shakespeare – have to rely on documentary evidence, such as is provided by legal records of many different kinds: church registers, parish records, court cases, memoirs, letters, wills, monuments, portraits, written accounts and anecdotes of varying degrees of reliability.

WRITING AND RE-WRITING SHAKESPEARE'S LIFE: A DISCUSSION

The major sources for Shakespeare's life have often been surveyed in works that inevitably grow out of date to varying degrees as new discoveries are made. *The Shakspere Allusion Book: A Collection of Allusions to Shakspere from 1591 to 1700*, published as long ago as 1909 (and badly in need of updating), remains useful. In 1946 E. K. Chambers published a little book called *Sources for a Life of William Shakespeare* based on lectures given to Oxford B. Litt. students and drawing on his experience in compiling his magisterial, wide-ranging but austere, two-volume *William Shakespeare: A Study of Facts and Problems*, dating back to 1930, which is still a useful, if synoptic, resource. B. Roland Lewis's massive, two-volume work *The Shakespeare Documents: Facsimiles, Transliterations, Translations and Commentary* of 1949 offers ampler commentary on individual life records as well as transcripts of the documents themselves. It is not totally superseded by S. Schoenbaum's magnificently produced *William Shakespeare: A Documentary Life* of 1974, which reproduces in scrupulous facsimile (but does not transcribe) a comprehensive range of documents accompanied by a highly readable if (or because) idiosyncratic narrative commentary. Its lesser-known successor, *William Shakespeare: Records and Images* (1981), casts the net wider. Launched in 2016, the website *Shakespeare Documented*, monitored by the Folger Shakespeare Library, offers a comprehensive range of facsimiles, transcripts and commentaries of 'source materials documenting the life of William Shakespeare (1564–1616), bringing together all known manuscript and print references to Shakespeare, his works, and additional references to his family, in his lifetime and shortly thereafter'.[1]

Documentary sources require authentication – notoriously, for instance, any that have passed through the hands of J. P. Collier are suspect. No less significantly, they are frequently subject to varying interpretation. The date of Shakespeare's baptism is recorded, but not that of his birth; knowledge that baptism normally followed within a few days of birth provides a reasonable basis for conjecture but does not definitively pinpoint a date. Even statements by Shakespeare himself may not be wholly reliable. The publication of *Venus and Adonis* in 1593 shows definitively that he had written the poem by this date, but does the statement in the dedication that it is 'the first heir of my invention' really mean that it is the first thing he wrote?[2] Most unlikely, if we believe, with A. J. Gurr, that Sonnet 145, with its apparent puns on the name of Anne Hathaway – '"I hate" from hate away she threw, / And saved my life, saying "not you"' (ll. 13–14) – was composed during Shakespeare's courtship.[3] On the other hand, we should acknowledge that the commonly held view that Shakespeare turned to composition of his narrative poems during 1593–4 because plague caused the theatres to close, though highly plausible, is speculation rather than fact. The poems could have been lying in his bottom drawer for years. Personally, I think it unlikely that the highly wrought poems antedate any of the plays (collaborative or not), but the possibility should not be ruled out.

Anecdotal evidence, whether from Shakespeare's own time or from later, is especially subject to suspicion. Maybe he did – as his contemporary John Manningham wrote in 1601– supplant Richard Burbage in an amorous assignation with a citizen's wife; maybe he poached deer at Charlecote; maybe he did die of fever after a drinking bout; maybe he was, as John Aubrey wrote several decades after Shakespeare died, at one time 'a schoolmaster in the country'; but none of these stories is backed up by evidence that would stand up in a court of law, and some of them conflict with other stories. But they are all part of what

---

[1] 'About Shakespeare Documented', *Shakespeare Documented*, www.shakespearedocumented.org/about.
[2] *William Shakespeare: The Complete Works*, ed. Stanley Wells, et al., 2nd edn (Oxford, 2005), p. 224. All subsequent Shakespeare quotations refer to this edition.
[3] A. J. Gurr, 'Shakespeare's First Poem: Sonnet 145', *Essays in Criticism*, 21 (1971), 221–6.

Chambers and others have called the Shakespeare mythos, and only the most austere of biographers would be likely to ignore them completely.

HOW HELPFUL IS IT FOR SHAKESPEARE'S WORKS TO BE RELATED TO ACCOUNTS OF HIS LIFE?

Margreta de Grazia

For me this question is really about what biography has to add to our knowledge and appreciation of his works. Shakespeare's works were being acted and read before there was any biography. It is not until after 1800 that anything that we would recognize as a Shakespeare biography exists, by which I mean something resembling a continuous cradle-to-grave narrative.

The little bits and pieces, those early anecdotes that we call biographical, were circulating in different kinds of texts and were being gathered together in antiquarian compendia. When Nicholas Rowe collected some of these, along with other points of reference, and put them at the front of his edition of Shakespeare in 1709, it marks the first time that an account of his life is placed at the threshold of his works. Rowe did that not because he thought that biography was important to the reading of Shakespeare but rather because his publisher, Jacob Tonson, had prefixed biographies to his editions of the ancients: Homer and Virgil, for example. By following the same format in printing Shakespeare, it was hoped that his status would be elevated to their level. A prefatory biographical account was the bibliographic marker of a classic.

Rowe is fascinating because he produced a biographical account but was uncertain how to bring it to bear on the works. He was not the only one. Think of Edmond Malone. He came much closer to writing something that, to us, resembles a biography, based on documentary evidence but working towards a comprehensive and continuous narrative. But his 500-plus page biography breaks just at the point when Shakespeare reaches London. He hasn't sufficient material to eke out Shakespeare's life during this period, from his arrival in London to his 'retirement' in Stratford, so he slots in what previously had been an independent essay: his attempt at a chronology of the works. He simply did not have enough verifiable facts about that key stretch to correlate with Shakespeare's works.

Biography still remains dependent on the devising of a chronology, nowhere more than in James Shapiro's two biographies. You take a year; things happen in that year; Shakespeare experiences them, as does his audience, and during that time he writes certain works. It's a chronology of the works that enables you to interrelate the works with both biography and historical events. Until you have such a chronology, even a conjectural one (and that is all we have ever had), the works cannot be interlocked with the life in a way that looks to us properly biographical. The fact that a chronology of Shakespeare's works is to this day uncertain and unstable renders the whole biographical enterprise fundamentally shaky. We know the latest possible date when a play could have been written but not the actual date of composition. In some cases, we might know when a play was first performed or first published, but that is not the same as knowing when it was composed.

WHAT CONSTITUTES SPECULATION, AND IS IT WELCOME?

Stanley Wells

I don't see how we can avoid speculation: speculation about what some people call the lost years, for example. It's perfectly natural that people should wonder about that and then provide a possible explanation: 'It might've been this, it might've been that.' Of course novelists do this all the time, and one interesting example is Anthony Burgess's *Nothing Like the Sun* (1964), a biographical novel, produced before he then wrote a Shakespeare biography (published in 1970), which is itself a biographical piece of fiction. At the end of one paragraph in the biography, Burgess writes, 'the whole of this paragraph is very unsound', and he's quite right too; it is.[4] In other words, he is acknowledging that speculation and fiction have helped to produce the biography.

The lives of creative writers pose special problems to their biographers. The works of art that they produce are certainly part of their life story, an index at least to their imaginations, to their inner lives – which after all is most likely to be why we are interested in those writers in the first place. I think it's important to try to consider the inner life of Shakespeare, a sort of spiritual biography. That, it seems to me, can only be discerned through the work, through his writings and the development of his imagination. A biographer may legitimately seek to interpret the works in relationship to external biographical facts but will need to exercise great sensitivity in so doing. In his plays, Shakespeare almost never writes as himself (prologues and epilogues may seem to be an exception). But no one can deny that he read extensively in composing them; so it is legitimate, for example, to portray him as studious and thoughtful, as well as a hard-working and observant man with a keen sense of humour. Shakespeare's works can only be ignored by biographers who are interested exclusively in his external life.

Some writers, seeking correspondences between situations portrayed in the plays and events in Shakespeare's life, find links between them; for example, between the death of his son Hamnet and the grieving of Constance over Prince Arthur in *King John*, or even between Shakespeare and Prospero – father, artist, reader, plotter. Other writers rigorously and vigorously deny the validity of such interpretative exercises.

It is possible too to write what may be described as partial biographies – books that focus on limited aspects of their subjects' lives. One example is Robert Bearman's *Shakespeare's Money*, subtitled 'How much did he make and what did this mean?' (2016). Another is Charles Nicholl's *The Lodger* (2007), centring on his life with the Mountjoys.

James Shapiro's *1599: A Year in the Life of William Shakespeare* (2005) and its successor *1606: William Shakespeare and the Year of Lear* (2015), combining biography with criticism, have had great success.

The situation becomes even more difficult when the subject of a biography writes in the first person, most conspicuously for Shakespeare in his Sonnets (or Charles Dickens writing from within his own experiences in *Great Expectations*). Do the Sonnets refer to identifiable if unnamed individuals, such as the Earl of Southampton or Emilia Lanier? Are they direct records of his emotional life or are they imaginary monologues, 'literary exercises' as the phrase goes, or are they perhaps a mixture of the two? And if so, how can we tell which are which?

WHAT PARTICULAR CONSIDERATIONS NEED TO BE BORNE IN MIND WHEN WRITING A BIOGRAPHY OF SHAKESPEARE?

James Shapiro

Anyone contemplating writing a life of Shakespeare must confront a familiar set of challenges. The first is 'What aspects of Shakespeare's life do existing biographies distort, ignore or simply get wrong?' I don't believe that you can write a compelling biography unless something genuinely disturbs you about the ways in which the story of Shakespeare's life has previously been told. You might, for example, imagine that the current portrait of Shakespeare is rooted too exclusively in his London life – and so, like Edgar I. Fripp in *Shakespeare: Man and Artist* (1938) or more recently René Weis in *Shakespeare Revealed* (2007), redirect attention to Shakespeare's life in Stratford-upon-Avon (which, on reflection, he never really left). Or you might feel that Shakespeare is regarded solely as a playwright (thereby slighting his body of work as a lyric poet). Or one who wrote for readers rather than playgoers. Or that religion

---

[4] Anthony Burgess, *Shakespeare* (London, 1970), p. 65.

played a greater (or lesser) role in his daily life than is ordinarily assumed. Since equal emphasis can't be given to everything, the first decision every biographer must make is what kind of story to tell, and that means highlighting some evidence and down-playing other aspects of his career. And there is inevitably a steep price paid for every choice.

Few fields in early modern studies are less theorized or historicized than Shakespeare biography. Too little work has also been done on the indebtedness of Shakespeare biography, taken as a whole, to other genres, including the *bildungsroman*, especially the highly influential and Shakespeare-saturated one by Goethe, *Wilhelm Meister's Apprenticeship* (1795–6), which has profoundly, and I fear permanently, muddied the relationship between the fictional and actual lives of the author of *Hamlet*.

It's also extraordinary how little reflection upon the refashioning of Shakespeare's life there has been, and the few exceptions to this have too often engaged in sniping rather than any kind of serious historical analysis. Why, for example, have biographies of him tended to flourish at certain moments — including the 1790s, the 1840s, and over the last few years — while languishing at others? What cultural forces account for these peaks and valleys? One possible explanation is that biography flourishes when the portrait of the artist falls out of alignment with contemporary values and scholarship. Take, for example, what has been published in the past twenty years. While there have been few archival discoveries about Shakespeare's life in these years, the many biographies written since the 1990s are clearly indebted to the great strides made in social and religious history, which have so radically transformed our understanding of Shakespeare's culture. Whenever the gap between our understanding of his fraught times and the familiar contours of his life have grown too great, biographers have scrambled to close that distance.

Another major consideration facing any Shakespeare biographer is form. Shakespeare is especially problematic for literary biographers working in the traditional form of the hefty cradle-to-grave biography, best exemplified in S. Schoenbaum's *William Shakespeare: A Compact Documentary Life* (1977) and Park Honan's *Shakespeare: A Life* (1998). These are both fine works, but, given how little is known of Shakespeare's formative as well as his final years, feel mighty thin at points (and both writers struggle, as other full-length biographers do, to resist the temptations of speculation, which inevitably reveals more about the biographer than his or her subject).

I'm far from the first biographer to recognize the pitfalls of the cradle-to-grave approach. Edmond Malone, the greatest researcher into Shakespeare's life, failed to complete his ambitious biography. The Victorian J. O. Halliwell-Phillipps tried to get around the problem of gaps in the life by penning what he called merely *Outlines of the Life of Shakespeare* (1881). Schoenbaum turned to writing the lives of those who tried (and largely failed) to pluck out the heart of Shakespeare's mystery in his *Shakespeare's Lives* (1988). And Katherine Duncan-Jones offers, as her subtitle indicates, only 'Scenes from His Life' in her *Ungentle Shakespeare* (2001). The quiet but necessary evasions of all these excellent biographers should give some sense of the problem of the so-called 'Lost Years' awaiting anyone pursuing a traditional approach.

I can think of some promising alternatives. Graham Holderness, in his *Nine Lives of William Shakespeare*, imaginatively, and in a variety of styles, explores many different possible lives (2011). And a richly rewarding approach has been put forward by Paul Edmondson and Stanley Wells in their collection *The Shakespeare Circle* (2015), which moves concentrically outward from the playwright's family to his friends, neighbours, colleagues and patrons. My favourite biography remains Charles Nicholl's *The Lodger: Shakespeare on Silver Street* (2007), which paints a vivid portrait of Shakespeare's life under the roof of the Mountjoys in the early years of the seventeenth century. It is an approach close to the one that I've pursued for the past quarter of a century, as I've tried to capture a slice of the life, first in *1599:*

WRITING AND RE-WRITING SHAKESPEARE'S LIFE: A DISCUSSION

A Year in the Life of William Shakespeare (2005) and then in *1606: William Shakespeare and the Year of Lear* (2015). One obvious advantage is that slice-of-life biographies can move more patiently and make potential connections otherwise impossible in works that must rush to cover a half-century of the writer's life.

The question of form is inextricably bound to that of audience. Are you writing a Shakespeare biography for fellow scholars? Or for a broader audience of general readers who might be interested in his life? It's not easy to do both, or do both well, since we've reached a point where academic and popular writing have drifted far apart. Those hoping to retell the story of Shakespeare's life will have to decide for whom, in the end, they are writing. So once again, tough choices need to be made, some of them practical: do you include extensive footnotes that risk alienating a public readership? Or, alternatively, do you provide instead of footnotes or endnotes a bibliographical essay, one that may leave scholars frustrated? Whatever you choose, prepare for strangers filling your inbox with emails expressing their disappointment in your choice.

WHAT MIGHT WE IDENTIFY AS THE BIOGRAPHICAL TRENDS OR INNOVATIONS IN THE LAST DECADE?

Katherine Scheil

One major trend is the desire to find ways to write about Shakespeare's life while avoiding the cradle-to-grave form of biography. Microbiographies have been a successful and insightful way to do this, focusing in-depth on a small period of time or on a single topic or angle. James Shapiro's *1599: A Year in the Life of William Shakespeare* (2005) and his prize-winning *1606: William Shakespeare and the Year of Lear* (2015) zoom in on single years in Shakespeare's lifetime alongside the events of that cultural moment, offering a depth of detail and analysis that a more traditional biography must eschew in service of the whole span of Shakespeare's life. Others have looked at a single topic, like Charles Nicholl's *The Lodger* (2007) or Robert Bearman's *Shakespeare's Money: How Much Did He Make and What Did This Mean* (2016), both of which isolate one aspect of Shakespeare's life as the organizing principle. Similarly, in *Finding New Place: An Archaeological Biography* (2016), Paul Edmondson, Kevin Colls and William Mitchell write a biography of Shakespeare's lost family home in Stratford as a way to illuminate the material realities of Shakespeare's life based on recovery of a key personal space. Another innovation is to examine the company that Shakespeare kept as a way to recreate his life experiences. Paul Edmondson and Stanley Wells's *The Shakespeare Circle* (2015) is an example of this trend, looking at the circle of intimate and more distant acquaintances, including friends, relatives, fellow actors, collaborators and patrons. It is worth pointing out that the various chapters in *The Shakespeare Circle* are allowed either to resonate with each other, or to create productive dissonances, so that readers can see the possibilities for multiple interpretations of the same thing – there is no overarching, agreed-upon party-line throughout the book. Without the imperative to tell a story from Shakespeare's birth to his death, biographical works are free to provide greater depth from specific angles, offering a much richer account of more targeted topics, periods or problems.

A related variation is to use Shakespeare biography to tell the life story of the author. Dominic Dromgoole's *Will and Me: How Shakespeare Took Over My Life* (2006) and Herman Gollob's *Me and Shakespeare: Adventures with the Bard* (2003) both attempt to present an author's memoirs in relationship to Shakespeare. Likewise, Michael Pennington, who described his relationship with Shakespeare as a 'long marriage', in *Sweet William: Twenty Thousand Hours with Shakespeare* (2012) explores Shakespeare's life and works through his own life as an actor.

Another trend in the last decade is a more overt acknowledgement of the role of fiction in Shakespearian biography. Graham Holderness's *Nine Lives of William Shakespeare* (2011) is the clearest example of this mode, where Holderness offers nine different versions of Shakespeare's life using the same material – writer, player, butcher-boy, business-man, etc. – followed by an imaginative work based on that chapter's emphases. The literary nature of Shakespearian biography was also a topic for Brian Cummings's 2014 lecture at the Folger Library in honour of Shakespeare's birthday. Entitled 'Shakespeare, Biography, and Anti-Biography', Cummings's lecture explored the roles of fiction, myth and memory in the various recreations of Shakespeare's life. The rapidly expanding field of biofiction also has embraced Shakespeare's life as vibrant subject matter. While biofiction is not the same thing as biography, it nevertheless draws on the same combination of historical material and imaginative material, only in a different ratio. From Grace Tiffany's *Will: A Novel* (2004) to Christopher Rush's *Will* (2007), a growing number of biofictional works have exploited the opportunity openly to fantasize about Shakespeare's life through this form, and the 'what if' mode of biofiction has unsettled many assumptions behind traditional biographies. Jude Morgan's novel *The Secret Life of William Shakespeare* (2014) was even described by Gary Taylor as 'better written, and more interesting, than any scholarly biography'.[5]

WHAT OTHER AREAS OF EXPERTISE WOULD YOU LIKE TO SEE BROUGHT TO BEAR ON SHAKESPEARIAN BIOGRAPHY?

James Shapiro

Open any popular and cradle-to-grave Shakespeare biography to the chapter discussing the year 1603 – a point roughly midway through Shakespeare's professional career – and you'll discover that there are not many pages left to read. In Park Honan's standard biography, you have arrived at the fifteenth of eighteen chapters. And in Peter Ackroyd's confident *Shakespeare: The Biography* (2005), you have reached the eighth of nine sections. But how can that be, given that such works as *Measure for Measure*, *Macbeth*, *King, Lear, Coriolanus* and later and no less great Jacobean plays, including *The Winter's Tale* and *The Tempest*, have yet to be treated? And Shakespeare's move to the indoor Blackfriars Theatre has not yet occurred! And the story of his co-authorship of plays with George Wilkins, Thomas Middleton and John Fletcher remains as yet untold?

My point here is that the Elizabethan Shakespeare has always received a disproportionate share of attention, in large part, I suspect, because biographers remain overly preoccupied with the formative personal, sexual and religious experiences that shaped Shakespeare's life (despite the fact that we know so little about these, except by reading the life out of the works, a dangerous and, to my mind, foolhardy thing to do, insofar as the works are bound to tell us what we ask of them).

I'm as guilty as the next biographer of unthinkingly describing Shakespeare as an 'Elizabethan' writer, having spent fifteen years of my life on what he was doing in the year 1599. After finishing that book, I realized how little I really knew about the sea-change in Shakespeare's Jacobean career in the decade or so after he became a King's Man in 1603.

I ended up co-authoring and then presenting a three-hour BBC documentary on Shakespeare's Jacobean career, then chose a representative and consequential Jacobean year – 1606 – and spent much of the next decade exploring what was distinctive about Shakespeare's work after the death of Elizabeth.

My decision to focus on what was different about the Jacobean Shakespeare was also part of a larger effort – implicit as well in my earlier book on Shakespeare's life in 1599 – to encourage biographers to focus on his creative years rather than devote so much attention to the years before he became an actor, poet and playwright, or to the last few years of his life, spent in Stratford-upon-Avon. I cannot really fathom why so much attention

---

[5] Gary Taylor, 'Review of Jude Morgan, *The Secret Life of William Shakespeare* (2014)', *The Washington Post*, 3 April 2014.

continues to be spent on subjects like the 'second best bed'. Nor does it much matter to me how Shakespeare died. I'd rather see biographers wrestling with crucial moments in his writing career that we have not collectively thought deeply enough about, such as his transition from actor to playwright; his collaborative relationships with musicians, fellow actors and fellow playwrights; how he navigated the terrible plague years of 1592/3 and 1603; whether he wrestled with the choice of a career as poet or playwright even how he first obtained enough money to join the Chamberlain's Men, and so on. While there are no doubt more archival discoveries to be made, surely there is more than enough material out there to enable biographers to sharpen our sense of Shakespeare at particular times and in particular places, in both Elizabethan and Jacobean England, if we are willing to sift through it patiently and carefully enough. I'm hoping that the coming years will see more biographies in this vein. And I hold out hope that I live long enough for a discovery to be unearthed that overturns much of what we have long believed about Shakespeare.

WHAT KINDS OF SOURCES CONSTITUTE A SUBJECT'S AFTERLIFE?

Katherine Scheil

The sources for an afterlife depend on the stories one wants to tell about the subject, and they can be much more eclectic than those used for a biography. Some sources have greater historical legitimacy than others, but the form of the afterlife privileges story over verity. Thus, the twelve words in Shakespeare's will regarding his wife, 'I give unto my wife my second best bed with the furniture', have a much more dominant presence in stories of Shakespeare's afterlife than the Latin epitaph on Anne Hathaway's grave, where she is described as a devoted and devout mother. While the epitaph dates from not long after Anne's death and was probably written by her daughter Susanna Hall, the salacious potential behind the 'second best bed' line of the will far outweighs the less provocative source that still remains on her grave.

The genre of the afterlife can take multiple forms with greater freedom, and the sources need not be comprehensive, often producing wildly divergent but highly entertaining results. Witness the story told in Avril Rowlands's two-act play *Mrs. Shakespeare ... The Poet's Wife* (2005), where Anne Hathaway is a work-at-home mother who manages her household and writes the plays of 'Shakespeare' in her spare time. While this version of Shakespeare's afterlife has little basis in fact, the story nevertheless suggests that Shakespeare's wife may have had an influence over his oeuvre and was not a passive figure. Archaeological discoveries at New Place have revealed a host of cottage industries that took place there during Shakespeare's lifetime, lending possible support to the germ of inspiration behind Rowlands's imaginative play.[6]

It is worth considering how some of the sources and documents that are missing from the Shakespearian archive can be imagined to create an afterlife. The absence of New Place in the landscape of Stratford-upon-Avon properties, for example, has encouraged a proliferation of afterlives about Shakespeare based on the Birthplace on Henley Street and on Anne Hathaway's Cottage but not as many afterlives about the end of his life. The reinstatement of New Place as a physical space will hopefully inspire more imaginings of Shakespeare's family home and about the lives of Shakespeare's family in that central space.

The Ireland forgeries in the 1790s illustrate the desire for sources particularly related to Shakespeare's private life. Ireland's forgery of love letters between William and Anne, complete with supposed locks of William's hair, betrays the desire for documentation of a romantic relationship between the Shakespeares but one for which no sources survive (and which may never have existed in the first place). Ireland's forged love-letters were reproduced to meet demand in the 1790s, further underlining the point that the sources used to

---

[6] Paul Edmondson, Kevin Colls and William Mitchell, *Finding Shakespeare's New Place: An Archaeological Biography* (Manchester, 2016); see, for example, pp. 166–9.

underpin an imaginary afterlife need not be actual historical sources. When I went to see Shakespeare's will on display at the Shakespeare Centre, I overheard a woman at the exhibit tell a companion that she always thought the 'second best bed' line in Shakespeare's will was a negative statement, until she read Carol Ann Duffy's poem 'Anne Hathaway'. She remarked that, after reading Duffy's sympathetic poem, she knew for sure that the 'second best bed' was a term of endearment. For this reader, and for many others, fictional works about Shakespeare's afterlife can be read back into the life and used for interpretation.

So, the sources for an afterlife can include both factual and historical documents, as well as fabricated sources for what we wish had survived but may never have existed in the first place.

DO WE EVEN NEED SHAKESPEARE BIOGRAPHY?

Margreta de Grazia

There is an extraordinary and undeniable appetite for Shakespeare biography among the general readership, and of course that should be satisfied. I don't happen to share that appetite, but I am interested in how it shifts and changes over time, and what that might tell us, for example, about the relation between how Shakespeare is studied in the academy and how he is absorbed by a general readership. We have no trouble recognizing the impact of New Historicism on James Shapiro's *1599* and *1606*. But what is it about readers outside the academy that want to see Shakespeare's creative output grounded in major historical events? New Historicism in the academy presently seems to be on the wane, giving way to more formalist or aesthetic approaches, with increased emphasis on Shakespeare as a poet rather than player and dramatist, with a stronger relationship to the classics as well as to his literary contemporaries, and an interest in shaping his own reputation, including after his death. Will future biographies emphasize this slant, playing down the more recent prioritizing of him as a man of the theatre with his finger on the pulse of contemporary events?

Recently, I've noticed and admired two very different kinds of Shakespearian biography, both using unfamiliar documents to new and imaginative ends. We tend to complain about the paucity of documents relating directly to Shakespeare's life but the appendix to an article by Lena Orlin lists 108 such documents, all of which name Shakespeare in his lifetime.[7] In this article, and in her forthcoming biography, *The Private Life of William Shakespeare* (Oxford), Orlin will be using them to approach Shakespeare's life indirectly, through parallel or cognate lives that intersected with Shakespeare's but are better documented. Adam Hooks, in *Selling Shakespeare*, also creates a different archive for his account of Shakespeare that is at once bibliographic and biographic, tracing Shakespeare's career through several stages of the production and reproduction in print of his works.[8] I'm wondering, too, if the dozen new depictions of Shakespeare's coat of arms discovered by Heather Wolfe in the College of Arms and elsewhere will prompt a new biographical slant.[9] Previously we had associated that bit of heraldry with his father John, but these depictions after 1600 suggest to Wolfe the degree to which his son William was invested in gentlemanly status, though we probably aren't very happy thinking of Shakespeare as a social climber. But it has to be said that there has always been some disappointment with what we know of Shakespeare's life. It seems incommensurate with his plays and poems. We regard his works as consummate achievements. But his life seems, on the face of things, quite ordinary and hardly inspiring.

---

[7] Lena Orlin, 'Anne by Indirection', *Shakespeare Quarterly* 65 (2014), 421–54.
[8] Adam G. Hooks, *Selling Shakespeare: Biography, Bibliography, and the Book Trade* (Cambridge, 2016).
[9] 'Shakespeare Coat of Arms', www.folger.edu/shakespeare-coat-of-arms-discovery?_ga=1.159955573.973260982.1475999586 (accessed 29 November 2016).

THE MERCHANT *IN* VENICE: RE-CREATING SHAKESPEARE IN THE GHETTO

SHAUL BASSI

'O Rh+'. The blood type is clearly legible on the tag placed on the bullet-proof vest of the tall, heavily armed policeman, 'nearest his heart' (4.1.251). He is here, along with another fifty servicemen, because of Shakespeare. They are here because of the Ghetto. Everything becomes solidly, inescapably real when I read that simple sequence of numbers and letters. 'If you prick us do we not bleed?' (3.1.59–60). *The Merchant of Venice* is going on stage in the Ghetto of Venice for the first time in history (Illustration 3), and we are minutes away from the opening. The sky in this late evening of the end of July 2016 is blissfully clear. The cicadas will start singing soon.

Other people have reviewed the Compagnia de' Colombari show.[1] My task here is to illustrate the premises and history of the production, the thinking underlying the project, the vision behind the first encounter between Shakespeare's *Merchant* and its ideal historical setting. The occasion was the coincidence of two landmark anniversaries in 2016: four hundred years since the death of Shakespeare, five hundred since 29 March 1516, when the Republic of Venice decreed that the Jews of the city, mostly newcomers and refugees, must be confined to a peripheral, churchless square, the 'Getto',[2] named after an abandoned copper foundry. At the intersection of the two historic dates (and strategically preceding the World Shakespeare Congress in Stratford and London), the Ghetto of Venice hosted the first ever promenade staging of *The Merchant of Venice* in a joint production by Ca' Foscari University and Compagnia de' Colombari, a project that was some years in the making.[3] The nexus between the play and the place is not obvious. Shakespeare does not mention the Ghetto (nor any Venetian site other than the Rialto), but the Ghetto is arguably presupposed in the text. In Ser Giovanni Fiorentino's *Pecorone*, Shakespeare's main source for the plot, the anonymous Jewish moneylender lives in Mestre, a town in the mainland domains of the Venetian republic. When the tale was written in the fourteenth century, Jews were not allowed to reside in Venice. Shakespeare, who almost certainly never visited Venice but read and heard a good deal about it, may have heard of that relatively new Jewish area, as had his countryman and contemporary Thomas Coryat, who, in the most accurate description of early seventeenth-century Venice left by a foreigner, made a point of visiting the Ghetto. This space legally constituted by the Republic enabled social and cultural dynamics that were impossible in England and are central in the play.[4] The interaction between Shylock and the Christian merchants, his ambivalent relationship with conviviality (the much discussed contradiction between 'I will not eat with you, drink with you' (1.3.34–5) and the invitation to dinner he accepts in 2.5), and above all the romance between Jessica and Lorenzo

---

[1] See, in particular, Carol Chillington Rutter's detailed and insightful article in this volume.
[2] Riccardo Calimani, *The Ghetto of Venice* (New York, 1987); Robert C. Davis and Benjamin Ravid, eds., *The Jews of Early Modern Venice* (Baltimore, 2001).
[3] All the details of the production are at www.themerchantinvenice.org.
[4] James Shapiro, *Shakespeare and the Jews* (New York, 2016).

3. *The Merchant in Venice*, final scene. On location in the Jewish Ghetto, Venice, directed by Karin Coonrod. Photograph by Andrea Messana.

are all the result of the creation of a defined and sanctioned area where Jews were simultaneously included in and excluded from the city. In this light, the Ghetto may be said to inform the Shakespearian text as an indispensable, non-literary *source*.

As I have proposed elsewhere, there are two antithetical interpretations of the function of Shakespearian settings.[5] The 'archaeological' position assumes that Shakespeare was intimately familiar with a specific locale, even physically present there. The opposite, 'allegorical' position is interested in locations only insofar as they operate as conveniently remote metaphors for real places that are too close to home to mention and/or epitomize certain moral or political features. Shakespeare's Venice resists both interpretations: while there is no evidence of (or need for) a Shakespearian journey to Italy, in spite of certain naive attempts to prove the contrary, the city is too overdetermined in the early modern cultural imagination to be just a stand-in for London.[6] The calculated construction and dissemination of a mythical image of itself on the part of Venice gained new momentum after the catastrophic defeat at the battle of Agnadello in 1509, the same crisis that propelled many Jews towards the city. It was under this 'state of exception' that the Ghetto was instituted:

[G]iven the urgent needs of the present times, the said Jews have been permitted to come and live in Venice, and the main purpose of this concession was to preserve

---

[5] Shaul Bassi, *Shakespeare's Italy and Italy's Shakespeare. Place, 'Race', Politics* (New York, 2016).

[6] David C. McPherson, *Shakespeare, Jonson, and the Myth of Venice* (Newark, 1990); Shaul Bassi and Alberto Toso Fei, *Shakespeare in Venice. Exploring the City with Shylock and Othello* (Treviso, 2007); Graham Holderness, *Shakespeare and Venice* (Farnham, 2010).

the property of Christians which was in their hands. But no god-fearing subject of our state would have wished them, after their arrival, to disperse throughout the city, sharing houses with Christians and going wherever they choose by day and night, perpetrating all those misdemeanours and detestable and abominable acts which are generally known and shameful to describe, with grave offense to the Majesty of God and uncommon notoriety on the part of this well-ordered Republic ... all the Jews who are at present living in different parishes within our city, and all others who may come here, until the law is changed as the times may demand and as shall be deemed expedient, shall be obliged to go at once to dwell together in the houses in the court within the Geto at San Hieronimo, where there is plenty of room for them to live.[7]

The words of the decree deserve to be quoted at length because the religious and social tropes around which the Ghetto was voted into existence, resonate powerfully in Shakespeare's play. The Jews who blend in with Christians and become agents of contagion, the necessary players for the economy and potential begetters of disorder, the people that good Christians go to when in urgent need. The charter of 1624, which restated rules established half a century earlier, clarifies the disparity between the actual conditions of moneylending and the astronomical sum of 3,000 ducats that constitutes Shylock's first words in the play: 'for the greater convenience of the poor, the Jews shall be bound to provide them with loans of 3 ducats or less in each pawn ticket, upon interest of 1 bagattino per lira per month and no more (= 5 per cent per annum)'.[8] Furthermore, the 1516 decree enjoined another binding condition: 'the Jews must pay a rent which will be higher by one third than that received at present by the landlords of the aforesaid houses'.[9] If someone was subjected to undue interest – usury – it was the Jews themselves.

This is the historical context in which Shakespeare imagined Shylock, and it is imperative that we constantly reiterate that Shylock is an imaginary Jew, the most influential imaginary Jew in Western culture. In 1555, Pope Paul IV decided to model new segregated Jewish quarters in papal territories on the Venetian plan and call them 'Ghettos'. From there the name extended in space and time to other ethnic enclaves and countless other physical, psychological, metaphorical forms of limitation and confinement. Today millions of people feel that they live in a 'ghetto', which has become, in sociological terms, a 'cognitive category', a signifier that has long relinquished its original loyalty to its Venetian signified.[10] And, as Shylock is a character in which a long history of critical and theatrical interpretations have sedimented, the Ghetto of Venice often becomes a screen where other future ghettos, especially the deadly ones of Nazi Europe, are projected, a palimpsest wherever new narratives are inscribed by different groups of visitors.[11] The least ostentatious landmark in Venice, it is its most opaque, intractable and indecipherable monument. In a city of arresting beauty, where each facade narcissistically doubles itself in the canals, the Ghetto was designed as an inward-looking place, where whatever was aesthetically precious – like its synagogues – had to be hidden from view. Following its desegregation in 1797, the Ghetto was excluded from the great literary myth of Venice forged by Byron, Ruskin, James, Mann, Proust and many others, and it remains the most misrepresented site in Venice. Bringing Shylock to the Ghetto, in the last analysis, was not an attempt to bridge the gap between fact and fiction, between the landscape of the theatrical mind and the cityscape of an iconic neighbourhood. On the contrary, *The Merchant in Venice* was predicated from the onset on a creative collision between the play and the place, in an attempt to see how two (early) modern myths could resonate with each other

---

[7] David Chambers and Brian Pullan, eds., *Venice. A Documentary History, 1450–1630* (Oxford, 1992), p. 338.
[8] Chambers and Pullan, *Venice*, p. 342.
[9] Chambers and Pullan, *Venice*, p. 338.
[10] Mitchell Duneier, *Ghetto: The Invention of a Place, the History of an Idea* (New York, 2016).
[11] Shaul Bassi and Isabella di Lenardo, *The Ghetto Inside Out* (Venice, 2014).

PRIDE OF PLACE

I vaguely remember hearing of the idea of staging the *Merchant* in the Ghetto at the time when Dustin Hoffman played a very proudly Jewish Shylock in New York in the 1980s, the same decade when the neighbourhood, after remaining marginal and invisible in the artistic and civic map of Venice, was becoming, once again, an important focal point. The installation of a Holocaust memorial turned it into a site of memory and a civic landmark; the publication of Riccardo Calimani's *The Ghetto of Venice* (prefaced by Elie Wiesel) put it back on the historiographical scene for a general readership; the renovation of the Jewish museum made it an increasingly popular tourist destination; the arrival of the Chabad movement reactivated, in a totally unexpected and initially disconcerting way for the local community, the cosmopolitan Jewish tradition of the area. For me, as a student and later scholar of English literature, Shylock was always the most direct, and never uncomplicated, *trait d'union* between my professional literary interests and my Jewish Venetian heritage, a connection made explicit by a grandfather whom I never knew, Gino Bassi, who in 1916 – the previous centennial – praised *The Merchant of Venice* as Shakespeare's demonstration of philo-Semitism.[12] Those were optimistic times for Italian Jews, building the new nation and forgetting the times where they had been ghettoized. Dying in the trenches of the First World War was the ultimate proof of loyalty on the part of these proud Italians 'of Israelite religion', an élan of patriotism that was surpassed only by the decision by some of them to join the Fascist party, that initially did not have an openly anti-Semitic agenda. My grandfather's expedient donning of the black shirt meant that the old liberal anglophile remained quintessentially Italian in deprecating Mussolini in private while becoming a party member to bolster his profession and support the family. This did not help when he and all other Italian Jews were declared an alien race in 1938. The family barely escaped deportation to the camps. If I indulge in these brief autobiographical remarks, it is because all these layers of personal and communal history have been intensely present in the decision to propose to my university that it led the project while asking the Committee for the 500 Years of the Ghetto (headed by my Jewish community, the moral authority over the place) that it endorse staging *The Merchant of Venice* in the Ghetto.

The Jewish community was fully supportive and *The Merchant in Venice* happened in the larger context of a rich programme marking the Ghetto quincentennial and being emphatically future-oriented. The programme included Simon Schama giving a plenary talk at the official ceremony on 29 March, a number of contemporary writers invited to reimagine the Ghetto in poetry and fiction, and a major exhibition at the Doge's Palace, the place where the Ghetto was voted into existence.[13] The accepted premise was that both the Ghetto and *The Merchant* are fundamentally *ambivalent* documents of Western civilization, in having been both instruments of intolerance and catalysts for cultural transformation. The guiding concept was that Shylock remains, no matter what, the most famous Venetian Jew of all times, and his ghost had haunted this place for a long time; it was high time he was exorcized. We were ready to add another layer to the palimpsest of the Ghetto. Predictably, the commemoration, and the Shakespeare production in particular, raised concerns that the Ghetto was being unduly glorified. Interestingly enough the terms of the debate were not markedly different from those set out by Salo Baron in his seminal essay 'Ghetto and Emancipation' (1928). Resisting the dominant narrative that Jewish emancipation had been 'the dawn of a new day after a nightmare of the deepest horror', a 'medieval' horror epitomized by the Ghetto, the Jewish historian maintained that in the specific historical circumstances there were relative advantages in an institution that 'grew up

---

[12] Gino Bassi, 'Nel terzo centenario della morte di Guglielmo Shakespeare', *Rassegna nazionale*, 16 April 1916, p. 11.

[13] For an overview of the programme: www.veniceghetto500.org.

voluntarily as a result of Jewish self-government' and only later brought about the situation that 'made it a legal compulsion for *all* Jews to live in a secluded district in which no Christian was allowed to dwell'.[14] Baron does not explicitly discuss Venice and only indirectly references it to locate in Pope Paul IV's bull *Cum nimis absurdum* (1555) the moment where the Ghetto assumes its 'extreme application'.[15] Baron's polemical edge against what he famously called 'the lachrymose theory' of Jewish history should be understood in its own geographical and historical context, and then alerts us to the circumstances of the Venice Ghetto commemoration. The main interpretative key of the quincentennial was one that aimed at emphasizing the agency of the Jews and their contribution to a city characterized by a long cosmopolitan and multi-ethnic tradition (the one that had clearly fascinated Shakespeare in both *The Merchant* and *Othello*), both before and after emancipation. This perspective, embraced by the quincentennial advisory board director, Donatella Calabi, and elegantly argued in her book *Venezia e il Ghetto*,[16] was opposed by its most vocal critic, who endorsed the lachrymose theory and excoriated the Shakespeare production as particularly inappropriate:

The Ghetto was a phenomenon of internal exile, three hundred years of segregation for a mass of people branded by the mark of difference, who were prevented from living full lives, like every other human being. To state that elsewhere life conditions were worse is no good reason to make people believe that that was, even then, a dignified life. It is truly embarrassing to witness celebrations and public events that have nothing to do with segregation, of which the Ghetto is an indelible sign and symbol.[17]

Such peremptory but ultimately marginal opposition deterred neither the community nor the committee, which officially approved the project. The university was willing to act as the main producer. The positive feedback and support was followed by, and subordinated to, the fundamental decision: which company could take up the challenge? Several leading Shakespearians were consulted, names were dropped, options were explored, preliminary contacts were established and harsh reality checks were made. An initial dilemma regarded the choice of language. Should we privilege the local audience and use Italian, or think more globally and adopt the original text? When Stanley Wells (an early and important supporter of the project) mentioned a festival devoted entirely to different versions of *Hamlet*, we briefly fantasized a panoply of *Merchants*, in many languages and styles.

Eventually, we – and at this point the plural pronoun is in order because the project had become inherently dialogic and collaborative – settled for English and for a production that could potentially draw the largest possible audience. Another cardinal point of the project was established from the start: this had to be a site-specific production. It would have been evocative to invite an existing production from a major international theatre, and perhaps interesting to re-enact the experiment of 1934, when Max Reinhardt adapted his successful version of *The Merchant* to the streets of Venice for the first edition of the Theatre Biennale. But the heart of our project was to make the Ghetto an essential component of the play from the very beginning. In an illuminating reading of *The Tempest*, Linda Charnes has defined Prospero's island as 'an entity in its own right, a place with a singular agency all its own … *the* major source of agency in the

---

[14] Salo Baron, 'Ghetto and Emancipation', in *The Menorah Treasury: Harvest of Half a Century*, ed. Leo W. Schwartz (Philadelphia, 1964), pp. 50, 55. Thanks to Jay Harris for pointing me to the essay.

[15] Baron, 'Ghetto and Emancipation', p. 55

[16] Donatella Calabi, *Venezia e il Ghetto: Cinquecento anni del 'recinto degli ebrei'* (Milano, 2016). For a recent survey of the historiographical debate on the Ghetto, see Gadi Luzzatto Voghera, 'A proposito della storiografia sugli ebrei di Venezia nel cinquecentenario della fondazione del Ghetto', *Quellen und Forschungen aus italienischen Archiven und Bibliotheken* 96 (2016), 2–8.

[17] 'Shakespeare 400. Umana (in)comprensione. Intervista a Dario Calimani', Venezianews, www.venezianews.it/index.php?option=com_content&task=view&id=8669&Itemid=338 (my translation).

play'.[18] The Ghetto has long been an important source of inspiration for Shakespeare actors and directors wishing to authenticate their Merchants and to reduce the distance between the stereotypical Shylock and the historical reality of Venetian Jews. This typically amounts to a sort of ethnographic fieldwork where the local expert – I have gratefully found myself in that position more than once – acts as a native informant. The central ambiguity of this approach is that making Shylock putatively more authentic warrants the interpretation that real Jews went about cutting off Christian pounds of flesh.[19] From the very beginning, we felt that to invite a major *Merchant of Venice* created elsewhere would not have been enough; only a production 'made in the Ghetto' could do justice to the occasion. Not a philological or archaeological gesture and let alone a sanitized, politically correct production of the play. At no point did we intend to turn Shylock into a nice individual to honour the memory of the Jews who were ghettoized and later persecuted here. At no point did we intend to recreate the illusion of travelling back into the sixteenth century. We would rather seek an event in which the Ghetto would not simply act as the backdrop of the action but would rather inspire, with its specific urban features and its multiple historical resonances, the action of the company. 'Place is something *all its own*' – Charnes continues – 'an entity that requires the participation of multiple modes of agency that include location, human perception, action and the passage of time. Through the alchemy of these elements, a Place can exert a powerful agency over its occupants and visitors. Unlike artful representation, Place can never be reduced to "the background of the phenomena it describes".'[20]

Unsurprisingly, there was another pressing factor. The genesis and early stages of the project coincided with a major political scandal in Venice, one that toppled the municipal government that had been supporting the Ghetto quincentennial and emptied the city coffers. With all my qualified sympathy for Shylock, I found myself in the position of Bassanio, seeking capital to pursue my labour of love. The intellectual debts in this adventure are too many to mention, but I want to acknowledge the precious advice given by James Shapiro, one of those rare scholars who successfully straddles the academic and theatrical worlds at the highest level. At a crucial moment, he cautioned me that some very famous actor could be genuinely tempted to accept the role of Shylock for this historic premiere, but that the forces of show business could also lure him away at any time (a prophecy that somehow materialized as regards a different role). In other words, with a compelling idea and no solid capital, we should seek somebody who would be artistically remarkable and flexible enough to accept the challenge of the place and time.

The stars aligned thanks to an intuition by another leading Shakespearian, David Scott Kastan. It was during a conversation with him and Kent Cartwright in late 2013 that the name of Colombari was first mentioned. A New York company with an Italian name, a multi-ethnic cast and a strong Shakespeare record seemed a perfect fit from the start. Born in Orvieto, Italy, in 2004, where the company re-imagined the medieval mystery plays and performed them in the streets and piazzas, the company describes its mission to 'generate theatre in surprising places' and to 'intentionally clash cultures, traditions and art forms to bring fresh interpretation to the written word – old and new ... Colombari brings performers and audiences together, thereby transforming strangers into community. Colombari is founded on the twin principles that the magic of great theatre can happen anywhere and be made accessible to everyone.'[21] A preliminary meeting in London

---

[18] Linda Charnes, 'Extraordinary renditions: Toward an agency of place', in *Shakespeare After 9–11: How Social Trauma Shapes Interpretation*, ed. Julia Reinhardt Lupton and Matthew Biberman (Lewiston, NY, 2010), pp. 68, 73.

[19] Shaul Bassi, '"The Christian will turn Hebrew": Converting Shylock on stage', in *Jewish Theatre: A Global View* (Leiden, 2009), pp. 113–32.

[20] Charnes, 'Extraordinary renditions', p. 76.

[21] See www.Colombari.org about-us.

with the visionary director Karin Coonrod, the driving force of the company, and her subsequent visits to Venice sealed the prospective collaboration. It may be a cliché but the whole project, which would eventually acquire the name *The Merchant in Venice*, in a small change of prepositions that alarmed many proofreaders but signified the singularity of the operation, evolved out of a close, continuing, curious, passionate dialogue across the continents.

The turning point happened with the Shylock project, a preparatory summer school held in Venice, at the Fondazione Cini, in June–July 2015, where the concept of the production was discussed with many project partners. The school was the platform where leading scholars and performers convened to explore Venice, the Ghetto and study *The Merchant of Venice* in a cross-cultural perspective. Forty international experts taught a group of twenty students and lectured to a general public.[22] Colombari came with a small cast of veterans of past productions, and the enthusiasm necessary to withstand the stifling heat of Venice summers (and perhaps the simultaneous presence of such a density of Shakespeare academics). Indeed, the graduate students, faculty members and Shakespeare lovers who attended the summer schools were treated to a smorgasbord of *Merchant of Venice* lectures, workshops, adaptations, field trips and performances. It was a tour de force that aimed at being at once a formative event in itself and a springboard for the production. Of the many aspects that one could mention of this rich experience is the fact that Coonrod had brought an exceptional Antonio with her but was still puzzling over her Shylock. It is the most ironical and sad episode of this story that Reginald E. Cathey, an extraordinary performer and generous individual, the catalyst of the company and protagonist of the summer, was wrenched away from the 2016 performance by his duties as a TV star in *House of Cards* (James Shapiro's prophecy). On the other hand, an experiment made during the same summer school while the director was still pondering whom she should cast as Shylock ended up being a signature of the production. There was going to be not one actor shouldering the responsibility of the key role. There were going to be five Shylocks.

'WHAT, ARE THERE MASQUES?' (2.5.28)

The Ca'Foscari/Colombari production did not intend to suggest any correct interpretation of the text or of the character as much as to offer a reading of the present of the Ghetto and of the topicality of the play. Colombari came to mobilize the dramatic potential of the play, its uncanny ability to dramatize anti-Semitism and to suggest ways out of it; it came to unsettle its audience with Shylock's own words: 'I am not bound to please thee with my answers' (4.1.64) (Illustration 4). To stage the play in the Ghetto was both to reactivate a forgotten tradition of the place as a performing space and to make a statement about Venice as a city that still produces and catalyses new culture and does not just display glamorous art and kitschy knick-knacks made elsewhere, whether in the art studios of New York or the sweatshops of Manila. Rather than choosing historical details, we chose historical metaphors. While emphatically not trying to recreate the atmosphere of the early modern Ghetto to authenticate the production, we definitely looked into that period to find a different kind of inspiration. Three episodes from the early seventeenth century highlight the Ghetto as a space of contact, exchange and confrontation, rather than of separation. The best-known one, often quoted in reference to *The Merchant*, is the visit of the English traveller Thomas Coryat to the Ghetto, who visits a synagogue and later engages in a theological dispute with a local Rabbi:

after there had passed many vehement speeches to and fro betwixt us, it happened that some forty or fifty Jewes flocked about me, and some of them beganne very insolently to swagger with me, because I durst reprehend their religion. Whereupon fearing least they would have offered me some violence, I withdrew my selfe by little

---

[22] The full programme at www.cini.it/events/shakespeare-in-venice-summer-school-the-shylock-project-3.

4. *The Merchant in Venice*, 4.1. On location in the Jewish Ghetto, Venice, directed by Karin Coonrod. Graziano (Sorab Wadia) berating Shylock (Ned Eisenberg) in the trial scene. Photograph by Andrea Messana.

and little towards the bridge at the entrance into the Ghetto, with an intent to flie from them, but by good fortune our noble Ambassador Sir Henry Wotton passing under the bridge in his Gondola at that very time, espyed me somewhat earnestly bickering with them, and so incontinently sent unto me out of his boate one of his principall Gentlemen ... who conveighed mee safely from these unchristian miscreants).[23]

The second episode concerns Sarra Copia Sullam, who, as a young Jewish woman with an extraordinary degree of self-confidence, published poetry, drama and philosophical works in an academy in the Ghetto where she hosted Jewish and Christian intellectuals. Sarra was embroiled in two controversies that ultimately forced her to abandon her public role and end her literary career. One provoked an inflammatory libel called the *Sareide*:

Thus at the end of the following month, August, the infamous libels were seen, the *Sareide* were read in the ghetto, insults were exchanged, abuses were shouted, threats of both passion and fury were hurled, all of them actions taken, understood, and viewed as a measure to turn a valiant, armipotent hero into an infamous trickster.[24]

Finally, I want to evoke an internal controversy, in which Rabbi Samuel ben Abraham Aboab excoriated a prominent member of the Jewish community for funding a theatre in the Ghetto:

He has degraded the crown and pride of the Torah to the earth. Within the holy camp [i.e. the Ghetto] he has built theatres and circuses, where men and women and

---

[23] Thomas Coryat, *Coryat's Crudities* (London, 1611). Modern edition: David Whittaker, ed., *Most Glorious & Peerless Venice* (Charlbury, 2013).

[24] 'Notices from Parnassus', from Sarra Copia Sulam, *Jewish Poet and Intellectual in Seventeenth-Century Venice*, ed. Don Harran (Chicago, 2009), p. 410.

children come together. Modest and chaste Jewish daughters sit together with profligate women of the streets, and all, great and small, violate the law of Moses ... If at least only adults went there. But what do they want of the little lambs? A great punishment awaits those who bring little children there. They lead them into temptation by having them sit with actors and listen to their obscene talk which poisons their young souls.[25]

I have singled out these three moments because, against any one-sided lachrymose view of Jewish history as well as any anachronistic and consolatory view of interfaith dialogue and post-enlightenment tolerance, they show the Ghetto not as a place of airtight separation, but as a contested space, a site of interrogation and conflict, one where Christians and Jews, much like in *The Merchant*, meet, fight and trade insults; where Jews quarrel among themselves over the uses and abuses of exogenous cultural forms; where Jews, locked in and subject to a curfew as they are, feel somehow empowered by the Ghetto. The unique conditions of the Ghetto made Venice a European capital of Jewish culture, and generated a cosmopolitan community that became very creative with the limitations imposed upon it.

ON LIMITS AND MISUNDERSTANDINGS

There is nothing new in suggesting that a theatrical production had very little space, very little time and very little money. And yet there is something special, if not welcome, in remembering that limitations were the defining condition of the Ghetto inhabitants, and that against and around these limitations they managed to be very creative, both in their everyday lives and in their influential cultural production. It is no accident that the word 'ghetto' has also long been associated with the idea of proud resistance to the condition of marginality and exclusion, of creative response to the severe limitations to which one is subjected. The production was a huge task that involved mixing people and acting styles, marshalling different organizational models, consulting with gondoliers for weather forecasts, respecting the Shabbat, dialoguing with the Jewish community and with the residents, working with the police, and courting and finding the very generous sponsors and donors who ultimately enabled a production that received no public funding whatsoever. The company really took advantage of the space of the Ghetto, crossing bridges, opening windows, projecting on synagogues and playing music on terraces. The physical and legal boundaries of the Ghetto became a source of inspiration. And the potential limit of not having a single iconic actor playing Shylock prompted the most creative, bold decision to have five different Shylocks acting in the show, splitting the part and making literal the multifaceted and somehow irreconcilable personality of the character. The role of Shylock as abandoned father and the deliverer of the 'Hath not a Jew eyes' speech was given to a woman, creating the most uncanny and powerful moment of dissonance in the production. Anti-Semitism was not eluded; it was summoned up. No Jewish Shylock, one could say, was allowed to usurp or supplant the real suffering borne by the Jews who were deported from Venice. And yet the prolonged howl of anguish uttered by the woman Shylock allowed for both empathy with Jewish suffering and for a more generalized identification with persecuted minorities.

Next to limitations, another concept may be key to interpret *The Merchant in Venice*. Citing the philosopher Vladimir Jankélévitch, the anthropologist Franco La Cecla writes that 'misunderstanding' is 'a moment of translation, a place where the essential incompatibility of individuals or cultures is negotiated' and, referring specifically to the Jewish case, that 'the ghetto is misunderstanding par excellence, because behind the negativity of the term hides something of advantage to both sides, those within and those without'.[26] I want to use this key to read a few aspects of the

---

[25] Cited in Erith Jaffe-Berg, 'Jewish theatre production in Venice during the Renaissance Venice before and during ghettoization', *Engramma* 136 (2016), www.engramma.it/eOS2/index.php?id_articolo=2895.

[26] Franco La Cecla, *Il malinteso. Antropologia dell'incontro* (Bari, 1997), pp. 9, 44.

play, showing both intentional and unintentional uses of misunderstanding.

A deliberate artistic choice was the incorporation of multiple languages in the production, echoing the multilingualism of the early modern Ghetto, which originated as a cosmopolitan community with Sephardic Jews from Spain and the Levant joining the Ashkenazi and Italian Jews who had first settled there, each 'nation' initially speaking their own language. Once again, there was less an attempt to reproduce such linguistic diversity as a 'reality effect' than an artistic gesture of punctuating the Shakespearian text with textual interpolations from traditional sources such as Commedia dell'Arte dialogue carefully selected by dramaturg Walter Valeri, and words and phrases from the play translated into Italian, Hebrew, Yiddish, Spanish and the Judeo-Venetian that developed inside the Ghetto. This linguistic carnival was made even more evocative by the diverse accents and inflections of an international cast of American, British, Australian, Indian and Italian actors from different regions. Mixing people, languages, acting styles and musical traditions – the composer Frank London also played with the expectation that he would draw on his celebrated Klezmer repertoire and created a soundscape more reminiscent of classic Italian film scores – was not only a tribute to a lesser-known aspect of local history but also a statement for our troubled present. An inattentive reviewer took issue with the uses of the words 'shabbat' and 'shalom' in the text, seen as a superficial smattering of Hebrew aimed at authenticating the scene. He would have been right, but he failed to register all the other, less obvious bits of Jewish languages that were deliberately worked into the play, with the assumption that they would *not* be understood (or to be more accurate, that different members of a very diverse audience would understand selectively).

A less premeditated misunderstanding originated during the summer of 2015, when the company left the island of San Giorgio, where so far they had been rehearsing, to give the Ghetto a try. As already suggested, the company did not come to make its Shylock and Jessica more authentic, or to learn the right colour of Shylock's hat. Rather, they came to learn the right colour of Venetian Jews' hats and decided that Shylock would remain bareheaded. As one can see in the BBC documentary *Shylock's Ghost*, the five Shylocks did perform a few scenes wearing a kippah, a skullcap bought from the Jewish museum. It was the easiest and fastest way to identify the character for the purpose of that little experiment, since nobody was wearing costumes. However, having myself written against the practice of authenticating Shylocks and having been told by some observers that the choice was not a wise one, I later raised the point with the director. The urgency of the detail was made even more evident by the last Italian production I had seen, where a modern dress and markedly comedic version saw Shylock (played by well-known film actor Silvio Orlando) wearing a pinstripe suit that made him indistinguishable from Antonio but donning a kippa and reciting a prayer at the very moment when he prepares to excise the pound of flesh. It was a perfect example of that return of the Jewish repressed typical of many well-meaning productions that are otherwise trying to defuse the anti-Semitism of the play. Having later been privileged to follow the early phases of preparation of the costumes, elegantly designed by Stefano Nicolao in close conversation with the director, I learned that the five Shylocks would be visually characterized by a yellow sash tied around their white costumes, in contrast with the red worn by the other Venetians over the same white costumes. It was a brilliant choice in many ways: it allowed actors to quickly switch between roles (each Shylock doubled as a different, Christian character) and it managed to evoke the colour that Jews had to wear (as a hat or as a badge) when they left the Ghetto during the day, while avoiding any pretence of realism. At that stage, I was also expecting the more customary choice of some caps of the same colour, in spite of the stifling July heat. Eventually the only players with heads covered were Portia, the Doge, Morocco and the musicians, leaving ironically the Jewish characters as the only bareheaded male performers. Had the director over-interpreted this specific concern over the use of the kippa? In a time of fierce controversies on the hijab, burka and 'burkini' as ethnic and religious markers pressing on the fragile European multiculturalism, the question of headwear remains open to debate.

THE SHOW MUST GO ON

The *Merchant in Venice* included a very special spin-off. The resonance of the event was such that we were blessed with a prestigious collateral event – a mock appeal to Shylock and Antonio presided over by the US Supreme court Justice Ruth Bader Ginsburg. Talking about misunderstandings, it was amusing to see how, early on, the news spread fast that she was actually going to perform in the play itself. In the imposing School of San Rocco, under the magnificent ceilings decorated by Tintoretto's dramatic revisitations of the Old Testament as harbinger of the New, after about two hours of arguments and twenty minutes of deliberation, the judges issued a unanimous ruling: the question of the pound of flesh was agreed to be 'a merry sport' that no court would enforce, Shylock was restored the 3,000 ducats and the demand of his conversion nullified. The judges also ruled that because Portia was 'an impostor' she be sentenced to attend law school. The lively pleadings by the lawyers were preceded by the 'Hath not a Jew eyes' speech passionately recited by F. Murray Abraham and followed by an exchange between James Shapiro and Stephen Greenblatt, adding up to a unique programme.[27] Three months later, Donald Trump was elected president of the US, advocating a political agenda and a public discourse antithetical to all the values and intellectual climate that the production and the mock appeal stood for.

Crucially, *The Merchant in Venice* also contained in itself the seeds of its afterlife. After five intense nights (and one late afternoon) in the Ghetto, the production continued with a challenging single performance at a prominent festival in Bassano, near Venice, which demonstrated that the actors had incorporated the Ghetto into the production and did not depend exclusively on the location.

And, in a highly symbolic occasion, an abridged version was performed inside a prison in Padua.

Another very important component was the multiple film projects associated with the production. Not only was the show video-recorded, but also the whole rehearsal process was documented by the sympathetic, perceptive and discreet presence of various filmmakers.[28] At a different level, *The Merchant in Venice* continues as the European Community-funded research project 'Shakespeare in and beyond the Ghetto', which is using the production as a springboard to make multiple resources available for future scholars, students and performers of the play.[29] A collaboration between Italian, German, Rumanian and British institutions that the Brexit vote will make impossible to replicate in the future.

The months preceding the show were marked by deadly terrorist attacks on European soil (Paris, Brussels, Nice), the escalation of the Syrian civil war, the 'failed coup' in Turkey that reduced the space of democracy, the Brexit referendum that separated the United Kingdom from the European Union, and a fierce debate on anti-Semitism in the British Labour Party. Pondering on the Ghetto as a performance space during the very early stages of preparation, I raised several questions, to which at least some tentative answers can be offered now. 'Is the project violating or infringing a sacred space? Does it impose the presence of the most hideous stereotypical alien? Is it forcing a global product on a local site?'[30] To this cluster of concerned questions, one can safely say, from the overall response and participation of all the agents at stake, that there was no sense of

---

[27] Rachel Donadio, 'Justice Ruth Bader Ginsburg Presides Over Shylock's Appeal', *New York Times*, 26 July 2016, www.nytimes.com/2016/07/28/theater/ruth-bader-ginsburg-rbg-venice-merchant-of-venice.html.

[28] *Perché Shylock*, documentary by Bruna Bertani and Felice Cappa (Rai 2016). Projects by the MIT Global Shakespeare programme directed by Diana Henderson and by Chicago filmmakers Ted Harding and Elizabeth Coffman are ongoing.

[29] 'Shakespeare in and beyond the Ghetto', www.shabegh.eu.

[30] Bassi, *Shakespeare's Italy*, p. 160.

violation and no tension. What is more important, though, is what lies ahead: 'Can the *Merchant* in the Ghetto add another narrative, a new critical layer?' Having discussed the prospects of the play, what about the future of the place? *The Merchant in Venice* was an experiment, an attempt to reconfigure the Ghetto for the future, respecting its role as religious centre, site of memory and tourist destination, but attempting to retrieve its vocation as meeting place, creative arena, contact zone between cultures and place of interrogation. The Ghetto remains an ordinary, fragile, vulnerable place. Over two summers we created temporary communities of scholars, students, actors, who gathered in Venice to prepare the play, and it was an intense, messy experience, affected by multiple uncertainties. I am so pleased that this production ends with all characters on stage and with an echoed question: 'Are you answered?' (4.1.61).

On one of the nights, when I was starting to relax while utterly unable to sit, I found my way upstage, under the arcade where the Banco Rosso, one of the Ghetto's pawnshops, has been reconstructed. From there, looking across the playing space, I could see the backs of the actors, the engrossed faces of the audience. I could see one of the Shylocks arriving ahead of his cue, warming up by stretching, while avoiding my glance of complicity – I was perhaps cultivating the fleeting illusion of really being part of the performance, while he did not want to lose focus. A group of children was sitting on the steps of a house and looking spellbound at the space. 'When is this going to be over?' – one of them whispered to me. 'Half an hour, I guess, why?' He pointed at his smartphone: 'There is a Pokemon in the middle and we need to catch him.' Five Shylocks and a Pokemon. Who would have thought it? The cicadas continued to sing.

SHAKESPEARE'S *THE MERCHANT OF VENICE* IN AND BEYOND THE GHETTO

CAROL CHILLINGTON RUTTER

When Sorab Wadia's Shylock stepped into the evening heat and started across the still-sweltering stones of the Campo del Ghetto Nuovo, shoulders hunched into something practised, like a shrug, as he considered 'Three thousand ducats. Well ... For three months. Well' (1.3.1–3), he was not just bringing home the most famous Venetian Jew who never lived. He was bringing to life a project that had been gestating for nearly a decade. It was the brainchild of Shaul Bassi of Ca' Foscari University of Venice. Realizing that the 400th anniversary of the death of William Shakespeare in 2016 would coincide with the 500th anniversary of the institution of the Jewish Ghetto in Venice,[1] Bassi conceived an idea to bring the playwright and the place into cultural confrontation with a production of *The Merchant of Venice* staged not just *in* Venice but, for the first time ever, *in* the Ghetto. *The Merchant of Venice* had been staged in Venice once before, in Max Reinhardt's sumptuous production of 1934 when Reinhardt used the campo in front of the church of San Trovaso along the Rio Ognisanti (which allowed entrances by gondola) as the playing space, 'improved' by the addition of staircases, false fronts and re-frescoed facades to set Antonio's house, Portia's villa and, on the far side of the Rio, Shylock's palazzo. In Italian, and fixing the city itself as the main protagonist of what Reinhardt directed as (unproblematically) a comedy,[2] that *Merchant* involved some 400 participants, sometimes 200 of them on stage together in a whirl of 'pageantry and moving crowds'. 'At one time', wrote the correspondent from the *Chicago Tribune*, 'there was the entrance of the prince of Morocco, little Moors bringing presents, musicians playing Arabian instruments. At another there was the pompous train of the prince of Aragon, accompanied by girl dancers playing upon their Basque tambourines.' Later, a 'great Venetian festival' was staged 'with sixteenth century

---

[1] As Bassi and Isabella di Lenardo note in 'The Ghetto Inside Out', this was the first such measure taken in Europe to segregate and protect 'a community identified on the basis of religion rather than geographical provenance'. They draw comparisons with other provisions in Venice to segregate foreigners, mainly 'merchants and political missions', by confining them to 'a designated quarter' of the city – the Protestant English ambassador Henry Wotton, arriving in La Serenissima in 1604, was directed to the remote sestiere of Cannaregio to find housing for his embassy – or to 'a "foreigners' house"', like the Fondaco dei Tedeschi', which sits on the Grand Canal just off the Rialto bridge but nevertheless 'constitutes a ready example of an architecture of segregation, control and at the same time of protection for one of the foreign "nations" most important to the mercantile life of the city' ('Fuori, dentro Ghetto', Occhi Aperti Su Venezia, Corte del Fontego (2013), translated by John Francis Phillimore, p. 8). The name 'ghetto' derives from the work done there in the fifteenth century, the 'terren del geto' being part of the public foundry where ordnance was cast.

[2] Elena Pellone in her unpublished MA dissertation, '*Merchant in Venice*: Community of Strangers', quotes Henry Kahane in 'Max Reinhardt's Total Theatre: A centenary lecture': 'The hero, focal point, heart, and essence of [Reinhardt's] performance is Venice. Not Shylock, but Venice. The ever-singing, ever-humming Venice. A city that rejoices with the lust of life, its pleasures and delights' (*Comparative Literature Studies* 12 (1975), 323–37). I am grateful to Elena Pellone for permission to quote freely from her dissertation, which includes 'insider' insights into the making of *The Merchant in Venice*. Pellone played Nerissa in the production.

gondolas... on the canal'. All this busy production came at a cost. Shakespeare's play got lost in the traffic: 'So lovely and impressive was it that it rather overshadowed the characters and plot of the play.'[3]

The dialogue between place and play that Shaul Bassi imagined was of a completely different order. Post-Holocaust, post a European future that Reinhardt in 1934 was beginning to experience but could hardly fully imagine, it could not have been otherwise. Shylock, by Bassi's reckoning, had been 'haunting' the Venetian Ghetto 'for centuries', 'overshadowing its real inhabitants'. It was time to bring him, in person, to his source site, to embody him in Shakespeare's writing, to give him a voice, to listen out for the 'controversial and inflammatory' in the play – not, thereby, to lay his ghost (though some might want him exorcized) but, better, to set him walking in a place where, by challenging the past, he could inform the future.[4] For Bassi, the place and the play operate as archives of memory. Anti-Semitism is recorded on the walls of the Venetian Ghetto as it is spat out of the mouths of the Jew-baiters in Shakespeare's play. Both the Ghetto and *The Merchant* persist as 'powerful sites' where 'the history of multicultural Europe is recapitulated'. Both 'have become global icons' from their origins as local phenomena. And both need to be seen as 'fundamentally ambivalent documents of Western civilisation in having been both instruments of intolerance and catalysts of cultural transformation'.

But recapitulation, in Bassi's terms, does not end by simply serving a memorial agenda. It proposes change. 'What's past is prologue' (2.1.258) as *The Tempest* puts it. Using the materials of memory, then, *The Merchant of Venice* in the Ghetto in July 2016 aimed ultimately to ask questions about the future: how people of different ethnic, religious, and cultural identity can live together; how the theatre and the arts can contribute to such coexistence.

In the end, however, the dialogue between place and play would not resolve anything, would not produce answers. Rather, the dialogue would end posing for the audience a profoundly disturbing question.

Elsewhere in this *Survey*, Shaul Bassi gives an account of the making of *The Merchant in Venice* and of the site-specific collaboration between the director Karin Coonrod, her New York-based company, Compagnia de' Colombari, and the polyglot cast of actors her visionary direction assembled, who, blown like Antonio's ships from every point on the compass, raised the production from the stones of Venice with just three weeks' rehearsal. Here, I am reviewing what spectators saw in the Campo del Ghetto Nuovo. It was a performance that began not with Shakespeare but with the raucous noise of Venetian carnival.

* * * * * *

We heard the actors long before we saw them. We – some three hundred of us – were packed into the steeply raked open-air bleacher seating that had been erected in the campo over the previous days. The playing space was marked out with waist-high crash barriers; at the centre, a tree gave the relief of some shade before the sun dropped behind the Ghetto's 400-year-old high-rises; stage right was a capped stone pozzo. Abandoned as a well, it would serve as all the 'furniture' of Portia's Belmont. Facing us, tucked into the corner of the campo, was the façade of the (modern) Museo Ebraico which exhibits the history of Jewish life in Venice; off left, under squat columns, the low entrance to the cramped Banco Rosso, the oldest-known surviving 'banco dei pegni', pawnbroking (along with the trade in second-hand furniture) being one of the only businesses permitted to the city's Jews. Further left, out of the corner of our eyes, we could see the bridge that connects the Ghetto to the Fondamenta degli Ormesini and the city 'beyond': in Shakespeare's day the Ghetto was an island, locked down at sunset. To our right, overlooking the playing space, were two sets of

---

[3] Lady Dunn, 12 August 1934. http://archives.chicagotribune.com/1934/08/12/page/66/article/reinhardt-sets-merchant-in-venice-locale/ (accessed 4 February 2017).
[4] These quotations of Bassi are drawn from the production programme (July 2016) and from the original Creative Europe funding bid (June 2014).

THE MERCHANT OF VENICE IN AND BEYOND THE GHETTO

5. *The Merchant of Venice*, Prologue. On location in the Jewish Ghetto, Venice, directed by Karin Coonrod. Francesca Sarah Toich as Lancillotto and full company. Photograph by Andrea Messana.

five windows (representing the books of the Torah) that belonged to two of the Ghetto's five synagogues: the Scuola Grande Tedesca and the Scuola Italiana. Behind us, but in the sightlines of the actors who faced them, were the two Holocaust memorials, one a bronze bas relief showing 'The Last Train' carrying deportees from the city in the summer of 1944; the other made of simple wooden planks, etched into them the names of the 247 Jews deported to Auschwitz-Birkenau from December 1943 to August 1944. Before we took our seats, sniffer dogs swept the campo. Fifty armed police patrolled the area. Even so, the vibrant quotidian life of the Ghetto continued on, oblivious, around us. School children, denied their normal pitch, ricocheted footballs off expensive PA equipment. Diners crammed the outside tables of Upupa where they could drink prosecco and rubberneck the show. Curious passers-by hung themselves over the crash barriers. (During the performance, they would chat with actors standing 'off'.) Locals dodged the congestion intent on somewhere else, mobile phones clamped to ears: 'Pronto!' Footfall beat on the pavement. Dogs barked.

Then, out of this white noise that composes the daily soundtrack of the Ghetto came another sound. Drums. Horns. Tambourines. Voices singing 'Amore an!': half shout, half musical caterwaul inviting us acoustically into carnival, into a comedy, from the direction of the Campo di Ghetto Vecchio. Louder and louder until a rowdy dancing procession of bodies appeared like, from the cut of their clothes, some visitation out of the Renaissance past or like the players arriving at Elsinore. Twenty-odd, they were led by a capering Arlecchino figure in a near-black leather 'Ruzante' mask, close-fitting white tumbler's tunic and leggings, and massive codpiece (Illustration 5). On closer inspection, though, these folk were clearly post-modern mash-ups.

The silhouettes of doublets and surcoats were superimposed on what might have been cargo pants worn over lace-up trainers. Patterns stencilled onto cotton masqueraded as woven brocade. Turned-up collars suggested standing ruffs. The colour palette – dull whites, smudged greys – suggested that these bodies had sprung out of the stone pavement they had just crossed. Other visual teases were on offer. The players wore a 'uniform' that established them both as an ensemble (who would stay in view across the performance) and androgynous. The women wore trousers. And waistcoats – in silk – styled like medieval breastplates. But elsewhere in this human scrum, a huge man in a piratical beard swirled in miles of 'girly' organza that floated over his trousers.

As the players came to rest in positions strewn across the playing space, the Arlecchino figure suddenly leaped over the footlights into the audience's space, confiding to us in a guttural growl (and in Judeo-Veneziano dialect): 'Àncuo in Hazer ghe se sta un gran tananai. Xe rivà do goym a far moscon al banco e i voeva tanti, *ma tanti*, magnod.'[5] Leaping back into the 'fiction' the *commedia* character launched into a prologue, a canzone version of Ruzante's tribute to carnal love in Angelo Beolco's *L'Anconitana*, the ballsy company belting out the chorus, 'Amore an!'. 'A ve vuogio far sentir', sang this Ruzante impersonator, 'un così bel straparlamento de amore come se n'è sentìo già mai' ('I want you to listen to the best love story anyone has ever heard. I've heard for a fact that Love, fearing the Turks might impale him during one of their manoeuvres, has left his home in Cyprus and he's come poking himself inside these city walls so he'll be safe inside a strong place; and he's making everyone fall in love'). 'Amore an! Ma chi cancaro parlarìa d'altro?' ('Love? Who the devil talks about anything else?'). And then, turning the focus onto the actor who would play Antonio (who held up his hands protestingly while the other Venetians hooted derisively, a gesture he would repeat later when Solanio concluded 'Why then you are in love!'), the masked character pointedly asked, 'L'Amore no se sa metere nei giovani e nei omeni in età da rason?' ('Doesn't love infect the mature man of sense just like the youth?').

Striking a *commedia* pose, Ruzante stripped off the mask to discover, to shouts of wonder, the body beneath to be Lancillotto (played, cross-dressed by Francesca Sarah Toich). Now, with that bawdy theme tune strutting around in our heads and prepping us for 'the best love story anyone has ever heard', Shakespeare's play began: 'In sooth, I know not why I am so sad'. In a single line, the up-beat nosedived.

So what kind of 'love story' were we in for? One that picked up on the fundamental binary, Jew vs Christian, that Shakespeare positions in this play as saturated cultural metaphor (as he had used blindness in *A Midsummer Night's Dream* or male friendship in *The Two Gentlemen of Verona*) to explore, here, 'profession' (in love, in life, in faith; in business, calculation, risk-taking) and to test the daunting challenge the leaden casket proposes: 'Who chooseth me' – that is, love – 'must give and hazard all he hath' (2.7.9)? In the event, Karin Coonrod's cut-down *Merchant* went for something smaller, but only slightly:[6] a love story that nursed broken hearts, both Jewish and Christian; hearts baffled by

---

[5] The lines were scripted by Shaul Bassi: 'Today in the Ghetto there was a great commotion. Two Christians came to the banco because they wanted a lot, but I mean *a lot*, of money.'

[6] Relying on her experience directing theatre in Italy to Italian audiences, Coonrod ('I know my chickens') cut the playing time to just over two hours. That meant that embellishment had to go – like the backstory to Bassanio's latest scrounging in 1.1 that establishes his prodigality and later the gorgeous duet between Portia and Bassanio, when, his prodigality made good in unpacking the riddle of 'hazard[ing] all', he accepts the miracle of the gift of her grace. Heavily edited though it was, the production did not in any way feel scrimped. Music (composed by Frank London, a klezmer expert) underscored with cellos (and mixing an acoustic that ranged from Neapolitan folk song to Jewish lament via opera canzone); a lighting design (by Peter Ksander) that slowly came up as the sky faded, throwing deep shadows across the campo then suddenly picking out a single window; and costumes by Stefano Nicolao (who heads the research-led Atelier Nicolao, designing historically informed creations) all produced richness of texture to enact Shakespeare's script in different media. Some of Coonrod's 'chickens' (among them Stanley Wells, Paul Edmondson, Carol Rutter) thought she was wrong: they would have watched this *Merchant* all night. But then, they were English.

betrayal, surprised by pain; a love story that cried out against a happy ending where everybody's boats come in. Except Shylock's. If Shakespeare's *Merchant*, then, sees 'Jew vs Christian' as abstracting notions of giving and hazarding all, Coonrod's 'Christian vs Jew' said something about history.

That is not to say that there was not wonder in this *Merchant*, though it made a delayed entrance. Men like Salarino (Hunter Perske: tall, broad-shouldered, bluff) and Salanio (Enrico Zagni: stocky, the permanent ironic tilt to his head suggesting he knew more than he was saying) were streetwise (and slightly soiled) urbanites whose laddish mocking of Antonio (Stefano Scherini: worn, a man you imagined living on espresso and fags) peaked when Bassanio turned up with Graziano and Lorenzo in tow. Meeting, these gallants were like cock-birds squaring. Left alone with Antonio, however, Bassanio (Michele Athos Guidi) began a story – 'In Belmont is a lady richly left' – drained of testosterone, one that left the grubby city behind as it soared into fairy tale. Guidi has a face by Veronese, and a Tuscan voice that, speaking English, caresses Shakespeare. As he spoke, the fairy tale came to life. Stage left, two women in trousers emerged from the ensemble. As they held out their arms like mannequins, the black-robed Angeli Neri – 'Black Angels' who served the production as silent onstage dressers and fixers, making the work of the play visible — removed their silk waistcoats and helped them into flowing organza fashioned as Renaissance surcoats that fastened at the breast but splayed open to show the trousers underneath, transforming them into Portia (Linda Powell: strong-built, serious-minded) and Nerissa (Elena Pellone: high-spirited, practised at poking fun at her mistress, goading her into gaiety).

Wonder underscored 3.2 (Coonrod's Scene 12), with Bassanio's wondrous 'What find I here?' (3.2.114) as he released Portia's portrait from the leaden casket. Coonrod had cut the Morocco (Matthieu Pastore: the big man in the dress, a peacock) and Aragon (Adriano Iurissevich: a cliché Spaniard in sombrero strumming a guitar) wooings of Shakespeare's 2.1, 2.7 and 2.9 into a single Scene 5, presenting the unsuitable suitors so hard on each other's heels that the 'business' of the lottery felt like waves of European invasion. Coonrod's directorial notion was that Belmont represented an 'island of the women' (Balthasar being cross-gendered as Balzarina: Monica Garavello) where opportunism, not love, was the name of the game and where the 'best story ... anyone has ever heard' was disillusioned, Portia's aim to keep control over her fortune and destiny. But as Linda Powell learned in rehearsal, 'You can push a concept only so far. Then Shakespeare's play asserts itself'.[7] Wanting Bassanio to 'tarry. Pause a day or two / Before you hazard' (3.2.1–2), playing for time by playing with discourse, 'Upon the rack' (3.2.25), she could not get past the line 'Beshrew your eyes!' (3.2.14) without discovering that Portia had discovered a love as deep as the unsounded bottom of the bay of Portugal. When Bassanio turned, as the scroll instructed, 'to where your lady is' (3.2.137) to 'claim her with a loving kiss' (3.2.138), Powell's Portia had to flee (her happiness; her terror?), putting the stone pozzo between herself and this man, momentarily suspended between her past and future, between her ambiguous freedom (while her fate was paradoxically locked in the caskets) and her destiny, 'lorded'. Then, in wondering tones, Portia literally put herself into Bassanio's awed hands with her complete giving of 'This house, these servants, and this same myself' (3.2.170). She handed them over with a ring – conditions attached. It was a wryly loaded object. A miniature time bomb waiting to go off. He took it joyfully, with no misgiving – and the moment passed, yielding to hurried exchanges first as Nerissa and Graziano coat-tailed their betters, then as more Venetians arrived, and with messages that drained 'the colour from Bassanio's cheek'. Bassanio's anguish was terrible, 'Ma / É proprio vero, Salanio, sono falliti /

---

[7] Powell shared her thoughts in a round-table discussion, 'Women in Shakespeare', held at the University of Warwick's Palazzo Papafava on July 29. It was chaired by Carol Rutter and also included Dr Boika Sokolova (Notre Dame in London) and actors Michelle Uranowitz and Elena Pellone.

Tutti i suoi investimenti? Non uno / Andato a buon fine? Da Tripoli, dal Messico . . . ?'[8]

Now it was the turn of the Venetians to wonder – but not romantically. Their astonishment was a reaction to the women's laughter that such heavy weather could be made of such a paltry debt: 'What no more? / Pay him six thousand and deface the bond; / Double . . . treble' (3.2.296–8). They had no experience of extravagance like this on the Rialto. They looked small. But then the tables turned. Portia insisted that Antonio's letter be read, viva voce. She heard Bassanio ventriloquize, 'If I might but see you at my death . . . if your love do not persuade you to come, let not my letter' (3.2.317–19). She stood rooted. 'Oh', she said. Flatly. 'Love.' She was making a new discovery about 'love'.[9] She turned on her heel, throwing over her shoulder, 'Dispatch all business and be gone' (3.2.320), no further mention of 'church' or 'wife' (3.2.301). Bewildered, Bassanio hesitated, and exited with the Venetians.

Wonder-damaged, Powell's Portia clearly found trouble in this scene. But it had arrived much earlier in the production. Jessica (Michelle Uranowitz: dark hair, dark eyes, her intense body bright, like a coal burning) was still a child, a child who still played cat's cradle and break-neck tig across the campo with Lancillotto, the lad she had grown up with and clearly adored, but a child bursting for adult life and love – and freedom from her father's house and discipline. What did she see in the whey-faced Christian with his thin chest and epicoene good looks (Lorenzo: Paul Spera)? The audience heard the catch in her voice apostrophizing her absent suitor, 'O Lorenzo, / If thou keep promise' (2.3.20), and they saw a chancer. It was not just the surly way he dismissed Lancillotto: 'Via!' Or the gloat in his voice, confounding Shylock's ducats and daughter, telling Graziano how Jessica 'hath directed / . . . I shall take her from her father's house, / What gold and jewels she's furnish'd with' (2.4.29–31). It was the fact that he arrived late for his tryst, leaving Graziano and Solanio to 'marvel' that 'he outdwells his hour' since 'lovers ever run *before* the clock' (2.6.3–4) and to cover for him with a *bel canto* tenor duet that reprised 'Amore an!' sung with Shakespeare's lyrics:

> O dieci volte più del vento volano i colombi
> Da Venere chiamati a suggelare nuovi amori
> Fedeli al nuovo incanto più che alla fede data.
>
> È sempre così: chi s'alza dal festino
> Con lo stesso appetito con cui s'era seduto?
> Le cose del mondo sempre si cercano
> Con più ardore che non si godano

Soaring, holding the high notes competitively to make a marvel of lung power, the voices were wonderful. But the lyrics blighted the moment. Was it always like this? Sempre così? Love 'got' never so sweet as love pursued? Was it true that 'All things' were 'with more spirit chased than enjoy'd' (2.6.12–3)? As the curtain-raiser to an elopement, this was bleak. And Lorenzo did not improve things, sauntering in, talking of 'affairs' that delayed him and joking with the lads about playing 'thieves for wives' (2.6.22–3). Then a spotlight hit a window high up on the façade of one of the houses lining the campo. Shutters were flung back. Jessica was there, throwing down not caskets but suitcases crammed with her father's wealth that sprang open when they hit the pavement, so that as she rushed down the stairs, out her father's door and into Lorenzo's arms, she found him scrambling for ducats. Thus was the Jew's wealth grabbed by Christian hands.

Uranowitz's Jessica did not see it. She was laughing, carrying the torch at the head of the jubilant gang of wife-thieves in carnival mode who began threading their way across the campo, picking up a crowd of masked revellers who shoved through a knot of five huddled figures, backs turned on the

---

[8] It was fundamental to Coonrod's vision for this production that several languages would be heard speaking Shakespeare's script, to make us hear its debates in the languages of custom in the Ghetto. Conceptually, the moves between languages were provocative. Practically, there was an even bigger pay-off, the extraordinary energy and muscularity released when actors whose native tongues struggled with Shakespeare were freed to speak him in their own language.

[9] Arden 2 (1955), edited by John Russell Brown, punctuates the line, 'O love! — dispatch all business and be gone.'

noise, all in knee-length kaftans. Before they had turned inwards into their self-protective circle, we had watched them belted in wide yellow sashes – yellow: the Jewish colour of stigma – by the Angeli Neri. Now, a low moan rose from them. Around them ugly voices mocked, hissed, spread toxic gossip as in some grotesque street urchin's game taunting them in a half dozen European languages: 'O mia figlia! O i miei ducati! Fuggita con un cristiano!'; 'Lo sporco Ebreo coi suoi strepiti / Non ho mai visto una furia sconclusionata.' The moan rose in volume. It reached a shattering wail like a damned soul's last howl. Silence. Shylock turned to face the tormentors.

In fact, five Shylocks turned to face the tormentors.

These five represented Karin Coonrod's boldest intervention in Shakespeare's script.[10] Here, they stood for the whole of Jewish experience in Venice, in the Ghetto. Earlier, taking on Shylock one by one, they had shown the Jew's part to be one of constant re-invention, constant re-negotiation with the Christians. Christian hypocrisies were a matter of profession; the Jew's, of survival. By multiple casting, then, Coonrod found a device to capture those points of contact, to play them to their scenic limits, thereby to test the theology underpinning this play as a love story where Christians profess giving and hazarding all. Because initially this *Merchant*'s Shylock wanted the Christians' love. As one of Coonrod's actors put it, 'It was a love bond that Shylock asked for, however perverse. He wanted his bond. He wanted his heart.'[11]

We watched the opening moves in that love story in 1.3 as Sorab Wadia's urbane, almost flirtatious Shylock wrong-footed Guidi's guileless Bassanio every step of the way with his practised shrug, his impeccable manners, his turn of phrase that teased Bassanio's desire, hanging the needy Venetian on his pauses. 'Three thousand ducats. Well.' It was his fastidious aloofness recounting some unpleasantness on the Rialto, 'You call me misbeliever, cut-throat dog, / … spit … spurn' (1.3.110–17), that provoked Scherini's Antonio to the vicious outburst, 'I am as like to call thee so again, / To spit on thee again, to spurn thee too' (1.3.128–9) that exposed the self-styled moderate man, 'I hold the world but as the world' (1.1.77), as the racist thug. But with that settled, Wadia's Shylock was genuine, offering Antonio 'I would be friends with you and have your love, / Forget the shames that you have stained me with' (1.3.136–7). He meant the bond as a 'merry sport', and though Guidi's Bassanio looked wild and objected, Antonio, laughing as Shylock also laughed, accepted the terms. But when Shylock offered his hand to seal the bargain, 'To buy his favour, I extend this friendship' (1.3.67), Antonio refused to take it. He would palm Shylock's ducats. But not his flesh. Thus, Shylock's proffered love was slapped down – without even touching him. It may have been meant as a rhetorical gesture, but the line Shylock aimed at Bassanio as a kind of 'ante up or fold' at the end of scene hung in the air after he exited: 'for my love, I pray you wrong me not' (1.3.169).

Wadia gave us Shylock on the Rialto; Adriano Iurissevich, Shylock 2, Shylock at home, a much older man, tetchy, even mean, a patriarch whose care of his daughter was austere, 'What, are there masques? Hear you me, Jessica, / Lock up my doors' (2.5.28–9). Shylock 3 was the father who discovered his girl gone, the Shylock who emerged from the wail. This Shylock was played by a woman (Jenni Lea-Jones), and in the keening of that voice that ended howling, we heard not only grief for a particular lost child but also grief reaching back into history, grief for the world's lost

---

[10] Unsurprisingly, given the international media event that this production represented, this casting decision was the most widely reported aspect of Coonrod's *Merchant*, seen as a device to put Shylock at the centre of attention, to generate sympathy for his victimization. As I aim to make clear here, letting us see Shylock in pieces, Shylock as a series of parts, Coonrod was doing something much more ambiguous and radical. She was unsettling continuity, a fixed interpretation of the role and ultimately the play. As she writes, Shylock is 'the whetsone of the play, not a victim' (personal communication, 3 January 2017).

[11] Elena Pellone, unpublished dissertation cited earlier, '*Merchant in Venice:* Community of Strangers'.

6. *The Merchant of Venice*, 3.1. On location in the Jewish Ghetto, Venice, directed by Karin Coonrod. Five Shylocks (Sorab Wadia, Adriano Iurissevich, Andrea Brugnera, Ned Eisenberg, Jenni Lea-Jones) wail the loss of Jessica. Photograph by Andrea Messana.

children (Illustration 6). This Shylock's challenge to Solanio and Salarino was chilling: 'You knew, none so well, none so well as you, of my daughter's flight' (3.1.23–4); the bid for likeness, 'Hath not a Jew eyes?' (3.1.54) gave us likeness as the ruin of humankindness, love's reverse: revenge. This Shylock was not just Rachel. He was Clytemnestra. But the bitter highmindedness of this scene did not survive into the next. Instead, picking up where Shylock 3 left off, Shylock 4 (Andrea Brugnera, who doubled Old Gobbo; shaggy, grey) played loss in commedia mode. His confusion of ducats and daughters, his frantic double-act with Tubal, his extravagant self-interest ('no ill luck stirring except what lights o' my shoulders, no sighs but o' my breathing, no tears but o' my shedding') were grotesque. Here was the caricature Jew embodying the racist stereotype. He was as loathsome as the louts we had watched baiting him.

A completely different Shylock walked into the courtroom – that was now packed with a jury brought out of the audience and invested in red stoles to stand behind the Duke, robed in red. There was nothing hysterical about Ned Eisenberg's compact, sure-footed Shylock. He had his bond. He had his oath. He knew the law. While others fretted and foamed at the mouth, he was impassive, answering the unanswerable with another unanswerable: 'How shalt thou hope for mercy, rend'ring none?' and 'What judgment shall I dread, doing no wrong?' (4.1.87–8). The Christian who had withheld his love would now be required to give his heart. The justice of the transaction pleased. But its literalism was terrible, not least when, rejecting mercy, 'On what compulsion must I?' (4.1.180), Eisenberg's Shylock called down merciless judgement upon himself, 'My deeds upon my head' (4.1.203). Here, we were watching some perverse love-test play out. The casket, this time, that contained the heart was made of human flesh. Shylock would never be closer to Antonio than for the long minutes when he held his knife's point against the Christian's body.

So, was 'Tarry a little' Shylock's salvation, saving him from killing, always a form of suicide in Shakespeare? Or did it simply repeat the punchline to a centuries' old anti-Semitic joke? When Eisenberg's Shylock stepped back, 'Why then, the devil give him good of it' (4.1.342), and threw down the knife, he and Antonio suddenly laughed. A reprise of that laugh they had laughed when they struck the 'merry bond' (1.3.172). One man had not, the other was not, killed. Stopped here, the merchant and the Jew of Venice might have ended things comically. But the Doctor of Law ploughed on. Howls of laughter from Graziano and the rest rose with each new discovery found in the law's fine print that brought fresh humiliation. Shylock's goods seized. Himself strangered, made an 'alien' (4.1.346). His life forfeit. 'Mercy' shown by the court assigning his wealth to his Christian son-in-law. Salvation imposed by shoving him onto his knees, forcing conversion. (The lawyer and 'his' clerk exchanged appalled looks: they had not expected Antonio's 'mercy'. Powell's Portia muttered to Pellone's Nerissa, 'Let's go home.') Shylock, half-smiling, was 'content'. He stood. Erect. He brushed the dirt of the courtroom from the knees of his trousers. He turned, saw a sea of red blocking his path. Then it parted. Not like the miracle in Exodus. Rather, like the operation of the city's Sanità. No one wanted to touch him. Meanwhile, the Duke and jurors disrobed, piling their gowns and stoles into a red heap that looked like a kind of human slaughter.

The aftermath played out. Bassanio kept his ring and his wife's promise – then capitulated to his friend's insisting that his 'love' be 'valued' against her 'commandment' (4.1.447–8). Back in Belmont, newlyweds gazed at the stars – and bickered. 'Pilgrims' returned home – just ahead of triumphant 'Jasons' who had notched up yet another 'fleece' (3.2.239). Day broke. Domestic rows broke out – resolving to wonder as rings were given a second time, argosies miraculously arrived in port, and 'manna' was dropped 'in the way / Of starved people' (5.1.294–5). We thought we were heading towards the bawdy quip that ends Shakespeare's play rhyming 'ring' with 'thing'. Then Coonrod took us somewhere else. Through the Belmont crowd pushed the five Shylocks. Speaking directly to us they reprised the monologue from the courtroom scene, sharing the lines so that the words came from every direction and ricocheted off every surface in the Ghetto (a speech we had to hear in full):

> You'll ask me why I rather choose to have
> A weight of carrion flesh than to receive
> Three thousand ducats. I'll not answer that,
> But say it is my humour. Is it answered?
> What if my house be troubled with a rat,
> And I be pleased to give ten thousand ducats
> To have it baned? What, are you answered yet?
> Some men there are love not a gaping pig,
> Some that are mad if they behold a cat,
> And others when the bagpipe sings i' th' nose
> Cannot contain their urine; for affection,
> Mistress of passion, sways it to the mood
> Of what it likes or loathes. Now, for your answer:
> As there is no firm reason to be rendered,
> Why he cannot abide a gaping pig,
> Why he a harmless necessary cat,
> Why he a woollen bagpipe, but of force
> Must yield to such inevitable shame
> As to offend himself being offended,
> So can I give no reason, nor I will not,
> More than a lodged hate and a certain loathing
> I bear Antonio, that I follow thus
> A losing suit against him. Are you answered?
>
> (4.1.39–61)

That final question, repeated by each Shylock, echoed across the campo. It was the last line of this *Merchant of Venice*. Then Jessica broke away. At full tilt she circled the campo; she wove among the Belmont crowd, staring into faces. She found her father; searched his face. Then, like Lancillotto at the beginning, she stepped across the footlights into our space, confronting us with a gaze that was as unsettling as Shylock's question. The sounds of several shofars called out. As she turned to look at the Ghetto from our point of view, high on the walls appeared words written in light. *Misericordia*. Mercy. רַחֲמִים.

This ending resolved nothing. Rather, it preserved the trouble this play makes for us in our own time. Promised a love story by the clown Lancillotto, the production gave us scenes of hazarding all that brought winning – Portia's, Jessica's — into terrible alignment with losing, losing that was given objective reality in the ruin of Shylock who had risked everything to test Christian 'profession': 'for my love, I pray you wrong me not' (1.3.169). In his reprise of the courtroom speech, then, how was he reframing the test? Refusing to 'answer' why he would 'rather choose to have / A weight of carrion flesh than to receive / Three thousand ducats', we heard him stunningly if ironically rejecting the commercial logic of the Rialto that underpinned Venetian life – and livelihood – whether it was the merchant's, the moneylender's, or the prodigal's. We heard him making daughters (represented in the courtroom in the proxy body of Antonio) much more valuable than ducats. But was he also, troublingly, attributing to the Jew a 'humour' or 'affection' beyond 'reason' that in him naturalized 'hate' and 'loathing'? Or then again, was he issuing a racial challenge, reframing his thoughts on 'likeness' to encompass all humanity, observing a deterministic ethical logic: 'Of force', that person who is 'himself . . . offended' 'Must yield to such inevitable shame / As to offend'. He had said before: 'The villainy you teach me I will execute.' So, in those long minutes in the courtroom when the knife was held against the human heart, who was the victim? The man about to die? Or the man who had been instructed in villainy, the man taught hate? And given the implacable logic of this stand-off, where did Mercy, *Misericordia*, רַחֲמִים fit in? Were they just lightshow projections to get us to gaze past the clutch of Shylocks challenging us with his perplexing discourse? Were they the means in Coonrod's production for the Ghetto to get the final word? As her last stage direction before 'Blackout' put it, 'The walls speak.' Were *they* the 'answer' to Shylock's 'Are you answer'd?' Or is the only 'answer' to the troubling questions Shakespeare's play proposes *in* and *beyond* the Ghetto our continuing engagement with the questions it refuses answer?

WHAT THE QUILLS CAN TELL: THE CASE OF JOHN FLETCHER AND PHILIP MASSINGER'S *LOVE'S CURE*

JOSÉ A. PÉREZ DÍEZ

An immediate problem for the study of English Renaissance drama and the history of its reception and early staging is the painful scarcity of handwritten witnesses of the theatrical trade. Promptbooks, authorial drafts, tiring-house plot charts, part scripts, bills of properties, company accounts, lists of members of theatrical troupes, doubling charts, presentation copies – all these are painfully scarce, and, problematically, what has survived may not be representative of more general practices. Paul Werstine, in his now seminal study *Early Modern Playhouse Manuscripts and the Editing of Shakespeare*, analyses twenty-two English play scripts extant from the period.[1] Tiffany Stern traces what we know of other theatrical documents, such as plot-scenarios, call-sheets, and actors' parts, in *Documents of Performance in Early Modern England* and, with Simon Palfrey, *Shakespeare in Parts*.[2] Other projects also try to offer a useful compilation of the available material in digital form. This is the case for the Henslowe-Alleyn Digitisation Project, directed by Grace Ioppolo, which offers unrestricted access to Philip Henslowe's and Edward Alleyn's papers preserved at Dulwich College, that amount to over 2,200 pages, including their personal correspondence and their account books and 'diaries'.[3] But the available documentation can only give a partial account of the ways in which theatre business was conducted. In particular, we still have a limited understanding of how dramatic and theatrical manuscripts operated and of the processes of textual transmission from authorial draft to final clean script, actors' parts, promptbooks and the textual witnesses behind printed publications. Bibliographers and textual critics have built useful, but sometimes misleading, models for the transmission and dissemination of dramatic texts in this period of English history, a case in point being the contested Gregian concept of 'foul papers' that Werstine has painstakingly tried to unpick. The thinness of the corpus can perhaps be attributed to the outbreak of the English Civil War of the 1640s and the subsequent eradication of theatrical performance in the country for almost twenty years. The change of dramatic taste in the Restoration may have done the rest. With the loss of these documents, which seems to have been very substantial indeed, we have lost as well the texts of a vast number of plays that might have survived in manuscript in various stages of development, as well as crucial information about those that are extant, including textual and external evidence that might have helped us date some of them more precisely or determine their authorship more accurately.

However, this is not the case for other European nations where theatrical performance flourished undisturbed throughout the seventeenth century

---

[1] Paul Werstine, *Early Modern Playhouse Manuscripts and the Editing of Shakespeare* (Cambridge, 2012).
[2] Tiffany Stern, *Documents of Performance in Early Modern England* (Cambridge, 2009); Tiffany Stern and Simon Palfrey, *Shakespeare in Parts* (Oxford, 2011).
[3] *Henslowe-Alleyn Digitisation Project*, King's College London, www.henslowe-alleyn.org.uk.

and beyond, and where documentary evidence of dramatic composition and theatrical practice is much richer. A particular case in point is Spain. For the comparatively few handwritten scripts preserved from the English Renaissance, there is a corpus of no fewer than 3,000 Spanish plays in manuscript that have survived from the period in libraries and archives across the continent. There is a centralized international project to catalogue these manuscripts in a scientific and systematic way: *Manos*, formerly *Manos teatrales*, a project sponsored by the Biblioteca Nacional de España and led by Alejandro García Reidy and Margaret Rich Greer.[4] In addition, a wealth of documentation around acting companies has survived in archives across the globe and has been painstakingly catalogued in a major reference work, the *Diccionario biográfico de actores del teatro clásico español* (DICAT; *Biographical Dictionary of Actors in Spanish Classical Theatre*), coordinated by Teresa Ferrer Valls at the University of Valencia. This database traces the professional careers of some 5,000 Spanish theatre makers of the sixteenth and seventeenth centuries, including actors, musicians, prompters and company managers.[5] My belief is that those of us concerned with the study of English plays from the Renaissance can learn much from these databases and from the corpus of plays and acting practices that they record, not just in terms of shared procedures in copying and revising playtexts, and in the composition and management of early modern theatre companies, but also in terms of the study of transnational literary influence.

I will therefore address what is the earliest and perhaps the most interesting case of direct textual influence of a Spanish *comedia* of the Golden Age on an English play of the same period: the extraordinary case of *Love's Cure, or The Martial Maid*, composed by John Fletcher and Philip Massinger, perhaps with a collaborator, most likely in the early months of 1615.[6] While the two subplots of this play are based on two Spanish picaresque novels that were well known and widely circulated in print across Europe,[7] the main plot derives unmistakably from a Spanish play written perhaps just a few years before: *La fuerza de la costumbre* (*The Force of Custom*) by the Valencian dramatist Guillén de Castro. The play presents the extraordinary case of a pair of siblings, a boy and a girl, who have been brought up separately as members of the opposite sex. The girl has grown up with her father among the Spanish troops in Flanders and has become a daring, brash young soldier. The boy has remained at home with his mother learning how to be a lady. Sixteen years later, the family is reunited and the siblings are instructed to take up the expected gender behaviour of their own sex. However, the two struggle to follow their parents' command, bringing about numerous farcical situations. In both versions, the socially anomalous situation is resolved by the intervention of heterosexual love in the form of a romantic attachment to another pair of siblings who represent traditional heteronormativity: Clara, the martial maid of the English play, falls in love with the boisterous womanizer Vitelli, while Lucio, the maidenly youth, finds his lost masculinity in his sudden infatuation with Vitelli's sister, Genevora, whom he defends at sword's point from another suitor, the duellist Lamoral. Except in some specific dramatic situations, and in some variation in the treatment of the topic of maidenly chastity, the Spanish original version tells exactly the same story: Doña Hipólita struggles to give up her military ways and to get used to wearing the garments expected of a gentlewoman of her rank, and she falls in love with Don Luis; meanwhile, Félix, her brother, wins the love of Luis's sister, Doña Leonor, by fighting a duel against the gallant Otavio. The inclusion of the misadventured parents separated by a family feud and by war, of a comic domestic servant, and of a good number of

---

[4] Freely accessible at https://manos.net/.
[5] Teresa Ferrer Valls, ed., *Diccionario biográfico de actores del teatro clásico español* (Kassel, 2008); see also www.reichenberger.de/Pages/b50.html.
[6] Martin Wiggins, *British Drama 1533–1642: A Catalogue*, 10 vols. (Oxford, 2015), vol. 6, entry 1779.
[7] *Lazarillo de Tormes* (1552; first surviving printing is from 1554) and *Guzmán de Alfarache* (*Primera parte*, Madrid, 1599; *Segunda parte*, Lisboa, 1604).

coinciding dramatic situations, complete the striking similarities between both versions of the story. Given his frequent interest in cross-dressing as a dramatic device, and his recurrent exploration of sexual politics, it is not hard to see why John Fletcher felt attracted to Castro's play. But there is a fundamental chronological problem: *La fuerza de la costumbre* was not printed until the spring of 1625 in a collection of twelve plays under the title *Segunda parte de las comedias de don Guillem de Castro*; Fletcher died from the plague in August of the same year.[8] This tight timescale makes it almost inconceivable that a copy of the collection could have travelled from Valencia to London in time for Fletcher to have had a hand in adapting one of the works for the English stage. However, the available evidence – a number of clear topical allusions as well as a remarkable lexical and stylistic proximity to other Fletcher plays of the same period – indicates that *Love's Cure* was composed in the early days of Fletcher and Massinger's writing partnership in the mid-1610s, most probably in the first months of 1615, as Martin Wiggins has suggested and my own editorial work on the play has corroborated.[9] If Fletcher had a hand in it – and the available authorship studies are unambiguous about this – then *La fuerza de la costumbre* must have made its way to England in manuscript form. Trying to defend his post-1625 dating of *Love's Cure*, attributing most of the play's text to Philip Massinger, George Walton Williams stated in the introduction to his magisterial edition of the play that 'it seems unnecessary to invent the thesis that a manuscript version had preceded the printed edition to England'.[10] Given the available evidence, there really is no other way.

The survival of no fewer than four extant manuscript copies of the Spanish *comedia* enables this theory, and, as we will see, the study of their textual and material features helps to understand the original reception of the play and its possible dissemination beyond the country where it was composed. The fact that so many copies of Guillén de Castro's play are extant is very unusual. There is no other play by Castro for which so many different manuscript versions have survived, not even of his most enduring and better-known works, such as *Las mocedades del Cid* (*The Youthful Deeds of the Cid*). Generally speaking, there are very few other Spanish plays from the period that have survived in so many versions. *Manos* contains very few examples from major Spanish playwrights of Castro's generation whose plays have survived in more than one or two manuscripts. For instance, among the extant *comedias* by Lope de Vega (1562–1635), out of more than 300 authenticated plays, only *La fortuna merecida* (*The Deserved Fortune*) and *El príncipe perfecto* (*The Perfect Prince*) survive in three manuscript copies. A greater number of manuscripts survive from the dramatists of the younger generation. For instance, *El gran príncipe de Fez, don Baltasar de Loyola* by Pedro Calderón de la Barca (1600–81) survives in no fewer than five manuscript copies but that is not a typical case. Four manuscripts is, therefore, a remarkably high number, which indicates that *La fuerza* was copied often for performance and private reading, probably due to an otherwise unrecorded popularity with its original audiences. Three of the manuscripts of *La fuerza* are held in the Biblioteca Nacional de España in Madrid, while the fourth was discovered by Margaret Rich Greer in the Biblioteca Palatina in Parma. The four extant manuscripts are the following:

BNE[1] Biblioteca Nacional de España, Madrid, MSS 15623. 49 folios.
BNE[2] Biblioteca Nacional de España, Madrid, MSS 17064, 28 folios.
BNE[3] Biblioteca Nacional de España, Madrid, MSS 15370, 49 folios.
BPP Biblioteca Palatina, Parma, CC★ IV 28033 Vol. 76, V 2, MS 4615, 55 folios.

---

[8] *Segunda parte de las comedias de don Guillem de Castro* (Valencia, 1625).
[9] Wiggins, *Catalogue*, vol. 6, entry 1779, pp. 465–6. My edition is being prepared for publication.
[10] John Fletcher and Francis Beaumont, *Love's Cure, or The Martial Maid*, ed. George Walton Williams, in *The Dramatic Works in the Beaumont and Fletcher Canon*, gen. ed. Fredson Bowers, 10 vols. (Cambridge, 1976), vol. 3, p. 5.

The only comprehensive study of the three manuscripts in Madrid and their relation to the text of the 1625 *Segunda parte* was undertaken by Melissa Machit in her 2013 doctoral dissertation at Harvard University, which remains the most up-to-date study of *La fuerza de la costumbre* as well as the only modern critical edition to have been attempted.[11] These three manuscripts vary substantially from each other and from the longer text in the *editio princeps*, and, as Machit observes, the relationship between them is not at all clear:

> It is difficult to establish a clear relationship or lineage among the three manuscript sources. I believe that the three manuscripts were copied before the 1625 publication or were based on texts that were, meaning that they were based on an unknown source, X. Some variants and omitted lines that are shared by all manuscripts suggest that revisions were made to the play before publication, with the heaviest alterations being made to Act III ... A stemma has not been possible because of the fact that there is no pattern of overlap between the manuscripts that is sustained throughout the whole text.[12]

The 1625 edition, carefully prepared by the dramatist, represents a fuller and more developed form of the play, and the manuscripts seem to contain earlier versions, connected in some form to a common ancestor. That the printed text is meant to supply a fuller dramaturgical representation of the stage business is evident from the stage directions, which are highly descriptive and supply visual and theatrical clues that would not be entirely necessary if the text were to be used as the basis of a performance. In general, all three manuscripts offer briefer stage directions that encode basic staging information but omit details that a theatre company might have been able to explore independently, those missing instructions on costume and acting choices might have been given in rehearsal instead of in the manuscript. For example, the first time Félix, the womanish boy, appears in male clothes, as opposed to the long feminizing habit he had been wearing previously, the 1625 version specifies what the actor would be wearing and how he would move: 'Sale don Felix vestido de corto, mal puesto quanto lleua, y el muy encogido' (sig. 2C4v; 'Enter Don Félix wearing a short doublet, all his garments in disarray, and he [walking as if he were] much shrunk').[13] At this point, all three BNE manuscripts omit the acting instruction (that he is moving in a certain way) and they alter or abbreviate the physical description: two say that he appears 'as a gallant' ('don felis galan', BNE[1]; 'felis de galan', BNE[3]) and the other one just specifies that he is wearing a short doublet ('don felix vestido de corto', BNE[2]). We can start to assume that some of these manuscripts, particularly BNE[1] and BNE[3], indicate some closer connection with performance than the more descriptive *princeps*.

We will now consider what we know of the provenance of these manuscripts and their material features and what they can reveal about their original purpose. The first two copies at the Biblioteca Nacional, BNE[1] and BNE[2], were part of the library of the Dukes of Osuna, acquired in 1886 by the Spanish state after the death of the 12th Duke, Mariano Téllez-Girón (1814–82), who had bankrupted the family.[14] It is unknown whether these two copies were already part of the collection in the seventeenth century. However, this seems a reasonable assumption, as Guillén de Castro and his family had strong ties to the House of Girón, heirs to the Dukedom of Osuna. From the time the dramatist moved to Madrid around 1618, he was under the patronage of Juan Téllez-Girón (1598–1656), the son of Pedro Téllez-Girón (1574–1624), 3rd Duke of Osuna, who had been

---

[11] Melissa Renee Machit, 'Bad Habits: Family, Identity, and Gender: Guillén de Castro's 1625 play, "La fuerza de la costumbre"' (unpublished PhD dissertation, Harvard University, 2013). The dissertation is free of embargo and is available through ProQuest, http://search.proquest.com/docview/1465065270.

[12] Machit, 'Bad Habits', p. 28.

[13] The exemplar cited is the copy at the Biblioteca Nacional, signature U/6740. It is available in full in the Biblioteca Digital Hispánica, http://bdh.bne.es/bnesearch/detalle/bdh0000079146.

[14] The date of the purchase appears in the catalogues that were compiled when Osuna's library arrived at the Biblioteca Nacional; the signature for the catalogue of printed books is MSS 18848, and for the manuscripts, MSS 21272.

the Spanish Viceroy of Sicily and Naples.[15] The *Gran Duque de Osuna*, as he was known, 'deeded a small farm and its income to [Castro] in 1619', though he had to mortgage it in 1623 to satisfy his ever-pressing debts.[16] In 1626, when his patron had become the fourth duke on his father's death, Castro married Ángela de Salgado, who was 'a member of the household of the Duchess of Osuna'.[17] According to Javier Ignacio Martínez del Barrio, the private library of the Duke of Osuna 'was formed thanks to the accumulation of books purchased following personal interests, as well as those dedicated to him'.[18] It is not unthinkable, then, that either or both of these manuscripts may have been presentation copies gifted by the dramatist to his wealthy patron.[19] It is also interesting to note that the only verified holograph in Castro's own hand, *Ingratitud por amor* (*Ingratitude for Love*), was also part of the Osuna collection.[20]

Both of these manuscripts are undated, though the hands are Spanish seventeenth-century italic. The most striking feature of BNE[2] is that the stage directions are very close in phrasing to those found in the 1625 *princeps*.[21] For example, the opening stage direction in the 1625 text, announcing the appearance of the womanish Félix and of his mother, is 'Salen doña Gostança, y don Felis en habito largo de estudiante' (sig. 2C1v; 'Enter Doña Costanza and Don Félix wearing the long habit of a student'), while in BNE[2] it is given as 'Sale doña constaça Y don felix / en auito de estudiantte' (fol. 1r; 'Enter Doña Costanza and Don Félix wearing the habit of a student'). The stage direction in the manuscript lacks the specification that the habit that Félix is wearing is long, which is an important fact, as the length of the costume is what makes it skirt-like and quasi-feminine. In any case, it is fuller and more descriptive than the other manuscripts of *La fuerza* and than other extant Spanish manuscripts with a provable theatrical provenance. The text, like the *princeps*, seems to be meant, therefore, primarily for private reading rather than performance. This copy, produced by a single hand, is remarkably clean, with no cancelled passages or emendations, and it uses a fairly consistent spelling in the etymological forms of some names: the Latinate *Felix* and *Constança* in numerous instances, instead of the relaxed variants *Felis* and *Costança* that prevail in the other manuscripts and in the *princeps*; this may indicate that it was produced by an educated person, perhaps a professional scribe. The dialogue, as Machit observed, is almost identical to the *princeps* in Acts I and II (only seventeen lines are missing from the manuscript), and it only differs significantly in Act III, where 124 lines are missing.[22] As the manuscript is undated, we cannot know whether it predates the 1625 *Segunda parte*, but if it does, as Machit suggests, then the coincidences in the phrasing of stage directions throughout the text might suggest that BNE[2] represents a version of the play that is closer than the others to the authorial manuscript that served as the basis of the *princeps*. Even if it did derive from a pre-1625 authorial source, the manuscript is not an autograph copy, as a comparison with Castro's handwriting and signature in the holograph of *Ingratitud por amor* reveals.[23] These features – its fuller text, its textual closeness to the authorial source, and the tidiness of the hand – are consistent with the supposition that this manuscript may have been a presentation copy commissioned by the dramatist to be given to the Duke of Osuna.

---

[15] Edward M. Wilson, *Guillén de Castro* (New York, 1973), pp. 14–15.

[16] Wilson, *Guillén de Castro*, pp. 14–16.

[17] Wilson, *Guillén de Castro*, p. 15.

[18] Javier Ignacio Martínez del Barrio, 'Educación y mentalidad de la alta nobleza española en los siglos XVI y XVII: la formación de la biblioteca de la Casa Ducal de Osuna', *Cuadernos de Historia Moderna* 12 (1991), 74; my translation.

[19] All details of the genealogy of the Dukes of Osuna are from Francisco Fernández de Béthencourt, *Historia genealógica y heráldica de la Monarquía Española: Casa Real y grandes de España* (Madrid, 1900).

[20] Biblioteca Nacional de España, MSS Vitr. 7, No. 2. It is reproduced in full in the Biblioteca Digital Hispánica, http://bdh.bne.es/bnesearch/detalle/bdh0000100307.

[21] BNE[2] is reproduced in full in the Biblioteca Digital Hispánica, http://bdh.bne.es/bnesearch/detalle/bdh0000198734.

[22] Machit, 'Bad Habits', p. 23.

[23] The holograph is at http://bdh.bne.es/bnesearch/detalle/bdh0000100307.

The other manuscript from the library of Osuna, BNE¹, is perhaps more interesting. It is also undated and, apart from the many textual variations in the dialogue, it differs significantly from both the printed text and BNE² in that the stage directions are scantier and much less detailed. For example, in the opening stage direction, the 'long habit' has disappeared: 'salen doña costanza y don felis destudiante' (fol. 1r; 'Enter Doña Costanza and Don Félix as a student').[24] It was produced mostly by a main scribe with a second hand completing the last two leaves and, among numerous other variants and omissions, it adds three passages: one that had been left out by the first scribe but that features in the 1625 text and BNE² (fol. 8r), and two new interpolations (fols. 10r and 12v). All in all, BNE¹ contains some 424 lines fewer than the *princeps*, and, as Machit describes, a whole character, Inés, is missing.[25] Machit also concluded that, when the scribe changed from fol. 48r, the textual source changed as well: the last line of the previous page is given at the top of the next in a completely altered form.[26] There is, therefore, some reason to think that the text was being prepared for performance: lines were cut, the dramatis personae was adjusted, additional passages were introduced and the stage directions give the minimum to clarify the basic traffic of actors on stage. If the copy behind it was a fuller manuscript, then the stage directions may have eroded when the text was copied out but it seems perhaps more plausible that it derives from an independent source predating by some years the revised text of the *princeps*.

The last manuscript in Madrid, BNE³, belonged to the bibliophile Agustín Durán (1789–1862), member of the Real Academia Española and director of the Biblioteca Nacional, whose personal papers and rich literary collection were donated by his widow to that library in 1863.[27] He noted the existence of the two other manuscripts of the play extant at the Biblioteca Nacional in his handwritten catalogue of the library of the Duke of Osuna.[28] However, in spite of his notable bibliographic care, he did not note the origin of BNE³ in any of the detailed catalogues of his personal library that survive among his papers. It is, by far, the most interesting of the three copies in Madrid. It was produced by two scribes who took turns at irregular intervals, using different spelling conventions even in the names of the characters. The text is generally clean, though there are several cancelled passages and crossed-out individual lines, as well as emendations, indicated either *currente calamo* by the same scribe or by a second hand at a later stage. Interestingly, as in BNE¹, the character of Inés is also entirely missing. Eduardo Juliá Martínez, who edited the play in 1927, noted its textual proximity to BNE¹ and suggested that this manuscript probably derives from the other, 'because it contains almost the same errors and the same lines are missing'.[29] Even conceding that it is likely that both manuscripts 'descend from a common source', Machit corrected Juliá Martínez's statement, saying that '[BNE³] presents lines that are consistent with [BNE²] and [the *princeps*] but omitted in [BNE¹], and [BNE¹] lacks twice as many lines as [BNE³]'.[30] The stemma is, again, unclear, but it seems likely that, as with BNE¹, the manuscript predates by some years the printed text. In addition, the stage directions are generally even briefer and less descriptive than those in BNE¹: for instance, the opening stage direction is simply given as 'felis y costansa solos' (fol. 1r; 'Félix and Costanza, alone'), without mentioning the crucial detail of costume. However, the most interesting feature of BNE³ is that it bears traces of

---

[24] BNE¹ is reproduced in full in the Biblioteca Digital Hispánica, http://bdh.bne.es/bnesearch/detalle/bdh0000099793.

[25] Machit, 'Bad Habits', p. 21. [26] Machit, 'Bad Habits', p. 22.

[27] BNE³ is reproduced in full in the Biblioteca Digital Hispánica, http://bdh.bne.es/bnesearch/detalle/bdh0000009298.

[28] *Catálogo de las comedias que existen en la biblioteca de la testamentaría de Osuna*, Biblioteca Nacional de España, MSS 21423/8. It must have been when compiling this catalogue that he added a loose sheet before the Osuna manuscripts indicating the author of the play in his own hand.

[29] Guillén de Castro, *Obras de don Guillén de Castro y Bellvís*, ed. Eduardo Juliá Martínez (Madrid, 1927), vol. 3, p. x; my translation.

[30] Machit, 'Bad Habits', p. 26.

having been prepared for a performance. Apart from the cancelled passages that may indicate theatrical cuts, there are a number of meaningful alterations, particularly on the first page, that modify some of the visual clues given in the text. For example, the substitution of the line 'trenzas de oro, entera saya' ('golden plaits, full smock'; line 6, crossed out) with 'a la ermosa rropa y saya' ('to the beauteous raiment and smock') could indicate that the line had to be changed because the actress playing Doña Costanza had dark hair.

A further proof of the theatrical origin of BNE³ is a statement found on the last page of the manuscript after the end of the play in the hand of the first scribe: 'escribiola Osorio y es suya a pesar de uellacos' (fol. 49v; 'It was written by Osorio and it is his/hers in spite of knaves').[31] It is a strong statement of ownership, rather than authorship, and it seems likely that this Osorio was one of the *autores de comedias* (company managers) of the period, rather than an actor or dramatist. If the identity of this Osorio could be ascertained, this detail could help to date the manuscript and establish whether this version of the play predates the 1625 *princeps*. However, a search on the DICAT database does not provide conclusive information: there were four *autores* with that surname who were active before 1625, and one, Diego Osorio de Velasco, who was active between 1623 and 1662. The four are Juan de Osorio, actor and *autor*, active in 1587–1606; Pedro de Osorio, actor and *autor*, active in 1609–25; Baltasar de Osorio, actor and *autor*, active in 1614–21; and Vicente Osorio, *autor*, active in 1614–20. It seems statistically more probable that it was one of the four, but we cannot know whether it might have been Osorio de Velasco before or after 1625 or indeed another *comediante* whose career has not been recorded. Given that the Spanish possessive pronoun 'suya' is common for male and female possessors, it is possible that the person alluded to was a woman, perhaps a female member of a theatre company. The possibilities, then, are four actresses, two on either side of the 1625 watershed: Mariana Osorio and Magdalena Osorio, both active in 1588–1607; Catalina de Osorio, active in 1621–33; and Eugenia Osorio, active in 1613–46. A much less likely candidate is the famous Elena Osorio y Velázquez, who was Lope de Vega's lover in the mid-1580s.[32] The data, however, remain inconclusive.

Apart from the textual features explained above, and Machit's claim that all three manuscripts in Madrid predate the *princeps*, there is only one piece of evidence that would date BNE³ to the early part of the century, and therefore before the publication of the *Segunda parte*. Agustín Durán provided an approximate date for this copy in one of his private catalogues: 'Fuerza (la) de la Costumbre = de D. Guillen de Castro / MS de la 1ª. 4ª pte del 17 =' (i.e. 'Manuscript from the first quarter of the seventeenth [century]').[33] Based on his extensive knowledge of Spanish Golden Age drama in print and manuscript, his acquaintance with his enormous collection of playbooks, his unlimited access to the holdings of the Biblioteca Nacional as its director, and his experience in cataloguing the other great collection of drama in Spain – the library of the Osuna family – Durán did not hesitate to assign a pre-1625 date to this manuscript. We cannot know, however, how he arrived at this conclusion, and we cannot take this estimation as an absolute dating of BNE³. But if Durán was right, this manuscript would have been copied between the composition of the play around 1610–15 and the publication of the *princeps* in 1625. If this copy is related to BNE¹, then it is also likely that that manuscript was in circulation in the relevant period.

I have only been able to see a small sample of pages from the manuscript in Parma (BPP), sent in digital form by kind permission of its director: fols. 1r, 5r and 54v, 55r, that is, the opening of the play and its final two pages. By the style of the hand, I can ascertain that the copy was similarly produced

---

[31] This image is available in the Biblioteca Digital Hispánica, http://bdh.bne.es/bnesearch/detalle/bdh0000009298.

[32] See Alonso Zamora Vicente, *Lope de Vega: su vida y su obra* (Madrid, 1961).

[33] *Colección de comedias manuscritas de varios autores, anteriores al año 1750*, Biblioteca Nacional de España, RES 122/10.

in the early seventeenth century, though, as far as I can see, it is also undated. *Manos* indicates that the manuscript contains corrections by the *Licenciado* Francisco de Rojas and that it may be an autograph copy, although I do not think this is the case, comparing it to the holograph of *Ingratitud por amor*. The opening stage direction is given as 'Sale doña Costança y don felix destudiante' (fol. 1r; 'Enter Doña Costanza and Don Félix as a student'), a minimal variation over BNE¹, to which it seems to be related. A comparison between the portion of the dialogue that I have been able to access and that of the other four witnesses reveals a notable coincidence of BPP with the text of BNE¹: most individual textual variants coincide in both texts, while, most importantly, four brief narrative passages in the opening scene are missing in both but present in the other three.³⁴ This confirms the proximity of BPP and BNE¹, although, interestingly, some individual readings are closer to the other versions: for example, in the fourth line of the play, the nun's habit that the matriarch, Doña Costanza, has been wearing is said to be 'pardo' ('brown') in the *princeps* and in BNE¹, while it is 'largo' ('long') in BNE²; in BNE³, the word 'pardo' appears crossed out and replaced with 'negro' ('black'), which is the reading in BPP. The textual variants and material features of this manuscript need further investigation if a complete edition of the play is to be attempted in the future. In any case, the manuscript at the Biblioteca Palatina seems to be intimately connected with BNE¹, and therefore with BNE³, so we can suspect that it also predates the 1625 edition, and it may also have been in circulation at the time of the composition of *Love's Cure*. We do not know how long the manuscript has been in Italy, but perhaps it was already out of Spain in the early 1610s.

In conclusion, there are three main implications of this study at large that are relevant to tracing the textual transmission of *La fuerza* and that support the interrelated dating of both plays that emerges from the available evidence. The first interesting implication is that the dating of Fletcher and Massinger's English adaptation to the early months of 1615 crucially establishes a lower limit for the date of composition of *La fuerza*. In the absence of any other external record, only one systematic study has attempted to date this *comedia* and the rest of Castro's canon. Courtney Bruerton, based on a statistical study of the patterns of versification throughout Castro's career, assigned the following dates: '1610?–20? (1610?–15?)'.³⁵ According to Bruerton, *La fuerza* was written at some point between 1610 and 1620, but the first five years of the decade seem more probable. This dating is thoroughly compatible with that of *Love's Cure*, and it seems likelier that *La fuerza* would have been composed towards the earlier part of the decade to allow for its circulation and dissemination beyond Spain. If at least three of the manuscript witnesses of *La fuerza*, if not all four of them including BNE², predate the *princeps* edition, then it is possible that the play was already in circulation in the early 1610s, facilitating Fletcher's access to its text.

The second implication is that the high number of extant manuscripts of this *comedia* allows for the assumption that there were many more in circulation in the early part of the seventeenth century. As Felix Raab memorably wrote, 'Manuscripts and printed books are like snakes: for every one you see there are a hundred others hidden in the undergrowth.'³⁶ No fewer than four copies have survived, and others may be still lurking in archives or private collections yet undiscovered. In fact, the extraordinary degree of interrelation and interdependence between the four extant manuscripts, and the difficulty in establishing a definite stemma due to this genealogical complexity, seem to suggest that the number of intermediary manuscripts that could explain how these specific four variants originated must have been very great indeed. The comparatively high number of surviving copies, and this inferred abundance of necessary

---

[34] In Machit's edition, lines 62–5, 69–72, 93–6, and 110–11.

[35] Courtney Bruerton, 'The chronology of the *comedias* of Guillén de Castro', *Hispanic Review* 12 (1944), 150.

[36] Felix Raab, *The English Face of Machiavelli: A Changing Interpretation, 1500–1700* (London, 1964), p. 53.

textual intermediaries, certainly enable the theory that Fletcher could have accessed this Spanish play in manuscript. Revising George Walton Williams's statement, I would say that it seems unnecessary to invent the thesis that the printed edition was the source of textual influence when the chronological evidence disables that theory and when the existence of these manuscripts enables the transmission of this *comedia* to an interested English readership in pre-printed form.

The third implication is that this relative abundance of textual evidence indicates that the play was very popular in its own time, clearly more so than the more celebrated and more frequently performed *comedias* in Castro's canon. An unrecorded early popularity of *La fuerza* with its first audiences in Spain may have brought the play to the attention of someone in Fletcher's circle. Of course, the name of James Mabbe, first translator of *La Celestina* and *Guzmán de Alfarache* into English, comes easily to mind. As secretary to John Digby, the English ambassador to the court of King Philip III of Spain, Mabbe had lived in Madrid from April 1611 until 1613, with possible shorter visits thereafter; his acquaintance with Fletcher is well attested by the fact that he contributed a prefatory verse to Mabbe's *The Rogue, or The Life of Guzmán de Alfarache* (1622).[37] Mabbe is not the only candidate, and further research is needed to try to ascertain the scope of some of the untraced networks of mutual literary influence in Europe through diplomacy, private travel and even household employment. For example, Don Diego Sarmiento de Acuña (1567–1626), the celebrated 1st Count of Gondomar, who served twice as the resident Spanish ambassador in London (1613–18 and 1620–2), had extensive contacts in the book trade and the theatre profession in Spain and in England, and he even employed two English librarians to curate the enormous collection of books held in his private residence at the Casa del Sol in Valladolid, the largest library in Spain at the time. The traffic of books in print and manuscript between his libraries in London and Valladolid was constant during his ambassadorship and it is not unimaginable that he may have granted access to his large collection of plays and other works of fiction to interested English parties, as was the case with his Spanish collection, demonstrably frequented by writers and scholars.[38] In any case, it seems reasonable to think that these available networks would have enabled an agent to acquire a manuscript copy of *La fueza* in Spain and bring it to London. Alternatively, that agent might have chosen to produce a closely worded written or verbal account of a performance of the play in Spain that the English dramatists could have accessed, perhaps with some distortion in the order of the episodes that the original play narrates, which may account for some of the structural differences. Jonathan Thacker is inclined to think that the transmission was not realized via a copy of the full text but rather through this kind of partial account of the play.[39] However, this theory would fail to explain the striking structural parallels between both plays, the similarities in the dramaturgical devices employed, the significant number of verbal echoes, and perhaps even the recurrence of the word *custom* as a textual *Leitmotiv* throughout *Love's Cure*, replicating the title of the *comedia*, and the recurrent use of the word 'costumbre' in its dialogue. Based on the available evidence, we cannot know in what precise form and in what specific circumstances the Spanish play travelled to England, but the existence of these manuscripts makes that process a real possibility, especially

---

[37] David Kathman, 'Mabbe, James (1571/2–1642?)', in *Oxford Dictionary of National Biography* (Oxford, 2004; online edn, 2010), www.oxforddnb.com/view/article/17319.

[38] See Carmen Manso Porto, *Don Diego Sarmiento de Acuña, Conde de Gondomar (1567–1626): erudito, mecenas y bibliófilo* (Santiago de Compostela, 1996); José García Oro, *Don Diego Sarmiento de Acuna, Conde de Gondomar y Embajador de España (1567–1626)* (Santiago de Compostela, 1997); Fernando Bartolomé Benito, *Don Diego Sarmiento de Acuña, Conde de Gondomar: el Maquiavelo español* (Gijón, 2005); and Juan Durán-Loriga, *El Embajador y el Rey: El Conde de Gondomar y Jacobo I de Inglaterra*, Biblioteca Diplomática Española, Sección Estudios 27 (Madrid, 2006).

[39] Public discussion at the Association for Hispanic Classical Theater conference, *The Comedia: Translation and Performance*, Theatre Royal, Bath, November 2013.

since one is found in Parma, outside the country where the play originated. If it travelled to Italy, it may have travelled elsewhere.

This kind of research, that only set out to address a long-standing chronological crux, does not constitute a methodology that can be followed with very many English Renaissance plays – after all, there are only three other plays which have been identified so far as having been based on Spanish dramatic material of the same period.[40] But it exemplifies the kind of comparative work that remains to be done and that can enrich and illuminate the dramatic history of Renaissance Europe by correlating data from different theatrical contexts and searching for the interrelations between different practices and traditions across the enormously permeable borders of the different nations. All too often we read scholarship of English Renaissance drama considered as an insular body of work, cut off from the continent by the seemingly impenetrable fogs of the English Channel. But the people who produced these plays were multilingual, educated and culturally open: men and women who were deeply engaged with a shared European theatrical and literary culture beyond the borders of their native England, a nation that was only then starting to become a global power and whose language was only beginning to gain a limited influence. And it may be more important now than ever to take up this cultural cosmopolitanism in the scholarly work that we do.

---

[40] Namely, Philip Massinger's *The Renegado* (1624), partially based on Cervantes's *Los baños de Argel*, and two plays by James Shirley: *The Young Admiral* (1633), based on Lope de Vega's *Don Lope de Cardona* (pub. 1618), and *The Opportunity* (1634), based on *El castigo del penséque* (1613–14) by Tirso de Molina.

WHAT IF GREG AND WERSTINE HAD EXAMINED EARLY MODERN SPANISH DRAMATIC MANUSCRIPTS?

JESÚS TRONCH

In this article, I seek to engage in the debate on the categories of 'foul papers' and 'promptbooks' as used by W. W. Greg, by bringing in evidence from the contemporary tradition of early modern Spanish drama. The names in the title of this article stand as representative of the opposing arguments in this debate. Greg hypothesized that the two most likely types of manuscripts which served as the basis of the early printed editions were 'foul papers' and 'promptbooks', and defined their respective textual characteristics by which editors could discern the nature of a printer's copy.[1] Paul Werstine, together with scholars such as Johan Gerritsen and William B. Long, argued that Greg's description of these categories did not correspond with the actual manuscripts and was therefore invalid.[2] The conclusions of both parties ultimately derive from the same evidence obtained from around one hundred manuscripts up to 1642,[3] a scanty and limited corpus of material compared to the presumed number of dramatic manuscripts in circulation during the period,[4] and even more limited when compared to the sheer abundance of extant manuscripts in the contemporary tradition of Spanish theatre: around 3,000 from the late sixteenth century to the early years of the eighteenth century.[5]

In an exercise in comparative textual criticism, I apply Werstine's method of analysis of twenty-one early modern English playhouse texts[6] to a selection of Spanish manuscripts in order to see whether this additional evidence confirms either Greg's position or Werstine's critique, and in particular Greg's proposal (put into practice by

---

This chapter was produced with the support of Research Project FFI2012–34347, funded by Spanish government through the *Plan Nacional I+D+i*, and of *Red del Patrimonio Teatral Clásico Español* FFI2015–71441-REDC, within the Spanish National Programme for Fostering Excellence in Scientific and Technical Research.

[1] W. W. Greg, *The Editorial Problem in Shakespeare* (Oxford, 1942; 3rd edn, 1952), p. 156.

[2] Paul Werstine, *Early Modern Playhouse Manuscripts and the Editing of Shakespeare* (Cambridge, 2013).

[3] This is the figure stated by Werstine, *Early Modern*, p. 4. Grace Ioppolo proposes between 100 and 125, in her *Dramatists and Their Manuscripts in the Age of Shakespeare, Jonson, Middleton and Heywood: Authorship, Authority and the Playhouse* (London, 2006), pp. 5–7.

[4] Some 13,000 manuscripts, as estimated by William Proctor Williams, '[Review of] *Early Modern Playhouse Manuscripts and the Editing of Shakespeare* by Paul Werstine', *Shakespeare Quarterly* 64 (2013), 473–45; p. 473.

[5] Margaret Greer, 'Authorial and theatrical community: Early modern Spanish theater manuscripts', *Renaissance Drama*, New Series 40 (2012), 101–12; p. 102. It is difficult to know how many Spanish manuscripts have survived in a more comparable period up to 1650. The standard inventory of manuscripts in the Biblioteca Nacional in Madrid, A. Paz y Meliá's *Catálogo de las piezas de teatro que se conservan en el departamento de manuscritos de la Biblioteca Nacional*, 2nd edn, vol. 1 (Madrid, 1934), occasionally provides a specific date or year (if included in the manuscript itself) and, for most entries, only indicates if the handwriting belongs to the sixteenth, seventeenth or eighteenth century. Margaret Greer and Alejandro García Reidy, the editors of the *Manos* open-access database (*www.manos.net*) estimate between 500 and 1,000 (private communication, 3 December 2016).

[6] Werstine, *Early Modern*.

many Shakespearean editors)[7] that it is possible to identify a printed play-text as based on 'foul papers' or on a 'promptbook' by discerning specific signs in the texts that denote each category.

Greg's study of dramatic manuscripts[8] was part of the New Bibliographers' programme to direct the study of early modern play-texts 'within the parameters of a properly scientifically-driven bibliographic approach',[9] which involved an analysis of the surviving evidence and of its material conditions. One of the tasks in this approach was to define a taxonomy of this evidence. Having no authorial manuscripts but only printed editions as witnesses, Shakespeare editors were compelled, as Alfred W. Pollard had already established, to identify the character of the lost manuscript underlying a quarto or folio text. As stated above, Greg summarized that 'the two most important sources of the extant texts are probably the author's foul papers and theatrical prompt-books'.[10] Although Greg generally formulated his proposals in rather tentative language,[11] and Fredson Bowers extended the kinds of sources to thirteen ('some of them speculative', including intermediate copies, authorial and scribal, as well as printed editions),[12] Greg's binary categorizations influenced the conceptual framework for Shakespeare textual studies to the extent that they 'ceased even to be thought of as hypotheses and assumed the statute of established facts'.[13] Their characteristics were cited almost systematically by most Shakespearean editors since the 1960s. An author's 'foul papers' would be characterized

by loose ends, false starts, textual tangles, unresolved confusions, and duplicated alternative versions of particular passages; by extensive inconsistency in the designation of characters in speech-prefixes and stage characters; by 'ghost' characters called for in stage directions, who never speak and are never spoken to; by extreme deficiencies in stage directions, particularly by repeated failure to provide entrances for characters, by the use of an actor's name (instead of character's) in stage directions and speech-prefixes.[14]

By contrast, 'promptbooks' would lack these authorial features and show rather more consistency and precision, together with additional stage directions and reminders necessary to guide the performance, as well as (but not always) the licence of the Master of the Revels.

However, as early as 1952, Gerritsen started to point out discrepancies between what was expected in 'foul papers' and 'promptbooks' and the actual readings in *The Honest Man's Fortune* both in the scribal manuscript transcribed by Edward Knight and in the 1647 Beaumont and Fletcher folio.[15] In 1985, Long showed that inconsistencies remained in a playbook used by the theatre company and questioned the use of stage directions in the task of identifying the printer's

---

[7] As observed by Barbara Mowat in 'The reproduction of Shakespeare's Texts', in *The Cambridge Companion to Shakespeare*, ed. Margreta de Grazia and Stanley Wells (Cambridge, 2001), pp. 13–29, pp. 23–5; and by Werstine, *Early Modern*, pp. 33–4.

[8] Mainly in W. W. Greg, *Dramatic Documents from the Elizabethan Playhouses: Stage Plots, Actors' Parts, Prompt Books*, 2 vols. (Oxford, 1931) but also in other articles. The application of his studies to Shakespearean textual criticism was set out in *Editorial Problem*, and in *The Shakespeare First Folio: Its Bibliographical and Textual History* (Oxford, 1955).

[9] Andrew Murphy, 'W. W. Greg (9 July 1875 – 4 March 1959)', in *Bradley, Greg, Folger: Great Shakespearians*, ed. Cary DiPietro (London and New York, 2011), p. 97. Appraisals of the significant contribution of Greg and the New Bibliography are F. W. Wilson, *Shakespeare and the New Bibliography*, rev. and ed. Helen Gardner (Oxford, 1970), and Gabriel Egan, *The Struggle for Shakespeare's Text: Twentieth-Century Editorial Theory and Practice* (Cambridge, 2010).

[10] Greg, *The Editorial Problem in Shakespeare*, p. 156.

[11] Just before the previous quotation, Greg warns his readers that his observations are 'impressions' that are 'exceedingly fallible' (*Editorial Problem*, p. 156).

[12] Fredson Bowers, *On Editing Shakespeare and the Elizabethan Dramatists* (Philadelphia, 1955), pp. 11–12. Bowers's extension can be seen as 'a formalization of the fluidity that was already acknowledged in Greg's simpler system made up of the binaries of foul and fair, theatrical and literary, authorial and scribal', as John Jowett qualifies it, *Shakespeare and Text* (Oxford, 2007), p. 102.

[13] Murphy, 'W. W. Greg', p. 106.

[14] Gary Taylor, 'General Introduction', in Stanley Wells and Gary Taylor, with John Jowett and William Montgomery, *William Shakespeare: A Textual Companion* (Oxford, 1987), pp. 1–68; p. 9, citing Greg, *Shakespeare First Folio*, pp. 114–21.

[15] Johan Gerritsen, ed., *The Honest Man's Fortune: A Critical Edition of MS Dyce 9 (1625)* (Groningen, 1952), pp. lxii–lxiii.

copy.[16] In subsequent articles, Long demonstrated that textual features characteristic of 'foul papers' were also found in surviving playhouse manuscripts (he advised against use of the term 'promptbook') which bear the intervention of bookkeepers, to the extent that they contradict any expectations of precision, neatness and consistency as Greg imagined promptbooks to be.[17]

In Early Modern Playhouse Manuscripts and the Editing of Shakespeare, Paul Werstine culminates his critique of the Gregian categories that had been expounded in a battery of articles since 1988.[18] In this monograph, defined as 'the most unapologetically field-redefining study' published in 2013,[19] and regarded by Werstine himself as 'an extended essay in New Bibliography',[20] Werstine submits the total corpus of those surviving play-texts that bear evidence of having been used as a guide to performance to a thorough analysis of its textual features in relation to Greg's assumptions, paying special attention to the interventions that were made and were not made in the playhouse observable in the evidence. The corpus in Werstine's study consists of eighteen manuscripts and three annotated quartos,[21] selected because of the consensus about their theatrical provenance and of their having 'annotations for stage production, usually, in the case of the MSS, in other hands than those in which the main text is inscribed'.[22] Werstine's taxonomy of the most common kinds of playhouse annotation in this corpus is as follows:[23]

A   Notation of actors' names
B   Notation of act division
C   Use of '*clear*' to note an empty stage
D   Passages cut
E   Roles entirely cut
F   Notation of props
G   Notation of sounds
H   Partial repetition of existing SDD
I   Full repetition of existing SDD
J   Addition of SDD
K   Warnings
L   SDD transferred from tops of versos to bottom of rectos
M   SDD transferred from tops of rectos to bottom of versos
N   Correction, change or addition of SPP

[16] William B. Long, 'Stage-directions: A misinterpreted factor in determining textual provenance', *TEXT: Transactions of the Society for Textual Scholarship* 2 (1985), 121–37; '"A bed for Woodstock": A warning for the unwary', *Medieval and Renaissance Drama in England* 2 (1985), 91–118.

[17] '*John a Kent and John a Cumber*: An Elizabethan Playbook and Its Implications', in *Shakespeare and Dramatic Tradition*, ed. W. R. Elton and W. B. Long (New York, 1989), pp. 125–43; and '"Precious few": English manuscript playbooks', in *A Companion to Shakespeare*, ed. David Scott Kastan (Oxford, 1999), pp. 414–33. Gabriel Egan, in his article 'Precision, consistency and completeness in early-modern playbook manuscripts: The evidence from *Thomas of Woodstock* and *John a Kent and John a Cumber*', *The Library* 12 (2011), 376–91, found Long's essays a 'necessary corrective to a prevailing editorial over-confidence in determining (with the aid of simplified rules from Greg) the manuscript provenance of early editions of plays', but he questions some of Long's inferences and concludes that the manuscripts 'contain conflicting evidence that is no better explained by Long's new orthodoxy than by the old one it replaced'.

[18] Paul Werstine, '"Foul papers" and "Prompt-books": Printer's copy for Shakespeare's *Comedy of Errors*', *Studies in Bibliography* 41 (1988), 232–46; and 'McKerrow's suggestion and twentieth-century textual criticism', *Renaissance Drama* 19 (1988), 149–73.

[19] Sonia Massai, 'Editions and textual studies', *Shakespeare Survey* 67 (2014), 484–6; p. 484.

[20] Werstine, *Early Modern*, p. 1.

[21] The eighteen manuscripts are: *John a Kent and John a Cumber*, attributed to Anthony Munday, Huntington Library MS HM 500; [*John of Bordeaux or the Second Part of Friar Bacon*], attributed to Robert Greene, Alnwick Castle MS 507; *Sir Thomas More*, attributed to Anthony Munday, Henry Chettle, revised by Thomas Dekker and probably by Thomas Heywood and William Shakespeare, British Library MS Harl. 7368; *Charlemange or the Distracted Emperor*, British Library MS Egerton 1994[6]; [*The First Part of the Reign of King Richard the Second, or Thomas of Woodstock*], British Library MS Egerton 1994[8]; *The Second Maiden's Tragedy* [or *The Lady's Tragedy*], British Library MS Landsdowne 807; *The Tragedy of Sir John van Olden Barnavelt*, by John Fletcher and Philip Massinger, British Library MS Additional 18653; *The Two Noble Ladies*, British Library MS Egerton 1994[11]; *Edmond Ironside the English King*, British Library MS Egerton 1994[5]; *The Welsh Embassador*, Cardiff Public Library MS 4.12; *The Captives*, by Thomas Heywood, British Library MS Egerton 1994; *The Parliament of Love*, by Philip Massinger, Victoria and Albert Museum MS Dyce 25.F.33; *The Honest Man's Fortune*, by Nathan Field, John Fletcher, and Philip Massinger, Victoria and Albert Museum MS Dyce 25.F.9; *The Soddered Citizen*, by John Clavell, Wiltshire and Swindon Record Office MS 865/502/2; *Believe as You List*, by Philip Massinger, British Library

	A	B	C	D	E	F	G	H	I	J	K	L	M	N	O	P	Q	R
Kent				√	√		√	√				√						
Bordeaux	√			√		√	√	√	√	√			√	√	√			
Moore	√			√	√	√	√	√	√	√				√	√		√	
Charlemagne		√		√			√	√	√	√		√					√	√
Woodstock	√	√		√			√	√	√	√	√			√	√	√	√	
SM/LT	√			√		√	√	√	√				√	√	√	√	√	√
Barnauelt	√			√	√	√	√	√		√		√		√	√	√	√	
Noble Ladys	√	√					√	√	√	√		√		√				
Ironside	√	√		√	√		√	√		√			√	√	√	√		
Embassador		√		√		√	√				√							
Captives	√	√	√	√		√	√	√	√	√	√			√	√	√		
Parliam^t		√		√		√	√		√						√	√		
HMF	√	√		√	√	√	√		√					√	√	√		
Looking glass	√		√	√	√	√	√			√		√	√	√	√	√		
Sodderd		√		√				√						√	√	√		
Beleeue	√	√		√		√	√	√	√	√	√	√		√	√	√	√	√
Lanchinge		√		√	√		√	√						√	√	√	√	√
Lady=mother	√	√		√	√	√	√			√	√			√	√	√	√	
Waspe	√	√		√	√	√	√	√	√					√	√	√		
Fleire		√		√	√	√				√				√	√	√		
Milk-Maids		√		√	√	√	√		√		√	√	√	√	√	√		

O Correction or change of dialogue
P Censorship by bookkeeper (or perhaps some other agent)
Q Censorship by the Master of Revels or his deputy
R Licence

Werstine provides a table (transcribed above) that visualizes the distribution of these annotations that 'reveal an intention to put these texts to use in the production of plays'[24] among the twenty-one texts in his corpus (listed in chronological order).[25]

In Appendix A of his monograph, Werstine details those features that Greg proposed as characteristic of 'foul papers' in each of the play-texts of the corpus. He arranges these presumed authorial features in nineteen categories, grouped into those dealing with 'naming' or character designations (categories 1 to 3), with speech prefixes (4 to 6), with stage directions (7 to 17), and with other features of dialogue (18 and 19):

#1. Multiple designations of the same character in SDD and SPP[26]
#2. Ambiguous character designations[27]

MS Egerton 2828; *The Launching of the Mary*, by Walter Mountfort, British Library MS Egerton 1994[15]; *The Lady Mother*, by Henry Glapthorne, British Library MS Egerton 1994; *The Wasp*, Alnwick Castle MS 507. The three printed texts are: *The Fleer*, by Edward Sharpham, British Library 11773.C.8; *A Looking Glass, for London and England*, by Thomas Lodge and Robert Greene, Regenstein Library at the University of Chicago PR2297.L8 160; *The Two Merry Milkmaids or the Best Words Wear the Garland*, attributed to John Cumber, Folger Shakespeare Library STC 4281 Copy 2.

[22] Werstine, *Early Modern*, p. 4.
[23] Werstine, *Early Modern*, pp. 239–43.
[24] Werstine, *Early Modern*, p. 241.
[25] Werstine, *Early Modern*, p. 243.
[26] As when the character named 'Emperor' in the first stage direction of *Bordeux* is later designated as 'fredrick' in the speech prefix at 15.1043 (Werstine, *Early Modern*, p. 359). References are keyed to W. L. Renwick, ed., *John of Bordeaux or the second part of Friar Bacon*, Malone Society Reprints (London, 1936).
[27] Again as when 'Emperor' in *Bordeux* designates the German emperor in the first speech prefix and 'Ambrothe the turke' at 3.128 (Werstine, *Early Modern*, p. 364). Other ambiguous designations are 'All.', 'Lady', 'Lord' and 'Lords', 'Ser.', '1.', '2.'.

IF GREG AND WERSTINE HAD EXAMINED SPANISH MANUSCRIPTS

	1	2	3	4	5	6	7	8	9	10	11	12	13	14	15	16	17	18	19
Non-theatrical																			
Bordeaux	√	√	√	√	√	√	√	√	√	√		√				√			√
Charlemagne	√						√		√			√							√
Ironside	√	√					√	√	√			√				√			√
SM/LT	√	√		√		√	√	√	√							√	√		√
Sodderd	√					√		√	√							√		√	√
Woodstock	√	√		√		√	√	√	√		√	√	√		√	√	√		√
Theatrical ones																			
Barnauelt	√	√			√	√		√	√	√						√	√	√	√
Embassador		√		√		√						√		√		√			
HMF	√	√						√								√	√	√	
Lady=mother	√	√		√		√	√	√	√							√		√	
Parliam^t	√	√		√			√		√							√			√
Authors																			
Beleeue	√	√			√		√	√	√		√					√		√	√
Captives	√	√		√		√	√	√								√	√		√
Kent	√	√		√			√					√	√		√				√
Lanchinge	√	√			√			√	√	√			√		√	√			√
Moore	√	√				√	√	√								√	√	√	√
Noble Ladys	√	√				√	√	√								√			
Waspe	√	√		√		√	√	√	√			√				√	√		
Printed texts																			
Fleire	√	√		√				√	√										
Looking glasse	√	√		√		√	√	√	√							√		√	
Milk-Maids	√	√		√			√	√	√	√		√				√			

#3. Dialogue errors in naming
#4. Erroneous SPP
#5. Misplaced SPP
#6. Missing SPP
#7. Missing entrances
#8. Indefinite entrances involving speakers[28]
#9. Other indefinite SDD[29]
#10. Omission of necessary characters from SDD
#11. Inclusion of unnecessary characters in entrance directions
#12. Mutes and ghosts
#13. Double entrances
#14. Erroneous SDD
#15. Petitory SDD[30]
#16. Missing exits
#17. Misplaced SDD, principally exits
#18. Marginal insertions of dialogue[31]
#19. Incomplete deletion[32]

The distribution of these 'foul papers' features among the playhouse texts is visualized in the table above

---

[28] Such as 'Enter offesers and rossaline' in *Bordeaux* (8.562), when at least one officer speaks at 565 (Werstine, *Early Modern*, p. 375). Other examples: '*the Clowns*', '*the rabble*', '*the lovers*'.

[29] Such as 'Enter all the presoners' in *Bordeaux* (18.1215); and imprecise designations such as '*attendants*', '*others*', '*other Nobles*', '*soldiers*' (Werstine, *Early Modern*, p. 379).

[30] Also called 'permissive' stage directions, as in *The Launching of the Mary*, 'there must appeare aloft, as many gallants & ladies as the roome Canne well hold' (5.1.2677–8) or in *Sir Thomas More* 'Enters Lord Maior, so many Aldermen as may ... ' (3.2.†954), quoted in Werstine (*Early Modern*, p. 386).

[31] Marginal additions that may cause confusion or mislineation if the manuscript is used as printer's copy because the insertions are not properly aligned as verse and/or properly signposted as to their intended location in the dialogue (Werstine, *Early Modern*, pp. 133 and 178).

[32] Causing confusions such as loose ends, false starts and duplications of dialogue (Werstine, *Early Modern*, pp. 178–90).

with titles listed according to kinds of text (manuscripts copied by apparently non-theatrical scribes, manuscripts copied by theatrical scribes, authorial manuscripts and annotated printed texts).[33]

This table clearly shows that playhouse texts (what Greg terms 'promptbooks') also contain variations in naming, loose ends, indefinite and permissive stage directions, etc., and are therefore not as orderly, precise and complete as Greg had proposed. In other words, Werstine's monograph exposes Greg's idealizations of 'foul papers' and 'promptbooks' by pointing out how Gregian characteristics of the former are present in the latter and therefore cannot be used to determine the provenance of a printed play-text.

Werstine is aware of one of the weaknesses of his argument: as pointed out above, the corpus of twenty-one theatre-related texts represents only a relatively small percentage of the number of manuscripts that must have circulated at that time. As Werstine himself acknowledges, his study is 'in no position to extrapolate from the proportions of scribal and authorial MSS that obtain among the extant MSS to make any claim about the proportions of such MSS that once existed in the early modern playhouses'.[34] At this point, I venture to supplement more evidence of play-texts annotated with a view to performance from the contemporary tradition of Spanish theatre and to analyse them in relation to Werstine's taxonomy of features of Gregian 'foul papers'.

The selection of Spanish manuscripts for my parallel corpus may seem an easy task at first, when most of the extant manuscripts are in general related to the theatre, while other kinds such as private transcripts are fewer and more difficult to locate. However, it is a well-founded assumption that a manuscript belonging to a theatre company does not necessarily imply that it was *used* with a view to performance. It is important to ensure that the documents under study show evidence of having been prepared for the stage, mainly by means of annotations in different hands and/or inks. To this end, I set up a list of textual features based on those that Hispanists recurrently cite to define a manuscript as 'theatrical' for its use to guide or assist in a production.[35] The most common feature is the so-called 'atajos', that is, cuts usually marked up by boxing the passage in question. These boxed fragments are often accompanied by warnings such as 'no', 'si' (= 'yes'), 'no se dice' (= 'not to be spoken'), 'dicese' (= 'to be spoken'), etc. Also common are the annotations in a different hand from that of the author, or of the main hand in a scribal copy, calling for a sound effect, such as 'musica', 'tocan' (= 'They play'), 'cajas' (= 'drums'), 'llaman' (= 'knock'), 'hagan ruido' (= 'make noise'). Other 'theatrical' annotations are changes in the designation of speeches to characters by crossing out the speech prefix and adding the new one right next to it, the occasional insertion of the personal name of actors, additions and corrections in stage directions, and scribal additions in the dialogue, sometimes by an *autor de comedias* or actor-manager of a theatre company. An obvious example of playhouse intervention is the warning directions, those drawing the theatre personnel's attention to some business that is to take place later in performance, for example, when 'Pdos' (an abbreviation of 'preparados' (= 'ready')) is inserted some lines earlier than an entrance.

Also indicative of the manuscript's use by a theatre company is the licence for performance, usually written at the end of the manuscript, as well as corrections in the dialogue carried out by the censor. By contrast, a very unusual feature is the repetition of a stage direction from the top of a verso or reverse page to the bottom of the preceding recto or obverse page (and similarly from bottom of a recto to the top of its verso). This duplication saved bookkeepers or prompters time in turning over a folio-sized page

---

[33] Werstine, *Early Modern*, p. 391.
[34] Werstine, *Early Modern*, p. 230.
[35] Among my sources of information (including many introductions to critical editions), I point out Manuel Sánchez Mariana, 'Los manuscritos dramáticos del Siglo de Oro', in *Ex libris. Homenaje al profesor José Fradejas Lebrero*, vol. 1, ed. José Nicolás Romera Castillo, Ana Freire López and Antonio Lorente Medina (Madrid, 1993), pp. 441–52; Marco Presotto, *Le commedie autografe di Lope de Vega: Catalogo e studio* (Kasel, 2000), pp. 46–9; and Milagros Rodríguez Cáceres, Elena E. Marcello and Felipe B. Pedraza Jiménez, eds., *La comedia española en sus manuscritos* (Cuenca, 2014).

(containing between fifty and eighty lines);[36] however, most of the Spanish manuscripts I have seen, or read descriptions of, are quarto size (accommodating between twenty-seven and forty-two lines per page).

The features of playhouse annotation explained so far generally coincide with those listed by Werstine.[37] Yet Hispanists also cite other characteristics. Added to the list of characters at the beginning of the play and/or of each act or 'jornada' can be found the names of players (often identifiable with those belonging to theatre companies) as well as crosses, circles, lines and other signs such as 'hase de sacar' (= '[an actor's part] to be copied out') used for the distribution of parts or other purposes.[38] Sometimes among the names of players appears that of the *autor de comedias*, who is also sometimes mentioned in the performance licence.[39] Some manuscripts bear an explicit reference to the *autor de comedias* or to an actor or actress for whom the copy was made.[40] Other features I have encountered are crosses added in the margins of the dialogue to draw attention to specific stage movements, to a stage direction or to corrections in the text;[41] numbers and sums related to production accounts, such as payment to actors,[42] or perhaps the number of lines for each act or 'jornada'; a cast with indications on how to double roles;[43] and a list of costumes and stage properties needed for the performance.

For my list of playhouse annotations in Spanish manuscripts, I keep Werstine's wording and their corresponding headings with capital letters for ease of comparison, but I add the following features:

[S] Scribal actors' names in cast list
[T] Crosses and circles in cast list
[U] Correction of SDD
[V] Actors' names in margin of dialogue
[W] Indication of *autor de comedias* or players related to a company
[X] Sums, lists of props

Finally, I omit Werstine's feature C (the use of '*clear*' to empty the stage) because it is not relevant as an outstanding annotation for Spanish theatrical practice.

For my parallel corpus of Spanish manuscripts, I carried out a pre-selection of likely candidates after reading the descriptions of five hundred manuscripts in the *Manos* database and of dozens of critical editions of plays that have manuscripts among their witnesses. I did not follow any special criterion other than the availability and the variety of playwrights. Some descriptions explicitly referred to evidence of use in a production; others did not categorize the manuscripts as such but the features described could well lead one to regard them as theatrical manuscripts. Many editors do not describe manuscripts in terms of categories such as drafts or

---

[36] Greg, *First Folio*, p. 138; Long, 'Precious Few', p. 416; Werstine, *Early Modern*, p. 240.

[37] Werstine, *Early Modern*, pp. 239–43.

[38] Presotto, *Le commedie*, pp. 37–8. Sometimes this distribution is authorial, as Presotto points out with reference to a number of Lope de Vega's autographs. For instance, on fol. 4r of manuscript Ms. 391 of Lope de Vega's *Estefanía la desdichada* at the Real Academia Española, these signs appear in the same ink as that used in many additional corrections in the dialogue (*sottolineature*), boxed passages, and 'no' and 'yes' annotations (Presotto, *Le commedie*, p. 236).

[39] Presotto, *Le commedie*, pp. 39–43.

[40] For instance, *La Santa Juana, Parte I* by Gabriel Téllez, BNE Res. 239; *La Serrana de la Vera* by Luis Vélez de Guevara, BNE Res. 101; and *El orden de Melquisedec* by Pedro Calderón de la Barca, manuscripts B2004 at the Hispanic Society of America (see corresponding entries in *manos.net*).

[41] The BNE 16564 manuscript of Lope de Vega's sacramental play *El hijo de la Iglesia* has small crosses in the margin of the dialogue on fols. 3r, 3v, 4r, 16v, 17v and 18r that seem to draw attention to stage movements, as explained in the entry for MS 3383 in Greer and García-Reidy's database *manos.net*.

[42] There are sums on fol. 3r of Lope de Vega's *Del monte sale quien el monte quema*, BNE Res. 94; and figures on fol. IIIv of BNE 16564 of Lope de Vega's *El hijo de la Iglesia*. Fol. 40v of manuscript BNE 16986 of Claramonte's *Púsoseme el sol* indicates that there are payments related to actors (see entry for manuscript 1513 in *manos.net*).

[43] For instance, on fol. 13v in the manuscript BNE 16058 of *Comedia a lo pastoril para la noche de Navidad* attributed to Pedro Díaz and Antón García, and on fol. 3r in the British Library manuscript MS Lansd. 760 of Diego Seron's *Garcilaso enamorado*; both described in their corresponding entries in *manos.net*.

stage copies but just as autographs or scribal.[44] Some differences between the two traditions need to be taken into account. While the English playhouse texts are confined to the period up to the closing of commercial theatres in 1642, the Spanish tradition does not have such a clear-cut chronological division and therefore I included manuscripts from the second half of the seventeenth century.

After discarding manuscripts that clearly showed no signs of theatrical use, my pre-selection resulted in an initial list of fifty manuscripts. I examined these texts to see if they complied with my list of annotations for stage production. I did not take the presence of a licence per se as indicative of use for performance but always in combination with other features, mainly annotations in a different hand from that of the main copyist (either author or scribe). Thus, for instance, I did not choose the BNE Vitr.7–5 autograph of Lope de Vega's *La dama boba*, which contains several licences on fol. 60v and also some actors' names in the *dramatis personae* on fol. 2r, but has only one boxed passage (of just four lines).[45] I also discarded the BNE Res. 134 manuscript of Lope de Vega's *El favor agradecido* since it lacks a performance licence and 'atajos' or boxed passages, although the *dramatis personae* shows crosses, and actors' names are added by an annotator in the margin of the dialogue. By contrast, I selected the BNE 15690 manuscript of *El valiente negro en Flandes* by Andrés de Claramonte, because of the 1651 licence and the boxed passages together with the non-authorial annotation of actors' names 'Lopez' (fol. 7v) and 'Cifuentes' (fols. 10r and 15r), actors who belonged to the theatre company managed by Toribio de la Vega in that year (Illustration 7).[46]

From these fifty manuscripts, I identified twenty-five which had clear evidence of annotations with a view to stage production and, as of December 2016, I have personally examined sixteen of them. The following are the references for these manuscripts, grouped into scribal and authorial copies – they include sigla, title, author, library shelfmark and, between parentheses, their date of performance and/or licence.

Scribal Copies

SM *El secreto en la mujer* by Andrés de Claramonte, BNE Res. 169 (early seventeenth century)[47]

MRR *El mayor rey de los reyes* by Andrés de Claramonte, BNE 17133 (early seventeenth century)[48]

PP *El príncipe perfecto* by Lope de Vega, BNE 15181 (earliest licence dated 1614)[49]

PSSL *Púsoseme el sol, salióme la luna* by Andrés de Claramonte, BNE 16986 (perf. 1642)[50]

VPS *El veneno para sí* by Juan Bautista Diamante, BNE 18316 (copied 1653)[51]

---

[44] And, of course, there are disagreements over the type of manuscript, as in the case of *La loca del cielo* (BNE 16568), which A. Paz y Meliá judges a draft, apparently an autograph (*Catálogo*, p. 314), while Margaret Greer disagrees (see corresponding entry in *manos.net*).

[45] Presotto remarks that 'non appaiono evidenti interventi per la rappresentazioni' (*Le commedie*, p. 184).

[46] See corresponding entry (manuscript 0137) in *manos.net*. For the connection of actors with the theatre company, see Teresa Ferrer Valls, dir., *Diccionario biográfico de actors del teatro clasico español (DICAT)* (Kassel, 2008). However, one wonders why a male actor's name ('cifuentes') is added next to a passage spoken by Doña Leonor, a female role played by an actress, as customary in early modern Spanish theatre.

[47] Alfredo Rodríguez López-Vázquez, ed., *El secreto en la mujer, by Andrés de Claramonte* (London, 1991). Paz y Meliá inserts a question mark over the autograph character of this manuscript (*Catálogo*, p. 506); Rodríguez claims that Claramonte dictated to a copyist and inserted marginal corrections himself (*El secreto*, p. 16); Greer suggests that the main hand could be that of a theatre manager or a prompter (see corresponding entry in *manos.net*).

[48] Paz y Meliá dates its handwriting to the early seventeenth century (*Catálogo*, p. 346). The modern edition I have consulted is that published by Real Academia Española in *Obras de Lope de Vega: Obras dramáticas*, vol. 7 (Madrid, 1930).

[49] Lope de Vega, 'El príncipe perfecto', ed. Judith Farré, in *Comedias: Parte XI*, ed. Laura Fernández and Gonzalo Pontón (Madrid: Editorial Gredos, 2012), vol. 1, pp. 921–1074.

[50] Paz y Meliá records its premiere as 1642 while the censorship is from 1655 (*Catálogo*, p. 459). Alfredo Rodríguez López-Vázquez, ed., *Púsoseme el sol, salióme la luna, by Andrés de Claramonte* (Kassel, 1985).

[51] Date indicated on fol. 33v. Paz y Meliá describes it as an autograph (*Catálogo*, p. 562) but this is questioned by Greer in the manuscript's entry in *manos.net*.

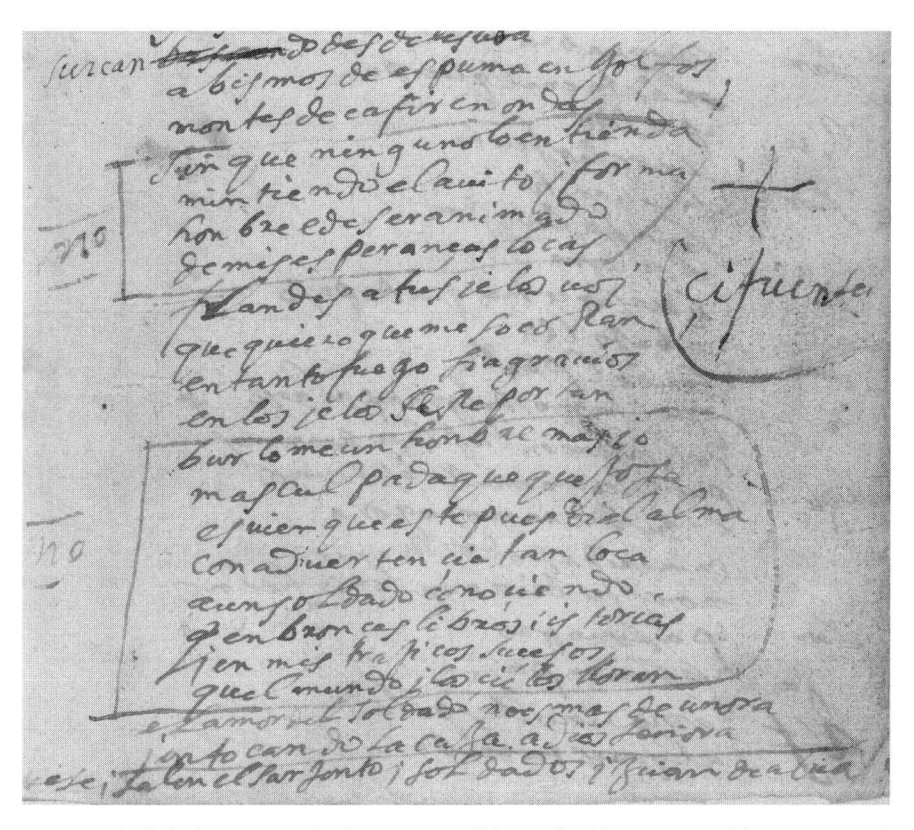

IF GREG AND WERSTINE HAD EXAMINED SPANISH MANUSCRIPTS

7. Claramonte's autograph of *El valiente negro en Flandes*, BNE 15690 (fol. 10r). © Biblioteca Nacional de España. Note also two boxed passages with 'no' instructions added.

DAL *Duelos de amor y lealtad* by Pedro Calderón de la Barca, BL Add Ms 33472 (late seventeenth century)[52]

GF *El galán fantasma* by Pedro Calderón de la Barca, BNE 15672 (copied in 1689)[53]

Autographs

PC *El cordobés valeroso Pedro Carbonero* by Lope de Vega, BNE Res. 166 (1603, lic. 1603)[54]

CM *La corona merecida* by Lope de Vega, BNE Res. 156 (1603, lic. 1608)[55]

PA *La prueba de los amigos* by Lope de Vega, BNE Res. 168 (1604, lic. 1608)[56]

BM *El bastardo Mudarra* by Lope de Vega, RAE Ms. 390 (1612, lic. 1612)[57]

SV *La Serrana de la Vera* by Luis Vélez de Guevara, BNE Res. 101 (1613)[58]

CPV *El Conde don Pero Vélez* by Luis Vélez de Guevara, BNE Res. 97 (early seventeenth century)[59]

[52] For its dating, see corresponding entry in *manos.net*.

[53] Noelia Iglesias, ed., *El galán fantasma*, by Pedro Calderón de la Barca (Madrid, 2015).

[54] Lope de Vega, 'Pedro Carbonero', ed. Alejandro García-Reidy, in *Lope de Vega: Comedias Parte XIV*, vol. 2, ed. José Enrique López Martínez (Madrid, 2015), pp. 1–199.

[55] Lope de Vega, 'La corona merecida', ed. Fernando Rodríguez-Gallego, in *Lope de Vega: Comedias Parte XIV*, vol. 1, ed. José Enrique López Martínez (Madrid, 2015), pp. 538–829.

[56] Jesús Gómez and Paloma Cuenca, eds., *Lope de Vega: Comedias, XIII*, Biblioteca Castro (Madrid, 1997), pp. 93–193.

[57] Lope de Vega, *El bastardo Mudarra y los siete infantes de Lara*, ed. Delmiro Antas (Barcelona, 1992).

[58] As dated by C. George Peale, 'Los textos y la fecha de *La Serrana de la Vera*', in *La Serrana de la Vera*, by Luis Vélez de Guevara, eds. William R. Manson and C. George Peale (Newark, 2002), pp. 41–9; p. 41.

[59] William R. Manson and C. George Peale, eds., *El Conde don Pero Vélez y don Sancho el Deseado*, by Luis Vélez de Guevara (Newark, 2002).

FEATURES COMMON TO SPANISH MANUSCRIPTS USED TO GUIDE PERFORMANCE

	A	B	D	E	F	G	H	I	J	K	N	O	P	Q	R	[S]	[T]	[U]	[V]	[W]	[X]
Scribal																					
SM			x				x	x				x									
MRR					x					x		x									
PP	?	x	x					x		x				x	x						x
PSSL			x									x							x	x	x
VPS						x	x	x				x									
DAL								x	x	x		x					x				
GF		x	x		x	x		x		x		x	x	x	x	x					
Autograph																					
PC			x		x					x	x		x	x	x				x		
CM			x		x						x		x	x	x						
PA	x		x					x		x	x	x	x		x			x			
BM			x		x				x	x	x		x	x							
SV				x				x						x					x		
CPV	x		x		x				x												
MF			x					x			x		x								
LE			x										x								
VNF		x	x										x		x		x				

MF *El mayorazgo figura* by Alonso del Castillo Solórzano, BNE 18.322 (1637)[60]
LE *Llamados y escogidos* by Pedro Calderón de la Barca BNE Res. 269 (lic. 1643)[61]
VNF *El valiente negro en Flandes* by Andrés de Claramonte, BNE 15690 (lic. 1651)[62]

One objection to my parallel corpus may well be that it is also limited (too limited when compared to the number of extant manuscripts in the Spanish tradition) and that the arbitrary criteria used for its selection prevent it from being representative. Yet I believe it may well serve as a test for the kind of comparative textual criticism in this article.

The table above shows the kinds of performance-oriented annotations I have found in the selected manuscripts that justify their inclusion in the parallel corpus. I will illustrate some of these features with examples from the manuscripts containing them. Notation of actor's names (feature A) occurs in Lope de Vega's autograph *La prueba de los amigos*, with 'luis truxillo' below a marginal entrance direction for Liselo and Justino on fol. 12v.[63] An example of feature D (Passages cut) can be seen on fol. 7r of in manuscript BNE Res. 269 of Pedro Calderón de la Barca's *Llamados y escogidos*, with several passages boxed, and several 'si' added by a different hand and ink replacing crossed-out 'no' annotations.

Notation of sounds (feature G) can be seen in the stage direction 'llaman' ('They knock') inserted by a

---

[60] For the date of 1637, see Ignacio Arellano, ed. *El mayorazgo figura by Alonso de Castillo Solórzano* (Barcelona, 1989), p. 53. The manuscript overwrites '8' on '7' (fol. 56v).

[61] Ignacio Arellano and Luis Galván, eds., *Llamados y escogidos*, by Pedro Calderón de la Barca (Pamplona and Kassel, 2002).

[62] Date of censorship on fol. 50v. Paz y Meliá inserts a question mark over the draft character of this manuscript ('Borrador original?', *Catálogo*, p. 556).

[63] Presotto, *Le commedie*, p. 339. An interesting case is the playwright's annotations, in *El conde Pero Vélez*, of the personal pronoun 'yo' (= 'I') in two moments, probably as indications to himself as an actor in the performance of 1615: in the margin of fols. 55v, as a warning direction for his next entrance onto the stage, and then, two sheets later, next to the speech assigned to the 'Secretario' (Manson and Peale, *El conde Pero Vélez*, p. 47).

8. Pedro Calderón de la Barca's *El galán fantasma*, BNE 15672 (fol. 71v). © Biblioteca Nacional de España.

different hand and in a different ink in fol. 71v of manuscript BNE 15672 of Pedro Calderón de la Barca's *El galán fantasma* (Illustration 8). An example of a warning direction (feature K) is 'Pdos Leonido y comparsa' (= 'Leonido and accompaniment be ready') inserted twenty-three lines before their entrance in Calderón's *Duelos de amor*, BL Add Ms 33472.

Censorship (feature Q) can be seen on fol. 21v of Calderón's *El galán fantasma* (BNE 15672) when 'alma' (= 'soul') is crossed out and 'fama' (= 'fame') is written next to it in a different ink by the censor (and playwright) Pedro Francisco de Lanini.[64]

Feature T can be exemplified by the crosses added, in a different (brownish) ink, next to each character in the *dramatis personae* on fol. 1r of *El valiente negro en Flandes* by Andrés de Claramonte BNE 15690 (Illustration 9).

A correction of a stage direction (feature U) can be seen in the addition of 'con luz' (= 'with a light') in a stage direction on fol. 67v of Calderón's *El galán fantasma*.

Finally, feature Y (figures and sums related to production accounts) appears in manuscript BNE 16986 of Claramonte's *Púsoseme el sol*, on fols. 21r and 21v, and fols. 40r, 40v and 41v.

Once this parallel Spanish corpus was justified as comprising examples of manuscripts employed to guide performance, I examined them to see whether they have any of the nineteen 'anomalies' or characteristics of Gregian 'foul papers' that Werstine analysed in his study. For the sake of economy, I will cite just one example for each feature.

#1. Multiple designations of the same character in SDD and SPP: in *El valiente negro en Flandes*, 'el negro' in a stage direction and 'Ju' (for Juan) in the speech prefix on fol. 7v (also 'Juan' in the stage direction on fol. 15v), for the play's protagonist Juan de Alba.

#2. Ambiguous character designations: in *La prueba de los amigos*, the speech prefix 'lis' for Liselo on fol. 13r, and for Liseno on fols. 54v and 55r.

#3. Dialogue errors in naming: in *El bastardo Mudarra*, the protagonist says 'Voy por mi prima' (= 'I'll fetch my cousin', fol. 51r/l. 2805) when it should be 'my niece', since on fol. 46v (l. 2525) Lope de Vega crossed out 'primo' (= 'cousin') and inserted 'tio' (= 'uncle'): Lope and the playhouse scribe failed to correct the relationship on fol. 51r.

#4. Erroneous SPP: in *El príncipe perfecto*, on fol. 38r, Ruy de Silva for Leonel at l. 1259, Leonel for Ruy de Silva at l. 1262, and Ruy de Silva for Leonel at l. 1266.

#5. Misplaced SPP: in *El secreto en la mujer*, fol. 10r.[65]

#6. Missing SPP: in *El secreto en la mujer*, Panfilo (fol. 32v/l. 2007)

#7. Missing entrances: in *El galán fantasma*, there is no entrance direction for Astolfo on fols. 42v and 74r (ll. 1752 and 3016 respectively).

#8. Indefinite entrances involving speakers: in *El bastardo Mudarra*, 'salgan algunos de los ynfantes' (= 'Enter some of the Infantes') on fol. 25r.

---

[64] Iglesias, *El galán*, p. 259.
[65] Rodríguez reassigns speech prefixes at l. 622 (*El secreto*, p. 65).

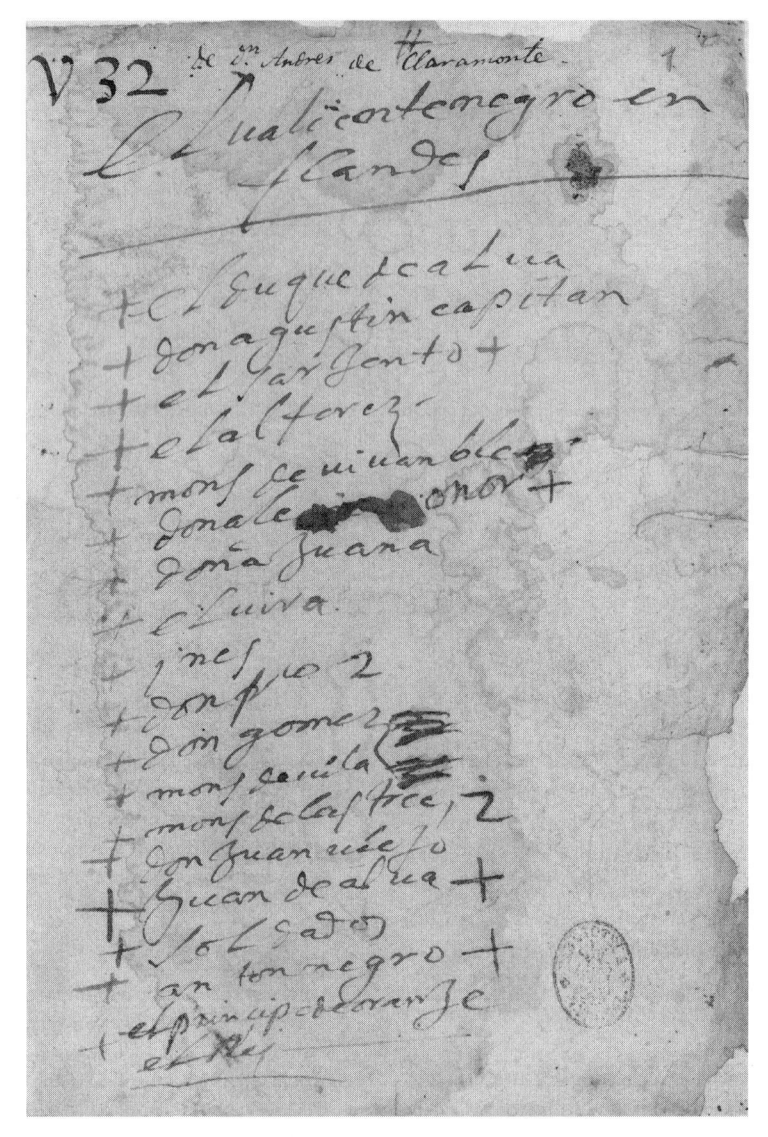

9. *El valiente negro en Flandes* by Andrés de Claramonte, BNE 15690 (fol. 1r). © Biblioteca Nacional de España.

#9. Other indefinite SDD: a very common feature, as in the initial entrance direction of *El valiente negro en Flandes*, 'y soldados' (= 'and soldiers') on fol. 2r.

#10. Omission of necessary characters from SDD: in *El mayorazgo figura*, Don Pedro is missing in an entrance direction (fol. 54v/l. 2623) though he speaks nineteen lines later.

#11. Inclusion of unnecessary characters in entrance directions: I have not found an example of this feature, but this circumstance is in consonance with the fact that Werstine records only one case among the twenty-one English playhouse texts.[66]

---

[66] A doubtful case in *Believe As You List* (1.1.2) since a leaf seems to be missing from the manuscript and it might have contained an entrance direction (Werstine, *Early Modern*, p. 384, quoting Greg, *Dramatic*).

IF GREG AND WERSTINE HAD EXAMINED SPANISH MANUSCRIPTS

FEATURES OF GREGIAN 'FOUL PAPERS' IN SPANISH PLAYHOUSE MANUSCRIPTS

	1	2	3	4	5	6	7	8	9	10	11	12	13	14	15	16	17	18	19
Scribal																			
SM		x	x	x	x	x		x	x	x					x			x	x
MRR									x										
PP		x		x					x	x					x			x	
PSSL	x														x				
VPS		x						x	x										
DAL		x							x										
GF						x	x		x				x	x	x		?	x	
Autograph																			
PC	x							x	x			x		x	x				
CM	x							x		x	?		x	x	x				
PA		x				x			x						x				
BM		x	x	?				x	x					x	x			x	x
SV	x	x			x			x	x	x					x			x	
CPV						x									x	x		x	
MF	x									x					x				
LE								x							x		x		x
VNF	x	x						x	x						x				

#12. Mutes and ghosts: in *Pedro Carbonero*, 'y con el tres compañeros' (= 'and with him three companions') but only two speak: Matías and Simón.

#13. Double entrances: in *El galán fantasma*, 'Entra ella primera y el tras ella ...' (= 'She exits first, and he after her ...', fol. 67r/l. 2800) and two lines later 'entrase' (= 'exit') in the same hand and ink.

#14. Erroneous SDD: in *El bastardo Mudarra*, 'Salga | d. Lanbra' (= 'Enter Doña Lanbra', fol. 14v), when this character does not intervene.

#15. Petitory SDD: in *Llamados y escogidos*, 'Canta dentro la fe y la voz aunque los de afuera ayuden a la música no importa' (= 'Faith and Voice sing within; although those outside help the music, it does not matter', fol. 23v/l. 1162).

#16. Missing exits: in *El bastardo Mudarra*, for Lope and Nuño (fol. 8r/l. 299).

#17. Misplaced SDD: in *Llamados y escogidos*, the entrance direction 'Salen el rey por una parte y la sinagoga por otra' (fol. 25r/l. 1224) seems to correspond to nineteen lines later.[67]

#18. Marginal insertions of dialogue: I have not found instances of marginal additions with mislineation of verse, but I have counted examples that at least disrupt the tidiness of the text, for example, in *El bastardo Mudarra*, Lope de Vega adds 'en esta pena dudosa / tienen mis ojos un bien' (fol. 47r/l. 2555).

#19. Incomplete deletion: in Lope de Vega's autograph *El bastardo Mudarra*, a different hand corrected Lope's line 'y que le ha quemar su casa dijo' by crossing out 'le' and 'su casa dijo', emending 'quemar' to 'quemado' and adding to 'a doña alambra, dijo' but forgot to delete the preposition 'de' (fol. 54r/l. 3019).[68]

As with Werstine's chart on page 391 of his monograph, the table above visualizes the results of my analysis by showing the distribution of 'foul papers' features among the Spanish playhouse-related manuscripts.

The first observation that should be made is that the Spanish manuscripts used to guide performance *also* contain features of 'foul papers' as Greg defined them. Yet there is a difference. This table of Spanish manuscripts is less dense in comparison to its equivalent in Werstine's study: there are fewer

---

[67] As Arellano and Galván point out, *Llamados*, p. 118.
[68] Antas, *El bastardo*, pp. 214–15.

111

'x's in this table than check marks in Werstine's chart (transcribed above). Although my corpus of Spanish plays cannot be taken as representative, the examples of scribal copies with one, two or even three 'x's, tell us something that cannot be overlooked: there were theatrical manuscripts in the Spanish tradition that were as orderly as Greg conceived promptbooks to be.

This is clearly the case with Claramonte's early seventeenth-century copy of *El mayor de los reyes*, which only has indefinite stage directions as characteristic of 'foul papers', while Calderón's *Duelos de amor y lealtad*, Claramonte's *Púsoseme el sol*, and Diamante's *El veneno para sí*, with two or three features of 'foul papers' only, are comparatively late manuscripts.[69] If Werstine concludes that the eighteen English surviving playhouse manuscripts are *not* characterized by 'orderliness and thoroughness', and 'are not finished texts',[70] the same statement cannot be made regarding all their Spanish counterparts, at least those in this parallel corpus.

However, these examples do not lessen the force of the majority of manuscripts analysed, which, in my opinion, back up Werstine's invalidation of the Gregian categories: the fact that these Spanish manuscripts bear features of both pre-theatrical 'foul papers' and of theatrical use to prepare a text for performance provides sufficient support to Werstine's contention that Shakespeare's editors can no longer rely on Greg's understanding of 'foul papers' and 'promptbooks' in order to discern the kind of manuscript from which a printed playtext derives.[71]

My analysis of Spanish manuscripts also supports Werstine's questioning of Gurr's theory of maximal and minimal texts associated with authorial 'foul papers' in Greg's sense and with trimmed performance scripts respectively.[72] Gurr postulates the maximal text as corresponding to the authorial version in a manuscript that would be licensed by the Master of the Revels and from which the theatre company would produce a cut version in a different manuscript. Werstine's counterargument is the evidence of *licensed* authorial manuscripts such as *Believe* and *Launching*. Similarly, all Spanish authorial copies in my parallel corpus (except *El conde Pero* Vélez) are licensed, bear features of playhouse cuts and changes, and therefore preserve both 'versions' in the same manuscript and not in different witnesses.

My close analysis of textual features in the selected Spanish manuscripts confirms the impression expressed by a number of Hispanists whom I asked: that the polarization of the Gregian types does not hold in the Spanish tradition. My conclusions are drawn from a confessedly limited corpus of manuscripts, as I remarked above, so it remains to be seen whether they would be further confirmed or would be questioned if more manuscripts were selected as evidence. To dispel this doubt, hundreds of Spanish manuscripts lie waiting for close examination in a comparative approach.

---

[69] In this respect, they are closer to the playhouse manuscripts from the Restoration period, as examined by Edward Langhans, *Restoration Promptbooks* (Carbondale and Edwardsville, 1981).
[70] Werstine, *Early Modern*, p. 242.
[71] Werstine, *Early Modern*, pp. 194 and 231.
[72] Andrew Gurr, 'Maximal and minimal texts: Shakespeare v. the Globe', *Shakespeare Survey 52* (1999), 68–87, pp. 76 and 85. A theory that Werstine qualifies as based on Greg's idealisation of authorial agency implicit in his notion of 'foul papers' and of theatrical agency in 'promptbooks' (*Early Modern*, p. 222).

EXIT MANUSCRIPTS: THE ARCHIVE OF THEATRE AND THE ARCHIVE OF PRINT

JOHN JOWETT

This article reaches towards a reconfiguration of our understanding of play manuscripts in ways that ultimately renegotiate the edge between Shakespeare's presence and absence in the text that we call Shakespeare. In doing so, it turns away from two existing models. The first lies in the distinction urged by the pioneering work of the New Bibliography in the earlier part of the twentieth century, between the purely authorial 'foul papers' and the theatre company 'promptbook' characterized by the presence of other hands. The second lies in the collapse of this distinction, at least as it was defined by W. W. Greg, a task that has been effected most influentially in the work of Paul Werstine. According to Werstine, the terminology is wrong and, more importantly, the category of 'foul papers', as Greg presented it, cannot be sustained. His case is firmly grounded in the evidence of surviving dramatic manuscripts. Werstine's *Early Modern Playhouse Manuscripts and the Editing of Shakespeare* is crucial as the first systematic study of the surviving early modern play manuscripts since Greg's pioneering work of the 1930s, and the most comprehensive ever.[1] The corpus that Werstine examines consists of all the surviving manuscripts of the period that were prepared with performance in view. All show evidence of onwards preparation by hands other than the dramatist's for performance on stage. All therefore are classified as playhouse manuscripts. But Werstine is concerned also with editorial theory and practice. My argument seeks to problematize the direct relationship Werstine and indeed many textual critics assume between the extant play manuscripts and the lost Shakespeare manuscripts that provided copy for the printers of his plays.

A play manuscript is made up of a set of leaves, each possessing width and depth, and therefore a three-dimensional physical object. This description contrasts with the representation of a manuscript in a stemma diagrammatically drawing the relation between manuscripts (or texts generally). The stemma represents a textual document as an entity that can be summarized as a point. This point takes form as one end of a line or as an intersection between more than one line. But the substance of a stemma is the line connecting point A with point B and with other points lying in the same direction or in a different one. I will suggest that the manuscript is itself a line, that is to say a text that exists not in its fixity but in its development through time. Reinstating the third dimension, I will therefore be considering such a manuscript also as a real object. As an object it serves practical functions, such as enabling the text to be read, copied or performed. If these functions are to be repeated, it will need to be conserved. If the text belongs to a group of texts designed to enable the same activities within an institutional setting, it will be conserved in an archive. I will propose a fundamental distinction between the archive of theatre and the archive of print.

Rather than being punctual in essence, a manuscript may be said temporarily to become

---

[1] Paul Werstine, *Early Modern Playhouse Manuscripts and the Editing of Shakespeare* (Cambridge, 2013).

punctual, or to become stemmatic, at any stage in its history at which it was copied. The early modern theatre manuscript that now survives is typically (though not quite always) a copy: a copy either in the hand of the author himself or in the hand of a company scribe. And one of the functions of this document is to supply 'copy', in the restricted sense of the source copied,[2] for the actors' parts, the documents from which the works were memorized and spoken in performance. The theatre manuscript thus has two attributes: it usually begins its existence as a transcript of an antecedent document and it exists as a vehicle for delivering performance by way of being copied itself. We can offer a general line of transmission:

Author's papers > theatre manuscript > actors' parts/ backstage plot > performance.

In fact, extant theatre manuscripts are also characterized by annotation. Textual scholars will have noted that the first two terms, 'author's papers' and 'theatre manuscript', in some way correspond with the 'foul papers' and annotated 'promptbook' of the New Bibliography. Essentially, this article is about that correspondence or the lack of it. But I turn first to the example of *Sir Thomas More*, the surviving manuscript that most richly illustrates how what we usually call a single manuscript developed through time. As will be seen, it complicates the schematic line of transmission in several ways, but even as it introduces reversions and exceptions, it illustrates the fundamental stages through which a theatre manuscript might pass. Though the overall richness and diversity of them makes the example unique, the changes introduced into the manuscript are individually typical of the processing of the text in and around the theatre.

It – and I refer here to the physical manuscript of *Sir Thomas More*, not the text – began its existence as a transcript in the hand of Anthony Munday of an entire play in a single hand. This singleness and completeness belies what is widely understood to be the collaborative nature of the authorial papers from which this document was derived.[3] The elegantly presented and legible script Munday prepared is known as the Original Text.[4] Though one or two leaves were removed when the play was revised and though the surviving leaves have been altered and supplemented, this 'original' manuscript can still be read. It offers the play (or, now, most of it) in a form that would have been authorially finished.

But the leaves of the Original Text themselves bear witness to subsequent alterations. The script was annotated by the Master of the Revels, Edmund Tilney, as censor. The various kinds of deletion marks he imposed in the first scene are extraordinarily persistent and heavy. The same script was annotated by two further hands. One of them was another dramatist, identified as Thomas Heywood, who wrote speeches for the Clown Betts in the margin. The other was the theatre functionary known only as Hand C, who, for example, duplicated a stage direction Munday had written in the right margin, 'Ent. Croftes', by copying it into the left, 'Enter Crofts'.

So far I have been describing only the leaves of the Original Text. Further interventions drastically reconstruct the basic physical components of the document: leaves were removed and six leaves containing revisions were added. After the main stage of this major restructuring had been undertaken, two slips were pasted into the Original Text. By examining one page (fol. 14a) and the paste-in that was affixed to it (Addition V), we can see directly, or detect with certainty, a highly stratified development:

---

[2] As in the publisher's claim on the title page that the Shakespeare First Folio was printed from 'True Originall Copies'.

[3] For the vexed and unresolved question of the authorship of the Original Text, see *Sir Thomas More*, ed. John Jowett, Arden 3 (London, 2011), 414–23, and previous work summarized there; Thomas Merriam, 'Moore the Merier', *Notes and Queries* 58 (2011), 242–7; Marina Tarlinskaja, 'Shakespeare among Others in *Sir Thomas More*: Verse Form and Attribution', in *Frontiers in Comparative Prosody: In Memoriam Mikhail Gasparov*, ed. Mikhail Lotman and Maria-Kristiina Lotman (Bern, 2011), 121–42.

[4] This designation, along with the numbering of the Additions and the labelling of the hands as 'Hand A', etc., derives from W. W. Greg, *The Book of Sir Thomas More*, Malone Society (Oxford, 1911).

THE ARCHIVE OF THEATRE AND THE ARCHIVE OF PRINT

1. Lost author's draft of the Original Text.
2. Extant transcript by Munday (the 'Original Text'; here the heavily cancelled fol. 14a).
3. Lost authorial draft of a revision of More's speech (the first manifestation of Addition V).
4. Extant transcript of More's speech by Hand C, as pasted into the Original Text.
5. Extant author's draft of the Messenger's speech by Heywood, as written in an unused portion of a page in a leaf found later in the sequence of manuscript leaves (fol. 16b).
6. Extant transcript of the Messenger's speech, as written sideways onto the left margin of both the original text and the paste-in slip by Hand C.
7. The further extant addition of a boxed stage direction by Hand C, written below the Messenger's speech towards the lower left corner, which names the actor Goodale (thus exemplifying another trait of theatre annotation).
8. The provision of an extant reference mark, a cross in a circle, within the stage-direction box, in order to link the stage direction to the passage that comes immediately before it in the revised sequence of text in Addition IV, at the end of which Hand C inserted a similar mark.

This is a vertical line of transmission, mostly within the manuscript itself, of extraordinary complexity. There is one other paste-in (Addition III), and Addition V is unusual for the recurrence of Hand C's interventions, but the stages of development are otherwise typical of this manuscript. Four dramatists authored the text found in the separate leaves containing the revisions. Some of the new material was transcribed by Hand C and in these cases the author's draft of the revision is lost. As noted already, Hand C also annotated the authorial script.

The manuscript of *Sir Thomas More* therefore contains a series of interventions falling under the headings of authorship, transcription and annotation. This document can broadly be described as the embodiment of two distinct versions of the play. One is constituted in the Original Text, the other in the revisions. It is most probable that the hand of Tilney acts as a separator dividing the two. The two textual versions roughly correspond to the physical, material constitution of the document. At the most fundamental level, the document as a whole is made up of two different stocks of paper into which the Original Text and revisions were written. In the writing inscribed into those stocks of paper, we can distinguish between the hand of Munday, who played no part in the revisions and so is confined to the leaves of the original document, and the hands of other dramatists, the revisers. But it is important to note that the materialities of paper and of penmanship do not coincide, because the inscriptions of the revising Heywood and Hand C are found on leaves of the Original Manuscript as well as the leaves of the revision.

Comparably, Wilhelmina P. Frijlink and William B. Long have shown how the manuscript of *Woodstock* underwent a series of alterations for various productions of the play over a number of years.[5] Although the date range is more restricted than they assumed,[6] and although the exact number of hands is difficult to determine, their demonstration of multiple strata remains valid. Thomas Middleton's *The Lady's Tragedy* was, like *Sir Thomas More*, transcribed from a lost precedent, censored by the Master of the Revels (then Sir George Buc), annotated for performance and revised by the addition of slips containing new text. The play manuscript therefore develops through time. The example of *Sir Thomas More* is extreme but the point is general: the variants between an early and a late manifestation of a play are much more likely to arise *within* a manuscript than they are to arise *between* manuscripts when the source manuscript is copied. A scribe is an agent of textual change, though only incidentally, as the primary task relates to copying and presentation;

---

[5] Wilhelmina P. Frijlinck, ed., *The First Part of the Reign of King Richard II or Thomas of Woodstock* (Oxford, 1929); William B. Long, '"A bed / for woodstock": A Warning for the Unwary', *Medieval and Renaissance Drama in England* 2 (1985), 91–118.

[6] As indicated by the Jacobean dating of the play established in MacD. P. Jackson, 'Shakespeare's *Richard II* and the Anonymous *Thomas of Woodstock*', *Medieval and Renaissance Drama in England* 14 (2001), 17–65.

a censor introduces major or minor changes without producing a new manuscript; and, in the context of the theatre, even a revising author in the first instance also more usually modifies an existing document through annotation or the addition of supplementary leaves rather than by preparing an entirely new document. Within the economic constraints of a commercial institution, paper was expensive, 'A London Scriueno^r is the deerest childe of his Mother Mony',[7] and transcription is time-consuming. These factors militate strongly against unnecessary transcription. Consequently, a single document could evolve over the course of time from one putative categorization to another. For example, if the author's papers were reasonably clean, they might be annotated to meet the needs of the theatre company and become the company's playbook. Even Heywood's untidy manuscript of *The Captives* was annotated.[8]

However, the surviving manuscripts are mostly transcripts. Whether they are authorial or scribal transcripts is a matter that is subordinate to the fact that the text has been copied from an antecedent document. Transcripts, insofar as they identify themselves as such, invariably present material and compelling evidence that there were manuscripts other than those that fortuitously happen to survive. Every transcript testifies to its antecedent. The directly or indirectly prior authorial manuscript is a necessary thing: the observation that no such document survives to the present is completely immaterial to the postulate that such documents historically existed. Greg's term 'foul papers' labelled such manuscripts. The term has the advantage that it is at least exampled in occasional usage in the period, alongside 'foul sheets'. The problem with the term lies in Greg's formalization of a word that was occasionally and imprecisely used to indicate any messy draft, so as to imply that a complete but unmodified authorial draft would routinely be submitted by the dramatist, copied out into a 'fair copy' that became the promptbook/playbook, and subsequently held in reserve by the theatre. This formalization of the term suggests a kind of knowledge that we do not have. But the evidence must be assessed for what it indicates indirectly as well as directly. We may not be able securely to infer too much from a surviving manuscript about the nature of a scribe's source document but transcription can safely be taken to imply prior foulness, however that is defined. According to Werstine, a manuscript 'would become "foul papers" only once it was transcribed or its transcription was at least envisioned', but the term nevertheless has 'a pejorative sense'.[9] The contradiction here between a judgement about a document's intrinsic features and a placement of that document within a process of transmission lies at the heart of the problem. But the term as in historical usage belongs above all to the world of the professional scribe, and it is in that world that the convergence presumably takes place between the professional activity of copying, so as to make the original document redundant, and a judgemental vocabulary vindicating that activity in terms of foul and fair.[10]

At some antecedent point the document that Greg called 'foul papers' existed. The terms by which such manuscripts may more satisfactorily be nominated are 'author's papers' or 'authorial draft'. It may be suspected that a substitution of terms is no more than a sleight of hand whereby the contrast between the originary document and the theatre document is maintained. But the proposed alternative, 'author's papers', has two simple and crucial differences. First, 'foul papers' were copied: they are described as foul in contradistinction to the fairness of the copy they elicit, as Werstine rightly argues. In contrast, it is an entirely open question as

---

[7] Anon., 'A Charector of a London Scriuenor', in the manuscript miscellany of *c.* 1620s–1630s, BL Add. MS 25303, fol. 183a, transcribed in Peter Beal, *In Praise of Scribes: Manuscripts and their Makers in Seventeenth-Century England* (Oxford, 1988), p. 198.
[8] See Arthur Brown's Malone Society Reprint (Oxford, 1953); Werstine, *Playhouse Manuscripts*, pp. 300–9; James Purkis, *Shakespeare and Manuscript Drama: Canon, Collaboration, and Text* (Cambridge, 2016), pp. 62–83.
[9] Werstine, *Playhouse Manuscripts*, pp. 99 and 98.
[10] Thus, whereas a manuscript that had been copied by hand might be designated as 'foul', this term would not be applied to designate the defining trait of a printer's copy manuscript.

to whether 'author's papers' were copied or not. They might, in principle at least, be developed towards performance by way of direct modification of the self-same manuscript. The manuscript of Heywood's *The Captives* is a likely case in point. The revisions in *Sir Thomas More* penned by the revising authors and annotated by Hand C are another. In other words, whereas 'foul papers' is a punctual term representing the imagined document as it stood at a fixed point in time (the moment of copying), the term 'author's papers' is fit for purpose in allowing for the possibilities of evolution within a single document, possibilities that are not exhausted at the point where the author relinquishes it. The term also allows for what seems to be the more usual outcome: that the manuscript that the dramatist delivered to the theatre company would be transcribed or was itself the dramatist's own transcript.

The second difference made by adopting the term 'author's papers' is that it negotiates a point deftly and astutely observed by Werstine: if the criterion for 'foul papers' is that they required a copy to be made to replace them, that criterion is not actually an authorial criterion at all, for '"foul papers" need not refer exclusively to authorial drafts'. For instance, a manuscript may as a result of adaptation in the theatre become messy and so require transcription. Werstine's examination of the manuscript of John Fletcher's *Bonduca* leads him to conclude: 'Contrary to Greg's assumption, "foul papers" need not refer exclusively to authorial drafts, whether these are messy or not; the term simply describes papers that, for whatever reason, are to be, are being, or have already been transcribed.'[11]

The force of the point is that foulness, far from depending on the single agency of the dramatist, might just as plausibly, or even more plausibly, result from the accretions of several hands other than those of the dramatist as sole author or co-author. Werstine's suggestion that 'foul papers' might refer to a manuscript in a post-authorial state where foulness has been superimposed by other hands, though it is logically sustainable, seems to be hypothetical. For in the case in point of *Bonduca*, the scribe Edward Knight refers very specifically to 'the fowle papers of the Authors' rather than a messy adapted script. If, notwithstanding, there is at least a hypothetical openness or ambiguity about the term 'foul papers', the same ambiguity does not apply to 'author's papers', which is more specific on the question of penmanship, whilst more mobile on the question of taxonomy.

The implication of Werstine's discussion is that if the author delivered a clean copy, and if it was heavily annotated in the theatre, the New Bibliographers were incorrect in identifying the inconsistencies characteristic of 'good quartos' as evidence of an unmodified authorial script. But these are very big 'if's. Werstine's analysis is effective in demonstrating that inconsistencies and ambiguities are to be found in playhouse documents and do not seem to have presented an obstacle to their utility in the theatre. But most of these inconsistencies and ambiguities are features of the initial authorial script.[12]

My account of Addition V in *Sir Thomas More* above shows the physical document becoming multilayered and complex. It is more than plausible to suggest that a fresh transcript would have been a good idea, and it is not unlikely that such a transcript was made. Nevertheless, Hand C took pains to ensure that the text of the play – as significantly distinct from the physical constitution of the document – was theatrically functional. The reference marks reflect his concern to ensure that despite the complexities of the document, the text was properly joined up. It is evident also in *Sir Thomas More* that the text in the leaves based on a transcription – whether the transcriber is Munday or Hand C – is more orderly than the text in the leaves that are probably uncopied drafts. The longest section of the

---

[11] Werstine, *Playhouse Manuscripts*, p. 98.
[12] Werstine points to examples of annotators introducing inconsistencies, though some of them, such as the alteration of Philip Massinger's 'Officers' to 'Guard' in *Believe as You List* (*Playhouse Manuscripts*, pp. 150–1), amount to clarifications rather than contradictions.

revisions in an author's hand is the 'Hand D' section attributed to Shakespeare;[13] the vagueness and variability of his speech prefixes and the inadequacies of his single stage direction are well recognized.[14] Hand C's failure to provide an entry for More himself is so spectacularly exceptional as to require some special explanation, but the overall tendency of his annotation is to produce clarity.

The second longest revision in the author's hand in *Sir Thomas More* is Heywood's Addition VI. It too illustrates the expected features of an authorial draft and shows most of them surviving after the play has undergone the annotations of Hand C. Like Shakespeare, Heywood did not supply an initial entrance. Nor did he provide an entrance for More in the middle of the passage. It was left to Hand C to add 'Enter a Servingman' and 'Enter Moore wth attendaunts w^{t} Purss & mace', thus progressing the authorial script towards theatrical intelligibility. In his speech prefixes, Heywood's practice is scarcely clear: the servingman is designated 'Man' and, more striking still, More himself is merely designated 'Lord' (even though Heywood refers to More by name in this passage).[15] The 'Incli.' of Munday's Original Text, identifying the role as the player of Inclination, is here called 'Vice' (another way of saying the Vice Inclination) or 'clo' (i.e. Clown). The latter identifies the role by type and suggests that Heywood envisaged that the actor might have been the one who played the Clown Bettes, a role for which he had particular responsibility in Addition II and in his annotations of the Original Text. Though Hand C reviewed the passage (as is evidenced by his added stage directions), he made no alterations to its irregular speech prefixes. Heywood's Addition VI also demonstrates a revealing example of the 'false start', where the author begins to write a passage and then abandons it and starts it afresh.[16] There is another such example in Munday's hand.[17] It offers evidence, by the simplest interpretation, that he might revise the play even as he transcribed it. Both Munday's and Heywood's false starts are clearly marked for deletion by the originating hand, so neither passage presents a duplication.

Werstine takes these various features as evidence that such inconsistencies and ambiguities are typical of playhouse manuscripts. According to him, Munday as author, for example, supplies 'regularity' in naming characters, a regularity that suffers through 'playhouse adaptation'.[18] But Munday's role in the extant document is in fact primarily that of scribe producing a fair copy of his and his collaborator's lost antecedent authorial papers. As for the revisions, in the first instance the typicality of some of them – those that introduce features associated with 'foul papers' – is absolutely that they display the features Greg associated with the authorial draft, because that is what they are. The distinctively 'playhouse' element is supplied

---

[13] See W. W. Greg, ed., *Shakespeare's Hand in the Play of Sir Thomas More* (Cambridge, 1923); Jowett, ed., *Sir Thomas More*, pp. 437–53, and work cited there; Gary Taylor and Rory Loughnane, 'The Canon and Chronology of Shakespeare's Works', in *The New Oxford Shakespeare Authorship Companion*, ed. Gary Taylor and Gabriel Egan (Oxford, 2017), pp. 417–602, specifically 'Sir Thomas More', pp. 548–53. For sceptical rejoinders, see James Purkis, 'Shakespeare's Singularity and *Sir Thomas More*', *Shakespeare Survey* 67 (Cambridge, 2014), 150–64, as reworked in *Shakespeare and Manuscript Drama*, pp. 191–246. Purkis draws on Paul Werstine's critique of the accumulation of allegedly 'unreliable' arguments found in Greg's collection, in Werstine's 'Shakespeare, More or Less: A. W. Pollard and Twentieth-century Shakespeare Editing', *Florilegium* 16 (1999), 125–45. Gabriel Egan notes that Purkis 'cited with approval Alois Brandl's claim that "a hundred unreliable arguments ... do not together make a reliable one"' (Purkis, 'Shakespeare's Singularity', 153). Strictly speaking this is true, but Purkis ought to have observed that it takes only a moderate reliability in the individual tests upon which arguments are built for the power of multiplication to make the accumulated reliability quickly mount up', in 'A History of Shakespearean Authorship Study', in *Authorship Companion*, ed. Taylor and Egan, pp. 27–47, p. 46.

[14] John Jowett, 'A Collaboration: Shakespeare and Hand C in *Sir Thomas More*', *Shakespeare Survey* 65 (Cambridge, 2012), 255–68.

[15] As noted in Purkis, *Shakespeare and Manuscript Drama*, pp. 164–5.

[16] On fol. 16a; compare Add.VI 21–35 with the expanded 36–55 in Greg's Malone Society transcript.

[17] On fol. 22a; compare ll. 1956–64 of the Original Text with the expanded ll. 1965–82 in Greg's Malone Society transcript.

[18] Werstine, *Playhouse Manuscripts*, p. 152.

elsewhere, in the annotations of Hand C. But the real point here is the inadequacy of binary labelling in *Sir Thomas More* as a work in progress, a progress with reversions along the way.

As the stratification of the manuscript manifests itself clearly, the passage of time can be halted at various points. At one such point, the manuscript would have defied the Werstinian concept of the universal category of playhouse manuscript characterized always by annotation. It is doubtful whether the Original Text had been at all annotated at the moment when it was submitted to and returned by the Master of the Revels. Thus, although at that point in time it would have held an inscription from the Master of the Revels, it would have failed to meet the one and only universal criterion identifying a 'playhouse manuscript': theatrical annotation.

Subsequent to this, the same manuscript would have defied the Gregian teleological progression from foul papers to promptbook. The document fair-copied by Munday and submitted to the Master of the Revels subsequently reverted to authorial draft as the revisions were compiled. Even within itself, the process of revision complicates both Gregian and Werstinian narratives. Of the six revisions added at this stage, various sections were transcribed by Hand C: parts of Addition II, all of Additions III and V, and most of Addition IV. But the remainder stands in the author's originating hand: Addition I, the larger proportion of Addition II, part of Addition IV, and all of Addition VI. Most of the Additions were annotated but Additions I and III were to remain without any annotation. The document defies a homogenizing label for the very reason that it, and the text it contains, pass through time and things happen to it.

What would have been the outcome if *Sir Thomas More* had provided copy for a quarto edition of the play? The question is not only hypothetical but also potentially misleading. Here, making an incidental nod towards stage business, I introduce the term 'exit manuscript'. This term does not refer to any defining characteristic intrinsic to the text in the document: an exit manuscript might be the author's papers, a playbook or a separate transcript of either of these. It might also be a manuscript characterized by what might be called off-script transmission, that is to say any form of transmission depending on speech or memory rather than document-to-document copying. The defining trait of an exit manuscript relates not to its content or history of penmanship but to its situation. It is that the manuscript leaves the environs of the theatre. Specifically, in the case of the Shakespeare printed plays set from manuscript, it migrates from the theatre to the printing house.

Many textual critics have been struck by the force of Fredson Bowers's observation that 'the printing of a quarto may be taken as implying the destruction of its manuscript'.[19] He went as far as to claim that it might even be destroyed. This is almost certainly an exaggeration, as various examples survive of manuscripts used as printer's copy; examples have been usefully catalogued and illustrated by J. K. Moore.[20] Nevertheless, a manuscript's journey to the realm of printed book culture can be taken to have been a one-way trip. In the usual course of publishing arrangements, the owner of a publishable manuscript, who in the case of Shakespeare and other early modern dramatists was the theatre company, would sell the manuscript to a publisher. The publisher would then own the manuscript absolutely and would seek entitlement to publish it. As Peter Blayney has described in exemplary detail, he would secure that entitlement by obtaining a licence from the Stationers' Company, and pay the appropriate fee.[21] For an additional fee he could have that entitlement recorded in the Stationers' Register

---

[19] Fredson Bowers, 'Authority, Copy, and Transmission in Shakespeare's Texts', in *Shakespeare Study Today*, ed. Georgianna Ziegler (New York, 1986), 7–36; p. 15.

[20] J. K. Moore, *Primary Materials Relating to Copy and Print in English Books of the Sixteenth and Seventeenth Centuries*, Oxford Bibliographical Society (Oxford, 1992).

[21] Peter W. M. Blayney, 'The Publication of Playbooks', in *A New History of Early English Drama*, ed. David Scott Kastan and John D. Cox (New York, 1997), pp. 383–422.

but in some cases he would save on this cost, as the Stationers' Company licence written into the manuscript itself was the primary evidence of entitlement. Thus for reasons relating to the publisher's entitlement as well as the bare fact of his proprietorial ownership, the manuscript would not return to the theatre. It had migrated definitively from the archive of the theatre company to arrive in the archive of a publisher.

The surviving playhouse manuscripts, in contrast, are not publishers' manuscripts; they are not exit manuscripts. All their characteristics identify them as part of the theatre archive. Clearly, that is how they originated; we may surmise further that that is how they survived. Some, indeed, may belong to the same present-day library archive because they originated in a single theatre collection. An example will illustrate the point. The British Library MS Egerton 1994 contains no fewer than fourteen sixteenth- and seventeenth-century plays, a very significant proportion of the whole body of surviving theatre manuscripts, along with a masque. It was evidently assembled by the actor and bookseller William Cartwright (1606–86) in the 1640s.[22] Cartwright's own access to the playbooks of the closed theatres was probably limited to those that had belonged to specific companies and it is statistically virtually certain that he obtained groups of plays from their archives. We can say with confidence that the surviving playbooks emanate from a generic archive that was different from the manuscripts behind Shakespeare's plays. Any assumption that there is an absolute equivalence between the extant playbooks and the manuscript copy for Shakespeare's printed plays cannot be sustained.

It might be objected that this terminology of the archives is a hair-splitting manoeuvre, on the grounds that, if we assume that Shakespeare (for example) wrote plays first and foremost to be performed, the printer's copy manuscripts were, directly or indirectly, from the theatre environment and therefore they are not in any meaningful way differentiable from the playbooks that remained in the theatre. But that misses the point. The point is that, if and when a play manuscript left the theatre environment, there must have been another different document that remained in the theatre. Unless the theatre company was facing dissolution (as during the civil wars), there could be no departure of a manuscript from a theatre without the theatre itself being sustained by the existence of a playbook that was a different document from the manuscript that departed.

For example, when the King's Men sold a very long manuscript of *Hamlet* to the publishers Nicholas Ling and Thomas Trundle in 1604, they retained a playbook so that they could continue to put their popular play on stage. We can take this to be a fact, because they did indeed continue to perform the play.[23] And, indeed, when the Folio was prepared in 1622–3 the publishers were able to print the play from a manuscript that was probably a copy of a playbook in use in the late Jacobean theatre. But actually the dichotomy between this theatrical manuscript and 'foul papers' does not work in this case. This is Werstine's point but it is also a point recognized by the New Bibliographers, who themselves realized that the printer's copy for the 1604–5 quarto of *Hamlet* was not a classic example of 'foul papers'. John Dover Wilson, in his classic study *The Manuscript of Shakespeare's 'Hamlet'* (1934) wrote that 'Q2 is almost entirely free from any trace of the prompter's hand.'[24] But 'almost free' and 'entirely free' are two different propositions, and Wilson knew it. He goes on:

There is only one piece of evidence which suggests that it may have been read with a view to performance, and that is the duplication of a stage-direction at 5.2.294. Here Q2 prints:

> *Drum, trumpet and shot.*
> *Florish, a peece goes off.*

---

[22] F. S. Boas, *Shakespeare and the Universities* (Oxford, 1923), pp. 96–110. Cartwright also collected the paintings depicting the actors Richard Burbage, Nathan Field and Richard Perkins: see Andrew Gurr, 'Cartwight, William (1606–1686)', in *Oxford Dictionary of Literary Biography* (Oxford), online by subscription.
[23] *Hamlet* was performed at Court in 1619.
[24] John Dover Wilson, *The Manuscript of Shakespeare's 'Hamlet'*, 2 vols. (Cambridge, 1934), p. 91.

And it seems likely that one of these directions... was added in the margin by the prompter when reading through the text.

W. W. Greg recognized the strength of the point and conceded a little more: 'At one or two points we may see the hand of the book-keeper taking notes.'[25] And the Arden 2 editor Harold Jenkins endorsed this conclusion, writing a subsection of his Introduction headed '*Playhouse marking of the manuscript*'.[26] In view of Werstine's demonstration of the kinds of variation and inconsistency that might survive into or be introduced into a playhouse manuscript, the suggestion regarding *Hamlet* originally put forward by Wilson is highly plausible.[27]

But Werstine does not only remind us of a point made long ago by Wilson, Greg and Jenkins. For *Hamlet* is not the only case where textual critics suggest the possibility that early Shakespeare quartos were printed from playhouse manuscripts. Werstine himself points out that the presence of actors' names is, in the extant manuscripts, always a provision introduced by an annotator rather than a dramatist. Such names are to be found in *Romeo and Juliet* (1599). In the cases of *Hamlet* and *Romeo*, the occasional indications of theatre annotation complicate, but do not invalidate, the more widely prevalent indication of the author's hand. The following, by way of contrast, are three examples in which the evidence of Shakespeare's hand in the printer's copy is far weaker and the hypothesis that the copy was a non-authorial transcript prepared for the theatre helps to resolve textual difficulties.

Example 1: the 1598 edition of *1 Henry IV* was always traditionally considered a 'good' quarto.[28] But it was probably printed from a non-authorial transcript, as was spelt out in considerable detail in the Oxford Shakespeare *Textual Companion* of 1987.[29] A transcript definitively is not 'foul papers', at least in the qualitative sense that it lacks foulness. Unfortunately, my textual introduction to this play, having erred on the side of excess in making the point about transcription, goes on to make a further inference rather too quickly: 'the stage directions are authorial in complexion, and it is not plausible that the manuscript served as a promptbook'. Here the conjunction 'and' is a weak snowbridge over a logical crevasse. In the light of Werstine's study, one must ask 'Why should such a manuscript not have served as a promptbook?' It is at least possible and it becomes still more plausible if one conjectures that the Chamberlain's Men would have needed a second playbook in which the offensive name Oldcastle was not merely altered (as it was in the quarto copy) but wholly removed.

Example 2: this also concerns censorship. The 1597 edition of *Richard II* is another 'good' quarto text that is recognized as having been printed from a manuscript too clean and well ordered to answer to the classical description of 'foul papers'. The quarto famously lacks the most crucial scene in the play's entire action, namely the deposition episode in which Richard reluctantly hands his crown to Bolingbroke. The removal of this episode is most widely and most plausibly attributed to theatrical censorship. But if the book-keeper or the Master of the Revels deleted the passage in the playbook, why does it not appear in a text which supposedly preceded the playbook? One answer would be that the manuscript was not a pre-theatrical authorial draft but the censored playbook.

Example 3: discussions of chronological priority of Quarto and Folio *Troilus and Cressida* have been bedevilled by the New Bibliographers' categories of foul papers and promptbook. They have led to

---

[25] W. W. Greg, *The Shakespeare First Folio: Its Bibliographical and Textual History* (Oxford, 1955), p. 311.

[26] Harold Jenkins, ed., *Hamlet*, Arden 2 (London, 1989), pp. 42–4.

[27] See also John Jowett, 'Textual Introduction' to *Hamlet*, in the New Oxford Shakespeare *Complete Works: Critical Reference Edition*, 2 vols. (Oxford, 2017), pp. 1115–26.

[28] Technically it is a reprint, as the survival of a copy of a single sheet of an antecedent quarto demonstrates.

[29] John Jowett, 'Textual Introduction' to *1 Henry IV*, in Stanley Wells and Gary Taylor, with John Jowett and William Montgomery, *William Shakespeare: A Textual Companion* (Oxford, 1987), pp. 329–32.

textual discussions attempting to attach one label to one text and the other label to the other; but there has been no agreement as to the line of development.[30] As this volatility of diagnosis implies, evidence for Shakespeare's hand in the printer's copy for either text is less than compelling. I suggest that the model of progression from foul paper to theatre manuscript is in the case of *Troilus and Cressida* dysfunctional. Instead, the two texts are probably divergent, reflecting separate revision from a common source, as is simply impossible if one of them has to be foul papers.[31]

There are doubtless other cases that could be adduced. But the advantages of rejecting a rigorous opposition between foul papers and promptbook will be clear enough from these. The immediate significance of the Folio texts for my present argument is that they reinforce the picture of the exit manuscript as a document that is distinct from and textually variant on the theatre company's retained playbook. The exit manuscript becomes copy for a quarto; the retained theatre manuscript eventually informs the Folio but stays in the theatre. Though I am sympathetic to Werstine's argument that 'good' quartos were set from theatre manuscripts, we lack the evidence that would enable us to make this a general position, as the ironic evidence of missing copies for transcripts testifies with dumb eloquence. The exit manuscripts are defined not as 'foul papers' or 'playbooks' but as manuscripts other than the company's playbook as it was retained for future use; in other words, they were 'foul papers' in the widest and most generic and most non-judgemental sense proposed by Werstine that, whatever their features might have been, they had been copied. I have recognized that in some cases the exit manuscript may have been a first playbook that was transcribed to make a second playbook before it was released to the printers. But, in some cases, there is relatively rich evidence indicating that the printed text's proximity to Shakespeare's hand, whereas, by comparison, the evidence for annotation is either lacking or insubstantial. As the extant playhouse manuscripts are almost all transcripts, there is no call for dogmatism as to the presence of theatrical annotation in the copies for Shakespeare's plays.

I propose the model of the two archives – the archives of theatre and of print – and I propose the category of the exit manuscript that moves from one archive to the other. It follows that the surviving manuscripts are not commensurate with the manuscripts that served as copy for the printing of Shakespeare's plays. This does not mean that they are consistently of a different kind. Indeed, the theatre archive repeatedly informs the First Folio, though the processes of transcription or annotation onto printed copy undoubtedly intervene. As for the quartos printed directly from a manuscript,[32] we can say that in various cases it is helpful to accept Werstine's suggestion gratefully and posit that they were or could have been set from a theatre playbook. But the separation between the theatre archive and the archive of print means that the New Bibliographers were right to understand that quartos might, sometimes at least, be printed from the lost but inevitably once actual manuscripts, of a kind that precedes the theatre manuscripts such as survive. This remains within the range of interpretative possibilities available to a textual critic. There is no justification for insisting that *all* printed Shakespeare quartos were set from annotated playbooks.

---

[30] A key intervention was Gary Taylor's '*Troilus and Cressida*: Bibliography, Performance, and Interpretation', *Shakespeare Studies* 15 (1982), 99–136, in which Taylor's conclusions reversed previous analyses by positing that the quarto of 1609 was printed from 'foul papers'.

[31] For details see John Jowett, 'Textual Introduction' to *Troilus and Cressida*, in *Critical Reference Edition*.

[32] As Werstine elsewhere deconstructs the distinction between 'good' and 'bad' quartos, there is no need to insist on it here, though, from another perspective, the extreme heterogeneity of the Shakespeare quartos remains a major issue for textual criticism. See Paul Werstine, 'Narratives about Printed Shakespeare Texts: "Foul Papers" and "Bad" Quartos', *Shakespeare Quarterly* 41 (1990), 65–86.

"SBLOOD!': HAMLET'S OATHS AND THE EDITING OF SHAKESPEARE'S PLAYS

LUCY MUNRO

Imagine, if you will, that it is the year 2416, and in a classroom somewhere far away, a teacher is working through the opening scene of *Hamlet*. For a variety of reasons, including intergalactic war, massive computer failure and the evolution of a particularly virulent paper mite, the only text of *Hamlet* that has survived is Richard Curtis's early 1980s parody *The Skinhead Hamlet*, a masterpiece of concise profanity that condenses Shakespeare's play to around 600 words, most of them variations on the word 'fuck'.[1] In the Arden fifteenth series edition that the teacher holds in her tentacle, the play opens like this:

1.1 The Battlements of Elsinore Castle.

Enter HAMLET, *followed by* GHOST.

GHOST   Oi! Mush!
HAMLET   Yer?
GHOST   I was fucked!   *Exit Ghost.*
HAMLET   O Fuck.   *Exit Hamlet.*[2]

The editor of this *Hamlet* has glossed the text thus:

1–4 **Oi** . . . **Fuck** The dialogue in this scene lacks the verse rhythms of later speeches (see, for example, the anapestic tetrameter of 3.1.2, 'I'll be fucked if I watch any more of this crap'), I have therefore lined it as prose.

1 **Oi** a common greeting
Mush man, 'bloke' (*OED* 1), a friendly form of address; the phrase could also refer to a prostitute's client (*OED* 2), and scholars have suggested that it reveals the Ghost's unspoken sexual desire for Hamlet, or his desire to exercise authority over him (see Fletcher, '*Hamlet's* Ghostly Longings').

2 **Yer** a colloquial form of *you*, perhaps expressing intimacy

3 **fucked** killed (see *fuck*, l. 4)
4 **Fuck** a strong oath alluding to sexual intercourse

The editor is more interested in the play's combination of verse and prose and its handling of issues of gender and sexuality than the precise impact of the term 'fuck' in late twentieth-century English, and has glossed this word and its cognates in a bland and somewhat perfunctory manner. Furthermore, when the word appears repeatedly in further scenes, in lines such as 'To fuck or be fucked' (2.1.5), 'Fuck off to a nunnery' (2.1.7) and 'She's fucking round the twist, in't she?' (4.2.2), she fails to take into account the many shifts of speaker, register, tone and context. The teacher in her classroom in 2416 is therefore unable to convey to her class the range of meanings that 'fuck' had at the time when this *Hamlet* was composed, such as its relationship to questions of gender, sexuality and social class or its affective capacity. Its true offensiveness is lost, along with its ability to do its cultural, aesthetic and emotional work.

This is, of course, a parody but my imaginary future editor of *The Skinhead Hamlet* is not very different from many of the editors who have worked with vocabulary that would have been truly offensive at the time when Shakespeare was

---

[1] *Not 1982*, ed. John Lloyd and Sean Hardie (London, 1981), n.p. (verso of pages for 3–6 December). Because this book is unpaginated and each scene is short, I will cite the text by act, scene and line number.
[2] This quotation is reformatted to Arden guidelines but the text is that printed in *Not 1982*.

writing. In Early Modern English, the most offensive words did not relate to the body and its operations; instead, they drew heavily on religious vocabulary and doctrine. These blasphemous oaths range from the comparatively mild 'Marry' and 'By the Mass' (by Shakespeare's time often associated with older people and nostalgic forms of Catholicism) to the highly inflammatory contracted oaths drawn from the fractured body parts of the crucified Christ – ''sblood', ''swounds' or 'zounds', ''sbodie', ''sfoot', ''slid', ''snails' – that appear to have emerged in the final decades of the sixteenth century. I am not, of course, suggesting that the bodily oaths available to English speakers today are directly equivalent to the religious oaths that they supplanted during the course of the eighteenth century.[3] Instead, I begin with the profanities of our own day in order to try to restore to early modern oaths some of their original emotional charge and to highlight the connections that they had to broader structures of behaviour and belief.

Profanity mattered in early modern England. It is well known that the Jacobean regime attempted to ban 'the great abuse of the holy Name of God in Stage-playes, Interludes, Maygames, Shewes, and such like' in 1606.[4] Equally, if not more important, are a series of attempts to legislate against swearing in general in the parliaments of 1610, 1614 and 1621, before 'An Act to Prevent and Reform Profane Swearing and Cursing' was finally issued in 1624.[5] Editors have been aware of these contexts for some time and many discuss in depth the differences in the treatment of oaths in quarto and folio texts of Shakespeare's plays, spurred by Gary Taylor's pioneering work on and around the first edition of the Oxford Shakespeare.[6] At the same time, however, they routinely underestimate the seriousness with which Shakespeare's contemporaries would have viewed words such as ''sblood' and ''swounds', and the treatment of these oaths in recent single-volume editions is highly erratic. Even when they work with plays such as *Hamlet*, *1 Henry IV* and *Othello*, where quarto editions preserve similar sets of oaths that appear to have been censored in the First Folio, editors approach profane swearing with very different priorities.

The contrast between editors' approaches to the swearing of Iago and Hamlet is instructive. Both characters use ''sblood' and ''swounds', but the treatment of these oaths in glosses and commentary notes is markedly different: while Iago's swearing is discussed in detail and his language connected with questions of characterization and censorship, commentary on Hamlet's swearing is often perfunctory and at times non-existent.[7] Iago's first use of the term ''sblood' comes in the play's fourth line, as he exclaims to Roderigo, ''Sblood, but you'll not hear me. If ever I did dream / Of such a matter, abhor me'.[8] This is how a series of editors gloss these lines:

4 '***Sblood***: God's blood. This and other oaths were omitted in F because of the new regulations against

---

[3] For an overview of this transition, see Melissa Mohr, *Holy Sh★t: A Brief History of Swearing* (New York and Oxford, 2013).

[4] An Acte to Restraine Abuses of Players, in *An[n]o regni Iacobi, regis Angl. Scotiae, Franc. & Hybern. viz. Angl. Franc. & Hybern. 3°. Scotiae 39° at the Second Session of Parliament Begun and Holden by Prorogation at Westminster the Fifth Day of November ... to the High Pleasure of Almighty God, and to the Weale Publique of this Realme, were Enacted as Followeth*, second impression (London, 1606), sig. H5r.

[5] See Hugh Gazzard, 'An Act to Restrain Abuses of Players (1606)', *Review of English Studies* 61 (2009), 495–528; p. 519.

[6] See, in particular, ''Swounds revisited: Theatrical, editorial and literary expurgation', in Gary Taylor and John Jowett, *Shakespeare Reshaped 1606–23* (Oxford, 1993), pp. 51–106.

[7] Iago uses 'sblood at 1.1.4 and 'swounds at 1.1.85, 1.1.107 and 5.2.216; elsewhere, 'swounds is used by the drunken Cassio at 2.3.141, the wounded Montano at 2.3.160, and Othello at 2.3.203, 3.3.157, 3.4.99 and 4.1.36. Hamlet uses 'sblood at 2.2.303 and 3.2.361 and 'swounds at 2.2.511 and 5.1.263. He is the only character to use either oath; Horatio, like Roderigo, uses milder oaths such as *tush* (1.1.29). Unless stated otherwise, all references to these plays are from E. A. J. Honigmann, ed., *Othello*, Arden Shakespeare Third Series, rev. edn with introduction by Ayanna Thompson (London, 2016) and Ann Thompson and Neil Taylor, eds., *Hamlet*, Arden Shakespeare Third Series, rev. edn (London, 2016).

[8] Honigmann, ed., *Othello*, 1.1.4–5. Honigmann here follows the text as it appears in the 1622 quarto.

HAMLET'S OATHS AND THE EDITING OF SHAKESPEARE'S PLAYS

profanity. Iago's oaths contrast with Roderigo's feeble *Tush*.[9]

4 **'Sblood,** that is, by Christ's blood; a very strong oath which F omits, in keeping with its policy of censoring the profanities that are found in Q1. See Textual Analysis, pp. 211–12 below.[10]

4 **'Sblood**: Christ's blood (a strong oath); **hear**: listen to[11]

4 **Sblood** God's blood, an oath expurgated in F (see p. 352)

4–5 **If ... matter** semi-proverbial (Dent, D592, 'He never dreamed of it')[12]

4 **'Sblood**: by Christ's blood; a strong oath, was omitted in the Folio text[13]

4 **'Sblood** God's blood. A strong oath expurgated from F.

5 **abhor** Stress on first syllable[14]

While only Michael Neill and E. A. J. Honigmann comment on other aspects of the exchange, each editor provides a gloss on the word ''sblood' and most note its omission from the folio text. Two of these scholars also refer readers to a more detailed discussion elsewhere in their edition, and Kenneth Muir highlights the structural relationship between Iago's oath and that of Roderigo ('Tush' is otherwise ignored by these editors). The editors similarly emphasize the power of Iago's oath: it is a 'strong oath' or a 'very strong oath'. Muir also comments on the way in which the use of profanity informs characterization in Shakespeare's plays, an approach developed in detail in Frances A. Shirley's important 1979 monograph, *Swearing and Perjury in Shakespeare's Plays*, a work to which recent editors of both *1 Henry IV* and *Titus Andronicus* refer when they term ''swounds' '[a] particularly strong oath' and 'one of the strongest oaths'.[15]

However, the treatment of the same oaths when they are uttered by Hamlet is notably different. In conversation with Rosencrantz and Guildenstern on the subject of Claudius's popularity in Act 2, scene 2, Hamlet declares, ''Sblood, there is something in this more than natural, if philosophy could find it out.'[16] This is how editors have glossed these lines in the same series as those quoted above:

365 ... **'Sblood**: By God's blood (in the eucharist).

366 **philosophy**: 'Natural philosophy' or (as we now call it) science.[17]

337–8 **more than natural ... find it out** that is, there is something abnormal about it as scientific investigation would show.[18]

363 **philosophy ... out** the philosophers could discover what it is[19]

390 **'Sblood**: an oath (by Christ's or God's blood)[20]

303 ... **'Sblood** abbreviation of 'God's blood'. F's omission is a likely expurgation.

304 **more than natural** outside natural laws, abnormal

philosophy science[21]

356 ... **'Sblood**: by Christ's blood.

357 **philosophy**: science, natural philosophy.[22]

All these editors include the word ''sblood' in their texts, even Philip Edwards and G. R. Hibbard, who otherwise base their editions on the folio text. Some do not gloss the word at all; others gloss it but without the intensifying adjectives such as 'strong' that feature in the *Othello* glosses. Only Ann Thompson and Neil Taylor draw attention to the omission of the oath in the folio and they are by far the most attentive of *Hamlet*'s recent editors to the use of blasphemous oaths, glossing ''swounds' as

---

[9] Commentary notes by Kenneth Muir (1968), in *Othello*, rev. edn (London, 2005), p. 157.

[10] Norman Sanders, ed., *Othello* (Cambridge, 1984), p. 65.

[11] Barbara A. Mowat and Paul Werstine, eds., *Othello*, Folger Shakespeare Library edn (New York, 1992), p. 6.

[12] Honigmann, ed., *Othello*, p. 119: these notes were originally published in 2003.

[13] Roma Gill, ed., *Othello*, Oxford Schools Shakespeare, 2nd edn (Oxford, 2002), p. 1.

[14] Michael Neill, ed., *Othello* (Oxford, 2006), p. 195.

[15] Frances A. Shirley, *Swearing and Perjury in Shakespeare's Plays* (London, 1979). See David M. Bevington, ed., *Henry IV, Part 1* (Oxford, 1987), p. 139; Eugene M. Waith, ed., *Titus Andronicus* (Oxford, 1984), p. 155.

[16] Thompson and Taylor, eds., *Hamlet*, 2.2.303-5. This is an edition of the 1604/5 second quarto text.

[17] Commentary notes by T. J. B. Spencer (1980), in *Hamlet*, rev. edn (London, 2005), p. 222.

[18] Philip Edwards, ed., *Hamlet* (Cambridge, 1985), p. 133.

[19] G. R. Hibbard, ed., *Hamlet* (Oxford, 1987), p. 222.

[20] Barbara A. Mowat and Paul Werstine, eds., *Hamlet*, Folger Shakespeare Library edn (New York, 1992), p. 104.

[21] Thompson and Taylor, eds., *Hamlet*, p. 290: these notes were originally published in 2006.

[22] Roma Gill, ed., *Hamlet*, Oxford Schools Shakespeare, rev. edn (Oxford, 2007), p. 54.

'a powerful oath' when it appears in Act 5, scene 2 (p. 430) where others either ignore it or provide only a minimal gloss. Hibbard, for example, annotates only Hamlet's second use of the term, noting that 'F's *Come* is an evident case of "purging"' (p. 333).

The strength of the editorial tradition of individual works is clear in the way that even the Folger and Oxford Schools editors, who work across the canon, gloss Iago and Hamlet's uses of ''sblood' differently. Furthermore, although *Othello* and *Hamlet* represent the extremes of editorial practice when it comes to profane swearing, the treatment of ''swounds' and ''sblood' is erratic elsewhere. L. A. Beaurline, for example, fails to gloss the Bastard's use of ''swounds' in his Cambridge edition of *King John*, while David Scott Kastan oddly refers to Falstaff's ''sblood' as a 'mild oath' in his Arden third series edition of *1 Henry IV*.[23] Why does this matter? If Iago's swearing deserves to be taken seriously and not to be elided or ignored, so does Hamlet's. Moreover, we should do more to place Hamlet alongside the range of characters that use ''swounds' and ''sblood' in Shakespeare's plays: Aaron in *Titus Andronicus*; Richard, Buckingham and the First and Second Executioners in *Richard III*; the Bastard in *King John*; Mercutio in *Romeo and Juliet*; Falstaff, Poins, Hotspur and Gadshill in *1 Henry IV*; Iago, Cassio, Montano and Othello in *Othello*. This is not, perhaps, the critical company that Hamlet generally keeps, but the list is suggestive of the complexity of the character as Shakespeare presents him in the first and second quartos.

In a broader context, swearing should also be understood as a speech act that had real force in pre- and post-Reformation England.[24] One especially powerful articulation of swearing's violent religious transgressions, Stephen Hawes's *The Conversion of Swearers* (1509), ventriloquizes Christ himself, pleading with swearers to leave his tortured body in peace:

> Tere me nowe no more
> My woundes are sore
> Leue sweryinge therfore and come to my grace
> I am redy
> To graunte mercy
> To the truely for thy trespace.[25]

On the printed page, the second part of each of the long, cross-rhymed lines floats in the margin next to the preceding line, and a series of flower or star motifs are scattered across the page. The fragmented text thus registers the terrible strain put upon Christ by the careless words of the swearer. While the emotive force of oaths such as 'marry' and 'by the Mass' may have diminished for Protestants in the mid- to late sixteenth century, the power of oaths sworn on the body of the crucified Christ survived the Reformation. Writing more than a century after the publication of *The Conversion of Swearers*, Abraham Gibson echoes Hawes in his description of

> *impious and fearefull Oaths*, which (me thinketh) I am afraid to mention, *blasphemous, horrible, terrible*, by the parts or adiuncts of *Christ*, as by his *life, death, passion, flesh, heart, wounds, blood, bones, armes, sides, guts, nailes, foote*, with many hundred more, which a gracious heart cannot but melt to heare, tremble to speake, quake to thinke and yet (good Lord) how common are they in the mouthes of the prophane sonnes of *Beliall* ... these instead of Crosse & Nailes, do between their owne teeth grinde him, and teare him[.][26]

For commentators such as Gibson, swearing enacts a parody not only of the crucifixion but also of the eucharist – itself the subject of intense controversy

---

[23] See L. A. Beaurline, ed., *King John* (Cambridge, 1990), p. 94; David Scott Kastan, *King Henry IV Part 1*, Arden Shakespeare Third Series (London, 2002), p. 154.

[24] On pre-Reformation swearing, see Lynn Forest-Hill, *Transgressive Language in Medieval English Drama: Signs of Challenge and Change* (Aldershot, 2000); Sandy Bardsley, *Venomous Tongues: Speech and Gender in Late-Medieval England* (Philadelphia, 2006), esp. pp. 95–9; Mohr, *Holy Sh★t*, pp. 88–128.

[25] Stephen Hawes, *The Co[n]uercyon of Swearers* (London, 1509), sig. A3v.

[26] Abraham Gibson, *The Lands Mourning, for Vaine Swearing: Or The Downe-fall of Oathes* (London, 1613), sigs D1v–D2r (pp. 34–5). For a similar account of swearing see John Downame, *Foure Treatises Tending to Disswade all Christians from Foure no Lesse Hainous then Common Sinnes; Namely, the Abuses of Swearing, Drunkennesse, Whoredome, and Briberie* (London, 1609), sig. D4v.

during the Reformation – in which swearers 'grinde' the body of Christ 'between their owne teeth', and their relationship with his body is violently reconfigured.

Isaac Barrow's 1678 collection of *Several Sermons Against Evil-Speaking* provides a detailed summary of the emotions that might drive people to swear:

Sometimes it ariseth from exorbitant heats of spirit, or transports of unbridled passion. When a man is keenly peevish, or fiercely angry, or eagerly contentious, then he blustereth, and dischargeth his choler in most tragical strains; then he would fright the objects of his displeasure by the most violent expressions thereof. This is sometime alleged in excuse of rash Swearing; (*I was provoked*, the Swearer will say, *I was in passion:*) but it is strange, that a bad cause should justify a bad effect; that one crime should warrant another; that what would spoil a good action, should excuse a bad one.

Sometimes it proceedeth from arrogant conceit, and a tyrannical humour; when a man fondly admireth his own opinion, and affecting to impose it on others, is thence moved to thwack it on with lusty Asseverations.

Sometimes it issueth from wantonnesse and levity of mind, disposing a man to sport with any thing, how serious, how grave, how sacred and venerable soever.

Sometimes its rise is from stupid inadvertency, or heady precipitancy; when the man doth not heed what he saith, or consider the nature and consequence of his words, but snatcheth any expression which cometh next[.][27]

Whether it is provoked by anger, conceit, wantonness or inadvertency, swearing reveals a speaker's emotional state and vulnerability to corruption; it can be an index of an individual's status within religious frameworks of salvation and damnation. But what makes the use of blasphemous oaths especially troubling is the idea that swearers might endanger their souls not through conscious transgression – as they might in committing adultery or murder – but through a failure to consider the implications of their words.

Swearing not only helps to reveal speakers' own emotional states but also has the potential to stir the emotions – be they sorrow, pity, reciprocal anger or wantonness – of those around them. I am reminded of the possibly apocryphal story of the viewer of the infamous interview between Bill Grundy and the Sex Pistols on Thames Television's *Today* show in 1976, who responded to hearing the words 'fucker' and 'fucking' by kicking his foot through his own television set. The viewer, a forty-seven-year-old lorry driver named James Holmes, was quoted as saying:

'It blew up and I was knocked backwards . . . But I was so angry and disgusted with this filth that I took a swing with my boot.

'I can swear as well as anyone, but I don't want this sort of muck coming into my home at teatime.'

Mr Holmes, of Beedfield Walk, Waltham Abbey, Essex, added: 'I am not a violent person, but I would like to have got hold of Grundy.'[28]

For James Holmes – or at least his representation in the popular press – listening to swearing provokes feelings of anger and disgust; even though he may use this kind of language himself, its invasion of his home and domestic space is enough to provoke him to violence.

For early modern writers, the angry spectator was, more often than not, God himself. In a much-reprinted anecdote, Philip Stubbes tells the story of a serving-man from Boothby in Lincolnshire, 'who had styll in his mouth, the vse to sweare, Gods precious blood, and that for verie trifles'. Although he is warned by his friends, he refuses to stop using this oath, with the result that God inflicts him with sickness. The serving-man refuses to give up swearing even in this extremity,

but hearing the Bell to towle, dyd most hardlie, in the verie anguishe of death, starte vp in his bedde, and sware by Gods blood, this Bell dooth towle for me, whereuppon immediatlie, the blood aboundauntly, from all the ioyntes of his body, as it were in streames, did issue out, most fearefullie, as well, from mouth, nose, wrestes, knees, heeles, and toes, with all other ioynts, not one left free: whereupon he most myserablie yeelded vp the ghost, whose iudgement I leaue vnto the Lord.[29]

---

[27] Isaac Barrow, *Several Sermons Against Evil-Speaking* (London, 1678), pp. 124–5.
[28] 'The filth and the fury', *Daily Mirror*, 2 December 1976.
[29] Philip Stubbes, *Two Wunderfull and Rare Examples, of the Undeferred and Present Approching Judgement of the Lord our God* (London, 1581), sigs A2r–A3r.

Like James Holmes, God responds to swearing with violent retribution and, like the *Daily Mirror*'s report, Stubbes's anecdote localizes and domesticates the swearer. This is not a figure from the Bible or classical myth, but someone from an identifiable town, the location of which is specified ('three myles from *Grathame*'); the events are said to have taken place 'in the moneth of *Iune*, last past' (sig. A2r). The swearer's horrific fate is thus made gruesome yet recognizable and applicable to a reader's own habits.

As Stubbes's anecdote suggests, the emotional charge of swearing drew some of its power from contemporary religious, cultural and educational contexts. For many Calvinist commentators the use of words such as ''sblood' or ''swounds' was a sign of the swearer's reprobate status as one of those damned before they were even born. One of the characters in Arthur Dent's dialogue, *The Plain Man's Path-way to Heauen* (1607), describes swearing as 'an euident demonstration of a Reprobate' and remarks, 'I neuer wist any man, truly fearing *God* in his heart, that was an vsuall and a common swearer'.[30] Similarly, in a sermon published in 1633, Samuel Otes attacks those who 'have a shew of religion, but they sweare like reprobates; they speake by the mouth of a greater beast, then themselves'.[31] In these statements, Dent and Otes suggest that swearing has the power to reveal the true or hidden self that is concealed by a display of religious zeal.

The question of how people learned to swear is also raised frequently in early modern texts and for many critics the fault lay within the household and family. In a collection of lectures revised for publication in the plague year of 1603, Henry Holland attacked his (implicitly male) readers for their failure to discipline the behaviour and speech of their dependents:

Teach & correct your vnruly seruants, keepe them from theaters and other abhominations, bring them to sermons more carefully, teach and correct your children for lying, swearing, & blasphemies ... But alasse, most of you miserable people, neither can teach, nor will learne any good: Nay, it is to be feared, you teach your wiues, children and seruants, all the euill you see, heare, & know, euery where practised in the world. They learn of you to sweare horribly, their wicked mouthes are full of othes: they learne of you to walke inordinately: for their liues are vngodly & prophane.[32]

Holland's reference to the theatres points to their uneasy place in this debate. For many religious and social commentators, plays were a site of moral and linguistic corruption, a place where spectators learned to murder, steal, fornicate and – not least – swear. As Brian Cummings suggests, one of the problems with the theatre was that swearing there was mimetic: in performing the role of a character who uttered profane oaths, actors were required to swear, and playgoers to listen to their profanities.[33]

Like Québécois French's 'sacres' – oaths drawing on religious vocabulary such as 'câlisse', 'osti', 'tabernak', 'crisse' and 'viarge' – English oaths based on the fragmented body of the crucified Christ had an affective power that has more in common with Present-Day English 'fuck' than 'for God's sake', 'Jesus Christ' or the descendants of religious oaths such as 'goddam', 'crikey' or 'blimey'.[34] Moreover, although it has sometimes been assumed that condensed or 'minced' oaths such as ''swounds' or ''sblood' were less transgressive than 'by God's wounds' or 'by God's blood', this belief was not shared by early modern commentators, who repeatedly insisted that condensed or euphemistic oaths were just as corrupting as any other form of swearing. The preacher Stephen Jerome, for example, encourages his readers to give up their 'Ridiculous and Childish Oathes, as by Fay,

---

[30] Arthur Dent, *The Plaine Mans Path-way to Heauen* (London, 1607), p. 137.
[31] Samuel Otes, *An Explanation of the Generall Epistle of Saint Jude* (London, 1633), p. 324.
[32] Henry Holland, 'The epistle to the reader', in *Spirituall Preseruatiues Against the Pestilence* (London, 1603), sig. A8r.
[33] Brian Cummings, *Mortal Thoughts: Religion, Secularity, and Identity in Shakespeare and Early Modern Culture* (Oxford, 2013), p. 154.
[34] The latter are nineteenth-century corruptions of 'Christ' and 'God blind me' respectively: see Jonathon Green, *Cassell's Dictionary of Slang* (London, 1998), s.v. 'blimey', 'crikey'.

HAMLET'S OATHS AND THE EDITING OF SHAKESPEARE'S PLAYS

Fakins, Trokins, Bodikins, Slid, Sounds, Cocke and Pye, with the like; whereby thou seekest to mocke and deceiue God, who will not be mocked.'[35] Such oaths may be 'ridiculous', but God will not be amused. Moreover, monosyllabic oaths seem to acquire a force and power of their own within early modern culture, perhaps in part because they were satisfying to say and suited to the violent expression of emotion.

For these reasons, to gloss ''swounds' or ''sblood' merely as 'an oath' or 'a strong oath' is to mislead readers as to the power of these words in their early modern contexts. Moreover, it also overlooks the odd things that were happening to these one-syllable oaths: they seem to have been becoming unmoored from the original promissory function of the oath, which Jonathan Gray, writing on oaths in the Reformation, calls 'a declaration or promise in which God was cited as witness to the truth of a statement'.[36] When Hamlet cries ''Sblood, there is something in this more than natural if philosophy could find it out', something of this function remains: the oath gives additional force to his declaration, underlining its truth from Hamlet's perspective. However, when Richard III asks 'Zounds, who is there?', upon Ratcliffe's interruption of his self-scrutiny just before the Battle of Bosworth Field, he is not making even an implicit promise; the oath is instead an expression of his shock and fear.[37] Similarly, when Aaron asks the Nurse 'Zounds, ye whore, is black so base a hue?', cradling his baby son, his oath underlines the force of his question in the face of her hostility.[38] Oaths here are not promises but expressions of extremes of emotion that are momentarily beyond articulate thought.[39]

Given all of these factors, juxtaposing Iago and Hamlet is again instructive. As scholars have recognized, the opening lines of *Othello* do important work in establishing the linguistic, social and ethical positions of the speakers:

RODERIGO   Tush, never tell me, I take it much unkindly
    That thou, Iago, who hast had my purse
    As if the strings were thine, shouldst know of this.

IAGO   'Sblood, but you'll not hear me. If ever I did dream
    Of such a matter, abhor me.   (1.1.1–5)

Roderigo's mild oath, 'Tush', is matched and exceeded by Iago's ''Sblood', an effect that is lost in the folio text, which omits both oaths.[40] The quarto's dialogue gives a vivid sense of Iago's impatience and vigour, which are underlined by the verbal force of his oath. The potential disrespect of the oath when addressed to his social superior is, however, balanced by other aspects of his language: Iago adopts respectful 'you' forms, whereas Roderigo, his social superior, addresses Iago as 'thou'. Iago's opening words could have jolted and disturbed early modern spectators, leaving them uncertain about Iago's social status, his character, and his relationship with Roderigo. Iago's swearing is also important because it establishes him as someone prepared to use a certain kind of language: he exhibits a transgressive verbal bravura; he perhaps even risks damnation. This quality is maintained as

---

[35] *Moses his sight of Canaan with Simeon his Dying-Song. Directing how to Live Holily and Dye Happily* (London, 1614), p. 434. For similar comments see also Anthony Anderson, *An Exposition of the Hymne Commonly called Benedictus with an Ample & Comfortable Application of the Same, to our Age and People* (London, 1574), fol. 25v; Walter Powell, *A Summons for Swearers* (London, 1645), sig. D4r.

[36] Jonathan Gray, *Oaths and the English Reformation* (Cambridge, 2012), p. 52. On the promissory functions of oaths, see also Cummings, *Mortal Thoughts*, esp. pp. 147–67; John Kerrigan, *Shakespeare's Binding Language* (Oxford, 2016); Beatrice Groves, 'New directions: The salvation of oaths: Grace, swearing and *Hamlet* in *The Revenger's Tragedy*', in *The Revenger's Tragedy: A Critical Reader*, ed. Brian Walsh (London, 2016), pp. 123–42.

[37] James R. Siemon, ed., *King Richard III*, Arden Shakespeare Third Series (London, 2009), 5.3.208.

[38] Jonathan Bate, ed., *Titus Andronicus*, Arden Shakespeare Third Series (London, 1995), 4.2.73.

[39] A similar use of oaths can be seen in *The Revenger's Tragedy*: for detailed commentary see Lucy Munro, '"'Cause I love swearing": Strong language, revenge and the body in *The Revenger's Tragedy*', in *The Revenger's Tragedy: The State of Play*, ed. Gretchen Minton (London, forthcoming 2017).

[40] See *Mr. William Shakespeares Comedies, Histories, & Tragedies Published According to the True Originall Copies* (London, 1623), p. 310.

the play continues. In addition to ''sblood' Iago also uses ''swounds', a word that becomes increasingly more prominent as the play progresses, and which appears to seep into the language of other characters as Iago's influence spreads.[41] As Shirley comments, 'we can measure the tensions to which he subjects others by watching them be moved, one by one, to stronger oaths'.[42]

In contrast, in *Hamlet*, only Hamlet himself uses oaths such as ''sblood' and ''swounds' – indeed, he is by far the play's most intense swearer – but swearing is again an index of character.[43] As noted above, Hamlet's first use of a blasphemous oath, ''sblood', appears in an exchange with Rosencranz and Guildenstern, his old friends from university in Wittenberg. The reduced popularity of the players in the city 'is not very strange', Hamlet comments,

> for my uncle is King of Denmark, and those that would make mouths at him while my father lived give twenty, forty, fifty, a hundred ducats apiece for his picture in little. 'Sblood, there is something in this more than natural if philosophy could find it out. (2.2.300–5)

The use of swearing here perhaps indicates heightened emotion, as Shirley suggests, and Hamlet's charged attitude towards his uncle.[44] But other factors may also be at work. It is noticeable that Hamlet's only other use of this oath also appears in a conversation with Rosencrantz and Guildenstern, after the performance of the 'Mousetrap' in Act 3, scene 2. At the end of the exchange during which Hamlet tries to persuade Guildenstern to play the recorder, he tells him:

> Why, look you how unworthy a thing you make of me: you would play upon me! You would seem to know my stops, you would pluck out the heart of my mystery, you would sound me from my lowest note to the top of my compass. And there is much music, excellent voice, in this little organ. Yet cannot you make it speak. 'Sblood! Do you think I am easier to be played on than a pipe? Call me what instrument you will, though you can fret me you cannot play upon me. (3.2.355–63)

Again, Hamlet's swearing suggests emotional disturbance – particularly, here, his growing irritation with Rosencrantz and Guildenstern, and their clumsy attempts to probe him. Yet it is significant that Hamlet uses ''sblood' twice in conversation with his old friends, and that these are the only times at which he uses this oath. This fact raises the possibility that the use of ''sblood' is part of his feigned madness, a way of signalling linguistic disorder, but other contexts should be considered. We might look, for example, to Thomas Nashe's description of 'some rufling Courtier, that sweares swoundes and bloud', in which he voices a common early modern assumption that those most likely to swear are high-status young men.[45] Using ''sblood' might therefore equally be part of a performance of laddish masculinity or posturing atheism, implicitly recalling the homosocial environment of their days in Wittenberg. Intriguingly enough, however, one of the most notorious swearers in the late sixteenth and early seventeenth century was Queen Elizabeth herself, whose fondness for the oath 'by God's death' was described by contemporaries and frequently alluded to in the years after her death.[46] The queen's swearing

---

[41] On this point, see Shirley, *Swearing and Perjury*, esp. pp. 100–2, 110–24; see also Giorgio Melchoiri, 'The rhetoric of character construction: *Othello*', *Shakespeare Survey* 34 (1981), 61–72; Sanders, ed., *Othello*, 202. Cummings offers an alternative reading, in which 'Othello is not contaminated by Iago's profanities, he swears of his own accord' and 'Othello's swearing is an index of an altogether deeper religious and political turmoil over language and belief within Elizabethan and Jacobean culture' (p. 156).

[42] Shirley, *Swearing and Perjury*, p. 102.

[43] For a survey of all of Hamlet's oaths and vows, see Shirley, *Swearing and Perjury*, pp. 102–10.

[44] Shirley, *Swearing and Perjury*, p. 103.

[45] Thomas Nashe, *An Almond for a Parrat, or Cutbert Curry-Knaues Almes Fit for the Knaue Martin* (London, 1589), sig. A2v.

[46] See, for example, the Spanish ambassador's report in July 1588 of her saying 'by God's death' in the aftermath of the defeat of the Spanish Armada, or John Speed's report of her response to an awkward ambassador who addressed her in Latin: 'Gods death my Lords (for that was her oath euer in anger) I haue been enforced this day to scowre vp my old Latine, that hath laine long in rusting.' See Bernardino De Mendoza to the King of Spain, 24 July 1588 (new style), *Calendar of State Papers, Spain (Simancas), Volume 4: 1587–1603* (London, 1899), p. 353; *The Theatre of the Empire of Great Britaine*

seems to have been a politically calculated action; as Shirley comments, 'Time and again I feel she swore to startle, knowing that she could back up what might have been mere bombast in a less powerful person.'[47] It is therefore also possible that Hamlet is pulling rank on Rosencranz and Guildenstern, deliberately using transgressive forms of language that they cannot use in return. The oath may reveal Hamlet's desire to alienate, snub, disturb or overpower his friends, or alternatively to disarm and bond with them, and its meaning may shift between the two scenes.

The picture is thickened and complicated by the other moments at which Hamlet swears. The term ''sblood' appears only in prose passages, where it might be expected as part of the representation of colloquial speech, but Hamlet's other potent oath, ''swounds', appears in speeches written in verse, and in rather different contexts, suggesting the care with which Shakespeare deploys swearing. The oath first occurs in Act 2, scene 2, in the soliloquy in which Hamlet ponders the Player's emotional response to the Hecuba story: 'Am I a coward?', he asks,

> Who calls me villain, breaks my pate across,
> Plucks off my beard and blows it in my face,
> Tweaks me by the nose, gives me the lie i'th' throat
> As deep as to the lungs? Who does me this,
> Ha? 'Swounds, I should take it. For it cannot be
> But I am pigeon-livered and lack gall
> To make oppression bitter, or ere this
> I should ha' fatted all the region kites
> With this slave's offal – bloody, bawdy villain,
> Remorseless, treacherous, lecherous, kindless villain.
> Why, what an ass am I: this is most brave,
> That I, the son of a dear murdered,
> Prompted to my revenge by heaven and hell,
> Most like a whore unpack my heart with words
> And fall a-cursing like a very drab,
> A stallion! Fie upon't, foh!   (2.2.506–22)

In this part of the soliloquy, Hamlet brings himself to an emotional climax in the lines that successively end in the word 'villain', and then suddenly deflates before building up again when he ponders his own linguistic excess. In the folio text, which omits the oath, the changes of tone are different in their effect, as a new half-line, 'O vengeance!' is introduced after 'kindless villain'. In addition, Thompson and Taylor's modernization of the folio's 'Who?' to 'Whoa!' creates a series of exclamations: 'O vengeance! / Whoa! What an ass am I! Ay, sure, this is most brave.'[48] The use of an oath in a verse soliloquy might seem to represent more genuine emotion than Hamlet's dialogue with Rosencrantz and Guildenstern. Yet Hamlet is still in some respects performing, if only to himself, and his use of ''swounds' in a soliloquy in which his status as the king's son is debated potentially carries a good deal of irony if we bear in mind the uses to which Elizabeth I appears to have put swearing.

Hamlet's later use of the word ''swounds' has a similarly performative quality, coming after his physical tussle with Laertes at Ophelia's grave:

> KING   O, he is mad, Laertes.
> QUEEN   For love of God, forbear him.
> HAMLET 'Swounds, show me what thou'lt do.
>   Woul't weep, woul't fight, woul't fast, woul't tear thyself,
>   Woul't drink up eisel, eat a crocodile?
>   I'll do't. Dost come here to whine,
>   To outface me with leaping in her grave?
>   Be buried quick with her, and so will I.
>   And if thou prate of mountains let them throw
>   Millions of acres on us till our ground,
>   Singeing his pate against the burning zone,
>   Make Ossa like a wart. Nay, and thou'lt mouth,
>   I'll rant as well as thou.
> QUEEN   This is mere madness.   (5.1.261–72)

Hamlet's speech here is framed by Claudius and Gertrude's assertions that he is insane; as in the exchanges with Rosencrantz and Guildenstern, disordered speech suggests real or feigned madness. However, the use of the word ''swounds' at the start of the speech also suggests Hamlet's hyperbolic performance of possessive grief. Rather than working up to the oath, he starts at that high point,

---

(London, 1612), p. 871. Shirley provides further examples: see *Swearing and Perjury*, pp. 9–10.

[47] Shirley, *Swearing and Perjury*, p. 9.

[48] Ann Thompson and Neil Taylor, eds., *Hamlet: The Texts of 1603 and 1623* (London, 2006), 2.2.576–7. See Shakespeare, *Comedies, Histories, & Tragedies*, p. 264.

transforming the physical violence of his struggle with Laertes into verbal violence. The extremes of swearing can, it seems, work as an emotional stimulant, as a performative example to oneself. This is, moreover, the scene in which Hamlet describes himself as 'Hamlet the Dane' (5.1.247), a rare assertion of his status as the heir presumptive to the throne. Again, Hamlet's use of oaths may be linked to a desire to assert his rank over those who appear to challenge or devalue it.

How should Hamlet's oaths, then, be glossed? Space on the page is obviously limited, even in the critical editions published by Arden, Oxford or Cambridge. But there should be room for editors to take into account the force and implications of profane oaths, in the way that recent series have encouraged their editors not merely to gloss sexual references only with euphemistic terms such as the classic 'a bawdy quibble' but to make a real effort to convey a word or phrase's meaning and effects.[49] Should this include the use of swearwords current in Present-Day English? There is a precedent, of sorts, for this approach in Brian Loughrey and Neil Taylor's 1988 edition of five plays by Thomas Middleton, in which modern expletives appear repeatedly in the commentary notes. Notes on Act 2, scene 1 of *A Trick to Catch the Old One*, for example, include these glosses: '32 *Medlar*: a medlar tree produces fruit which is only eaten when over-ripe. "Medlar" was slang for both "cunt" and "whore" ... 57–8 *go down*: return home/fuck/perform fellatio'.[50] As in these examples, expletives are used mainly – and somewhat misleadingly – in the notes on sexual obscenity, where they often give innuendo an edge of violence that is only rarely present in Middleton's text. In contrast, Loughrey and Taylor's notes on profane oaths are rather bland – in the same section of *A Trick to Catch the Old One*, 'Cud's me' is glossed as 'an oath corrupted from "God save me"'.

Of course, simply to gloss ''Sblood' with 'fuck' or 'fucking hell' would be as blunt an instrument as glossing 'go down' as 'fuck', and would not take into account the residual promissory function that many of Shakespeare's blasphemous oaths retain. Yet an alternative approach, using religious oaths that have largely lost their force, such as 'goddam' or 'blimey', similarly fails to convey the effect of early modern religious oaths. The editor of an early modern English play faces a similar problem to that of the translator of twentieth-century Québécois texts into English, which has been much discussed in relation to the works of Roch Carrier and Michel Tremblay.[51] Vivien Bosley, for example, argues that when English translations of the phrases 'Ah ben, câlisse!', 'y'a pas une crisse de vue française' and 'Maudit cul' in Tremblay's *Les Belles-soeurs* all involve the use of 'god damn', the lack of specificity is 'a sign of distance from the religious fact, and linguistic impoverishment thereby'. However, deliberately avoiding religious language also fails to provide 'the impression of having the church as a constant living presence in one's life, such that it is absorbed into the familiar world of everyday speech and understood as a reference to a dominant truth of existence'.[52] Although similarities between the *sacres* and Early Modern English swearing should not be exaggerated, these remarks also hold true of late Elizabethan society, and they need to be taken into account when oaths are glossed.

Taking all these factors into consideration, it would in theory be possible to gloss Hamlet's first oath like this, making use of a modern oath but not

---

[49] On this issue see Helen Wilcox, 'The character of a footnote ... or annotation revisited', in *In Arden: Editing Shakespeare*, ed. Ann Thompson and Gordon McMullan (London, 2003), pp. 194–208; Stanley Wells, *Shakespeare, Sex and Love* (Oxford, 2010).

[50] Brian Loughrey and Neil Taylor, *Five Plays: Thomas Middleton* (Harmondsworth, 1988), p. 15.

[51] See Renate Usmiani, 'Tremblay opus: Unity in diversity', *Canadian Theatre Review* 24 (1979), 26–38; Vivien Bosley, 'Diluting the mixture: Translating Michel Tremblay's *Les Belles-soeurs*', *TTR: traduction, terminologie, rédaction* 1 (1988), 139–45; Agnes Whitefield, ed., *Writing Between the Lines: Portraits of Canadian Anglophone Translators* (Waterloo, ON, 2006), esp. pp. 172, 184–5, 271–3; Louise Ladouceur, *Dramatic Licence: Translating Theatre from One Official Language to the Other in Canada*, trans. Richard Lebeau (Edmonton, 2012), esp. pp. 79–82.

[52] Bosley, 'Diluting the mixture', pp. 142–3.

suggesting that the two words are directly equivalent:

'Sblood a corruption of 'by God's blood', a religious oath with a similar emotional force to *fuck* in twenty-first century English.

However, there are problems with this approach. First, readers who are not native speakers of English may have trouble assessing the degree of emotion that attaches itself to words such as 'fuck'. Second, it is hard to imagine a student-orientated edition of the play – or even a full-scale Arden edition – using profanity in this way, given the general level of sensitivity to swearing that still prevails in Anglophone societies. Loughrey and Taylor's Middleton edition is a Penguin paperback, regularly used by students, and it was apparently published to little outcry;[53] but Middleton does not have the levels of educational and cultural prominence that Shakespeare retains. Simply put, it still matters more if you swear in a Shakespeare edition than in a Middleton one.

Taking these objections into account, here is another attempt at glossing Hamlet's use of ''sblood', referring to modern swearing in general rather than to specific words:

'Sblood a corruption of 'by God's blood'. Swearing on the body parts of the crucified Christ was the most extreme form of profanity available in early modern English and it had a similar force to the sexual and excremental oaths of twenty-first century English.

Better, perhaps, but a little wordy, and the word 'excremental' feels overblown. More importantly, this gloss does not tell us why Hamlet swears here, or precisely what the impact of his swearing might be. So we might adjust things:

'Sblood a corruption of 'by God's blood', one of the powerful and transgressive religious oaths that had a similar force to bodily oaths in twenty-first-century English. Hamlet uses *'sblood* twice (see 3.2.361, where it is also addressed to Rosencrantz and Guildenstern), and he also uses a similar oath, *'swounds* (2.2.511 and 5.1.263). In addition to conveying strong emotion, such oaths were often associated with youth, masculinity, high status and religious transgression.

So far, so good. But we might also want to say something about the censorship:

'Sblood a corruption of 'by God's blood', one of the powerful and transgressive religious oaths that had a similar force to bodily oaths in twenty-first-century English. Hamlet uses *'sblood* twice (see 3.2.361, where it is also addressed to Rosencrantz and Guildenstern), and he also uses a similar oath, *'swounds* (2.2.511 and 5.1.263). In addition to conveying strong emotion, such oaths were often associated with youth, masculinity, high status and religious transgression. These oaths were censored in F.

This note is getting bulky, perhaps too long even for an Arden edition. And I have yet to mention other aspects of profanity in *Hamlet*, such as the promissory function of oaths, the connection that is forged through language use between Hamlet and characters such as Iago, Falstaff or Mercutio, or the ways in which oaths might be animated and adapted in performance and translation. So perhaps this is the inevitable solution:

'Sblood a corruption of 'by God's blood', one of the powerful and transgressive religious oaths that had a similar force to bodily oaths in twenty-first-century English. On the uses of swearing in the play see the Introduction, pp. 30–40.

It is always easier to criticize than to offer solutions. Yet experimenting with ways of glossing Hamlet's swearing is useful because it reminds us of the role of the editor in conveying not simply meaning but also the broader social and cultural associations of words in Early Modern English. For many readers, a gloss on a word such as ''sblood' in an edition of *Hamlet* may be their only point of access to sixteenth- and seventeenth-century debates about the status of specific kinds of language or the

---

[53] Reviewing the edition, S. McCafferty praised the notes in particular: 'The footnotes to the plays are excellent for the general reader and offer a concise and modern interpretation, particularly of some of Middleton's more colourful oaths and sexual double meanings' (*Notes and Queries*, 37.1 (March 1990), 89–90; p. 90). However, Ann Thompson informs me that the publisher received at least one complaint.

relationship between language and broader structures of thought. It is therefore incumbent on editors to think outside the traditions of glossing that may attach themselves to specific plays, and to foreground the kinds of connections that may have been obvious to early modern spectators and readers but are obscure to us. We render Shakespeare's oaths silent and inarticulate if we fail to listen to them or to pay attention to their range of potential meanings.

In *The Skinhead Hamlet*, the Prince of Denmark's final words are 'I'm fucked. The rest is fucking silence' (5.2.13). The word 'fuck' and its cognates are crucial to the meaning of Curtis's parody: if readers do not know what it means, or understand something of its broader cultural associations, they will be wholly unable to comprehend or interpret this text. I do not make the same claim for *Hamlet* itself, or any of Shakespeare's plays. But swearing provides us with an important guide to the ways in which Shakespeare may have viewed his unruly protagonist, and it also alerts us to the broader network of ideas about language, society and faith with which he engages throughout his plays.

ANTIHONORIFICABILITUDINITATIBUS: *LOVE'S LABOUR'S LOST* AND UNTEACHABLE WORDS

ADAM ZUCKER

The 'Shakespeare's Unteachable Words' session at the 2016 World Shakespeare Conference came into being, as many good things do, during a conversation I had with Lucy Munro. We wondered together if we could imagine a panel that could combine my interest in pedantry with her current research on oaths, and it became a bit of a game to find a conceptual framework that was broad enough to contain our multitudes. Since, as the article that follows here will make clear, my own writing was beginning to revolve around difficult words (such as *honorificabilitudinitatibus*) and nonsensical constructions in the early printings of *Love's Labours Lost*, the idea of language that resisted ordinary acts of teacherly explication started to rise to the surface. Could there be such a thing, we asked ourselves, as a word or a class of language that was in some sense resistant to standard pedagogical practice? Do early modern oaths have a power that we can no longer identify or reasonably transmit? Do Latinate nonsense and scholastic in-jokes have a reasonable place in our world any more? And, as Indira Ghose went on to ask as she joined us in our efforts, is there any way to properly locate for our students the language of 'honesty' and 'honour' so central to early modern England's nascent ideas about class? These questions are all subsidiary lines stemming from what became our central theme: did Shakespeare write any unteachable words?

My own approach to this problem was directed in part by a few of Jacques Rancière's ideas about pedagogy, set out in the early pages of *The Ignorant Schoolmaster*. For Rancière (writing, admittedly, from a subject position defined by the French academy of the 1980s), the classroom is a scene of enforced stupidity or 'stultification', the term translator Kristen Ross uses for Rancière's '*abrutir*'. While those of us who are firmly interpellated into pedagogical scenarios by our own lifetimes of teaching and learning might see the act of teaching as a gift, or as a process of endowment, Rancière's analysis finds darker tones in the meeting of two minds:

> There is stultification whenever one intelligence is subordinated to another. A person—and a child in particular—may need a master when his own will is not strong enough to set him on track and keep him there. But that subjection is purely one of will over will. It becomes stultification when it links an intelligence to another intelligence. In the act of teaching and learning there are two wills and two intelligences. We will call their coincidence *stultification*.[1]

While this assessment is perhaps less directly applicable to the often conversational, dialogic classrooms of the early twenty-first century Anglophone world, the premise is worth holding up as a refractive lens for the problem of pedagogy in Shakespearean

---

[1] Jacques Rancière, *The Ignorant Schoolmaster: Five Lessons in Intellectual Emancipation*, trans. Kristin Ross (Palo Alto, CA, 1991; 1987), p. 13. For a useful condensed overview of that longer work, see Jacques Rancière, 'On ignorant schoolmasters,' in *Jacques Rancière: Education, Truth, Emancipation*, ed. Charles Wright and Gert J. J. Biesta (London, 2010), pp. 1–24.

contexts. We (and by that I mean today's classroom leaders) would not consider ourselves to be enforcing stupidity upon our students. But as we teach Shakespeare's works, we are always putting on display our own 'intelligences' – that is to say, our scholarly aptitudes, our personal or digital archives, our reservoirs of fact and practice that inform our work in our classrooms. That display, according to Rancière, can be useful as a process of explanation, but explanation itself always produces the stratifying distances that bring the idea of stupidity into being.

I would imagine that some readers of this chapter will respond to this idea the way I did when I first encountered it. 'That's not how I teach', I thought to myself. My own self-reflexive, self-conscious pedagogy, I would like to think, counteracts this stultifying effect. But Rancière would argue otherwise. The ignorant schoolmaster, in his model, begins teaching from a perspective devoid of expert knowledge. Students learn by being given materials to decode but they are not told how to decode them. They learn, in the Rancièrean hypothetical, without being told anything at all.[2]

What follows here is in no way an endorsement of this pedagogical model, though I do find it to be provocative in useful ways. I became a teacher in part because I take comfort from the solidifying fictions I can build out of facts, and I enjoy showing others how those fictions act on us in literary contexts. But while I am and always have been more than willing to share this process openly with my students, the explanation or narrating of fact itself has played an odd, secret role in my pedagogy and in my own teacherly psychology. The moment when a student clearly cannot understand something that I myself know, the moment when I say something like 'well, what Shakespeare means here is . . . ' or 'Actually, there's a joke about sixteenth-century animal husbandry here' or something along those lines, that 'teaching moment' is crucial, but it enacts over and over again the process that Rancière critiques in the *Ignorant Schoolmaster*. It is a moment that reminds everyone in the room that I know things and that they do not. Our relative intelligences are created in those moments, no matter how often I let them know that I, too, rely on marginal glosses and past classroom lessons to guide me through semantic problems as I wend my way through *Hamlet* for the 700th time. Horrifyingly, the practical conversations I use to put my students at ease about ignorance simply reinforce the point: I know a lot about how to learn Shakespeare. Rancière's terms are rough, but necessary and clarifying. Even at my charming professorial best, I stultify.

Out of all Shakespeare's comedies, *Love's Labours Lost* may be the one that is most interested in the relationship between ignorance and pedagogy. From the almost immediate failure of the King's Academy to the jests that are volleyed back and forth and forth and back again between lords and ladies and foresters and pages and clowns, nearly everyone in the play gets a chance to enact the Rancièrian exchange. Even the character named 'Dull' gets in a decent zinger at one point. And in what may be the clearest sign of the play's pedagogical engagements, a long list of critics have used the play to discuss the relative intelligence of Shakespeare himself, sorting through its classical in-jokes in pursuit of the school-boy life of Stratford's natural genius.[3] Of course, the focal points of all this in the play are the pedantic, pretentious, scholar-figures of Holofernes and Nathaniel, both of whom love nothing more than to explicate everything around them and every hard word they hear. These two characters are exemplary models for a certain kind of glossorial authority that we in our own roles as scholars, teachers, and editors often adopt as we curate or present Shakespeare's texts for readers and students. What follows here rests on the premise that we can

---

[2] Rancière's ur-Ignoramus is Joseph Jacotot, who, in the 1820s 'taught' a group of Flemish speakers French despite his inability to speak Flemish. He gave his students a bilingual translation of *Telemaque* and told them to learn what they could. Within six months, the story goes, they all understood French.

[3] See, most famously, the work of Thomas Spencer Baynes, *Shakespeare Studies* (London, 1894), and T. W. Baldwin, *William Shakspere's Small Latin and Lesse Greeke*, 2 vols. (Urbana, 1944).

learn quite a bit about our own silent assumptions pertaining to related forms of editorial and scholarly authority by pursuing the parallel courses that appear between our work and those of the ludicrous scholars in the forest of Navarre. We can, I will suggest, think more clearly about our own pedagogical biases if we look to the words or phrases in Shakespeare's plays (and especially in *Love's Labour's Lost*) that resist explanation, that may be unteachable in some way, and that mock us, as we push back against them.

EMPTY WORDS

The boundaries between stupidity and intelligence in *Love Labour's Lost* are often drawn by the material diversity of language, by unusual transactions between words that do things with their semantic content and words that mean nothing but do things just by simply being there.[4] Characters across the play's social spectrum use meaningless phrases to prove themselves in battles for the momentary currency of cleverness. In the first act, for example, Berowne ends a set of manly rhyme-wrestling within the newly forged Academy of Navarre with a phrase that no one around him understands:

KING.   How well he's read, to reason against reading.
DUMAINE. Proceeded well, to stop all good
    proceeding.
LONGAVILLE.   He weeds the corn and still lets grow
    the weeding.
BEROWNE.   The spring is near when green geese are
    a-breeding.[5]   (1.1.94–7)

When questioned about his joke, Berowne agrees with Dumaine that the phrase is 'In reason nothing', but it has just enough substance 'in rhyme' to fit into place. It is formally decorous, in other words, but it lacks functional semantic content. This combination turns out to be a deeply effective one. Berowne wins the boys' game by enacting, illustrating and exaggerating its meaninglessness. The ornate, lyrical wit most loved by the Academy is powerfully punctuated by Berowne's ability to stop making sense.

As a result, his nonsense helps construct a central organizing feature of the play's social hierarchy: Berowne's privilege is marked out, in part, by his ability to deploy semantically empty (and novel) language without being stained by it.[6]

At the other end of the play's imagined spectrum lies Costard, usually named in the early texts' speech-headings as a rustic 'Clown', whose job in the play is mainly to mis-deliver letters, misunderstand elaborate diction and get caught canoodling with Jaquenetta. Costard is also, however, the speaker of the linguistic equivalent of the pedantic Holy of Holies, the longest latinate term in all of Shakespeare and, indeed, one of the sixteenth century's favorite emblems of ludicrous suffixization: *honorificabilitudinitatibus*.[7] The literal meaning

---

[4] The most influential work for my thinking here includes William Carroll, *The Great Feast of Language in Love's Labour's Lost* (Princeton, 1976); Keir Elam, *Shakespeare's Universe of Discourse: Language Games in the Comedies* (Cambridge, 1984); Malcolm Evans, *Signifying Nothing: Truth's True Contents in Shakespeare's Texts* (Athens, GA, 1986), pp. 50–67; Patricia Parker, 'Preposterous reversals: *Love's Labor's Lost*', *Modern Language Quarterly* 54.4 (1993), 435–82; and Lynne Magnusson, 'Armado and the politics of English in *Love's Labour's Lost*', in *Shakespeare and the Cultures of Performance*, ed. Paul Yachnin and Patricia Badir (Burlington, VT, 2008), pp. 53–68.

[5] Unless otherwise noted, all citations from *Love's Labour's Lost* are taken from H. R. Woodhuysen, ed. *The Arden Shakespeare* (London, 1998).

[6] Occasionally, critics will mistake the social logic of the play for the true state of things. Here is one editor on the play's novel diction: 'Armado and Holofernes between them are responsible for the majority of these new words; but Biron is the third most important contributor to the total and, while their new words smell of the inkhorn, his do not. They appear as natural growths from the native soil of plain English usage. They need no gloss and have never needed one.' G. R. Hibbard, ed. *Love's Labour's Lost* (Oxford, 1990), pp. 36–7. What does an inkhorn smell like?

[7] For a (the?) thoroughgoing survey of the appearance of *honorificabilitudinitatibus* in medieval and Renaissance contexts, see the entry on the word on, strangely enough, Wikipedia.com. https://en.wikipedia.org/wiki/Honorificabilitudinitatibus (accessed May 2016). Thank you, anonymous contributors. Also relevant: Noel Malcolm's discussion on 'Macaronics, word-coining, gibberish, and coining' in the introduction to *The Origins of English Nonsense* (London, 1997), where he points

of the word is something like 'the state of being able to accept honours', but, importantly, this definition has absolutely nothing to do with the word's effect in the text. While there are many people in the play who speak Latin (more or less), Costard is definitively not one of them (see 3.1.132–6, where he decides that 'Remuneration' is 'the Latin word for three farthings'). Costard uses *honorificabilitudinitatibus* not to indicate someone's honorificabilituditnity, but rather to tell a joke about Moth's size:

I marvel thy Master hath not eaten thee for a word, for thou are not so long by the head as honorificabilitudinitatibus. Thou art easier swallowed than a flapdragon.
(5.1.38–41)

Costard works with *honorificabilitudinitatibus* like a modern English-speaking child works with *antidisestablishmentarianism*: to him, it means no more and no less than 'extremely long word'. It is a sound to be spoken with as many syllables as possible and then, figuratively, to be eaten.

There is, of course, a joke here for learned audience members or readers who might have encountered the word in other contexts, since the less-than-scholarly Costard would not be expected, from their perspective, to speak this way. Patricia Parker argues that moments like these in *Love's Labour's Lost* critique the values and language of elite culture by deflating or 'deforming' them.[8] This is true, but a differently valenced leveling effect is also at work. Audience members and readers (both in Shakespeare's time and in ours) need no particular education to laugh at the sound or sight of a huge word. Difficult Latin, in other words, can be funny to audiences who do not speak a word of it. It can be absolutely empty of content but still do its job.

Now – a bit of scholarly explication. If one wanted to be especially pedantic (and of course, I do), one could present a series of philological facts pertaining to this word. It appears in mainly scholastic contexts with varying degrees of irony beginning in the eighth century; it is used, most famously, by Erasmus in his *Adages* to poke fun at someone who loves long words and it had become by the later sixteenth century a clear marker for jokes about pedantry and ludicrous latinate terms. Fair enough. But while I am interested in all this, I am not sure it helps us understand the power of the term in *Love's Labour's Lost*. By the time we get to Shakespeare's day, the word's meaning or distant historical context has little to do with its purposes. John Marston, for example, uses it in *The Dutch Courtesan* in 1605 to let Crispinella compare another character's annoying 'discourse' to 'the long word *honorificabilitudinitatibus*: 'a great deale / Of sound and no sence'. Erasmian jokes and clerical winks are besides the point. No one seems to care what the word means at all.

The gigantic hollowed-out space of *honorificabilitudinitatibus* makes it seem a bit like a container waiting to be filled when it appears in *Love's Labour's Lost*. As a result, it has a fairly strange position in the work of people who feel that empty spaces should not exist in Shakespeare's plays. The term, most strikingly, became an elaborate staging ground for believers in the Baconian hypothesis. Following Isaac Hull Platt, Edward Durning-Lawrence and others saw in *honorificabilitudinitatibus* a central clue in the all-too-obvious ciphers that Sir Francis had left behind in the plays [Illustration 10].[9] Elizabethan courtiers certainly enjoyed playing games with anagrams but, as

---

out the link between Latinizing word games and Rabelais (p. 105). See also Anne Prescott, *Imagining Rabelais in Renaissance England* (New Haven, 1998).

[8] Parker's argument in 'Preposterous Reversals' (cited above) is worth quoting at length: 'If from the perspective of the higher social orders in this play, the appropriate response to Costard's (or Armado's) imperfect mastery of "manner and form" is mockery and ridicule, from another perspective these deformations, turnings, and varyings reflect on far more than the lower orders in the play: the "high" is brought "low" not only by the iterations of parodic mimickry but through exposures (such as the cheeky servant Moth's) of how open to manipulation are the forms themselves (how "preposterously" led by bodily desire, rather than, more loftily, the other way around), when such turning or varying becomes a means through which the pretensions of the aristocrats are themselves deflated' (p. 439).

[9] Sir Edward Durning-Lawrence, Bt. *Bacon is Shake-Speare* (London, 1910), p. 102. See also Isaac Hull Platt, *Are the*

> and that therefore the true solution of the meaning of the long word "Honorificabilitudinitatibus," about which so much nonsense has been written, is without possibility of doubt or question to be found by arranging the letters to form the Latin hexameter.
>
> HI LUDI F. BACONIS NATI TUITI ORBI
>
> These plays F. Bacon's offspring are preserved for the world.
>
> It is not possible to afford a clearer mechanical proof that
>
> THE SHAKESPEARE PLAYS ARE BACON'S OFFSPRING.
>
> It is not possible to make a clearer and more definite statement that
>
> BACON IS THE AUTHOR OF THE PLAYS.
>
> 10. Sir Edward Durning-Lawrence, Bt, *Bacon is Shake-Speare* (London, 1910), p. 102.

a tool of argumentation in this context, they are useless. Indeed, if we read the word as some kind of anagrammatic clue, we would have to consider the possibility that Shakespeare was trying to send us other messages about his identity such as 'I: A Fictitious Hindi Bobtail Urn' or 'Ti-Hi! A bobcat in a fur dilution is I' or even the rather more cryptic 'Lo! I hid a rabbinic unit! It is tofu', all of which are *also* complete anagrams of *honorificabilitudinitatibus*.[10]

Rabbinic ciphers aside, I do think the appearance of this word in the early printed editions of *Love's Labour's Lost* is a kind of clue – just not the sort that Durning-Lawrence and his co-religionists wanted it to be. The 1598 Quarto of *Love's Labour's Lost* (Q1) does, in fact, draw attention to the non-semantic force of the word by emphasizing its material letter-forms. Nearly every bit of Latin in the play is set in italics. Costard's honorificabilitudinitatibus is a notable exception.[11] Typographically speaking, in other words, the word does not perform as ordinary Latin. And why would it need to? The

Shakespeare Plays Signed by Francis Bacon? (Philadelphia, 1897), pp. 6–7.

[10] These anagrams (along with hundreds of thousands of other possibilities) can be revealed through tedious weeks and months of letter-arranging, or by visiting the Internet Anagram Server at http://wordsmith.org/anagram/ which does the job in three seconds or so.

[11] A qualification: the appearance of this word in roman type may have its roots in the exigencies of typesetting, rather than being a bit of print-shop or scribal interpretation – it is the final word on a line of prose, and there is no room for it on the next one down. It's possible that setting the word in italic type would have made it too long for the text block. It is also possible that the shop was running low on italic letters when they set this Latin-heavy forme. That said, the effect of the decision, whatever its cause, is to visually set this particular bit of Latin apart for a reader. For an excellent recent discussion of typographical variation in the printing of non-English in early modern playbooks, see Marjorie Rubright, 'Dutch impressions: The narcissism of minor differences in print', in *Doppelganger Dilemmas: Anglo-Dutch Relations in Early Modern English Literature and Culture* (Philadelphia, 2014), pp. 110–61. Thanks also to Claire Bourne for directing me toward the typographical oddities of early printings of *Love's Labour's Lost*.

nonsensical quality of the word is just as funny as its more abstruse scholastic reference – and for today's audiences it is certainly funnier. If we grant as much, Costard's joke performs in type and in sound as a levelling mechanism, inviting all kinds of people, learned and not, to laugh at its thirteen syllables. Sixteenth-century jokes that are organized by Latin and pedantry, in other words, are not only aimed at people who have spent time in school. The satirical thrust of nonsensical language does not always map onto or reinforce the kinds of social stratification that people invested in educational competencies sometimes take for granted in the Shakespearean text. Lynne Magnusson's ideas about the pleasures of linguistic multiplicity in *Love's Labour's Lost* and Parker's sense of the play's preposterous effects hold true even, or perhaps especially, when words themselves do extra-semantic work.[12]

These ideas might help shed light on one of the oddest editorial cruxes in *Love's Labour's Lost*. It is found in the conversation between Holofernes (here, 'Peda', for the stock figure 'Pedant') and Nathaniel (here, 'Curat') about Don Armado, whose ornate rhetorical stylings are simply too 'peregrinat' for their taste (square brackets indicate my insertions):

PEDA.   I abhorre such phanatticall phantasims, such insociable and point devise companions, such rackers of ortagriphie, as to speake dout sine [b], when he should say doubt; det when he shold pronounce debt; d e b t, not det: he clepeth a Calfe, a Caufe: a halfe, haufe: neighbour *vocatur* nebour; neigh abreviated ne: this is abhominable, which he would call abbominable, it insinuateth me of inf [s?]amie: *ne inteligis domine*, to make frantique lunatique?

CURAT.   *Laus deo, bene intelligo.*

PEDA.   *Bome boon for boon prescian*, a little scratcht, twil serve.[13]   (1598, F4r)

There are many typographical and syntactical mysteries in this passage (including the most ironic weird spelling in the Shakespeare canon – 'ortagriphie'), but it is the final bits of Latinesque nonsense that interest me here. '*Bome boon for boon prescian, a little scratcht twill serve*' is a showpiece of a textual tangle, and most editors view it as having

been unravelled. Theobald, in his edition of 1733, decided that Holofernes was responding to and correcting an error in Nathaniel's speech. He emends the line to '*Bone? Bone* for *bene*; Priscian, a little scratch; 'twill serve' (where 'Priscian' refers to the author of a well-known Latin grammar text).[14] Of course, all this assumes that Nathaniel has actually made the mistake of *saying* 'bone' for 'bene' one line earlier, which is not the case in Q or F. In order for Theobald to make sense of Holofernes's line, he had to un-edit Nathaniel's line and insert a grammatical error of his own into it. Bad Latin abounds, even when things look to have been set aright.

But I am more interested in the text's obvious problems than in their solutions. Where did this jumble come from? Was it the product of someone's mistake? If so, what is the nature of the error that led to it? These are not easy questions to answer with any certainty. The chain of transmission for the playtext is, as always, a bit of a mystery. There is general agreement that Q1 was based on the kind of manuscript we have come to call authorial 'foul papers', but even if this was definitively proven to be the case, we would have no idea how many people were involved in the series of events that led to the Bome-ing and the booning.[15] Did someone in William White's print shop misread the manuscript copy? Did someone mis-transcribe a playhouse or authorial manuscript

---

[12] See Parker, 'Preposterous' and Magnusson, 'Politics of English'.

[13] I've amended 'u' to 'v' but otherwise kept the spellings in Q1.

[14] On the pre-twentieth-century editorial history of this passage, see Horace Howard Furness, ed., *A New Variorum Edition of Shakespeare: Love's Labour's Lost* (Philadelphia, 1904), pp. 210–13.

[15] On the difficulties inherent to the designation 'foul papers' along with other terms used to describe lost print-shop manuscripts, see John Jowett's brief discussion in 'Editing Shakespeare in the twentieth century', in *Shakespeare Survey* 59 (Cambridge, 2006), pp. 1–19; pp. 9–13; and Paul Werstine's more thorough critique of those terms as they were set out by W. W. Greg, *Early Modern Playhouse Manuscripts*, esp. p. 50.

when he made a copy for the publisher? Was Shakespeare himself the source of the mess? Or was some other reviser, editor, actor or transcriber part of the chain of transmission? Exactly whose stupidity are we dealing with here?

Since we will never positively know the answer to this question, it might be worth lingering on the fairly solid premise that whoever set the type for the 1598 and Folio versions of *Love's Labour's Lost* likely did not see erroneous stupidity here. The extant copies of Q1 *Love's Labour's Lost*, as Paul Werstine has demonstrated, show evidence of stop-press corrections and, while it is unclear whether or not the forme that contains '*Bome boon for boon prescian*' was ever corrected (no variant states have been found), Werstine suspects that whoever dealt with the typesetting for *Love's Labour's Lost* had some knowledge of Latin.[16] With that in mind, he suggests the play's many extant errors in Latin case, number and spelling might have been left uncorrected on otherwise corrected formes because they were assumed to be part of the conventional, stage-pedant satire aimed at Holofernes and Nathaniel.[17] And while other kinds of errors in Q1 *Love's Labour's Lost* were changed when the Folio text was set (possibly, though not certainly, from a corrected or supplemented version of Q1), the strange passage was reprinted as is – and it was retained in F2 (1632), in which other errors in foreign languages that were retained in F1 were amended.[18] For at least a few early readers of *Love's Labour's Lost*, then, '*Bome boon for boon prescian*' seemed like a perfectly reasonable thing for Holofernes to say. That inexplicable line at that moment seemed to them to be as intelligent or, at the very least, as intelligible as anything else in the text they were creating. Scholars, apparently, sometimes say absolutely meaningless things.

POETIC NONSENSE

The kinds of questions Stephen Orgel pursues in his foundational brief essay 'The Poetics of Incomprehensibility' are clearly relevant here, though in a slightly different key. What if our impulse to make sense out of nonsense hides an important facet of a Shakespearean text? What if our 'commonsense' decision to perform our/Shakespeare's learnedness by clarifying obscurity and emending the impossible interferes with other kinds of meaning that shaped the reception of Shakespeare's plays in print and performance? For Orgel, these questions are inspired by cruxes caused by unclear diction or obscure constructions, not outright nonsense (e.g. Hermione's odd phrase 'strength of limit' in *The Winter's Tale*).[19] As a result, even in the midst of his brilliant critique of modern editors' Burkhardtian assumptions that the English Renaissance existed as 'an integrated culture that still spoke a universal language', Orgel has a tendency to preserve, if only partially, an underlying authority in the person of an intelligent Shakespeare: in every bit of textual obscurity, he suggests, 'the playwright must ... have meant something'.[20] As we have seen, however, in the case of *Love's Labour's Lost*, it is in no way clear that the earliest readers of the play would have felt this way. '*Bome boon for boon prescian*' is not obscure,

---

[16] Paul Werstine, 'Variants in the First Quarto of *Love's Labour's Lost*', *Shakespeare Survey 12* (Cambridge, 1979), 35–47. Werstine's supposition is based on the skill showed by White's shop with printing Latin text in other books, in addition to his observation that Latin goes uncorrected on formes which show evidence of careful proofreading elsewhere. This was, in his assessment, a case of educated non-correction.

[17] Werstine, 'Variants in the First Quarto', pp. 42–5.

[18] On F *Love's Labour's Lost*, see Stanley Wells, 'The copy for the Folio text of *Love's Labour's Lost*', *Review of English Studies*, n.s. 33, 130 (1982), 137–47 along with the critique of Wells's conclusions by Sonia Massai in *Shakespeare and the Rise of the Editor* (Cambridge, 2007), pp. 144–9. It is worth noting, too, that the title page of the 1598 edition advertises that the play has been 'Newly corrected and amended', suggesting that there may be a lost earlier edition of the play (Q0). If so, then this odd passage in the 1598 edition *might* have already survived one round of edits – though since we have no idea what the text of Q0 looks/looked like, it is impossible to say for sure.

[19] Stephen Orgel, 'The Poetics of Incomprehensibility', *Shakespeare Quarterly* 42 (1991), 432–7.

[20] Orgel, 'The poetics of incomprehensibility', pp. 437 and 436.

exactly. It does not prove an emotional state or confuse for the purpose of plot development. It is more like a bearer of non-signification, unlearned and not smart, yet passed over or accepted in edition after edition, meaning be damned.

There may, in fact, be a potentially learned reason for this nonsensical phrase to have seemed properly, even artfully, placed in the lines of Holofernes. There was a healthy tradition of poetic nonsense in the period, a tradition that sat adjacent to the satirical portraits of pedants and needless Latinate complexity in early modern England. Here, for example, is a commendatory poem written by Thomas Randolph for the 1630 edition of James Shirley's play *The Gratefull Servant*. The voice Randolph adopts borrows more than a bit from the figure of the stage-pedant:

> I cannot fulminate or tonitruate words;
> To puzz'le intellects my ninth lasse affords
> No sychophronian buskins, nor can straine
> Gargantuan lines to Gigantize thy veine,
> Nor make a iusiurand, that thy great playes
> Are terra del fo'gos or incognitae.
> Thy Pegasus in his admir'd carreere
> Curvets on Capreolls of nonsence here.[21]

Randolph's jokey fustian pedantism is an offshoot of the rich vein of seventeenth-century nonsense poetry documented at some length by Noel Malcolm in his anthology *The Origins of English Nonsense*.[22] Much of this poetry dances along the borderline of referential intelligence, though it is always, in the end, meaningless. Take this snippet from a John Taylor poem printed in his pamphlet *Sir Gregory Nonsense: His Newes from no place*:

> Then did the Turnetripes on the Coast of *France*
> Catch fifteen hundred thousand Grashoppers,
> With fourteene Spanish Needles bumbasted,
> Poach'd with the Egges of fourescore Flanders Mares,
> Mounted upon the foote of *Caucasus*,
> They whorld the footeball of conspiring fate[23]

Given this ludicrous mess, it might not be surprising to learn that Taylor's epistolary preface in *Sir Gregory Nonsense* begins with a familiar salutation to the pamphlet's entirely imaginary dedicatee, Master Trim Tram Senceles: 'Most *Honorificabilitudinitatibus*' (A3r). Nearly ten years earlier, Taylor had experimented with pedantic nonsense verse in a text that explicitly named the 'no place' from which Sir Gregory hailed: *Odcomb's Complaint: Or CORIATS funeral Epicedium ...*, which was printed in London, despite the mock colophon at the foot of the title page, 'Printed for merrie recreation, and are to be sold at the salvation in *Utopia*. 1613.' This pamphlet opens with a verse apology that makes Taylor sound at times like Berowne expounding upon the formal decorousness of his meaningless 'green geese' crack: 'I know my Dactils, and my Spondees well; / My true proportion, & my equal measure' (A3r). The point is more or less proven by the pamphlet's collection of nonsense poems written, ostensibly, to mourn the death of Thomas Coryate, author of the infamous travel text *Coryats Crudities* (1611). That book, in turn, is a veritable mother lode of nonsense verse that sounds quite like the impossible Latin of Holofernes. Among its many prefatory poems, *Coryats Crudities* contains several written in authentically structured nonsensical foreign languages. The most famous of the bunch is titled 'In the Utopian tongue', by Henry Peacham, and it begins with this truly mystifying couplet: 'Ny thalomin ythsi Coryate lachmah babowns / O Asiam Europans Americ-werowans.'[24] Not to be outdone, Taylor included an 'Epitaph in

---

[21] James Shirley, *The Gratefull Servant* (London, 1630), A3r. The text gives 'sychophronian'; pedants of my stripe will like to know that this is a misreading for 'lychophronian'.

[22] Malcolm, *Origins of English Nonsense*; for more on Taylor's nonsense projects, see Rebecca Fall, 'Popular nonsense, according to John Taylor and Ben Jonson', *Studies in English Literature* 57.1 (2017), 87–110; Carla Mazzio, *The Inarticulate Renaissance: Language Trouble in an Age of Eloquence* (Philadelphia, PA, 2009), esp. pp. 1–93; and, in a different vein, Stephen Booth, *Precious Nonsense: The Gettysburg Address, Ben Jonson's Epitaphs on His Children, and Twelfth Night* (Berkeley, 1998).

[23] John Taylor, *Sir Gregory Nonsence: His Newes from no place* (London, 1622), sig. B6r.

[24] Thomas Coryate, *Coryats Crudities* (London, 1611), sig. I1r.

the Utopian tongue' in *Odcomb's Complaint*, which begins 'Nortumblum callimūquash omystoliton quashte burashte, / Scribuke woshtay solusbay perambulatushte' (B3r).[25] That poem sits alongside an 'Epitaph in the Barmooda tongue, which must be pronounced with the accent of the grunting of the hogge' (a brief sample: 'Animogh trogh deradrogh maramogh hogh Flondrogh calpsogh' (B2v)).[26]

These experiments in quasi-exotic, placelessly foreign nonsense poetry tempt the scholar in all of us by being almost language. Like *Bome boon for boon prescian*, the Utopian or 'Barmoodan' lines of Taylor and Peacham arrange phonemes in believable sequences, luring readers (and editors) into trying to solve the puzzle of translation. The few times I have presented these poems on slides in public lectures, I have poked fun at my audience members, knowing that many of them were doing their best to parse them out or solve their seeming mysteries (I asked – they were). But as far as I can tell, the pieces of these puzzles add up to no more and no less than a particularly effective kind of scholar bait, an emptiness that acts on us, that jibes at us, that tests us with its nothing. If words can have agency, these are just begging to be glossed.

On at least one occasion, they were. One nonsense poem in *Coryats Crudities* presents its own helpful scholar in its margins, like Spenser's 'collaborator' E. K. in the *Shepheardes Calendar*. But whereas E. K. generally makes sense, the glossing voice in John Hoskins's 'Cabalisticall verses' intervenes in an entirely meaningless context, defining in some detail the word 'Gymnosophist,' but leaving unexplained the remainder of the poem, including, for example, its reference to 'your equinoctial pasticrust / Proiecting out a purple chariot wheele'.[27] Hoskins's marginal gloss on 'Gymnosophist' holds the gesture of annotation up to the satirical gaze, manipulating and exposing scholarly credit by ironizing it.[28] The joke here not only pokes fun at pedants who take their classical vocabularies a bit too seriously, but it also brings its wide range of readers into a knowing community that might now recognize, whatever their level of education, that there are different styles or dispositions in the social field defined by what Carsten Madsen has called the 'hermeneutic gesture' of the gloss.[29] There is, again, a joke for more learned readers built into the accessible premise – the first 'Utopian' poem, which appeared in the earliest editions of Thomas More's *Utopia*, contains the word 'Gymnosophoan' in the midst of its own nonsense language. But as is the case with Costard's 'honorificabilitudinitatibus', one does not really need to be formally educated to learn from this glossing joke. A marginal definition of nothing can function quite well as a joke on its own terms. We do not need to be experts on noplace for it to do its work.

SENSIBLE IN THE DULLER PARTS

Modern editors and teachers tend to not engage with this kind of contextual nonsense when they decide how to handle obscure, meaningless passages in Shakespeare. Generally speaking, we share Theobald's assumption that something as disorganized as '*Bome boon for boon prescian*' could not be

---

[25] The tilde in 'callimūquash' stands in for the printer's mark indicating that the word has been shortened to save space on the line (usually an N or M has been omitted). But in this case, it is hard to know exactly what is missing here. What is the longer version of this imaginary, non-existent word? Ask John Taylor.

[26] For recent work on Coryate and the prefatory poems that appeared in (and out of) his *Crudities*, see Michelle O'Callaghan, *The English Wits: Literature and Sociability in Early Modern England* (Cambridge, 2007), pp. 102–52; Anthony Parr, *Renaissance Mad Voyages: Experiments in Early Modern English Travel* (Burlington, VT, 2015), pp. 165–76; and Katharine Craik, 'Reading *Coryats Crudities* (1611)', *SEL* 44 (2007), 43–69.

[27] Coryate, sig. e6r. Sir Andrew Aguecheek uses similar language as he recalls Feste joking around about 'the Vapians passing the equinoctial of Queubus' (2.3.23).

[28] On the ways in which authors and readers sort through and create meaning in glosses, see Jane Griffith, *Diverting Authority: Experimental Glossing Practice in Manuscript and Print* (Oxford, 2015).

[29] Carsten Madsen, 'The Rhetoric of Commentary', *Glossator* 3 (2010), 19–30.

a purposeful or, at the very least, a meaningful element in a Shakespearean text. There are, I have suggested, good reasons for our resistance to nonsense of this sort. But as we pursue attempts to undo textual tangles, we should do so for reasons other than the less-than-clear idea that they (and their entanglers) interfere with our access to the performance of Shakespeare's learnedness. If we use the Shakespearean text as a screen onto which we project our most knowledgeable selves, if we ignore the cultural place of obscurity or nonsense, we run the risk of reproducing Holofernes's and Nathaniel's own pedantic errors in *Love's Labour's Lost*. Those imaginary scholars are infuriated by nonsensical constructions which disrupt their fantasy of an ideal, cogent style. Nathaniel's assessment of Dull's capabilities sets out the broader social logic at play here. Listen for the echoes of Rancière's stultified brute:

Sir, he hath never fed of the dainties that are bred in a book. He hath not eat paper, as it were; he hath not drunk ink. His intellect is not replenished. He is only an animal, only sensible in the duller parts. And such barren plants are set before us that we thankful should be – which we of taste and feeling are – for those parts that do fructify in us more than he. (4.2.24–9)

Shakespeare here simultaneously enacts and mocks the familiar pattern in which one person's presumably poor performance is used to set off the skills possessed by 'we of taste and feeling'. Nathaniel does it to Dull. We all do it to Nathaniel, when we laugh at his pretentions. But as we critique the figure of the pedant, and as we seek to identify or clarify the errors of Holofernes or Nathaniel or Shakespeare or a compositor both in text and in sociable performance, we should be clear that a larger set of relationships is at stake. The satirical figure of the pedant always offers more than just a satire of pedantry. The gloss always offers more than a helpful explanation. Both help create our understanding of the practice of teaching and learning in which different styles and textual markers structure a larger field. Our classifications or ranked judgements of teachers, students, texts, and modes of education can mask (if we adapt a Bourdieuvian frame) a wider network of economic or political relationships that subtend or structure the limits of stylistic possibility built into the educational field.[30] When we read the pedant in *Love's Labour's Lost*, when we teach the outlines of the early modern educational field, when we separate out the stupid labour of a print-house compositor from a hypothetically intelligent Shakespearean copytext, and when we explain the true meaning of a meaningless phrase, we are likewise contributing to the history of our own emplacement within educational institutions and their corollary networks. This process should be named as such.

As I hope I have begun to suggest here, our own performances of knowledge in these contexts are deeply pressured by the incomprehensible hybrid Latinglish in the early printings of *Love's Labour's Lost*. When we work to erase it, to render the words of our pedants sensible, we draw lines that do not simply reveal the differences between the stupid and the smart, or the knowing and the unknowing, but rather bring those categories into being.[31] It is all too easy to use these categories to fill the empty spaces of St Paul's churchyard with shadowy compositors and scribes, all standing between us and Shakespeare's educated genius. It is easy, too, to fill our classrooms with imagined students who cannot understand what our own fine brains have to offer. But rather than honoring ourselves, what if we attempt to find a bearing marked by being *antihonorificabilitudinitatibus* in these scenarios? Complex knowledge and explication is never the only route to textual, semantic or comic clarity. We do not have to be masters of figure and trope and Latin to understand the joke of the pedant figure; we do not have to be well-versed in *sententiae* culled from Horace or Cicero or simple school-room dialogues to enjoy *Love's Labour's Lost*; we do not have to have been taught by

---

[30] See, for example, Pierre Bourdieu, *The State Nobility: Elite Schools in the Field of Power*, trans. Lauretta Clough (Palo Alto, CA, 1996).

[31] Cf. Rancière, *The Ignorant Schoolmaster*, p. 6.

a ponderously self-obsessive language-twister or a terrible punster to get the mockery that is aimed at Holofernes. The point of all these difficult terms, especially in performance as words float into being, is not just to wink at audience members who have been in school. Satirical pedantry, like other forms of art or text that depict differences based on cultural competencies, can incorporate new knowledge communities in audiences and readers, regardless of their previous experience with school-room pedantry itself. If early modern drama really was able to inflect the political life or affiliations of its participants, if drama could re-form social communities into new arrangements without explicitly setting out to do so, stage pedants might be seen as exemplary figures in that process. I hope that lesson can still be learned by us, as we think about our own places in contemporary life as teachers of a subject and, more particularly, of an author who is on the one hand a standard-bearer of privileged culture but is also on the other hand a metonymic figure for a caricatured pedantry within the academy.

In the classroom, we might perform Shakespeare's unteachable words in ways that permit them to be just that. We might hold up their incomprehensibility not as something that always needs to be squashed out of existence in an edition or explicated into sense but use them rather as the tools they are, use them to animate comic scenarios in which teachers and students share in the pleasure of befuddlement. In our time of deep confusion, we might find ways to let a comic fog do its job, even as we clarify for ourselves and our communities the political stakes of knowledge and our struggle to put it to good ends.

SHAKESPEARE AND WHO? AESCHYLUS, *EDWARD III* AND THOMAS KYD

GARY TAYLOR, JOHN V. NANCE, AND KEEGAN COOPER

What we call 'objectivity' might be better understood as the practical application of ignorance. An 'objective' investigation begins by acknowledging that there are things that the investigators do not know but *want* to know. Objectivity is always motivated and hence subjective; we can thus always deconstruct the binary implicit in any claim to objectivity. But in pursuit of a packet of desired knowledge, 'objective' investigators construct an experiment that carefully preserves and contains their ignorance, so that the ignorance does not leak out and contaminate the results. Such contamination is what we call 'bias'. Bias is simply ignorance masquerading as knowledge. Objectivity instead unmasks, frames and uses its own ignorance.

For instance: we do not know who wrote most of *Edward III*. A strong, long-lasting, expanding consensus among attribution specialists and editors makes us confident that Shakespeare wrote the sequence in which the Countess of Salisbury resists the adulterous advances of King Edward.[1] But we have no such confidence about the authorship of the rest of the play. The plural pronoun 'we' in the preceding sentence refers to the community of Shakespeare scholars, generally, but also in particular to the three authors of this chapter. When we began our investigation, we did not have any opinions about who wrote most of *Edward III*.

But Brian Vickers knows. He is adamant that most of *Edward III* was written by Thomas Kyd.[2] He also knows that Kyd wrote most of *1 Henry VI*, and all of *Arden of Faversham*, *Fair Em* and *King Leir*. His certainty is enviable and hard to resist; his global claims are exciting. If Vickers is right, then he will, with a single hypothesis, have solved a whole series of important attribution problems and thereby reshaped our understanding of the rise of English commercial drama in the late 1580s and early 1590s. His claim would also make all five plays more interesting: it would relate them to each other and to the Kyd canon. It would enable us to tell good new stories about five plays that are currently seldom discussed or taught at all. There is already strong, widely accepted evidence for Shakespeare collaborating with George Peele (in *Titus Andronicus*), Thomas Nashe (in *1 Henry VI*), and Christopher Marlowe (in various scenes of the *Henry VI* plays); adding Kyd to the roster would make the group portrait of Shakespeare's early collaborators more diverse and complete. Like Gary Taylor's enthusiasm for Thomas Middleton, Vickers's advocacy of Kyd attempts to reshape the intellectual and literary landscape by insisting on the importance of an underappreciated artist.

Nevertheless, the methods used by Vickers to defend his expansion of the Kyd canon have been cogently challenged by other attribution

---

[1] For an overview of scholarship on Shakespeare's presence, see Will Sharpe, 'Authorship and Attribution', in *William Shakespeare and Others: Collaborative Plays*, ed. Jonathan Bate et al. (New York, 2013), pp. 663–70.

[2] Brian Vickers, 'The Two Authors of *Edward III*', in *Shakespeare Survey 67* (Cambridge, 2014), pp. 102–18.

scholars.[3] Although they may seem complex, his arguments all depend on a simple algorithm, that is, a prescribed sequence of precise actions:

1. Decide/intuit who the author of an anonymously published or disputed target text is most likely to be.
2. Search that target text for parallels with the work of that expected author (using plagiarism software).
3. Take the list of parallels you find in step two, and check them against a large database (a private database of fifty-five plays).
4. Count the number of parallels that result from steps 2 and 3.
5. Declare that the result is 'a sufficient number'.
6. Use that 'sufficient number' as a baseline to establish the authorship of other test samples.

Unfortunately, no number supplied by this method would be sufficient to establish the authorship of any text, because the initial step predetermines the chosen candidate. The larger database is used only to identify which of the chosen parallels is most unusual. The Vickers algorithm is unreliable because it does not provide comparable figures for all other potential candidates – a much more daunting task. To avoid such self-defeating circularity, we use a different algorithm:

1. Do not assume that you know the author of the anonymously published or disputed target text (in this case, passages from *Edward III* that are not widely attributed to Shakespeare).
2. Use databases and search engines that are publicly available, so that other scholars can replicate your methods and check your reported results.
3. Find a method that correctly identifies the known author of a sample of dramatic writing comparable to the target text, distinguishing the known author from all other candidate playwrights working in the relevant period.
4. Apply the same method to the target text of unknown authorship.

The advantage of our method is that it frames and contains our ignorance. The database does not know, or care, who is the real author and neither does the search engine. People did not design the databases or search engines to prove that Kyd or Marlowe or Shakespeare or anyone else wrote certain parts of certain texts.

In this case, we have chosen as our target text the material in *Edward III* to which Vickers devotes most of his article: the passage from the second entry of the Mariner, to the end of his long speech reporting the defeat of the French navy (4.137–84). That is, we have let Vickers choose the target sample, to ensure that our results can be easily compared with his. In testing that sample, we have used publicly available databases and search engines (Literature Online and EEBO-TCP) to identify sequences of two to four consecutive words ('n-grams') or juxtapositions of two or more semantically significant words within ten words of one another ('collocations'). These databases and methods have, in previous studies, successfully identified the known author of dramatic passages by Shakespeare, Marlowe and Peele (all known to have been writing for the commercial theatre before 1595), and by Dekker, Jonson, Heywood, Middleton, Rowley, Webster and Wilkins (all known to have been writing plays after 1594).

However, it is possible that this method would not work for Kyd, simply because less of his undisputed dramatic writing survives. Kyd's name is confidently associated with only three plays: *The Spanish Tragedy*, *Solyman and Perseda* and *Cornelia* (a loose translation/adaptation of a French play by Robert Garnier). At the outset of this investigation, we simply did not know whether Kyd's three plays were a canon large enough to produce reliable results in any test that depends on rare n-grams and collocations. In fact, earlier studies have established that differences in canon size can warp the results of some tests.[4] Because Vickers concentrates on the relationship between *Edward III* and *Cornelia*, we decided to take our control sample from *Cornelia*. It is the only

---

[3] See MacDonald P. Jackson, *Determining the Shakespeare Canon* (Oxford, 2014), and essays by Gabriel Egan and MacDonald P. Jackson in *Shakespearian Authorship: A Companion to the New Oxford Shakespeare* (Oxford, 2017).
[4] See Gary Taylor, 'Empirical Middleton: *Macbeth*, adaptation, and micro-attribution', *Shakespeare Quarterly* 65 (2014), 239–72.

play attributed to Kyd in his lifetime; as a translation, it would seem the least likely to supply reliable proof of authorship, so if *Cornelia* can be correctly identified, then anything else by Kyd should also be identifiable by the same methods. Because Vickers focuses on the literary and theatrical genre of the 'messenger speech', we chose for a control test the long messenger speech from *Cornelia* that he links, stylistically, to the Mariner's speech in *Edward III*. Because other tests have used sample sizes of 173 consecutive words, we tested the first 173 words of the messenger speech in *Cornelia* (5.47–79, 'Caesar, that ... marcht on'). In order to maximize Kyd's chances, we limited our database to plays written in the ten years from 1585 (widely considered to be the earliest possible date for *The Spanish Tragedy*) to 1594 (the year of his death, and of the publication of *Cornelia*).[5] We found twenty-four parallels unique to one other play first performed in those ten years.[6] Eight are linked to playwrights with a single unique parallel. Shakespeare and Marlowe each have two; Lodge has two or three (depending on his share of the collaborative *Looking Glass*); two anonymous plays, *Leir* and *Locrine*, have two apiece. Obviously, a single unique parallel, or two unique parallels, is not sufficient to determine authorship. Only two playwrights indisputably have more than two parallels to this passage: Peele with three, and Kyd with five. The majority of Kyd's parallels (three) come from *The Spanish Tragedy*. One play by Kyd has as many parallels as the entire dramatic canon of the nearest alternative candidate.

This control sample from *Cornelia* tells us that the test can successfully identify Kyd's writing, and it provides us with an empirical basis for a prediction of the results we should expect to find in the comparable messenger speech from *Edward III*, if it is indeed Kyd's work.

This *Edward III* passage could be tested in a variety of ways. We began by examining the first 173 words of the Mariner's speech; these results were reported at the World Shakespeare Congress in August 2016. Subsequently, we tested the whole passage, dividing it in half (184 words to 183 words), or into two samples of 173 words with an uncounted residue. But the results were always the same. Whether we consider this as one long sample, or two standard-sized samples, or two equal samples, it does not in any way resemble the control passage from *Cornelia*.

Marlowe is the most likely author, though he is not far ahead of Shakespeare. There are nineteen unique parallels in Marlowe's uncontested work, and another eleven in texts that he probably wrote (*Dido*, the 1616 text of *Faustus*, *1 Henry VI* 5.4 and 5.7, and *2 Henry VI* 4.5). By contrast, there are only sixteen uncontested Shakespeare parallels. No recent attribution scholarship gives Shakespeare the Marlovian scenes in *1 Henry VI*, so removing those from the Marlowe column would not put them in the Shakespeare canon. Vickers does not accept Marlowe's authorship of any of the Cade scenes in *2 Henry VI* but that only affects one parallel, and three different kinds of empirical evidence have all independently pointed to Marlowe's authorship of 4.5.[7] As Taylor and Nance noted in 2015, Marlowe and Shakespeare resemble each other, lexically, more than either resembles any other playwright of the period 1576–95.[8] So it would not be surprising that

---

[5] We used the dates in Martin Wiggins and Catherine Richardson, *British Drama 1533–1642: A Catalogue*, vols. 2 and 3 (Oxford, 2014), except in a few cases where the New Oxford Shakespeare, more recently, reaches different conclusions. We did not include closet plays by writers (like Mary Sidney) not associated with the commercial theatres.

[6] Due to the spatial constraints of this volume, we are unable to list the parallels here. Full data for our tests of *Cornelia* and *Edward III* are available from the authors.

[7] See Hugh Craig's chapter on *Henry VI* in Hugh Craig and Arthur Kinney, *Shakespeare, Computers, and the Mystery of Authorship* (New York, 2009), pp. 69–77; John V. Nance, '"We John Cade": Shakespeare, Marlowe, and the Authorship of *2 Henry VI* 4.2.33–189', *Shakespeare*, http://dx.doi.org/10.1080/17450918.2015.1102166 (published online 17 December 2015); Santiago Segarra, Mark Eisen, Gabriel Egan and Alejandro Ribeiro, 'Attributing the authorship of the *Henry VI* plays by word adjacency', *Shakespeare Quarterly* 67 (2016), 232–56.

[8] Gary Taylor and John V. Nance, 'Imitation or collaboration? Marlowe in the early Shakespeare canon', in *Shakespeare Survey 68* (Cambridge, 2015), 32–47.

a passage written by Marlowe would also contain many Shakespeare parallels (but fewer than Marlowe). No passage indisputably by Shakespeare has been shown to have fewer Shakespeare than Marlowe parallels.

But even though Shakespeare probably did not write this passage, he is a much more plausible candidate than Kyd, whose nine parallels barely separate him from Peele or Greene. Peele has eight uncontested parallels, and one probable but uncertain one; there are also two unique parallels in *Troublesome Reign*, which Vickers assigns to Peele.[9] If Vickers is right about *Troublesome Reign*, then his own hypothesis there argues against his claim for Kyd's authorship here. Greene, with seven undisputed parallels, and another two that are less certain, may also equal Kyd's total. This whole pattern radically differs from the *Cornelia* control sample.

The results are equally clear if we look, not at overall totals, but at the clustering of parallels in individual plays. A focus on individual plays should work to the advantage of a playwright with a small canon. Twelve different plays, by at least seven different authors, have three unique parallels apiece. Obviously, in a sample this size (367 words), three parallels in a single play are not remarkable, and do not constitute reliable authorship evidence. In contrast, eight plays have more than three unique parallels: *Richard III* (nine), *2 Tamburlaine* (seven), *1 Tamburlaine* (six), *1 Henry VI* (six), Marlowe and Nashe's *Dido* (four), and the anonymous *Famous Victories* and *Locrine* (four each). Four parallels in a single play do not look like good evidence either. But Shakespeare's *Richard III* has as many as all Kyd's plays put together. It has three times more than any single play by Kyd, Peele, Green, or Nashe; both Marlowe's *Tamburlaine* plays have twice as many. In the collaborative *1 Henry VI*, only one parallel can be confidently attributed to Shakespeare; the rest all come from scenes demonstrably not Shakespearian, and probably written by Marlowe. Like the total number of parallels overall, the evidence of parallels clustered in a single play strongly points to either Shakespeare or Marlowe as author of the Mariner episode. The largest ratio of parallels to word totals would point to two plays by Marlowe; the largest concentration of plays with high numbers would also point to Marlowe.

Another way to analyze this evidence would be to give greatest weight to parallels that, in addition to being unique in plays written between 1585 and 1594, do not appear in any non-dramatic texts printed in that decade. Marlowe has five such parallels (three in *Edward II*, two in *Jew of Malta*). By contrast, Shakespeare has only two (both in *Richard III*), as do Kyd and Peele. Two such exceptionally rare parallels in a single dramatic canon is, self-evidently, not reliable evidence. Nor is two such parallels in a single play (as happens in both *Richard III* and *Jew of Malta*). But only one play contains more than two, and only one dramatic canon has more than three overall, and both exceptions point to Marlowe.

We might also consider cases where more than one play in the decade contains a parallel with this passage, but both such plays were written by the same author: the parallel is then not unique to a single play, but is unique to a single author. If we included such parallels, Kyd would gain nothing, but Peele would add two parallels (putting his total higher than Kyd's), *David and Bethsabe* and *3 Henry VI* would both move into the category of plays with more than three unique parallels, and the non-Shakespearian, probably Marlovian scenes of *1 Henry VI* would have six parallels (as many as *1 Tamburlaine*). Marlowe's overall total would rise to thirty-two and Shakespeare's to eighteen (more than double Kyd's).

Finally, we might consider cases where there is no unique parallel in the drama of that decade, but there is a unique parallel in non-dramatic works searchable in EEBO-TCP. Most of those parallels are clearly irrelevant but a small number were written by authors who were also working in the

---

[9] Brian Vickers, 'The *Troublesome Raigne*, George Peele, and the date of *King John*', in *Words that Count: Essays on Early Modern Authorship in Honor of MacDonald P. Jackson*, ed. Brian Boyd (Newark, 2004), pp. 78–116.

commercial theatres. One such parallel for Peele would increase his lead over Kyd. But the four unique non-dramatic parallels provided by Lodge make him the most conspicuous playwright in this list, in contrast to writers with large canons of poetry and prose published in the decade (Greene, Peele, Nashe and Shakespeare). Shakespeare's two long narrative poems should, in this test, give him an advantage over Marlowe, none of whose poetry was published by 1594. But it does not.

Attention to unique non-dramatic parallels also bears other, unexpected fruit. The collocation 'were … to give them way' does not appear in any of the plays of the decade but does show up in a single non-dramatic text: the English translation of Petruccio Ubaldini's *A discourse concerninge the Spanishe fleete inuading Englande in the yeare 1588* (STC 24481, 1590). Karl P. Wentersdorf identified this as a source of the play, and in particular of the Mariner's reference to 'the *Nonpariglia*, that braue ship' (4.177).[10] No such ship is identified in any of the sources for the naval battle in Edward III's reign, but Ubaldini refers to 'the ship called the *Non Pariglin*' (sic, bottom of page 12). The New Oxford Shakespeare accepted Wentersdorf's evidence that this scene alludes to the English defeat of the Spanish Armada but was sceptical about the relevance of the 1590 pamphlet; after all, the 1588 victory must have been a topic of conversation and gossip among most Englishman.[11] Nevertheless, the Ubaldini translation follows its reference to *The Nonpareil* with the sentence 'the Spaniards were all enforced to giue them waie' (p. 13). This is a uniquely strong parallel for the Mariner's following 'That we perforce were fain to give them way' (4.182). It therefore seems to establish that the author of the Mariner's speech did indeed get details of the 1588 naval battle from the 1590 pamphlet and hence was writing after 13 October 1590 (when the Ubaldini text was entered in the Stationers' Register).

The issue of the scene's sources is also important to its attribution. Vickers devotes much of his argument to establishing parallels between the Mariner's speech and Senecan messenger speeches, as though the influence of Seneca itself was evidence for Kyd's authorship. He is not alone in making that assumption, which in fact goes back to Edmond Malone.[12] But Martin Wiggins identifies Seneca as an influence on nineteen dramatic texts, besides *Edward III*, composed in 1585–94.[13] Eleven are plays written for the commercial theatre, including two by Shakespeare, two by Marlowe, two by Greene, and the only extant play by Kyd (*Spanish Tragedy*). Of those other Senecan plays, one has the most unique verbal parallels to this passage (Shakespeare's *Richard III*), and another has the most verbal parallels that are unique both among dramatic and non-dramatic texts (Marlowe's *Edward II*). The Senecan aspects of the Mariner's speech, analyzed by Vickers, are entirely compatible with authorship by Shakespeare or Marlowe – or Greene, Nashe, Peele and Anonymous.

However, Seneca did not invent the theatrical convention of the epic narrative speech by an anonymous messenger describing tragic offstage events, including battles. That goes back to the earliest extant Greek tragedies.[14] Indeed, the most obvious classical source for this episode in *Edward III* is Aeschylus's *Persae* ('The Persians'), performed in 472 BCE.[15] In both plays, a messenger narrates, from the perspective of defeat, and the perspective of the enemies of the play's audience, the events of a disastrous offstage naval battle. Both messengers report the result of that battle before depicting it. This places the

---

[10] Karl P. Wentersdorf, 'The date of *Edward III*', *Shakespeare Quarterly* 16 (1965), 227–31.
[11] Gary Taylor and Rory Loughnane, 'Canon and chronology', in *Shakespearian Authorship*, p. 505d.
[12] See the critique of Malone's assumption that 'Senecan' means 'written by Kyd' in Terri Bourus, *Young Shakespeare's Young Hamlet: Print, Piracy, and Performance* (New York, 2014), pp. 159–64.
[13] Wiggins, *British Drama*, items 783, 797, 810, 813, 839, 848, 854, 857, 865, 885, 904, 914, 915, 927, 928, 938, 941, 943, 950.
[14] James Barrett, *Staged Narrative: Poetics and the Messenger in Greek Tragedy* (Berkeley, 2002), pp. 56–102.
[15] H. D. Broadhead, ed., *The Persae of Aeschylus* (Cambridge, 1960). The most poetically interesting modern translation is Aeschylus, *Persians*, trans. and ed. Janet Lembke and C. J. Herington (New York, 1981).

dramatic emphasis on description – or, the poetics of making the invisible visible – as opposed to a purely informational account to move the plot. These structural similarities might, theoretically, be coincidental, the result of different playwrights, confronted with similar historical materials, independently solving a dramatic problem by similar means. However, before the battle King John compares his invading army to that of Xerxes: 'By land, with Xerxes we compare of strength, Whose soldiers drank up rivers in their thirst' (4.56–7). Xerxes is the protagonist of the Athenian tragedy. Only two English playwrights working in 1585–94 refer to him: Lodge in his non-dramatic *Catharos*, who imagines Xerxes talking with Hannibal, and Marlowe, whose Tamburlaine compares his future army to 'The host of Xerxes, which by fame is said / To drink the mighty Parthian Araris' (*1 Tamburlaine* 2.4). Marlowe's is obviously the closer parallel to *Edward III*.

Marlowe's knowledge of Xerxes might have come from a variety of historical sources. But King John more specifically boasts that the French navy has 'a thousand sail' (4.1). This number contradicts the play's historical sources: Holinshed reports that the French 'assembled a nauie of foure hundred ships'.[16] But 'a thousand' matches the size of Xerxes's invading Persian fleet in Aeschylus: 'For the whole number of the ships of Hellas amounted to ten times thirty, and apart from these, there was a chosen squadron of ten. But Xerxes, this I know, has under his command a thousand.'[17] Not all the historical sources agreed with this number: Plutarch's *Moralia*, available in an Elizabethan translation, gave Xerxes '1200', a number which also appears in many other classical authors. But Aeschylus, Ctesias and Plato all refer to one thousand, and a playwright who could read any of those Greek authors would be most likely to choose the playwright Aeschylus.[18] So the author of the Mariner's speech in *Edward III* seems to have presented the French navy defeated at Sluys not only in terms of the Spanish fleet defeated by the English in 1588 but also in terms of the Persian fleet defeated by the Athenians at Salamis in 480 BCE.

Historically, both victorious navies made tactical use of a narrow waterway and night operations. But at Sluys the French were trapped in a harbour; at Salamis the battle was instead confined to the channel between an island and the mainland, and *Edward III* likewise refers not to a harbour but to 'the sea whose channel filled' (4.161). *Edward III*, unlike Holinshed or Herotodus (or Ubaldini), does not focus on the importance of military tactics; instead, like *Persae*, it turns those aspects of the battle into occasions for atmospheric poetry:

when the sun had ceased to illumine the earth with his beams, and darkness had covered the precincts of the sky, they should bring up in serried order the main body of the fleet ... When the light of the sun had faded and night drew on ... When, however, radiant day with her white coursers shone over the land ... Ships had been crowded in the narrows ... hemmed them in and battered every side ... The hulls of our vessels rolled over and the sea was hidden from our sight, strewn as it was with wracks and slaughtered men. The shores and reefs were crowded with our dead ... and groans and shrieks filled the open sea until the face of sable night hid the scene.[19]

> Then 'gan the day to turn to gloomy night,
> And darkness did as well enclose the quick
> As those that were but newly reft of life...
> Purple the sea whose channel filled as fast
> With streaming gore that from the maimed fell...
> Then might ye see the reeling vessels split
> And, tottering, sink into the ruthless flood
> Until their lofty tops were seen no more.

---

[16] Raphael Holinshed et al., *The Third Volume of Chronicles* (1587), 358.

[17] *Persae*, 341 (*xilias*); translation from Aeschylus, *Persians*, ed. and trans. Herbert Weir Smith, Loeb Classical Library (Cambridge, MA, 1988), 139. Aeschylus continues with a subordinate clause ('while those exceeding in speed were twice a hundred, and seven more'). But this supplementary distinction is ambiguous and confusing, and it is easy to understand why later writers sometimes ignored it, producing the simple round number 'a thousand'.

[18] Plato, *Laws*, III.699; the *Persica* of Ctesias is only partially preserved in Photius's *Epitome*.

[19] *Persae*, 382–428; Smith, *Persians*, 343–5.

An essential component of the Aeschylean messenger speech is its invocation of the language of the epic tradition.[20] For an Elizabethan playwright, there were classical and specifically epic precedents for associating the carnage of battle, and specifically blood spilt in the course of war, with the colour purple. Arthur Hall's 1581 translation of the *Iliad* – the only English translation before Chapman's partial translation in 1598 – includes four images of this type: the bigram 'purple gore' occurs twice and blood is twice described as 'purple'. The translator accurately reflects Homer's uses of *porphura* (from which 'purple' is etymologically derived). These and many other Elizabethan examples demonstrate that there is nothing particularly remarkable about the use of 'purple' here in *Edward III*, or the similar use of 'purple gore' in the General's speech in *The Spanish Tragedy*.[21] We have included 'purple NEAR gore' among parallels linking this speech to Kyd but in *Edward III* 'purple' describes 'the sea', whereas *Spanish Tragedy* has the much more conventional bigram 'purple gore' (describing a land battle). In *Edward III* 'purple' and 'gore' are ten words apart, at the very edge of the 'NEAR' search-function; the unique parallel with *Spanish Tragedy* is much less impressive than the unique parallel between 'Purple the sea' and 'the purple sea' (in *Dido*). The specific purple coloring of the violence of combat in these plays could be Homeric, derived from Hall's translation, but it could also stem from the classical Latin of Virgil's *Aeneid* that was known to anyone with a grammar school education (and which is the primary source of *Dido, Queen of Carthage*). But although 'purple' in *Edward III* could reflect the influence of Homer and Virgil, it might also echo Aeschylus. The Persian messenger reporting on the defeat at Salamis uses 'porphura baphe' to describe blood, metaphorically, as 'purple dyes' (*Persae* line 317): the blond beard of Matallos, one of the leaders of the Persian fleet, is dyed purple by his blood, as 'the sea' is dyed purple by 'steaming gore' in *Edward III*.

Seneca was familiar to most Elizabethan playwrights and by 1581 all his plays were available in English translations. But *Persae* had not been translated into English when *Edward III* was written or published. More significantly, it had not been translated into Latin; if Latin translations existed, they had not been printed anywhere in Europe.[22] Therefore, the author of this passage in *Edward III* could read ancient Greek well enough to translate, for himself, the notoriously clotted, difficult, archaic style of Aeschylus. Shakespeare displays no comparable indebtedness to ancient Greek and neither does Kyd. We would expect such knowledge to be limited to the so-called University Wits, the Elizabethan playwrights with a Cambridge or Oxford education: Marlowe, Greene, Peele, Lodge, Nashe and Watson. Marlowe, who translated and adapted Musaeus, certainly read Greek; so did Thomas Watson (who translated Sophocles's *Antigone* into Latin, and cited Greek authors in the commentary to *Hekatompathia*). When an undergraduate at Oxford, Peele wrote a lost translation of Euripides's *Iphigenia*, praised by the Latin playwright William Gager. Greene was indebted to the Greek romances of Heliodorus and Longus. Lodge translated the Greek works of Josephus. In contrast, Gabriel Harvey mocked Nashe's 'ignorance of Greek'; Harvey was hardly an objective judge but nothing in Nashe's extant work suggests that he was capable of reading Aeschylus in the original.

Of these candidates, Marlowe is the one most strongly represented in unique verbal parallels and much more likely than Greene or Peele. The sheer verbal and theatrical power of the speech – demonstrated by James Newcomb's performance in the Chicago Shakespeare Theatre's 2016 adaptation of *Edward III* and other Shakespeare histories in the cycle *Tug of War: Foreign Quarrels* – is also more

---

[20] Barrett, *Staged Narrative*, pp. 550–5.
[21] Braunmuller's observations that the Mariner's speech 'closely imitates' the General's 'messenger speech' in *The Spanish Tragedy* partly relies on this shared image. See *Edward III*, ed. Giorgio Melchiori (Cambridge, 1998), note to 3.1. 144–83.
[22] We base this claim on USTC, the online Universal Short Title Catalogue, which does not record any sixteenth-century Latin translations.

likely to suggest Marlowe than his lesser contemporaries. The accounts by both Holinshed and Aeschylus specify the names of combatants and victims; by contrast, the Mariner's speech is a compelling poetic evocation of anonymous mass death, a subject that fascinated Marlowe.[23] Nevertheless, Lodge, Nashe and Watson could have read Aeschylus and cannot be ruled out. Like Nashe, Lodge has only a single extant play of uncontested single authorship; Watson has no known surviving English plays.[24]

We return, then, to the importance of acknowledging ignorance. The conventional 'Messenger Speech' is an epistemological paradigm. The listener is ignorant. The messenger has knowledge about something that has already happened, which he – and in its traditional form the knowledgeable messenger is always male – delivers to the listener. This is also a traditional paradigm for scholarship: the singular scholar gives the ignorant reader an authoritative true account of the past.

But Vickers, despite his scholarly credentials, is wrong about this messenger speech: Kyd did not write it. Because this speech is the linchpin of his argument, we suspect that Vickers is wrong about the whole play. But the compelling evidence that Kyd did not write the Mariner episode does not, in itself, prove that Kyd wrote nothing in *Edward III*. He might, theoretically, still have written most of the play. However, no good evidence of his authorship of the rest of the play has been published. Kyd is therefore just one of the untested potential candidates. Moreover, even if Kyd turns out to be the likeliest candidate in other scenes, Vickers would still be wrong in insisting on 'The Two Authors of *Edward III*'. If Kyd collaborated on *Edward III*, he was one of three (or more) co-authors.[25]

The laboriously collected, detailed data required by our own tests are, necessarily, focused on a small amount of text: they cannot make claims about a full-length play or even half of one. These tests might be compared to ice-core samples, used to study the history of glaciers (and of the planetary climate) over geological stretches of time. A single ice-core sample can tell us only about the history of a particular spot on a particular glacier; but the more samples we have, the more confident we can be of the global history we are trying to recover.

The ice-core samples from this passage of *Edward III* demonstrate that it cannot have been written by Kyd and is very unlikely to have been written by Shakespeare, Peele or Greene. Marlowe is a very strong candidate. But more research is needed. No one has yet discovered a reliable empirical method for identifying the work of Lodge, Nashe or Watson in a passage of this size. Until such a method is developed, we cannot disqualify those three candidates. This is a problem not just for this passage of *Edward III* but also for many other anonymous or collaborative plays that survive from 1585–94. As long as we remain ignorant about Nashe, Lodge and Watson (and Munday), we cannot be certain about Marlowe, Shakespeare or much of the decade of theatrical history that preceded the formation of the Chamberlain's Men.

---

[23] For a recent articulation of this tendency in Marlowe, see Patricia Cahill, 'Marlowe, death-worlds, and warfare', in *Christopher Marlowe in Context*, ed. Emily C. Bartels and Emma Smith (New York, 2012), pp. 169–80.

[24] For Watson as a commercial playwright between 1583 and his death in 1592, see MacDonald P. Jackson, *Determining the Shakespeare Canon* (Oxford, 2014), 119–20.

[25] Computational stylistics does not identify Marlowe or any other major playwright as the sole author of all the non-Shakespearean scenes: see Timothy Irish Watt, 'The authorship of *The Raigne of Edward III*', in *Mystery*, ed. Craig and Kinney, pp. 116–33. Shakespeare could have worked with more than one collaborator, or the Mariner episode (and the rest of the play) might have been written by Lodge, Nashe and/or Watson. Watt's statistical techniques are unreliable for small samples, like those analyzed here.

AUTHORIAL ATTRIBUTION AND SHAKESPEAREAN VARIETY: GENRE, FORM AND CHRONOLOGY

HUGH CRAIG

Traditionally, Shakespeare is celebrated for the profusion and diversity of his writing and for the elusiveness of his creative personality. Jonathan Bate notes that contemporaries singled Shakespeare out for 'the variety of his modes and moods'.[1] Samuel Johnson thought the plays displayed 'good and evil, joy and sorrow, mingled with endless variety of proportion and innumerable modes of combination'.[2] Shakespeare is one of W. B. Yeats's chief exemplars of the 'emotion of multitude', which Yeats finds lacking in much of modern drama.[3] Shakespeare is often seen as one of those creators who is 'invisible, refined out of existence', in the words of Stephen Dedalus.[4] Matthew Arnold's much-quoted formulation is that 'Others abide our question. Thou art free.'[5]

These general notions about exceptional variety and the absence of a recognisable voice run counter to the requirements for authorship attribution, among which consistency and distinctiveness are paramount. The more an author's writing changes from work to work, scene to scene, or character to character, the more difficult it is to judge whether a disputed work, scene or character should be assigned to that author or away from them. The fainter the authorial voice sounding through every work and section of a work, and transcending internal changes and contrasts, the less confident we can feel when we sense the presence or absence of that voice in a given passage.

Fortunately, the same attribution methods which give a new focus to these traditional questions about variety and consistency also offer new answers. The estimation of variability is a foundational aspect of statistics, which has developed numerous ways to summarise it and to take account of it in seeking genuine rather than apparent differences between observations. We can use these methods to compare the degree of internal variation in a writer's style with the extent of the contrast between that style and another writer's. This can help establish a proper sense of the reliability of quantitative work in various situations.

There is another more general interest in the topic. The quantitative approach analyses dramatic texture and dramatic construction in the plays of Shakespeare and his contemporaries from first principles. It may seem unduly abstract and mechanical to treat plays as counts of constituent words, but this approach does offer a view without too many preconceptions and with a wide sweep of attention. The answers it provides on the relative

---

[1] Jonathan Bate, *The Genius of Shakespeare* (Oxford, 1998), p. 21.
[2] Samuel Johnson, *Preface to Shakespeare*, in *Samuel Johnson: Selected Poetry and Prose*, ed. Frank Brady and W. K. Wimsatt (Berkeley, 1977), pp. 303–4.
[3] W. B. Yeats, 'The emotion of multitude', in *The Collected Works of W. B. Yeats: Volume IV: The Early Essays*, ed. Richard J. Finneran and George Bornstein (New York, 2007), pp. 159–60.
[4] James Joyce, *A Portrait of the Artist as a Young Man*, ed. Seamus Deane (New York, 1992), p. 233.
[5] Matthew Arnold, 'Shakespeare', in *The Oxford Authors: Matthew Arnold*, ed. Miriam Allott and Robert Super (Oxford, 1986), p. 8, l. 1.

importance in Shakespeare's style of genre, form and chronology cannot claim any absolute objectivity. They hold only within the particular constraints and parameters of the chosen system of samples, variables and procedures. Yet to the extent that the system is well designed and safeguarded against obvious sources of bias, these answers can stimulate broad-based comparative thinking about the plays. They can challenge established dogmas and prompt new ideas.

In a recent article, Joseph Rudman puts the case that competing factors are so strong and so hard to deal with in Shakespeare texts that what he calls 'non-traditional' authorship studies are invalid even before they begin. He notes that 'It has been shown in many studies that genre trumps authorship – there is a greater stylistic difference between one author in different genres than between two authors writing in the same genre.'[6] This claim, which, if true, puts authorship attribution into doubt, is the starting point for this chapter.

There are twenty-eight plays most people agree are Shakespeare's unaided work and, within the twenty-eight, there are eight tragedies and twelve comedies (as opposed to six history plays and two tragicomedies), according to one standard division.[7] So the largest pairing available is eight versus eight, the eight tragedies and a group of eight of the comedies, which we can select randomly.[8]

We then find sets of comedies by others to make authorial comparisons. In my corpus four of these are available: Chapman, Jonson, Middleton and Fletcher.[9] We then have the comedy-tragedy difference within Shakespeare to compare to the external comedy to comedy comparison, Shakespeare to others, precisely in the terms set by Rudman. Is the difference between Shakespeare comedies and Shakespeare tragedies greater than the difference between Shakespeare comedies and a set of comedies by other writers?

My test for difference is going to be the number of words from a list of 100 very common words that are used at different rates in one eight-play group compared to in another eight-play group.

We are looking for genuine difference, persisting through local variation, and for this we rely on the *t*-test, which provides a way of accommodating the three factors of the difference in average counts, the variation within the sets, and the number of samples.[10] The *t*-test can place a particular comparison in a range between a difference that is probably only illusory and a difference in the samples that we can be confident is genuinely marked and consistent. In the first case the averages are much the same, there is wide internal variation, and we only have a few samples to judge from. In the second case there is a marked difference in averages, the counts do not fluctuate much, and we have

---

[6] Rudman does not name any of these studies in his article. Joseph Rudman, 'Non-traditional authorship attribution studies of William Shakespeare's canon: Some caveats', *Journal of Early Modern Studies* 5 (2016), 307–28; esp. p. 318.
[7] For genre classifications I rely on Alfred Harbage and S. Schoenbaum, *Annals of English Drama, 975–1700* (Philadelphia, 1964).
[8] The Shakespeare tragedies I use are: *Antony and Cleopatra, Coriolanus, Hamlet, Julius Caesar, King Lear, Othello, Romeo and Juliet* and *Troilus and Cressida*. The Shakespeare comedies are: *All's Well that Ends Well, As You Like It, Comedy of Errors, Love's Labour's Lost, Merchant of Venice, Merry Wives of Windsor, A Midsummer Night's Dream, Much Ado About Nothing, Taming of the Shrew, Tempest, Twelfth Night* and *Two Gentlemen of Verona*. For the editions used, mostly early printed versions, see the supplementary materials for this article available on the publications page of the Centre for Literary and Linguistic Computing website at the University of Newcastle, Australia (www.newcastle.edu.au/research-and-innovation/centre/education-arts/cllc/publications).
[9] The Chapman comedies are: *All Fools, Blind Beggar of Alexandria, Gentleman Usher, Humorous Day's Mirth, May Day, Monsieur d'Olive, Sir Giles Goosecap* and *Widow's Tears*. The Fletcher comedies are: *Captain, Chances, Monsieur Thomas, Pilgrim, Rule a Wife, Wild Goose Chase, Wit without Money* and *Woman's Prize*. The Jonson comedies are: *Alchemist, Case is Altered, Cynthia's Revels, Epicene, Every Man in his Humour, Every Man out of his Humour, New Inn* and *Tale of a Tub*. The Middleton comedies are: *Mad World My Masters, More Dissemblers Beside Women, Nice Valour, No Wit No Help Like a Woman's, Trick to Catch the Old One, Phoenix, Widow* and *Your Five Gallants*.
[10] See George W. Snedecor and William G. Cochran, *Statistical Methods*, 8th edn (Ames, 1989), pp. 53–8. I use the heteroscedastic version, known as Welch's *t*-test.

abundant samples. The summary statistic for the *t*-test is a probability, expressed as a decimal fraction, that the two sets come from the same parent population. At one extreme this would be close to zero, at the other close to one.

'Different' means that it is the sort of difference that only comes up once in a hundred trials using randomly assembled groups.[11] There will always be some differences, but they have to be reasonably marked and consistent to count here. If we have 100 words, as in this set, one word is likely to get above the threshold merely through chance fluctuations. If there is more than one word significantly higher or lower in one group than in the other, we are justified in regarding the groups as different in style.

The 100 words are

the, I, and, of, a, you, is, my, to [infinitive], it, in [preposition], not, to [preposition], will [verb], me, your, be, but, with, have, this, he, for [preposition], his, as, what, all, him, thou, that [relative], are, shall, if, do, that [demonstrative], now, thy, we [true Plural], by [preposition], no [adjective], or, that [conjunction], thee, they, at, she, would, so [adverb Degree], then, am, was, here, how, from, there, our [true Plural], her [adjective], o, them, more, their, on [preposition], well, her [personal Pronoun], may, for [conjunction], must, when, yet, one, which [relative], us [true Plural], so [adverb Manner], were, why, can, should, too, ye, had, than, upon [preposition], such, an, these, out, never, some, hath, where, like [preposition], up [adverb], did, much, most, mine, nor, any, has and *no[exclamation]*

They are marked to separate the grammatical functions of some of the words, for example *no* as an adjective and *no* as an exclamation. Why choose these words? They look innocuous but the way they vary in rates of use has been proved over and over again to be revealing about style across the range of factors that interest readers and scholars. There are just over 84,000 different words in my corpus but these 100 of them account for 53 per cent of the word total. They dominate numerically and they represent the skeleton of style, the syntactic framework of the language. If the claim Rudman quotes as a caveat is generally true, they ought to be more different in genres within an author's work than in cross-author groups of the same genre.

There are three words from the set of 100 that are different enough in usage in the Shakespeare comedies compared to the tragedies to cross the chosen threshold: *a, for* as a preposition and *I*. *A* and *I* are higher in the comedies and *for* as a preposition is higher in the tragedies. The expectation with randomly assembled play groups would be for one word to cross the threshold, so evidently Shakespeare comedy and tragedy do have more than a random difference. We can then test the differences between the Shakespeare comedies and the four sets of comedies by other writers and put them alongside the internal comedy-tragedy difference (Illustration 11).

There are many more words used differently between the pairs of authors, ranging from seven for Chapman to thirty-four for Fletcher. The experiment set up to estimate genre difference compared to author difference shows that author difference is much greater – at least with these variables, these genres, these authors and these play sets.

Play dialogue is spoken by characters, which, for many dramatic purposes, need to be distinguished from each other. Shakespeare characters, as already mentioned, are celebrated for their variety. This inherent diversity in character styles gives a particular interest to the character version of the genre question already posed, that is, are Shakespeare comedy characters more different in their styles from Shakespeare tragedy characters than Shakespeare comedy characters are from comedy characters created by other authors? Sceptics of computational approaches sometimes refer to this diversity as a reason to question the reliability of authorship attribution by quantitative means, arguing, for instance, that the dialogue of characters in plays 'may tell you something about the characters but cannot reliably indicate authorship'.[12]

---

[11] This is usually expressed as 'p <.01'.

[12] Brian Vickers, 'The marriage of philology and informatics', *British Academy Review* (November 2009), pp. 41–4; esp. p. 42.

AUTHORIAL ATTRIBUTION AND SHAKESPEAREAN VARIETY

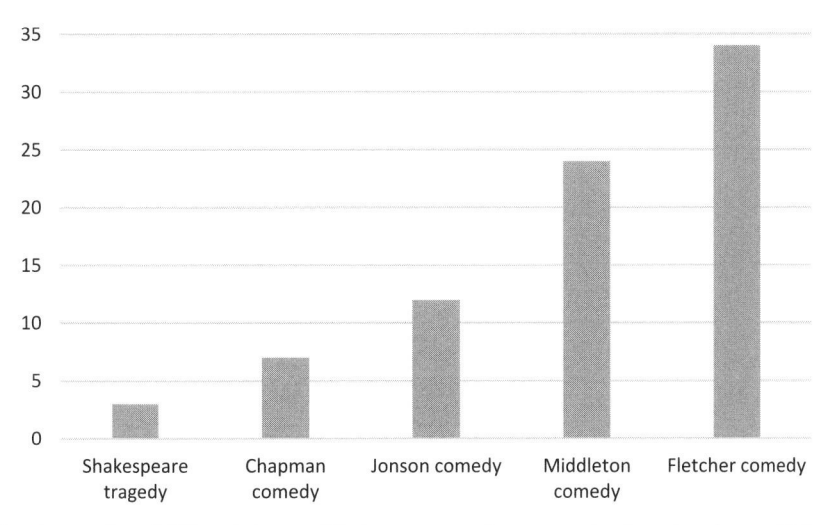

11. Number of function words used differently in a set of Shakespeare comedies compared to five other play sets. Eight plays in each set; 100 very common function words tested; threshold for a significant difference, Welch's *t*-test p <.01.

To test this empirically, we can assemble a set of eight Shakespeare comedy characters, eight Shakespeare tragedy characters and eight characters from Chapman, Fletcher, Jonson and Middleton comedies and compare the level of differences.[13]

As before, I ask the question, how many of a set of 100 very common words are used differently in Shakespeare comedy versus tragedy, and how many in Shakespeare comedy versus the comedy of other writers? Illustration 12 shows the number of words that are judged to be used differently in the five comparisons.

One word (the word *what*, as it happens) is used differently in the Shakespeare tragedy characters, whereas there are between three and twelve words used differently in the sets of comedy characters by other writers. The internal Shakespeare contrast in style according to genre is always less than the external contrast with other writers, though the gap is not as great as with whole plays. The samples are smaller, for one thing, allowing more internal variation. It is possible that if we continued to experiment with all the variations possible in the eight-character sets, internal Shakespeare comedy-tragedy differences might equal or exceed one or other of the authorial contrasts. The overall pattern of author

---

[13] I selected randomly from characters who speak 3,000 words or more of dialogue, and chose only one from each play. The Shakespeare comedy set is: Benedick (*Much Ado about Nothing*), Berowne (*Love's Labour's Lost*), Duke (*Measure for Measure*), Parolles (*All's Well that Ends Well*), Portia (*Merchant of Venice*), Proteus (*Two Gentlemen of Verona*), Rosalind (*As You Like It*) and Sir John Falstaff (*Merry Wives of Windsor*). The Shakespeare tragedy set is: Brutus (*Julius Caesar*), Claudius (*Hamlet*), Cleopatra (*Antony and Cleopatra*), Iago (*Othello*), King (*King Lear*), Menenius Agrippa (*Coriolanus*), Romeo (*Romeo and Juliet*) and Troilus (*Troilus and Cressida*). The Chapman comedy set is: Rynaldo (*All Fools*), Irus (*Blind Beggar of Alexandria*), Vincentio (*Gentleman Usher*), Lemot (*Humorous Day's Mirth*), Quintiliano (*May Day*), Monsieur d'Olive (*Monsieur d'Olive*), Momford (*Sir Giles Goosecap*) and Lysander (*Widow's Tears*). The Fletcher comedy set is: Don John (*Chances*), Juletta (*Pilgrim*), Laelia (*Captain*), Michael Perez (*Rule a Wife*), Mirabell (*Wild Goose Chase*), Petruchio (*Woman's Prize*), Thomas (*Monsieur Thomas*) and Valentine (*Wit without Money*). The Jonson comedy set is: Amorphus (*Cynthia's Revels*), Carlo Buffone (*Every Man out of His Humour*), Face (*Alchemist*), Fitzdottrell (*Devil is an Ass*), Quarlous (*Bartholomew Fair*), Thorello (*Every Man in His Humour*), Truewit (*Epicene*) and Tucca (*Poetaster*). The Middleton comedy set is: Allwit (*Chaste Maid in Cheapside*), Duchess (*More Dissemblers Beside Women*), Follywit (*Mad World My Masters*), Goldstone (*Your Five Gallants*), Mistress Low-water (*No Wit, No Help Like a Woman's*), Phoenix (*Phoenix*), Pieboard (*Puritan*) and Quomodo (*Michaelmas Term*).

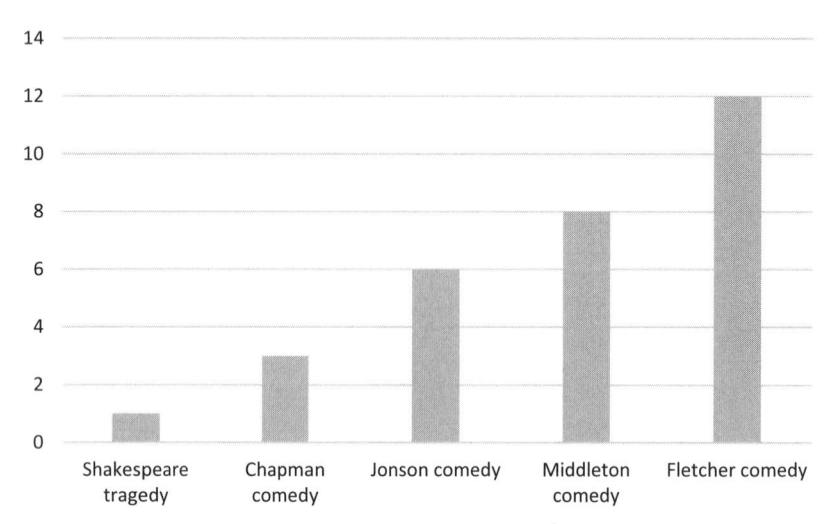

12. Number of function words used differently in a set of Shakespeare comedy characters and in five other sets of characters. Eight characters in each set; 100 very common function words tested; threshold for a significant difference, Welch's *t*-test p <.01.

differences trumping genre differences is clear nevertheless.

In order to generalise more widely, we need to assemble some larger sets. If we make a fourteen-play multi-author comedy set, as well as multi-author tragedy and history sets of fourteen, we can compare each with each to get a sense of how much genres differ from each other generally.[14]

Fourteen is an arbitrary number but it is about as large as we can achieve with reasonably 'pure' samples (or very well mixed ones), given that we want a number of different kinds of texts to compare with each other. We want large sets to account for variation within a category, but there is only so much concentration in any one area available in my corpus (243 professional-company plays, 1580–1642) and there is only so much available anywhere from the surviving plays. Only a handful of playwrights have fourteen well-attributed, single-author plays to their names. We sometimes forget how unusual the Shakespeare canon is. Shakespeare was involved in forty plays, twenty-eight of them as sole author.[15] James Shirley is credited with thirty-one plays and four collaborative ones but after that the next highest is Middleton, with eighteen single

[14] The mixed-author comedy set is: George Chapman, *Humorous Day's Mirth*; John Cooke, *Greene's Tu Quoque*; John Day, *Humour out of Breath*; Thomas Dekker, *Old Fortunatus*; Nathan Field, *Amends for Ladies*; John Fletcher, *Monsieur Thomas*; Robert Greene, *Friar Bacon and Friar Bungay*; William Haughton, *Englishmen for My Money*; Thomas Heywood, *Wise Woman of Hogdson*; Ben Jonson, *Volpone*; John Marston, *What You Will*; Thomas Middleton, *Chaste Maid in Cheapside*; Henry Porter, *Two Angry Women of Abingdon*; and William Shakespeare, *Comedy of Errors*. The mixed-author tragedy set is: George Chapman, *Byron's Conspiracy*; Henry Chettle, *Tragedy of Hoffman*; Robert Daborne, *Christian Turned Turk*; John Fletcher, *Bonduca*; Ben Jonson, *Sejanus*; Thomas Kyd, *Spanish Tragedy*; Christopher Marlowe, *Jew of Malta*; John Marston, *Antonio's Revenge*; Thomas Middleton, *Revenger's Tragedy*; William Rowley, *All's Lost by Lust*; Thomas Heywood, *Woman Killed with Kindness*; William Shakespeare, *Romeo and Juliet*; Cyril Tourneur, *Atheist's Tragedy*; and John Webster, *White Devil*. The mixed-author history set is: *Captain Thomas Stukeley*, *Edmond Ironside*, *Edward the Third* and *Thomas Lord Cromwell*, all anonymous; Thomas Dekker and John Webster, *Sir Thomas Wyatt*; John Ford, *Perkin Warbeck*; Robert Greene, *James the Fourth*; Thomas Heywood, *Edward the Fourth Part 1*; Thomas Heywood, *If You Know Not Me You Know Nobody Part 1*; Christopher Marlowe, *Edward the Second*; George Peele, *Edward the First*; Samuel Rowley, *When You See Me You Know Me*; William Shakespeare, *Henry the Fourth Part 1*; and William Shakespeare, *Richard the Third*.

[15] See the table of contents of the *The New Oxford Shakespeare*, ed. Gary Taylor, John Jowett, Terri Bourus and Gabriel Egan (Oxford, 2016).

AUTHORIAL ATTRIBUTION AND SHAKESPEAREAN VARIETY

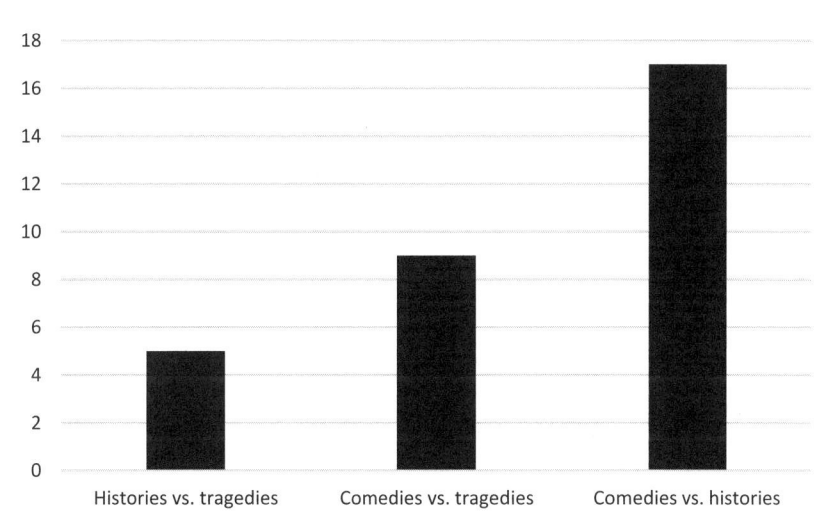

13. Number of function words used differently in pairs of genre play sets. Fourteen plays in each set; 100 very common function words tested; threshold for a significant difference, Welch's *t*-test p <.01.

author plus seven collaborative.[16] The data are limited. It is not likely we will find any more whole plays of Shakespeare's among the surviving anonymous plays, for instance.

Illustration 13 shows the results for the genre comparisons. Comedies versus histories shows the greatest difference. Seventeen words are used at significantly different rates. Tragedies and histories are the least different, with five of the 100 words this time crossing the threshold.

Now we do the same thing with authors: make up sets of fourteen plays, as mixed as possible in terms of genre. Shakespeare, Fletcher, Middleton and Jonson have large enough canons to make this possible, though in some cases like Jonson's we are limited in the mixing – twelve comedies and two tragicomedies is the best we can do. As usual, we find how many of the 100 words are differently used one author to another. There are thirty-two in the case of Shakespeare to Jonson, and thirty-eight in the case of Shakespeare to Middleton (Illustration 14). Generally, focusing on Shakespeare, it seems that authorship trumps genre rather than the other way around.

This is one author compared to one other author. What happens if we take a 'comedy-plus' Shakespeare set – twelve comedies and two tragicomedies – and compare this to a set of twelve comedies and two tragicomedies each by a different author of the period when Shakespeare was having plays performed?[17] We now have Shakespeare versus the world, all in one slightly extended genre (Illustration 15).

There are far fewer differences. Shakespeare versus one other author is strikingly different – thirty-eight

---

[16] See the list on the 'James Shirley's Works' page on the website *The Complete Works of James Shirley*, Durham University, and the table of contents of Thomas Middleton, *The Collected Works*, ed. Gary Taylor and John Lavagnino (Oxford, 2007).

[17] The Shakespeare comedies and tragicomedies are: *All's Well that Ends Well*, *As You Like It*, *Comedy of Errors*, *Cymbeline*, *Love's Labour's Lost*, *Merchant of Venice*, *Merry Wives of Windsor*, *Midsummer Night's Dream*, *Much Ado about Nothing*, *Taming of the Shrew*, *Tempest*, *Twelfth Night*, *Two Gentlemen of Verona* and *Winter's Tale*. The comedies and tragicomedies by other authors are Robert Armin, *Two Maids of More-Clack*; Francis Beaumont and John Fletcher, *King and No King*; George Chapman, *Blind Beggar of Alexandria*; John Cooke, *Greene's Tu Quoque*; John Day, *Isle of Gulls*; Thomas Dekker, *Honest Whore Part 2*; Richard Field, Philip Massinger and John Fletcher, *Honest Man's Fortune*; William Haughton, *Devil and his Dame*; Thomas Heywood, *Wise Woman of Hogdson*; Ben Jonson, *Epicene*; John Lyly, *Woman in the Moon*; John Marston, *What You Will*; Thomas Middleton, *Michaelmas Term*; and Edward Sharpham, *Cupid's Whirligig*.

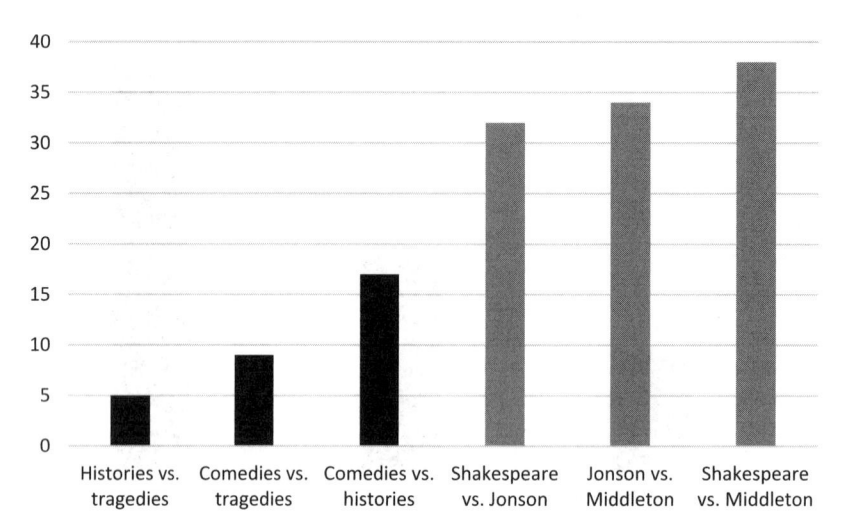

14. Number of function words used differently in pairs of genre and author play sets. Fourteen plays in each set; 100 very common function words tested; threshold for a significant difference, Welch's *t*-test p <.01.

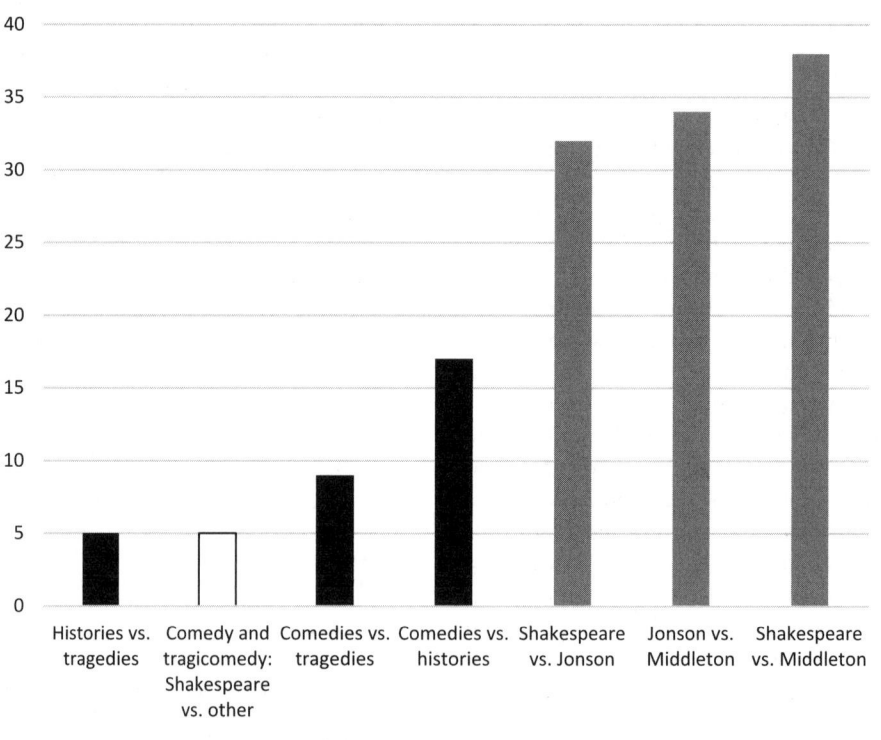

15. Number of function words used differently in various pairs of genre and author play sets, including Shakespeare and non-Shakespeare comedy-tragicomedy sets. Fourteen plays in each set; 100 very common function words tested; threshold for a significant difference, Welch's *t*-test p <.01.

AUTHORIAL ATTRIBUTION AND SHAKESPEAREAN VARIETY

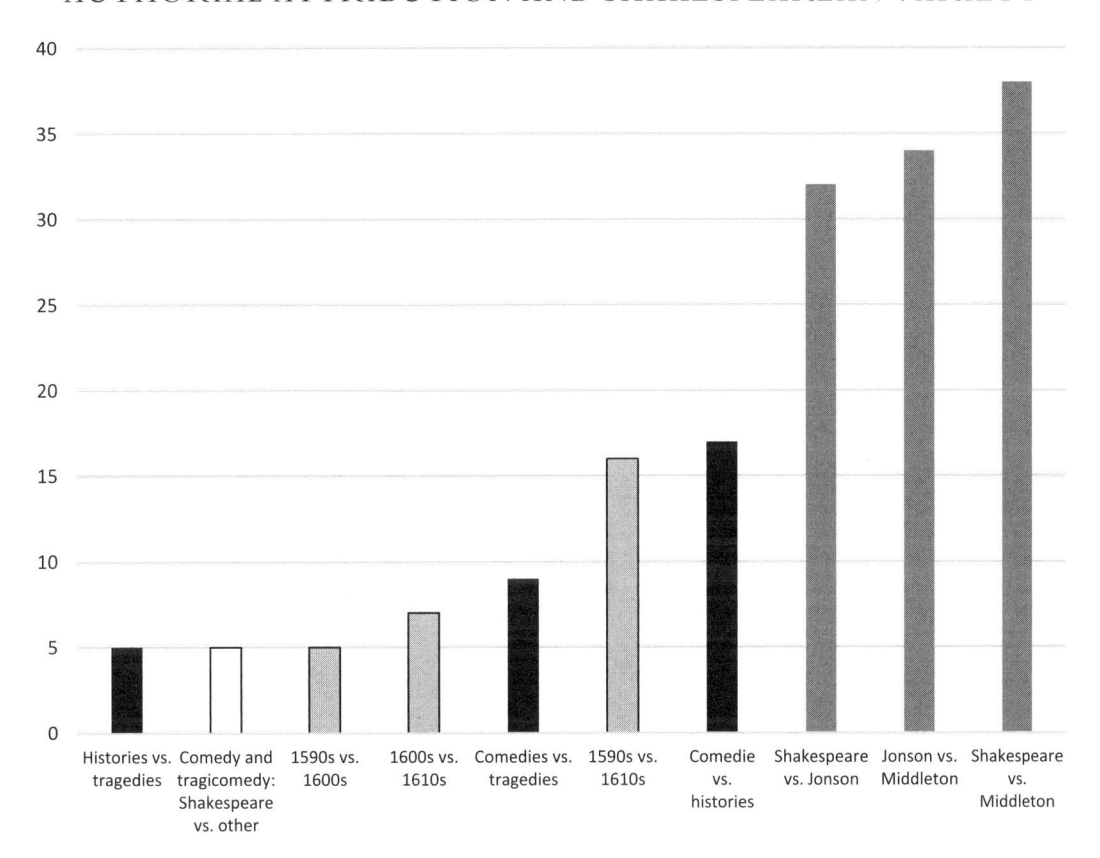

16. Number of function words used differently in pairs of play sets, including pairs of sets by decade. Fourteen plays in each set; 100 very common function words tested; threshold for a significant difference, Welch's t-test $p < .01$.

of the 100 words are markedly higher or lower in Shakespeare in the Middleton comparison we saw earlier. Shakespeare comedy-tragicomedy versus comedy-tragicomedy in general is not so different – five of 100 words are different, the same for the lowest genre comparison. Here authorship does not trump genre. Shakespeare comedy-plus is close to a general comedy-plus grouping of his time. In this case Shakespeare emerges as more balanced and representative than extraordinary. He fits closely the practice of his time. Rudman's caveat proves to be applicable in the case of comparing Shakespeare to other authors in general. Careful selection of the variables and control sets to be used would be necessary to overcome the potential influence of other factors in this more ambitious kind of testing.

What about time periods? How do they rate in terms of overall, generalised difference? I made up sets of plays from three decades (as many different authors represented as possible, and mixing genres also) and compared them (Illustrations 16–17).[18]

---

[18] The plays were allotted by date of first performance, according to the *Annals of English Drama*. The 1590s set is: Anonymous, *Knack to Know a Knave*; Anonymous, *Look About You*; George Chapman, *Blind Beggar of Alexandria*; George Chapman, *Humorous Day's Mirth*; Thomas Dekker, *Old Fortunatus*; Thomas Dekker, *Shoemaker's Holiday*; William Haughton, *Devil and his Dame*; William Haughton, *Englishmen for My Money*; Ben Jonson, *Case is Altered*; Ben Jonson, *Cynthia's Revels*; John Lyly, *Mother Bombie*; John Lyly, *Woman in the Moon*; William Shakespeare, *Comedy of Errors*; and William Shakespeare, *Taming of the Shrew*. The 1600s set is: Anonymous, *Every Woman in her Humour*; Robert Armin,

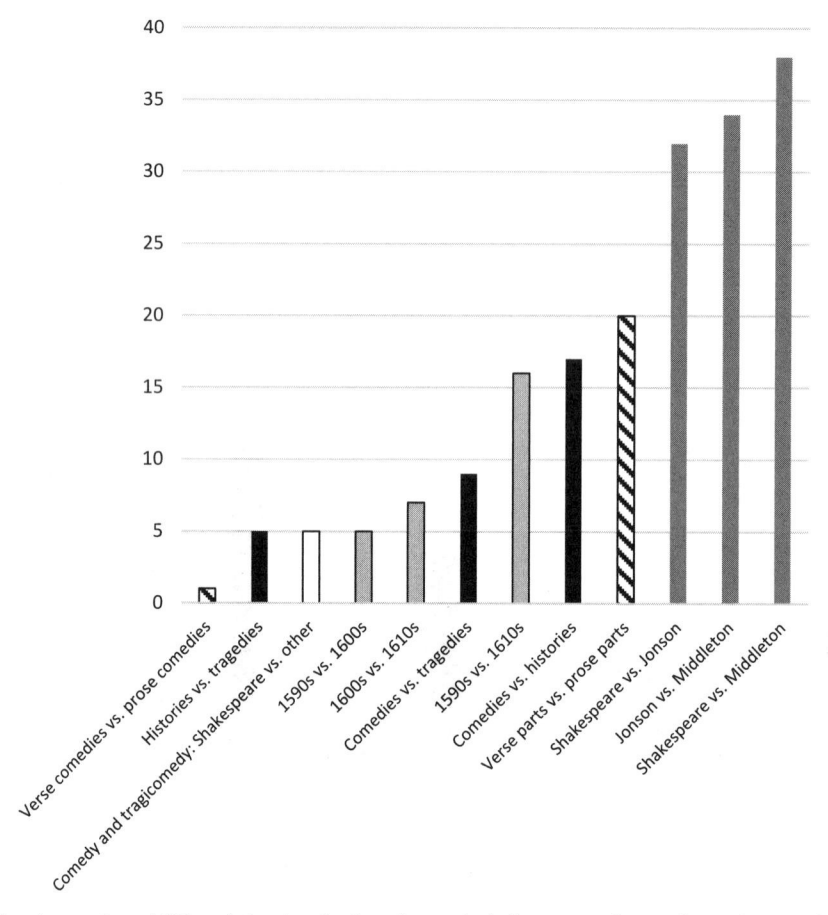

17. Number of function words used differently in pairs of various play sets, including verse and prose plays and verse and prose play parts. Fourteen plays in each set; 100 very common function words tested; threshold for a significant difference, Welch's t-test p <.01.

Not much happens in adjacent decades, 1590s to 1600s, and 1600s to 1610s, but we find sixteen words different when comparing 1590s to 1610s — which would encompass early and very late Shakespeare. This is still not close to the level of differences between authors, but it comes close to the strongest genre difference.

Another difference often mentioned as an obstacle for author attribution is the stylistic difference between verse and prose. It seems logical that there must be constraints in writing in verse compared to prose. As a result, practitioners of authorship attribution often assume that the prose–verse difference is a confounding variable in authorship and limit

Two Maids of More-Clack; George Chapman, *All Fools*; George Chapman, *May Day*; John Day, *Isle of Gulls*; Thomas Dekker, *Honest Whore Part 2*; Thomas Heywood, *Wise Woman of Hogdson*; Ben Jonson, *Poetaster*; Lewis Markham and Gervase Machin, *Dumb Knight*; John Marston, *What You Will*; Thomas Middleton, *Phoenix*; William Shakespeare, *All's Well that Ends Well*; William Shakespeare, *Twelfth Night*; and Edward Sharpham, *Fleire*. The 1610s set is: John Cooke, *Greene's Tu Quoque*; Thomas Dekker, *If It Be Not Good, the Devil Is In It*; Nathan Field, *Amends for Ladies*; John Fletcher, *Woman's Prize*; John Fletcher, *Chances*; John Fletcher, *Captain*; John Fletcher, *Monsieur Thomas*; Ben Jonson, *Devil is an Ass*; Ben Jonson, *Bartholomew Fair*; Thomas Middleton, *No Wit No Help Like a Woman's*; Thomas Middleton, *More Dissemblers Beside Women*; Thomas Middleton, *Chaste Maid in Cheapside*; William Rowley, *New Wonder, A Woman Never Vexed*; and William Shakespeare, *Tempest*.

themselves to samples in one or the other mode: to dramatic and non-dramatic verse, for example, or to dramatic verse in one metre.[19] This aspect is explored in a forthcoming study using the same methodology as above.[20] Fourteen comedies in verse were compared with fourteen comedies in prose, with no more than three plays by any one author included in either set and with any of remaining prose in the verse comedies, such as letters, and any remaining verse in the prose comedies, such as songs, deleted.

Surprisingly, they are not very different at all. Among the 100 words tested, just one difference crosses the threshold for significance, what one would expect from random groups compared with each other. It seems that playwrights when working entirely in verse or entirely in prose are capable of creating a full range of effects from low comedy to high seriousness within the chosen form.

This same study also examines the case of comedies that mix verse and prose. The verse parts and prose parts of fourteen comedies of this mixed type are compared. Twenty words are used differently this time. It seems that when playwrights are working in prose and verse in the same play, they specialise – clowns and the middling sort in prose, for instance, and kings and lovers in verse. That brings about a divergence in style, a divergence similar to an extreme genre contrast like comedy and history.

Generally, authorship trumps the other obvious factors in style with common-words analysis in the trials presented here. With one-on-one author comparisons, there are more words crossing the threshold for significant difference in the lowest author to author comparison than in the highest comparison for genre, era or mode. This suggests that attribution is possible, and Rudman's caveat is weakened in force. But genre, date and mode also are present stylistically, and we need to take account of their potential for bias and watch out for extreme genre effects (e.g. comedy vs history), extreme date effects (widely separated decades) and extreme form effects (prose and verse where they both appear in the same play).

As samples get smaller all these effects will be accentuated because there is more chance of local concentration and less chance of their being balanced out. With other kinds of evidence, the picture might be different. No doubt more lexical words would reflect genre more strongly, for instance.

However, from this study we can draw some conclusions. When looked at as discourse, one insistent thing a passage from a Shakespeare play says to us is 'this is by Shakespeare'. It also says 'this is a comedy or a tragedy'. After that it says, a little less loudly, 'this is early or late' and in some cases it may also say 'this is prose or verse'.

This is a distant reading of Shakespearean drama. It gives a starting point for the business of interpretation, which would not be available any other way. We can check assertions that are made a priori and *ex cathedra* and provide responses that have a kind of truth – relative to the specific conditions of the tests – for those who are interested in the truth. The methods are capable of providing surprises and can stubbornly refuse to give the expected answer, which is salutary.

In one aspect it invites us to think about prose and verse as sometimes neutral stylistically and sometimes intensely specialised. It reveals sharp differences between the styles of authors when compared one on one. In contrast, when differences within the non-Shakespearean are suppressed and we contrive a maximally mixed 'other' to Shakespeare comedy, we find Shakespeare not so different after all, a one-playwright comedy everyman matching the composite everyman we created. And at another level the analysis shows that all

---

[19] See Ward E. Y. Elliott and Robert J. Valenza, 'Oxford by the numbers: What are the odds that the Earl of Oxford could have written Shakespeare's poems and plays?', *The Tennessee Law Review* 72 (2004), 323–453, and John V. Nance, 'From Shakespeare "To ye Q."', *Shakespeare Quarterly* 34 (2016), 204–31.

[20] Hugh Craig and Brett Greatley-Hirsch, *Style, Computers, and Early Modern Drama* (Cambridge, forthcoming 2017).

playwrights moved together to create a 1610s style collectively different from a 1590s style.

We knew all these things, but the common-words frequency analysis gives them a definite shape and even puts a number on them. It then falls to the interpreter to work out if and how these numerical results relate to what happens when actors speak this dialogue and audiences listen. For Shakespeareans in the twenty-first century, that is perhaps one of the more inviting challenges around.

APPENDIX

	# words out of a set of 100 with significant differences
8-play sets	
Shakespeare comedy vs Shakespeare tragedy	3
Shakespeare comedy vs Chapman comedy	7
Shakespeare comedy vs Jonson comedy	12
Shakespeare comedy vs Middleton comedy	24
Shakespeare comedy vs Fletcher comedy	34
8-character sets	
Shakespeare comedy vs Shakespeare tragedy	1
Shakespeare comedy vs Chapman comedy	3
Shakespeare comedy vs Jonson comedy	6
Shakespeare comedy vs Middleton comedy	8
Shakespeare comedy vs Fletcher comedy	12
14-play sets	
Comedies vs tragedies	9
Comedies vs histories	17
Histories vs tragedies	5
Shakespeare vs Jonson	32
Shakespeare vs Middleton	38
Jonson vs Middleton	34
Comedy and tragicomedy: Shakespeare vs other	5
1590s vs 1600s	5
1600s vs 1610s	7
1590s vs 1610s	16
Verse comedies vs prose comedies	2
Verse comedy parts vs prose comedy parts	20

'MY MOTHER'S MAIDS, WHEN THEY DID SEW AND SPIN': STAGING SEWING, TELLING TALES

HESTER LEES-JEFFRIES

Thomas Wyatt's poem, of which the first line is quoted here, has nothing to do with sewing or spinning. Its sources are well known, primarily Horace's *Satire* 2.6, but also Aesop and many subsequent reworkings. Although it is usually termed a satire, it is also slyly dramatic in its construction: the reader, or hearer, may well first picture a nostalgic scene of feminine domestic labour but then must attend to the first person utterances of two anthropomorphized rodents and their moralizing narrator, and, in the poem's last third or so, reconfigure their attentiveness to the poem and its voices to include (perhaps even to become?) Wyatt's familiar interlocutor, John Poynz.[1] This article thinks about the relationship between the evocation and, especially, the staging of scenes of textile-making by women, and what might be termed traditional stories, broadly interpreted. It suggests that such moments can occasion reflection on the processes of literary and dramatic making, and of performance, positing multiple models of poetic and dramatic construction.

The connections between spinning, weaving, sewing and other forms of textile labour and writing are axiomatic and, especially since Rozsika Parker's *The Subversive Stitch* and more recently Susan Frye's *Pens and Needles*, the idea of needlework as a form of women's textuality has become familiar.[2] The discussion here builds on much work in the field of early modern textile culture, especially by Natasha Korda, Catherine Richardson, Peter Stallybrass and Ann Rosalind Jones; recent work by Chloe Porter and Jonathan Gil Harris has also influenced it, although less visibly.[3] Nearly twenty years ago, Lena Cowen Orlin's 'Three ways to be invisible in the Renaissance' forcefully set out what it termed 'a cultural ideology of the everyday occupation of

---

I am grateful to Helen Cooper for inviting me to participate in the panel on 'Shakespeare and traditional stories' at the WSC and for her generous comments on the revised version of my paper.

[1] Greg Walker is unusual in not simply noting its Horatian source but also emphasizing that it is 'a work song, a *chanson de toile*, recalled from [Wyatt's] childhood'; he suggests that it begins 'with a series of effects which problematize its connection to [Wyatt's] own inventive mind . . . seek[ing] to disguise the originality of the work, and downplay its claims to literary authority' (*Writing Under Tyranny: English Literature and the Henrician Reformation* (Oxford, 2005), p. 308). Editors tend not to comment on its domestic frame; Patricia Thomson (who does) notes that 'The hypothetical song could not possibly account for the form and structure of "My mothers maydes", which is an unsonglike narrative and moral satire' (*Sir Thomas Wyatt and His Background* (London, 1964), p. 267).

[2] Rozsika Parker, *The Subversive Stitch: Embroidery and the Making of the Feminine* (London, 1984); Susan Frye, *Pens and Needles: Women's Textualities in Early Modern England* (Philadelphia, 2010).

[3] Natasha Korda, *Labors Lost: Women's Work and the Early Modern English Stage* (Philadelphia, 2011); Catherine Richardson, *Shakespeare and Material Culture* (Oxford, 2011); Ann Rosalind Jones and Peter Stallybrass, *Renaissance Clothing and the Materials of Memory* (Cambridge, 2000); Chloe Porter, *Making and Unmaking in Early Modern English Drama: Spectators, Aesthetics and Incompletion* (Manchester, 2013); Jonathan Gil Harris, *Untimely Matter in the Time of Shakespeare* (Philadelphia, 2009).

needlework'.[4] This article both makes a case for the particularity of textile scenes and references in drama and resists too neat an equivalence of sewing and writing, which sees needlework above all as women's self-expression. Such an equivalence flattens out the distinctiveness of needlework, not as product so much as process: that it is very communal and collaborative, that its materiality is constituted in extended temporalities, that it could be pieced together, in terms of both its sources and its actual material, by many hands. The singular line of the thread, the voice of the shuttle (it might be termed) is a seductive conceit. But, all too easily, it can suggest and become elided with the linear narrative or the single author or with a teleological drive to a moment of reading and unified interpretation: even Philomel's sampler can become tedious (*Titus Andronicus* 2.4.39).[5] Fascinating work has been done on printed pattern books but needlework was still quite literally *handi*work.[6] And it also remained thoroughly embedded in oral culture, not least because it was so strongly associated with songs and with storytelling. As Adam Fox observes, 'Most of the oral culture which can be recovered from sixteenth- and seventeenth-century England is adult male culture.'[7] Textile artefacts can therefore be material traces of the rich oral cultures of women, even if they are no longer fully or easily legible. In addition, and especially in a dramatic context, they can signify and evoke as activities as well as things.

In 2.4 of *Twelfth Night*, Orsino calls for music, a song that he first describes to Cesario as 'old and antic' (2.4.3). When Feste appears to sing it, Orsino comments further:

Mark it, Cesario, it is old and plain.
The spinsters, and the knitters in the sun,
And the free maids that weave their thread with bones,
Do use to chant it. It is silly sooth,
And dallies with the innocence of love,
Like the old age.   (2.4.42–7)

Writing about poor women in Shakespeare, Fiona McNeill points out that the lacemakers evoked by Orsino, who are making bone or bobbin lace, are chanting because lacemaking involves complicated counting; work songs have strong rhythms and repetitions which facilitate this. Yet, as McNeill also notes, the song that Feste eventually sings, 'Come away, death', does not seem to be a lacemakers' counting song or 'tell', as they were known, at all.[8] The socio-economic history that she elucidates is fascinating and important but it does not tell us much directly about the work that this song, and especially the way in which it is introduced and framed by Orsino, is doing in this scene.

Like Wyatt's poem, Orsino's speech conjures a nostalgic scene of female making as the context for song or tale. Unlike Wyatt's poem, the song which follows is not a fable or a satire, yet it does not fit or reflect the terms in which it has been introduced either. Its lyric content ventriloquizes the narcissistic Orsino, melodramatically 'slain by a fair cruel maid' (2.4.53). What the scene will go on to do, however, is invoke and then suppress another woman's story, that of Cesario's sister, who both is and is not Viola, who 'never told her love', whose history remained 'a blank' (2.4.110). One of the things that Orsino's frame does is to introduce and then frustrate or occlude a feminine mode of making and telling stories, anticipating the scene's later and more poignant female absent presence. Orsino's household is apparently an entirely male one, and one which, for all its music and lyricism, privileges the individual – no one has

---

[4] Lena Cowen Orlin, 'Three ways to be invisible in the Renaissance: Sex, reputation, and stitchery', in *Renaissance Culture and the Everyday*, ed. Patricia Fumerton and Simon Hunt (Philadelphia, 1999), pp. 183–203; p. 184. Orlin's essay began as a paper at the World Shakespeare Congress in 1996.
[5] Quotations from Shakespeare are from *William Shakespeare: The Complete Works*, ed. Stanley Wells, *et al.*, 2nd edn (Oxford, 2005).
[6] For work on printed pattern books, see, for example, Jones and Stallybrass, 'The needle and the pen: Needlework and the appropriation of printed texts', in their *Renaissance Clothing and the Materials of Memory*, pp. 134–71.
[7] Adam Fox, *Oral and Literate Culture in England, 1500–1700* (Oxford, 2000), p. 173.
[8] Fiona McNeill, *Poor Women in Shakespeare* (Cambridge, 2007), pp. 48–51.

ever loved like me, says Orsino – over the communal: there seems to be no room here for an alternative model of female speaking and subjective narration that might enable Cesario's sister to tell. And, as editors point out, although Orsino's companion Curio is identified by name in the dialogue, his colleague Valentine is only named as such in the speech prefixes. It is easy to find Ovid in *Twelfth Night*,[9] but Valentine and Orsino-Orson,[10] like Wyatt's mice, also belong, at least in name, to the more folkloric world of the lacemakers, the knitters and the spinsters.[11]

Sewing is one of the very few forms of making that can readily be staged. It does not require fire or heavy equipment; unlike cooking, it is not messy. (Also unlike cooking, it can be indefinitely extended as a staged process, rather than performing an action which must be completed in order to signify fully: a garland must be fully woven; a bow-tie tied, claret decanted, sandwich made. With sewing, timing is usually not an issue.)[12] Staged needlework could have a novelty value, especially in plays performed by the children's companies: Lois Potter cites *Ralph Roister Doister*, probably written by Nicholas Udall, probably for performance by schoolboys, in the mid-1550s, which includes

[an] elaborate scene in which the maidservants – Madge Mumblecrust, Tib Talkapace and Annot Alyface – sing while performing three different female occupations, sewing, spinning and knitting ('So shall we pleasantly bothe the tyme beguile now, / And eke dispatche all our works ere we can tell how'). The resulting song for three voices, the most popular form in this period, shows the women competing to see who can work fastest ('Sewe Tibet, knitte Anot, spinne Margerie, / Let us see who shall winne the victorie': lines 314–15).[13]

She suggests that 'This scene of manual labour by boys playing women must have looked as charming to spectators as it does to Ralph Roister Doister, who watches it'.[14] She also notes Bunch the Botcher, played by the clown, in *The Weakest Goeth to the Wall*, perhaps performed by the Earl of Oxford's boys in 1599 (and printed in 1600). The clown enters 'with a paire of sheares, a handbasket with a crossebottome of thread, three or foure paire of old stockings, peeces of fustian and cloath, &c' and proceeds to mend a stocking as he sings, so 'imitat[ing] the kind of basic mending that many men probably did themselves'.[15] Potter suggests that Dekker's *Shoemakers' Holiday*, with its workshop scenes, may have spawned imitators: Dekker himself made his Patient Grissil one of a family of basket-weavers and included a scene of such weaving: 'The task is partly symbolic: the easily bending osier stands for social and marital obedience.'[16]

Needlework can economically establish both setting (the private domestic interior, as in the examples discussed below) and character (the

---

[9] See Jonathan Bate, *Shakespeare and Ovid* (Oxford, 1993), pp. 144–51, and Hester Lees-Jeffries, *Shakespeare and Memory* (Oxford, 2013), pp. 122–4.

[10] 'Valentine and Orson' is a story of separated twins, the former raised as a knight at court, the latter in the forest by bears. It was probably French in origin, but there were versions in many other European vernacular languages, and an English version was printed in 1550; there was a play of the name performed in 1598. On the popularity of 'Valentine and Orson', see Helen Cooper, *The English Romance in Time: Transforming Motifs From Geoffrey of Monmouth to the Death of Shakespeare* (Oxford, 2004), esp. pp. 1, 36, 428–9.

[11] 'Tales of the supernatural were just some among the repertoire of yarns woven by wives and mothers as they sat and worked or sewed around the evening hearth. The Elizabethan, John Florio, was dismissive of the kind of "flim-flam tale, as women tell when they shale peason", or "ould wiues tales as they tell when they spinne"', Fox, *Oral and Literate Culture*, p. 189. 'Yarn', meaning 'story' seems to be nineteenth-century and possibly nautical in origin (OED, yarn, 2a).

[12] These examples are drawn from Rupert Goold's production of *Macbeth*, with Patrick Stewart (Chichester, London, New York, from 2007), filmed for BBC4 in 2010.

[13] Lois Potter, 'Skills, qualities, and practice', *Shakespeare Studies* 43 (2015), 27–34; p. 29.

[14] Potter, 'Skills, qualities, and practice', p. 29.

[15] Potter, 'Skills, qualities, and practice', p. 30.

[16] Potter, 'Skills, qualities, and practice', p. 30. See also the discussion of the basket-weaving scene by Tom Rutter, *Work and Play on the Shakespearean Stage* (Cambridge, 2008), pp. 112–13; he discusses *The Shoemakers' Holiday* at length.

good, sometimes dull, woman: 'In *Eastward Ho*, stitchery is stage shorthand to establish character: the unassuming Mildred is first seen "*sewing*"').[17] And needlework, and textile work more generally, can also focus attention on process, the making rather than the made. On stage, the stitches cannot easily be seen but the activity, and the repeated movements which constitute it, can be made visible. Even more than letters and other papers, staged or invocated sewing can act as a focusing mechanism for the audience: it demands a particular kind of real or imaginative attention to small or even invisible things and the precise and delicate movement of the hands. More than simply being the visual equivalent of asking characters or audience to listen, it can itself signal that request, and one of the things to which it perhaps invites more careful attention is a plurality of voices and the stories that do not necessarily get heard or written down. For an early modern audience in particular, sewing scenes might readily be associated with attentive listening. Frye notes women recording what they heard read aloud as they sewed in their diaries: Elizabeth Hoby noted Foxe, Latimer's *Sermons* and Bright's *Melancholy*, as well as other Protestant works, but Anne Clifford heard Ovid, Spenser and Montaigne.[18]

Ophelia has been sewing in her closet when she is visited and frightened by the apparently mad Hamlet in the episode she describes to her father in 2.1. Orlin describes this as her 'moment of greatest innocence', noting that 'Sewing scenes are often strategically employed in the interest of heightened dramatic contrast, to establish a woman's impregnable purity just before it is assailed or before she encounters some other form of jeopardy.'[19] In early modern dress at least it would not be incongruous for Ophelia still to be clutching her work when she describes the episode to Polonius and it would underscore that this can also be one of Ophelia's moments of quasi-dramaturgical power in the play, vividly describing and perhaps even performing Hamlet's appearance, gestures and actions. She is a maker, unfolding a tale (the textile metaphor resonates) analogous to that promised by the Ghost, who has, perhaps, himself been loosed out of hell. This moment's negative counterpart can be found in her mad scenes, her performance of ballad fragments, scraps of feminine oral culture.[20] The herbs and flowers that she distributes, if they were staged as such, could also recall such embroidery and specifically the 'slips', the individual motifs, frequently floral, which were one of the most common forms of embroidery worked by elite women: 'Once worked in a canvas ground, these slips could be cut out and sewn onto a woven fabric such as velvet, and they are found adorning all types of furnishings and clothing in the period, from gloves to wall hangings and bed curtains.'[21] When sent by her father and the king to intercept Hamlet in the lobby, however, Ophelia is given a book as camouflage. The book marks her solitariness as much as her needlework might stand for her participation in an unseen community of women but it also marks her inscription and incorporation into patriarchal narratives of paternal and political control.[22]

Early modern education was strongly gendered and further marked by the considerations of social class: Latin, especially Ovid, connoted public, masculine literacy; needlework evoked feminine private oracy.[23] Wendy Wall cites Anthony Munday's

---

[17] Orlin, 'Three ways to be invisible', p. 192.
[18] Frye, *Pens and Needles*, pp. 123–5.
[19] Orlin, 'Three ways to be invisible', pp. 192–3.
[20] See my discussion of Ophelia's madness as fragmentation and collection in *Shakespeare and Memory*, pp. 163–9.
[21] Whitney Trettien, 'Isabella Whitney's slips: Textile labor, gendered authorship, and the early modern miscellany', *Journal of Medieval and Early Modern Studies* 45 (2015), 505–21; p. 506.
[22] 'Only in *All Fools, 1 Edward IV, The Launching of the Mary, The Shoemaker's Holiday, The Wisdom of Doctor Dodypoll*, and *A Woman is a Weathercock* does a woman sit alone to sew ... Elsewhere, however, the group [sewing] scenes of the moralists are the rule.' Orlin, 'Three ways to be invisible', p. 193.
[23] Frye sets out the problems with the interpretation of this as a straightforward binary: 'The first misconception is that only women were associated with the needle and only men with the pen – a misconception held despite repeated attempts to complicate this binary by scholars as well as by early modern people themselves. The second misconception is that the needle was only associated with drudgery, while the pen

Fedele and Fortunio (1585), at the end of which Pedante proposes to Medusa with the suggestion

> I'll set up a great grammar schoole by and by,
> We shall thrive well enough, it will tumble in roundly.
> I'll teach boyes the Latin tongue, to write and to read,
> And thou, little wenches, their needle and thread,

suggesting that he 'dwells on needles as a sign of segregated schooling'.[24] Girls were trained in needlework because it offered them a means of earning an independent living, albeit an impoverished one, as well as contributing to a household economy. And plain sewing skills were needed for the manufacture of family clothing and household linens; all housewives needed to have basic embroidery skills so as to be able to mark their linens if they were being sent out for laundering, as was often the case. Amy Louise Erickson notes that

> Needlework alone – without reading – was available to very poor girls. Widows on poor relief in Ipswich at the end of the sixteenth century had daughters of between 7 and 11 who were at 'skoole to knyt' or who 'goeth to knitting schole'. An accomplished knitter could make 2s. a week, whereas these girls' mothers picked oakum for 4d., or made bone lace for 9d. a week.[25]

For these women, it was a means of survival, not simply a domestic or more ornamental accomplishment.

In *A Midsummer Night's Dream*, Helena's memories of her long friendship with Hermia are grounded in a similar identification of women's education with needlework, albeit in a much more elite context:

> O, is all quite forgot?
> All schooldays' friendship, childhood innocence?
> We, Hermia, like two artificial gods
> Have with our needles created both one flower,
> Both on one sampler, sitting on one cushion,
> Both warbling of one song, both in one key,
> As if our hands, our sides, voices, and minds
> Had been incorporate . . .
> And will you rend our ancient love asunder,
> To join with men in scorning your poor friend?
> (3.2.202–9, 216–17)

Elsewhere in the play, Hermia and Helena's friendship has been characterized as one shaped by shared confidences and conversations; their history is an oral one. And here, Helena parallels that with the recollection of shared embroidery: the women have grown up together in and through their shared production of needlework; they have sewn, sung, spoken their intertwined identities as women into existence. Jones and Stallybrass point out the speech's celebration of the 'inventive power' of the needleworkers, 'artificial gods' engaged in quasi-divine acts of creation, and the language of bodily incorporation which recalls the marriage service.[26] The ancient love being 'rent' is at least residually that sampler, destroying not simply a beautiful thing but the shared project and process, in time, of its creation.

What Helena is specifically remembering is probably a spot sampler, described by Frye as akin to a commonplace book, a way of recording and, more importantly, of sharing patterns and motifs which, she suggests, 'manifest lifetimes of connection among women'.[27] The sampler is a reminder that the traditional is that which is literally passed on and which, crucially, concerns process as well as product, skill as much as content. As Elizabeth Spiller puts it, discussing early modern making more generally, 'being able to make something was an act of knowledge; knowing something involved knowing how to make it'; she describes the work of early modern artisans as 'an alternative knowledge tradition'.[28]

---

was only associated with intellectual work. To a certain extent the needle represented women's obedience to a rigid insistence on sexual difference, but it is an unstable signifier and, as an object, it is small but phallic, penetrating as well as penetrable, conveying activity, even violence, as well as creativity' (*Pens and Needles*, p. 16).

[24] Wendy Wall, *Staging Domesticity: Household Work and English Identity in Early Modern Drama* (Cambridge, 2002), p. 65.

[25] Amy Louise Erickson, *Women and Property in Early Modern England* (London, 1995), p. 58, citing John Webb, ed., *Poor Relief in Elizabethan Ipswich* (Ipswich, 1966), pp. 126, 128, 133–5, 138.

[26] Jones and Stallybrass, *Renaissance Clothing and the Materials of Memory*, p. 153.

[27] Frye, *Pens and Needles*, p. 126.

[28] Elizabeth Spiller, 'Shakespeare and the making of early modern science: Resituating Prospero's art', *South Central Review* 26 (2009), 24–41; p. 27, cited by Porter, *Making and Unmaking in Early Modern English Drama*, p. 33.

Although she does not discuss women's making in these terms, the suggestion that women's textile work is less the opposite of masculine Latinity, or of a particular kind of narrative mode, defined as such by its (non) textuality, and more an alternative form of knowledge is an appealing one.

The connection between women, the construction of feminine identity, especially virtuous femininity, and needlework is a strong one in early modern literature and culture. In the Bisham entertainment, staged for Elizabeth I in 1592, Elizabeth Russell's daughters Isabella and Sibylla converted Pan to virtue and the service of the queen by describing the samplers that they were working on as they spoke. The samplers depicted 'the follies of the Gods, who became beastes, for their affections ... The honour of Virgins who became Goddesses for their chastity', with 'Mens tongues, wrought all with double stitch' and 'Roses, Eglentine, harts-ease, wrought with Queenes stitch, and all right'.[29] As Sara Mueller has suggested, 'The girls demonstrate their mastery not only of different kinds of stitches, hence displaying their sound education and hard work at mastering their craft, but they also reveal their mastery of the precepts of feminine virtue.'[30] In the poem's 'argument', Shakespeare's Lucrece is 'spinning amongst her maids'; in the poem, Tarquin is given momentary pause by 'Lucretia's glove wherein her needle sticks' (317) on his way to her chamber: the needle pricks his finger as he picks up the (conventionally erotic) glove, 'as who should say "This glove to wanton tricks / Is not inured. Return again in haste. / Thou seest our mistress' ornaments are chaste"' (320–2). Later in the period, Ford's incestuous Annabella calls for her work when she is alerted to the approach of her father, enabling her to strike 'a recognised pose of virtuous industry'; it is a 'talisman' or 'badge' of virtue.[31] In *Pericles*, Marina's virtue is indeed attested by her textile skills:

> [she] weaved the sleided silk
> With fingers long, small, white as milk;
> Or when she would with sharp nee'le wound
> The cambric ... (15.21–4)

Both her sewing and her singing are vastly superior to her rival Philoten and it is her combination of musical and embroidery skills that enables her to escape the brothel and earn an honest living teaching others (as well as silencing the voices of educated masculine authority):

> Deep clerks she dumbs, and with her nee'le composes
> Nature's own shape, of bud, bird, branch, or berry,
> That e'en her art sisters the natural roses.
> Her inkle, silk, twin with the rubied cherry;
> That pupils lacks she none of noble race ... (20.5–9)

Of course, *Pericles* itself is 'a song that old was sung' (1.1); its virtuous heroine, who sings and stitches, operates as a kind of romance *mise en abîme* if it is imagined that she too sings the old songs as she sews. One way of reading Gertrude's account of Ophelia's death might be as a further act not so much of ekphrastic reinscription but of a kind of embroidery that is not just rhetorical, embroidery that reincorporates both Ophelia and Gertrude herself into the familiar textile narratives of decorative female virtue, which make such songs acceptable, or bearable.[32] Gertrude, as it were, assembles the slips; she ornaments even as she conceals a solitary, sad little death.

* * *

Orlin explores the way in which textile work itself makes women invisible, and needlework itself is so closely identified with the feminine, especially the admirable feminine, that it becomes unremarkable; it does not need to be referred to directly, let alone to be made explicit in stage directions, for its onstage presence to be inferred. It could perhaps more readily be assumed that pairs or groups of women in Shakespeare's plays are sewing or carrying their needlework and therefore that the silent,

---

[29] *Speeches delivered to her maiestie this last progresse, at the right honourable the Lady Russels, at Bissham* ... (1592), A3r.
[30] Sara Mueller, 'Domestic work in progress entertainments', in *Working Subjects in Early Modern English Drama*, ed. Michelle M. Dowd and Natasha Korda (Farnham, 2011) pp. 145–59; p. 152.
[31] Orlin, 'Three ways to be invisible', pp. 183, 184, 185.
[32] To 'embroider' in a narrative sense, embellishing or elaborating a story in the telling, is just emerging at this time. OED, 'embroider', 2b, 2c.

unremarked presence of that work itself can sometimes perform work in narrative and dramaturgical terms. Needlework scenes focus attention on the making and telling of both stories and plays in performance and on the status of both plays and stories as dynamic made things.

The two sewing scenes which Shakespeare definitely stages are in *Coriolanus* and *Henry VIII*. The *Coriolanus* scene straightforwardly reflects classical models of domestic virtue and includes a usefully full stage direction:

Enter Volumnia and Virgilia, mother and wife to Martius. They set them down on two low stools and sew (1.3.0)

It is both the activity and the low stools that make this scene domestic: the actors would presumably carry their stool in one hand and their work in the other, and their proximity to the ground and to each other narrows the focus of the scene. It creates a tableau of domestic harmony and virtuous feminine industry, albeit one that is immediately distorted by Volumnia. (An early modern audience might note the contrast with *Antony and Cleopatra* 2.5, in which, awaiting news of Antony, Cleopatra calls first for music, then suggests billiards, then angling. Antony's first wife Fulvia is, presumably, an able seamstress, if Enobarbus's extended textile metaphor on hearing news of her death in 1.2.153–62 is any indication.)

The scene in *Henry VIII* is more interesting. The stage direction is briefer, '*Enter Queen Katherine and her women, as at work*' (3.1.0), but with the *Coriolanus* example in mind, it can be inferred that the women at least have stools, with perhaps a chair for the queen. The scene has Holinshed as its starting point, wherein the queen is described as having 'a skeine of white thred about hir necke', apparently sewing in her privy chamber.[33] (There were excellent examples of needlework scenes, featuring both Katherine of Aragon and Anne Boleyn, in the BBC adaptation of Hilary Mantel's *Wolf Hall* and *Bring up the Bodies* (2015).)

Katherine asks that their needlework be accompanied by music:

Take thy lute, wench. My soul grows sad with troubles.
Sing, and disperse 'em if thou canst. Leave working.
(3.1.1–2)

The song begins thus:

> Orpheus with his lute made trees,
> And the mountain tops that freeze,
> Bow themselves when he did sing.
> To his music plants and flowers
> Ever sprung, as sun and showers
> There had made a lasting spring. (3.1.3–8)

This scene of textile-making is accompanied by a classical lyric extolling other forms of aesthetic creation. The periodic syntax suggestively delays the verb so that, in its opening, the song announces that 'Orpheus with his lute made trees, and the mountain tops'. The 'plants and flowers' 'ever sprung' and the 'sun and showers ... made a lasting spring' suggest a moment frozen in time, image rather than text or melody. Orpheus was a frequent subject in early modern needlework.[34] The scene is interrupted first by a gentleman and then by the two cardinals, Wolsey and Campeius. As in Holinshed, Wolsey begins in Latin but Katherine exhorts him to speak in English and in the hearing of her attendants.

This scene is therefore one of competing and conjoined discourses and narratives and this is reinforced by its also being a sewing scene. It matters that the joins, the processes of making, show, as public is set against private, domestic against political, Latin against English, masculine against feminine. The inset lyric, the invocation of Ovid, the closeness of the chronicle source, emphasize the madeness of this dramatic artefact, as does the general editorial agreement that this is a Fletcher scene and that the song is recycled from another of Fletcher's plays. *Henry VIII* often draws attention to its own strangeness and hybridity, mingling masque and versified chronicle, pageant, prophecy and myth. A sewing scene, no matter how closely

---

[33] Raphael Holinshed, *The Third Volume of Chronicles* (1586), Rrrr2v.
[34] See above for Ovid's *Metamorphoses* being read aloud while women sewed.

based in historical fact, is one way of staging the possibility of different kinds of story and different kinds of storytelling, and here, also, the insufficiency of the textual, the Latin, the public.

Paralleling the sewing scene in *Henry VIII*, an implicit sewing scene in another late play can be posited. In many contemporary productions of *The Winter's Tale*, 2.1, in which Hermione is accused and arrested by Leontes, is staged as if Hermione and her ladies are putting the child Mamillius to bed, presumably because the idea of the bedtime story still inheres with affective nostalgia in the way that a sewing scene does not, especially if Mamillius (as seems almost compulsory) wears blue-striped pyjamas.[35] But there is nothing in the text to suggest that bedtime setting; rather, a domestic *mise en scène* of stools and chair seems more likely, an intimate, harmonious, benign world of women and children into which Leontes and his lords intrude. This could be very easily reinforced in a performance in early modern dress by having Hermione and her ladies sewing; such a context would be entirely logical for the tale-telling promised by Mamillius. A sewing scene would give a material form to the play's interest in fabrication, both narrative and aesthetic, and is perhaps further indicated by Hermione's instruction to her son, 'Pray you sit by us' (2.1.23): Hermione at least is sitting down, and presumably her women are too. In modern dress a bedtime setting can succeed very well in affective terms, but any sense of women's making and of craft is lost.

There were many men involved in textile trades: most tailors were men, as were most professional embroiderers. Henslowe's accounts suggest that running repairs and at least some costume making or alteration were undertaken by the in-house tireman.[36] Most people, men or women, would have been able to mend their own clothes at the level of sewing on a point or applying a patch. The needlework imagined and perhaps staged in these scenes, however, was one of the defining accomplishments of socially elite women. To speak of the performance of gender and of gender itself as performative is unremarkable: needlework is a very particular kind of performativity

and one that, as an activity of making, draws a particular kind of attention to itself as both performative and constitutive. In thinking about boy actors, it has become usual to dwell, as Jones and Stallybrass have suggested, on the body beneath[37] or perhaps to think about their musical abilities, recalling contemporary accounts of the musical skills of the children's companies, the Willow Song and other lyrics apparently performed by boys in the adult companies,[38] or even the enduring fetishization of the boy treble. In watching adolescent boys performing women's parts, in companies such as Edward's Boys, one's attention is sometimes drawn to the tendency to gangly wristiness and awkward outsize hands (not as easily concealed as outsize feet) that can characterize boys in their mid-teens.[39] But what about what those hands had to do? Did boys playing women's parts *commonly* sew on stage, in the same way as they wore wigs and painted their faces, and to the same end, the performance of a simulacrum of femininity? It seems not unlikely: if they could do it, mandated by stage directions in *Coriolanus* and *Henry VIII*, they could do it in *The Winter's Tale* (and elsewhere).[40]

Like the story of Cesario's sister, Mamillius's winter's tale, with its fairy-tale promise of sprites and goblins, remains unheard. When, at the play's conclusion, Paulina fears that any account of Hermione's being alive might well be 'hooted

---

[35] In the Propeller production (dir. Edward Hall, 2005, 2011–12), and at the RSC in 2006 (dir. Dominic Cooke) and 2009 (dir. David Farr).
[36] See Jean MacIntyre, *Costumes and Scripts in the Elizabethan Theatre* (Edmonton, 1992), pp. 96–7.
[37] Jones and Stallybrass, 'Transvestism and the "body beneath": Speculating on the boy actor', in *Renaissance Clothing and the Materials of Memory*, pp. 207–19.
[38] For example, 'Take, O take those lips away' in *Measure* 4.1, where the singer is 'Boy'.
[39] Edward's Boys is an ensemble of students from King Edward VI School in Stratford-upon-Avon which, since 2005, has performed plays written for the boys' companies under the direction of Perry Mills. See www.edwardsboys.org.
[40] In a longer version of this article (in progress), I explore the possibility that the 'English lesson' scene in *Henry V*, 3.4 is also a sewing scene.

at / Like an old tale' (5.3.117–18) without the material proof of the thing itself, she overlays such a tale with the Pygmalion narrative and with biblical narratives of resurrection.[41] Both the putative sewing scene and the statue scene stage different ways of telling and narrating and different kinds of making and made-ness, material and theatrical. The statue scene does not come out of nowhere: it is partly anticipated by this earlier scene of a tale that has to be taken on trust by both actors and audience, whispered by a child in his mother's ear, and the needlework with which the good queen and her maids might hypothetically, but legitimately, be equipped.

Left only with the products of women's textile labour, it is all too easy to treat them as texts, to go source hunting, and to read them as finished expressions of identity and ideology. Literary critics have tended to privilege elite textile productions, often with narrative content drawn from the Bible or from Ovid, frequently via the intermediary of Dutch engravings. Yet the sampler, the cushion, the hanging, even if it is as elaborate as those created by Bess of Hardwick, Mary Queen of Scots and their women, is only part of the story. It is the static finished product, not the process or the scene of making; it is the printed text rather than the play in performance, dynamic, plastic, collaborative, spatio-temporally constituted. Something like a hanging made from 'slips', 'a play was pieced together out of a collection of odds and ends: it was not a single whole entity';[42] as Chloe Porter has pointed out, to 'piece', as it is used in the Prologue to *Henry V*, for example ('Piece out our imperfections with your thoughts', 23), is at least partly textile in its referents.[43] The chorus invites the audience to *make* with him.

The associations between textile labour, especially needlework, the fashioning of femininity, and different forms of story, often primarily oral and traditional, are therefore mutually reinforcing in Shakespeare's plays. Needlework is marked by time, by song, by story, even before it becomes (in Jones and Stallybrass's resonant term) the materials of memory. Textile work marks time more than writing does, whether through its nostalgic evocation of the past or because it is rhythmically made. It need not have figurative content, to be 'story work', so-called, to be the material trace of a lost world of story and song. Like the stories that are not necessarily found in Holinshed, or Plutarch, or Ovid, needlework is dynamic, communal, memetic, handed down, not always written down. And it is certainly not to dismiss the customary equivalence between writing and needlework to suggest that dramatic writing might be a particularly dense instantiation of this: performed and experienced in time and space, an embodied practice, a communal activity. Like stories and like theatre itself, textile making is grounded in the possibility of remaking and recycling, of continuing future activity, retelling, re-creation.

---

[41] See, for example, Lees-Jeffries, *Shakespeare and Memory*, pp. 193–5.
[42] Tiffany Stern, *Documents of Performance in Early Modern England* (Cambridge, 2009), p. 1.
[43] See Porter, *Making and Unmaking in Early Modern English Drama*, pp. 28–30.

WHY PROSPERO DROWNED HIS BOOKS, AND OTHER CATHOLIC FOLKLORE

HELEN COOPER

This is an article about the role of cultural memory and the shaping of the imagination – in particular, Shakespeare's imagination – in Reformation England. It attempts to study the persistence of memory and habit, and the preservation of memories with the help of old books: specifically, the collection of saints' lives known as the *Golden Legend*. The original compilation was made around 1260 by Jacobus de Voragine, archbishop of Genoa, in Latin, from which it was translated into numerous European vernaculars. There were a number of versions adapted or derived from it in Middle English, which often added in additional saints, usually English ones, and saints' lives remained a staple of the early years of English printing.[1] Jacobus's entire collection was translated by way of a French intermediary by William Caxton and printed as a substantial folio in 1483. As was normal in these early prints, it had no title page but the colophon announced it as 'the legende named in latyn legenda aurea', and it was as the *Golden Legend* that later generations knew it. It was an immediate success: there were some ten editions down to 1527, each of them with variations in contents – additional biblical stories or a greater emphasis on English saints – until foreshadowings of the Reformation finally closed in on such works. More striking still is how many copies still survive: at least 130, perhaps many more.[2] Given the number of occasions when there would have been incentives to destroy copies – not just at the Reformation itself, but under the Commonwealth or any of the later anti-Catholic or pro-rationalist movements in England, quite apart from the effects of normal wear and tear – there must have been many more copies still around in the sixteenth century. Books are durable assets and the *Golden Legend* had been an expensive one too. It is evident that many – hundreds – of people did not just throw their copies away in response either to Cranmer's reforms of the Church or the Anglican Settlement, even if they blacked out the descriptor 'pope' from the index or crossed through sections of legends that they found particularly offensive.[3] Those fierce anti-Catholic and anti-superstition polemicists Reginald Scot and Samuel Harsnett

---

[1] See Eamon Duffy, *The Stripping of the Altars: Traditional Religion in England 1400–1580* (New Haven, 1992), pp. 77–9. The most popular of the medieval adaptations, John Mirk's *Festiall* or *Liber festivalis*, went through twenty-three editions between 1483 and 1532.

[2] The number of copies in major libraries collected for the *Electronic Short Title Catalogue* comes to over 130, but there are likely to be others in smaller or private libraries that have not yet been noted. The number of editions depends on how variant editions are counted.

[3] This is the case with around half the copies reproduced on EEBO; of particular interest in showing how the affiliation of successive owners might change is the EEBO copy of the 1521 edition, STC 24879.5, which has a marginalium hoping that the author was well-intentioned (f. 1), 'pope' both deleted and then re-inserted by hand in the 'Tabula' of saints' lives, and the life of St Thomas of Canterbury removed altogether. The British Library 1527 Wynkyn de Worde edition (STC 24880) has similar deletions in its 'Tabula' of lives, f. liii–iiii[v], and the Translation of St Thomas Becket, f. clxvii[v]. This is the copy used in this article, as the 1527 edition has the largest number of copies known to survive. Cited hereafter as [*Legend*]; none of the editions carries a title page.

both included it in their armoury, and Archbishop Matthew Parker's copy still survives.[4] It is also the kind of book that recusants would have been particularly likely to preserve, including quite possibly Shakespeare's Catholic Arden cousins and, in view of the number of copies still extant, there might well have been others in Stratford itself, perhaps in the church, perhaps in the ownership of men such as the town's schoolmasters who had Catholic sympathies or connections, perhaps also in conformist households that were happy to keep it on a shelf with appropriate deletions of less favoured passages.[5]

In any case, knowledge of its stories was not limited to the printed text. Although there is a range of early sources for them, some claiming eyewitness testimony or recorded by careful historians such as Eusebius, they also travelled by word of mouth along the network of roads radiating out from Rome and beyond. Oral transmission in turn encouraged both elaboration on the originals and new stories loosely modelled on the old but which often resembled romances much more than sober accounts of persecution or exemplary perseverance.[6] Their dissemination was given institutional support by the inclusion of appropriate readings (*legenda*, texts to be read) in the liturgy proper to the particular saint's day, by the importance of shrines dedicated to individual saints, and by relics held there, in parish churches or as part of the devotional paraphernalia in royal treasuries or private houses. The whole cult was encouraged further by the practice of ascribing specific areas of action to each saint, so that one selected a saint as the addressee of prayer depending on whether one were a shoemaker or a tailor or whether one suffered from toothache or impotence. Such legends had thus been familiar in oral as well as written form for centuries, not least because they were very good stories; the entertaining often indeed outdid the edifying. The *Legend* has been described as 'a religious Arabian Nights entertainment for every day of the year', and its stories are still often told to children in Catholic countries.[7] That Catholicism was so closely integrated into everyday life made for a lively oral culture alongside the official practices of the Church. Jacobus incorporated a good deal of such culture into his own legends, and the proliferation of both that and of material too implausible, or too local, for him to include carried through unbroken into the early modern era.[8] This kind of subject-matter caused embarrassment even within the Roman church and led to the Bollandists' rewriting of hagiography from the Counter-Reformation forwards,[9] but there was common ground on both sides of the confessional gulf in that both Catholics and Protestants embraced a marked division between more illiterate communities who preserved and encouraged such a proliferation of legend and the literate elite who decried it.[10]

The 'folklore' in the title of this chapter is meant to serve as an indicator of the popularity of such material. It is only possible to access oral culture through the written record and, so far as identifying any writer's sources is concerned, unequivocal proof is likely to come only through verbal similarity. We can be quite sure, however, that neither Shakespeare nor anyone else in England needed to have read the *Golden Legend* in order to know about St George and the dragon: Stratford was by no means alone in having a pageant that featured

---

[4] See Reginald Scot, *The Discoverie of Witchcraft* (1584), pp. 163–4, 459, and his dismissal of it along with Adam Bell and Friar Rush, 'Discourse vpon Diuels and Spirits', p. 498; Samuel Harsnett, *A Declaration of Egregious Popish Impostures* (1603), p. 118; and Parker's copy held in the Parker Library, Corpus Christi College, Cambridge.

[5] Alison Shell, *Oral Culture and Catholicism in Early Modern England* (Cambridge, 2007), pp. 85–7.

[6] Helen C. White, *Tudor Books of Saints and Martyrs* (Madison, WI, 1963), pp. 4–14.

[7] Donald A. Stauffer, *English Biography before 1700* (Cambridge, MA, 1930), p. 22.

[8] Shell, *Oral Culture*, pp. 20–1. For a collection of hagiographic material too weird for Jacobus, see C. Grant Loomis, *White Magic: The Folklore of Christian Legend* (Cambridge, MA, 1948).

[9] The Jesuit Bollandists set out in the early seventeenth century to produce a scholarly set of saints' lives, so excising the popular and ahistorical elements that Jacobus had incorporated into his *Legenda*; the work is still incomplete.

[10] Shell, *Oral Culture*, p. 56.

him (it was suppressed under Edward VI but revived under Mary). St Margaret's somewhat different dragon would be equally familiar, along with the story of St Christopher's carrying of the infant Christ; and St Barbara's flight through the air might have come not so far behind.[11] The *Golden Legend* included not only stories of this kind, with a good proportion of strong-minded women, but also various legends of more obscure women saints who entered monasteries disguised as men and were then accused, by lustful women whose sexual advances they refused, of either rape or of fathering a child.[12] Cross-dressing, in fact, was nothing new for sixteenth-century readers and perhaps for storytellers too. It is too easy to think of Protestantism as the official form of religion in England from the 1530s onwards and to overlook the revival of Catholicism under Mary in the 1550s. Everyone just ten years older than Shakespeare would have had vivid memories of an England with a full Catholic culture, and whatever his parents' view on religion may have been, they would have had abundant experience of that active Catholicism. Famously, John Shakespeare, as town bailiff of Stratford, was responsible for getting the wall paintings in the Guild Chapel whitewashed over in the year before Shakespeare was born: paintings that included not only the Last Judgement over the chancel arch but also various saints from the *Legend* including St George and St Thomas Becket.[13] It is of course impossible to prove that anyone described to the young Shakespeare what was under the whitewash, but it seems implausible that they would not have done so that those newly blank white walls would not have been filled in by spoken stories.

That is hypothetical – and so is this article. I set out to try to answer the question – 'Did Shakespeare know the *Golden Legend*?', and I have failed to answer it either positively or negatively: it remains a 'perhaps'. There are sufficient similarities between Caxton's book and Shakespeare's own works to keep open the possibility that he knew it but they are neither close enough nor consistent enough to prove that he did. The points where his works come closest in verbal similarity are also the moments of striking imagery or phrasing such as might remain in the imagination, not least a child's imagination, from oral readings or retellings of its stories. Whether or not he had any direct knowledge, the *Legend* and its lives were still part of that wide context of narrative, that sea of stories, in which he grew up. We perpetually look at the official, humanist reading matter of the sixteenth century that he encountered from his schooldays onwards, Ovid and Plautus in the classroom, Plutarch and Holinshed in adulthood; we too easily forget how much else was around and available to him. Mothers and nursemaids, as the humanists never failed to complain, brought up their children on very different literary fare. Stories told around the fireside or to children at bedtime, in Stratford or anywhere else, were not Ovidian or Plutarchan. We know that Shakespeare knew, or read (because he quotes it) the much-reprinted romance of Bevis of Hampton, originally composed in the early fourteenth century; and he alludes to a good number of other such romances. He knew the medieval story collection entitled the *Gesta Romanorum* and Caxton's pedagogically more demanding *Recueil of the History of Troy*. Furthermore, he read all of those, and a good many other things too, in prints dating from before 1565, even when later editions were available; and his Chaucer, which first makes its presence strongly felt in the mid-1590s in *A Midsummer Night's Dream*, and his Gower, used first in *The Comedy of Errors* before it dominated *Pericles*, were likewise old editions.[14]

---

[11] [*Legend*], St George's dragon, f. cxi^v; St Margaret, ff. clxvi–vii; St Christopher, ff. clxxvi–viii; St Barbara's flight, f. cccxvii.

[12] [*Legend*], St Marina, f. cxxxiii; St Theodora, ff. clxi^v–xiii; St Eugenia, f. ccxl; St Pelagia (also known as St Margaret), ff. cclxvii^v–viii (the second of two successive saints with the same alternative names; the previous one ended her life cross-dressed as a hermit).

[13] A. G. Harmon argues that a cultural familiarity with the story of Becket's martyrdom, perhaps encouraged by his commemoration in the Guild Chapel, lies behind the end of *Richard II* ('Shakespeare's carved saints', *Studies in English Literature* 45 (2005), 315–31).

[14] Helen Cooper, *Shakespeare and the Medieval World* (London, 2010), pp. 168, 176–9, 204–6, 221.

They were thus all things that he could have read in his childhood or teens; and so a *Golden Legend* from the 1520s is not out of line with his other reading patterns. Various people within Shakespeare's circle might have had these books: in addition to the Ardens, perhaps his neighbours the Fields, whose son Richard was sufficiently book-mad to be sent off to London to be apprenticed to a printer and later took over the business. It is highly likely, indeed, in view of the printing history of many popular works, that the Shakespeares themselves had a few books in the corner of a cupboard. Many of the cheap prints of medieval texts were the standard fare of households of any degree of literacy: quarto editions of those metrical romances or broadside ballads of Robin Hood. Books, especially more substantial books, were passed down from one generation to another or bought second-hand. We have no idea what the house in Henley Street may have contained but absence of evidence is not evidence of absence – and the many allusions in Shakespeare's works add up at least to circumstantial evidence that they had *something*.

The evidence for Shakespeare's acquaintance with the *Golden Legend* is scattered throughout Caxton's translation. One of the most striking instances is a passage in the Life of St James the Greater (the More), in which there is a collocation of a number of things that also occur in *The Tempest*: a staff with magical powers; a magician who can render people immobile but who later repents of his magic; and a boat 'without sayle or rother', like the boat with no 'tackle, sail, nor mast' in which Prospero was cast adrift.[15] None of those is especially uncommon in widespread Elizabethan reading matter of various kinds, though they are not often found together, and the Life of St James furthermore disperses them across two separate episodes and uses them to tell a different story. In themselves, they would make the *Golden Legend* no more than a soft analogue, that is, an item that contains analogous material but which is not close enough to be defined as a source. More significant, however, is that the magician, named Hermogenes, once reformed, has to drown his books, not burn them – drown them, apparently in order that the demons they contain will not be able to escape in the smoke or at least so that people will not believe that they might have done so:

Than he went & brought to þe apostle all his bokes of his false crafte & enchauntynge for to be brent. But saynt Iames bycause that þe odour of þe brennynge myght do euyll or harme to some fooles / he made them to be cast in to the see.   (f. clxiii^v)

This drowning of books of magic is very unusual indeed. That they should be burned is authorized, if not commanded, in the Acts of the Apostles (19.19), which was commonly cited in medieval and early modern texts in relation to the Old Testament prohibition on divining, astrology, enchantment, consultation with familiar spirits and necromancy (Deuteronomy 18.10–12). The burning of such books was a standard practice in the sixteenth century as in the Middle Ages, alongside an increasing concern both to suppress necromantic magic (i.e. involving supernatural powers) and to deny its efficacy.[16] Demonic magic was especially condemned, but the more superstitious end of Christian magic such as involved charms or talismans was also deplored by the Catholic church hierarchy as well as by the Reformers.

The official aim of book-burning was to prevent the dissemination of the ideas the books contained

---

[15] Most of these appear in the apocryphal episode concerning the magician Hermogenes, plus the miraculous transportation of the saint's corpse in a rudderless boat, [*Legend*], ff. clxiii–vi. See also *The Tempest*, 1.2.147, 3.3.67–8, 5.1.7–11, 61, 255–6 (*William Shakespeare: The Complete Works*, ed. Stanley Wells, *et al.* (Oxford, 1986)). Prospero's staff is not mentioned until 5.1.54, but its presence is implied in his drawing of a circle on the ground, and it is likely elsewhere; it has a regular role in the performance history of the play.

[16] See, for instance, James Mason, *The Anatomie of Sorcerie* (London, 1612), pp. 89–90; *Witches, Devils, and Doctors in the Renaissance: Johann Weyer, De praestigiis daemonum*, ed. George Mora, trans. John Shea, Medieval & Renaissance Texts & Studies (Binghamton, NY, 1991), p. 484; Richard Kieckhefer, *Magic in the Middle Ages* (Cambridge, 1989), pp. 156–93; on the increase in concern, see also Corinne Saunders, *Magic and the Supernatural in Medieval English Romances* (Cambridge, 2010), pp. 71–7.

but that segued easily into the more popular belief that the figures or spells written in them carried their demonic power with them and that those powers extended from the figures to the material on which they were inscribed.[17] The existence of such a belief is witnessed principally by the number of refutations it invited from more orthodox clerics.[18] The polemicist Johann Weyer describes a belief that 'evil demons' listed in one book have promised obedience to it, so that the book is 'scrupulously guarded lest it be used for some unauthorized purpose'.[19] Caliban is convinced that Prospero will lose all his powers if his books are burned, for

> without them
> He's but a sot as I am, nor hath not
> One spirit to command   (3.2.93–5)

– phrasing that suggests that the books contain more than words alone: he could learn the charms by heart but he needs the books if the spirits are to manifest themselves. For those who took a more material view of the magic, however, burning might still not be a wholly efficacious way to dispose of the demons that such books contained. A spell or curse inscribed on a cloth that was then buried near a victim's house could be reversed by destroying the material on which it was written, by digging up and burning the cloth and then throwing the ashes into running water – a double destruction of the magic.[20] Reginald Scot, in the *Discourse vpon Diuels and Spirits* appended to his *Discoverie of Witchcraft* of 1584, describes how the occultist Fascitus Cardanus (Fascizo Cardano) continued to be pestered by his 'familiar diuell' even after burning his books; the only change was that the devil now gave false answers.[21] The notion in the legend of St James that demons might in some way be present in 'þe odour of þe brennynge' is presumably related to demons' well-known affinity with the smoke of fumigation, a standard element in their conjuration.[22] Folk belief, however, persisted despite all the propaganda to the contrary, and stories such as that of Hermogenes did not do much to quell it. Shakespeare is careful not to associate Prospero too directly with devils and the whole supernatural machinery of the play is overtly fictional. But the elves and others through whom he operates the 'rough magic' that he finally abjures are far from being beneficent.[23] His ability to raise storms, as we first encounter him doing, and his ability to summon the dead are regular features of demonic magic. So he has good reason to dispose of his book; but that he drowns it rather than burning it is something that he seems to share only with the *Golden Legend* life of St James, and that turns the story from a soft analogue into something that commands more serious consideration as a possible source.

The idea that Shakespeare might have had some acquaintance with the *Golden Legend*, or that there are some marked similarities between it and his own works, is not original to this article. One recent example is Lawrence Warner's claim that the legend of the mother of Thomas Becket was the source for the courtship of Othello and Desdemona.[24] Becket's mother, according to legend (in both senses: it seems likely to have been a story transferred, quite possibly orally, from similar tales current in romance culture), was a Saracen princess, who fell in love with an English crusader named Gilbert Becket after he had

---

[17] Recommended writing surfaces included the skin of deer, cat, hare or female dog (Kieckhefer, *Magic*, pp. 9, 191, 171, 7).

[18] It is noted, for instance, by St Thomas Aquinas, *Summa contra Gentiles* III.II.105,10: magical symbols and characters are just signs, and there is no inherent power in either the symbol itself or 'the bodies on which these figures are put' (dhspriory.org/Thomas/ContraGentiles3b.htm, accessed 18 October 2016). For an early modern example, see Mora, *Witches, Devils, and Doctors*, pp. 402–5.

[19] Mora, *Witches, Devils, and Doctors*, p. 112.

[20] Kieckhefer, *Magic*, pp. 163–4 – though in this instance the object was to set the devils free from the cloth.

[21] Scot, *Discourse*, in his *Discoverie of Witchcraft*, p. 497. Elsewhere in the *Discoverie*, Scot treats Cardano as a fellow sceptic.

[22] Kieckhefer, *Magic*, pp. 6, 7, 157, 166.

[23] *The Tempest*, 5.1.50–1.

[24] Lawrence Warner, 'Desdemona's wooing: Towards a pre-1538 *Othello*', in *Word and Self Estranged in English Texts, 1550–1660*, ed. Philippa Kelly and Liam Semler (Aldershot, 2010), pp. 121–34.

been captured by her father. She hears them talking together,

> by whiche conuersacyon it fortuned þᵗ the doughter of this prynce had especyall loue vnto this Gylberte / & was familyer with hym. And on a tyme she disclosed her loue to hym. (f. lx)

Gilbert promises to marry her if she will convert to Christianity but he escapes back to England; she follows him to London, is duly converted, and gives birth to Thomas.[25] The Saracen princess who falls for a Christian knight is a common motif in early romance, and the pressure to have a hero born under very special circumstances is universal; the appearance of both in the Becket legend may well have been an instance of an oral story adopted into the written culture.[26] The similarities between the legend and *Othello* seem to me again to fall short of proving that it is a direct source – conversations with a father, for instance, are not the same as courtship by storytelling; but it is at worst an interesting analogue, and it is closer than the other suggested sources cited by Warner, Aeneas's recounting of the fall of Troy being the favourite.

Other of the saints' legends contain episodes strongly suggestive of the plays. St Agnes, like the Marina of *Pericles*, is put in a brothel, in her case by a wicked provost and, like Marina, she converts all the young men who come to have sex with her, though since she is a strenuously virgin saint, when the son of the provost arrives 'for taccomplysshe his euyll wyll', he is instantly strangled by the devil – an act of divine vengeance such as is reserved in *Pericles* for the tyrant Antiochus and his daughter.[27] Some legends share their structure with Shakespeare's plots, notably those of families rediscovering each other. The legend of St Clement tells of a woman shipwrecked with her three sons, who, believing them drowned, is given shelter and a home by kind people in the country where she comes ashore. She hears that her husband is also dead but refuses to marry again; and meantime her husband is told by his wicked brother that she had been unfaithful to him. Finally, however, they are all reunited, and the husband accepts his wife as being truly faithful – all told with much circumstantial detail.[28] It is a kind of mix of the *Comedy of Errors*, *Pericles* and *The Winter's Tale*. The story of Apollonius of Tyre, in various redactions (especially Gower's), was the immediate source for the frame of the *Comedy* and of all of *Pericles* but the legend of Clement shows how familiar that story outline was. St Clement was by no means unknown in England, too: witness the two churches dedicated to him in London (St Clement Danes and St Clement Eastcheap) and, for evidence of the wider dissemination of the story in the Midlands, a fifteenth-century wall painting in a house at Piccotts End, Hertfordshire, in which he is identified by his iconographic symbol of an anchor on his shoulder.[29] Further close parallels with *Pericles* appear in the life of Mary Magdalene. It has long been recognized that the Digby play of *Mary Magdalene* of *c.* 1500 is curiously like *Pericles*; the *Golden Legend* tells the same story in a form much more widely accessible, even though it does not offer any of the parallels of stagecraft.[30] It includes an episode in which a husband and wife (the equivalents of Pericles and Thaisa) go to sea, and in the course of their voyage encounter

> a grete tempest & orage. / & the wynde encreased & grewe ouer hydous / in suche wyse that this lady whiche was grete & nygh the tyme of her chyldynge began to wexe feble / & had grete anguisshe for the grete wawes &

---

[25] [*Legend*], f. lx. The story first appears as an interpolation in a Latin life of Becket of the late twelfth or early thirteenth century.

[26] On the predominance of the Saracen princess motif, see Judith Weiss, 'The wooing woman in Anglo Norman romance', in *Romance in Medieval England*, ed. Maldwyn Mills, Carol Meale and Jennifer Fellows (Cambridge, 1991), pp. 149–61.

[27] [*Legend*], f. lxxv. [28] [*Legend*], ff. cccxviiiᵛ–xxxiᵛ.

[29] Simon Schama, *The Face of Britain: The Nation through its Portraits* (London, 2015), pp. 22–5. St Clement appears in the far right, somewhat damaged, panel of the five-panel painting.

[30] See Joanne M. Rochester, 'Space and staging in the Digby *Mary Magdalen* and *Pericles, Prince of Tyre*', *Early Theatre* 13 (2010), 43–62.

troublynge of þe see / & soone after began to trauaille & was delyuered of a fayr sone by occasyon of þe storm & tempeste / and in her chyldynge dyed.[31]

As in the play, the sailors refuse to keep the corpse on board; but the legend, like the play, ultimately has a happy ending, with the wife brought back to life and the father recovering both wife and child. As in the case of St Clement, this belongs with the realm of folklore, of a sea of stories common to the whole Mediterranean region that emerges alike in the Apollonius story and in the saints' lives: legends where apparently miraculous recoveries are indeed just that, miraculous.[32] Again, whether or not Shakespeare had read these, they provide a context for the reception of his plays.

Beyond these episodes, there are also instances of phrasing in his work that might suggest a knowledge of the *Golden Legend*. The devil is at one point described as the Prince of Darkness, the same phrase that Tom-o-Bedlam uses.[33] The immediate source of the phrase may well have been Samuel Harsnett's *Declaration of Egregious Popish Impostures*, from which Shakespeare acquired the names of Tom's devils, but Harsnett, as a knowledgeable polemicist, shows a familiarity with a good many saints' lives, and it is possible that he had himself picked the phrase up from what he calls 'the golden legend booke'.[34] In another story the devil leads a lustful young man 'into a derke valley / & there he waded ouer waters & dyches, myres & hedges', and ultimately into a 'foule myre', again like Poor Tom.[35] There are other smaller details too. Although the existence of guardian angels was widely recognized, it is harder to find a source for the idea of a personal evil angel such as appears in Sonnet 144, 'Two loves I have'; but the *Legend* knows all about them, 'To euery man ben gyuen two aungelles / one euyll for to styre hym to yll / & one good to kepe hym.'[36] It was not necessary to know the *Legend* to be familiar with the idea, but the work does give authority for it. More specific might be Katherine of Aragon's vision before her death of 'six personages clad in white robes, wearing on their heads garlands of bays, and golden visors on their faces', who do homage to her, and she describes how their 'bright faces / Cast thousand beams upon me, like the sun'.[37] St Clare has a comparable vision before her death of 'a grete company of virgyns ... all cladde with white clothes / & eche of them bare a crowne of golde on theyr hedes', who likewise do homage and whose leader (in fact the Blessed Virgin, though for obvious reasons she is not mentioned in *Henry VIII*) lights up the whole room with 'a right grete clerenes ... that it semed þᵉ nyght to be clere daye'.[38] A vision of this kind might sound as if it should be commonplace but the passage from the *Legend* is much closer to the play than the parallels in Revelations (4.4, 14.4) most often cited as its source.

Whether Shakespeare, or his collaborators in the jointly authored plays, knew the *Legend* directly or whether some of these ideas and imagery flowed out into the general culture, into memory, is impossible to know. By the time he was writing *Henry VIII*, Catholicism was not so much of a taboo area as it had been under Elizabeth. In 1620, Massinger and Dekker dramatized the death of St Dorothy in *The Virgin Martyr*, including the legend that in midwinter, after a man had challenged her to bring him the roses and apples of Christ that she had spoken of, a holy child came to her with a basket full of them to give to him.[39] A play of St Christopher, now lost, was famously offered to a recusant household in Yorkshire in 1609 as an alternative to plays of Lear and Pericles

---

[31] [*Legend*], f. clxviiiᵛ.
[32] Peter Womack, 'Shakespeare and the sea of stories', *Journal of Medieval and Early Modern Studies* 29 (1999), 169–87, suggests that the Apollonius story was itself the source for the legend of Mary Magdalene and that sacred and profane stories formed a 'common repertoire' (p. 172). That the Apollonius story itself had still earlier precursors is by no means impossible.
[33] [*Legend*], f. lxviiiᵛ; *The Tragedy of King Lear* (folio text), 3.4.134.
[34] Samuel Harsnett, *A Declaration of Egregious Popish Impostures* (1603), pp. 147, 168, 118; Geoffrey Bullough, ed., *Narrative and Dramatic Sources of Shakespeare*, vol. 7 (London, 1973), pp. 414–20.
[35] [*Legend*], f. cxᵛ; cf. *Lear*, 3.4.48–50, 124–5.
[36] [*Legend*], f. cclvii. [37] *Henry VIII* [*All is True*], 4.2.82–9.
[38] [*Legend*], f. cccxiiiᵛ. [39] [*Legend*], ff. cccxlii–iii.

by a company of travelling Catholic players, in a dramatization that told the story of the saint as found in the *Legend* in a much fuller version of his life than the amputated limb of it that is generally known now.[40] It was the additional anti-Protestant satire added to the story, not the legend itself, that incurred the particular wrath of the Star Chamber and which led to its entering the records. Other sources for Christopher's story, as for many of its saints, are possible but the *Golden Legend* was both accessible and still familiar, and it at least prepared potential audiences for dramatizations of wonder stories that would have had some ring of familiarity about them – stories whose elements and structures would have been known.

Oral culture and popular memory such as shaped storytelling in the early modern era are notoriously hard to recover, and so are reading practices within the household or outside formal education, especially if the reading matter fell beyond the range of approved texts. It was there, however, that the young Shakespeare's imagination was shaped. We still cannot be sure whether the *Golden Legend* itself was a part of that cultural memory, though the possibility remains open. What we can be sure of is that wonder tales of the sort that the *Legend* contains were a part of the popular culture in which he grew up and they in due course became part of a shared bond with his audience.

---

[40] See Phebe Jensen, 'Recusancy, festivity and community: The Simpsons at Gowlthwaite Hall', in *Region, Religion and Patronage*, ed. Richard Dutton, Alison Findlay and Richard Wilson (Manchester, 2003), pp. 101–20. She notes its closeness to the *Legend* version of St Christopher and argues that the play may have been intended to 'replicate medieval theatrical culture' (pp. 107–9).

WHY DID THE ENGLISH STAGE TAKE BOYS FOR ACTRESSES?

PAMELA ALLEN BROWN

English professionals used skilled boys and youths to play female roles until the Restoration, many decades after their Continental counterparts began to use actresses. The nagging question is why. Did audiences prefer female impersonation by males or did the structure and economics of the theater business delay the advent of actresses?[1] Sophie Tomlinson offers another persuasive argument: English dramatists feared 'the threat of the actress in performance [that] lay in the potential for presenting femininity as a vivid and mobile force: the spectacle of the woman-actor summoning up a spectre of the female subject'.[2] When Queen Henrietta Maria and her ladies took speaking roles in court drama, Caroline writers responded with plays that treat performing women with satiric hostility, striving at the same time to avoid open criticism of the queen.

Tomlinson's analysis is acute but I want to argue that the English players had faced such a 'threat' before. In the 1570s, the challenge came from Italian actresses instead of a French queen. Actresses first joined itinerant commedia dell'arte troupes in Italy in the 1560s, and by the 1570s the first great divas and their troupes were crossing national borders and becoming royal favorites outside Italy, especially in France and Spain. Some mixed-gender troupes even visited remote England to play at Elizabeth's court and for popular audiences. In the same period the English opened their doors to their first paying audiences. Faced with the constant demand for new plays, love stories and romances, writers pressed into service the materials and methods of the Italian players – plots featuring blocking fathers and rebellious daughters; star scenes of poetic improvising, sung laments and madness; and playmaking via *contaminatio* of theatregrams – while derogating their rivals as vulgar clowns and whores only capable of farces and jigs.[3]

The Italification of English plays meant many more roles for women. Before 1578 half of all adult plays in the repertory had no female speaking parts at all. After that date not one play lacks a female role.[4] Female leading parts grew longer, more exotic and more complex, with star scenes that called on players to show their acting skill. Many of these roles bear the marks of the diva, but instead of using women to play them the English imitated (and often satirized) the *innamorata* the foreign actress helped invent. The evidence lies in the

---

[1] Michael Shapiro, 'The introduction of actresses in England: Delay or Defensiveness?', in *Enacting Gender on the English Renaissance Stage*, ed. Viviana Comensoli and Anne Russell (Champaign, IL, 1999).

[2] Sophie Tomlinson, 'She that plays the king: Henrietta Maria and the threat of the actress in Caroline culture', in *The Politics of Tragicomedy: Shakespeare and After*, ed. Gordon McMullan and Jonathan Hope (London, 1992), 192.

[3] Thomas Nashe sneered at the Italians for using 'whores and common courtyzans to play women's parts', *Pierce Penniless His Supplication to the Diuell* (London, 1592), 90–1. Thomas Heywood dismissed their repertory: all plays 'that frequent are / In Italy and France, even in these dayes, / Compar'd with ours, are rather jiggs than Playes' (from the Prologue, *A Challenge for Beautie* (London, 1636)).

[4] David Mann, 'Appendix: Female characters in the adult repertory, 1500–1614', *Shakespeare's Women: Performance and Conception* (Cambridge, 2008), 241–5.

plays of the most innovative playwrights, including John Lyly, Christopher Marlowe, Thomas Kyd, William Shakespeare and John Webster. These writers managed to create marketable substitutes for the star actress using boys to simulate her hypertheatrical foreign glamour.

How has this debt remained invisible for so long? Despite the transnational turn in early modern studies, few Shakespeareans take any interest in any form of theatre but the London professional stage. Thus they fail to note that the Italian scripted and popular drama, which playwrights constantly plundered for plots and roles, was irrevocably altered by the advent of the *innamorata* actress in the professional troupes of the period. English travellers and writers noticed her, even if we do not. The advent of the actress in Italy occurred sometime in the mid-century, with the first record of a woman in a troupe list dating to 1564. The *commedia dell'arte* had been all-male since its inception twenty years earlier, as were the amateur groups that performed regular comedy and the occasional tragedy. The professional women players proved enormously popular. The comici quickly changed their offerings, adding plays that focused on the unmasked lovers and enlarging the *innamorata* role in particular. Some literary playwrights did the same, exploiting the dramatic potential of the newly articulate, appealing leading woman and devising ways to move her to center stage, away from the windows and doors which had been the domain of the passive *virgo* of earlier plays. Divas such as Vincenza Armani, Vittoria Piissimi, Barbara Flaminia and Isabella Andreini took aim at other genres besides comedy, distinguishing themselves in scenes of high pathos, both in pastorals, which often featured attempted suicide and tearful laments, or in tragic performances of madness, suicide and murder.

The impact of actresses on drama extended beyond Italy in the form of roles and plots featuring active, voluble young women whose deeds, choices and fates became increasingly important in all three Renaissance genres: comedy, pastoral and tragedy. Their multi-generic versatility made them sought-after stars and elevated the prestige of their companies, enabling them to establish playing routes and patronage networks all over the map.[5] Very rapidly, the *innamorata* role expanded in both improvised and scripted drama, carried across the Continent by the itinerant comici and by the foreign players and writers with whom they came in contact. Over time actresses proved an innovation that was nothing short of revolutionary. Their charisma and skills spurred groundbreaking experiments in pastoral tragicomedy and musical drama, prompting the composers of *intermedi* and the first operas to feature them in their works.[6] The first actresses also carved out an important new identity for women as paid artisans, and established a space for women to speak and act in the public sphere.

The English first heard about this dazzling novelty from ambassadors to France, who wrote excitedly about the Italian troupes that had entertained the court in 1571 and 1572. Throughout the 1570s Queen Elizabeth showed a lively appetite for Italian plays and players, even commissioning her own Italian comedy. Individual Italian entertainers had crossed the Channel to play at court and in London since the days of Henry VIII but now full companies began to arrive. In 1574 one company presented an avant-garde pastoral with nymphs, goddesses and a satyr for the queen on her summer progress, and in 1577–8 actors and actresses in the troupe of Drusiano Martinelli came for months, performing comedies and acrobatic shows at court and in London, possibly at Burbage's new Theater.[7] Reports about Italian companies abroad flowed in from travellers such as Fynes Moryson, George Whetstone, Philip Sidney, Thomas Coryate and George Sandys, and from touring

---

[5] Pamela Allen Brown, 'The traveling diva and generic innovation', *Renaissance Drama* 44, 2 (2016), 249–67.

[6] Emily Wilbourne, *Seventeenth-Century Opera and the Sound of the Commedia dell'Arte* (Chicago, 2016), pp. 51–91; Anne MacNeil, *Music and Women of the Commedia dell'Arte in the Late Sixteenth Century* (Oxford, 2003), pp. 11–20, 149.

[7] Robert Henke, 'Back to the future: A review of twentieth-century commedia-Shakespeare studies', *Early Theatre* 11 (2008), 227–40.

English players who brought home news about the comici and their craft. The English learned much and stole much from the Italians whose material and methods of playmaking helped them meet the incessant demand for new plays week after week, especially comedies and romances in the Italian style. Playwrights translated or adapted whole plays from Italy but more often they re-used familiar 'theatregrams' (roles, plot elements, speeches and scenes) they found in five-act humanist plays and in the *arte*'s improvised and scripted three-act plays drawing on them.[8] This new kind of drama placed romantic lovers front and centre, and thus the *innamorata* part honed by the actresses grew in size and importance.

In England, actress-driven roles first appear in children's plays at court. Lyly worked in the shadow of Tasso, whose career and poetry Elizabeth avidly followed. Tasso called on the famous Gelosi company and their actresses to play in early performances of *Aminta* (1573), a phenomenal success. The influential *Aminta* spurred new pastorals in courts across Europe, including the pastoral that the Italian players presented to Elizabeth in 1574. As Tasso's choice suggests, the skilled divas proved far more compelling in pastorals than cross-dressed amateur youths and they quickly redefined its specialized erotic, poetic and musical vocabulary. Playing nymphs and goddesses in their sheer classicizing gowns, foreign actresses played up their attractions in Arcadian settings that allowed a far greater scope for female passion and action than Renaissance comedies set on the city street. (When the diva Isabella Andreini wrote her pastoral *Mirtilla* in the mode of Tasso, she featured a clever nymph who tricks, binds and beats a rapine satyr.)

Like the Italians, Lyly enlarged the scope for female mimesis by creating protean and passionate women: the hapless Queen Sapho, who runs mad with desire under Venus's spell in Lyly's *Sapho and Phao*, for example, and the charismatic Pandora of *The Woman in the Moon*, whose beauty makes the gods both envious and vengeful, but who quickly converts all to desperate lovers who vie for her favors. Lyly's boyish women remain elegantly androgynous, befitting their Italianate courtly audiences but, when playwrights faced the open arenas and vast audiences of the new popular stages, they created a bolder, more aggressive diva. In *The Spanish Tragedy*, the first great hit of the public stage, Kyd creates a single-minded actress-avenger in Bel-Imperia, who schemes to gain her will, flirts poetically, soliloquizes often and finally destroys her prey with a stellar performance in the final play-within-the-play. Recruiting her for the role of Perseda, Hieronymo praises Italian tragedians for their extemporal playing and for their actresses: 'For what's a play without a woman in it?' Taking the low road of exploitative satire, Anthony Munday vulgarized the *innamorata* role in *The Two Italian Gentlemen*, his adaptation of Luigi Pasqualigo's *Il Fedele*. His Victoria is positively courtesan-like, more musical and more murderous than her Italian original.

Shakespeare's adaptations were varied and complex: he drew on a varied repertoire of traits for his actress-types, including hyper-theatricality, literariness, expressive complexity and protean versatility. These show up within roles in his earliest comedies, from the cross-dressing Julia and idealized Silvia in *Two Gentlemen of Verona* to the proud, Latin-speaking, improvising Bianca of *The Taming of the Shrew*. Not just textual sources but Italian performative models provided templates for the extemporal witplay and theatrical verve of Rosalind, Viola, Portia and Helena. In *Romeo and Juliet*, Shakespeare's first great tragedy, he offers spectators a stunningly original diva in Juliet, a theatrical prodigy whose magnetic persona blends

---

[8] Louise George Clubb, *Italian Drama in Shakespeare's Time* (New Haven, 1989). English playwrights imitated scenes and speeches of the newly central, passionate and complex actress-driven *innamorata*, which featured in both *commedia dell'arte* scenarios and in Torquato Tasso's *Aminta*, Battista Guarini's *Pastor Fido*, Girolamo Bargagli's *La Pellegrina*, Grazzini's *La Spiritata* (adapted by John Jeffere as *The Bugbears*), Luigi Pasqualigo's *Il Fedele* (adapted by Anthony Munday as *Feidele and Fortunio*) and Piccolomini's *Alessandro* (adapted by George Chapman as *May Day*), among others.

aspects of the subaltern boy and the sublime *innamorata*, and whose art conceals art.

The diva type also had to be spectacular. With the proper wig, make-up, gown and props, the players might impress audiences with a dazzling vision of Cleopatra or Queen Elizabeth. Brilliant staging went only so far in simulating an *innamorata* in the style of the diva, however: the success of the sleight-of-hand depended on the talent and charisma of the boy who played her and the writer who provided his lines. The actress could project a confident elegance and pull off quick-witted improvisations because of her long professional training, backed up by her star power. The roster of boys talented and experienced enough to pull off a role such as Juliet was always limited, yet playwrights continued to create them in the vein of the celebrity diva. Though the boy actor had painfully acquired Latin literacy and training in memorization, vocal delivery, singing and musicianship, these skills were put to the test when he had to deliver the greatness of Cleopatra in her death scene or to play witty Rosalind playing Ganymede, with all her improvisatory flair. Ambitious actresses today covet such complex leading roles, which spur them to surpass their own limits as players. The young actor handed such past might feel actorly pride and ambition, but it is even more likely that he feared getting hissed and even beaten if he failed at producing the illusion of stardom (not just womanhood) on stage. The chances of finding a talented boy player up to the challenge was low and the risks of failure were high, for both actor and writer.

This brings us to the question Stephen Orgel posed long ago: 'Why did the English stage take boys for women?'[9] Many Shakespeareans might answer that they were barred by law from using women or that there were simply no women players that the professionals could draw on. Both are false assertions. No law regulating the gender of actors has ever come to light but ample evidence does exist that women performed at court, in the streets, at great houses, in parish halls and, on rare occasions, the London professional stage.[10] As I have shown, Italian troupes with actresses crossed the Channel to play in London and at court, and we know that later on French actresses played in Caroline London. In other words, the all-male stage was surrounded by spheres of public and private performance that included girls and women in significant numbers, playing for audiences high and low. Some played speaking roles and many were trained in singing and music. These performing women, and this rich history, have never been judged noteworthy because English culture and history 'had an interest in rendering them unnoticeable'.[11]

Thanks to the efforts of feminist scholars and the increasing interest in the transnationality of early modern theatrical culture, the phenomenon of women performing has become harder to ignore. Interpreting this evidence has attracted debate and controversy. Dympna Callaghan argues that, even if many women did perform in places other than the professional stage, it does not alter the fact that Shakespeare's theatre deliberately excluded women, creating a felt absence that affected every moment, every role, every play.[12] The men who controlled this womanless stage were deeply homosocial, like English culture at large, far more comfortable with the same-sex male love and affection than with female sexuality or men's desires for women; it follows that all female dramatic roles on that stage are products of masculinist projection and ventriloquism, blocking out female desire and

---

[9] Stephen Orgel, 'Nobody's perfect: Or why did the English stage take boys for women?' *The South Atlantic Quarterly* 88 (1989), 7–29.

[10] 'Introduction', Pamela Allen Brown and Peter Parolin, eds., *Women Players in England, 1500–1660: Beyond the All-Male Stage* (Aldershot, 2005); Jessica Schiermeister, 'The false issue of "illegality" of female performance', *The Shakespeare Standard*, http://theshakespearestandard.com/false-issue-illegality-female-performance/.

[11] Stephen Orgel, *Impersonations: The Performance of Gender in Shakespeare's England* (Cambridge, 1996), p. 9.

[12] Dympna Callaghan, *Shakespeare Without Women: Representing Gender and Race on the Renaissance Stage* (London, 2000). In a similar vein, David Mann refutes the idea that women spectators affected characterizations of women, which he calls largely masculinist projections, in *Shakespeare's Women: Performance and Conception* (Cambridge, 2008).

subjectivity. Other scholars take the view that female pleasure, desire and fantasy were important factors in theatrical success, forces that pushed dramatists to offer plays and characters that pleased not only men but women and offered new textures and contradictions in female impersonation.[13] What is certain is that wooden depictions of 'good' and 'bad' women and satiric caricatures played by boy-puppets in drag appealed to some audiences for a limited period, but these female roles have largely vanished from memory.

A handful of brilliant diva-style roles by Shakespeare and his contemporaries continue to attract great actors and to move audiences of all kinds, quite a feat considering they were written four centuries ago and 'created' (in theatrical parlance) by boy players whose talents are generally underestimated and whose profession was equated with whoring and idleness. Part of the audience's pleasure then and now was seeing a charismatic female character burn up the stage, just as they love seeing the theatrical showmen Hamlet, Falstaff and Richard III do the same. With hyper-theatrical roles tailored for star performances, the player's actual gender is not as important as a great performance and, as Shakespeare teaches us, a diva such as Cleopatra or Viola can be played by a male or female. That is one of the distinctive qualities of a diva role: it summons not an ordinary woman and everyday gender identity but a professional player possessed of verbal eloquence and wit, volatile passions, histrionic self-awareness and love of centre stage.

Many scholars have written on the erotic appeal and sexual identity of the boy player of female roles. While this work is important, I believe the field should focus less on the boy's homo- and hetero-erotic appeal and more on his skills and professional standing, since these are highly relevant to the meaning of his performed role and the plays in which he appears.[14] At the same time, we need to demolish the premise that the English stage practices were totally isolated from Continental developments. Too often the English theatre business is cordoned off as an insider world dominated by male writers, segregated from cosmopolitan aspirations and transnational theatrical and courtly networks which prominently featured performing women. The approach I advocate avoids the Scylla of essentialism that results from reducing players to the presumed erotic appeal stemming from their gender; and it steers clear of the Charybdis of treating Shakespeare as an exclusively English genius who did not need or learn anything from the Italians – an opinion expressed more often than you would think. What is missing is a more cosmopolitan view of the Shakespearean stage, which traded in exotic wares and competed for the favor of a knowing and demanding courtly clientele. Shakespeare's theater shows a fascinated, edgy awareness of actresses that tempered and moulded his female roles. He and his peers knew that glamorous actresses playing women in love might well have an edge over boys who impersonated them. Their response was to adapt and imitate the diva's trademark role, and in many cases the stratagem worked.

Seeing the skilled and attractive boy-*innamorata* as a stand-in for the virtuosic actress allows us to make some headway with Orgel's unanswered question. The English stage took boys for actresses because they wanted everything the actress offered, except the player herself. They took and used what the new actresses and their co-players offered freely: engaging, exciting young women in love, riveting passions, woman-centered plots and compelling star scenes that pleased both Italophilic courtly audiences and the crowds in the new arena theaters. Despite growing curiosity about

---

[13] On the debate see Natasha Korda, 'Women in the theatre', *The Oxford Handbook of Early Modern Theatre* (Oxford, 2011) and Orgel, *Impersonations*, 11. Also see Clare McManus and Lucy Munro, 'Renaissance women's performance and the dramatic canon: Theatre history, evidence, and narratives', *Shakespeare Bulletin* 33 (2015), 1–7.

[14] Important studies focused on the training and 'enskilment' of the boy actor include Evelyn B. Tribble, *Cognition in the Globe: Attention and Memory in Shakespeare's Theatre* (Basingstoke, 2011) and Scott McMillin, 'The sharer and his boy: Rehearsing Shakespeare's women', in *From Script to Stage in Early Modern England*, ed. Peter Holland and Stephen Orgel (Basingstoke, 2004), 195–230.

the Italians and their actresses among elites and tours of Italian players in London, the English players managed to stem the tide, making England an anomaly by 1600. These professionals were fully aware of the mixed-gender stage but, without coordinating their efforts, they delayed the advent of professional actresses by decades, by inventing spectacular Italianate women and pressing talented boys to play them. With renewed attention being paid to character and the rising interest in performing women and girls in England and abroad, it is time to return to the study of women's roles but with more cosmopolitan eyes and a keener attention to gender-as-performance. While no foreign diva invented Bel-Imperia, Juliet, Portia or the Duchess of Malfi, the diva's generic versatility, artistry and charisma shadow these and other stellar *innamorata* roles. When we open out the study of female mimesis to the transnational sphere, we see that women *did* participate in the making of theatre and in the creation of new roles, a phenomenon that put pressure on writers to create a new brand of woman-centered drama, even on the all-male stage. The irony is that the skilled labours of the lowly boy player and the foreign diva figure so large in that now forgotten history.

ACTING AMISS: TOWARDS A HISTORY OF ACTORLY CRAFT AND PLAYHOUSE JUDGEMENT

SIMON SMITH

In 1598, theatre enthusiast and future playwright John Marston published a scathing verse satire, in which he imagines a caricatured, gullish and obsessive playgoer named Luscus. Besides speaking '[n]aught but pure *Juliat* and *Romio*', this memorable figure is particularly recognizable for his tendency to reflect at length on the respective merits of his favourite actors:

> Say, who acts best, Drusus, or Roscio?
> Now I have him, that nere of ought did speake
> But when of playes or Plaiers he did treate.[1]

This playful and somewhat slippery text attests to the fashion for theatregoing in the late 1590s, as well as to a range of anxieties about playgoers and their behaviour rather more nuanced and subtle than those articulated by anti-theatricalists in preceding decades. Perhaps most striking of all, however, is what playhouse reception seems to involve for Luscus: for him, playgoing is about judging the craft of the early modern actor just as much as engaging with fictional worlds created upon the stage.

In 1598, Marston had long been part of an Inns of Court milieu famous for passionate theatre attendance, his own father later bemoaning his 'delight in plays and vain studies and fooleries', yet his career actually writing for the professional stage appears to have begun after the clamp-down on satire and Bishops' Ban of 4 June 1599, which saw *The Scourge of Villainie* publically burned.[2] His fictional account of a playgoer's relentless theoretical and critical reflection on the art of playing is thus the product of his experiences amongst audiences, this exaggerated character embodying glimpses, fragments and echoes of 1590s playhouse engagements from the perspective of paying customer rather than company member. In this light, it is telling that Marston sees Luscus stereotypically and hyperbolically as a playgoer precisely *because* he loves to offer critiques of actorly technique, discoursing enthusiastically and indefinitely on the topic at the slightest invitation.

It is not entirely unexpected to find Marston imagining a fellow playgoer who reflects on the process of play-making; after all, for many early modern subjects it was the skill of the Lord Chamberlain's or King's Men that created Shakespeare's plays, transforming fragmentary sets of texts – parts, letters, songs, backstage plots – into dramatic performances.[3] Working under strikingly

---

I am grateful to the Leverhulme Trust Early Career Fellowship scheme for supporting my research for this chapter. I am also extremely grateful to Kara Northway, Lois Potter, Lyn Tribble, Emma Whipday, Deanne Williams and Sue Wiseman for their comments on earlier versions.

[1] John Marston, *The Scourge of Villanie* (London, 1598), sig. G7v. Excellent actors are often labelled with the names of Classical forebears like Drusus and Roscius in the early modern period.

[2] Marston's father made this remark, later deleted, in a will of 24 October 1599. The National Archives (TNA): PROB 11/166/71; James Knowles, 'Marston, John (bap. 1576, d. 1634)', in *Oxford Dictionary of National Biography* (Oxford, 2004), www.odnb.com (accessed 13 November 2016).

[3] These textual fragments are discussed in: Tiffany Stern, *Documents of Performance in Early Modern England* (Cambridge, 2009), pp. 120–231; Simon Palfrey and Tiffany Stern, *Shakespeare in Parts* (Oxford, 2007), pp. 15–79.

different conditions of rehearsal and repertory from those of the twenty-first century commercial stage, and trained with an entirely different set of theoretical principles in mind, the players who brought drama into being at the Globe and Blackfriars drew upon a substantial set of professional competencies and collective skills. Perhaps, then, it is all the more surprising that from a late modern critical perspective, Luscus's fascination with technical accomplishment actually highlights a significant lacuna: scholarly accounts of the early modern theatre generally have very little to say about audience members' attention to actorly skill.

It is well established that the craft of his fellow actors was both crucial to the realization of Shakespeare's plays and, in all probability, central to the dramatist's very conception of his work as he wrote. However, rather less attention has been afforded to early modern play*goers*' awareness of the skills that this involved. Despite renewed interest in the practicalities of acting from Tiffany Stern, Evelyn B. Tribble and others, scholars have generally pursued investigations of actors separately from studies of playgoers.[4] What, then, might we deduce from the textual record about how, or how far, a less caricatured late Elizabethan might be expected to engage with actorly skill? Does Marston's poem present a figure who gets playgoing wrong or simply one who takes characteristic playhouse behaviour to extremes? Was it odd, in 1598, for a playgoer to consider 'who acts best' or is Luscus only a bore because the player's craft is his sole topic of conversation? The critical tendency towards separate histories of actors and of playgoers, whilst productive in many ways, leaves these and many other questions about playgoer engagements with actorly skill requiring further investigation.

John Astington wonders whether such a separation may be for the best, arguing that, whilst 'there would have been a lively tradition of talk about plays and players, then, our impression today, based on surviving texts, is that contemporary dramatists were the chief critics and theorists of the arts of theatre, performance included'. He notes, too, that Simon Forman makes no mention of particular actors performing in the various plays he saw at the Globe in 1611 nor of 'the immediate and particular effects of their performances'.[5] It is certainly true that there was a strong tradition of early modern dramatists (often those who were themselves players) reflecting upon plays and playing – in paratexts for stage and page, in the dialogue of plays themselves, in dedicated tracts such as Thomas Heywood's *Apology for Actors* – but the converse implication that the textual record has little to offer regarding playgoers' critical and theoretical engagements with actors and acting – or indeed that such engagements may not have taken place at all – is challenged by eyewitness accounts and a range of other sources.

This article examines playhouse attention to the craft of the early modern actor in order to test two related hypotheses. The first is that playgoers habitually reflected upon and judged actorly skill, often whilst taking pleasure in the fictional worlds and characters created by that very craft. If accepted, this claim would not only require us to revise histories of playgoing to take account of judicious engagements with performers' technique but would also demand reconsiderations of the wider relationship between playgoers and performers, and of methods for interrogating early modern theatrical culture: if actorly craft was the explicit subject of audiences' attention, is it therefore necessary to interweave playgoing and acting more closely in accounts of theatre history, rather than treating them as separate topics of investigation?

---

[4] See: John Astington, *Actors and Acting in Shakespeare's Time: The Art of Stage Playing* (Cambridge, 2010); Andrew Gurr, *Playgoing in Shakespeare's London*, 3rd edn (Cambridge, 2004); B. L. Joseph, *Elizabethan Acting*, 2nd edn (Oxford, 1964); Jeremy Lopez, *Theatrical Convention and Audience Response in Early Modern Drama* (Cambridge, 2003); Joseph R. Roach, *The Player's Passion: Studies in the Science of Action* (Newark, 1985); Tiffany Stern, *Rehearsal from Shakespeare to Sheridan* (Oxford, 2000); Evelyn B. Tribble, *Cognition in the Globe: Attention and Memory in Shakespeare's Theatre* (Basingstoke, 2011); Charley Whitney, *Early Responses to Renaissance Drama* (Cambridge, 2006).

[5] Astington, *Actors and Acting*, pp. 10–11.

The second, broader suggestion, considered in the later part of this article, is that the particular combination of judicious regard for actorly skill with imaginative, potentially playful engagements with fiction is itself indicative of a wider culture of playgoing that treated pleasure and judgement not as alternative modes of response but as simultaneous aspects of playhouse experience. This would represent a significant challenge to the current picture of early modern drama and its reception, in which a critical tradition with roots in Ben Jonson's polemical paratextual distinctions between 'popular delight' and 'be[ing] censur'd by th'austerest brow' has often treated judicious criticism and unthinking pleasure as distinct modes of engagement, sometimes associating each response with separate subgroupings within a typical audience.[6] In pursuing playhouse engagements with actorly craft, then, this article begins to sketch an alternative account of early modern theatrical experience predicated upon a widespread *expectation* that one could take pleasure in many aspects of a dramatic performance even whilst remaining critically engaged – in short, a culture of playgoing in which drama by Shakespeare and his contemporaries was expected to delight and to provoke censure in equal measure.

We can begin by turning to some early modern accounts of playgoing – both real and imagined – that record playhouse attention to actors' technical skill. One of the few first-hand testimonies of Shakespearian performance before 1642 is that of Henry Jackson. His reflections in Latin upon several plays performed by the King's Men at Oxford in 1610, including *Othello* and *The Alchemist*, survive in a letter held at Corpus Christi College Library. His observation that Desdemona could 'move ... spectators' pity with her very expression' is well known and often explored in accounts of how gender may have been performed on the early modern stage. Less commonly quoted, however, are his more general remarks on how the King's Men 'held tragedies which they acted decorously and aptly', moving the audience to tears 'not only by what they said but also by what they did'. Jackson represents himself as part of the crowd that packed out the venue for these performances, referring to 'Desdemona slain before *us*' (my emphasis).[7] In so doing, he frames his account as that of an eyewitness deeply engaged with the technical craft of dramatic performance. Strikingly, even as Jackson describes powerful emotional responses of sorrow and pity – and even whilst referring to 'Desdemona' rather than the actor playing this role – he is quick to comment on the players' skill that allows them to move playgoers in this way. He identifies 'what they did' as well as 'what they said' as key technical accomplishments, an explanation of *how* the King's Men are able to shape and control the responses he observes in other playgoers and, at times, in himself. Jackson seems to be just as interested in the actorly skill required to evoke aesthetic effects as he is in what those effects might be.

Jackson's letter is extremely valuable as apparent eyewitness evidence of a specific early modern performance, but in isolation this source cannot demonstrate widespread playhouse critiquing of actorly craft. Beside the fact that it is only a single text, as a senior member of an Oxford college, writing in Latin, Jackson is scarcely representative of the full range of attendees to be expected in a London theatre. Other evidence is required, if we are to speculate that Jackson's critical instinct reflects broader conventions of playhouse response to drama. Indeed, eyewitness accounts may not be the most revealing form of evidence, if

---

[6] Ben Jonson, *The Comicall Satyre of Every Man Out of His Humor* (1600), sig. B2r; *Sejanus his Fall* (1604), sig. ¶2r. Recent work in this tradition includes Gurr's distinctions between '[t]he wiser sort' and 'audiences ... in the mass as passive tasters of what was set before them', building on Alfred Harbage's account of how 'the average' playgoer and 'the exceptional member of the audience – the "judicious" spectator' are separated, at least in the view of certain dramatists. Gurr, *Playgoing*, pp. 116, 129; Alfred Harbage, *Shakespeare's Audience* (New York, 1941; repr. 1961), pp. 125–6.

[7] Henry Jackson, Letter to D. G. P. dated September 1610, Oxford, Corpus Christi, MS 304, fols. 83v–84r. Translated by Patrick Gregory in *Records of Early English Drama: Oxford*, ed. John R. Elliott, Alexandra F. Johnston, Alan H. Nelson and Diana Wyatt, 2 vols. (Toronto, 2004), vol. 2, pp. 1037–8.

we are interested in wider cultural expectations of playgoers' behaviour rather than specific instances. In contrast, oblique sources are often particularly helpful to the study of historically distanced cultures for their capacity to highlight the familiarity that allows a given idea – in this case playhouse judgement – to serve as a tangential reference point in work not otherwise interested or invested in that matter. Passing references may therefore indicate not how a specific individual responded at a given performance but whether critical engagement with the player's craft was a broadly recognized component of playgoing, a cultural expectation perhaps analogous to judging when to boo a pantomime villain or verbally abuse a referee in more recent popular entertainment contexts.

Such evidence includes one early modern text entirely unrelated to practical playhouse performance: lines set as a madrigal by Orlando Gibbons, published in 1612 and probably written by Walter Ralegh whilst imprisoned in the Tower in the first decade of James's reign.[8] The poem, widely circulated in manuscript with attribution to Ralegh, takes the playhouse not as its historical subject but as an extended point of comparison:

> What is our life? a play of passion,
> Our mirth the musicke of diuision,
> Our mothers wombes the tyring houses be,
> Where we are drest for this short Comedy,
> Heauen the Iudicious sharpe spectator is,
> That sits and markes still who doth act amisse,
> Our graves that hide vs from the searching Sun,
> Are like drawne curtaynes when the play is done,
> Thus march wee playing to our latest rest,
> Onely we dye in earnest, that's no iest.[9]

The *theatrum mundi* trope, beloved of early modern writers, typically compares the performances required of playing companies with those required in life, either itemizing the many roles performed between birth and death, like Jacques in *As You Like It* (2.7.139–66), or, like Francis Quarles, enumerating the various kinds of performance encompassed by a play, from dumb show (a baby's first breath) to epilogue (death), via prologue (a baby's first cry) and inter-act music (life's many distractions).[10]

Ralegh draws upon both traditions but also, unusually, populates his *theatrum mundi* with an audience: Heaven sits as a spectator, presumably in an upper gallery, noting 'who doth act amisse'. In choosing this metaphor for the watchful and judgemental eye of God, Ralegh reveals his expectation of what spectators do at a play: they sit, view and censure. Yet this is not censure of the play itself, often discussed in prologues and epilogues by dramatists hoping their work will receive a favourable reception; rather, this spectator is judging how each performer 'doth act'. Gibbons's setting has Heaven 'mark[ing]' the quality of the acting, whilst other versions of the same poem circulating in manuscript describe the celestial critic 'behould[ing]', 'not[ing]', or simply 'view[ing] whosoere doth Acte amiss'.[11] Strikingly, in every text, the imagined playgoer attends in order to assess the craft of the performers, not even making reference to the quality of the play itself, and this in turn facilitates a slightly laboured pun on God's judgement of the 'act[s]' of a person's life. Edward Burns asks whether Ralegh's poem might 'trivialise heaven' by 'present[ing] it as one of those critical spectators often mocked in plays as one of the playhouses' most recognisable types', but Ralegh's Heaven has little to do with the negative playhouse censuring of plays remarked upon in

---

[8] See Mark Nicholls and Penry Williams, 'Ralegh, Sir Walter (1554–1618)' in *ODNB*.

[9] Sir Walter Ralegh?, 'What is our Life?', in Orlando Gibbons, *The First Set of Madrigals and Mottets of 5. Parts apt for Viols and Voyces* (London, 1612), sig. C1v. Words repeated for musical reasons have been omitted.

[10] Francis Quarles, 'On the Life and Death of a Man (1630?)'; transcribed in Gurr, *Playgoing*, p. 285. On the range of elements that might be considered part of the dramatic performance in an early modern playhouse, see: Tiffany Stern, 'Before the beginning; after the end: When did plays start and stop?', in *Shakespeare and Textual Studies*, ed. Margaret Jane Kidnie and Sonia Massai (Cambridge, 2015), pp. 358–74.

[11] *The Poems of Walter Raleigh: A Historical Edition*, ed. Michael Rudick (Tempe, AZ, 1999), pp. 69–70 (poems 29A–C).

dramatic paratexts, and far more to do with a separate tradition of expected and desirable judgements concerning the skill of the dramatic performers.[12] As an incidental account of a playgoer judging actorly skill, the poem provides a significant step in reconstructing the cultural familiarity of such judgements.

Another *theatrum mundi* poem, published, coincidentally, in the same year as Gibbons's setting, makes a similar observation. The poet mirrors Ralegh's relatively unusual addition of an audience to his allegorical playhouse, this time the heavenly 'Iehoue', who

> doth as spectator sit.
> And chiefe determiner to applaud the best,
> And their indeuours crowne with more then merit.
> But by their euill actions dommes the rest,
> To end disgrac't whilst others praise inherit.[13]

Again, it is explicitly actors rather than plays that are to be judged, those performers displaying 'euill actions' damned to disgrace whilst the 'best' are rewarded with 'praise' for their 'indeavours'. This time the pun is sharp, the actor's gestural skill mapped precisely onto God's judgement of a person's actions. Significantly, the pun relies upon the assumption, shared with Ralegh's poem, that playgoers attend the theatre in order to judge the performers' technical abilities, again emphasizing the cultural familiarity of this expectation in earlier seventeenth-century England.

The lines are the work of a playwright and actor, serving as the author's dedication 'to his Booke' in Heywood's 1612 defence of his profession. Taken in isolation or in conjunction with the paratextual and other reflections of practising actors and dramatists, Heywood's poem might read as the view of producer rather than consumer, a fantasy of the audience reaction an actor might hope for, or indeed fear, particularly given that the lines preface a text explicitly intended to praise and glorify actors. Yet when placed in relief with Marston's early satire and, particularly, Ralegh's *theatrum mundi* poem – the latter the work of a man far removed both socially and professionally from the world of commercial dramatic production – a rather different reading emerges. All three texts take as an assumption – and critically, in the cases of Ralegh's and Heywood's poems, this assumption is tangential to their central concerns with heavenly judgement – that the censuring of actorly technique is a playhouse behaviour recognizable to their intended readers. This suggests familiarity well beyond those with a professional investment in the technical competence of dramatic performers: Heywood's conceit is not an insular and ultimately questionable actorly fantasy but rather the rehearsal of an expectation about playhouse behaviour that appears to have been relatively commonplace in early modern London. In this light, his text can contribute to a history that places rather less emphasis on 'contemporary dramatists' as 'chief critics and theorists of the arts of theatre' than might otherwise be expected.[14]

The observations of Marston, Jackson, Ralegh and Heywood all suggest strongly that the player's craft was an expected target of playgoer censure, but questions of precisely how such judgements were made, and what exactly playgoers thought actorly skill involved, require further investigation. Indeed, audience members' opinions on the subject could differ considerably from those of early modern play-makers and may likewise be distinct from accounts developed, for instance, through social-scientific and cognitive models by later scholars. In recent years, research by Tiffany Stern on the significance of actors' parts to the process of rehearsal and performance has fundamentally reshaped understandings of how early modern dramatic performance worked, whilst Evelyn B. Tribble's interrogation of players and the playhouse space through the lens of Distributed Cognition has offered a new view of the enskilment of early modern players and playing

---

[12] Edward Burns, *Character: Acting and Being on the Pre-Modern Stage* (London, 1990), p. 127.
[13] Thomas Heywood, *An Apology for Actors* (London, 1612), sig. a4v.
[14] Astington, *Actors and Acting*, p. 10.

companies.[15] It does not necessarily follow, however, that early modern subjects encountering plays from a relatively casual consumer's perspective would typically have thought in terms of the textual fragmentation encountered materially by members of an acting company or the socially distributed professional competencies experienced as embodied knowledge by the actors themselves. We must look again to the early modern textual record, then, in order to trace exactly how ideas of actorly craft circulated amongst playgoing non-specialists.

Of relevance here is a slightly older tradition of scholarship that traces the ways in which the skill of acting was discussed and theorized in the early modern period, when models derived largely from Cicero and Quintilian emphasized the primacy of well-chosen 'action' (*actio*) and 'accent' (*pronuntio*) in both oratory and dramatic performance.[16] It seems that many early modern subjects were familiar with the idea that skilful dramatic performance involved apt gesture, facial expression, gait and other movements – all encompassed by 'action' – as well as judicious uses of voice, emphasis and other aspects of verbal delivery, encompassed in turn by 'accent'. Importantly, as Tribble reminds us, the actor's task combines rather than opposes these elements, for gesture is 'not simply decoration' but has 'deep links with speech', links as explicit in early modern manuals noting the hand's 'naturall competency to express the motives and affections of the Minde' as they are fundamental to recent scientific studies of language, gesture and cognition.[17]

Several of the texts already encountered directly frame judgements of actorly craft through the categories of action and accent. Henry Jackson's admiration for 'what [the King's Men] did' as well as 'what they said' when performing at Oxford in 1610 posits the formal categories of *actio* and *pronuntio* as the basis of these actors' skill. Likewise, Thomas Heywood's fictional Jove is explicitly concerned with 'euill actions', drawing on the same conceptual framework as Jackson but focusing in particular on gesture for the sake of a pun on 'actions'.[18] Another epistolary account that, unlike Jackson's, relates to performance in London's commercial playhouses proceeds similarly. In August 1624, when Thomas Middleton's *A Game at Chess* was staged at the Globe, John Chamberlain wrote to Sir Dudley Carleton in an attempt to convey something of the commotion that the play had caused; this hubbub of discussion related principally to the drama's political resonances, and to the King's Men's sheer impudence in staging such material publically.[19]

Yet despite being faced with the outrage of players personating living political figures, Chamberlain's astonishment is nonetheless marshalled by a judgement upon the skill of the King's Men, framed through action and accent: he notes how the players and, in particular, one actor were judged to have 'counterfeited' the Spanish ambassador Gondomar's 'person to the life, with all his graces and faces'.[20] Here, Chamberlain reports widespread admiration of the skills required to personate Gondomar so effectively. In particular, the actor's facial expressions – a key element of early modern gesture – and his 'graces' are picked out for praise, the latter potentially encompassing characteristic modes of speech as well as deportment, and thus requiring the performer to demonstrate skilled

---

[15] Stern, *Rehearsal*; Palfrey and Stern, *Shakespeare in Parts*; Tribble, *Cognition in the Globe*.

[16] See, in particular, Joseph, *Elizabethan Acting*, pp. 1–24; Roach, *Player's Passion*, pp. 23–57.

[17] Tribble, *Cognition in the Globe*, p. 97; John Bulwer, *Chirologia: Or the Naturall Language of the Hand* (London, 1644), sig. B2v. See Susan Goldin-Meadow, *Hearing Gestures: How Our Hands Help Us Think* (Boston, MA, 2003); Adam Kendon, *Gesture: Visible Action as Utterance* (Cambridge, 2004); David McNeill, *Hand and Mind: What Gestures Reveal About Thought* (Chicago, 1992), *Language and Gesture* (Cambridge, 2000).

[18] Jackson, 'Letter to D. G. P.', p. 1037; Heywood, *Apology*, sig. a4v.

[19] See Thomas Howard-Hill, *Middleton's 'Vulgar Pasquin': Essays on 'A Game at Chess'* (London, 1995), p. 109 and *passim*.

[20] John Chamberlain, 'Letter to Sir Dudley Carleton, Saturday 21 August 1624', in *Thomas Middleton and Early Modern Textual Culture: A Companion to the Collected Works*, ed. Gary Taylor and James Lavagnino (Oxford, 2007), pp. 870–1.

accent as well as action.[21] Even while principally concerned with the precedent for public comment on contemporary politics set by the King's Men's performances (and by the authorities' anticipated response), reactions to *A Game at Chess* still apparently took in the question of the actors' technical accomplishment, treating such judgements as an expected or integrated aspect of playhouse engagement with dramatic performance. Whilst the model of action and accent was – like any theory – at times tested and stretched in practice, it is to these twin categories that early modern playgoers habitually turned when seeking to expound actorly craft.[22]

Why might early modern playgoers have been so interested in a matter as technical and specialized as the skill of a commercial player, and so quick to turn to *actio* and *pronuntio*? Certainly, there appears to have been a general culture of censure in the early modern playhouse, where 'in a sense, audiences were jurors', and everything from the decoration of the theatre to the pre-show music, via the dramatist's writing and the narrative itself, was subject to value judgements.[23] But there may be yet more specific reasons why actorly craft was a particular locus for censure. For those privileged enough to have attended grammar school or received private tuition as a child – and it is important to note from the outset that such a subset of playgoers excludes many, particularly women and those of lower social status – the apt use of action and accent would have been a central pillar of their education.[24] As Astington has recently explored, Cicero's *De Oratore* and Quintilian's *Institutio Oratoria*, 'both, especially the first, recommended as school reading', outline the proper development of action and accent as part of rhetorical training with specific reference to playing.[25]

Not only do Quintilian and Cicero present the specific skills of *actio* and *pronuntio* as common to oratory and acting but both also advocate the use of actors as models for students in their oratorical training. Cicero suggests of 'delivery' that 'the orators ... have abandoned this entire field', leaving 'the actors, who are only imitators of reality' as the best exemplars of *pronuntio*. Likewise, in relation to *actio* – specifically facial expression – he refers approvingly to the renowned Roman comic actor Roscius, a reference point later adopted, as we have seen, by Marston in *The Scourge of Villainie*.[26] Quintilian shows particular interest in how pupils should develop skill in accent with reference to players, suggesting '[t]he comic actor' could provide a source for the 'future orator['s] ... knowledge of Delivery', with the qualification that the performance of 'drunkenness', 'cringing manners' and 'the emotions of love, greed, or fear' are to remain strictly absent from the curriculum (for '[f]requent imitation develops into habit'). Like Cicero, he warns against the 'staginess' of 'some kinds of gesture and movement' used by 'comic actors' but nonetheless notes that 'the orator must indeed master both to a certain extent'. In order to differentiate between stage actions suitable and unsuitable for oratorical imitation, pupils are reminded that the 'first rule' of the art of action 'is not to seem to be art'.[27]

---

[21] See 'grace, *n.* 13.a–c', in *Oxford English Dictionary*, 3rd edn (Oxford, 2013), www.oed.com (accessed 13 November 2016).

[22] On skill at the limits of action and accent, see: Tom Bishop, 'Boot and schtick', *Shakespeare Studies* 43 (2015), 35–49; Richard Preiss, 'John Taylor, William Fennor, and the "Trial of Wit"', *Shakespeare Studies* 43 (2015), 50–78.

[23] Laurie Maguire, 'Audience-actor boundaries in *Othello*', *Proceedings of the British Academy* 181 (2012), 123–42; p. 124. Gurr gathers accounts of many such judgements in: 'Appendix 2: References to Playgoing', in *Playgoing*, pp. 247–301.

[24] For a recent account of the social make-up of grammar school pupils, see: Lynn Enterline, *Shakespeare's Schoolroom: Rhetoric, Discipline, Emotion* (Philadelphia, 2012), pp. 15–18.

[25] Astington, *Actors and Acting*, pp. 44–5. On the teaching of rhetoric, see Quentin Skinner, *Forensic Shakespeare* (Oxford, 2014), pp. 25–47 and *passim*. T. W. Baldwin's monumental study of the sixteenth-century English grammar school curriculum remains the standard reference work on the broader topic: *William Shakspere's Small Latine & Lesse Greeke* (Urbana, 1944).

[26] Marcus Tullius Cicero, *Cicero: On the Ideal Orator (De oratore)*, trans. and ed. James M. May and Jakob Wisse (Oxford, 2001), III.214–5, 221, pp. 291–4; Marston, *Scourge of Villanie*, sig. G7v.

[27] Quintilian, *The Orator's Education*, trans. and ed. D. A. Russell (Cambridge, MA; London, 2001), I.xi.1–3, pp. 236–9; Cicero, *De oratore*, III.220, p. 294.

This Classical connection – via action and accent – between the skills of oratory and acting is widely rehearsed in vernacular early modern texts. In the Caroline period, Sir Richard Baker writes in response to William Prynne that '*Gracefulness* of *action*, is the greatest pleasure of a Play, seeing it is the greatest pleasure of (the Art of pleasure) *Rhetorick*: in which we may be bold to say; there never had been so good Oratours, if there had not first been Players.'[28] Significantly, Baker draws upon a long-standing and culturally familiar trope in order to make this argument, the connection even extending to the classroom performance of drama. Charles Hoole's *New Discovery of the Old Art of Teaching School* (1661) encourages schoolmasters to provide students with 'an Act or Scene that is full of affection, and action', to be learned and then acted 'first in private among themselves, and afterwards in the open Schoole before their fellowes; and herein you must have a main care of their pronunciation, and acting every gesture to the very life'. Such performance is apparently an 'especiall remedy' for 'subrustick bashfulnesse and unresistable timorousnesse', which if not corrected by dramatic performance is 'apt in riper yeares to drown many good parts in men'.[29] Hoole rehearses a long-established view of the value of dramatic performance in grammar school education, Thomas Wilson having noted some hundred years previously that '[t]here are a thousand such faults among men both for their speech and also for their gesture, the which if in their young years they be not remedied, they will hardly be forgot when they come to man's state'.[30] Early modern playgoers with such an education, then, would certainly have studied the theory and probably have practised the craft of dramatic performance, bringing a body of theoretical and embodied knowledge about action, accent and other actorly skills to their engagements with performance.

The knowledge of actorly skill from school could have had a direct bearing upon playgoers' interest in an actor's technique. Early modern audiences, and indeed audiences at the reconstructed Globe that stands on Bankside today, have often been likened to football crowds, although as scholars including Paul Prescott have traced, straightforwardly suggesting equivalence between the two groups is not always particularly productive.[31] However, an analogy concerned with the theoretical and embodied knowledge of individuals rather than the behaviour of whole crowds may have more potential to elucidate the relationship between playhouse response and prior knowledge and experience.

Today, those who spent their childhood kicking footballs around school playgrounds and local parks are often quick to venture opinions on exactly which players bring certain technical qualities to the England national team, or on the efficacy of the '4–4–2 Diamond' formation, given the positional competencies of the players currently available for selection. For such fans, embodied and theoretical knowledge based on childhood experience frames a mode of engagement that could also obtain for early modern playgoers with similarly embodied and theoretical knowledge of *actio* and *pronuntio*. Guillemette Bolens has recently explored how embodied knowledge can shape responses to skilled bodily actions through kinaesthetic empathy: 'I may infer … kinesthetic sensations on the basis of the kinesic signals I perceive in [someone else's] … movements. In an act of kinesthetic empathy, I may internally simulate what these inferred sensations possibly feel like via my own kinesthetic memory and knowledge.'[32] Thus, playgoers' judgements of an actor's technical ability could be rooted in their own understanding *and*

---

[28] Sir Richard Baker, *Theatrum Redivivum, or, the Theatre Vindicated* (London, 1662), sig. D1v–D2r.
[29] Charles Hoole, *A New Discovery of the Old Art of Teaching Schoole* (London, 1661), pp. 142–3.
[30] Thomas Wilson, *The Art of Rhetoric (1560)*, ed. Peter E. Medine (University Park, PA, 1994), pp. 242–3.
[31] See, for instance: Paul Prescott, *Reviewing Shakespeare: Journalism and Performance from the Eighteenth Century to the Present* (Cambridge, 2013), pp. 163–5; Andrew Gurr, *Rebuilding Shakespeare's Globe* (London, 1989), p. 53; *The Shakespearean Stage, 1574–1642*, 4th edn (Cambridge, 2009), p. 279.
[32] Guillemette Bolens, *The Style of Gestures: Embodiment and Cognition in Literary Narrative* (Baltimore, 2012), p. 3.

experience of actorly enskilment, a means of connecting personal experience with professional performance. Indeed, such a connection may go so far as providing a mode of playhouse self-reflection, closer aligning an audience member's perspective with that of an actor and his part.

In truth, the technique of one of the King's Men's player-shareholders was probably far removed from that of schoolboys attempting a comic scene for the benefit of their subrustic bashfulness; indeed, the skill of the early modern professional actor was far more complex, social and environmentally distributed than the model of action and accent could possibly hope to acknowledge, as Astington, Tribble and Lois Potter have variously demonstrated.[33] Yet as we have seen, playgoers repeatedly make judgements about actorly skill, their conclusions perhaps shaped by their own understandings – based partly in experience – of what skilful acting looks and sounds like, even if Ciceronian concern for *actio* and *pronuntio* provides them with somewhat limiting paradigms.

It would be easy to suggest that playhouse censure of actorly skill was the particular preserve of those who had access to a grammar school education or private tutor, a view that would generally limit such engagements to males of a certain social status and thus a relatively circumscribed subsection of Shakespeare's audience. Moreover, Heaven and Jove were both explicitly sitting, as opposed to standing in the yard, as they made their judgements, just as, in real life, John Holles sat in the gallery of the Globe as he determined that *A Game at Chess* was 'more wittily penned, then wysely staged' in 1624.[34] Yet this may not be the whole story. Both Baker and Heywood – in vernacular texts directly concerned with commercial drama rather than Classical theory – describe judgements upon actorly craft that hint at a wider cultural movement of the ideas of action and accent, perhaps in oral as well as textual form. Recent studies of topics as diverse as human–animal transformations and musical performance suggest that we underestimate the capacity of complex ideas and practices to circulate amongst less educated or illiterate early modern subjects at our peril.[35]

A refracted and tentative glimpse of less privileged playgoers censuring actorly skill appears in a printed paratext slightly removed from actual playhouse practice. In 1589 Thomas Nashe addressed a somewhat cantankerous passage to 'the gentlemen Students of Both Universities', complaining, among other things, of

how eloquent our gowned age is growen of late; so that euerie mechanicall mate abhorres the english he was borne too, and plucks, with a solemne periphrasis, his *vt vales* from the inkhorne: which I impute not so much to the perfection of arts, as to the seruile imitation of vainglorious tragœdians, who contend not so seriouslie to excell in action, as to embowell the cloudes in a speach of comparison; thinking themselues more than initiated in poets immortalitie, if they but once get *Boreas* by the beard and the heauenlie bull by the deaw-lap.[36]

Nashe's concern is to flatter the university educated and, ultimately, to set up a separate complaint about playwrights themselves. Yet his image of 'mechanical[s]' spouting Latin or Latinate phrases in approving imitation of 'vainglorious Tragedians' suggests that any playgoer, regardless of background or education, could be perfectly confident in their own capacity to judge – and imitate – the craft of the early modern actor, not to mention being enthusiastic about doing so. This combination of judgement and imitation appears to relate to verbal construction and perhaps accent, given that the tragedians they mimic are accused of an excessive focus on choice words over apt action.

---

[33] Astington, *Actors and Acting*, pp. 76–149; Tribble, *Cognition in the Globe*, pp. 111–50; Lois Potter, '"Nobody's perfect": Actors' Memories and Shakespeare's plays of the 1590s', in *Shakespeare Survey 42* (Cambridge, 1990), pp. 85–98.

[34] John Holles, 'Letter to the Earl of Somerset, Wednesday 11 August 1624', in *Middleton and Textual Culture*, ed. Taylor and Lavagnino, pp. 867–8.

[35] Susan Wiseman, *Writing Metamorphosis in the English Renaissance, 1550–1700* (Cambridge, 2014); Christopher Marsh, *Music and Society in Early Modern England* (Cambridge, 2010), pp. 32–70.

[36] Thomas Nashe, 'To the gentlemen students of both universities', in Robert Greene, *Menaphon Camillas Alarum to Slumbering Euphues* (London, 1589), sig. 2*2r.

The Cambridge-educated Nashe displays an anxiety that such modes of censorious engagement with actorly skill might be widespread amongst playgoers of lower social status. Moreover, his apparent discomfort at a mechanical mate's approving appropriation of a professional player's 'solemn periphrasis' and, perhaps, *pronuntio* hints at a culture of judgement not limited to former students of Cicero. Whilst the nature of the textual record generally allows more precise accounts of privileged playgoers' knowledge, their experience and their possible motivations for censure, it is just as important to attend to the patchy evidence concerning other audience members, for such material offers glimpses of playhouse judgement as a less elite and more democratic mode of engagement with early modern drama in performance. Such glimpses may even serve to warn more generally against attending only to fuller materials, given the risk of replicating the socially myopic nature of many of the most forthcoming early modern sources.

Having traced playhouse judgements upon actorly craft through eyewitness accounts and wider discussions, and speculated as to the possible motivations for such judgements, the final part of this article turns to consider how actorly judgement might fit into a wider history of early modern responses to drama. Playgoers are often presented as experiencing pleasure at the theatre, from the lascivious delight that Stephen Gosson fears 'slye' onstage 'whordome' will evoke, to the gratification that, at the end of *Twelfth Night*, Feste promises the Lord Chamberlain's Men will 'strive' to provide on a daily basis (5.1.404).[37] At first glance, these responses may seem distinct from the kinds of distanced reflection that might be associated with censure, yet, if we attend to a full range of surviving textual evidence, it is striking how often pleasure and judgement are not just represented as occurring simultaneously but actually framed as interlinked parts of the same response.

One such conjunction of pleasure and judgement appears in accounts of playgoers pleased by the quality of a performer's *actio*. Mary Wroth, author of an important closet drama, *Love's Victory*, did not write for the commercial stage but she does make passing reference to a playgoer's awareness of actorly skill, framed in precisely these terms, in *The Countess of Montgomery's Urania* (1621). In the first book of her expansive prose romance, a lustful and somewhat duplicitous queen takes a keen interest in a particularly well-proportioned and attractive gentleman visiting her court; while not the tallest, he was 'farre from being low' and his beard was 'something inclind to yellow'. She seeks his love with 'all passionate ardency' but, despite her best efforts, he is 'no further wrought, then if he had seene a delicate play-boy acte a louing womans part, and knowing him a Boy, lik'd onely his action'.[38] The very point of the analogy is a playgoer's archetypal awareness of a performer's artifice, even whilst admiring the veracity of his personation: she assumes that her readers will unproblematically recognize the playhouse practice of assessing how skilfully a boy player 'usurp[s] the grace, / Voice, gait and action of a gentlewoman' (*Shrew*, Induction 1.129–30). Moreover, Wroth suggests that this hypothetical playgoer takes pleasure of some kind in the 'play-boy['s] . . . action', implying that playhouse censure of *actio* and *pronuntio* occurred not as an alternative to or substitute for emotive engagement with performance but rather as a simultaneous, mutually informing response, a pleasure perhaps resulting in part from the playgoer's approval and thus interwoven with the act of judgement.

Such a combination of pleasure and judgement also appears when Thomas Platter describes how 'very pleasingly performed' the Julius Caesar play was that he saw on 21 September 1599, probably Shakespeare's at the Globe but possibly another on the same subject at the Rose.[39] Significantly, the very notion of pleasing performance suggests both a positive judgement upon the craft of the

---

[37] Stephen Gosson, *Playes Confuted in Fiue Actions* (London, 1582), sig. C5v.

[38] Lady Mary Wroth, *The Countesse of Mountgomeries Urania* (London, 1621), pp. 59–60.

[39] Translated in Ernest Schanzer, 'Thomas Platter's observations on the Elizabethan stage', *Notes and Queries* 201 (1956), 465–7; p. 466. Schanzer also discusses the identity of the play (pp. 466–7).

performance and pleasure in watching it. A similar blend of discretion and satisfaction in relation to a very specific kind of gesture or movement also seems present in Platter's further comment on how 'admirably and exceedingly gracefully' the company danced at the end of the play, dressed as men and women. Indeed, the Swiss visitor seems particularly interested in this specific skill, also noting how 'gracefully' a second troupe of players danced at the end of a performance at the Boar's Head or the Curtain.[40] Once again, the very act of judgement upon actorly craft – both in the laudable action of the players' dancing and in their more general pleasing performance – seems itself to be pleasurable, this time for a historical eyewitness of the London playhouses.

We might also return to Henry Jackson's account of the King's Men's performances in 1610, where emotive responses of 'pity' and 'tears' were inextricably bound up with precise and measured censuring of the players' action and accent, discharged 'decorously and aptly'. Jackson's 'moved' playgoers are further suggestive of a culture of playhouse response in which critical scrutiny and emotive responses – including but not limited to pleasure – were not considered mutually exclusive playhouse behaviours.[41]

Descriptions of actorly censure interwoven with emotive engagement also chime with accounts of playgoing not directly concerned with the player's craft. John Manningham's approving reference to the 'good practise' used to gull Malvolio in *Twelfth Night* is both a reflection upon Shakespeare's apt dramatic construction and a record of one witness's pleasure in this stagecraft; likewise, the 'wytt & mirthe' in *Love's Labour's Lost* that Sir Walter Cope reports will 'please' the queen 'exceedingly' brings together critical reflection on the quality of the play's 'wytt' and pleasure in the 'mirthe' that Shakespeare's comedy is expected to provoke in Queen Anna.[42] These tantalizing passing references to pleasure and judgement hint at rich and multifarious playhouse engagements, quite comfortably encompassing a range of seemingly contradictory responses of censure and delight in a single visit to a venue such as the Globe, and of relevance far beyond the particular issue of actorly skill.

This article has taken steps towards a history of actorly craft and playhouse judgement, tracing references to the censuring of players' technical skill, examining playgoers' potential motivations for judging actors and placing these considerations in wider contexts of early modern theatrical response. What emerges has clear ramifications for understanding playgoers' motivations and behaviour and for assessing the paradigms within which early modern drama was performed and written, as well as indicating new directions in studies of Shakespearian performance and early modern playhouse culture. Most immediately, this investigation has offered considerable support for the hypothesis that actorly craft was indeed an explicit topic of playhouse attention, something just as significant to early modern subjects' engagements with drama in performance as was narrative structure, apt characterization, a playhouse's capacity for visual and aural stagecraft or the poetic abilities of playwrights themselves.

A history of judicious playgoing has further implications, not least for the ways in which Shakespeare and other dramatists would have anticipated audiences engaging with fictional worlds created for the commercial stage. Playgoers keen to reflect upon the practicalities of performance even as they engage more imaginatively with dramatic narratives and characters would provide strikingly idiosyncratic target audiences for the King's Men and their dramatists, and, crucially, would require texts written with precisely these audience expectations in mind. Unlike some later theatrical contexts, the early modern stage is renowned for requiring audience

---

[40] Schanzer, 'Thomas Platter's Observations', p. 466; Gabriel Egan, 'Thomas Platter's account of an unknown play at the Curtain or the Boar's Head', *Notes and Queries* 245 (2000), 53–6.
[41] Jackson, 'Letter to D. G. P.', p. 1037.
[42] *The Diary of John Manningham of the Middle Temple, 1602–1603*, ed. Robert Parker Sorlien (Hanover, NH, 1976), p. 48; Sir Walter Cope, Letter to Sir Robert Cecil (1604), Hatfield House Library and Archives, MS CP 189/95.

members themselves to participate in the creation of drama through the forces of imagination. If, as this study suggests, playgoers were also quite consciously attentive to the means of theatrical production – in this case, the technical craft of the performers – then we must acknowledge an additional element of self-reflexivity: early modern playgoers not only participated in the creation of Shakespeare but even dwelt upon the practicalities of that creation as it took place.

This in turn affects critical approaches to play-texts written for theatres such as the Globe and Blackfriars. Plays such as *Hamlet* or *Antony and Cleopatra* read rather differently if we imagine a playwright composing in conscious anticipation of close engagement with the technicality of a role as expansive as Hamlet or as tonally complex and virtuosic as Cleopatra. Perhaps, too, the sheer number of technically demanding parts in plays such as *Twelfth Night* or *King Lear* needs to be understood differently, if Shakespeare constructed these ensemble pieces fully expecting playgoers to engage closely with the question of 'who acts best' amongst the performers of Lear, Cordelia, Edgar, Edmund, the Fool, Gloucester, Regan and Goneril or amongst the many substantive roles that populate Illyria.[43] Theatre history is not simply concerned with what happens to texts after they emerge from a playwright's pen but bears directly upon the conditions under which Shakespeare and his contemporaries wrote, requiring us to take its suggestions into account when reading early modern drama closely, just as when attending to the history of Shakespearian performance.

What is also clear from the textual record is the need to locate playhouse judgements as precisely as possible within wider early modern discourses of actorly skill. The ubiquity of *actio* and *pronuntio* in educational contexts certainly indicates one significant sphere of discussion shaping engagements with commercial players but the sheer range and number of sources suggesting widespread familiarity with action and accent implies that these categories were also familiar to subjects neither part of elite circles nor privy to a grammar school education. Whilst texts are often more forthcoming about the experiences of some playgoers than others, there is nonetheless clear scope for further investigation of just how widely models of actorly craft predicated upon action and accent may have circulated and thus how relevant these versions of technical skill are for examining playhouse engagements with the work of Shakespeare and his contemporaries.

The second, wider hypothesis tested in this article, that delight and censure were not alternative modes of engagement but intertwined features of playhouse response in early modern England, has also proved productive. A thoroughgoing history of playgoing, pleasure and judgement before 1642 lies beyond the scope of this article, although such a study is certainly required. Nonetheless, this account of the pleasures and judgements invited specifically by actorly skill demonstrates the need to reconsider the potential interaction of the two responses from the ground up, moving away from neater distinctions between 'the wiser sort' and 'audiences ... in the mass' that have held sway in previous theatre histories and returning to the textual record with an open mind as to the potential complexity, entanglement and variety of early modern playhouse engagements with drama.[44]

---

[43] Marston, *Scourge of Villanie*, sig. G7v.
[44] Gurr, *Playgoing*, pp. 116, 120.

'WHAT IMPORTS THIS SONG?': SPONTANEOUS SINGERS AND SPACES OF MEANING IN SHAKESPEARE

ELISABETH LUTTEMAN

'Has this fellow no feeling of his business that a sings at grave-making?' exclaims Hamlet as he comes across the singing sexton in Act 5 of the play (5.1.65–6). The singing gives rise to an immediate response, causing Hamlet to notice the gravedigger and pause longer in the graveyard. It provides the dramatic impulse for, as well as a backdrop to, the prince's musings to Horatio, leads into his subsequent conversation with the gravedigger and participates in a voicing and reformulating of some of the play's core concerns. The scene points to several of the many dramatic functions songs can be argued to have in early modern drama – participating in the characterization of both singing and listening characters; in setting the scene, creating an ambience or changing the tone or mood; and in the action, prompting characters to act or preventing them from acting.[1] In 'appropriating' or referring to extant, well-known lyrics and tunes, they can also form a link to the world outside the playhouse that may draw attention to the play's status as play.[2] They may communicate simultaneously within the framework of the drama and outside it, sending signals about character emotions, relationships and motivations as well as about dramatic conventions and agreements. Frequently, several functions and layers interact, making moments of song multifaceted, theatrically rich events in the drama.

In the following, I will explore possible spaces of meaning created by song in relation to three characters from Shakespeare's *Hamlet* – the gravedigger, Ophelia and the eponymous prince – drawing also on *King Lear*. The two plays share a concern with issues of essence and appearance, identity and disguise, madness and sanity, sense and nonsense, truth-telling and performance – themes voiced also in the moments of song. I am concerned specifically with appropriated or popular songs, and with spontaneous singing, a term I base on W. H. Auden's distinction between 'called-for' and 'impromptu' song – that is, instances of song requested by one character and performed by another, or instances of a character singing of his or her own accord.[3] I will consider the ability of song to create an intimate, self-contained space and at the same time ripple out through the play as a whole, its potential to open up a space of ambiguity and unstable meaning both on and off stage, meaning simultaneously in relation to multiple characters and themes, and its capacity to create

---

[1] Explored and discussed for instance in David Lindley, *Shakespeare and Music* (London, 2006); John H. Long, *Shakespeare's Use of Music: The Histories and Tragedies* (Gainesville, 1971); Peter J. Seng, *The Vocal Songs in the Plays of Shakespeare: A Critical History* (Cambridge, 1967); F. W. Sternfeld, *Music in Shakespearean Tragedy* (London, 1963); Richmond Noble, *Shakespeare's Use of Song* (Oxford, 1923).

[2] Stephen Orgel, 'Introduction', in Ross Duffin, *Shakespeare's Songbook* (London and New York, 2004), p. 13; Jacquelyn Ann Fox-Good, *Let Rich Music's Tongue Unfold: A Study of Shakespeare's Songs* (Ann Arbor, 1998), p. 156.

[3] W. H. Auden, 'Music in Shakespeare', in *The Dyer's Hand and Other Essays* (London, 1962), pp. 511, 522.

an intertextual, metatheatrical space where meaning stretches beyond the stage.

Hamlet's initial response to the gravedigger, who sings while he finishes his work and waits for his companion to return with 'a stoup of liquor' (5.1.60), is that the singing is inappropriate. Looking at the song's text, however, it is pertinent in many ways. It refers to a lyric by Lord Vaux, 'I Loathe That I Did Love', which appeared in the collection *Tottel's Miscellany* in 1557. As Ross Duffin suggests, the gravedigger's text draws on the first, third and eighth stanzas of the Vaux poem. I would add to these three the next to last stanza, which seems to have a part in the gravedigger's second verse. The last Vaux stanza also resonates with the graveyard scene as a whole: 'And ye that bide behind, / Have ye none other trust: / As ye of clay were cast by kind, / So shall ye waste to dust.'[4] The re-working or garbling of lines of an extant lyric displayed in the gravedigger's song is a recurring characteristic of spontaneously singing characters in Shakespeare and one that places the song between stage and the world outside the playhouse, making it resonate in both spaces. The garbling might be seen as a representation of a faltering memory or the process of oral transmission but it is also a dramatically pertinent adaptation of the song to character-specific needs and circumstances. Richmond Noble notes how the changes make the ballad more relevant to the work the gravedigger has at hand: the 'house' of Vaux's poem becomes the 'pit' he is himself standing in; the 'spade' he is holding is given a more prominent place through repetition.[5]

The song's theme of death and dust ties in well with the gravedigger's work. As a song of old age, however, it also ironically highlights the fact that death in *Hamlet* is always untimely – in a politically tense court and a time of madness and impending war, its cause is assassination, battle or suicide. The scene and its song pick up on the theme voiced by Gertrude and Claudius at the very beginning of the play: 'all that lives must die, / Passing through nature to eternity' (1.2.72–3). The same theme is subsequently voiced by Hamlet in the speech before his duel with Laertes: 'If it be not now, yet it will come' (5.2.167–8). With the inevitability of death as one of the few remaining constants in the play's world, the gravedigger's singing may be heard to participate in the development of central thoughts in Hamlet as a character, nuancing and modulating his earlier comment 'Ay, madam, it is common' (1.2.74).

The gravedigger's singing is focused on the stark reality and inevitably common experiences of the human condition. In the fifteenth-century play *Mankind*, Janette Dillon recounts, the character with the same name enters with a spade – an object implying, she suggests, a link to the first man, Adam, and through him to all mankind – 'announcing that "we" ... are derived "Of the earth and of the clay"'.[6] The gravedigger's song is about earth, sung from the earth and also resolutely down-to-earth. The graveyard emerges as a space of conflation: the king and the beggar become one and the same; the nobleman, the lawyer and the mad rogue share a tomb. A blurring or reversal of categories is also in a sense inherent in the mode of song itself – it is a conflation of a personal, individual voice with the fictive voices of a story as well as with many other voices that have sung and are singing the song. At the same time, the gravedigger's punning dialogue with his companion, which prefigures the song, has highlighted the hierarchical structure of the play's world. The song's stanzas, interspersed with Hamlet's thoughts on the transience of life and sovereignty, thus participate in opening up a field of tension between conflicting, but equally real, realities of life.

A space of more deliberate commentary is opened up through spontaneous singing in *King Lear*, where the Fool, from his first appearance on stage, employs snatches of rhymes and songs to critique Lear's actions.[7] The reference in Act 1, scene 4 to the

---

[4] Duffin, *Shakespeare's Songbook*, p. 212.
[5] Noble, *Shakespeare's Use of Song*, p. 120.
[6] Janette Dillon, *The Cambridge Introduction to Early English Theatre* (Cambridge, 2006), p. 101.
[7] There are no stage directions for song in *Lear*, but the Fool's character, the lyrics and the markers in the dialogue have all led editors to add directions for song to many of his snatches. As the description of the jester Yorick in *Hamlet* suggests, it would not be unexpected for a fool figure to sing.

spiritual ballad 'Some Men For Sudden Joy'[8] shows the same kind of claiming of an extant lyric as that discussed in relation to the gravedigger. The original ballad text, on sin, repentance and forgiveness, brings into play the theme of failing to serve and obey God 'according to [one's] kind',[9] something that resonates with the questioning of Lear's decision to give up his kingdom. Here, too, the re-working makes the text pertinent to the situation and the character singing – the Fool's stanza substitutes the last two lines, making them relate to the king, and also changes the perspective of the ballad line 'some in sorrow sing' to the more personal 'I for sorrow sung' (1.4.157). However, the Fool aims to make a point to a specific listener and the stanza about the king 'go[ing] the fools among' (1.4.159) is integrated perfectly into his critique, tying in with a larger theme of reversed roles that is present in the madness and disguise on the heath and still reflected in Cordelia's care for her 'child-changèd father' near the end of the play (4.6.15). Indeed, for F. W. Sternfeld, '[t]he dramatic function of the songs' has 'been fulfilled when arrogant Lear has become "wise enough to play the fool"'.[10]

A reversal of sorts may also be heard in the way popular song itself functions. As David Lindley states, 'it is not the least striking feature of the play that the popular music which elsewhere carries with it suggestions of subversion should here be an image of truthful perception'.[11] The nature of this truth perceived by the Fool is related to the bank from which he draws his commentary and paradoxical wisdom as well as to the ties that Lear's actions break at the beginning of the play. Lawrence Danson suggests that the 'bond' represented by Cordelia, 'expressive of traditional values, shared beliefs', constitutes 'the cornerstone of the play's society'. In rejecting and breaking this, Lear also tears the fabric of the play's social and political worlds.[12] The Fool, on the other hand, expresses himself through a mixture of 'wise saws, riddles, and fragments of ballads' that, John H. Long argues, 'suggest a moral or comment on an action by reminding Lear and the audience of analogous situations in the folk-histories'.[13] He is heard, appropriately, to employ the collective voice of proverbs and songs to point to a breach of social structures and 'shared beliefs' brought about by Lear, and subsequently by Goneril and Regan.[14] In this sense, any regeneration in *King Lear* is intimately connected to a sense of return. What Danson terms the 'new order' or 'new world', 'struggling to be born among the outcasts on the heath',[15] is equally an old world forgotten – something manifest in the echoes of old proverbs and songs that is reconnected with, rediscovered and restated largely through the Fool's particular discourse and relation to song.

The Fool's punning and riddling may interrogate the line between meaning and meaninglessness, but his nonsense, as Kent points out, is rarely 'altogether fool' (4.146). An important dimension of the way in which his fragmented discourse works as a space of critique is that of suggestion and indirection.[16] Significantly, the ambiguity of intention and meaning, similar in puns and snatches of song,[17] opens the commentary to the associations of the listeners, allowing possible meanings to proliferate, and

---

[8] Duffin, *Shakespeare's Songbook*, p. 376.
[9] Duffin, *Shakespeare's Songbook*, p. 375.
[10] Sternfeld, *Music in Shakespearean Tragedy*, pp. 166–7.
[11] David Lindley, 'Shakespeare's provoking music', in *The Well Enchanting Skill: Music, Poetry and Drama in the Culture of the Renaissance*, ed. John Caldwell, Edward Olleson and Susan Wollenberg (Oxford, 1990), p. 90.
[12] Lawrence Danson, *Tragic Alphabet: Shakespeare's Drama of Language* (New Haven, 1974), p. 166.
[13] Long, *Shakespeare's Use of Music*, p. 164.
[14] See Lindley, *Shakespeare and Music*, p. 162, for a suggestion that the collective voice present in the Fool's discourse may be heard to remind the king of the people and 'world outside the ceremonies of court', of which he has '"ta'en too little care" (3.4.32–3)'. This, too, potentially resonates with the reference to 'Some Men For Sudden Joy' and a failure to perform properly the duties of 'one's kind'.
[15] Danson, *Tragic Alphabet*, pp. 171–2.
[16] Since his licence for free speech had its limits, indirection emerges as characteristic of the stage fool's discourse, Long suggests (*Shakespeare's Use of Music*, pp. 64–5).
[17] To play with words, Nathalie Roulon points out, is to be sensitive to the musical qualities of language, its rhythm and sounds, as much as, or more than, to its capacity to signify (*Les femmes et la musique dans l'oeuvre de Shakespeare* (Paris, 2011), p. 119). According to Sternfeld, *Music in Shakespearean Tragedy*, p. 162, a lyric in its entirety may be seen to '[border] on a pun', since it is often connected to the surrounding dialogue or prose by 'a single word whose sound evokes' it.

creating a reflective surface in which they perceive what they believe to be there. This aspect of the dramatic representation of the fool is remarkably similar to that of the madwoman or madman, and Ophelia's scenes in Act 4 of *Hamlet* indicate several ways in which moments of song are open to interpretation or application on the part of audiences both onstage and off.

As Gertrude's comment shows – 'what imports this song?' (4.5.27) – Ophelia's onstage listeners struggle to understand her. What is more, pinning down meaning is important to them: the possible threat or danger perceived in her madness and mad singing appears to be linked mainly to the uncertain way in which the songs signify, their ability to 'strew / Dangerous conjectures in ill-breeding minds' (4.5.14–15).[18] Their interpretations focus on her grief for Polonius but, as Peter Seng's discussion shows, her songs may be heard to point simultaneously in several directions, enabling singer and individual listeners to understand them in different ways,[19] and raising questions about whether meaning can or cannot be contained by interpretation. The first song, 'How should I your true love know', appears in its first four lines to be a reference to 'Walsingham', a ballad of an abandoned, aged lover looking for his lost love, striking up a conversation with a pilgrim on the road.[20] Ophelia's version draws on both the pilgrim's and the lover's parts of the dialogue, emphasizing how multiple perspectives are brought into play by the song. The stanza is concerned with appearances and intentions, echoing the play's larger concern with seeming, 'trappings' and 'suits' (1.2.86), and potentially questioning the reliability of exterior attributes, such as the pilgrim's cockle hat. It resonates with Ophelia's own experience – Seng remarks on Polonius's advice to her not to take Hamlet's 'tenders' of affection 'at face value' and on her 'confused' response, 'I do not know, my lord, what I should think' (1.4.104).[21] If seen as directed specifically at the Queen, referring to Old Hamlet,[22] the song also resonates strongly with Hamlet's speech in her bedchamber about the difference between the old king and Claudius, this 'Hyperion to a satyr' (1.2.140). Lamenting the fickle nature of particularly women's affections, the ballad story further resonates with Gertrude abandoning love and grief for the old king and with Hamlet's previously expressed views on female 'frailty' (1.2.146).

Like the gravedigger's lyric and the Fool's snatch, Ophelia's stanza seizes on relevant lines or thoughts from an extant song and adapts them. The focus on death, burials and mourning in the following stanzas opens up a theme that also resounds through her subsequent songs and raises questions about whether Ophelia has been unable to 'cast away moan' (4.5.196) and grieved herself into madness – unable, like Hamlet, to follow the advice of the king and queen when they tell him to 'cast [his] nighted colour off' (1.2.68). The songs, and Ophelia's state in singing them, might enforce the stance of Gertrude and Claudius, chiding Hamlet's inability to moderate his grief, but it could just as well enforce Hamlet's view, chiding the royal couple for being so quick to lay off grieving. Both views are, from the standpoint of the other, guilty of a breach of custom.

Mark W. Booth suggests that song forms 'a vital bridge between what passes in separate lives and what endures in community experience'.[23] When spontaneous singers turn to ballads and popular songs, they tune in on or connect with a collective expression, an accumulated experience. This is one way in which the songs mean – they are intended to be recognized and identified with. They may be heard as suggestive of the fictive communities to which characters belong, like the community of women Nathalie Roulon suggests is

---

[18] Amanda Eubanks Winkler, *O Let Us Howle Some Heavy Note: Music for Witches, the Melancholy, and the Mad on the Seventeenth-Century English Stage* (Bloomington, 2006), p. 88; Lindley, *Shakespeare and Music*, p. 156.

[19] Seng, *The Vocal Songs*, pp. 131–56.

[20] Duffin, *Shakespeare's Songbook*, p. 423.

[21] Seng, *The Vocal Songs*, p. 147.

[22] Long, *Shakespeare's Use of Music*, p. 115; Seng, *The Vocal Songs*, pp. 133–4.

[23] Mark W. Booth, *The Experience of Songs* (New Haven, 1981), p. 201.

invoked through the 'Willow Song' in *Othello*.[24] In forms of song like the catch or the ballad, singing is also in practice a collective activity that joins individual voices. Ophelia's attempt to get her listeners to sing the burden-like 'Down, a-down' (4.5.171) can be heard to emphasize her isolation and her singing in the wrong place at the wrong time but also possibly to point to the fact that the community she is invoking through her songs is missing where she sings them.[25] Several critics have traced a loss of meaning in rituals of different kinds in *Hamlet*, commenting on how 'rites' – from mourning to prayer – are repeatedly 'broken or interrupted'.[26] Ophelia's songs echo this and the many voices sounding through and together with her voice may be heard to point to a failure to adhere to communal values and to a loss of common human experience.

In the moments considered here, song emphasizes a series of tensions between isolation and community, individual and collective, the expression and the loss of self.[27] There is an inherent tension, too, between self and assumed identities and voices, as song allows, even demands, a certain taking on of roles. The singer takes on the voice of a fictive character and steps into another subject position,[28] and at the same time, the song's persona is given voice in the moment of song, becoming an expression of the emotion and experience of the spontaneous singer. In otherwise spoken drama, song also stands out as a distinct mode of expression and communication – particularly spontaneous song, which is not framed as a performance within the play – and this in itself may be one way in which it means on stage.[29] Within the drama, the possibility of communicating or of assuming a voice through song means that it can be employed by characters as a conscious means of disguise or aid in the acting out of a role and, in this context, I would like to turn to the eponymous prince in *Hamlet*, exploring song as part of his assumed 'antic disposition' (1.5.173). As a developing dramatic convention in the representation of madness,[30] metatheatrically employed by the potentially singing prince, song draws on attitudes to singing in relation both to the world outside the playhouse and to the stage, meaning across plays and characters, making it possible for spontaneous singing to confuse or upset onstage listeners while making perfect dramatic sense to the audience.

In the midst of Hamlet's mad conversation with Polonius in Act 2, lines from the ballad 'Jepha Judge of Israel' are seamlessly integrated into the spoken dialogue. There are no stage directions specifying song,[31] but the phrases in the dialogue are strikingly consistent with the original ballad stanza and might easily be sung. Q1 shares the orthography 'Jepha' with the ballad and also calls it a 'godly ballet' rather than the 'pious chanson' of Q2 and F, strengthening the link to its ballad source, not only to the biblical story.[32] Hamlet's first two lines after introducing 'Jephthah' into the

---

[24] Roulon, *Les femmes et la musique*, p. 223.
[25] The 2016 production of *Hamlet* at the RSC, directed by Simon Godwin, showed Ophelia temporarily succeeding in making the king and queen sing but this, too, emphasized the characters' different experiences of the situation.
[26] R. A. Foakes, *Hamlet Versus Lear: Cultural Politics and Shakespeare's Art* (Cambridge, 1993), p. 173.
[27] This is pertinent in relation to 'mad song', since madness might be read either as an excess of self, as suggested by Danson's discussion of a 'solipsistic language', or as an 'absence' of self. Danson, *Tragic Alphabet*, pp. 176–7; Carol Thomas Neely, 'Did madness have a Renaissance?', *Renaissance Quarterly* 44, 4 (1991), 776–91; p. 779.
[28] Bruce R. Smith, 'Ballads within, around, among, of, upon, against, within', in *The Acoustic World of Early Modern England: Attending to the O-factor* (Chicago and London, 1999), p. 176.
[29] Winkler, *O Let Us Howle*, p. 10; Auden, 'Music in Shakespeare', p. 511. For a discussion on song as a mode 'opposed to speech', see Leslie C. Dunn, 'Ophelia's songs in Hamlet: Music, madness, and the feminine', in *Embodied Voices: Representing Female Vocality in Western Culture*, ed. Leslie C. Dunn and Nancy A. Jones (Cambridge, 1994), pp. 50–64; p. 52.
[30] See for instance Winkler, *O Let Us Howle*, p. 86; Lindley, *Shakespeare and Music*, p. 154.
[31] *Hamlet, First Quarto 1603*, Shakespeare Quarto Facsimiles No. 7 (London, 1951); *Hamlet, Second Quarto 1604–5*, Shakespeare Quartos in Collotype Facsimile Number 4 (London, 1940); *Mr William Shakespeares Comedies, Histories, & Tragedies: A Facsimile of the First Folio, 1623* (London and New York, 1998).
[32] Duffin, *Shakespeare's Songbook*, pp. 226–9.

conversation could be imagined as a spoken or partly sung reference to the ballad, his 'Nay, that follows not' (2.2.413) as a comment on Polonius missing the reference, and the subsequent lines as full-fledged song, interrupted, as Ophelia's singing will later be, by spoken comments. I agree with Lindley's suggestion that 'there is no obvious reason' why Hamlet should not sing here.[33] Singing would encourage Polonius to draw the conclusion that Hamlet has gone mad, and the appropriation of this particular ballad encourages his theory that the reason is unrequited love for his daughter. Hamlet might thus be seen to employ the ballad both to give the impression of madness and to suggest an interpretation of its cause to his onstage listener. The scene also hints at the ability of song to open up a space of unstable meaning not only by being ambiguous and difficult to interpret but also by constituting a refusal to communicate in expected and accepted ways, working as critique, mockery or resistance by being a reflective surface that deflects comments.

Hamlet could also be interpreted as a spontaneous singer in Act 3, scene 2, after the interrupted performance of 'The Mousetrap'. When the king has hastily exited, Hamlet, left alone with Horatio on the stage, has two rhymed four-line stanzas in ballad metre, 'Why, let the strucken deer go weep' and 'For thou dost know, O Damon dear'. Both stanzas have possible connections to other texts and to tunes – the first, in Duffin's reading, to the poem and ballad tune 'If Care Do Cause Men Cry'; the second to a song from Richard Edward's play *Damon and Pithias*, also registered separately as a song and with a tune called for by other ballads.[34] As in the *Jepha* scene, singing seems possible in a performance context both because of the musical hints surrounding the passages and because of the dramatic moment in the play. If he were to sing here, just as he has found his uncle's guilt proved, Hamlet would display one of the characteristics of spontaneous singers: the expression of emotion, excitement or anxiety through song. Like the scene immediately following his encounter with the ghost, this passage shows Hamlet in an ambivalent state of mind, making the question of his feigned madness ambiguous. Singing would further increase the ambiguity and could potentially enforce interpretations of Hamlet's conscious taking on of roles as well as of his own distraught state of mind.

It seems probable that the *Damon* reference would bring to mind the story, play or ballad of the friendship between Damon and Pythias in relation to Hamlet and Horatio. Similarly, the *Jepha* story, where the father sacrifices his daughter, might influence the perception of the relationship between Polonius and Ophelia, and, as Duffin seems to suggest, hint to the playhouse audience that things were not looking good for Ophelia.[35] Ways in which the texts or stories of appropriated songs may resonate with the themes of the plays have also been suggested above in relation to 'I Loathe That I Did Love' and 'Some Men For Sudden Joy'. Links and hints brought into play by appropriated songs can turn both on words and on the music itself, which means together with the lyrics as well as on its own.[36] In the case of ballads, a suggestive web of meaning is created, encompassing the experience of the tune itself as well as the different stories sung to it. Even a brief reference to a tune or ballad title might activate such a web, allowing the audience to make connections to a range of previous experiences both in and outside the playhouse.[37]

Such recognition creates a space both intertextual and metatheatrical, where song may simultaneously encourage immersion and highlight the play's status as fiction and where stage and

---

[33] Lindley, *Shakespeare and Music*, p. 159. See also Long, *Shakespeare's Use of Music*, p. 113, who, seeing Hamlet as 'acting the court jester', suggests that singing would be 'in character'.

[34] Duffin, *Shakespeare's Songbook*, pp. 463–4, 117.

[35] Duffin, *Shakespeare's Songbook*, p. 228.

[36] See Christopher Marsh, *Music and Society in Early Modern England* (Cambridge, 2006), pp. 288–327.

[37] In relation to 'I Loathe That I Did Love', another ballad with similar imagery calls for a tune with this title some twenty years after the publication of the miscellany where one of two musical settings suggested by Duffin first appeared, hinting at a possibility of a connection between tune and theme (*Shakespeare's Songbook*, pp. 212–13).

audience, play and outside world meet and interact. The moments of song are also metatheatrical in potentially pointing to ways in which the theatre itself works. In speaking through puns, songs and indirection the plays, too, adopt a particular mode of expression and communication and, as a whole, they may be seen as reflective surfaces similar to the songs and discourse of the spontaneous singers explored here. Like a character assuming a voice or role through song, the theatre may be a dressed-up critic of society. It can also be society's licensed fool, entertaining, mocking and commenting. Further, as Dunn suggests music to be 'like the "madwoman" in language, releasing subversive powers of self-expression',[38] so the theatre may claim licence that has not been given, highlighting the possibility of an audience making 'dangerous conjectures' based on what they see and hear. In this sense, the spontaneously singing characters, their songs and the spaces of meaning created by them participate in the plays' larger concern with their own theatrical status.

I have considered here some of the ways in which song can open up spaces of meaning in two of Shakespeare's plays, both onstage and off. The graveyard scene in particular shows how a moment of song may create an intimate, self-contained space and at the same time ripple out through the play, connecting to its larger themes. Both the gravedigger's and Ophelia's singing points to how it may participate directly in the dramatic movement of the play while at the same time temporarily halting the action, allowing multiple and contradictory meanings to resonate, linger and proliferate. All the instances suggest that song may open up an in-between space of unstable, ambiguous meaning, intention and interpretation. Precisely because it is musical, the space created also emerges as a possible site of alternative, non-verbal meanings. Ophelia's scenes further show how songs may mean simultaneously in relation to several different characters and themes. In these instances, songs can be heard to embody a simultaneous movement in more than one direction both in terms of meaning and dramatic structure or action. Both Ophelia's scenes and Hamlet's possible employment of the dramatic convention of mad song suggest that singing may mean differently to onstage listeners and offstage audiences. In their appropriation and reconfiguration of extant lyrics and tunes, the instances of song also point to how stage songs participate in a web of meaning stretching beyond the stage, in an intertextual, metatheatrical space where play and outside world, as well as stage and audience, meet and interact.

A space of reversal has been explored in relation to song, resonating with the shared concerns of the plays, and the genre of popular song has been heard to significantly contribute to the nature of the commentary, criticism or truth offered by the plays' singers. *Hamlet* and *Lear* both point to the possibility of speaking truth through the assumed voices of song, and of finding it not only in madness, folly and nonsense but also in playacting or disguise. Similar to the dramatic spaces of the graveyard and the heath, song emerges as a space of conflation, blurring boundaries between individual and collective, self and role, between sense and nonsense; between high and low, nobleman and beggar. By doing so, it also emphasizes tensions in the characters and the plays' worlds. Song further creates a space of conflation between stage and outside world, drama and everyday life. This may be linked to the use of popular song but also to the mode of singing itself, representing a blending of multiple voices both past and present. Significantly, it emerges as a space of human experience and, in this, the singers and their songs find a place at the thematic, dramatic and emotional core of the two plays.

---

[38] Dunn, 'Ophelia's songs', p. 59.

SHAKESPEARE'S DEPRIVING PARTICLES

RUTH MORSE

Affixation does not get much attention nowadays, although Charles Barber observed years ago that in the early modern period 'affixation alone produces more new words than loans from all languages' and illustrated this lexical expansion with examples of what adding a prefix or a suffix could do.[1] This short article explores what Shakespeare achieved with a particle of a word and why it might matter. In brief, he clusters prefixes in ways not dissimilar from strong images or those fingerprint groups first analysed by Caroline Spurgeon and Edward Armstrong, among others, but Shakespeare uses them to convey the simultaneous absence or negation of an evaluative-descriptive noun.[2] Their purpose is, further, to create unease about the characters who speak them; that is, they have an ethical function, as my examples demonstrate. I focus on the Anglo-Saxon derived 'un-', with a reference or two to the Latin/French 'diss-', which does slightly different work. These 'depriving particles', sometimes called 'privatives', create 'particular moments of recusatory dismay',[3] embedding the values they lack or negate, thus emphasizing what they contradict; for example, 'unthought' and 'dishonour'.

However acutely we hear, however closely we read, it is not easy to catch the work of the depriving particles as they fly by, subliminally undermining a noun that looks like a sceptical observation, sounds like a rebuke, is criticism – but not always quite what one might expect a character to say. Certain of Shakespeare's words become carriers of signification easy to miss, without that stopping their doing their subliminal or unconscious work. By emphasizing a lack or negating a positive, Shakespeare's characters – the politicians (in the early modern English sense), the ambitious, the cheats and the liars various – reveal flaws and intentions they might prefer to remain hidden. They group them more than do other characters. Ordinary characters and bit-part characters often use one or two privatives, many of which are anodyne, such as 'unhappy' or 'unpleasing', but theirs do not carry the same reflexiveness upon the speaker. In the work in progress that follows, I shall suggest how and why these words require attention and what functions they perform.

To begin with the vocabulary of analysis, the use of 'privative' belongs to the world of philosophical analysis in Latin: OED's first citation is *c.* 1398, in the sense linguistics still uses, in John Trevisa's translation of *On the Properties of Things* by Bartholomeus Anglicus of about 1240. *OED* begins, 'Consisting in or marked by the absence or loss of some quality or

---

In memory of Russ McDonald. With thanks to A.E.B. Coldiron and Jonathan Hope for help along the way and to Stefan Collini for close and careful reading.

[1] In his *Early Modern English*, The Language Library (London, 1976), pp. 184ff. Barber was particularly interested in suffixes, which created more new words than prefixes did. My work confirms his discovery that 'un-' is the most important of the prefixes. We agree that the use of French loan 'in-' is a particularly close variant; I would add the variant 'im-'.

[2] Caroline Spurgeon, *Shakespeare's Imagery and What It Tells Us* (Cambridge, 1935); E. A. Armstrong, *Shakespeare's Imagination: A Study of the Psychology of Association and Inspiration* (London, 1946). Also in Ruth Morse, 'Unfit for human consumption: Shakespeare's unnatural food', *Shakespeare Jahrbuch [West]*, 119 (1983), 125–43. In retrospect there is a certain irony to my title, whose two 'un-' prefixes I entirely missed.

[3] I owe this phrase to A. E. B. Coldiron (personal communication).

attribute that is normally present; (more generally) designating a negative quality or condition'. James Mill is clearer, 'It is usual to reserve the term Privative for names which signify not simple absence, but the absence of something usually present, or of which the presence might have been expected.'[4] I shall offer a contrast between the clustered value-engaged privatives of dangerous characters with a rudimentary control group of everyday, common privatives – 'unhappy' or 'untimely', for example – used by a variety of other kinds of characters, including some of the anonymous figures – attendant lords and ladies, gardeners, scriveners, servants whose moral compasses are more straightforward as well as less characterized than the central agents. But mainly I concentrate on wicked schemers, indicating a spectrum of usage and function. A second category, etymology, has turned out to be more surprising, though it should not have been.

That Shakespeare makes certain characters condemn themselves is well known: they give less or more excuse for choosing evil and know themselves wicked, such as Richard III or Macbeth, who share a tortured sense of their conduct with *Hamlet*'s Claudius. There has been enough argument in Shakespeare criticism about the place of such characters and what Shakespeare is 'really' doing, usually referring to contemporary social order. The kind of close reading I am doing here used to take weeks as one reread and spotted more related keywords, which were then checked against a paper concordance. Methodologically, even at the earliest stage of what became this article, I opted for prefixes, and read down the columns of OED. My choices were not fortuitous but I admit unashamedly that prefixes are necessarily easier to find than suffixes. Without the powerful searching programs now available, the collection of terms becomes a pachyderm nigh on to impossible to manipulate. Additionally, keyword searching depends on knowledge, insight and contextual understanding. In my recent experience working on attitudes to land, the unexpected payoff of frequency lists was that they also revealed etymologies of emotional attachment, unattachment and detachment.[5] Robert Watson's article demonstrates this for *Coriolanus*.[6]

As a case study, let me illustrate the problems of keyword searching, or searching for a defined combination of letters, in this case 'un★'. The software is a close reader but it cannot distinguish homonyms, different meanings or dismiss words such as 'unfold', which is frequent throughout the corpus, nor 'until' or such 'unders' as '-take' and '-stand'. One advantage of human slow reading is that in looking for occurrences of words, concepts or semantic fields, the questions change and modify the argument because, if you look up and down the columns of a concordance from each example of the word you are searching for, clusters begin to appear, which contain associated words that may not be immediately identifiable as related. Caroline Spurgeon emphasized this. While computational stylistics has the advantage that the computer does not get bored, an alert human eye remains a necessity in order to recognize and sort context, etymology and patterns. I had from Jonathan Hope a list of the number of hits for 'un+' by play, a list in which *Richard III* came top, with 159 hits, followed closely by *2 Henry VI*, and then the other English history plays. *Hamlet* logs in with 124. Meanwhile, bottom of the league table,

---

[4] Bartholomeus, surprisingly, combines sensation (taste) and grammar: 'The nynþe sauour hatte werischnesse or vnsauerynesse. And þat may be yseyde in tweye wise, pryuatif or positif. Priuatif is ycleped vnsauery if þe sauour þerof may nought be knowe by þe taste', and 'Nounes adiectiue tokeneþ somwhat positif affirmynge [adiectiua nomina quae aliquid connotant positiue], for somme tokeneth þerwith effect in creatures and somme respect'. *On the Properties of Things, John Trevisa's Translation of Bartholomaeus Anglicus De Proprietatibus Rerum, a Critical Text*, ed. M. C. Seymour, *et al.*, 3 vols. (Oxford, 1975), vol. 2, p. 1316. Text is edited from BL Add. 27944 and appears in chapter 52 of the 19th book; James Mill, *Analysis of the Phenomena of the Human Mind*, new edn (London, 1869), vol. 2, p. 99n.

[5] Ruth Morse and David Schalkwyk, 'This earth, this land, this island', *Archiv für das Studium der neueren Sprachen und Literaturen* 167 (2015), 394–415.

[6] See Robert N. Watson, 'Coriolanus and the "common part"', in *Shakespeare Survey 69* (Cambridge, 2016), pp. 181–97.

Dream has only 39. This was not puzzling for long: the kings Henry IV and V had many brothers, more than Edward IV's two. The initially striking disproportion of 'un' in *Richard III* is, alas, due to 'uncle', entirely the result of philoprogenitive families of sons who have nephews and nieces.

Additionally, keyword searching cannot help by distinguishing the ways the un-words are used by bad or good or merely indifferent characters or by distinguishing very common words that characters of all kinds employ without particular stress. It cannot say much about who is speaking in what circumstances to which other character. Even so, jokes and limitations aside, *Richard III* is indeed high in privatives that set a tone of inexorable tragedy, and its most wicked of wicked uncles shares linguistic attributes with Uncle Claudius. It is Claudius with whom I shall begin.

I have already referred to the importance of etymology and Shakespeare's consistent preference for Anglo-Saxon monosyllables at moments of high emotion, as opposed to Latinate polysyllables to heighten register. Some of these normal privatives form a category of unremarkable words: unfit, unhappy (meaning 'unfortunate'), unjust, unkind, unknown, unlawful, unquiet, unsafe, untimely, untold, unwilling/ness, unworthy. Nothing calls particular attention to them and they are used by all kinds of characters. My opening intuition was that privatives work at high-octane strength where characters of evil intent use them to impress their onstage interlocutors but where, also, the whole play speaks *through* its interlocutors to condemn such characters and warn spectators or readers of their dangerous intentions. But that is not all.

When Claudius takes Hamlet to task for excessive grief he says,

> 'Tis sweet and commendable in your nature, Hamlet,
> To give these mourning duties to your father;
> But you must know your father lost a father;
> That father lost, lost his; and the survivor bound
> In filial obligation for some term
> To do obsequious sorrow. But to persever
> In obstinate condolement is a course
> Of **impious** stubbornness, 'tis **unmanly** grief,
> It shows a will most **incorrect** to heaven,
> A heart **unfortified**, a mind **impatient**,
> An understanding simple and **unschooled**;
> For what we know must be, and is as common
> As any the most vulgar thing to sense,
> Why should we in our peevish opposition
> Take it to heart? Fie, 'tis a fault to heaven,
> A fault against the dead, a fault to nature . . .
> . . . We pray you throw to earth
> This **unprevailing** woe.[7]

Obviously, what 'impious', 'unmanly', 'incorrect', 'unfortified', 'impatient', 'unschooled' and 'unprevailing' have in common is the lack of the ordinary values the nouns preserve: pious, manly, correct, fortified, patient, schooled and prevailing – as James Mill observed. Claudius is doing something that many of Shakespeare's ethically dubious characters do; in effect, he provides us with those right values by absenting them. Unsavoury characters would do better to eschew them altogether. But they do not. The only non-romance words in the list are school and man; the others seem to create high register. As Claudius reaches his peroration he uses more Anglo-Saxon monosyllables, that habit of Shakespeare's for emotional seriousness. Why, however, 'unprevailing', if not that Claudius accuses Hamlet of behaving like a woman, as Laertes blames himself when he weeps for his sister? The two cases should feel different and they do. Evidently, the presence of these privatives, even in such a cluster, is not the only effect we note in Claudius. The king is prone to orotund polysyllables ('obstinate condolement'), to rhetorical repetitions, which hammer at his point. Here, as elsewhere, Claudius makes so much noise it is hard to concentrate on what he actually says. He is a scheming politician, would-be statesman, potential tyrant and, of course, drunk. He corrupts what he touches or, perhaps, attracts the corrupt to himself: neither Laertes nor Polonius is resistant to the use of the 'un-' privative.

---

[7] *Hamlet*, 1.2.87–107. Quotations from *Hamlet* are taken from *William Shakespeare: The Complete Works*, ed. Stanley Wells, et al., 2nd edn (Oxford, 2005).

In this play, with its variety of styles and registers, Hamlet himself is a particularly alert critic, ready to pounce on pretentious misuses of, say, court speech but also ready to appreciate old-fashioned verse that is part of the audience's past, if they remember Marlowe or the even older rhythms of the play-within. We are the audience of an audience, watching courtiers responding with approbation to the king's speeches and decisions. Shakespeare invites us to disapprove, or, at least, he offers us the possibility of disapprobation, to see through the fraudulence and dishonesty of men such as Claudius. We may be carried away by the delights of the depraved but there are warnings in the air. So let us listen to the Ghost, just for a moment, when a second example in juxtaposition will carry more force:

> Thus was I, sleeping, by a brother's hand
> Of life, of crown, of queen at once dispatched,
> Cut off even in the blossoms of my sin,
> **Un**houseled, **dis**-appointed, **un**aneled,
> No reck'ning made, but sent to my account
> With all my **im**perfections on my head.
> O horrible, O horrible, most horrible!
> (*Hamlet*, 1.5.74–80)

Fratricide and regicide are indeed horrible. And this time the variety of 'un-' prefixes indicates lack, with the negative 'dis' indicating a kind of ante-mortem destruction. The question here becomes our attitude to this apparition, this unready sinner, murdered unabsolved. What is missing in this picture is any hint of repentance. That ought to set warning lights going. Othello is more generous as he worries about Desdemona's need to repent, working, as he does, with a presumption of guilt. *Hamlet*'s Ghost is an egotist of the first water. In **un**folding his fate to Hamlet, he simultaneously **un**folds it to himself, reliving his **un**hap, his **mis**fortune, lamenting the **un**timeliness of the murder which prevented it and presenting the reckoning of the account of its '**im**perfections' – plain English 'sins'. Is Shakespeare condemning this suffering spirit? At this point we cannot know, and at no point can we intuit an answer if we do not read slowly and stay alert.

Once we notice, the trawl of privatives begins to contribute to groups and categories that work from play to play. Forms of 'untimely' will be plentiful in what follows, and I shall return to these patterns as I edge towards serious ethical questions, not just What Happens in Hamlet, which seems so contradictory. Is the Spirit seducing Hamlet, who is certainly susceptible to revenge killings? Claudius may lie in order to seduce Laertes, but Laertes the poisoner is beforehand with his revenge. For good measure let us consider Polonius-the-spy, a feeble shadow of the killer kings and princes. To his children he uses 'unproportioned' (1.3.60), 'unfledged' (1.3.65), 'unsifted' (1.3.102), not many, but choice. 'Sift' and 'fledge' stand out among the romance majority. To Reynaldo he uses 'incontinency' (2.1.31), 'unreclaimèd' (2.1.35) – not much, but nothing to do a father honour.

So let me turn to *Richard III*. I have habitually used the Riverside Shakespeare and the Harvard Concordance; for this work I used the MIT text for my first survey, because it is convenient; then I turned to John Jowett's exemplary Oxford Shakespeare.[8] I acknowledge the problems of more than one text but, at this early stage, it does not make a huge difference. So let us survey some categories of words in 'un-' as a feature of common speech, that is, not clusters by the wicked but ordinary word choices. In the following examples, then, it is not Richard – so obviously one of history's most deplorable wicked uncles, at least before Henrys VII and VIII – but a three-tier distribution of bit parts, 'also cast' and minor roles.

The bit parts offer the commonest of common usages, such as the nameless Messenger's 'unknown' (2.4.51) or Brackenbury's 'unfelt imagination' (1.4.73). Brackenbury is more present than his few lines suggest to a reader. The Scrivener, who is less present than Brackenbury but who has a fourteen-line speech of the kind we know from both the Welsh Captain and the Gardener in *Richard II* – those characters who speak

---

[8] Line numbers refer to this edition. John Jowett, ed., *The Tragedy of King Richard III* (Oxford, 2000).

to a situation and represent the good sense of ordinary men – adds his legal jargon 'untainted' and 'unexamined' (3.6.9). Stanley gives us 'unwise' (4.1.47). Shading into 'also cast', Lady Anne is a great one for the depriving particles that underpin the world of Yorkist England. We hear her but we do not hear her long. Elsewhere, the play's women, to whom we have finally learned to pay attention, join her in the tolling knells of absence where something ought to be, would normally be, present. She speaks of an 'untimely fall' (1.2.4) and a child 'untimely brought to light' (1.2.21). When their time is out of joint she gives us 'unnatural' three times (1.2.22, 58, 59), as well as 'unhappiness' (1.2.23 n), 'unworthy' (1.2.86), 'unwillingness' (4.1.53), 'unfit' (1.2.107), and 'unpleasing news' (4.1.32). The cursing women have few but, again, choice examples. Margaret has not many, but they include 'untimely' twice (1.3.198; 4.4.65), 'unlooked accident' (1.3.211) and 'unpitied end' (4.4.69). So also the Duchess of York, including 'unrest' (4.4.23), 'unquiet' (2.4.58), 'unhappy' (2.2.4), 'unmoaned' (2.2.63) (for her loss of false, fleeting, perjured Clarence). These are almost all etymologically Anglo-Saxon.

The minor men who run afoul of Richard include characters such as Buckingham, Hastings and some more or less anonymous bit-part servants. As Richard's supposed advisers watch him frame Hastings, we have Lovell's 'unsuspected Hastings' (3.5.21), and Hastings himself is 'unprepared' (3.2.63) and 'unprovided' (3.2.73) but assured of his 'untroubled' soul (5.3.136). Just as well. Buckingham's criticism includes 'ungoverned' twice (3.7.105),[9] 'unwilling' (3.1.173) and 'unlawful' (3.7.173). Rivers only has 'unjustly' (3.3.20), Ratcliff 'unarmed, and unresolved' (4.4.354); the slightly more loquacious Dorset has 'unviolable' (2.1.27), 'unthankfulness', 'ungrateful'[10] and 'unwillingness'.[11] The scale tips only slightly towards Anglo-Saxon derivation.

We are left with the other kings, Edward IV, his son (briefly), as well as Richard III himself. Of these King Edward has three: 'unfeignedly' (2.1.22), 'unjustly' (2.1.124) and 'ungracious' (2.1.126); his precocious sons have other things to say; and Richard brings us towards the end. About his brother, the king, Richard says, 'unsatiate Edward' (3.5.85, indicating sexual incontinence), 'unswayed' (4.4.387), 'unpossessed' (4.4.388). About himself – just the privatives, again – he uses 'deformed' (1.1.20), 'unfinished' (1.1.20), 'unshapen' (1.2.235), 'unwittingly' (2.1.55), 'unadvisedly',[12] 'untainted' (3.1.7), 'unmindful' (4.4.362), 'unfashionable' (1.1.22), 'unavoided' (4.4.207), 'unfit for state and dignity' (3.7.187), 'unknown reasons' (1.2.203), 'unrespective boys' (4.2.28), 'untired' (4.2.43). His privatives are frequent and scattered throughout the play, enough so that we can pity him and judge him, understand his insistence upon the failure of love around him and his self-hatred, discontent and envy. We think of him as always lying, one way or another, except in one scene – the night before the battle – and at this point we come full circle, back to ghosts, with the terrors of Richard's final, sleepless night, in which he is visited by unrelenting figures from the Other World. The chorus of 'despair and die' urges Richard to damn his own soul (5.3.128). They ring a change on the purgatorial ghost of old Hamlet.

So, to an unsatisfactory inconclusiveness. First result: which character has the highest number of 'un'+a positive value? That slimey toad, Claudius. Hamlet's ghost is up there, too, but not so many. First additional problem: the samples are too small for statistical analysis, which, in any case, cannot tell us about who is speaking, to whom, or at what point in a play nor whether a character's word choices form clusters. First additional critical point: some of the rhetorical strength of any prefix is repetition, a kind of anaphora, but not always at the beginning of sentences or phrases and, second, the obvious use of sound to infiltrate audiences' unconscious can be dealt with by a brief

---

[9] See Appendix E in Jowett's edition, l. 5, for the second instance of 'ungoverned'.
[10] See Appendix D in Jowett's edition, ll. 2–3.
[11] See Appendix D in Jowett's edition, l. 4.
[12] See Appendix M in Jowett's edition, l. 5.

observation, such as the repetitions of 'ears' in *Hamlet* or the amount of, say, 'unfolding' that does and does not happen in *Othello*. Second additional critical point: my examples note prefixes related to 'un', such an 'in' and 'im', which Shakespeare uses alongside 'un'. I cannot at this point give a viable report on the thickness and frequency of the 'un-' clusters, and I am not sure what to do about the etymologically different status of the Latinate prefixes. Third critical point: *Hamlet* in particular suggests the question whether, if a character uses ethically negating privatives, that implies at least a possibility that the character is, *ipso facto*, morally tainted.

SHAKESPEARE'S COMEDY OF UPRIGHT STATUS: STANDING BEARS AND FALLEN HUMANS

LAURIE SHANNON

On the heels of Darwin's confirmation, in *The Descent of Man*, that the principles of natural selection outlined earlier in the *Origin of Species* applied to humans as well as other animals, Sir Leslie Stephen said he was 'glad to see the poor beasts getting their revenge'.[1] Stephen noted that the philosophical tradition, itself an index and sometimes handmaiden for the species presumptions of human exceptionalism, had designated beasts 'nothing better than machines'; he clearly had Descartes in mind as a belated object of the virtual 'tooth and claw' of animal vengeance.[2] Confronting the full human implications of natural selection, Darwin outlined what he vividly called 'a community of descent', a commons extending across species; he insisted there were, in his words, 'no separate acts of creation'.[3] Here, the spectacular, preening and myopic view of a stand-alone humanity and of human self-authorship ('I think therefore I am') suffers a historic trip-and-fall. That flipped sense of a 'descent', an abrupt and downward trajectory from towering upright stature, will lure us back to Shakespeare's most irresistible stage direction, '*Exit, pursued by a bear*' (3.3.57, s.d.), and finally to what it means, in a comic theory of humanity, to lie down in *The Taming of the Shrew*.[4]

Where, or how, may we say that Darwin and Shakespeare touch, for purposes of historical analysis? Might the two thinkers be said to share a common question? Or a meaningfully parallel approach to the perennial question, the question of 'life' – a question joined anew in our time of genetic politics and the population science of biopower? As many new maps of creaturely relatedness as have intervened between them, Darwin and Shakespeare *do* share a cogently similar conception of 'creaturely life', a concept with roots in Genesis and revived by Michel Foucault, Giorgio Agamben, Eric Santner and others. The mode of thought that Shakespeare draws upon and that Darwin's inquiry still practised engages in what we might call a natural–historical method, one based on the observable bodily specifications of animals and also the sense that each kind's earthly existence is legitimate: *warranted by some good law*. Natural history

---

I am very grateful to Randall Martin for prompting us to consider the question of 'Shakespeare and Darwin' for our panel of that name at the 2016 World Shakespeare Congress; I also thank him and Scott Maisano, as my fellow-panelists in pursuit of the relation between the two thinkers, and Andreas Höfele, who so generously chaired our session.

[1] Leslie Stephen, 'Darwin and divinity', *Popular Science Monthly* (June 1872), p. 191.

[2] René Descartes, *The Discourse on Method*, trans. Donald Cress (Indianapolis, 1998), p. 19; Alfred Lord Tennyson, *In Memoriam A. H. H.* (1850), Canto 56. ('Tooth and claw' predates Tennyson's formulation. Note also Tennyson's influence by notions of the 'transmutation of species' that had been presented in Robert Chambers's anonymously published *Vestiges of the Natural History of Creation* (1844).)

[3] Charles Darwin, *The Descent of Man, and Selection in Relation to Sex* (London, 2004), p. 43.

[4] For *The Taming of the Shrew*, quotations will be from *The Taming of the Shrew*, ed. Barbara Hodgdon, The Arden Shakespeare, third series (London, 2010). Quotations from other plays are from *William Shakespeare: The Complete Works*, ed. Stanley Wells, *et al.*, 2nd edn (Oxford, 2005).

subordinates the particulars of mechanism, categoricalism and functionalism to the larger shape of narrative form; creatures are the protagonists of a history, a genealogical account in which they star as actors and agents. Prefiguring Darwin's 'community of descent', one early modern historian of animals harmonized classical natural history and Christian doctrine, referring equivocally to Nature or God as 'our common parent'.[5] This narrative encoding of a genealogical relation enables *some* ethic to hold, both across species and inside 'humankind'.

Darwin opposed the vivisection of other animals, and his 1871 publication of *The Descent of Man* was much motivated by an abolitionist stance. Shakespeare and contemporaries drew on an interpretation of the creation narrative and on classical natural history with some similar ethical effects. Reading the Hexameron, Renaissance writers grasped a *relative* animal entitlement or membership within a system of 'political' relatedness across kinds (as opposed to a radical ontological difference precluding those relations). As I have detailed elsewhere, in such a cosmopolitics, humankind appears as a fallen sort of tyrant-species, genealogically descended *and* morally descending from the proper stewardship Genesis first assigned us.[6] These fallen relations were ratified only equivocally and in retrospect by the imposition of 'fear and dread' of man among animals, when Noah's landing demoted them to devourable subjects (Genesis 1.26, 9.2–3). At the same time, schooled in the positive, classical natural–historical 'specs' of animal embodiment and capacities, writers perceived a bodily integrity in animals that not only made them perfect 'in their kinds', but also cast doubt on the psychic integrity, bodily endowment and overall constitutional sufficiency of humankind *as a kind*.

A passage from Pliny's *Historia naturalis* served as the *locus classicus* for this idea. Listing the rich provisioning Nature gave to all the other animals, Pliny makes humankind a cosmic orphan:

of all other living creatures, man she hath brought forth all naked ... To all the rest, given she hath sufficient to clad them everie one according to their kinde: as namely, shells, cods, hard hides, prickes, shagge, bristles, haire, downe feathers, quils, skailes, and fleeces of wooll ... against the injuries both of heat and cold: man alone, poore wretch, she hath laid all naked upon the bare earth [in Pliny's Latin phrasing, *nudus in nuda terra*].[7]

I have traced the intellectual legacy of this idea of our bodily exposure and cosmic vulnerability to the extreme conditions of the naked ground elsewhere, arguing that early modernity harboured a 'human *negative* exceptionalist' view alongside its more predictable human exceptionalist presumptions.

For Darwin and for Shakespeare, the human failure actually to achieve total exceptionality had a certain ethical traction, whether it elevated animals or lowered humans – in the scale of being or to the ground. Aspects of the debate, for both thinkers, were legibly inscribed in the human body itself, especially, as we will see, in the notoriously high-stakes territory of our upright stature. This article explores some occasions where the fuzzy math of two-footedness and four-footedness poses classificatory tangles, with implications for our claims of literal 'tenure' on the earth. In Shakespeare's hands, the vulnerability of human uprightness – to both precipitous falls and periodic prostration – can lead us, further, to an inquiry into comedy and kind, or even 'comedies of kind'.

A keystone in Darwin's case for natural selection in the 'descent' of man, upright posture is an adaptation that, he argues, 'sufficed to raise man to his present high position in the organic scale'.[8] The rise of man for Darwin is an opportunistic bodily ascent; the human story tells, in other

---

[5] Edward Topsell, *The Historie of Foure-Footed Beastes* (1607), Epistle Dedicatory, p. iii, my pagination.

[6] Laurie Shannon, 'The law's first subjects: Animal stakeholders, human tyranny, and the political life of early modern genesis', in *The Accommodated Animal: Cosmopolity in Shakespearean Locales* (Chicago, 2013), pp. 29–81.

[7] Pliny (the Elder), *The Historie of the World, Commonly called, The Naturall Historie of C. Plinius Secundus*, ed. and trans. Philemon Holland (1601), Proeme, Book 7, p. 152; Pliny, *Natural History*, ed. and trans. Horace Rackham *et al.*, vol. 2 (Cambridge, 1942), Book 7, p. 506.

[8] Darwin, *The Descent of Man*, p. 85.

words, a descendant's narrative about standing up. Indeed, Darwin calls the 'erect attitude' one of man's 'most *conspicuous characters*'.[9] In 'throwing a stone or spear, and in many other actions', Darwin points out, 'a man must stand firmly on his feet'.[10] While Darwin understood all features of embodiment as non-unique and at least potentially present in other creatures who might face an adaptive situation where uprightness gives an advantage, a chorus of Renaissance commentators celebrated that 'conspicuous' uprightness of the human body as, instead, an exclusive index of human exceptionality.

C. A. Patrides wryly noted that 'few commonplaces of thought have been so enthusiastically supported by authorities of the first magnitude and, in close pursuit, by a legion of lesser talents'.[11] Helkiah Crooke's 1615 *Microcosmographia*, for example, asserts that 'Man onely [*sic*] is of an upright frame and proportion'; this, so that man 'might behold and meditate on heavenly things'.[12] After all, pursuing firm-footedness similarly to Darwin on spear-throwing, Crooke asks, 'who can write, ride, live in a civill and sociable life, erect Altars unto God, builde shippes ... throwe all manner of Darts, and practise other infinite sorts of excellent Artes; *eyther groveling with his face downward, or sprawling on his backe with his face upward*?' Crooke's comic invocation of human form, tipped off its proper axis, protests a little too much. His ludicrous image of crashed humanity triggers too firm a denial when he reasserts that '*onely* man amongst all other creatures' possesses this verticality, denying several kinds of facts – most obviously that some other animals *do* walk upright (as commentators from Montaigne to Thomas Browne pointed out) and that humans, sometimes, do not.

Specifications of two- vs four-footedness posed recurring troubles for classification. Apes knocked constantly at the door, and the privilege, of two-footedness. Natural historians laboured to confine them to the quadruped column, with sometimes heady consequences for counting up hands and feet. In *The Historie of Foure-Footed Beastes*, Edward Topsell writes that 'their hands ... are like a mans ... their feet are ... not like mans ... for they are like great handes [and also] ... they use their feete both for going and handling'. Facing the ape's difference from 'other Quadrupeds', Topsell convolutedly argues that apes '*grow out of kinde*[:] ... They live more downward than upward, like other foure footed Beasts, [yet] ... they have no taile, like 2-legged creatures.'[13] By Topsell's accounting, apes prove difficult to measure as two-footed, four-footed, or maybe even four-handed. To 'live more downward than upward' – and yet to lack a tail (!) – frays the normal sciences of the upright and the prone.

Apes thus posed boundary problems well before Darwin, as Kenneth Gouwens and Scott Maisano have shown.[14] Let us turn next to consider the 'figure' of the Renaissance bear. Topsell's chapter reckons the bear's character: 'armed, filthy, deformed, cruel, dreadful, fierce, greedy ... bloody, heavy, night-ranging ... menacing ... headlong, rauening, rigid and terrible'.[15] There is

---

[9] Darwin, *The Descent of Man*, p. 71, my italics.
[10] Darwin, *The Descent of Man*, p. 69.
[11] C. A. Patrides, '"With his face towards Heaven": The upright form of man', in *Premises and Motifs in Renaissance Thought and Literature* (Princeton, 1982), pp. 83–9; p. 85. Patrides reviews the endorsements of Plato, Aristotle, Cicero and Ovid; of Christian commentators Justin, Augustine, Basil, Gregory, Ambrose, Boethius and Calvin, and of a host of Renaissance English and Continental writers.
[12] Helkiah Crooke, *Microcosmographia: A Description of the Body of Man* (1615), pp. 4–5 (all quotations are from these pages). Crooke's ideological blinkers on this point lead him, further, to defy Aristotle's formulas for bodily specifications in animals and defend bodily order itself as singularly human, claiming that 'onely man amongst all other creatures ... hath his parts distinct, the upper, the neather, the fore, the backe parts, those on the right hand, and those on the left hand; the rest of the Creatures either have them not at al, or very confused'.
[13] Topsell, *Historie of Foure-Footed Beastes*, p. 4, my italics.
[14] For excellent accounts of the cultural work of the ape in Renaissance humanism, see Kenneth Gouwens, 'Human exceptionalism', in *The Renaissance World*, ed. John Jeffries Martin (London, 2007), pp. 415–34 and Scott Maisano, 'Shakespearean primatology: A diptych', *Postmedieval: A Journal of Medieval Cultural Studies* 1.1 (2010), 115–23.
[15] Topsell, *Historie of Foure-Footed Beastes*, p. 36

much to work with here, but for present purposes I highlight 'armed' and 'headlong'. In Topsell's book, as sometimes happens, the image of a horizontally rendered animal is rotated to optimize it on the page, and this one evokes a bear standing on its 'hind legs'; viewed either way, its hand-like fore-paws (with vivid curving nails) are raised aloft, *the better to raven you with*. Alert to the special 'quantity of body' bears present, Topsell stresses their 'great' or 'huge' 'stature'. The concept of *stature*, of course, encodes bodily magnitude, uprightness and some sovereignty too — and that is as it should be with a bear. As Topsell notes, 'his feete are like handes'; these virtual hands feed into the bear's 'greatest strength', when the 'heavy' bear sets 'himselfe vpright vppon [his] hinder legges'. Contradicting their much-heralded ferocity, one anecdote tells of a beloved pet bear, who 'with her hand or foote' would scratch on a 'chamber doore to have it opened, when she was hungry'. When a bear faces 'an armed man', Topsell continues, the bear 'standeth vpright and taketh the man betwixt his forefeet'.[16] Indeed, if we recall the visual representations of Renaissance bears (scenes of hunting; of bears baited, or dancing; emblem book imagery), we might venture to call the uprightness of bears downright 'conspicuous', to borrow Darwin's term. Renaissance representations of bears reverse Topsell on apes; they tell us that bears 'live more upward than downward'.

This brings us to *The Winter's Tale*. Much consideration of its electrifying stage direction (so very remarkable on its face and, strikingly, warranted by the play's earliest edition) has concerned the puzzle whether a real Bankside bear could have been cast as the marauder who pursues Antigonus offstage. As Michael Bristol's wonderful elucidation of the play summarizes its *bear problem*, this 'has been addressed primarily as a practical and contingent question of theater history, an aspect of the play as spectacle. Was it a real bear or a man in a bear suit? ... [and, relatedly] Was it supposed to be funny, or was it intended to frighten the audience?'[17] Andreas Höfele has documented the extremely generative symbolic and cultural proximity of stake and stage. While insufficient evidence has emerged by which to confirm a real bear's onstage appearance, Höfele notes the distinction of Shakespeare's failure to give notice of the bear in advance speeches and yet to insist on the bear in the unusual stage direction.[18] Barbara Ravelhofer has scoured archival materials pursuing the Thames-side bears, finding abundant evidence of the charges for and the humans in charge of their keeping. In particular, she establishes the trainability of bears to perform elaborate routines and the 1609 arrival of two polar-bear cubs (captives from Greenland) among the other bears already kept in Henslowe's Bankside domain; the pair triggered a vogue of literary reference to white bears in the years around *The Winter's Tale*.[19] In the absence of certainty, and the certainty of radical proximity, the bear's performance lingers as a magical *perhaps*.

Either way, however, it must be said that bears figured ambivalently in early modern London; they serve as emblems of ferocity but also as dancing entertainers, and Ravelhofer suggestively mentions what she calls '*the double life of bears* ... as clowns and gladiators'.[20] And so I pose another bear problem, one likewise answerable only by decisions made for performance, past or future. Whether we imagine a real bear or a costumed man (a 'bear suit'), which bear is it who shows up onstage? The clown or the gladiator? Should the 'beare' performer be cued-up to perform its culturally 'conspicuous' uprightness? Or enter on all fours? Would upright stature make the bear look more ferocious (that is, poised to kill) or more funny by exaggeration, as if imitating a conventionally villainish, *human* performance of predatory threat – itself a theatrical bodily stance that is perhaps just our imitation of the threatening bear?

---

[16] Topsell, *Historie of Foure-Footed Beastes*, pp. 38, 41, 39.

[17] Michael Bristol, 'In search of the bear: Spatiotemporal form and the heterogeneity of economies in The Winter's Tale', *Shakespeare Quarterly* 42 (1991), 145–67; p. 159.

[18] Andreas Höfele, *Stage, Stake, and Scaffold: Humans and Animals in Shakespeare's Theatre* (Oxford, 2011), pp. 31–2.

[19] Barbara Ravelhofer, '"Beasts of recreacion": Henslowe's White Bears', *English Literary Renaissance*, 32 (2002), 287–323.

[20] Ravelhofer, '"Beasts of recreacion"', p. 317; my italics.

Finally, where might prospects of the bear's uprightness point us, in turn, concerning species-definitions in and for comedy, with its characteristic or 'conspicuous' address of what we might well pivot to call the 'problem of the human'?

To end this consideration, I swerve towards the exit by pursuing comic stakes for uprightness in the 'Induction' of *The Taming of the Shrew*. In addition to posing a real puzzle for Shakespeare's editors, the 'Induction' holds out a shimmering lure for considerations of comic theory, humanness and kind or membership.[21] It memorably involves Christopher Sly, a lowly 'rogue' with a high tavern bill, on whom a vertical identity prank will be played by a Lord. Sly's narrative is a story of literal ups and downs. It opens with a vituperative quarrel with a Hostess; a gendered controversy, about Sly's descent or station, sets up an opening for an inquiry into species. Issuing a curse that will rebound on him very shortly, he condemns the Hostess to a 'cold bed' (1.8–9). Only fourteen lines into the play, the intoxicated tinker with an uncivil tongue gives in to gravity and *hits the ground*, not running but falling down drunk. Prostrate outdoors, Sly poses a strict classificatory challenge to the Lord, who enters with men and dogs returning from the hunt and in the very midst of some real, insider analysis of virtues and praise of excellence in hunting dogs. The Lord and his followers appear as engaged participants already in the assessment of kinds. The Lord asks, 'What's here?' (not who), 'One dead, or drunk?', he asks if Sly is breathing (1.30).[22] A huntsman confirms this and sarcastically recycles Pliny's bare-earth notion to comment that the ground is 'a bed but cold to sleep so soundly' (1.32). The Lord stresses the species corrosiveness of Sly's roll in the dirt, exclaiming 'how like a swine he lies!' (1.33). With this tableau of a *de minimis* man who has violated the decorum of species and made an open bed of the bare ground, the game begins.

The Lord's 'practise' on this lowly and lowered man enacts, first, an amendment of his inappropriate bedding. The Lord commands his men to 'Carry him gently to my fairest chamber', where he will be 'conveyed to bed' (either head-first or feet-first, but not by walking) and 'wrapped in sweet clothes' (1.45, 36–7). The Lord itemizes the many 'goods' marking pre-eminence within the human: rings for Sly's fingers, a banquet ready, 'wanton pictures' on chamber walls (1.46), distilled water, juniper incense, flowers and so on. After inventorying these props, the Lord punningly reiterates: 'Take him up gently and to bed with him' (1.71). As Sly is carried up, a troop of players arrive whom the Lord recruits to the jest. In the exchange with the players, the Lord tells them of his special guest, introducing him pointedly as one who 'yet... never heard a play' and might respond to one like 'the veriest antic in the world' on seeing a comedy (1.95, 100). The ruse goes forward.

When Sly awakens and is offered a choice of clothes, he rebuts the question itself, retorting by means of an inventory of his body: 'Ne'er ask me what raiment I'll wear, for I have no more doublets than backs, no more stockings than legs, nor no more shoes than feet — nay, sometime more feet than shoes' (2.7–10). The Lord protests that Sly is 'a mighty man *of... descent*' (2.13, my emphasis) and that the furnishings and tokens of privilege belong to him. Sly vociferously denies this notion that he is 'of descent' and offers instead to 'score' himself 'up' in other terms as 'old Sly's son... by birth a pedlar, by education a cardmaker, by transmutation a bear-herd, and... by present profession a tinker' (2.17–19, 22). But Sly accepts the transformation, remarking simply that fifteen years in bed is 'a goodly

---

[21] In her edition, Barbara Hodgdon details the editorial issues surrounding the jostling texts (*The Taming of the Shrew / The Taming of a Shrew*) and the under-integrated Induction and Sly passages to conclude, very reasonably, that 'the' play might be best understood as 'representing different stages of an ongoing theatrical "commodity" that was formed at some point in the early 1590s and has been undergoing mutations ever since' (p. 36).

[22] The encounter evocatively prefigures the episode when Stephano encounters Trinculo and Caliban hiding (sheltering half-exposed beneath Caliban's cloak) on the open beach in *The Tempest*: 'What's the matter? Have we devils here?... I have not scaped drowning to be afeard now of your four legs. For it hath been said: "As proper a man as ever went on four legs cannot make him give ground"' (*The Tempest*, 2.2. 57–62).

nap' and thanking god for his 'good amends' (2.79, 95). His first response to this amendment is to hail the cross-dressed page who plays his 'wife': 'Madam, undress you and come now to bed' (2.114). When the page puts off this encounter, Sly remains flat in bed but offers the punning sexual complaint that 'it stands so that I may hardly tarry so long' (2.122). But Sly seems never to stand back up. For all the calls for walking, riding and coursing, he stays in bed; indeed, in some productions where Sly has remained onstage for the whole play, they have left him in bed for the duration.[23]

As an extension of these horizontal tendencies, the form of Sly's resistance to comedy evidences his liminal humanity. He never enacts the advertised 'antic' response the players were warned of (which at least would have its legible place in the universe of theatre). When they offer him the chance to hear 'a pleasant comedy' for his health (2.126), he glares, 'Is not a comonty a Christmas gambol or a tumbling trick?' or 'household stuff?' The better-informed page replies to gloss it 'a kind of history' (2.133–6). We might reverse this to say, too, that comedies give a 'history of kind', considering their core inquiry into the nature of belonging and membership, if we cast the question at the species level and consider the community that is being calibrated there. On the one hand, the apparent remnants of the Induction do seem textually fragmentary. But, on the other, they dramatize Sly being sidelined and left out of membership; like an unravelled thread or a line that just runs out in extinction, he fails to be incorporated. Exactly as a host of Renaissance commentators had warned, in a drama of decision-making about humanity as an act of choice and identification, Sly's relapsing shortfall in the humanity test of upright stature indexes his failure to join. In his brief reappearance at the end of the first scene of the play proper, a servant prods the drooping Sly, saying 'My Lord, you nod; you do not mind the play' (1.1.247); Sly asks, 'Comes there any more of it?' (1.1.249). The knowing Servant points out ''tis but begun' but Sly laments 'would 'twere done' (1.1.250–2). His head is falling down, again. As bears seem to live 'more upward than downward' (to repeat Topsell's metric), some people seem to live more downward than upward.

As Darwin himself considers the very process that Sly resists, the key values of comedy emerge to shape his account. At the end of the discussion of upright stature as the penultimate step to crowning human descent-as-ascent, Darwin takes up the old natural–historical idea of man's incapacity that had been relayed forward since Pliny. 'It has often been objected', he writes, 'that man is one of the most helpless and defenceless creatures in the world.'[24] All the familiar details of Pliny's arraignment return, as Darwin rehearses them: 'the naked and unprotected state of the body, the absence of great teeth or claws for defence, the small strength and speed of man ... [, and] to these deficiencies there might be added ... more'.[25] Darwin accepts these characterizations of the human animal, but he reverses the logic to stress something counter-intuitive: *there is a natural advantage to being small and weak*. Had we been descended from animals of greater size, strength and ferocity, he writes, we 'would not perhaps have become social' and so might have failed to develop 'sympathy and the love of ... fellows'. For this reason, Darwin concludes 'it might have been an immense advantage to man to have sprung from some comparatively weak creature', because it favoured the 'social qualities which lead [man] to give and receive aid from his fellow-men'. With his tendency to live more downward than upward, his misrecognition of comedy and his persistent refusal to *join* its social choreographies, Sly, in his way, *just says no* to the evolutionary adaptations of sociability and membership.

---

[23] Hodgdon, *The Taming of the Shrew*, 2.138n.
[24] Darwin, *The Descent of Man*, p. 83.
[25] Darwin, *The Descent of Man*, p. 84. All subsequent quotations from Darwin are from this page.

'WORTH THE NAME OF A CHRISTIAN'?: THE PARABOLIC ECONOMY OF *THE TWO GENTLEMEN OF VERONA*

MARGARET TUDEAU-CLAYTON

In his attack on players, *A Mirrour of Monsters* (1587), William Rankins comments: 'Folly so bleareth mens eyes, that they take playes to be profounde Scripture.'[1] Taking as insight, this indictment of blindness – which furnishes further support for Jeffrey Knapp's thesis about the religious purposes of playing[2] – this article takes as its focus the one instance in the Shakespearean canon of the word 'parable' in what may be (as the Oxford editors propose) the first performed play: *The Two Gentlemen of Verona*. An 'unjustly neglected comedy' as Kiernan Ryan has commented,[3] *Two Gentlemen* tends to be treated dismissively as 'apprentice work' by critics and editors who thus avoid the challenges posed by its perceived 'excesses' – the 'excess' of verbal play throughout and the 'excess' of forgiveness at its close.[4] My purpose is to show how, viewed from the place of the word 'parable' (2.6.35) – in what is itself an apparently redundant scene – these excesses may be taken together as functions of a parabolic economy which finds expression in the content as well as form of the play.

As I discuss in a first part, the word 'parable' is introduced by the figure of the servant clown Lance in relation to verbal play and to the signs emitted by his dog Crab, a live figure of the unpredictable and indeterminate 'excesses' of 'life' which, like verbal play and like 'the parable', elude definitive understanding and so tend to the multiplication of possibilities of meaning. Crab is, moreover, the protagonist of a serio-comic parable told by Lance towards the end of the play (4.4) in explanatory anticipation of the 'excess' of forgiveness at its close, as I show in the third section. A parable of (canine) straying and redemption, this is analogous to the biblical parables of the lost sheep and the prodigal son, which, as I discuss in the second section, are explicitly evoked by the two servant clowns, Speed and Lance, again in instances of verbal play, at their respective first entrances. The first of these is particularly telling as it signals a structural parallel with the liturgical script of *The Book of Common Prayer* (1552) in which the two biblical parables are embedded, as I discuss. The structural parallel serves to highlight the turn made by the servant clowns away from the moral 'straying' of the liturgical script to verbal straying, or 'mistaking' as it is called. Bringing together the comic and sacred in instances of

---

[1] William Rankins, *A Mirrour of Monsters: wherein is plainely described the manifold vices, & spotted enormities, that are caused by the infectious sight of playes,* ... (London, 1587), sig. Ciir. In quotations from early modern texts u/v i/j spellings are normalized throughout.

[2] Jeffrey Knapp, *Shakespeare's Tribe: Church, Nation and Theater in Renaissance England* (Chicago, 2002). Knapp quotes a similar claim in the first printed attack by John Northbrooke (?1577) that people 'shame not to say and affirm openly ... that they learn as much or more at a Play, than they do at God's word preached' (Knapp, *Shakespeare's Tribe*, p. 5).

[3] Kiernan Ryan, *Shakespeare's Comedies* (New York, 2009), p. 55.

[4] Park Honan, *Shakespeare: A Life* (Oxford, 1998), p. 55; 'Introduction' in William Shakespeare, *The Two Gentlemen of Verona*, ed. William C. Carroll (London, 2004), p. 30. References throughout will be to this, the third Arden edition.

what Peter Berger calls 'redeeming laughter'[5] these 'mistakes' summon a complex response of pleasure in a release from the 'law' and in iteration, at the level of language, of the comic parabolic plot of straying and reparation. As I discuss in the third section, Lance's parable likewise prompts such laughter, though here at the level of content rather than of form, even as it draws attention to the extraordinary character of the economy of God's gift of redemption by alluding to another specific parable – of 'the debt'. As this parable foregrounds, and the New Testament repeatedly insists, the just response to this extraordinary, inexhaustible debt-gift economy is 'charity'. It is precisely this ethical and spiritual ideal that, in the scene of the 'parable', is evoked by Lance as that which renders one 'worth the name of a Christian' (2.5.46–7). Illustrated in this scene by unlimited 'welcomes' offered the stranger, this ideal is illustrated in the final scene by a general, unlimited (and to modern minds scandalously excessive) forgiveness. Tellingly, as I shall show, the movement to this close is overtly aligned with the liturgical script of Holy Communion in *The Book of Common Prayer* (1552).

'BUT BY A PARABLE' (2.5.34–5)

It is perhaps because there is just this one instance that the word 'parable' is not included by Chris Hassel in his dictionary, *Shakespeare's Religious Language*, although it is mentioned by Naseeb Shaheen in his earlier collection of biblical references.[6] Certainly, the self-conscious specificity with which it is used in *Two Gentlemen* would justify its inclusion. The relevant scene opens with Speed's reassuring welcome of Lance on his arrival as a stranger in Milan, as I take up below. He then proceeds to endeavour to extract an answer to the question whether Lance's master Proteus and Julia are to marry. Lance evades a direct reply and, in response to Speed's frustrated 'I understand thee not' (2.5.22), digresses into verbal play at once on 'understand'/'stand under' and on staff/lance (his name) (23–9). Speed reverts to his question – 'will't be a match?' (30) – only to be referred to Lance's dog Crab: 'Ask my dog. If he say "Ay", it will; if he say "No", it will; if he shake his tail and say nothing, it will' (31–2). Speed presumes this means the answer is 'it will', but Lance refuses to say: 'Thou shalt never get such a secret from me but by a parable' (34–5). Richmond Noble and James Sims as well as Naseeb Shaheen have drawn attention to the verses in the gospel of Matthew in which Christ is said to speak only in parables (Matthew 13.34) in fulfilment of the prophecy in Psalms 78.2: 'I wil open my mouth in parables, & wil utter the things which have bene kept secret' (Matthew 13.35). However, while Noble makes no further comment, Sims sees merely a comically incongruous association of Lance with Christ.[7] Neither comments on the relation to what goes before – the evasive verbal play on 'understand' and the reference to the enigmatic signs emitted by the non-speaking animal, both modes of signification which might be described as 'mystical and dark, or far-fetched'. This is how the figure of the '*Parabola*, or Resemblance Mystical' is described in *The Art of English Poesy* (1587) by George Puttenham, who gives as his principal instance 'all the preachings of Christ in the Gospel'.[8] Eminently poetical then as well as scriptural, the 'parable' – to recall Rankins –

---

[5] Peter L. Berger, *Redeeming Laughter. The Comic Dimension of Human Experience* (New York, 1997).
[6] R. Chris Hassel, *Shakespeare's Religious Language: A Dictionary* (London, 2015) (first published 2005); Naseeb Shaheen, *Biblical References in Shakespeare's Comedies* (London, 1993), p. 32.
[7] Richmond Noble, *Shakespeare's Biblical Knowledge* (London, 1935), p. 141; James H. Sims, *Dramatic Uses of Biblical Allusions in Marlowe and Shakespeare* (Gainesville, 1966), p. 31. Remarkably, Noble asserts here that 'Biblical references are remarkably few' in *Two Gentlemen*. Many, if not all, have been collected by Shaheen, *Biblical References*, pp. 32–6 where differences between the various English Bibles are given. I refer throughout (in parentheses) to the Geneva Bible (Geneva, 1560). It is worth noting that, if 'incongruence' is recurrently evoked in theories of the comic, it is specifically central to Berger's notion of 'redeeming laughter' in which sacred and comic perspectives *meet* in a shared 'diagnosis of the world as a mass of incongruences'. (Berger, *Redeeming Laughter*, p. 43).
[8] George Puttenham, *The Art of English Poesy*, ed. F. Whigham and W. A. Rebhorn (Ithaca, 2007), p. 330.

is 'profound' in the sense that it both conceals and reveals, a 'riddling' mode of discourse that lends itself to a multiplication of possible meanings.[9] In this it is not only like 'poesy' (see note 9), but also like verbal play and the non-verbal 'signs' emitted by the non-speaking animal, a live figure of the excess to meaning of the unpredictable contingencies of 'life'.[10] Indeed, introduced into the theatre through this figure, these contingencies may prompt a straying into 'live' improvisation by the actor who plays Lance (in early performances probably Will Kemp) and who risks being upstaged by Crab.[11]

The apparently redundant exchange – Speed never gets an answer to his question – is framed by talk of the alehouse to which the two repair at the close of the scene. At the outset Speed reassures a pessimistic Lance of the welcomes he will receive in the alehouse 'where, for one shot of five pence, thou shalt have five thousand welcomes' (2.5.8–9). Though unnoticed, or at least not recorded, this is surely another biblical reference: to Christ's feeding of the five thousand by the multiplication of five loaves. Indeed, this narrative is to be found in the very next chapter of Matthew and, in the Geneva Bible, the header 'Five thousand fed' (sig. CCir) faces the header 'Parables' (sig. BBiiiiv).[12] In his influential *Paraphrases* (placed by royal injunction in all parish churches in England), Erasmus calls this an 'evangelicall feaste', a feast, that is, which epitomises the distinctive character of the Christian religion, including its implications for social justice – 'that no man should lacke and no man have to muche' – even as it shows Christ 'the feastemaker' as 'a feaster and a feder' of bodies as well as of souls.[13] In the spirit of this gloss, the narrative is turned as a parable by Speed who, specifically, turns the loaves to money (anticipating a much later sense of 'bread') which, once invested, multiplies in a yield of 'welcomes', even as he transfers the site of multiplication to the alehouse – a place at once of social and bodily nourishment. It is a turn that may glance at (in order to defend) the contested traditional practice of 'church ales', which were occasions for the generation of collective funds (for redistribution, like the five loaves) as well as community fellow feeling, occasions, in short, for 'promoting love and Christian charity', as the defenders of the practice put it.[14] This is underscored at the close of the scene when Speed's idea is taken up by Lance who suggests that their going 'to the ale' together is proof of the 'charity' that makes them 'worth the name of a Christian' (45–50). Glancing in 'worth' at the divisive issue of justification by faith or works, Lance suggests that the distinctive character of

---

[9] That the 'poetic' character of Christ's parables was widely recognized during the period as, for instance, in England by Philip Sidney, is noted by R. W. Maslen who cites Bacon's description of them as 'divine poetry'. Philip Sidney, *An Apology for Poetry*, ed. R. W. Maslen (Manchester, 2002), pp. 165–6. Brian Cummings has argued that for Erasmus Christ's parables imply a theory as well as a defence of literature (Sidney's 'poesy') see 'Erasmus on Literature and Knowledge' in *Knowing Faith: Literature, Belief and Knowledge in Early Modern England*, ed. Subha Mukherji: and Tim Stuart-Buttle (Basingstoke, 2017), forthcoming. I discuss again below Erasmus on the 'riddling' character of Christ's parables.

[10] Quintilian specifically states that this figure of comparison ('parabole') may be drawn from dumb creatures ('mutis'). He is echoed in the influential handbook by the Renaissance humanist Joannes Susenbrotus (Zürich, 1540), which Shakespeare may have known. See Quintilian, *Institutio Oratoria, The Orator's Education* ed. and trans. Donald A. Russell, repr. (Cambridge, MA, 2001), p. 443 (5.11.23); Joseph Xavier Brennan, *The Epitome Troporum ac Schematum of Joannes Susenbrotus: Text, Translation, and Commentary* (Illinois, 1953), pp. 97–8. If the parable is consistently treated in classical and Renaissance handbooks as a rhetorical/poetical figure of comparison, I also consider it as a narrative genre.

[11] Carroll, 'Introduction', p. 75. Crab's name may itself be a playful instance of such riddling discourse for if, 'like a crab', it goes backwards (cf. *Hamlet* 2.2.205), it forms bare/k, a turn like that made in *Love's Labour's Lost* where a reversal of the AB of the hornbook summons the noise of 'a silly sheep' (5.1.45–8). Carroll suggests 'the dog's manner of walking may resemble a crab's' (note to 2.3.0.1).

[12] In the other three gospels the headers in the Geneva Bible are: 'Of the five loaves' (Mark 6) (sig. EEiiiir); 'the five loaves' (Luke 9) (sig. HHiiiiv); 'the five loaves' (John 5) (sig. MMir).

[13] *The first tome or volume of the Paraphrase of Erasmus upon the Newe Testamente*, trans. N. Udall (London, 1548), fol. lxxxiv.

[14] François Laroque, *Shakespeare's Festive World*, trans. Janet Lloyd (Cambridge, 1993), p. 160.

a Christian – specifically contrasted with 'a Jew', metonym for the Old Testament 'law' – lies in 'charity', an ethical as well as spiritual ideal which eliminates the faith/works opposition even as it fulfils 'the law' insofar as it is conceived (as it is by Paul, Augustine, Erasmus and Tyndale amongst others) and practised as the 'just' human response to the inexhaustible debt-gift economy of God's universal redemption in Christ. Here this response finds expression in generous and generative hospitality towards Lance, a stranger in Milan who fears he is 'not welcome' (2–3). That hospitality is due especially to strangers is urged in the Old as well as the New Testament and reiterated by Shakespeare, most explicitly in his contribution to the book of *Sir Thomas More*.[15] To the stranger's anxious concern that he is 'not welcome' Speed responds with a reassuring reminder of the many 'welcomes' he will receive, recalling as he does so the narrative of Christ's multiplication of five loaves, which he turns as a parable of an occasion for the expression of (unlimited) charity. Itself parabolic in mode then, this scene invites understanding of the affinity of the play to the scriptural – and, like comedy, domestic – genre it explicitly invokes in association with other elusive modes of signification, which likewise tend to the multiplication of possible meanings. This is underscored by the self-reflexive instance of the biblical narrative of the multiplication of loaves turned parable of the multiplication of 'welcomes' that illustrate the 'charity' that makes one 'worth the name of a Christian'.

'A SHEEP DOTH VERY OFTEN STRAY' (1.1.74) AND 'THE PRODIGIOUS SON' (2.3.3): BIBLICAL PARABLES OF STRAYING AND REDEMPTION IN TWO GENTLEMEN

The affinity of the comedy and its recurring verbal play with the figure/genre of the parable is highlighted by the two biblical parables evoked, again in instances of verbal play, by the two servant clowns at their respective first entrances in 1.1. and 2.3: the parables of the lost sheep and the prodigal son. Analogous parables of the recovery of what has been lost – the comic plot of redemption – and the attendant affective yield, which the parables call joy, the two parables are told, together with the parable of the lost coin, in Luke 15. In a striking structural parallel with the liturgical script of morning/evening prayer in which the two parables are embedded, as I take up below, Valentine's servant Speed, on his first entrance, responds to information from Lance's master Proteus that Valentine has 'shipped' for Milan by playing on 'ship' and 'a sheep' that 'doth very often stray' (1.1.74). This triggers a digression of some fifty lines of verbal play, which suspends linearity (both of plot and of language) as well as the social hierarchy of master/servant in an instance of the release from the 'Symbolic law' that is procured by joking according to psychoanalytic theories (Freud, Purdie).[16] As it happens, this is the very passage cited by Park Honan to illustrate the 'verbal excesses' with which Shakespeare was 'enamoured' in 'his apprentice work', a dismissive treatment which thus avoids the challenge of such 'excesses' to those for whom such digressive play yields little or no pleasure (let alone joy).[17] Such play does indeed abound in *Two Gentlemen*, especially in the exchanges between Speed and Lance who himself later quibbles on 'ship' in another instance

---

[15] See Margaret Tudeau-Clayton, '"This is the stranger's case": The utopic dissonance of Shakespeare's contribution to *Sir Thomas More*', in *Shakespeare Survey 65* (Cambridge, 2012), pp. 239–54.

[16] The nuance made to Freud's argument by Purdie that joking is a 'marked' transgression of the Symbolic law' which constitutes the joker as a 'master' of discourse', underscores the levelling social dimension to such digressive verbal exchanges between master and servant. Susan Purdie, *Comedy. The Mastery of Discourse* (New York, 1993), p. 5 (emphasis in original). Kiernan Ryan makes a fine case for the pervasive verbal play in *Two Gentlemen* as 'an obstructive strategy', a form of resistance to the 'power of a dominant discourse' (Ryan, *Shakespeare's Comedies*, pp. 48–9).

[17] Honan, *Shakespeare: A Life*, p. 55. Honan is not alone, of course, only particularly explicit in expressing what is a characteristically 'modern' distaste for verbal play and display, as I discuss further in *Shakespeare's Englishes: Against Englishness* (forthcoming).

of what Speed calls his characteristic 'vice': 'mistake the word' (3.1.278).[18] In such deliberate 'mistaking', which depends for its effect on near simultaneous recognition and correction of the mistake, the comic parabolic plot of straying and reparation – lost and found – is reiterated at the level of language.[19] In another telling instance, on his first entrance, Lance likens himself, on the point of his departure for Milan, to 'the prodigious son' (2.3.3). Like the earlier play on ship/sheep, this 'mistaking' reference to the parable of the prodigal son prompts what Peter Berger calls redeeming laughter in which sacred and comic perspectives meet to generate a complex yield of pleasure – at once in a release from the 'law' (of 'proper' cultural and linguistic forms) and in a reiteration, at the level of language, of the comic parabolic plot of straying/loss and reparation.[20]

If Lance's verbal 'mistake' has consistently been dismissed as mere 'malapropism', as I have indicated (note 18), the parable he references has been recognized as of 'relevance to *Two Gentlemen* as a whole'.[21] This relevance is, however, taken to be only at the level of the plot, as it is at this level that the parable – the most frequently cited in the Shakespearean canon – has been taken to be relevant to the other plays in which it is evoked.[22] It is, indeed, at this level that the parable tends to be reproduced in the (very many) appropriations of it in early modern culture, as, in their respective work on drama and narrative fictions, Alan R. Young and Richard Helgerson have shown.[23] Where an abstract level of meaning is evoked, moreover, it is not so much in a 'Resemblance Mystical', as in a moral lesson of transgression, repentance and mercy, as when Philip Sidney gives 'the lost child's disdainful prodigality, turned to envy a swine's dinner' as the memorable image which carries this 'instructing' parable's moral lesson of 'disobedience and mercy'.[24]

It is in a script of transgression and repentance, which contains their possibilities of meaning, that both parables – of the lost sheep as well as of the prodigal son – are embedded, from 1552, in the order of morning/evening prayer in *The Book of Common Prayer*, a 'performative book', as Brian Cummings pertinently comments, 'like a playtext'.[25] This liturgical script opens with penitential sentences to be read by the minister, which include the expressed penitence of the prodigal son (Luke 15.18), followed by a general confession in which members of the

---

[18] Speed's comment indicates that Lance's 'mistaking' is conscious play rather than the unconscious slips of an uneducated, socially aspirational and inept figure, which is what is signalled by the (anachronistic) use of the label 'malapropism' (by, for example, Carroll in his note to 'prodigious' [2.3.3]). The problem of distinguishing conscious verbal play from unconscious mistaking has been discussed by linguistic historians, notably Norman Blake, who points out the (often) class inflected bias of editors who make the category distinction (Norman Blake, 'Shakespeare's language: Past achievements and future directions' in *Proceedings of the XIXth International Conference of AEDEAN*, ed. Javier Pérez-Guerra, M.Teresa Caneda Cabrera, Marta Dahlgren, Teresa Fernandez-Colmeiro and Edouardo J. Varela (Vigo, 1996), pp. 21–35; p. 27).

[19] Interestingly, 'repair' is the term used in interactional linguistics for the correction of recognized errors in speech; see Celia Kitzinger, 'Repair' in *The Handbook of Conversation Analysis*, ed. Jack Sidnell and Tanya Stivers (Chichester, 2013), pp. 229–56. My thanks to Oliver Morgan for this reference.

[20] Berger, *Redeeming Laughter* (see above notes 5 and 7). In a pertinent comment David Martin suggests that for Berger it is 'in the incongruities of the comic' which reveal how 'we are double natured, lost and found' that the 'epiphany' of a transcendent 'other' or 'counter' world lies (David Martin, 'Berger: An appreciation', in *Peter Berger and the Study of Religion*, ed. Linda Woodhead (London, 2001), pp. 11–16; p. 15). In a brilliant deconstructive analysis of *The Comedy of Errors*, Barbara Freedman suggestively writes of 'meaning . . . lost and found . . . like the prodigal son', though she is referring to the protagonist's subjective experience, not verbal play (Barbara Freedman *Staging the Gaze. Post Modernism, Psychoanalysis, and Shakespearean Comedy* (Ithaca, 1991), p. 85).

[21] Carroll, 'Introduction', p. 35.

[22] Noble, *Shakespeare's Biblical Knowledge*, p. 277.

[23] Alan R. Young, *The English Prodigal Son Plays: A Theatrical Fashion of the Sixteenth and Seventeenth Centuries* (Salzburg, 1979); Richard Helgerson, *The Elizabethan Prodigals* (Berkeley, 1976).

[24] Sidney, *An Apology*, p. 91.

[25] Brian Cummings, 'Introduction', in *The Book of Common Prayer*, ed. Brian Cummings (Oxford, 2011), p. xxxiv. I refer throughout in parentheses to this invaluable edition (henceforth *BCP*).

congregation are summoned into the (abject) subject position of the penitent son to confess, in the language of the analogous parable, 'we have erred and straied from thy waies, lyke lost sheep' (*BCP*, p. 103). Speed's echo of these words at the outset of the play establishes a structural parallel between the two playtexts, which renders highly telling the swerve of the second from moral to verbal straying, or mistaking. For, instead of the abject subject position of the penitent into which participants are summoned by the liturgical script, spectators are offered the liberating pleasure of 'redeeming laughter' in the 'excesses' of verbal play.

The liturgical script is not, however, jettisoned altogether. On the contrary, it is pointedly evoked in the main plot in which Lance's master, the straying, inconstant Proteus, leaves his father's home to betray his mistress and his friend before finally attempting rape on his friend's mistress. This is a prodigal, indeed prodigious, straying that Proteus himself recognizes early on as a 'false transgression' (2.4.194) before making his confession in Act 5 in language which echoes the liturgical general confession, though not of morning/evening prayer but, significantly given what follows, of 'the Lordes Supper, or holy Communion' (*BCP*, p. 124).

> My shame and guilt confounds me.
> Forgive me, Valentine; if *hearty sorrow*
> Be a *sufficient ransom* for offence,
> I tender' it here.   (5.4.73–6, emphasis mine)

In what is again a structurally parallel moment Proteus here takes the position of participants in the general confession who together say, 'we do earnestly repente, and bee *hartely sorye* for these our misdoinges' and who thus prepare to receive communion in remembrance of Christ's '*sufficient* sacrifice' made 'for our redemption' (*BCP*, pp. 134, 137 emphases mine).[26] The 'if' here, together with 'sufficient', bears out Sarah Beckwith's point that the 'question of sufficiency haunts penitential discourse' after the abolition of the sacrament of penance,[27] while the reminder of the 'sufficient sacrifice' of Christ signals that penitential sorrow alone is not sufficient, that what is needed too is the (unlimited) grace of forgiveness procured by this sacrifice. Indeed, the double sense of 'sufficient' here anticipates, if ambiguously, the 'grammar of forgiveness' that Beckwith discerns in her very fine analysis of the (in some ways similar) closing scene of *The Winter's Tale* where the expression of repentance and the receiving of the grace of forgiveness are entwined in a single movement.[28]

Proteus's expression of penitential sorrow prompts an immediate response of unconditional forgiveness from Valentine – 'satisfied', as he says, 'by repentance' as all should be who are of 'heaven' or 'earth' (79–80). His lines may echo, as Noble suggests, the first of the penitential sentences of morning prayer (Ezekiel 18.21–2).[29] More importantly, however, they begin the movement of the play towards the 'Resemblance Mystical' of the biblical parables and the second 'excess' which disturbs modern critics and playgoers, including the third Arden editor William Carroll, who comments how 'the more extraordinary and generous' 'Valentine's forgiveness seems' the more '*consequently* objectionable' it is.[30] It was indeed for its 'Resemblance Mystical' to God's extraordinary free, unlimited and universal gift of forgiveness in Christ, which 'exceeds the requirements of those who stand in need of it', as Calvin puts it in his commentary, that the parable of the prodigal son was dear to protestant exegetes for whom it illustrated 'the whole work of our redemption'.[31] The Anglican minister

---

[26] The structural parallel is highlighted by the fact that, as Cummings helpfully points out, the confession was moved in the 1552 version to a place just prior to consecration 'as part of the preparation for worthy receiving of the Communion, rather than as part of the rite' (*BCP*, p. 731).

[27] Sarah Beckwith, *Shakespeare and the Grammar of Forgiveness* (Ithaca, 2011), p. 132. My thanks to Pippa Berry for pointing out the pertinence of Beckwith's work to my discussion of this passage.

[28] Beckwith, *Shakespeare and the Grammar of Forgiveness*, pp. 140–2.

[29] Noble, *Shakespeare's Biblical Knowledge*, p. 142.

[30] Carroll, 'Introduction', p. 30, emphasis mine.

[31] Calvin's comment on the parable is paraphrased and Samuel Gardiner's overview (1599) is quoted in Young, *The English*

Samuel Purchas goes so far as to invite comparison between the prodigal son and Christ who left 'his Fathers house' to undertake a journey 'to recover that which was lost', an unusual, perhaps (to recall Puttenham) 'far-fetched' interpretation which exemplifies how the parable as figure/genre lends itself to multiple possible meanings as well as how this instance is taken to illustrate the 'superadmirable bounty' of God's inexhaustible gift of redemption in Christ.[32] More usually, the comparison is drawn (as, for instance, by Calvin) between God and the figure of the father whose unconditional welcome (Luke 15.20) pre-empts the son's rehearsed speech of penitence (Luke 15.18–19) which, when spoken (21), is ignored by the father – ironically, we might add, given its place in the liturgical script. In the analogous parables of the lost sheep and the lost coin too the focus is on the recovery of that which was lost and the attendant affective yield of joy.

This focus is still more evident in the version of the parable of the lost sheep in Matthew (18.12–13) which makes no mention at all of repentance and which is immediately preceded by Christ's declaration that 'the Sonne of man is come to save that which was lost' (18.11). Tellingly, the next parable here is not of the prodigal son but of 'The dette' as it is called in the header in the Geneva Bible (sig. CCiiir), which faces the header 'The lost shepe' (sig. CCiiv). This parable is told by Christ in implicit explanation of his response to Peter's question, which comes between the two parables, as to the number of times he should forgive his brother – 'seventie times seven' (Matthew 18.22) – a response which is glossed in the Geneva Bible where it features again (Luke 17.4): 'manie times: for by a certaine number he meaneth an uncerteine' (or indeterminate) number (sig KKivr) The parable tells of a master who cancels the large debt of a servant who in turn refuses to cancel the much smaller debt of a fellow servant and is consequently punished by the master. It thus illustrates the logic of the unlimited debt-gift economy of God's redemption in Christ, which calls for unlimited forgiveness as the 'just' response: 'forgive from your hearts, eche one to his brother their trespaces' (Matthew 18.35). This logic is reiterated throughout the New Testament, notably of course in the words of 'the Lordes prayer' 'forgeve us our trespasses as we forgeve them that trespasse against us' (*BCP*, p. 104), translated more accurately, it is worth noting, in the Geneva Bible and the King James Bible (which cross references the parable): 'forgive us our dettes, as we also forgive our detters' (Matthew 6.12).[33]

It is the challenge (or scandal) of this economy that is staged at the close of the main plot of *Two Gentlemen*. Not only is the repentant prodigal Proteus forgiven (if more explicitly by his friend Valentine than by the two women he has wronged) but the figure of the law, the Duke of Milan, 'forget[s] all former griefs' and '[c]ancel[s] all grudge' against Valentine (5.4.140–1) and, at the request of Valentine, 'forgive[s]' the outlaws 'what they have committed here' now that they are 'reformed' (152–4). To underscore the point the thrice reiterated 'one' of the closing line – 'One feast, one house, one mutual happiness' (171) – expresses the achieved reconciliation in liturgically resonant language, which recalls the at-one-ment offered by the 'thre ... in one' God 'for our redemption', remembered at Holy Communion (*BCP*, pp. 136, 137). This highlights how, in rehearsing the comic plot of straying and reparation the theatre too (or alternatively) might represent a 'place of reconciliation', like the rite of Holy Communion, before as well as after the Reformation – a function, it is worth noting, which became all the more important, as Beckwith observes, once expression of penitence was incorporated into the liturgical script of

---

Prodigal Son Plays, pp. 19, 22. For the exegetical tradition to which these comments belong and which treats the parable as '*Evangelium in Evangelio*' (i.e. as an epitome of the New Testament), see Lytta Bassett, *La Joie Imprenable* (Geneva, 1996), pp. 64–72; p. 66.

[32] Samuel Purchas, *Purchas his pilgrimes In five bookes* (London, 1625), pp. 49–50.

[33] I have not seen a satisfactory explanation of this turn from 'debt' to 'trespass' but it must be connected to the development of early modern capitalism and the protestant ideology of money.

The Book of Common Prayer.[34] Overtly echoed in the main plot, this script is evoked only to be turned by the servant clowns whose verbal 'mistaking' nevertheless speaks to the inexhaustible debt-gift economy of redemption inasmuch as it reiterates the comic plot of straying and reparation at the level of language even as it offers a release from the law of 'proper' forms – including the 'proper' form of the liturgical script – and summons unlimited possibilities of meaning. In this the servant clowns are joined by the mute figure of the indeterminate contingencies of 'life', which likewise summon unlimited possibilities of meaning. Together, they prompt 'redeeming laughter' in which, as Berger comments, there is 'a profound discovery of freedom'.[35]

'HOW MANY MASTERS WOULD DO THIS FOR HIS SERVANT?' (4.4.28–9): LANCE'S PARABLE OF STRAYING AND REDEMPTION

Just prior to the final act – and in explanatory anticipation of the close – Lance tells the audience a second tale, or rather a number of related tales, precisely about this mute figure, his dog Crab (4.4.1–38). As his first tale turned around the figure of the son who leaves his family, like the parable of the prodigal son (2.3.1–30), these tales turn around the figures of master and servant, like the parable of the debt. Crab is again rebuked for his indifference, though here not towards human emotions (as in the first tale), but towards human social hierarchies and norms of behaviour as well as towards what the master has done for his 'servant', as Lance calls Crab (1). Kiernan Ryan has pointed out the delightfully subversive character of the tale of an 'errant pet' that steals 'a capon's leg' from Silvia's table before taking a piss as he earlier pissed on her petticoat.[36] This is not, however, the whole story. For Lance begins by recalling how he 'saved' Crab 'from drowning' (3), before proceeding to tell of the recent occasion when he took 'a fault upon [him] that [Crab] did' (13–14) – the fault of pissing under Silvia's table for which a death sentence was pronounced by the figure of the law, the Duke of Milan: 'Hang him up', says the Duke' (21–2). Taking Crab's place by declaring ''twas I did the thing you wot of' (26), Lance suffers the punishment (of whipping) due to Crab as, he claims, he has suffered before, saving Crab from being 'executed' (31) as he saved him from drowning. After these tales of recurrent substitutive redemption(s) – in which the master saves the servant by taking his place – Lance turns to the audience (and/or to Crab) to pose the (rhetorical) question: 'How many masters would do this for his servant?' (28–9). Like the domestic figures of master and servant, the (rhetorical) question is a recurrent feature of the parable, as in the parables of the lost sheep and the lost coin, which begin respectively: 'What man of you having an hundredth shepe . . . ?' 'what woman . . . ?' (Luke 15.4, 8). Both thus invite hearers to identify with the figure that recovers what has been lost and to imagine their joy. Lance's question has a different effect, summoning as it does recognition of the gap between ordinary masters in the real world of the theatre audience and the (extraordinary) master of the New Testament who becomes a servant in order to deliver those under the death penalty of the law for their 'faults' in a substitutive redemption like that performed by Lance for Crab. Crab's indifference/ingratitude is thus associated with the 'unjust' response – of masters as well as servants – to the prodigal/prodigious act of this extraordinary master/servant. As the play signals, the just response is rather the 'charity' which renders 'worth the name of a Christian' and which finds expression in the generous and generative 'welcomes', especially of strangers, evoked in the earlier scene, and in the general, unlimited forgiveness staged at the close.

In telling his parable Lance does not once 'mistake the word'. It is the tale itself that prompts redeeming laughter rather than the reiteration in verbal play of the plot of straying and redemption,

---

[34] Beckwith, *Shakespeare and the Grammar of Forgiveness*, p. 134. See, too, Arnold Hunt, 'The Lord's supper in early modern England', *Past and Present* 161 (November 1998), 39–83.
[35] Berger, *Redeeming Laughter*, p. 43.
[36] Ryan, *Shakespeare's Comedies*, pp. 45–6.

lost and found. His parable is, however, as elusive as verbal play – the meaning sketched here has eluded critics – and as 'deliciously subversive'.[37] Indeed, it likewise offers pleasurable release from the 'law' (of social forms and hierarchies), even as it evokes the prodigal, inexhaustible debt-gift economy of redemption to which the domestic genres of comedy and parable and the analogous instances – of straying sheep, son and dog – testify.

CONCLUSION

In *The Stage Acquitted* (1699), as Jeffrey Knapp points out, the 'theatre's earlier spiritual pretensions' – pretensions evoked even as they are dismissed by William Rankins in the quotation with which I began – are reaffirmed in the assertion that 'a bare Precept is less touching than *Example*', which suggests, as he comments, that 'players' exerted a more 'lively' influence over an audience than preachers.[38] For Elizabethan spectators whose responses may have been dulled by repeated obligatory participation in the liturgical scripts of the church-state apparatus, *Two Gentlemen* offers a 'lively', and perhaps quickening, parable about what makes one 'worth the name of a Christian', a 'recreation' in both senses of the word which, as Erasmus claims in his *Paraphrases*, Christ sought to work on 'the people' by speaking in 'riddelles and cloudes of parables' 'to thyntent that he might both excite and stirre their minds with darke speakyng and make them desirouse to learne'.[39] Challenged to enquire whether they measure up to the proposed criterion of 'charity', exemplified by unlimited 'welcomes' and unlimited forgiveness, as the just response to the extraordinary, unlimited debt-gift economy of God's universal redemption in Christ, they are at the same time invited to rediscover the liberating release from 'the law' and the joy attendant on the plot of redemption through the laughter prompted especially by verbal 'mistaking' and by the mute figure of the indeterminate excesses to meaning of 'life'. Indeed, this invitation to liberating 'redeeming laughter' bears out the reluctant admission of William Rankins that playgoers looked to plays 'to unloade [their] heavy harts' rather than to Scripture and the figure of Christ, 'bounde to sette us free'.[40]

---

[37] Ryan, *Shakespeare's Comedies*, pp. 45–6.

[38] Knapp, *Shakespeare's Tribe*, p. 21.

[39] *The first tome or volume of the Paraphrase of Erasmus*, fol. lxxviiir. It is worth noting that in his long comment on Matthew 13 Erasmus not only reiterates the point that the purpose of the parables was to 'provoke ... the desyre of learnyng and searchyng' (fol. lxxvir), but also that Christ thus avoided causing offence (fol. lxxvir) and allowing others a 'holde' over him (fol. lxxviiir) – a poignant testimony to the pragmatic prudence as well as the desire for freedom motivating evasive or riddling discourse, which is as pertinent to the author of the *Praise of Folly* at the beginning of the sixteenth century as it is to the author of *Two Gentlemen* at its end.

[40] Rankins, *A Mirrour of Monsters*, sig. Giiiir–Giiiiv. In playing on two senses of 'bound' here Rankins may recognize at some level the freedom latent in such play. Indeed, for whatever (perhaps more mundane) reasons he later turns playwright himself. See S. P. Cerasano, 'Rankins, William', *Oxford Dictionary of National Biography*, Oxford, 2004; online edn, Oct 2006 [www.oxforddnb.com/view/article/23134, accessed 29 Dec 2016].

'TITUS, UNKIND': SHAKESPEARE'S REVISION OF VIRGIL'S AENEAS IN *TITUS ANDRONICUS*

MEGAN ELIZABETH ALLEN

In the opening scene of Shakespeare's *Titus Andronicus* (1588–93), Titus's eldest remaining son, Lucius, demands 'Give us the proudest prisoner of the Goths, / That we may hew his limbs' (1.1.96–7), in recompense for the loss of his brothers. The bodily violence and dismemberment done to Alarbus overtly represent the disintegration of Gothic power and society following their military defeat, at least in the society represented by the Gothic ruling family. In the face of Tamora's pleas, Lucius callously puns on the metaphor of the family tree, suggesting that the sacrifice of Tamora's eldest son is necessary to the proper maintenance of her family or, more precisely of her family as a metonym for her society. The promise of this scene, swiftly broken, is that Alarbus's sacrifice will repair relations between Roman and Goth, that this impiety will somehow restore a pious Rome.

Shakespeare, in his portrayal of kinship in *Titus Andronicus*, focuses on the collision of the political and the domestic, and how kinship is affected by the ideologies underlying *romanitas*. The concept of *romanitas*, so exhaustively analyzed by critics, clarifies how early modern conceptions of Roman ideals acted as models to be imitated and how that imitation affected early modern kinship structures.[1] While the term *romanitas* itself was not current in early modern England, I follow recent critics in using the term to describe the range of practices and beliefs ascribed to fictional portrayals of Romans by early modern English people, which ascription Warren Chernaik calls the Elizabethan 'myth of Rome'.[2] In an earlier but still current definition, Robert S. Miola describes the early modern concept of *romanitas* as a 'military code of honor that encompasses the virtues of pride,

---

[1] Though the genre of the 'Roman play' was first identified by Mungo MacCallum in *Shakespeare's Roman Plays and Their Background* (New York, 1910), MacCallum excluded *Titus* from his definition of 'Roman-ness', as did James Emerson Philips, *State in Shakespeare's Greek and Roman Plays* (New York, 1940); Maurice Charney, *Shakespeare's Roman Plays* (Cambridge, 1961); D. A. Traversi, *Shakespeare: The Roman Plays* (Stanford, 1963); J. L. Simmons, *Shakespeare's Pagan World* (Charlottesville, 1973); P. A. Cantor, *Shakespeare's Rome* (Ithaca, 1976); and Michael Platt, *Rome and Romans According to Shakespeare* (Lanham, MD, 1983). Robert S. Miola is the first to include *Titus*, seeing the Roman plays, including *Lucrece* and *Cymbeline*, as connected by the ideals of 'constancy, honor, and pietas' in *Shakespeare's Rome* (Cambridge, 1983), p. 17. More recent critics accept *Titus* as a Roman play, such as Anne Sophie Refskou, 'Compassionate perception and touching experiences in Shakespearean drama', *Critical Survey* 29 (2015), 60–84; Leonard Tennenhouse, 'Playing and power', in *Staging the Renaissance*, ed. David Scott Kastan and Peter Stallybrass (New York, 1992, 2013); W. W. Weber, 'Shakespeare after all?: The authorship of *Titus Andronicus* 4.1 reconsidered', *Shakespeare Survey* 67 (Cambridge, 2014), 69–84; S. Emmerichs, '"Thou map of woe": Mapping the feminine in *Titus Andronicus* and *King Lear*', *English Studies* 97 (2016), 546–67; even Paulina Kewes, '"I ask your voice and your suffrages": The bogus Rome of Peele and Shakespeare's *Titus Andronicus*', *The Review of Politics* 78 (2016), 551–70 is questioning the accuracy of the portrayal of Rome, not whether this is a Roman play.

[2] Warren Chernaik, *The Myth of Rome in Shakespeare and His Contemporaries* (Cambridge, 2011).

courage, constancy, integrity, discipline, service, and self-sacrifice'. Writing about *Titus*, Miola argues that Titus attempts to 'identify personal and civil welfare'; that identification causes the violent collision of competing values as elements of the political and the domestic fail to behave in ways explicable to Titus.[3] Titus's status as the most Roman of the Romans is established very quickly in the play and the context of the establishing lines emphasizes Titus's attempt to be a proper model for imitation, that is, to embody an imitable space. As G. K. Hunter critically noted, *romanitas* was a set of ideals transmitted to the Tudors 'in a series of images of virtue held up as models or secular *mirabilia*'.[4] Starting from the realization that Titus's Roman-ness appeals to a larger cultural tendency to see Roman-ness as ideal and imitable, I argue that Shakespeare creates the model Roman in Titus in order to demonstrate the dangers of systems of imitation while also critiquing Roman ideologies and their reception in early modern England. One of the key virtues comprising *romanitas* was *pietas*, conveyed to England primarily through the figure of Aeneas. Titus's identification with Aeneas establishes his suitability for imitation; however, further investigation of Titus's model reveals the violent complications in Titus's piety.

Titus's role as a model of Roman ideals is founded on his identification with Aeneas, who is often given the adjectival epithet 'Pius' throughout Virgil's *Aeneid*. That identification is actually established shortly before Titus's entrance, when his brother Marcus interrupts the succession argument between the emperor's two sons with the news that 'Andronicus, surnamèd Pius' (1.1.23) has been chosen as the next emperor. Titus evidently earned his new name in battle, having returned as 'Renownèd Titus, flourishing in arms' (1.1.38), but the reference to his surname opens up a range of allusions which emphasize Titus's role as a model of Roman virtue. The Captain introducing Titus identifies him as

> The good Andronicus,
> Patron of virtue, Rome's best champion,
> Successful in the battles that he fights,
> With honour and with fortune is returned
> From where he circumscribed with his sword
> And brought to yoke the enemies of Rome.
> (1.1.64–9)

This introduction establishes Titus as the ideal Roman, the embodiment of martial honour, moral virtue and well-deserved fame. Paired with this description, the pointed reference to his surname 'Pius' identifies him as a character devoted to higher ideals. 'Pius' was 'the honorary epithet bestowed by Virgil on Aeneas, and by Aeneas on his deserving successors. Titus himself, by virtue of his ten-year defense of Rome against the Goths . . . proclaims his descent from that heroic ancestry'.[5] That is, Shakespeare accesses commonplace understandings of Aeneas as a model of virtue derived from early modern humanist educational practices, which emphasized the imitation of these noble Romans. As Charles Martindale notes, 'To the humanists the *Aeneid* was a guide to right living, and *pius* Aeneas a prime exemplary hero . . . in Jonson's words, "the reading of Homer and Virgil is counseled by Quintilian as the best way of informing youth, and confirming man" (*Discoveries* 2240)'.[6] The exemplarity of Aeneas, especially in

---

[3] Miola, *Shakespeare's Rome*, p. 45. Sharon Emmerichs attributes his failure of understanding to his attempt to unite the personal with the civil specifically 'through Lavinia's proposed marriage to Saturninus', noting that Shakespeare generally portrays 'the dangers of treating women as territory, as landscapes to be conquered, and as blank spaces waiting for a masculine hand to map her boundaries', in '"Thou map of woe": Mapping the feminine in *Titus Andronicus* and *King Lear*', *English Studies* 97 (2016), 546–67; pp. 555, 547. While this argument is compelling, I am not as convinced that his mistake is a strictly gendered one, as he similarly unites both realms in his treatment of his son Mutius, discussed below.

[4] G. K. Hunter, 'A Roman thought: Renaissance attitudes to history exemplified in Shakespeare and Jonson', in *An English Miscellany Presented to W. S. Mackie*, ed. Brian S. Lee (Oxford, 1977), p. 94.

[5] Jacques Berthoud, Introduction, *Titus Andronicus* (London, 2005), p. xli.

[6] Charles Martindale, 'Shakespeare and Virgil,' in *Shakespeare and the Classics*, ed. Charles Martindale and Albert Booth Taylor (Cambridge, 2004), p. 95.

terms of his association with *pietas*, elucidates Shakespeare's choice to create his own model of the ideal Roman, Titus, in Aeneas's image.

Shakespeare's ideal Roman is designed as a critique of Roman and Elizabethan English values, constructed to highlight the violent exaggerations within the norms of *pietas* and *virtus* as received and understood by early moderns.[7] The relationship between Titus's familial violence and his identification with Aeneas has been misunderstood by critics, who note that Titus does not seem to behave with piety. Berthoud calls the sacrifice of Alarbus 'the limiting point of the lineage-family because to that family it is the fulfilment of its identity (the link between the dead and the living is preserved) while representing its contradiction (one family's piety is another's atrocity)'.[8] Many critics emphasize that Titus, the embodiment of Roman virtue, kills not one but two of his children: 'Mutius, in the name of absolute paternal authority ... and Lavinia, in the name of female chastity.'[9] Titus's indifference to 'natural' blood ties is further emphasized when, ignoring Tamora's impassioned pleas, Titus orders the sacrifice of her eldest son and heir. Tamora, captured queen of the Goths, presumably a barbarian and Other to Rome's civilized virtues of *pietas* and *virtus*, responds to Titus's lack of mercy by clearly identifying his major fault: 'O cruel irreligious piety!' (1.1.130). The phrase has been read in terms of its foreshadowing of the downfall of Rome, with many critics identifying this moment as leading to, even causing, Rome to become a 'wilderness of tigers' (3.1.53).[10] While earlier critical readings identified this moment as the crucial abandonment of civilized Roman values that cause the downfall of the civilization, more recent critics complicate Shakespeare's relationship with Roman cultural capital by noting that this moment is a critique of both systems, reading both Roman *romanitas* and English appropriations as corrupt claimants to a perverse normativity.[11] However, critics supporting both arguments tend to claim that Titus's understanding of *pietas* is flawed in some way, and that his claim to embody *pietas* is contradicted by his killing Mutius, demanding the blood sacrifice or ignoring a mother's plea.

In a departure from this critical consensus, I examine Shakespeare's use of Virgil's *Aeneid* to construct Titus's understanding of *pietas*, which reveals that Mutius's murder in the name of *pietas*

---

[7] In a recent article, Paulina Kewes argues that the lack of historical accuracy, identifiable source, or stable political structure are not the result of 'ignorance or ineptitude', but 'a deliberate ploy to heighten relevance and encourage transhistorical and transcultural comparisons while deflecting all too likely criticism if this were a "real" story', in '"I ask your voices and your suffrages"', 553–4. J. K. Barret, on the other hand, dismisses the issue of accuracy on the grounds that 'Shakespeare's play constructs its present tense on literary historical terms', in 'Chained Allusions, Patterned Futures, and the Dangers of Interpretation in Titus Andronicus', *ELR* (2014), 452–85; p. 453.

[8] Berthoud, 'Introduction', p. 33. For similar readings, see also Lindsey Scott, '"Groaning shadows that are gone": The ghosts of Titus Andronicus', *English Studies*, 96 (2015), 403–23; pp. 403–4.

[9] Berthoud, 'Introduction', p. 28. See also Carolyn Sale, 'Black Aeneas: Race, English literary history, and the "barbarous" poetics of *Titus Andronicus*,' *Shakespeare Quarterly* 62 (2011), 25–52; p. 47. Emmerichs attributes Lavinia's death to Titus's interference in her marital choices, a redrawing of her boundaries which 'sets the stage for another masculine and foreign invasion to penetrate the two feminine focal points in his life—Rome and Lavinia' ('"Thou map of woe"', p. 555).

[10] See, for instance, Jo Eldridge Carney, '"I'll find a day to massacre them all": Tamora in *Titus Andronicus* and Catherine De Medicis,' *Comparative Drama* 48 (2014), 415–35; p. 427.

[11] For Jacques Berthoud, 'Introduction', p. 33, Coppélia Kahn, *Roman Shakespeare: Warriors, Wounds and Women* (London, 1997), p. 51, and Andrew Hadfield, *Shakespeare and Republicanism* (Cambridge, 2005), p. 159, this moment is a failure of *pietas*. As Carolyn Sale argues, Shakespeare's presentation of barbarous Romans and vengeful Goths seems to criticize Roman imperial dogma as a 'dehumanizing code', 'Black Aeneas', p. 45. By portraying Tamora's violence as 'a response to Roman barbarity and the violence of the Roman response as excessive', Sale argues, the play 'pushes back against unquestioning veneration of ancient Rome or its culture', 'Black Aeneas', p. 43. Grace Starry West makes a similar argument, suggesting that 'Shakespeare is exploring the relationship between Roman education—the source of all the bookish allusions—and the disintegration of the magnificent city which produced that education', in her 'Going by the book: Classical allusions in Shakespeare's *Titus Andronicus*', *Philology*, 79 (1982), 62–77; p. 65.

is not so incongruous as it appears.[12] As St Hilaire notes (uniquely among literary critics), the problem is not that 'Titus's behavior is inconsistent with Rome's historical practices but rather that Titus's sacrifice is entirely consistent with a similarly appalling scene in a Roman text.'[13] That is, the *pietas* displayed by Titus is consistent with the *pietas* displayed by Aeneas, in that both versions of *pietas* portray ideal and excessive moments that reveal the violent currents beneath English *and* Roman norms.

When Shakespeare was writing *Titus*, monarchy had been revealed to be a system which had the potential to *fail*. In the lifetimes of many pondering this question during the succession crisis, the monarchy had produced sons that did not resemble their fathers, daughters that resembled their fathers but were unfruitful, or no sons at all. This context of failure and potential failure makes the ideal of stability through continuity, and continuity through reproduction, an extremely appealing ideal as well as a potentially fragile reality.[14] The focus on stability represents one of the key ideals underpinning primogeniture. Titus attempts to solve Rome's succession crisis by upholding that value. In his first appearance, Titus upholds the virtues of primogeniture in a short speech that reveals his assumption that the son will resemble the father (1.1.224–7). That assumption is almost immediately proven false when Mutius, one of Titus's sons, fails to support Titus's decision to marry Lavinia to Saturninus. The play features repeated failures of resemblance and, from the first, these failures prompt in Titus an excessive form of *pietas* that demands the destruction of, to borrow a term from Sara Ahmed, the 'unhappy object'.[15] That is, the *impia* child becomes an obstacle to Titus's ability to think about his own *pietas* unproblematically. Mutius disrupts Titus's attempt to create peace and in doing so inadvertently casts himself in the 'determinately un-Roman role of the Rutulians, Rome's first enemies'.[16] In failing to behave according to Roman precedents, Mutius also fails to resemble his father. Titus's response to obstacles is to decide that the obstacle, even if it is his own son, must then be destroyed. This overreaction to the 'unhappy object' reveals that Titus's enactment of *pietas* is excessive, an exaggeration of an already violent normative virtue.

In the very first scene of the play, Titus's portrayal of *pietas* seems counter to traditional humanist and critical understandings of the virtue. During Lavinia's first rape, when Bassianus absconds with his covert bride, Mutius, one of Titus's many sons, bars his father's way. When Titus is faced with his sons' disobedience, he

---

[12] Scholarly examinations of Shakespeare's use of classical sources tend to address Ovid and Seneca, mostly regarding 'allusions to other Roman authorities, such as Virgil and Horace, and local embroidery on the wholecloth of Ovid' in Heather James, *Shakespeare's Troy: Drama, Politics, and the Translation of Empire* (Cambridge, 1997), p. 42. See also Charles Martindale, 'Shakespeare and Virgil', p. 89. Even if Shakespeare had not had access to the Latin, the *Aeneid* was 'Englished' by Henry, Earl of Surrey, and published after his death as *Certain bokes of Virgiles Aeneis turned into English meter by the right honorable lorde, Henry Earle of Surrey* (London, 1557). There was also an earlier translation by Gavin Douglas, *Eneados* (1513).

[13] Danielle A. St Hilaire, 'Allusion and sacrifice in *Titus Andronicus*', *Studies in English Literature*, 49 (2009), 311–31; p. 314.

[14] Susan Doran suggests that 'the number of succession tracts produced during this period is powerful evidence of the urgency of the debate', such as *A Conference about the Next Succession to the Crown of England* by the Jesuit Robert Persons, in 'Three Late-Elizabethan Succession Tracts', in *The Struggle for the Succession in Late Elizabethan England*, ed. Jean-Christophe Mayer (Montpellier, 2004), 91–117; p. 115.

[15] Sara Ahmed, 'Happy objects', in *The Affect Theory Reader*, ed. Melissa Gregg and Gregory J. Seigworth (Durham, 2010). Ahmed argues that the idea that 'we share an orientation toward the family as being good, as being what promises happiness in return for loyalty' means that family 'shapes what we do; you have to "make" and "keep" the family, which directs how you spend your time, energy, and resources', p. 38. Titus's maintenance of what he counts as 'family' manifests in the violent removal of 'affect aliens' (39), the figures that do not share his orientation toward this specific 'family'. While I do not address affect theory as a whole in this argument, I find Ahmed's critique of affective attribution strikingly relevant to Titus's behaviour in the scenes in which he decides which children count as belonging to this family.

[16] St Hilaire, 'Allusion and sacrifice', p. 320.

responds by denying the familial bond in an act of non-recognition: 'Nor thou nor he are any sons of mine. / My sons would never so dishonour me' (1.1. 290–1). That is, these could not be his sons, because his sons would never disobey him.[17] Moreover, Titus strengthens his non-recognition claim when denying Mutius a place in the family tomb:

> Traitors, away, he rests not in this tomb.
> This monument five hundred years hath stood,
> Which I have sumptuously re-edified.
> Here none but soldiers and Rome's servitors
> Repose in fame, none basely slain in brawls.
> Bury him where you can; he comes not here.
> (1.1.346–51)

This speech encapsulates the play's focus on familial resemblance as a political issue. Titus does not recognize Mutius as his son because Mutius does not fit the very specific criteria associated with the right to be buried in the family tomb. This is an exclusive monument, dedicated only to 'soldiers and Rome's servitors'. Mutius, classified as 'basely slain in brawls', is rejected from the family tomb and therefore is fated to become another one of the 'unappeased' (1.1.100) shadows Alarbus's death was meant to prevent. Coppélia Kahn, in her *Roman Shakespeare* (1997), notes that 'The two filicides [Alarbus and Mutius] are paralleled: both sons are sacrificed in the names of the fathers, according to a piety that seems not only cruel and irreligious but also a perversion of *virtus*.'[18] However, because Titus enters the play as the victorious Roman general and is consistently associated with the martial values of honour and service, Titus's speech contains the assumption that he belongs to this kin group of soldiers and servitors, faithful citizens who put the city before themselves and their families.

Titus enters the play having won fame as a soldier of Rome, and his martial- and honour-based criteria for disinheriting (and perhaps disinterring) Mutius suggest that his problem is that Mutius does not resemble his father's martial prowess or familial honour. Having died in what Titus calls a 'brawl', Mutius has failed to imitate the family's 'honourable' tradition of dying in military combat for the protection of the city and the family name. Titus is the family's representative of those martial- and honour-based virtues; Mutius's failure of imitation is an indictment of his father's ability to inculcate his children with the family's values. As historian John Sommerville notes, 'the state grew up around the family and the clan and consciously depended on them to raise the kind of children they considered necessary to Rome's survival and power'.[19] With his son's public and catastrophic failure to support both his father and, by extension, his state, Titus's only available response is to deny that Mutius was ever his son, lest his own culpability in Mutius's actions receive too much attention. Moreover, this moment may not represent an impiety because, according to Roman law, Titus has 'the right of the father to "give or take life" from a rebellious child ... Rome gives this right to fathers in gratitude for their commitment to Rome'.[20] That is, Mutius's death is perfectly in line with the possibilities contained within the concept of *pietas*, rendering the filicide normative and therefore *pietas* horrific. Because Titus is consistently associated with *pietas*, his deadly reaction to Mutius's failure of resemblance encapsulates the play's critique of both aspects of *romanitas*: *virtus* and *pietas*. The apparent contradiction of this scene, Titus's tendency toward sacrificing sons in the name of a virtue that should logically support the preservation of his sons, is actually the key to understanding Shakespeare's purpose in identifying Titus with Aeneas.

In the act of not just killing Mutius but also denying their kinship, Titus establishes an understanding of *pietas* in which the claims of duty transume the claims of emotion. Titus exaggerates the

---

[17] Emily Detmer-Goebel, '"Then let no man but I / Do execution on my flesh and blood": Filicide and family bonds in *Titus Andronicus*', *Medieval and Renaissance Drama in England* 28 (2015), 110–22; p. 111. See also Raymond Westbrook, 'Vitae Necisque Potestas', *Historia: Zeitschrift fur Alte Geschichte* 48 (1999), 203–23; p. 207.
[18] Kahn, Roman Shakespeare, p. 49.
[19] John Sommerville, *The Rise and Fall of Childhood* (Beverly Hills, CA, 1982), p. 37.
[20] Detmer-Goebel, 'Filicide and family bonds', p. 112.

necessity of putting duty before emotions in ways that intensify his identification with Pius Aeneas. While *pietas* is the structuring virtue of the *Aeneid*, Aeneas's embodiment of that virtue seems to disintegrate in the second half. Aeneas is not uncritically praised, and his actions toward the end of Book 10 emphasize not his devotion to duty but his savagery in revenge. Upon hearing of the death of Pallas, Aeneas captures 'four sons of Sulmo, / fighters all, and the same number reared by Ufens: / Aeneas takes them alive to offer Pallas' shade / and soak his flaming pyre with captive blood' (10: 613–16).[21] The resemblance to the fate of Tamora's son Alarbus is striking and, as Nicholas R. Moschovakis claims, 'It is in part because of his insistence on such rites that Titus has earned Aeneas's own epithet, "Pius" (1.1.23).'[22] This understanding of Virgil's portrayal of *pietas* reads the devotion as well as the vengeance as aspects of the virtue; for instance, St. Hilaire reads Titus's sacrifice of Alarbus as 'not a falling away from or perversion of Virgilian piety but the fulfillment of it'.[23] However, I want to modify St. Hilaire's claim to note that this moment is an exception in Aeneas's usual behaviour. Far from 'depict[ing] human sacrifice as an element in the cult of Rome's heroic founders',[24] Virgil portrays Aeneas's perversion of ideal *pietas*.

By rendering Aeneas's *pietas* violent and vengeful, Virgil creates a vision of *pietas* in decline, and Shakespeare's sensitive reading recognizes that this is not the ideal *pietas* of most of the poem but *pietas* at its most extreme and most perverse. Identifying Pius Titus with Pius Aeneas is a deliberate appropriation of exactly the extreme, grotesque reading of *pietas* at the heart of Books 10 and 11 of the *Aeneid*. Titus's role as model of Roman virtues emphasizes the cyclical nature of the imitative ideal – as son becomes father, imitator becomes imitated – but his role as imitator of Aeneas's exaggerated *pietas* implicates the structure of imitation in the play's critique of received values. Powell's important new reading of the *Aeneid* argues that Aeneas acts in the name of *pietas* when avenging Pallas, which, he notes, highlights the 'fact that filial loyalty in [them] conflicted spectacularly with the claims of filial virtue in other Romans'.[25] When Aeneas is faced with a severe blow to his own *pietas*, he responds by 'mocking the *pietas* of others'.[26] Applying Powell's insight to my reading of *Titus*, I argue that while Titus does imitate Aeneas's version of *pietas*, it is the extreme, perverse *pietas* that turns on itself with savage mockery and brutal violence.

Tamora questions her sons' sacrifice, attributing to their actions in war the same *pietas* for which they are murdered:

> But must my sons be slaughtered in the streets
> For valiant doings in their country's cause?
> O, if to fight for king and commonweal
> Were piety in thine, it is in these.
> Andronicus, stain not thy tomb with this blood.
> (1.1.112–16)

Dickson argues that 'Titus, in this formulation, should live up to his emulation of Roman virtues and show mercy and honour to the warrior Alarbus.'[27] However, I would argue that in the

---

[21] All quotations taken from Robert Fagles, trans. *The Aeneid* (New York, 2008).
[22] Nicholas R. Moschovakis, '"Irreligious piety" and Christian history: Persecution as pagan anachronism in *Titus Andronicus*', *Shakespeare Quarterly* 53 (2002), 460–86; p. 464.
[23] St Hilaire, 'Allusion and sacrifice', p. 314.
[24] Moschovakis, '"Irreligious piety"', p. 464.
[25] Anton Powell, *Virgil the Partisan: A Study in the Re-Integration of Classics* (Swansea, 2008), p. 67. The critical consensus has been to ignore most aspects of Octavian's reputation among his contemporaries; Powell's text makes the compelling argument that the triumviral period is as important to Virgil's poems as the Augustan Rome toward which they look.
[26] Powell, *Virgil the Partisan*, p. 66.
[27] Vernon Guy Dickson, '"A pattern, precedent, and lively warrant": Emulation, rhetoric, and cruel propriety in *Titus Andronicus*', *Renaissance Quarterly* 62 (2009), 376–409; p. 397. Dickson's overall argument is that too-close imitation of classical sources leads to the violence of Lavinia's rape and later her murder at Titus's hands; for a similar argument, see William W. Weber, '"Worse than Philomel": Violence, revenge, and meta-allusion in *Titus Andronicus*', *Studies in Philology* 112 (2015), 698–717; p. 701; and Mariangela Tempera, 'Shakespearean outdoing: *Titus Andronicus* and Italian Renaissance tragedy', *Shakespeare and*

context of Book 10, *pietas* is associated with just this kind of pitiless revenge. Titus's response to Tamora's plea would seem to argue that Roman familial values are more important than the familial values of foreigners and enemies of the state, reaffirming his dedication to the city rather than to attempting to establish his own hereditary monarchy. Titus's insistence on the sacrifice of Tamora's son in exchange for his own makes him a closer model to Aeneas.[28] Nevertheless, Shakespeare by no means intends the comparison to reflect favourably on Titus or, for that matter, on Aeneas. Shakespeare rather uses Virgil's portrait of Aeneas to portray an exaggeration of *pietas* caused by vengeance, a morbid *pietas* that leads to increasing levels of violence, and ultimately to the destruction of the very values that lead these men to seek revenge.[29]

Shakespeare uses Aeneas as a model for Titus and it is crucial that he uses *all* of Aeneas's character, following Virgil's attempts to reconcile the contradictory pious and impious actions of his founding hero.[30] However, Shakespeare uses that attempt at reconciliation to suggest that the contradictions are inherent to *pietas* itself.[31] That is, Shakespeare repeatedly portrays a character insistently associated with *pietas* performing impious acts in the name of piety. 'Pius' Titus sacrifices his enemy's eldest son to balance the martial deaths of his own sons, murders one of his own sons for disobeying him, and murders his daughter because she has been raped and mutilated. Lavinia's murder has been amply discussed by critics. What I want to emphasize is that these killings have in common a perversion or exaggeration of *pietas*: Tamora's son is killed to put Titus's sons' souls to rest in a scene that strikingly recalls Aeneas's revenge for Pallas's death in Book 10 of the *Aeneid*; Mutius is killed because he failed to uphold the pious value of filial obedience; and Lavinia is killed to restore the family's honour in fine Roman tradition. Titus's tendency toward impious sacrifices in the name of *pietas* may not have been common practice in Rome but Virgil attributes the practice to the founder of Rome.[32] The association of his sacrificial *pietas* with revenge strips some of the ritualistic logic from the play's opening scene, turning a society-mending funeral into a destructive sacrifice.

Titus's return to Rome is triumphant; his murdered sons are another visible sign of his virtue carried onto the stage for a very pointedly public funeral. Titus's support of *romanitas* is not just established but exaggerated from his first appearance. Newly returned from the wars that have been threatening Rome for at least forty years, bearing home twenty-one of his twenty-five sons to be buried in the family tomb, bearing the scars of his service to Rome that, unlike Coriolanus's wounds, do not seem to need to speak for him, Titus establishes *pietas* as a value that underpins political manoeuvres:

> Stand gracious to the rights that we intend.
> Romans, of five-and-twenty valiant sons,
> Half of the number that King Priam had,
> Behold the poor remains, alive and dead:
> These that survive, let Rome reward with love;
> These that I bring unto their latest home,
> With burial amongst their ancestors.
> ...
> Titus, unkind and careless of thine own,
> Why suffer'st thou thy sons unburied yet
> To hover on the dreadful shore of Styx?

Renaissance Literary Theories: Anglo-Italian Transactions, ed. Michele Marrapodi (Farnham, 2011), 75–88.

[28] Dickson, "'A pattern, precedent, and lively warrant'", p. 398.

[29] Powell describes Virgil's portrait of Octavian-as-Aeneas, *Virgil the Partisan*, p. 49–51.

[30] Cora Fox notes that Renaissance readers would have come to the poem with knowledge of its Augustan context, able to understand the 'critique of abuses of power to which the poem obsessively returns,' in *Ovid and the Politics of Emotion in Elizabethan England* (New York, 2009), p. 12.

[31] St Hilaire notes that the 'sacrifice of Alarbus is thus not a break from Roman tradition but rather is rooted deeply in that tradition, in Rome's foundational text', 'Allusion and sacrifice', p. 315. However, my argument is slightly different from St Hilaire's in that I identify the continuities in the underlying ideologies that create both ideal and violent versions of pietas, rather than taking Aeneas's violence as simply the norm itself.

[32] Discussed above, see also M. Owen Lee, *Fathers and Sons in Virgil's Aeneid: Tum Genitor Natum*, (New York, 1979), pp. 85, 185.

Make way to lay them by their brethren.
There greet in silence, as the dead are wont,
And sleep in peace, slain in your country's wars.
O sacred receptacle of my joys,
Sweet cell of virtue and nobility,
How many sons hast thou of mine in store
That thou wilt never render to me more!
(1.1.78–95)

This speech encapsulates Shakespeare's thinking about how familial relationships, and inheritance systems, structure political conversations about the transmission of rule. In setting out the terms of his procession-cum-funeral, Titus attempts to establish himself as the ideal Roman in a *political* setting by highlighting the magnitude of his *personal* sacrifice to Rome's wars.[33] The sacrifice of his sons is a sacrifice of parts of himself and of potential guarantors of his own immortality. With so few sons remaining, the succession of his house is imperilled. As St Hilaire argues, 'the loss of twenty-one sons is immense, and suggests the vulnerability of Titus's Rome at the play's outset'.[34] To further mark himself as avatar of *virtus* and *pietas*, Titus also aligns himself with the Trojan king and patriarch Priam, perhaps best known for retrieving Hector's mistreated body through an appeal to *pietas*.[35] However, the allusion to Priam must also invoke stories that he witnessed the murder of another of his sons before the family altar, before being murdered himself in a particularly graphic scene in the *Aeneid* featuring the failure of an appeal to *pietas*.[36]

In spite of its ambivalent associations, the reference to Priam could represent a conflation of obedience to father and to state: Priam is specifically the Trojan king *and* patriarch, as famous for his fatherhood as for his kingliness. Titus embraces this conflation in his assumption that authority resides in the father; in requiring his children's obedience, he draws on the received idea that his own authority is natural by using paternalistic terms. But, also like Priam, Titus survives his children; that survival further cements his association with the broader version of *pietas* as exemplified by a patriarch from a different tradition: the paternal and the violent Aeneas. Aeneas abandons his efforts to fight the Greeks, his beloved wife, his new love Dido, and several men he thinks of as sons in order to establish Rome.[37] Every sacrifice was for the future of his lineage. The point of sacrificing self and certain family members to duty is to preserve the family line as a whole. As Robert Miola notes, Rome's inhabitants 'often live and die according to [the city's] dictates for the approval of its future generations'.[38] In spite of its profound lack of pity, *pietas* is essentially a preservative virtue; to the men who adhere to the ideal form of the virtue, *pietas* ascribes the responsibility to preserve sons' heritages.[39] Titus, however, sacrifices the future of his lineage to preserve its past.

When he first appears on stage, Titus takes a moment in his triumphal speech to reprimand himself for not immediately burying his sons, calling himself 'Titus unkind' (1.1.86), that is, devoid of natural feeling or undutiful. The term 'unkind' also indicates a breakage of family ties – as Hamlet sarcastically notes, the terms kin and kind should be, but are not always, closely related. Titus seems to be calling himself back from service to the city to a broken or unfulfilled loyalty to kin. The exaggerated *pietas* portrayed by Titus, and by Aeneas in Book 10, involves a fixation on the proper burial of family members and the most *impia* actions in the *Aeneid* make some aspect of that burial impossible. When Aeneas is on his quest for vengeance, and actively mocking the *pietas* of others, he tells one of his victims, 'Now lie there,

---

[33] In thinking about the impact of politics on the familial but also about the impact of the familial on politics, it is worth noting that the commonplace that the family is the 'natural' metaphor for the state elides the violence placed by political pressures on familial emotions. However, as Peter Lake notes, what we term the 'public' and 'private' are anachronistic; see *The Anti-Christ's Lewd Hat: Protestants, Papists and Players in Post-Reformation England* (New Haven, CT, 2002), p. 100.
[34] St Hilaire, 'Allusion and sacrifice', p. 312.
[35] Lisa Hopkins, *The Cultural Uses of the Caesars on the English Renaissance Stage* (Aldershot, 2008), pp. 18–19.
[36] Lee, *Fathers and Sons*, pp. 38–40.
[37] Lee, *Fathers and Sons*, p. 32, notes that Virgil calls the men *Aeneidae*.
[38] Miola, '"Thou map of woe"', p. 17.
[39] Lee, *Fathers and Sons*, p. 52.

you great horrific sight! / No loving mother will bury you in the ground / or weight your body down with your fathers' tomb. / You'll be abandoned now to carrion birds or plunged / in the deep sea and swept away by the waves and / ravening fish will dart and lick your wounds!' (10:660–5).[40] Killing one brother, he says to the other who pleads for his life, 'die! No brother deserts a brother here!' (10:708). All of his victims in this section are not random but 'unfortunates who appeal to him in the name of *pietas*'.[41] His revenge takes the form of denying proper burial, preventing that particular expression of *pietas*. However, Aeneas is recalled to himself upon witnessing the sacrifice of a son for his father: 'this picture of love for a father pierced his heart', causing him to once again respect another family's *pietas*, stating 'I give you back to your fathers' ash and shades' (10:74, 79). Aeneas's momentary exaggeration of *pietas* into murder and vengeance is portrayed as an aberration brought on by grief, even madness. Titus begins the play in a similar state of grief, having lost most of his sons; however, as a virtue in *Titus*, *pietas* is exaggerated in every character. Lucius responds to his father's grief by calling for Alarbus's sacrifice. Tamora pleads with Titus to respect her own family's *pietas*; when he does not, when he murders her eldest son in a ritual of 'cruel, irreligious piety' (1.1.130), she determines to 'raze their faction and their family' (1.1.448). Titus recognizes his own unstable relationship to his family, and especially to his family tomb, but in a passing aside ('Titus unkind') that seems incapable of affecting his responses to Mutius's disobedience or Tamora's plea. That relationship to family is consistently set aside, while the relationship to the family tomb is pushed to the forefront.

Many critics have noted Titus's apparent obsession with his family tomb, and by extension proper familial burial, which dominates the stage, physically and symbolically, during his first scene. Coppélia Kahn describes Titus's obsession as an 'exaggerated investment in the patriarchal order ... The tomb thus represents not simply the continuity of the family so much as the subordination of the family to the military needs of the state – the original and hallowed medium of *virtus*.'[42] Kahn reads Titus's devotion to *virtus* as merely part of his extreme *romanitas* but it is worth teasing out the subtleties of this scene. Titus does indeed value *virtus* over ideal *pietas*, and in doing so misunderstands one vital aspect of Virgil's *pietas*: in the *Aeneid*, *pietas* is consistently treated as more important than *virtus*, martial valour.[43] However, Titus focuses on his martial duty to Rome above all else. The claims of the city transume the claims of the family, as Titus overemphasizes the necessity of putting duty before emotions. Titus does not just put the cause first; he actively sacrifices the majority of his sons.

Shakespeare obsessively reminds the audience of Titus's emotional losses, juxtaposing them against his intensified devotion to duty. The play focuses on the family's faltering future generations in Titus's first scene, establishing the very emotional cost of Rome's wars – Titus's 'five-and-twenty valiant sons' (1.1.79) – and making their 'poor remains, alive and dead' (1.1.81) the central issue of his hero's return. Titus references 'thine own' and 'thy sons' (1.1.86, 91), his 'joys' (1.1.92), and his 'sons' (1.1.94) again, returning continually to his family's sacrifices for (or to) the war effort. The effect of repeated emotional appeals cast as appeals to duty serves to emphasize Titus's focus on city above family. What should be an emotional issue, the loss of his sons, is redirected toward his duty to Rome. The same burial he impiously denies to Tamora's sons he frets over withholding from his own sons even temporarily.

While the loss of his sons is redirected toward his devotion to duty, the emotional core to the scene, for Titus, is his family's past. Titus refers to 'their ancestors' (84), 'their brethren' (1.1.89), 'the dead' (1.1.90), and the other sons 'in store' (1.1.94), that

---

[40] It irresistibly recalls Tamora's fate, which is discussed below.
[41] Lee, *Fathers and Sons*, p. 85.
[42] Kahn, *Roman Shakespeare*, p. 52.
[43] Powell, *Virgil the Partisan*, pp. 32–3.

is, in the family tomb, establishing a link to the family's past generations. The grave becomes a site of values, a concrete 'cell of virtue and nobility' that materializes his family's reputation and makes enduringly visible the worth of his lineage. The tomb is also capable of housing Titus's emotional response to the loss of his sons. It is only the buried sons Titus refers to as his 'joys', restricting emotion to the dead and duty to the living. In Titus's view, the family as an institution is focused on maintaining ties to the valorized past through the effective burial of the dead. As Paul Kottman theorizes, each family member is entombed so that the connection to both past and future generations is made visible and concrete.[44] The 'continuity of their [family] history'[45] creates and ratifies Titus's authority with each funeral.

However, the opening scene reveals that, because the burial ritual is susceptible to indecorum and interruption, its power is fragile; it sometimes fails to bind and can become incapable of knitting the scattered corn of Rome into 'one mutual sheaf' (5.3.70). Titus's murder of his son Mutius and denial of his place in the family tomb reveals an inherent instability in this symbol of familial unity and continuity. If sons can be denied a place in the family tomb, the family itself is revealed as a contingent and potentially brittle institution.[46] The family is denaturalized, though paternal authority over the constitution of the family is thereby enhanced. The application of familial metaphors to politics consequently renders political stability equally fragile, a necessary condition for the enhancement of the authority of the political ruler.

Titus's obsession with the tomb materializes his excessive, morbid *pietas*. What should be Titus's emotional losses are actually registered numerically – we never learn the names of the twenty-one (1.1.195) or twenty-two (3.1.10) sons out of twenty-five lost to the wars, and Titus seems more emotionally affected by Mutius disobeying him (1.1.380–3) than by his own filicide and the deaths of nearly two dozen other sons. And Titus confirms, 'For two-and-twenty sons I never wept, / Because they died in honour's lofty bed' (3.1.10–11). After Titus refuses to bury Mutius in the family tomb, Marcus recalls Tamora's accusation of 'irreligious piety', stating 'My lord, this is impiety in you' (1.1.352), noting again the incompatibility of the institution of *pietas* as practised by Titus and the 'natural' kinship bond. Mutius goes on to make the case overtly that blood ties are natural and should therefore supersede the ideals that comprise *romanitas*, especially *pietas*: 'Brother, for in that name doth nature plead—', and Quintus continues, 'Father, and in that name doth nature speak—' (1.1.367–8). It has been suggested that the discrepancies in Titus's count come out of collaborative work between Shakespeare and George Peele.[47] While Titus's characterization may have been the result of a mistake, he nevertheless refers to varying numbers of lost children rather than their names, overall giving an impression of a 'by the numbers' relationship with his sons. Also, while the play might indeed have been written collaboratively, that would not necessarily affect audience perception of Titus's character. Titus states that he had 'five-and-twenty valiant sons, / Half the number that King Priam had' (1.1.79–80); alternatively, changing the count of dead sons from twenty-one to twenty-two could indicate his reacceptance of Mutius, earlier repudiated and murdered for his disobedience. If Titus is using the altered count to indicate his forgiveness of his son, then the mistake is no mistake at all and actually a means of apologizing without ever acknowledging his own mistake aloud.

---

[44] Paul A. Kottman, *Tragic Conditions in Shakespeare: Disinheriting the Globe* (Baltimore, 2009), p. 60.

[45] Berthoud, 'Introduction', p. 23.

[46] Cynthia J. Bannon, *The Brothers of Romulus: Fraternal Pietas in Roman Law, Literature, and Society* (Princeton, NJ, 1997), p. 27.

[47] While critical opinion is divided on whether the play is actually collaborative, the research in Brian Vickers's *Shakespeare, Co-Author: A Historical Study of Five Collaborative Plays* (Oxford, 2002) is reliable and seems to indicate a collaborative effort. More recent critics, such as Paulina Kewes, accept as a given that the play was cowritten by Peele and Shakespeare. Weber provides an extremely thorough overview of this debate, '"Worse then Philomel"', pp. 703–4, though he argues against Vickers, p. 704.

Both republican and imperial Romans in this play, and people in early modern England, 'distinguished those who were related by blood and ascribed to them a deep sense of identity', and idealized blood kinship and 'its power to generate affection and duty'.[48] The ideal of *pietas* was often cast against duty to the state in other Roman authors critical of Augustus's disregard of familial relationships.[49] Shakespeare uses Virgil's portrayal of Aeneas's vengeful *pietas* to criticize early modern arguments about the role of kinship in the state. The necessity of violence to buttress political action casts *pietas*, and a particularly early modern model of kinship, as endangered by a predatory political system in spite of its adoption of kinship metaphors to describe political actions and actors.

Parodying the debate between hereditary and electoral systems exposes both as the product of corrupt ideologies, casting a different light on the third iteration of this argument at the end of the play. Titus's eldest son and heir, Lucius, is named the elected Emperor of the city he would need to restore. However, if Lucius is meant to be the play's hero, then Shakespeare's condemnation of both systems is only intensified.[50] The same Lucius that demands the barbarous sacrifice of Alarbus restores justice and peace to Rome, an almost ludicrous solution to the play's dilemma. The play ends by returning to the *Aeneid*:

> as erst our ancestor,
> When with his solemn tongue he did discourse
> To love-sick Dido's sad-attending ear
> The story of that baleful burning night,
> When subtle Greeks surprised King Priam's Troy.
> Tell us what Sinon hath bewitched our ears,
> Or who hath brought the fatal engine in
> That gives our Troy, our Rome, the civil wound.
>
> (5.3.79–86)

The allusive request for elucidation only increases the negative foreboding that attends Lucius's rise to power: if Lucius has taken his father's place as the play's avatar of Aeneas, then the reference to Dido recalls her abandonment and suicide in terms that preclude us from viewing Lucius as the unproblematic saviour of the play. The reference to Priam reminds us of Lucius's father, body still warm, destroyed by his dedication to Roman values. If the 'fatal engine' has been brought in, no matter by whom, it is already too late for the characters and for the city. While presented as Titus's heir, Lucius is elected to the throne after Saturninus 'thereby acceding to the position to which Bassianus' merit entitled him, and thus also in a sense succeeding and replacing him'.[51] However, Lucius is also replacing Saturninus and either replacement foils the purpose of primogeniture as an inheritance structure: the replication and replacement of his father. Lucius is replacing the wrong man.

Tamora asserts that her marriage to Saturninus has made her 'incorporate in Rome, / A Roman

---

[48] Bannon, *The Brothers of Romulus*, p. 62, p. 5.
[49] Powell, *Virgil the Partisan*, ch. 2: 'The theft of *pietas*', especially pp. 64–75.
[50] Whether Lucius's accession to the throne represents a positive ending to the play is hotly debated among critics. Yates argues that 'the good empire returns with Lucius', in Frances A. Yates, *Astrea: The Imperial Theme in the Sixteenth Century* (Routledge, 1975, reprint 1999), p. 75. Grace West argues that Lucius, in Marcus's speech at the end of the play, is the play's model of 'our ancestor' Aeneas, 'Going by the book', p. 75. Lucius also models Aeneas in that his succession marks him as indicated in another Virgilian allusion to triumvirate politics: for Powell, 'Julius Caesar, like Anchises, had made a somewhat erratic start, flawed both in calculation and in morality. In each case it was the son who would transcend the father's virtues and would found (or refound) gloriously and to last', *Virgil the Partisan*, p. 76. However, as Vernon Guy Dickson notes, 'Lucius's final acts of judgment reify the accepted cultural stereotypes of the play, especially in the pitiless treatment of Aaron and Tamora ... [and his] judgments programmatically replicate Roman tradition, following Titus's example at the play's beginning', '"A pattern, precedent, and lively warrant"', p. 404. Like Moschovakis and Bate, Brower observes that 'the saving of Rome by Lucius, traditionally first of the British kings and descended from their "ancestor" Aeneas, in Reuben Arthur Brower, *Hero & Saint: Shakespeare and the Graeco-Roman heroic tradition* (Oxford, 1971), p. 194. However, Moschovakis also notes the difficulty of regarding 'Lucius Andronicus, a ritual butcher, as a magnet for the nostalgia of Protestants hoping to Restore the English rite to its primitive state', '"Irreligious piety"', p. 466.
[51] Clifford Chalmers Huffman, '*Titus Andronicus*: Metamorphosis and renewal', *MLR*, 67 (1972), 730–41; p. 740.

now adopted happily' (1.1.459–60). In an act of purgation, the Goth who has been taken into the city is cast out in the play's final denial of another family's *pietas*. While Lucius honours Aaron's request to preserve his son's life (5.1.69), Tamora, 'that ravenous tiger', is denied the burial that would appease her spirit and honour her kin: 'No funeral rite, nor man in mourning weed, / No mournful bell shall ring her burial, / But throw her forth to beasts and birds of prey' (5.3.194, 195–7). Jonathan Bate notes that this was the fate of executed felons in Elizabethan England and therefore an accurate punishment for her crimes within the play; this moment also irresistibly recalls Aeneas's refusal of burial rites to his enemies in the moments after Pallas's death.[52] His refusal to allow his victims proper burial in their 'fathers' tomb' (10:664) is part of his programme of vengeance; while Lucius is meting out justice for Tamora's crimes in this scene, he is also denying her family the rites and respect he demands for his own.[53] Aeneas's exaggeration of *pietas* into violence was the momentary lapse of a grief-stricken father; the one moment in which Lucius respects another family's *pietas*, however, is equally temporary and he ends the play as he began, demanding the fulfilment of his own family's *pietas* at the expense of another's.

The play features repeated failures of resemblance and, from the first, these failures prompt in Titus a form of *pietas* that demands the destruction of the *impia* child, who becomes an obstacle to Titus's construction of the ideal Roman family. Mutius's failure to behave according to Roman precedents, and therefore to resemble his own father, renders him an obstacle that Titus must destroy in order to maintain his vision of his family as emblems of the primary values of *romanitas* – *pietas* and *virtus*. Moreover, this overreaction to Mutius's rebellion reveals that Titus's enactment of *pietas* is excessive, an exaggeration of an already violent normative virtue, and this exaggeration demonstrates the destructive effects of political and ideological interventions on familial relationships. The imbrication of such relationships in the political matters of the play, from the initial succession debates to Lucius's final inheritance, further suggests their ability to undermine political institutions and complicate ideological systems. Titus's exaggerated *romanitas* makes visible his complete adoption of Roman political ideals, but the completeness of that adoption destroys the very institutions he supports, suggesting that the instability revealed by his actions is inherent to politics and family alike.

---

[52] Jonathan Bate, *Titus Andronicus*. Arden Shakespeare Third Series (London and New York, 1995), p. 277, ft. 197.

[53] Elizabeth D. Gruber emphasizes the role of the 'unappeased shadows' in emphasizing 'rupture and crisis', and in 'thoroughly complicating even the most basic questions of identity (such as the seemingly impermeable boundary between the living and the dead)', in 'Building the necropolis: Killing mother/nature in *The Spanish Tragedy* and *Titus Andronicus*', *Lit: Literature Interpretation Theory* 25.4 (2014), 271–90; p. 273.

'CUT HIM OUT IN LITTLE STARS': JULIET'S CUTE CLASSICISM

JULIA REINHARD LUPTON

In 'What is a classic? Is Shakespeare a classic?', Sean Keilen counterposes monumental constructions of artistic permanence with Ovidian figures of mutability and vitality as conduits of classicism. Keilen ends with an appeal for a critical practice that would relinquish authority in order to cultivate receptivity:

For those of us who are open to the idea of thinking about these topics with Shakespeare, the invitation that he makes in his late plays to compare his art and Ovid's myths, without determining what the outcome of that comparison will be, gestures to forms of reflective composition that were excluded from English literary studies when it became an academic discipline at the end of the nineteenth century. I mean writing that sets aside a belief in authority and the desire to persuade others to adopt a point of view — writing that approaches criticism as an opportunity to hold oneself open to art's presence, undergo change, and share the experience of wonder with a reader.[1]

Keilen takes up Jonson's line, 'Thou art a monument without a tomb', from his poem on Shakespeare in the First Folio to explore the classicizing dynamic between vitality and petrification. Jonson's eulogy ends with another image that belongs to the same complex of critical-creative issues:

> But stay, I see thee in the hemisphere
> Advanc'd, and made a constellation there!
> Shine forth, thou star of poets, and with rage
> Or influence, chide or cheer the drooping stage.
> Which, since thy flight from hence, hath mourn'd like night,
> And despairs day, but for thy volume's light.[2]

At first glance the image of Shakespeare as a constellation or star fixed in the firmament for all to see appears to belong to the monumental theory of classicism. Stellification was the reward given to heroes (Castor and Pollux, Hercules, Alcestis) and then to kings and emperors (Aeneas, Romulus, Julius Caesar, Augustus). Deification through stellification easily merged with the Nativity star in Christian iconographies of sacred kingship; by the middle of the seventeenth century, Charles I would be celebrated in an epideictic star writing that condensed sovereignty, poetic power and divinity.[3] As Heather James has noted, Shakespeare's literary stellification was preceded by that of Sir Philip 'Astrophil' Sidney, whose apotheosis as a soldier-

---

I delivered a version of this article for a panel, '"Cut him out in little stars": Romeo and Juliet Among the Arts' at the World Shakespeare Congress 2016. Many thanks to my co-panellists Joseph Campana and Viola Timm and to the organizers of the WSC. I also develop a line of thought in this article that appears in the special issue 'Cute Shakespeare', *Journal of Early Modern Cultural Studies* 16.3 (2016), which I co-edited with Thomas P. Anderson.

[1] Sean Keilen, 'What is a classic? Is Shakespeare a classic?', in *Routledge Research Companion to Shakespeare and Classical Literature*, ed. Sean Keilen and Nick Moschovakis (London, 2017, forthcoming).

[2] Ben Jonson, 'To the memory of my beloved the author, Mr. William Shakespeare', in *Ben Jonson and the Cavalier Poets*, ed. Hugh Maclean (New York, 1974), pp. 85–8, ll. 75–80.

[3] Sytithe Pugh, *Herrick, Fanshawe, and the Politics of Intertextuality: Classical Literature and Seventeenth-Century Royalism* (London, 2010), pp. 54–8. On stellification as a conceit in court entertainments, see Martin Butler, 'The early Stuart masque', in *The Stuart Court and Europe: Essays in Politics and Political Culture*, ed. Malcolm Smuts (Cambridge, 1996), pp. 81–2.

courtier-poet drew on the imperial motifs that allowed Virgil and Ovid to hitch their own artistic immortality to the tail of Caesar's star.[4]

Constellation offers more than the singular glamour of cosmic visibility, however; it also sketches relationships among poets, who begin to cohere in a canon and suggest a 'stellified community'.[5] When Jonson says that Shakespeare has been 'made a constellation', the passive voice admits multiple agents into the process of astral projection, including the efforts of Jonson himself along with the editors, future readers and theatrical users of the First Folio.[6] If Shakespeare, in Jonson's famous phrase, was 'Soul of the age', it was because his brighter star could be configured into a pattern with 'our Lyly', 'sporting Kyd' and 'Marlowe's mighty line' while sharing sky space with ancient authors. Constellations, like historical periodization, involve acts of pattern recognition that require consensus. As maps that enable navigation, moreover, constellations are used as well as read: literary constellations might draw together different kinds of knowledges (theatrical, hermeneutic, interpersonal) in order to orient reading choices that train judgement, cultivate sympathy, build attention or direct action. When Jonson writes that Shakespeare's star can 'with rage / Or influence, chide or cheer the drooping stage' (ll. 29–30), influence in the astrological sense begins to release its modern meaning of inspiring new art, naming the retroactive rhythm through which time-bound works are reborn as classics. What is classical in the stellification motif is its promise of an immortality conferred by the fruits of human capability; in the words of Hannah Arendt, for the ancients, 'the task and potential greatness of mortals lie in their ability to produce things – works and deeds and words – which would deserve to be and, at least to a degree, are at home in everlastingness, so that through them mortals could find their place in a cosmos where everything is immortal except themselves'.[7] In her estimation, first the philosophers and then Christianity mucked up the courage at the heart (*coeur*) of the classical cult of fame by replacing 'the striving for immortality, the way of life of the citizen, the *bios politikos*' with an eternal *nunc stans* outside of rather than produced by human affairs.[8]

Arendt, Benjamin and Adorno used the figure of the constellation, with its diagrammatic emphasis on the lines among points and its inherent dialectic between imaginative projection and objective components, to describe the 'history of the relations and influences that affect an object for at least as long as the object exists'.[9] Jonson's poem, with its epochal mapping of literary influence and its mythopoetic treatment of canon formation, can itself be constellated with the Arendtian line of thinking with and about classicism.

In this article, I take up the stellification motif in Juliet's glorious 'Gallop apace' monologue, in which she promises immortality to her beloved in a fantasy of stellar cutwork (3.2.20–5). Itself an adaptation of earlier sources and motifs, Juliet's image of stellification predicts the fashioning of the lovers into the souvenirs and icons of a global brand for teen love. But of course Juliet is no Caesar. Or we could say that she is a 'Cute Caesar', even 'the Caesar of Cute': the name 'Juliet' is a Julian diminutive, and Shakespeare's resetting of the play in July rather than Brooke's December asserts the Julian dimension of the play's Romanesque world.[10] In 'Cute Shakespeare', a special issue of the *Journal of Early*

---

[4] Heather James, *Shakespeare's Troy: Drama, Politics, and the Translation of Empire* (Cambridge, 1997), p. 8.
[5] Pugh uses the phrase 'stellified community' in her reading of Herrick's *Hesperides* (*Herrick, Fanshawe, and the Politics of Intertextuality*, p. 55).
[6] On readers as users, see Bradin Cormack and Carla Mazzio, *Book Use and Book Theory, 1500–1700* (Chicago, 2005).
[7] Hannah Arendt, *The Human Condition*, 2nd edn (Chicago, 1998), p. 19.
[8] Arendt, *The Human Condition*, p. 20.
[9] Deborah Cook, *Theodor Adorno: Key Concepts* (Oxon, 2014), pp. 59–60.
[10] I use the word 'Romanesque' here to name the simultaneously classical and medieval stamp of Shakespeare's play, with its origins in Latin poetry (Pyramus and Thisbe, Orpheus) and Italian local narratives. In local lore, the Romanesque Basilica di San Zeno houses the crypt where Romeo and Juliet were married. On the Italian character of *Romeo and Juliet*, see new work by Julian Jiménez Heffernan, 'Romeo's Earliness', in *Renaissance Drama* (forthcoming); and Shaul Bassi, 'The names of the rose: Romeo and Juliet in Italy', in *Romeo and Juliet: A Critical Reader*, ed. Julia Reinhard Lupton (London, 2015), pp. 177–98.

Modern Cultural Studies, a group of us used Sianne Ngai's *Our Aesthetic Categories: Zany, Interesting, Cute* to feel out the contours of a 'cute' aesthetic in the Renaissance.[11] Although Ngai associates cuteness with the commodity, she refuses to restrict her analysis to a critique of consumerism, instead finding in various experiments with small things (Gertrude Stein's *Tender Buttons*, Winnicott's transitional objects) a minor aesthetics attuned to the remainders of infantile object orders. The essays in our volume identify a distinctive brand of Shakespearean cuteness that merges care, aggression and intimacy via tactile investigation, sumptuary pleasure and the post-secular dialectic of re-enchantment. In these pages, I further explore Juliet's stellification fantasy as one moment in a suite of Ovidian, festive and domestic references that affiliate Juliet's creative capacities with fabric arts, votive tendencies and memorial miniaturizations. Thinking with Keilen about Juliet's poetry, I would like to pose the question 'Can classicism be cute?' How might a part-object eroticism, extreme youth and the *energeia* of anticipation recolour the elegiac and heroic impulses of stellification into a more feminine and handheld poetics of praise that curates minor effects over major monuments?

In attending with care to Juliet's effulgent image gallery, I aim to follow Keilen's request that we approach criticism 'as an opportunity to hold oneself open to art's presence, undergo change, and share the experience of wonder with a reader'. Whereas Keilen focuses on the heroes of late Shakespeare and their middle-aged capacity to 'free themselves from their convictions and by changing, to live a new life' my pendant piece looks at the freshness and courage of the adolescent imagination and the ability of girls to clothe sexual adventure, which is also political adventure, in the diaphanous fabrics, festive rhythms and instant images of daily life. Juliet's cute classicism partakes not in the wonder of Leontes and Prospero, who accept what Keilen calls, citing Bacon's definition of wonder, a 'broken knowledge', but in a form of receptivity that I would characterize as 'tender': vulnerable, receptive, donative, transitional and untested. Juliet's stellification fantasy, I am suggesting, offers a star map showing how we as readers, teachers and auditors of Shakespeare can tune into the play's minor classicism in order to renew our relationship to a play that scholars have tended to love neither wisely nor too well.

Juliet's epithalamium begins in the heavens, with Ovid, cosmic bodies, teen risk and the traces of elegy:

> Gallop apace, you fiery-footed steeds,
> Towards Phoebus' lodging. Such a wagoner
> As Phaeton would whip you to the west
> And bring in cloudy night immediately.[12]
>
> (3.2.1–4)

It is an inauspicious analogy to say the least. Jettisoned from his rash *translatio imperii* by a thunderbolt from Jove, Phaeton is compared by Ovid to a shooting star: 'But Phaeton (fire yet blasing stil among his yellow haire) / Shot headlong downe, and glid among the Region of the Ayre / Like to a starre in Winter nights (the weather cleare and fayre) / Which though it doe not fall in deede, yet falleth to our sight.'[13] This lingering simile is all that remains from a stellification procedure (into the constellation Auriga) that Ovid leaves out of his version of the story.[14] Ovid's simile associates cosmic light with a certain optics, a phenomenology of appearing that precedes and 'influences' art by providing a model of the image in nature. Perhaps ironically, Ovid's epic simile evokes the stellification of Caesar, whose 'shyning starre ... drew a greate way after it bryght beames like burning heare'.[15] In both passages, the image of burning hair traces the memory of movement into the receptive sky,

---

[11] Sianne Ngai, *Our Aesthetic Categories: Zany, Interesting, Cute* (Cambridge, MA, 2012).

[12] Citations from *Romeo and Juliet* are from René Weis, ed., *Romeo and Juliet*, Arden Shakespeare Third Series (London, 2012).

[13] Jonathan Frederick Nims, ed., *Ovid's Metamorphoses: The Arthur Golding Translation of 1567* (Philadelphia, 2000), II.404–7.

[14] Robert P. Merrix, 'The Phaëthon allusion in *Richard II*: The search for identity', *English Literary Renaissance* 17 (1987), 279.

[15] Nims, ed., *Ovid's Metamorphoses*, xv.955–6.

like Aby Warburg's 'accessories in motion' (*bewegte Beiwerke*), the fabric, ribbons, hair and leafy boughs that communicate motion in Renaissance entertainments and their pictorial transcription.[16]

Whereas Caesar is going up, Phaethon is coming down, as Richard II notes in his appropriation of the trope:

> Down, down I come, like glist'ring Phaëton,
> Wanting the manage of unruly jades.
> In the base court? Base court where kings grow base
> To come at traitors' calls and do them grace.
> In the base court? Come down? Down court, down king!
> For night-owls shriek where mounting larks should sing.[17]   (3.3.178–83)

Anticipating the lark/nightingale exchanges of *Romeo and Juliet*, also delivered 'aloft at the window' (SD 3.5.0), Richard II is a petty/pretty Caesar whose orchestration of his descent unfolds both mythopoetically and architecturally, as he prepares to descend from the balcony to the stage below. In both plays, classical myth provides a syntax as well as a semantics that place the characters in 'a spatial environment whose vertical and horizontal perspectives it simultaneously remodels'.[18] In both plays, the allusion becomes a vector graphic that orients the players in a world of competing virtues, physical movements and emotional arcs, communicating the glamour of what appears to fall but does not (the sovereign who will rise in memory as he declines in power, the lovers who will enter the firmament of immemorial fame even as they rashly begin the descent towards their deaths). In neither case could we call Phaeton 'cute', exactly, but the story's easy assimilation to anecdotes about teenagers borrowing Dad's car places it in a YA cosmos that Juliet is helping to constellate.[19] Phaeton's confrontation with constellations turned into epic monsters has a mock-heroic cast, while his sisters the Heliades' amber mourning for him introduces a topos of liquid inclusion that memorializes the minor and the miniature, like Queen Mab's own 'gallop[ing]' in the insect world (1.4.70, 77).[20] Juliet is a classic Girl, whose pirouettes on the threshold between childhood and womanhood activate ancient myths of adolescent development (Persephone, Thisbe and Hero, but also Phaeton). Adolescence *is* metamorphosis, an Ovidian truth tapped in this play and taken up in school curricula as well as tween and teen adaptations.

Stars return in Juliet's explicit reference to stellification two-thirds of the way through the monologue:

> Come, gentle night, come, loving black-browed night,
> Give me my Romeo, and when I shall die
> Take him and cut him out in little stars,
> And he will make the face of heaven so fine
> That all the world will be in love with night
> And pay no worship to the garish sun.   (3.2.20–5)

Stellification usually supports elegiac and memorial projects, and Juliet's fantasy certainly points forward to the death of the lovers and their afterlife in theatre, art and culture. Yet she keeps mourning at bay by setting the image in an epithalamion, with its breathless movement 'apace' towards erotic consummation: as editors have pointed out, Q1 and F's bold 'I shall die' emphasizes orgasm rather than mortality, and Juliet retools stellification in order to picture herself 'seeing stars' in the moment of erotic bliss.[21] The image treats Romeo's body as a kind of fabric or cloth of gold worked into a constellation of glittering shapes on the velvet

---

[16] Aby Warburg, 'Sandro Botticelli', in *The Renewal of Pagan Antiquity* (Los Angeles, 1999), pp. 88–156, and commentary by Phillippe-Alain Michaud, *Aby Warburg and the Image in Motion*, trans. Sophie Hawkes (New York, 2004).

[17] Charles R. Forker, ed., *Richard II*, Arden Shakespeare Third Series (London, 2002).

[18] Janice Valls-Russell, 'Erotic perspectives: When Pyramus and Thisbe meet Hero and Leander in *Romeo and Juliet*', in *Shakespeare's Erotic Mythology and Ovidian Renaissance Culture*, ed. Agnès Lafont (Farnham, Surrey, 2013), p. 78.

[19] On *Romeo and Juliet* and YA (young adult) fiction, see Greg M. Colón Semenza, '*Tromeo and Juliet*, teen films, and the cinematic aesthetic of un-cuteness', *Journal of Early Modern Cultural Studies* 16.3 (2016), 13–29.

[20] On the Heliades, amber and the poetics of mourning/memorialization, see Shannon Kelley, 'Amber, the Heliades, and the poetics of trauma in Marvell's "The Nymph Complaining"', *Studies in English Literature* 55 (2015), 151–74.

[21] Weis, ed., *Romeo and Juliet*, p. 249n.

canopy of the night sky. Unhae Langis connects the passage with the Neoplatonic idea of the astral body, 'made of very fine, lucent stuff ... corporeal but subtle'.[22] 'Cute' derives from 'acute' and originally concerned keenness, sharpness and cunning (OED cute, adj: 1).[23] Juliet imagines the night cutting her lover out in 'little stars', a project that is as much miniaturizing as monumentalizing.

Juliet's imaginative work with fabric runs through the monologue as a whole. She introduces night as a 'close curtain' and then as a 'black mantle', whose welcome darkness will enhance the haptic pleasures of erotic exploration, before picturing Romeo as 'thou day in night' (3.2.17) who will 'lie upon the wings of night / Whiter than new snow upon a raven's back' (3.2.18–19). These fabric images are tactile as well as visual, communicating the thermal glow cast by lovers who 'can see to do their amorous rites / By their own beauties' (3.2.8–9) along with the softness and shelter afforded by the heavy bedclothes (coverlet, canopy, curtains) that made the Renaissance bed into a room within a room. Juliet's invocation to night ends with a scene of dress-up:

> So tedious is this day
> As is the night before some festival
> To an impatient child that hath new robes
> And may not wear them. (3.2.28–31)

Juliet wants to put on Romeo as she would don fresh new party clothes, not a gown so much as a wrap, a velvet surround for two; note the strikingly soft imagery here and throughout. The reference to holiday brings us back to Brooke's original Christmas setting and its Nativity star, while the image of Juliet as an 'impatient child' exaggerates her youth in the passage's most marked realization of a cute aesthetic. Her erotic imagery favours the entwining embrace and the languid lull over the thrust and the parry; the irony, of course, is that unbeknownst to Juliet, Romeo has already chosen sword play over 'sweet Juliet', whose beauty has made him 'effeminate / And ... softened valour's steel' (3.1.115–17).

Belonging to this fabric flow, the stellification trope tenderly buttons the speech's manifold pleats to interior design and festival costuming. Compare, for example, the appliqué projects of Bess of Hardwick, which feature 'cloth of gold facades ... inset with panels of deep blue velvet embroidered with gold twist and tiny spangles'.[24] These hangings operate the same set of affordances tapped by Romeo when he says that Juliet seems to hang 'upon the cheek of night / As a rich jewel in an Ethiop's ear' (1.5.44–5). In both cases, the contrast is not only between light and dark, but between gloss and matte; compare Sidney's image of stars that 'spangle the black weeds of night' in *Astrophil and Stella*.[25] Closer in subject matter, and with related light effects, is this inlaid panel illustrating the story of Pyramus and Thisbe, which uses the black Lydian stone to set off glimmering inlays of mother-of-pearl, marble and ivory (Illustration 18). The sky hosts a floral swag in the place of stars, highlighting the decorative character of the panel and diminishing the story's tragic impact.[26] At 81 x 68 centimetres, this intimate piece invites tactile as well as visual exploration and celebrates its own crafty cut-work with semi-precious materials.

Juliet's Romeo cut-outs may also carry a whiff of Christmas cookie and gingerbread boy; note that marzipan is on the menu for the Capulet ball. Many holiday sweets began their lives as votive offerings, gifts dedicated to a saint or deity in fulfilment of

---

[22] Unhae Langis, 'Love and death: *Discordia Concors* in *Romeo and Juliet*', MS p. 6, citing D. P. Walker, 'The astral body in Renaissance medicine', *Journal of the Warburg and Courtauld Institutes* 21.1–2 (1958), 121–2.
[23] See Ngai, *Our Aesethetic Categories*, p. 87, on the etymology of 'cute' and Bruce R. Smith, *Shakespeare | Cut: Rethinking Cutwork in an Age of Distraction* (Oxford, 2016), on a range of meanings and uses that accrue to the cut in Shakespearean drama.
[24] Santina M. Levey, *The Embroideries at Hardwick Hall: A Catalogue* (London, 2008), p. 134.
[25] Astrophil and Stella, in *Sir Philip Sidney: Selected Poems*, ed. Kathrine Duncan-Jones (Oxford, 1973), Sonnet 26, l. 6.
[26] The exchange of stars for flowers belongs to the courtly entertainment tradition, such as Jonson's Chloris/Flora masque, *Chloridia*, which ended with 'the stellification of the earth with flowers to make it a second heaven' (Douglas Brooks-Davies, *The Mercurian Monarch: Magical Politics from Spenser to Pope* (Manchester, 1983), p. 100).

18. Pyramus and Thisbe, mother of pearl and marble inlaid into Lydian stone, Dirck van Rijswijck, Amsterdam, 1659, Rijksmuseum. Public domain (www.rijksmuseum.nl/en/collection/BK-16468).

a vow and as an act of thanksgiving.[27] Whereas sacrifice involves offering up a human or animal victim who will die in the process of purifying or redeeming a community, votive offerings are tokens brought to a temple or church not for slaughter but for display and deposit (artwork, altars, vases, furniture) or immediate use (flowers,

[27] My thanks to Viola Timm for her work on votives and ex votos in the context of medical humanities. See her 'Religious culture and health promotion: Care, practice, object', *Revista Brasileira em Promoção da Saúde* 28 (2015), 149–50. She defines votive practices as 'the linguistic performative act of ontologization supporting existence ... care as in Arendt's caritas, and the organization of the future', p. 150.

candles, oil, cakes). A sacrificed animal might be reproduced as a model, picture or baked good, while perishable offerings such as fruits or biscuits might be duplicated as charming figurines. At periods of transition, children might dedicate their playthings to the temple, and often it is difficult to distinguish a toy from a trophy.[28] These diminutive offerings contribute to a 'cute classicism' gathered up in the vortices of gratitude and healing. The votive offering is neither sacrifice nor fetish; it is a gift of love, an expression of thanks and a token of healing and repair. If a narrative of sacrifice drives the movement of *Romeo and Juliet* as a whole, a more votive kind of offering comes into play in this passage, with its festive leftovers and spirit of affirmation. The cults around the lovers in present-day Verona partake in votive practices, such as the sticky notes and love padlocks that visitors leave near the gold statue of Juliet or the letters left at her tomb and answered by a team of votaries.[29]

Juliet's stellification fantasy is at once sex game, light show, velvet canopy and banqueting stuff, a star-spangled banner that transforms radical bodily dispersal into a new coherence that promises duration. The stellified Romeo functions like one of D. W. Winnicott's transitional objects, the teddy bears and security blankets that install a prehistory of art into the 'holding environment' or 'potential space' of play.[30] In Viola Timm's compelling use of Winnicott in our Cute Shakespeare project, transitional objects help constellate rich internal spaces for creative and empathic commemoration, curatorial zones open to receiving gifts from outside: the kind of imaginative work that Juliet ventures in the poetics of her speech and the forms of craft and scenography implied by her interior designs. To cut Romeo into little stars is to translate the supine lover laid out *on* the bed into himself a kind of bedding, a soft canopy or sheltering heavens of desire billowing into memory through the work of cutting and appliqué. Read through Winnicott, this work becomes a gesture of care – care for the other, but also for the world – rather than an act of destruction. Transitional objects institute zones of intimacy but also tools for separation: it is Romeo who is stellified, not the two lovers together, and Juliet is symbolizing the separation between them implied by their mutual acknowledgement.[31]

Ngai writes of 'the apparent ability of the [cute] object to withstand the violence that its very passivity seems to solicit'.[32] Juliet's imagined dismemberment of her lover exults and preserves him in the other space of art: as Hugh Grady argues, love is 'defeated by power and patriarchy, but triumphant in a precisely aesthetic, utopian sphere', and he suggests that these lines in particular perform an 'aesthetic embedding and revaluation' that 'charms us with its baroque union of opposites'.[33] Grady's characterization of the passage as 'charming' moves us towards the minor aesthetics of cuteness, while the word 'embedding' suggests the softscape in which I am hanging Juliet's little stars. Like the glove that re-anchors Romeo's own astral flights in the touch of Juliet's cheek (2.2. 24–5), the immortality promised in Juliet's votive cutwork studs imperial stellification programmes with the 'small things ... dog and cat and flowerpot' that Arendt disparages as a bourgeois weakness.[34] This velvet surround of intimate pleasures wrapped within gently handled losses yields

---

[28] William Henry Denham Rouse, *Greek Votive Offerings: An Essay in the History of Greek Religion* (London, 1902), pp. 18, 250, 70.
[29] Bassi, 'The names of the rose', pp. 195–6.
[30] Bonnie Honig has linked Winnicott's transitional object to forms of democratic resilience; see, for example, her 'The politics of public things: Neoliberalism and the routine of privatization', *No Foundations: An Interdisciplinary Journal of Law and Justice* 10 (2013), 66–83. See also Bonnie Honig, 'What kind of a thing is land? Hannah Arendt's object relations, or: The Jewish unconscious of Arendt's most "Greek" text', *Political Theory* 44 (2016), 307–36; and Bonnie Honig, *Public Things: Democracy in Disrepair* (New York, 2017).
[31] Paul A. Kottman, 'Defying the stars: Tragic love as the struggle for freedom in *Romeo and Juliet*', *Shakespeare Quarterly* 63 (2012), 1–38.
[32] Ngai, *Our Aesethetic Categories*, p. 89.
[33] Hugh Grady, *Impure Aesthetics* (Cambridge, 2011), pp. 206, 217–18.
[34] See Arendt, *The Human Condition*, p. 52; and reparative commentary by Ngai, *Our Aesthetic Categories*, p. 69, and Honig, *Public Things*, p. 68.

'the sweetness — the wordless, imageless utopia' that Adorno attributed to *Romeo and Juliet*.[35]

What, then, would a cute classicism look like, and what forms of attention and response might it cultivate? In cute classicism, the decorative arts and Warburg's accessories in motion wrap the harder practices of monumental museology in their mobile drift, drape and swag, encouraging a hermeneutics of entanglement and mutual embrace. The devotional motives of cute classicism are votive rather than sacrificial, preferring figurines, sweets and hair to the binding, bloodletting and scapegoating of tragic narrative. Cute classicism's miniaturizing metaphors (boy as glove, bird, star, frock, confection) support an eroticism of part objects, haptic play and transitional toys. Finally, cute classicism supplements the wonder of the late plays with an aesthetics of tenderness. Tenderness implies extreme youth, vulnerability and softness (2.0.4), and it solicits attention, affection, attachment and concern (1.5.95; 3.1.70). 'Is love a tender thing?', Romeo asks, and then answers, 'It is too rough, / Too rude, too boisterous, and it pricks like thorn' (1.4.25–6), a response that solicits the very comportment of care he seems to deny.[36] Tenderness involves sensing vulnerability, acknowledging separation and embracing loss even while practising the intimate mergings of touch. Juliet's cut-out stars are 'tender things', trembling, twinkling images of pleasure given in the receiving and already remembered in the making, inviting us as readers to lay down fresh paths among vernacular knowledges, festive practices, literary texts and theatrical-technical regimes in order to heighten and tune our capacities for tenderness.

How do you stage stellification? In Barry Kosky's 2016 production of Jean-Philippe Rameau's *Castor and Pollux* at the Kömische Oper in Berlin, two shimmering columns of glitter channelled the stellification of the brothers. Specks of gold fell from above like snow and collected in piles on the stage while the surviving (and abandoned) wife/sister, Télaire, circled miserably around the shimmering memories of her raptured beloveds. Like the Orpheus myth that *Castor and Pollux* shares with *Romeo and Juliet*, Rameau's opera traces a loop between *katabasis* (descent to the underworld) and apotheosis (memorialization as poetry and constellation); in Kosky's staging, Télaire is an earthbound Eurydice, doomed not to a second death but to bereft survival, a casualty of the classical memorialization project in both its downward dip and its upward arc. There is nothing cute about Kosky's elemental production, which heaped a huge burial mound of earth at the centre of the stage to depict the underworld, but the final tunnels of glitter recall children's crafts and Christmas snow globes, and in this share something with Juliet's 'little stars'. Juliet is Castor to Romeo's Pollux but she is also Eurydice to his Orpheus, as he misreads her vital signs in the crypt and precipitously kills himself.

Stellification also beckons in less literal forms; for example, in the ode to Griffith Observatory and classic Hollywood film in Damien Chazelle's 2016 *La La Land* and in the intergalactic avowal of love and loss in Denis Villeneuve's 2016 *Arrival*. *La La Land* is closer in spirit to early Shakespeare and *Arrival* to late Shakespeare; both films use visions of the cosmos to achieve endings that are in no simple sense happy yet cannot be called tragic, either: in both films, lovers part and, in *Arrival*, a child dies, yet their protagonists approach immortality by honouring persons, times and time through the self-conscious handling of art (*La La Land*) and language (*Arrival*). Although their moods and methods belong to different universes, both the late romances and *Romeo and Juliet* insistently move beyond comedy and tragedy into a mode that is best called dramatic poetry. In these experimental works, genre lays out a zone in which the unknown can be encountered within the bounds of the known; ultimately, the rules and expectations of received forms cannot exhaust the achievements of plays that test so many human

---

[35] Adorno, cited by Grady, *Impure Aesthetics*, p. 206.
[36] Other compositions of exemplary tenderness in the play include the scene of weaning recounted by the Nurse and the sonnet duet, which includes Romeo's promise to smooth the rough touch of his hands with 'a tender kiss' (1.5.95).

emotions, virtuous capacities, developmental stages and environmental constraints in the ever-reconstellating field of their shifting relations. As Paul Kottman argues in his counter-generic defence of Shakespeare, 'formal rules for storytelling are no help for a body of drama . . . that has to solve for itself, again and again with each new play and performance, what a drama *is* and what it might become'.[37] As she gallops apace into the contracting horizon of her future, Juliet simultaneously enacts and memorializes her life story in all of its tender precocity, donating her Instragram gallery of quick bright things to a minor classicism that continues to gleam and twinkle in the fluid firmaments of film, dance and dream.[38]

---

[37] Paul A. Kottman, 'Why think about Shakespearean tragedy today?', in *Cambridge Companion to Shakespearean Tragedy*, ed. Claire McEachern (Cambridge, 2013), p. 245.

[38] On Juliet's 'quick bright things' as protests against the stillness of monumentalization, see William N. West, 'Romeo and Juliet's understudies', in *Romeo and Juliet: A Critical Reader*, ed. Reinhard Lupton, p. 135. On Instagram aesthetics, see Lev Manovich, 'Designing and living instragram photography: Themes, feeds, sequences, branding, faces, bodies', *Manovich*, http://manovich.net/index.php/projects/instagram-and-contemporary-image (accessed 1 January 2017).

THE WILL OF CAESAR: CHOICE-MAKING, THE DEATH OF THE ROMAN REPUBLIC AND THE DEVELOPMENT OF SHAKESPEAREAN CHARACTER

KATHARINE EISAMAN MAUS

There is a critical consensus that at the very end of the sixteenth century Shakespeare suddenly improves. In *A Year in the Life of Shakespeare: 1599*, James Shapiro states the commonplace succinctly: 'at age thirty-five, Shakespeare went from being an exceptionally talented writer to being one of the greatest who ever lived'.[1] Of course the nature of this leap of genius is a matter of debate. Most agree, however, that Shakespeare seems to develop an apparently more profound conception of human nature in the plays he writes in these years and the years following. They also agree that *Julius Caesar*, written immediately after *Henry V*, is the play in which this new conception emerges: a play in which, as Andrew Hadfield claims, 'the main characters appear more "rounded" and have greater psychological depth than those in Shakespeare's earlier plays'.[2]

So what, exactly, is new in *Julius Caesar*? The play shares *Henry V*'s concerns with empire-building, with regime change and with the staging of spectacular events from history. Yet, of course, one difference is the Roman setting, different in many respects from the medieval England that preoccupied Shakespeare in his previous nine political plays. Andrew Hadfield has elucidated Shakespeare's engagement with the political legacy of Rome in the revival of republican thought in the late sixteenth century. Shakespeare was also likely aware of Rome's long legal shadow: Roman law provided the basis of the 'civil law' used on much of the Continent, and the relationship between the civil law and English common law was an important topic of debate in intellectual circles at the turn of the seventeenth century.[3] In this article, I shall argue that a new character-conception in *Julius Caesar* is related to, and perhaps inspired by, the move from English to Roman historical material, and by the way Shakespeare imagines the relationship between a character's inner life and the options provided by his political and legal environment. The ancient Roman setting, I believe, encouraged Shakespeare to attend to processes of choice-making and to find innovative means for representing those processes onstage.

I would like to thank Rachel Holmes and Douglas Clark for their comments on this article, as well as audience members at Johns Hopkins University, Washington and Lee University, the World Shakespeare Conference 2016 and the Shakespeare Association of America 2017.

[1] James Shapiro, *A Year in the Life of Shakespeare: 1599* (New York, 2005), p. xxii.

[2] Andrew Hadfield, *Shakespeare and Republicanism* (Cambridge, 2005), p. 161.

[3] Bradin Cormack draws attention to Shakespeare's evident awareness of these competing legal systems in *A Power to Do Justice: Jurisdiction, English Literature, and the Rise of Common Law 1509–1625* (Chicago, 2007).

I

In a pivotal moment in *Julius Caesar*, Mark Antony displays and reads from Caesar's last will and testament: it is the climax of his bravura eulogy and the juncture at which the Roman populace decisively turns against Caesar's assassins. The speech itself – indeed, the entire scene in which Brutus and Antony successively address the citizenry – is a Shakespearean invention which develops hints from his sources, Plutarch's *Lives* of Antony, Caesar and Brutus.[4] Interestingly, Shakespeare's re-imagining of the historical events emphasizes a way in which Rome would seem especially alien to Shakespeare's original audience, since one important difference between medieval/early modern England and republican Rome was their systems of inheritance. Inheritance protocols may seem dry legal matters, yet they instantiate the way a person and his affiliations are defined physically and temporally, the way a person's scope of power may be imagined and legally enforced. In other words, Antony's revelation of Caesar's will is not merely a brilliant piece of political incitement. It also reflects different possibilities for the self, its agency and its freedom than were available in the English history plays Shakespeare had written in the late 1590s.

In any political system, and in any system of property-holding, the death of a ruler or owner creates a crisis. Who will assume the power of the deceased over the resources he used to control? An orderly transfer from the dead to the living requires rules. Yet those rules vary widely. In some societies, the succession of property and status is prescribed by law or custom, so that the wishes of the property-holder have little or nothing to do with the destination of his wealth after his death. Sometimes the decision is up to the person who dies, the 'testator', who is empowered to leave an oral or written will specifying who might inherit and under what conditions. In such cases, the agency of the property-holder survives his physical body, his whims or plans binding his survivors in the future.

How do Roman methods for determining inheritance, succession and legacy differ from English methods? Under medieval and early modern English common law, wealth is divided into two kinds: 'moveables' or chattel property on the one hand, and on the other hand 'real' property, that is, land, including the things firmly attached to it like houses and barns. Chattels could be disposed of by will but the succession to land wealth, upon which most political power rested in the medieval and early modern period, is much more tightly specified. While, by the late sixteenth century, it is possible to dispose of some land by will or sale, in practice much of the land held by elite families is held in 'tail', with the succession predetermined to 'heirs of the body' or 'heirs male of the body' in a specified order. In the paradigmatic case of an elite family, the eldest legitimate biological son succeeds to all or almost all of his father's landed property and to his father's titles of honour upon his father's death. This system is meant to ensure the continuing power of a noble family by keeping its wealth intact; it also heads off potential conflict among the survivors by indicating, as unambiguously as possible and as far as possible in advance, the 'heir apparent', an individual who will rightfully inherit both the land and the title that accompanies it. This individual is supposed to be the person who most closely resembles the current property-holder, imagined as his copy in the next generation. The heir, in the evocative phrase of early modern lawyers, 'stands in the shoes of his ancestor', assuming his father's territories upon his father's death and taking over his father's social place.

The English entail system strongly prefers to designate the heir by purely structural means. Except in the most extreme cases – for instance, when the heir apparent is insane or an outlaw – the choices and character traits of either the father or the son have no effect over the succession of the

---

[4] Plutarch claims that Antony incited a riot by lamenting his dead friend in a 'pathetic' and 'commiserating' speech and he also notes that Caesar left bequests to the people in his will. But in none of the three source lives does he have Antony displaying and reading from the will over Caesar's dead body, in response to Brutus's speech defending the assassination.

property. The eldest son inherits not because the father loves him best nor because he exhibits any particular merit but simply because of his sex and birth order. In the *Henry IV* plays, King Henry IV is deeply apprehensive about the suitability of his heir apparent, wishing, for instance, that it could be proved that the fairies had switched his eldest son at birth with the seemingly more capable Hotspur. But he cannot dislodge Prince Hal from his position as heir apparent; in fact, the Prince's deliberate obscuring of his own merits is an effective strategy for the Prince only because both father and son are aware of the son's impregnable position. The mightiest man in England – the one person who might arguably be above the law – seems powerless to change the order of succession.

There were plenty of problems with the English way of doing things and the nine history plays Shakespeare writes between 1592 and 1599, as well as several of his comedies, display them pretty comprehensively. In an age of high mortality, the statistically most common problem is the failure of the line: what happens when a landholder had no surviving sons or no surviving children at all? What happens when the father dies too soon, when his heir is too young to take his place, or lingers too long, so that his son is biologically adult but unable to assume his destined social position? If all, or the majority of, the property devolves upon the eldest legitimate son, how are widows, younger sons, daughters and bastards to be provided for? What happens if the eldest son is not biologically the child of his mother's husband but the offspring of an adulterous interloper? Rules develop to cope with all these permutations and in addition there evolve ways to evade the rules when occasion warrants, so that the custom of primogeniture is not quite so ironclad in practice as it might seem from a reading of the law books. But interestingly, the most pressing difficulty in Shakespeare's history plays is not those with which the lawyers preoccupy themselves. The most obvious problem of inheritance in this series of plays is that despite the legal assumption that the heir is his father's replica (a fantasy also elaborated in Shakespeare's procreation sonnets), very often the son is nothing like his parent.[5] While King Richard III's brothers were 'two mirrors' of their father's 'princely semblance', the deformed Richard is, according to his mother, a 'false glass' (2.2.51–3).[6] The son of the warlike and prudent Black Prince and the grandson of the victorious King Edward III is the feckless King Richard II. Even the peaceful succession of power from Henry IV to Henry V highlights the differences between father and son. Over the course of the *Henry IV* plays, the heir apparent's excellence is represented as a highly idiosyncratic swerving from the paternal pattern. King Henry V's combining of self-interest with care for his subjects, and of performative skill with moral obliviousness, is a matter of unique personality traits and unique youthful opportunities, such as access to Falstaff. These circumstances are not likely to be repeated in the next generation. And they are not. In the final scene of *Henry V*, Henry proposes to Katherine: 'Shall not thou and I, between Saint Denis and Saint George, compound a boy, half-French half-English, that shall go to Constantinople and take the Turk by the beard?' (5.2.204–7). Henry envisions a crusading Plantagenet offspring who will amplify his own ambitions for conquest and finally bring to fruition his own father's most cherished, and unrealized, dream. But Henry VI has his own inexplicably different personality – gullible, pious and conflict-averse.

Roman inheritance law offers an entirely different set of opportunities and pitfalls. While social class in the Roman Republic is determined by property entitlements, office is not. In other words, political power is not enmeshed with landholding as it is for an English peer, and titles of honour and offices are not handed down from one generation to the next.

---

[5] For more extended discussions of this issue, see Katharine Eisaman Maus, *Being and Having in Shakespeare* (Oxford, 2012), pp. 40–56 and Michelle Dowd, *The Dynamics of Inheritance on the Shakespearean Stage* (Cambridge, 2015), pp. 117–27.
[6] Shakespeare quotations are taken from *William Shakespeare: The Complete Works*, eds. Stanley Wells, *et al.*, 2nd edn (Oxford, 2005).

Roman law makes a clear distinction between *imperium*, the power of the magistrate, and *dominium*, power over one's property and domestic establishment: a distinction that the English system tends to elide. Partly because of this difference, there is no system of entailed property in Roman law as there is in medieval and early modern England, nor any assumption of primogeniture. In other words, there is no 'heir apparent' whose right to the estate is virtually unassailable. It is routine, in fact, for prosperous individuals to encourage the dutiful behaviour of potential heirs by keeping them guessing as to the destination of their wealth after their death. If a man dies intestate, his wealth is divided equally among his children irrespective of birth order or sex. However, most property-holders dispose of their wealth by means of a written will. And the law gives them a very free hand in devising that document. As Richard Saller writes: 'The Roman law of succession provided testators with a remarkable array of options in distributing their property, unstructured by conventions of primogeniture or ultimogeniture.'[7] Thus the fate of Roman property is decided by the property-holder, rather than determined by his kinship relationship to his heirs or by his children's sex and birth order.

Of course, just because Romans can leave their wealth to anyone does not mean they did; in the majority of cases the heirs are the children and dependents of the paterfamilias. Wealthy and prominent Romans, however, concerned to secure their public reputation into the future, like to leave legacies and public bequests outside the immediate family circle.[8] Julius Caesar's will is an especially splendid instance. In his funeral speech, Mark Antony reads his stipulations:

> To every Roman citizen he gives –
> To every several man – seventy-five drachmas.
> ...
> Moreover he hath left you all his walks,
> His private arbours, and new-planted orchards,
> On this side Tiber. He hath left them you,
> And to your heirs forever – common pleasures
> To walk abroad and recreate yourselves.
> Here was a Caesar. When comes such another?
>
> (3.2.236–45)

Because the terms of a Roman will are almost entirely unconstrained by law, this kind of posthumous bounty becomes an expression of, a literal *testament* to, the unique character of the property holder: 'Here was a Caesar! When comes such another?'

To a sceptic such as Brutus or Cassius, Caesar's propensity to shower goods on the people who support him simply encourages their venal eagerness to trade ancient political freedoms for material comforts. And yet the terms of the will suggest a sophisticated conception of the *res publica*. Caesar attends to the good of the Roman citizenry both as individuals – he leaves 'every several man' a bequest of seventy-five drachmas – and as a community, which acquires his 'walks, / His private arbours, and new-planted orchards' in perpetuity, as 'common pleasures / To walk abroad and recreate yourselves'. Caesar's will magnifies his agency in two ways. First, because his bequests are choices, they reveal the character of the will-maker (spectacularly generous, committed to the public good) in ways that guarantee that he will be fondly remembered by his beneficiaries. Second, his will constrains what will happen to his property in the future, beyond the death of the choice-maker. This posthumous constraint may operate in a different direction from the one the testator had originally envisioned – in the event, the effect of Caesar's choices is not to establish a public park 'on this side Tiber' but to start a civil war. Yet the power of the testator manifests itself nonetheless. The will is a version of the ghost that will appear later in the play in Brutus's tent at Philippi, an obscure but potent force from beyond the grave.

In Caesar's case, the dispersion of his property is especially salient because he has no legitimate children, a deficiency highlighted in 1.2, in which he asks Antony to touch Calphurnia in the

---

[7] Richard Saller, *Patriarchy, Property, and Death in the Roman Family* (Cambridge, 1994), pp. 161–2.

[8] This form of magnanimous ostentation was so popular that in the reign of Augustus the Lex Fulcidia eventually required that a man with living dependents leave them at least a quarter of his property.

Lupercalian footrace: 'for our elders say / The barren, touchèd in this holy chase, / Shake off their sterile curse' (9–11). In this situation, too, Roman practice diverges from English custom. Both societies endure high mortality and frequent dynastic failure. In England, the solution is to resort to ever more distant relatives in a carefully specified order. In Rome, the solution is adoption, a means of creating kinfolk not recognized by English law until 1926. Because Roman adoption is explicitly designed as an inheritance strategy, it has a different social function from nowadays. As Hugh Lindsay explains:

> Today in the Western world, adoption is seen as a means for couples who are unable to have children to experience parenthood ... people with a strong commitment to raising children will be able to take over children whose situation is in some way substantially impaired. In Roman society, by contrast, adoption was an absolutely routine way of ensuring the succession of property and the continuation of a family line.[9]

Because the rationale for adoption is the survival of the family, an entity defined in legal rather than in blood terms, Roman women cannot adopt; although women can own property, only the paterfamilias is imagined to have this kind of legal interest in perpetuating a dynasty. For that reason, too, adults are more frequently adopted than are fragile children and they are often adopted not during the testator's lifetime but in the testator's will. In essence, then, the testator insists that, as a condition of receiving his property, the heir continue the testator's family, taking his name and promising to fulfil his religious obligations to the testator's ancestors rather than to his own blood relatives.

If a Roman property-holder has much greater freedom to designate his heir or heirs than an English property-holder does, so too do the potential recipients of the estate. In practical terms, of course, the efficacy of the progenitor's 'last will', which seems to propel his agency beyond death, is dependent upon the good faith of his executors. In *Julius Caesar*, only two scenes after his moving revelation of Caesar's extraordinary generosity, Mark Antony is planning to circumvent his provisions: 'Fetch the will hither, and we shall determine / How to cut off some charge in legacies' (4.1.8–9). Yet even in less dodgy circumstances, inheritance is not an automatic process. Since the heir inherits the testator's debts as well as his goods, and because, in the case of adoption, he needs to relinquish his original family affiliation in order to take up the new one, it is sometimes not in his interest to accept the inheritance. (Although he does not dramatize this episode in *Julius Caesar*, Shakespeare may have known from reading Suetonius that Octavius's mother advised him not to permit himself to be adopted as principal heir by Julius Caesar's will, on the grounds that he would thus be making himself vulnerable to Julius's enemies.) If the Roman law provides almost unlimited options to testators in determining who will inherit their property, it also allows heirs the choice of electing or repudiating their own ancestry. Inheritance is a choice on both the giving and the receiving end.

II

The Roman system of making one's own heirs and ancestors, in other words, emphasizes the liberty of the participants to an extent that seems extraordinary in comparison to the more constrained English system. Moreover, it is only one of a suite of ethically approved options available to the elite Roman male that were unavailable to his Christian counterpart in the Middle Ages or at the end of the sixteenth century. He could decide to divorce his wife. He could elect to end his own life, committing suicide with honour. In *Julius Caesar*, as in classical political and legal theory generally, the 'liberty' of the male Roman citizen in such matters is sharply distinguished from the situation of the slave, who is subject to the bidding of another, and likewise from the situation of the woman, who is imagined to be compliant by

---

[9] Hugh Lindsay, *Adoption in the Roman World* (Cambridge, 2009), p. 1.

nature. The exercise of this liberty is what makes Romans Roman, and men men. The more elite, the more 'honourable' the man, the more aggressively he asserts this freedom to choose. Asked why he refuses to come to the Senate House, Caesar declares imperiously, 'the cause is in my will; I will not come' (2.2.71).

The Roman Republic emphasizes the scope of choice in public affairs as well as domestic ones: its officials are elected to their positions, not installed in them by God and ancestry. In Roman political theory, revived by 'neo-Roman' theorists of liberty in the Italian Renaissance and circulating widely in England in the late sixteenth century, personal and political liberty are typically assumed to be tightly bound together, so that assaulting the one is tantamount to assaulting the other. This assumption is in fact questionable, since many Roman liberties (of testation, of divorce, of suicide) survive the death of the Republic and are even enhanced under the emperors. Yet in order to understand the fear with which the conspirators regard the apparently debile and amiable Caesar, we need to realize that they assume that an assault on one kind of freedom is automatically an assault on all of them. That is because although the proud expression of wilfulness seems to be the proper emanation of the noble Roman, one man's will, if entirely unfettered, threatens to swamp everyone else's. The danger presented by Julius Caesar, according to republicans such as Cassius, is that his self-assertion will reduce everybody else to the status of bondmen: Cassius maintains that the potential for domination, even if it is not exercised, is the equivalent of enslavement. This is one of the features of republican thought that would be controversially revived in the early modern period: Quentin Skinner remarks that, for the mid-seventeenth-century republican political theorist Algernon Sidney, 'it is the mere possibility of your being subjected with impunity to arbitrary coercion, not the fact of your being coerced, that takes away your liberty and reduces you to the condition of a slave'.[10] Brutus shares this way of thinking, acknowledging that Caesar has not yet actually abused his power, but he is worried that he might abuse it in the future:

Then lest he may, prevent. And since the quarrel
Will bear no colour for the thing he is,
Fashion it thus: that what he is, augmented,
Would run to these and these extremities;
And therefore think him as a serpent's egg
Which, hatched, would as his kind grow mischievous,
And kill him in the shell.   (2.1.28–34)

The challenge for Roman Republican society, then, as Shakespeare presents it in *Julius Caesar*, is the policing of choice, the keeping of each individual's treasured and vigorously asserted liberties within bounds that are perceived to be legitimate.

In classical republican theory as articulated by Cicero and others, those restraints upon choice are provided by a law that treats all citizens equally. Yet legal institutions have little purchase in Shakespeare's play. Instead, the circumscription of the individual will seems to be achieved by competition. Cassius provides an analysis that duplicates Plutarch's remarks in his *Life of Julius Caesar*:

When went there by an age since the great flood,
But [Rome] was famed with more than with one man?
When could they say till now, that talked of Rome,
That her wide walls encompassed but one man?
Now is it Rome indeed, and room enough
When there is in it but one only man.   (1.2.153–8)

Once Julius Caesar eliminates his main competitor, Pompey the Great, his ascendancy becomes dangerous, because the liberty of the republican Roman is both constrained and produced by jostling against the freedoms of others. We see how the jockeying of wills hems in those wills in a moment before the battle of Philippi between Mark Antony and Octavius:

ANTONY.   Octavius, lead your battle softly on
                    Upon the left hand of the even field.
OCTAVIUS.   Upon the right hand, I; keep thou the left.
ANTONY.   Why do you cross me in this exigent?
OCTAVIUS.   I do not cross you, but I will do so.
                                                    (5.1.16–20)

---

[10] Quentin Skinner, *Liberty Before Liberalism* (Cambridge, 1998), p. 72.

THE WILL OF CAESAR

Here Octavius picks a quarrel with Antony, meaningless on the face of it, purely in order to assert his own competing will and thus to limit the scope of Antony's.

Because *Julius Caesar* is full of such apparently pointless conflicts, Wayne Rebhorn has persuasively argued that the failure of the Roman Republic is the result of fatally destructive homosocial competition among elite men.[11] Yet it is important to recognize that the clash of wills is not merely destructive; it is a feature of the policy debates we see so often in this play, especially between Cassius and Brutus. It seems to be part and parcel of their republican inheritance: to assert their conflicting opinions and subject the matter in question to negotiation and settlement. In fact, when competition ceases and the powerful align their choices, the results can be terrifying, as in 4.1 when Antony, Octavius and Lepidus condemn hundreds of their compatriots to death without process of law, merely upon personal whim. The play presents the excesses of tyranny as merely Roman liberties writ too large, because too uncontested. Thus the assassination of Caesar might be seen – in fact, is described by Brutus both in his discussions with his fellow-conspirators and in his address to the plebeians – as a reassertion of competing wills, a way of rebalancing the *res publica* and preventing tyranny by eliminating Caesar's outsize self-assertion.

III

So Roman Republican law and custom, in its emphasis upon 'liberty', draws attention to choice-making in both its liberatory and its dangerous aspects. What does all this have to do with Shakespeare's methods of characterization in *Julius Caesar* and with what is perceived to be his great leap forward into psychological realism and depth? Stephen Greenblatt writes of a breakthrough he sees in this play: of Brutus's great soliloquy in 2.1 he writes 'it has something new: the unmistakable marks of actual thinking . . . his words have the peculiar shorthand of the brain at work'.[12]

More precisely, I would argue, Brutus's soliloquy shows its speaker in the process of making what I would call a 'constitutive decision': the kind of choice that will not only determine his immediate course of action but also determine the kind of person he will be able to become in the future and the kind of world he will find himself living in. In many of the earlier plays Shakespeare elides the actual process of mulling over such a course of action, merely displaying its effects. For instance, in *Richard II*, an earlier play about usurpation and regicide, Richard's momentous decision to exile Bolingbroke happens in an off-stage consultation with his peers; even more saliently, Bolingbroke's later decision to seize the throne from Richard is entirely occluded. The future Henry IV arrives in England claiming to come '[b]ut for his own' (*Richard II* 2.3.148), the duchy of Lancaster confiscated by Richard after the death of John of Gaunt, Bolingbroke's father. Yet Bolingbroke quickly monopolizes the support of lords and commons and in 4.1 announces that 'In God's name I'll ascend the regal throne' (104). Shakespeare at no point shows us Bolingbroke in the process of deciding upon his course of action. Whether Bolingbroke initially feigns more limited aims in order to gather supporters around him, whether his advisors need to persuade him to accept the crown, or whether he is merely carried along by events, remains unclear. Another clarifying comparison is with *The Merchant of Venice*, written after *Richard II* but two or three years prior to *Julius Caesar*. Here three suitors are asked to pick from one of three caskets – gold, silver and lead – and each one is afforded a monologue explaining his rationale for his selection. But the casket test does not elicit a 'constitutive decision' of the kind Brutus is making in 2.1 of *Julius Caesar*. The casket test reveals who the suitors already are, not what they might potentially become. Each

---

[11] Wayne Rebhorn, 'The crisis of the aristocracy in Julius Caesar', *Renaissance Quarterly* 43 (1990), 75–111.
[12] Stephen Greenblatt, *Will in the World* (New York, 2004), p. 301.

suitor, because of the traits he possesses and the value system to which he adheres, could not have selected otherwise. The casket test is a test of worthiness, not an invitation to personal development.

By contrast, in *Julius Caesar*, Brutus begins his soliloquy uncertain about how he will act and, in the process of brooding, convinces himself to ally himself with the conspirators in their plot to murder Caesar. Both he and we are aware that he is making a profoundly effectual decision: it could go either way but, whatever way it goes, there will be profound consequences for himself and for Rome. In this scene, then, Shakespeare focuses upon the gap between beginning to form an intention and the action that will eventually issue from that intention. He slows down and zeroes in on the process of choice-making. At the end of the soliloquy, Brutus comments upon the opening of this gap:

> Between the acting of a dreadful thing
> And the first motion, all the interim is
> Like a phantasma or a hideous dream.
> The genius and the mortal instruments
> Are then in counsel, and the state of man,
> Like to a little kingdom, suffers then
> The nature of an insurrection. (2.1.63–9)

Brutus's remarks make explicit the analogy between psychological upheaval and political turmoil, tying his inward turbulence to the civil war that will follow, and follow from it. But Shakespeare is not just interested in the political consequences of Brutus's decision; he is fascinated by what Brutus calls 'the interim' itself, the period that intervenes between the 'first motion' and the 'acting of a dreadful thing'.

This decision-making interim is, on the face of it, hardly an obvious subject for dramatic representation, since it is generally a silent and internal process. Shakespeare makes it visible and vivid by torqueing the convention of the soliloquy, which as James Hirsch has plausibly argued is imagined in early modern drama as a form of articulate self-address rather than a direct representation of inner thoughts.[13] In doing so Shakespeare has a partial anticipation in Christopher Marlowe's *Doctor Faustus*, another play that stages the mullings-over of a solitary protagonist. But part of Marlowe's point is that Faustus himself elides the moment of choice, pretending to himself that the decision has already been made and could not be made otherwise, and therefore jumping into sin and self-deception so recklessly that he horrifies even his tempting devil, Mephistophilis: 'O, Faustus, leave these frivolous demands, / Which strikes a terror to my fainting soul!'[14]

The closest analogue to what Shakespeare is doing with Brutus's soliloquy in 2.1 is not, in fact, a monologue from an earlier play by him or by another dramatist. The nearest precedent is in Shakespeare's own 1594 non-dramatic poem, *The Rape of Lucrece*. Though the story of the rape of Lucrece and its aftermath is full of violence, when Shakespeare writes his poem he sequesters most of the plot in a prefatory prose 'Argument' and in a couple of tumultuous stanzas. The rest of this long poem is devoted to the ruminations of first Tarquin, then Lucrece, as they slowly and hesitantly puzzle out to themselves a course of action. Their choices, like Brutus's, could go either way and, like Brutus's, their choices have profound personal and political consequences. It is not coincidental, I think, that Shakespeare associates these constitutive choices with the Roman Republic: with its birth in *Lucrece* and with its death in *Julius Caesar*. For the kind of soliloquizing in which his characters engage is an internal version of deliberative rhetoric, the free speaking for and against a course of action typical of participation in a democracy or representative assembly.

---

[13] James E. Hirsch, *Shakespeare and the History of Soliloquies* (Madison, NJ, 2003). The question that preoccupies Hirsch for most of his monograph, whether the soliloquy is 'spoken' or 'thought', is not really germane to my point, which is that Shakespeare is focusing on a particular stage in the process between first impulse and eventual action. But Hirsch's analysis is useful in that it demonstrates that the soliloquy is imagined in Renaissance drama as a 'speech to the self', and therefore it is not surprising that it should have the same features as a deliberative speech addressed to an assembly.

[14] Christopher Marlowe, *Doctor Faustus*, ed. David Scott Kastan (New York, 2005), p. 66, 1.3.79–80.

Just because Shakespeare is fascinated by the mechanisms of choice, however, does not mean that he unreservedly celebrates choice-making, nor is he necessarily sanguine about the exercise of what the republicans would call 'liberty'. Tacitus, writing *A Dialogue on Oratory* under the Emperor Domitian, argues that the famous rhetorical skills of Athens and of Republican Rome reflect not the superior wit and skill of those living under those regimes but the turbulent nature of their politics:

The great and famous eloquence of old is the nursling of the licence which fools called freedom; it is the companion of sedition, the stimulant of an unruly people, a stranger to obedience and subjection, a defiant, reckless, presumptuous thing which does not show itself in a well-governed state.[15]

For Tacitus, far from being a pinnacle of human achievement, the exercise of choice and the arts of persuasion that enable those choices are merely exhausting and error-prone. Whatever his interest in the psychological complexities of choice-making, Shakespeare seems to share some of Tacitus's scepticism about its efficacy. The protagonists of both *The Rape of Lucrece* and *Julius Caesar*, after tortuous efforts at deliberation, go ahead and make terrible decisions.[16] And this proneness to error is not merely a problem when the process of deliberation is a mental struggle within a single character or when an issue is argued pro and contra before the weak and easily swayed plebeians. In *Julius Caesar*, Cassius again and again proposes a course of action – to kill Antony, to prevent him from speaking to the plebeians, to refrain from confronting Octavius and Antony at Philippi. Brutus, however, out-argues him and prevails and then, in the course of events, his proposed course of action turns out to be disastrous.

These disasters are, to some extent, traceable to Brutus's tendency to argue from principle rather than from expediency; his 'noble' refusal to attend to self-interest ultimately harms his cause. But they are also due to unforeseeable contingencies, the inevitable limitations of the evidence available to any choice-maker. Brutus understands these limitations: he cannot know for sure, for instance, that if Julius Caesar becomes king, he will prove an intolerable tyrant. 'He would be crowned. / How that might change his nature, there's the question' (2.1.12–13). Much of his soliloquy in 2.1, in which he struggles to decide whether to join the conspiracy to assassinate Caesar, is an attempt to answer that question, to make predictions. For when anyone makes a choice, he or she implicitly develops a theory about what the future might bring and about how one's own course of action might conceivably alter that state of affairs: 'O that a man might know / The end of this day's business ere it come' (5.1.123–4).

In *Julius Caesar*, the necessity and difficulty of discerning the future is captured in a pervasive fascination with omens: if one could read the omens correctly, one could presumably discover the shape of the future and use that knowledge to make better choices. Yet in *Julius Caesar*, omens never deliver on their promise. The Soothsayer is dismissed, Calphurnia's dream reinterpreted. A slave's hand burns without being consumed, a lion roams free in the Capitol, men with fire walk the streets, and yet their purport at the time is obscure: 'men may construe things after their fashion, / Clean from the purpose of the things themselves' (1.3.34–5). Only in retrospect, apparently, do such warnings become readable: their meanings perhaps obvious from the belated perspective of Shakespeare and his audience but not from the perspective of the characters. Moreover, even as omens seem to offer a way to improve choice-making, they also – insofar as they emanate from a supernatural apparently beyond human agency – undermine the centrality of that choice-making by suggesting that the real determinants of history are elsewhere, and that one's fate is

---

[15] Tacitus, *Dialogus de Oratoribus (English)*, Perseus Digital Library, Dial.16.40, http://perseus.uchicago.edu/perseus-cgi/citequery3.pl?dbname=PerseusLatinTexts&query=Tac.%20Dial.%2040.4&getid=1.

[16] For a more extended discussion of the process of decision-making in *Lucrece*, see Katharine Eisaman Maus, 'Taking tropes seriously: Language and violence in *The Rape of Lucrece*', *Shakespeare Quarterly* 37 (1986), 66–82.

ineluctable. Not only might 'liberty' produce bad decisions; it may be, in the last analysis, an illusion.

IV

This article began with a discussion of inheritance law but, as I have already indicated, matters of succession are only one domain in which Roman patricians had more scope for choice than their counterparts in medieval and early modern England. Moreover, as I have also already noted, the freedoms of Roman will-making are not as tightly bound up with republican, deliberative politics as it might initially seem: for under the emperors, although choice-making withers as a public activity, some of the liberties of the Roman citizen, including freedom of testation, survive. So why did I focus initially upon the more specific matter of testamentary freedom? One reason is that Brutus's choice-making is tied up in a conception of what it means to be the heir to a legacy of republican political engagement. Because the Roman heir must actively accept his inheritance, rather than passively receiving it, Brutus conceives his relationship to the past as a choice. It is a mantle that must be voluntarily assumed by, not simply conferred upon, the heir who will wear it. In the midst of Brutus's deliberations, his servant Lucius brings him a letter:

He opens the letter and reads
'Brutus, thou sleep'st. Awake, and see thyself.
Shall Rome, et cetera? Speak, strike, redress.' –
...
'Shall Rome, et cetera?' Thus must I piece it out:
Shall Rome stand under one man's awe? What, Rome?
My ancestors did from the streets of Rome
The Tarquin drive when he was called a king.
(2.1.46–54)

The letter is provocative and deliberately vague: Brutus must 'piece it out' with his own conjectures. Hesitating over whether to join the conspirators, he must decide not only whether Caesar is a tyrant or potential tyrant but also, if so, how he needs to understand his own political inheritance. He construes himself as the heir of his ancestor and namesake, Lucius Junius Brutus, ouster of Tarquin and founder of the republic, rather than as the friend (and Plutarch suggests, the illegitimate son) of Julius Caesar. Inheritance in other words, is not automatic, but an effortful deliberative process, a commitment to a past that implies choices about the future.

The other reason to emphasize issues of chosen succession in *Julius Caesar* is that they might help clarify the relationship between *Julius Caesar* and Shakespeare's next play, *Hamlet*. Like the Roman Republic, the Denmark of *Hamlet* is a polity in which primogeniture is evidently not the rule: upon the death of old Hamlet the monarchy falls not to his son but to his brother. The reason for this apparently anomalous state of affairs is left obscure until almost the end of the play, when we learn from Hamlet that Denmark chooses its monarchs and that Claudius '[p]opped in between th'election and my hopes' (*Hamlet* 5.2.66). Yet the remark about the king's election is only one of Hamlet's complaints about Claudius, almost an aside or an afterthought, not as Hamlet's main reason for wanting to dislodge him. Instead, in *Hamlet* Shakespeare focuses on what Brutus calls the 'little kingdom', the individual in the process of settling upon a course of action. Hamlet is famously 'a man who could not make up his mind' but, in fact, he is a man who does make up his mind – he merely spends four acts getting there. In other words, Shakespeare's interest in the choice-making process, evident especially in Brutus's soliloquy in *Julius Caesar* 2.1, expands to fill practically the whole play in *Hamlet*. And Hamlet likewise imagines this decision as a way of coming to terms with his relationship with a forbear: a relationship that is not given or conferred but must be actively chosen by the heir. But that will have to be the topic for another article.

'AS FOR THAT LIGHT HOBBY-HORSE, MY SISTER': SHAKESPEAREAN INFLUENCES AND POPULAR DISCOURSES IN *BLURT MASTER CONSTABLE*

NATÁLIA PIKLI

But stay, I see thee in the Hemisphere
Advanc'd, and made a Constellation there!
Shine forth, thou Starre of Poets, and with rage,
Or influence, chide, or cheere the drooping Stage...[1]

Ben Jonson described Shakespeare in the 1623 Folio with the early modern metaphor of planetary influence, but can we talk about such a 'vertical' and hierarchical interpretation of his influence after the scholarly findings and less cultic attitude of the twenty-first century? Recent digital research has fostered a renewed interest in authorship and consequently in the debated notion of influence or 'sources'. Bullough's positivistic idealism in charting the relationship between Shakespearean texts and their 'sources' appears, by now, outdated, and a more complicated model of 'traffic' or mutual influencing seems useful, with a strong focus on both lateral and reciprocal relations as well as on the shared cultural context of the age. The original Latin meaning of the word 'influence' ('influere': 'flow'), however, might still prove helpful in metaphorically describing the intricate ways ideas and phrases circulated in the vibrant cultural world of the late sixteenth and early seventeenth centuries.

Shakespeare was as much influenced by others as he influenced his contemporaries. In early modern England, writers' words and ideas flew into works of different statuses and genres almost without any restrictions, especially in the booming theatrical business, and this process was further complicated by the easy two-way traffic between the elite and popular cultural discourses of the time. Therefore, hard evidence for one writer or work influencing another is difficult to establish with absolute certainty and often proves inadequate in some respect. On the other hand, the complex interaction among a number of texts and authors offers a challenging testing field for examining the circulation of several clusters of ideas and images in a given age.[2]

Non-canonical plays and non-dramatic popular texts provide a challenging field for research since they are free of the cultic status of Shakespearean–Marlovian–Jonsonian works, and they may remind us of a wider cultural context

---

I would like to thank the convenors (Christy Desmet, Paola Pugliatti, Donatella Pallotti, Robert Sawyer) and participants of the seminar 'Shakespeare: Visions and Revisions' for the highly inspiring sharing of ideas regarding this topic at the Shakespeare World Congress.

[1] Ben Jonson, 'To the memory of my beloved, The Author', First Folio (1623), http://firstfolio.bodleian.ox.ac.uk/book.html, sig. A4r.

[2] Jan Assmann's theory of cultural memory also argues that cultural texts and phenomena of a given age exist in 'circulation', interpersonal communication establishing and re-producing the social identity of the group, keeping the 'symbolic worldview' of the community in constant motion. See Jan Assmann, *Religion and Memory: Ten Studies*, trans. Rodney Livingstone (Stanford, 2006).

influencing (by now) canonical texts. Several centuries of literary cults may often distort our understanding of canonical works, with layers of meaning added by centuries of criticism. Therefore, a phenomenon that was simply a part of the common cultural discourses and theatrical practices of the age may be attributed to and recognized in Shakespearean plays only (e.g. the 'bed-trick'). With this inverse effect, non-canonical texts and plays of the age are capable of illuminating aspects of canonical works hitherto less clear. On the other hand, the frequent practice of quickly crafting a good-enough play with some basic dramaturgy resulted in plays like *Blurt Master Constable* (performed by the Children of Paul's), which also informs us about the expectations of target audiences in different theatrical contexts. Such instant satisfaction of demand often called for plays that may be described by the term 'medley imitation', their authors capitalizing on the devices and dramaturgical tricks of successful plays in public playhouses, 'patching a play' with little motivational characterization or coherence of structure.[3]

In examinations of the intricate web of interrelated influences and the circulation of ideas, clusters of evocative metaphors and phrases prove exceptionally useful. Research on cultural discourses regarding taming unruly women and horses, and the stigmatization of unbridled female sexuality, may be brought into focus with the polysemous word 'hobby-horse', referring to a breed of horse, the toy hobby-horse on a stick, the Morris hobby-horse, and to a whore, or a fool (*OED*, hobby-horse, *n*.).[4] Where the pejorative use of the word is dominant, referring to loose women, it often appears as part of a cluster of other pejorative words and phrases (fairy queen, quean, hackney, minx, 'flax-wench that puts to / Before her troth-plight' in *The Winter's Tale* (1.2.279–80)),[5] which together act as evocative calling rhymes in a larger cultural context of female unruliness. This more wide-ranging issue is in tangential relationship with the ambiguous gender of the Morris hobby-horse in texts of the age – it was originally conceived of as a tourney-style costume of a man riding a horse, dancing, leaping and frolicking with girls and women during the dance and also pulling them under its 'skirt', signifying the fertility aspect of the Morris in carnivalesque, life-celebrating rituals. This male-gendered (ritual) meaning, however, was transformed in later textual/dramatic use, when the 'hobby-horse' referred to wanton women and whores, which process may have been partly instigated by popular discourse associating women and horses, either taming unruly women and horses or 'riding' them in a sexual sense.[6] The hobby-horse will also appear

---

[3] Although imitation formed a major part of Humanist education, I suggest that this rather mercantile practice of the quick 'patching of a play' must be differently understood.

[4] See also pictorial representations of the Morris hobby-horse in the so-called Betley window (a stained glass window of the early sixteenth century from a house in Betley, Staffordshire, and now on display at the Victoria and Albert Museum) and Morris dancers with a hobby-horse along the Thames near Richmond in a *c*. 1620 detail of the Dutch artist Vinckenboom's *Thames at Richmond, with the Old Royal Palace*, now at the Fitzwilliam Museum in Cambridge. These images and the emblem book appearances of hobby-horses were examined in Natália Pikli, '"Such flirts as they": The hobby-horse in Early Modern Emblem Books', in *The Power of Words: Papers in Honour of Tibor Fabiny's Sixtieth Birthday* (Budapest, 2015), pp. 305–16. The same Morris hobby-horse also appeared in a court performance for Queen Elizabeth by the Children of Paul's under the mastership of Westcott on 2 February 1575. Martin Wiggins, *British Drama 1533–1642. A Catalogue*, 7 vols. (Oxford, 2012), vol. 2, p. 122, entry 572 records, '*Play of Vanity* (lost) Revels Accounts ... VANITY, prob. a male character, two CITIZENS, PROPS: Animals: two hobby-horses (made of hoops and wire), with riders' boots and spurs on the sides, and bits with bosses'.

[5] Unless otherwise specified, Shakespeare quotations are from *William Shakespeare: The Complete Works*, ed. Stanley Wells, *et al.*, 2nd edn (Oxford, 2005).

[6] A number of studies and articles attest to this association of women, horses and fools in early modern England. See, for example, Bruce Boehrer, *Shakespeare Among the Animals* (New York, 2002). Hungarian popular libellous poems of the same period also shared this association. See Natália Pikli, 'Across cultures: Shakespeare and the carnivalesque shrew', *European Journal of English Studies* 14 (2010), 235–48.

in the following analysis of the non-canonical play *Blurt Master Constable* with a look at parallels in Shakespeare and in a non-dramatic text by Nicholas Breton. I share Tiffany Stern's recently suggested approach to drama history and her conviction that 'the printed non-play is a huge untapped resource of theatrical data, particularly when the non-play is written either by a playwright or by a writer known to have been interested in the theatre'.[7] In this light, both Dekker and Breton are good case studies, Dekker himself being a famous 'play-patcher'.[8]

Blurt Master Constable is an exciting play with regard to philological issues. We have a good published playtext in the quarto of 1602 (with minor print variations but no major differences)[9] and ample evidence for a performance at the Children of Paul's in late 1601, attested by the title page and other extraneous sources as well, like Pudsey's manuscript commonplace book of theatrical quotes.[10] The play was entered in the Stationers' Register to Edward Allde (Aldee) on 7 June 1602, and it appeared in quarto in the same year. The text is divided into scenes but not acts; the copy behind the 1602 quarto appears to be authorial; stage directions are at once literary and elaborate. As for its authorship, although Kirkman attributed the play to Middleton, and for a longer while the collaboration of Middleton and Dekker was supported, by now Dekker's single authorship seems to be verified, so much so that not only Wiggins's recent *Catalogue* but also the latest Middleton critical edition confirm Dekker's single authorship.[11] (Not to speak of the fact that plays written specifically for the Children of Paul's were always single-authored, as Gair's list confirms.[12]) What is even more important, though, is the fact that the play was conceived for the Children of Paul's, a theatrical context that defines its mood. As Berger claims, 'it is a coterie play: satirical, bawdy, amorous, cynical, and non-idealistic',[13] a world apart from the romantic comedy performed by adult companies for a wide and varied public and providing a rather saucy theatrical

[7] Tiffany Stern, 'Re-patching the play', in *Script to Stage in Early Modern England*, ed. Peter Holland and Stephen Orgel (New York, 2004), pp. 151–77; p. 153.

[8] George Wither refers to playwrights who are 'men only wise enough, / Out of some rotten old worme-eaten stuffe / To patch up a bald witless Comedy' in his *Abuses Stript and Whipt* (1613), qtd. in Stern, 'Re-patching the play', p. 154. Since he also uses hobby-horse (and theatrical) references in a complicated way, Wither, with this satire and his emblem book *A Collection of Emblems* (1635), will also appear in my monograph, *Forgotten and Remembered: The Cultural Memory of the Early Modern Hobby-Horse*.

[9] See Thomas Leland Berger, *A Critical Old-Spelling Edition of Thomas Dekker's Blurt Master Constable* (1602) (Salzburg, 1979). This critical edition is based on the eight copies of the 1602 quarto. I will refer to this edition (though with an eye to the quarto copy I could consult), providing act, scene, line numbers in text for easier reference.

[10] Additionally, Cyrus Hoy supports Dekker's authorship based on Edward Pudsey's manuscript. Cyrus Hoy, 'Notes to *Satiromastix*', in *Dramatic Works of Thomas Dekker*, ed. Fredson Bowers, 4 vols. (Cambridge, 1980), vol. 4, pp. 179–80, 197. Lazarillo's 'lecturing' to the courtesans on marriage is also based on the *Le quinze hoyes de marriage*, which Dekker translated and published in 1603 as *The Bachelor's Banquet*.

[11] For a historical account until 1979, see Berger, *A Critical Old-Spelling Edition of Thomas Dekker's* Blurt Master Constable (1602), pp. 1–30. See also Wiggins, *British Drama 1533–1642*, vol. 4, pp. 347–51, entry 1311, which lists *Blurt* and re-affirms Dekker's authorship. Wiggins's best guess for performance is winter 1601. See also MacDonald P. Jackson and Gary Taylor, 'Works excluded from this edition', in *Thomas Middleton and Early Modern Textual Culture: A Companion to the Collected Works* (Oxford, 2007), pp. 444–8.

[12] Reavley Gair, *The Children of Paul's: The Story of a Theatre Company, 1533–1608* (Cambridge, 1982), pp. 186–7.

[13] Berger, *A Critical Old-Spelling Edition of Thomas Dekker's* Blurt Master Constable (1602), p. 37. Kathleen E. McLuskie, *Dekker and Heywood: Professional Dramatists* (New York, 1994), p. 107, also describes this audience as 'a sophisticated élite, confident of its urbane values, appreciating drama which mocked and parodied the styles of the other popular theatres'. Gair's detailed study, *The Children of Paul's*, offers a more nuanced look at this audience based on the make-up and affluence of the neighbouring parishes and the ubiquitous presence of lawyers in the cathedral, adding that the minimal 2d entry fee (in 1601, based on data from Pery's 1601 play *The Cuckqueans and Cuckolds' Errants*) was not so high considering that one did not have to pay the boatman to get to Southwark. But basically Gair also attests to a rather closed, club-like audience (according to his reconstruction of the playhouse with only 50–100 seats) See Gair, *The Children of Paul's*, pp. 44–74, 170–1. Bart van Es,

experience of a more elite bent, one in which child actors ('little eyases, that cry out on the top of question', *Hamlet* 2.2.337–8)[14] played courtesans, lovers, clowns and braggarts for an audience with a more refined (or libertine) taste. The quarto title page also attests to this closed circle popularity ('As it hath bin sundry times privately acted'), which defines the general mood of the comedy.

Blurt Master Constable, or the Spaniard's Night-Walk neither is, nor was, a particularly good and popular play, though it must have enjoyed local success with the Children of Paul's since it not only quite heavily exploited the specific singing and dancing talents of the young choristers (in 1601 most probably aged between 8 and 14 years) as well as the parodistic allure of young boys performing in adult male and female roles,[15] but also appealed to an audience well-informed in the contemporary theatrical world.[16] The episodic structure is based on dramaturgical elements already made successful by a number of earlier plays, most notably Kyd's *The Spanish Tragedy* and especially Shakespeare's *Love's Labour's Lost* and *Much Ado About Nothing*, to which the play appears to be the most heavily indebted, although we also find a number of other allusions to *Romeo and Juliet*, *As You Like It* and Marston's *Antonio's Revenge*.[17] Besides imitating these chronological forerunners, the author of *Blurt* uses typical *commedia dell'arte* figures and situations and other common dramaturgical clichés, and the play also capitalizes on the evocative phrases of popular misogynistic discourses, like the ones surrounding the hobbyhorse. However, without the profound character-conception and dramaturgical coherence of either Kyd or Shakespeare, the play remains amusing, but instant and superficial, entertainment. On the other hand, precisely because Dekker, a notorious 'dresser of plays about town',[18] wrote it hastily, it becomes a good specimen for illuminating the workings of early modern show business, as well as the circulation of contemporary cultural and theatrical discourses, and it also informs us about the specific demands of the audience and the circumstances of the Children of Paul's theatre.

The story is a hodgepodge of a romantic plot of love complications and the rather carnivalesque comic storyline of courtesans tricking two stupid suitors, an old Venetian pantaloon, Curvetto, and a Spanish braggart soldier, Lazarillo,[19] with the added humour of the stupid constable Blurt and

---

'The children's companies', in *Shakespeare in Company* (Oxford, 2013), pp. 192–231, also supports this idea.

[14] References to *Hamlet* are taken from Harold Jenkins, ed., *Hamlet* (London, 1982). These lines appear in the 1603 Q1 and the 1623 Folio text of *Hamlet*; however, they gibe at the rival boy actors' company, the Children of the Chapel, performing at the Blackfriars with great success after Michaelmas 1600. Although the Children of Paul's was the first boys' company to enjoy a popular revival after late 1599, they were on friendlier terms with the Lord Chamberlain's Men, taking the same side in the War of the Theatres against Jonson and at times even sharing plays and playwrights, for example, Dekker's *Satiromastix* in 1602, which was performed by both companies. See Gair, *The Children of Paul's*, pp. 133–8. However, the acting style of the two young companies must have been rather similar.

[15] Gair, *The Children of Paul's*, p. 169.

[16] Gair, *The Children of Paul's*, pp. 170–1.

[17] Dekker's theatrical success relied more on his instinct for appeasing the popular demand and his colourful language than on his ability to produce a coherent plot. The contemporaneous and single-authored *The Shoemakers' Holiday* is also 'rather clumsily constructed'. See Daryll Grantley, 'Thomas Dekker and the emergence of city comedy', in *The Cambridge Companion to Shakespeare and Contemporary Dramatists*, ed. Ton Hoenselaars (Cambridge, 2012), pp. 83–96; p. 90.

[18] Jonson's gibe at Demetrius/Dekker in *Poetaster*. Grantley, 'Thomas Dekker and the emergence of city comedy', pp. 84, 85, 90, also confirms that Dekker could make money not primarily because of his education but thanks to his 'ability to gauge the taste of audiences and to craft products to appeal to those tastes', which clearly shows in his huge and varied oeuvre. Dekker was a collaborator or sole author in over forty-five plays, eighteen of which survive, and eight are written by him alone, with three more usually ascribed to him (among them, *Blurt*). Between 1598 and 1602 Dekker was especially active, with his hand in about twenty-three plays.

[19] Although braggart soldiers (from Plautus to Shakespeare's Falstaff) and stupid constables (Tophas in Lyly's *Endymion*, Bobadill in Jonson's *Every Man In His Humour*) are staples of the cultural memory of the age, the following analysis will reveal a closer kinship between these specific Shakespearean and Dekkerian counterparts.

his company, modelled on Dogberry, Verges and their watch. As neither of the plots takes obvious precedence, it is hard to say which is the main plot – very much like in *Much Ado About Nothing*. The story of potentially tragic love affairs is mostly modelled on Kyd's play (there is even a tongue-in-cheek reference to 'olde Jeronimo' in 4.1.54 when the courtesan Simperina sends away the tricked Curvetto); however, it definitely shows signs of Shakespearean influence as well – the secret marriage of Romeo and Juliet by a Friar is echoed in the Venetian young woman Violetta and the French prisoner-of-war Fontinell's clandestine marriage, though this time it is not the fathers and families who oppose their love but Violetta's wild and boisterous brother, Hippolito, and his friend Camillo, who is Fontinell's rival and who originally captured the Frenchman and brought him home as a prisoner of war and 'love token' for his beloved.[20]

The plotlines and characters meet in Imperia's hothouse. Imperia seems to rule over not only the brothel in Venice but also everyone's emotions (or, rather, desires). She appears as an omnipotent empress, verifying her name and simultaneously parodying Kyd's chaste and tragic heroine, Bel-Imperia. She is the stereotypical Venetian madam and triumphant courtesan, desired by almost all men, and she also recalls such characters in Roman comedy. Hers is the star part, with many lines and opportunities for improvisation and singing (indicated by many 'Fa la las'). Hippolito, also an admirer of hers, enraged because of the sudden love between his sister Violetta and Fontinell, sends the Frenchman's picture to Imperia to make her fall in love with the fair prisoner. He succeeds but Imperia's 'falling in love' with Fontinell never truly hinders her powers, and she appears rather unfazed when the angry and jealous Violetta bursts into the brothel demanding her husband. Imperia is quickly persuaded to play her part in the bed-trick, sending Violetta into her own bedroom where Fontinell is waiting for Imperia's amorous rewards. Although it is not clear whether Violetta and Fontinell plotted this earlier (for which there is only Frisco a page boy's aside as proof, earlier in Act 3), or whether it is only Violetta's sudden whim, an idea meant to save both of them after she has learned about her husband's affair (character description and motivation being rather sketchy), the trick contributes to the happy ending, presided over by the Duke, who appears rather as *deus ex machina*. Imperia then gets a reward kiss from Hippolito with words echoing those triumphant patriarchal figures in Shakespeare who silence unruly women ('Puncke you may laugh at this, / Heet's trickes, but mouth Ile stop you with a kisse' 5.3.133–4)[21] and, although Curvetto does not want to marry her, a 'puncke, a whore', disobeying the Duke's direct order, Imperia does not appear to be fazed at all; she is defiant ('I will be burnt to ashes first') and leaves the scene victorious.

The bed-trick, made necessary after the marriage, is a common and favoured theatrical device of the age and its biblical, mythological and folklore predecessors were also well known. It appears in around forty plays of the time, from Rowley to Marston, even though the Shakespearean instances in *Measure for Measure* and *All's Well That Ends Well* are the most well known; however, we must keep in mind that the theatrical efficacy of this element must have been recognized by each playwright, so a search for direct influences is unnecessary. On the other hand, the

---

[20] In the quarto edition that I also consulted, his name is spelled as Fontinell, Fontanelle, Fontenell, etc. See *BLVRT Master-Conſtable, OR The Spaniard's Night-walke. As it has bin ſundry times priuately acted by the Children of Paules* (London, 1602), Early English Books Online.

[21] Compare to '(*kissing her*) Peace, I will stop your mouth' in *Much Ado* 5.4.97. Although the stage direction is by Theobald, and both the 1600 quarto and 1623 folio give the speech prefix as 'Leon.' (Leonato), we might agree with the editors in attributing this line to Benedick, a plausible conclusion, since Petruchio and the other 'lover' characters are more apt to use this phrase in such a situation than an uncle. However, Claire McEachern's argument is also plausible. McEachern sees Leonato's words coming from a re-established powerful patriarchal position. See Claire McEachern, ed., *Much Ado About Nothing*, Arden 3 (London, 2006), pp. 108, 316.

stupid constable Blurt is very similar to Dogberry from *Much Ado About Nothing* and the fantastic Spanish knight, Lazarillo, is quite a clear imitation of Don Armado from *Love's Labour's Lost* – but again, we cannot completely disregard the fact that stupid constables and *commedia dell'arte* braggarts do appear in a number of other contemporary works as well. What might seem clear echoes of Shakespeare from a distance of 400 years come to us slightly distorted by the current cultic attitude towards Shakespeare. These instances may only be manifestations of a commonly shared storehouse of motifs and devices, even though the undeniable contemporary popularity of Shakespeare's plays and of the performances of the Lord Chamberlain's Men make the claim that his plays had a great impact on the writer of *Blurt*, whose dramaturgical skill never reached his, plausible (though never certain).

In such a play it is no wonder that references to women are less subtle and rely on stereotypes. Male and female characters show no signs of psychological motivation but appear, rather, as theatrical types (mostly taken from *commedia dell'arte*)[22] or as a cluster of embodied clichés themselves, often with a harsh misogynistic edge.[23] Violetta even refers to herself in such terms, which seems odd if we take her as a full-fledged dramatic character but makes sense in the original performative context, where a young boy plays an adult woman in love, rather in caricature fashion: 'besides I have a womans reason, I will not daunce, because I will not daunce' (1.1.176–8). At times, however, Violetta echoes the witty comic heroines of Shakespeare, imitating the euphuistic bantering style of Beatrice from *Much Ado* in maxims like 'troth I thinke he is not a sound man that wil dye for a woman, and yet I would never love a man soundlie, that would not knocke at deathes doore for my love' (1.1.103–4). And she also shares their 'loose tongue', but her enraged defiance of her brother and of his friend's love when Camillo is trying to serenade her is presented in a rather macho register, which surpasses Shakespeare's shrewish Katherine Minola by far:

Hip. You will not leave my friend in this poore taking?
Viol. Yes, by the velvet brow of darknes.
Hip. You scurvey Tyt: s'foote scurvey anything; Do you heare *Susanna*: you puncke, if I geld not your Muske-Cat; Ile doo't by Iesu; lets goe *Camillo*.
Viol. Nay but pure swaggerer, ruffin; doe you thinke To fright me with your bug-beare threates? goe by;
Harke, tosse-pot in your eare, the French-man's mine,
And by these hands Ile have him. (3.1.150–8)

This tone remains the dominant one between the main characters, Hippolito and Violetta, although there are lighter moments of sibling rivalry with some echoes of Beatrice and Benedick's banter, especially at the beginning, when Hippolito and Camillo return from the war and Violetta is mocking her brother's bragging tale of war. The first scene clearly echoes *Much Ado*, as the young men return from battle to give themselves over to nicer pleasures of love (romantic on Camillo's part, carnal on Hippolito's) and banqueting:

Viol. Faith brother, how many did you kill for your share?
Hip. Not so many as thou hast done with that villainous eye by a thousand.
Viol. I thought so much, that's just none. (1.1.34–7)

Beatrice displays a similarly sceptical attitude to Benedick's military prowess when she says 'I pray you, how many hath he killed and eaten in these wars? But how many hath he killed? For indeed I promised to eat all of his killing' (*Much Ado* 1.1. 40–3). Although this association is proverbial in the age, the dramaturgical context and register support Shakespearean influence.[24] However, as we saw

---

[22] This is confirmed verbally as well: 'zanies' appear in the masked dance (SD 2.2), and Hippolito calls his friend, Camillo a 'decayed concupiscentious *Inamorato*' (3.1.8).
[23] See Camillo's comment, 'women are strange fooles, and will take any thing' (1.1.208).
[24] McEachern's footnote, p. 152, refers to Dent.

earlier, although Violetta might display, at times, the witty and sophisticated mocking tone of Beatrice, it is never consistent – she often lapses into a more openly aggressive register. Her character and diction show a different kind of influence, which I call 'medley imitation', a phenomenon in which a less talented and original playwright picks up bits and pieces from contemporary plays popular in the theatre and uses them without dramaturgical distinction, that is, in creating characters and situations without an overarching coherence to either. Such medleys might contribute (at least partially and economically) to a successful theatrical performance but not to lasting good drama.[25] Other dramaturgical tricks in *Blurt* also imitate *Much Ado* in a similarly fragmented way: not only the situations and tone at the beginning but also the end resolution seem to be modelled on the earlier play. After the bed-trick, Violetta (the abused bride) appears masked and Fontinell has to 're-marry' (or 're-acknowledge') her, as is the case for Claudio and Hero. Fontinell and Claudio both resort to similar categories for describing the loathed mistress. Fontinell first swears of his love towards Violetta with the words in the counterpoint simile 'some negro geldering' (3.1.74) and then compares Violetta to a 'blacke Negro' (5.2.16), while Claudio promises to marry the substitute wife, 'I'll hold my mind, were she an Ethiope' (5.4.38). Although the darkness of a loathly lady was part of the common storehouse of images, the number of similarities suggests a more direct (conscious or unconscious) imitation.

In such a dramatic context, the lines containing the hobby-horse will necessarily have a harsher edge, one more condemning for women. In this scene, the young Venetian men, 'all weapon'd' and led by Hippolito and Camillo, prepare to take revenge for a number of things simultaneously, as summarized in a fifteen-line rant by Camillo: they want to retaliate for Violetta's falseness in falling in love with Camillo's prisoner of war, whose life he saved; for the 'Ignoble marriage'; and also for the ensuing betrayal of Violetta by Fontinell, who is now doting on 'a painted Curtizan', an act 'in scorne of our Italian lawes, our familie' (5.1.1–15). Such a heap of hurts might appear psychologically incoherent from the mouth of Camillo but it nicely prepares the way for the harsh words of a brother who intends to kill his sister in his rage:

HIP. As for that light Hobby-horse my Sister, whose foule name I will race out with my Poniard, by the honour of my Familie (which her lust hath prophaned) I sweare (and Gentlemen be in this my sworne brothers), I sweare that as all *Venice* does admire her beautie, so all the world shall be amazed at her punishment: follow therefore. (5.1.18–23)

Not only does a noble-born brother intend to kill his sister for having married someone in secret but he calls her a 'hobby-horse' (a whore) in public, a meaning strengthened by the adjective 'light', which is pejorative when referring to women. Furthermore, the following dialogue confirms Violetta's positioning even further – both metaphorically and literally:

VIRGILIO. And kill'd [Fontinell], to hang out his reeking bodie at his Harlots window.[26]
CAMILLO. And by his body, the strumpets.
HIPPOLITO. And between both, my Sisters.

(5.1. 29–32)

The scene closes with Hippolito's oath: '*Catso*, Saint *Marke*, my Pistoll, thus death flyes' (5.1.40), in which 'catso' is the Italian slang word for penis,

---

[25] Stern, 'Re-Patching the Play', claims that most plays were written and used in a fragmentary way, with easily detachable parts like epilogues and songs akin to a rope like structure made with removable or added threads, so there is a general patchwork nature to them. I mostly agree, though my contention is that the differences between more and less coherent dramaturgical structures are worth highlighting with reference to authorial and contextual factors.

[26] This supposed discovery, imagined in the curtained discovery area of Paul's playhouse, is a direct reference to Piero's bloody corpse shown hanging in Marston's *Antonio's Revenge*, a play just preceding *Blurt*. See Gair, *The Children of Paul's*, p. 130.

a term also appearing in Marston's plays written for the same company.[27] The whole play attests to a more generalized and debasing view of women, heaping theatrical and popular misogynistic or sexual clichés onto one another, from speaking names to plot twists, without providing sufficient motivation for either plot or characters. Female sexuality is treated with a cynical edge in both plays but to a different extent. 'Nothing' may refer to 'vagina' in the title of Shakespeare's play (and also 'noting'); however, Fontinell's sonnet, read and sung by the courtesans, makes it unmistakably clear that the answer to the question, 'In a faire woman what thing is best?' is not only a 'hart most chaste' but rather the other 'thing', which 'in a woman's middle it is plaste' (2.2.50–65).

Blurt Master Constable seems to be heavily indebted to the Shakespearean plays preceding it a couple of years: *Love's Labour's Lost* and *Much Ado About Nothing*. Although the exact nature of the influence could never be known, interesting parallels and differences can be pointed out, which in the case of *Love's Labour's Lost* are mostly focused on the figure of the Spanish 'fantastic' and braggart soldier Don Armado and his dialogues on love with the pert page-boy, Moth. On the other hand, Blurt, the stupid constable strongly recalls Dogberry; additionally, his helper, Slubber, is modelled on Dogberry's helpers, especially on Verges from *Much Ado*, with Slubber combining the roles of the sidekick and the scrivener as well, since he is the only one of the two who can read (though Blurt puts on his spectacles 'To see that hee read right', 2.2.122). The first comic scene in the play is 2.2, where Blurt establishes himself by echoing Dogberry's officiousness and claiming to be 'the Duke's own image', 'the Duke's own grace' (and later his 'Cipher'). *Blurt*'s Lazarillo, the Spaniard's name, is already an unashamed borrowing from the picaresque novel of the same title. He introduces himself as '*Lazarillo de Tormes* in *Castile*, cozen Germaine to the *Adolantado* of *Spaine*',[28] and Blurt instantly misinterprets his name with a Dogberry-like common sense malapropism: 'Has a good name, *Slubber* set it downe: write, *Lazarus* in torment at the Castle, and a cozening *Germaine*, at the signe of the Falantido diddle in *Spaine*' (1.2.148–9, 151–3).

Blurt and *Love's Labour's Lost* have even clearer echoes. When we first meet Don Armado, he enters and asks his page about the signs of melancholy, referring to himself ('Boy, what sign is it when a man of great spirit grows melancholy?', *Love's Labour's Lost* 1.2.1–2)[29] – just like Lazarillo ('Boy, I am melancholy because I burne', 2.1.1). Of course, both Spaniards allude to their being in love,[30] but the difference in tone is felt from the beginning – Armado and Moth engage in a witty and rhetorically well-versed and erudite discussion of great men being in love from Hercules to Samson, Moth finally 'defining' female beauty in a song. Lazarillo, by contrast, pines after 'laced mutton', that is, a prostitute (Imperia), and his desire is countered instantly by Pilcher the pageboy's down-to-earth hunger ('Plaine mutton without a lace would

---

[27] The quarto gives 'At so', but I agree with Berger's claim that the compositor substituted this for a term unknown (or too indecent) to him in order make some sense of it (Berger, *A Critical Old-Spelling Edition of Thomas Dekker's* Blurt Master Constable (1602), p. 141). Plus, Marston liked to sparkle with his Italian in such a way – in *Antonio and Mellida*, his first play for the Children of Paul's in 1599, two page boys are called Dildo and Catso, both slang terms for the penis in Italian. See Gair, *The Children of Paul's*, p. 28.

[28] The Spanish picaresque novel of *Lazarillo de Tormes* (1554), in English translation by David Rowland, was a popular book; it ran to four editions before the end of the Tudor era. Although there are data about a 1567 edition, the earliest remaining edition is that of 1586. See Beatriz Rodríguez Rodríguez, 'David Rowland's *Lazarillo de Tormes* (1586): Analysis of expansions in an Elizabethan translation', *Sederi Yearbook* 18 (2008), 81–96.

[29] Quotations taken from H. R. Woudhuysen, ed., *Love's Labour's Lost*, Arden III (Walton-on-Thames, 1998).

[30] We also have to consider that melancholy, heart-burn lovers are a staple of the age from Overbury's and Burton's descriptions to Rosalind's mocking of Orlando and Benedick's changes after being tricked into love with Beatrice. In *Blurt*, Violetta's page boy, Truepenny, mocks Fontinell with similar expectations (2.2.14–20), and the list is almost endless. However, with regard to the two Spanish fantastic braggarts, the similarities are wider reaching.

INFLUENCES AND DISCOURSES IN *BLURT MASTER CONSTABLE*

serve me' 2.1.8).³¹ Shakespeare's play mostly uses subtler references to female sexuality – like 'green goose' (4.3.72) and 'light wench' (1.2.117) – and although the hobby-horse reference in the dialogue between Armado and Moth (3.1.27–9) is bawdy, it is accurately positioned, coming from Moth, a saucy clever pageboy, and not from his noble brother. Moth is like a licensed fool, who is free to run his mouth at large and enjoys the liberty of being untouched by love (like Puck or Mercutio); therefore, he is more easily given to a detached, sarcastic and stereotypically misogynistic attitude to women:

ARMADO: But O – But O –
MOTH: 'The hobby-horse is forgot.'
ARMADO: Call'st thou my love a 'hobby-horse'?
MOTH: No, master. The hobby-horse is but a colt, and your love perhaps a hackney.   (3.1.26–30)

Moth's cluster of horse metaphors strengthens Jaquenetta's status as a loose woman: the sexual liberty of the Morris hobby-horse, symbolizing the fertility aspect of the Morris dance,³² is recalled with a phrase that resounds in these decades with the force of a proverb and is uttered with a bawdy innuendo, since 'O' is a frequent slang reference to the vagina.³³ Moth wilfully misinterprets Don Armado's sighs and transfers them to this register, and he does not let us remain in doubt about his opinion of Jaquenetta: 'colts', young horses, have been regarded as unruly and untamed and have been likened to lascivious young women for centuries, starting with Chaucer's Wife of Bath, and 'hackney', a hired horse ridden by whoever pays for it, is a term brought into ready parallel with prostitutes.³⁴

Moth's words leave no room for doubt as to the moral nature of Jaquenetta and the strongest actualized meaning of the polysemous word. However, the hobby-horse reference in *Much Ado About Nothing* is more complex: Benedick uses it to address Claudio and Don Pedro as dim-witted fellows, fools,³⁵ but interestingly, the immediate context, in which they make jokes at Benedick's expense, alludes to the (rhetorically amusing) discussion of love, melancholy and female sexuality again:

CLAUDIO.   That's as much as to say the sweet youth's in love.
D. PEDRO.   The greatest note of it is his melancholy.

---

[31] Imperia also resorts to the same stock idea in her entrée, though with bawdy associations, complaining about her gown being too tight in the middle: 'In good troth, if I bee not sicke I must be melancholye then: this same gown never comes on, but I am so melancholie, and so hart-burnt'; this makes her 'bend in the backe', which is 'the fault of the bodie' (3.1.18–20, 32).

[32] For more detail, see John Forrest, *The History of Morris Dancing 1458–1750* (Cambridge, 1999) or Alan Brissenden, 'Shakespeare and the morris', *The Review of English Studies* 30 (1979), 1–11; p. 6, who writes of 'the use of the hobby-horse in fertility rituals, with the death of the year and its resurrection at spring'. He notes that 'the costume of the hobby-horse, with its protruding head offers ample opportunity for symbolically phallic action' by pulling girls under the skirt/costume.

[33] *OED* confirms this idea ('proverbial from a lost old ballad'), as do most glossaries in critical editions.

[34] All glossaries and sexual dictionaries attest to this meaning. The same clear association between whores and hobby-horses can be found with a different dramaturgical significance in *Othello*, where the prostitute Bianca rejects Cassio's handkerchief indignantly: 'This is some minx's token, and I must take out the work. There, give it the hobby-horse. Wheresoever you had it, I'll take out no work on't' (*Othello*, 4.1.150–3). 'Minx' works in the same way as 'hackney', confirming the word's association with loose women, just like 'flax-wench' in *The Winter's Tale*, though this late play employs this association for tragic ends, as Leontes's insane and ungrounded jealousy causes the destruction of his family: 'My wife's a hobby-horse, deserves a name / As rank as any flax-wench that puts to / Before her troth-plight' (*Winter's Tale*, 1.2.278–80).

[35] The shift in meaning seems understandable as the Fool was another traditional figure of the Morris dance, and both the hobby-horse and the Fool were responsible for a close interaction with the audience, collecting donations and frolicking with audience members, the Fool beating them with his bauble or pig's bladder, the hobby-horse pulling girls under its costume. This association is made clear by Ben Jonson when he writes: 'But see the Hobby-Horse is forgot. / Foole, it must be your lot, / To supply his want with faces / And some other Buffon graces. / You know how' (Ben Jonson, *Entertainment at Althrope* (1603), ll. 286–90). For a more detailed discussion see Pikli, '"*Such flirts as they*"'.

CLAUDIO. And when was he wont to wash his face?
D. PEDRO. Yea, or to paint himself? – for the which I hear what they say of him.
CLAUDIO. Nay, but his jesting spirit, which is now crept into a lute-string, and now governed by stops.
D. PEDRO. Indeed, that tells a heavy tale for him. Conclude, conclude, he is in love.
CLAUDIO. Nay, but I know who loves him.
D. PEDRO. That would I know too. I warrant, one that knows him not.
CLAUDIO. Yes, and his ill conditions, and, in despite of all, dies for him.
D. PEDRO. She shall be buried with her face upwards.
BENEDICK. Yet is this no charm for the toothache. Old signor, walk aside with me. I have studied eight or nine wise words to speak to you, which these hobby-horses must not hear. (3.2.48–66)

The references to making love ('buried face upwards', 'dies for him', both evoking 'die' as the most well-known Elizabethan slang expression for orgasm) foreground Beatrice's sexuality. Although she is not a loose woman de facto, the discussion of her sexual activity by two men unrelated to her pushes Beatrice towards an association of looseness and wantonness. The primary meaning of the 'hobby-horse' here is that of a foolish person but that meaning is stratified and complicated by the context, which calls for a palimpsest interpretation considering the evocative images of the Morris hobby, the fool and the whore.

This pattern of a more nuanced use of the word along with references to popular culture is characteristic of Shakespeare in general. Despite Moth's jokes, sexual innuendo in *Love's Labour's Lost* is subtler and more sophisticated than in *Blurt*. Although Woudhuysen, the editor of the Arden Three edition, emphasizes and glosses every possible double entendre in the play, they never become as conspicuous as the ones in the Venetian play, which work with ruder and more easily made associations. Besides quality, quantity becomes a distinguishing feature as well. Characters with speaking names appear in both but, by their sheer number in *Blurt*, the message of associating these characters with low life and worthless trivia is hammered in. As opposed to Anthony Dull, the stupid constable, Costard (large apple, 'stupid head', rustic) and Moth in *Love's Labour's Lost*, Dekker's play abounds with such characters. Blurt, the constable, blurts out his malapropisms with gusto; his watchmen are called Woodcocke (a foolish bird, easily netted, and hence a simpleton), Gulch (a glutton or drunkard), Kilderkin (a cask for liquids or fish),[36] Pissebreach, Cuckoe and Garlicke, all references to carnivalesque associations with plenty of food, drink, foolery, bodily functions and sexual freedom.[37] The many pert page boys (all major characters have one), comfortably suiting a young boys' company's casting possibilities, are only distinguished by speaking names and not character: Doyt (a Dutch coin, half a farthing, a worthless sum), Dandiprat (a small coin worth three half pence, a dwarf, a page), Pilcher (a small dried fish or a term of abuse), Truepenny (a trusty fellow, used also in the popular register in *Hamlet*, 1.5.158–9)[38] and Frisco (a caper in a dance). Besides carnivalesque and 'vulgar' names, scatological practical jokes form a major part of the subplot: Curvetto, the old pantaloon and suitor to courtesans is doused with water (or rather urine) by Simperina when he comes to the brothel at night and pulls the rope of the bell; Lazarillo is made to believe that evil spirits haunt the rooms of the brothel, and he falls into an ordure pit in his

---

[36] See the glosses in Berger, *A Critical Old-Spelling Edition of Thomas Dekker's* Blurt Master Constable (1602), p. 168, which are based on *OED*.
[37] See Mihail Bakhtin, *Rabelais and His World*, trans. H. Iswolsky (Bloomington, IN, 1984); Peter Stallybrass, '"Drunk with the cup of liberty": Robin Hood, the carnivalesque, and the rhetoric of violence in Early Modern England' in *The Violence of Representation: Literature and the History of Violence*, ed. N. Armstrong and L. Tennenhouse (London, 1989), pp. 45–76.
[38] The note in Jenkins, ed., *Hamlet*, p. 225, confirms the popular register of this term, which is further supported by the fact that both quartos have 'Ha, ha' instead of the folio's more elite 'Ah ha'. *Ralph Roister Doister* also had a trusty servant by that name.

nightshirt.[39] And the characters do not hold back when it comes to verbal abuse to express their hurt. Curvetto calls these women 'damn'd whores', 'punckes, punkateeroes, nags, hags' (4.1.25) or Frisco a 'cunny-catching slaue' (4.3.39). Such openly and unashamedly rude and carnivalesque verbal and stage actions are rarer in Shakespeare – and they usually form an integral part of either the character or the given situation, like Mercutio's 'open-arse' references[40] or Kent's threat to daub the wall of a privy with Oswald's remains in *King Lear*.[41]

As opposed to these easily decipherable names and stage actions, it only takes a small leap for the educated audience of the Children of Paul's to have a good laugh at the courtesans' names: Trivia and Simperina. Although they sound Latinate, and therefore elite, the typically early modern English attitude and word use are clear. 'Trivial', 'base' and 'vulgar' reflect the distancing attitude of the more educated and aspiring middling sort, when they refer to aspects of popular culture (as described by Burke and Lamb),[42] and Simperina goes back to the verb 'simper', which was a frequent word from the mid-sixteenth century used to denote coy, affected, flirtatious behaviour. Although the verb was used to refer to men as well (e.g. in the epilogue of *As You Like It*),[43] it was more readily used to refer to light wenches (and horses), as Nicholas Breton's contemporary pamphlet *Pasquils Mistresse* (1600) affirms. Breton describes the unworthy mistress:

> But if that she can simper like a Mare
> And like a Hobby horse can holde her heade
> Prate like a Parrat, like on Owlet stare,
> And sleepe and snort before she goe to bed,
> And in her pocket haue a crust of breade,
> And play the wanton on a wooden bench,
> Who would not casst his gorge for such a wench?[44]

Nicholas Breton's satirical pamphlet describes the worthy woman in brief and the unworthy mistress at length, giving a full list of such wenches in facile rhyme royal stanzas, heaping clichés upon clichés. As a second-rate but prolific author, the stepson of George Gascoigne and allegedly a tavern friend of Shakespeare himself,[45] Breton, like Dekker, tended to capitalize on the most popular and easily recognizable topics and images; therefore his works present a storehouse of cultural stereotypes of the time. His list of the wenches who are 'unworthy mistresses', that is, not fit to make good wives, includes references to the unworthy woman being not only bestial – described in terms of

---

[39] Lazarillo's falling into the pit carries a further bawdy reference, based on the popular association of 'hell' and 'vagina', for example, in Shakespeare's sonnets. Lazarillo says, 'I am dung wet: I fell like *Lucifer*, I thinke, into hell, and am in worse pickle than my leane Pilcher: here about is the Hothouse of my loue, ho, ho? why ho there?' (4.3.70–3). Although this incident might be familiar from Boccaccio (*Decameron*, 2.5, as Berger, *A Critical Old-Spelling Edition of Thomas Dekker's* Blurt Master Constable (1602), p. 34, claims), in my opinion this seems a more general carnivalesque incident, the inclusion of which in the general rough merriment of the comic plot is more indicative of 'medley imitation' than the influence of a given text.

[40] 'O Romeo, that she were, O that she were / An open-arse, and thou a popp'rin' pear' (2.1.37–8).

[41] Kent (to Oswald): 'Thou whoreson Z, thou unnecessary letter – my lord, if you'll give me leave I will tread this unbolted villain into mortar and daub the wall of a jakes with him' (*Lear*, 2.2.63–6). This carnivalesque scatology is manifest in only verbal abuse, which attests to a more sophisticated dramaturgical use of the carnivalesque than having smelly and dirty Lazarillo on stage freshly coming from a dungpit.

[42] Peter Burke, *Popular Culture in Early Modern Europe* (Aldershot, 2009); Mary Ellen Lamb, *The Popular Culture of Shakespeare, Spenser and Johnson* (New York, 2006).

[43] Rosalind: 'And I charge you, O men, for the love you bear to women – as I perceive by your simpering none of you hates them' (*As You Like It*, 5.Epilogue). However, one must note here that this passage in Shakespeare is the most confusing from the perspective of gender: a boy-actor is speaking these lines in a meta-theatrical situation, where there is an oscillation between his original male self and his 'female' persona as Rosalind (who also played the male Ganymede, who played the part of Orlando's female lover). Shakespeare further strengthens this gender ambiguity by keeping up the conditional throughout ('If I were a woman').

[44] Nicholas Breton, *Pasquils Mistresse: or The Worthie and Unworthie Woman, With the Description and Passion of that Furie, Jealousie* (London, 1600), sig. D1r, Early English Books Online.

[45] His short biography is given in Jean Robertson, ed., *Poems by Nicholas Breton* (Liverpool, 1952), pp. xi–xxx.

animals, her unruliness expressed in pictures of untamed horses – but also associated with lowly pastimes like Morris dances, Robin Hood games, or sitting and gossiping on benches. She is also predominantly false: a 'picture of a painted face'.[46] This appears in numerous texts in the age, for instance in Hamlet's derogatory words to Ophelia: 'I have heard of your paintings well enough. God hath given you one face and you make yourselves another' (3.1.144–6). Breton's unworthy mistress is cozening and can appear as a female rogue, a pickpocket, a pandar – she can 'Diue in a pocket, or can picke a locke'[47] and can use cunning words as 'a conny-catching queane' to 'make her copper seeme good currant coyne', that is, to fool men.[48]

Breton's work indicates that such clusters of phrases stigmatizing non-standard female behaviour were very popular around the turn of the century. He was quite well-known as a poet by that time, mentioned in Puttenham's *The Arte of English Poesie* (1589), mocked by Nashe in his preface to Sidney's *Astrophel and Stella* (1591), and listed among other poets such as Spenser, Daniel, Drayton and Shakespeare in Francis Meres's *Palladis Tamia* (1598). He became especially popular with his Pasquil quartos, a number of amusing verse pamphlets in satirical vein published in 1600 (*Pasquils Mad-Cap; The Second Part of Pasquils Mad-cap Intituled: The Fooles Cap* in two editions; *Pasquils Passe, and passeth not, Pasquils Mistresse: Or the Worthie and vnworthie woman*).[49] As we have seen, the last one, dedicated to the soon-to-be-married 'Lustie Humfrey' (the historical Humfrey King, tobacconist) is focused on the virtue, but even more on the vices, of women – deviation being always more interesting than the 'rare phoenix' of the virtuous woman.[50] The publishing context for this pamphlet is highly interesting and confirms the probably close links between Breton and Shakespeare. The quarto was printed by Thomas Fisher between June and October 1600, the year he set up his shop. The title page bears the device of Fisher, which is the same kingfisher image that appears on the first quarto of '*A mydsommer nights Dreame*', entered in the Stationers' Register on 8 October.[51]

Breton's list of all kinds of unworthy mistresses witnesses a commonly used and easily recognized storehouse of images regarding female deviation from the norm. As a very prolific and money-hungry writer, he knew what triggered popular applause and ready money: misogyny in an amusing way.[52] The hobby-horse fits this context perfectly in a number of senses, disregarding the gender confusion – it is rather unclear whether in the quoted stanza the half-man half-horse hobby-horse of the Morris dance acts as one part of the simile, thus evoking the ritualistic fertility aspect of the image, or if it is a more direct reference to female wantonness, meaning that the mistress who holds her head high is likened to an actual (proud) whore. In addition, the connotations of foolishness and 'vulgar' country pastimes cannot be removed from possible reception either, especially because, I would suggest, these denotations do not annul each other but interact in contemporary readers' minds, creating a salacious palimpsest of meanings.

Reading dramatic and non-dramatic, canonical and non-canonical texts side by side may appear to be a crude patchwork of a scholarly enterprise. However, once we recognize the intricate web of interrelatedness between

---

[46] Breton, *Pasquils Mistresse*, sig. B3v.
[47] Breton, *Pasquils Mistresse*, sig. D1v.
[48] Breton, *Pasquils Mistresse*, sig. D2v.
[49] Robertson, *Poems by Nicholas Breton*, pp. lxxi–lxxvii.
[50] Breton, *Pasquils Mistresse*, sig. B3r.
[51] There are a good number of interesting verbal and thematic echoes between this work and the quasi-contemporaneous *Hamlet*, like the use of the word 'beautify' and a parallel to Ophelia's song about the seduced and then abandoned maiden girl.
[52] In this respect, it is quite interesting that after Salohcin Treboun dedicates the book to Humfrey (Salohcin Treboun is an anagram of Nicholas Breton), he addresses readers and then the women separately (Breton, *Pasquils Mistresse*, 'Pasquil, in generall, to women', sig. A4v). The phenomenon of women readers being the target audience for texts treating unruly female behaviour in a rather misogynistic way will be addressed in my monograph.

cultural and commercial products and figures in this vibrant age, new windows may open on theatrical, cultural and authorial questions. Hopefully this analysis focusing on *Blurt Master Constable* and its foolish characters will help shed new light on complicated problems and truths, and we may agree with Borachio that 'What your wisdoms could not discover, these shallow fools have brought to light' (*Much Ado* 5.1. 225–6).

MESSIANIC UGLINESS IN *A MIDSUMMER NIGHT'S DREAM* AND *THE WINTER'S TALE*

NAOMI BAKER

'God's works always appear deformed'
(Martin Luther, *Heidelberg Disputation*)

I

Recent philosophical interest in St Paul has brought renewed focus to the radical potential of the apostle's thought, demonstrating the extent to which his teachings upend the violent hierarchies of the ancient world.[1] For Paul, after all, counter to ancient orthodoxies,

God hath chosen the foolish things of the world to confound the wise, and God hath chosen the weak things of the world to confound the mighty things, and vile things of the world, and things which are despised, hath God chosen, and things which are not, to bring to nought things that are.

(1 Corinthians 1:27–8, 1599 Geneva Bible)

Paul's elevation of the 'things which are not' over the 'things that are' constitutes a challenge not only to the Gnostic wisdom he confronts in the Corinthian community but also to the very foundations of Greek metaphysics.[2] In Platonism, being is equated with the divine and thus with that which is fixed, beautiful and good: being, in other words, is the ultimate ideal. Not-being, on the other hand, signifies the lack, corruption, transience and ugliness of the material order, that which only the foolish would prize. Flying in the face of such principles, Paul's messianic message locates the divine in the midst of the ugliness and privation of temporal existence. No wonder, then, that Nietzsche claims that it is 'beauty above all [that] hurt [the] eyes and ears' of the apostle he terms the 'first Christian'.[3] As Nietzsche recognizes, to his horror, Paul launches an attack on the most cherished aesthetic and philosophical values of antiquity.[4] Rather than testifying to the apostle's 'hate-filled' vengefulness, as Nietzsche claims, however, Paul's rejection of Greco-Roman values constitutes a radical critique of the hierarchically structured ancient cosmos, a critique that illuminates the links between beauty and rigid, oppressive forms of law and identity.[5] In this article,

---

Many thanks to Gideon Baker, Anke Bernau and Jo Carruthers for their comments on earlier versions of this chapter. I presented aspects of this research at the Renaissance Society of America annual meeting in Berlin, the University of Bristol and the World Shakespeare Congress in Stratford-upon-Avon. I am grateful for the responses of the participants in all those seminars.

[1] See, for instance, Alain Badiou, *Saint Paul: The Foundation of Universalism*, trans. Ray Brassier (Stanford, 2003); Jacob Taubes, *The Political Theology of Paul*, trans. Dana Hollander (Stanford, 2004); Giorgio Agamben, *The Time That Remains: A Commentary on the Letter to the Romans*, trans. Patricia Dailey (Stanford, 2005).

[2] See Jacob Taubes, 'The justification of ugliness in the early Christian tradition', in *From Cult to Culture: Fragments Toward a Critique of Historical Reason*, ed. Charlotte Elisheva Fonrobert and Amir Engel (Stanford, 2010), p. 85.

[3] Friedrich Nietzsche, *The Antichrist, Ecce Homo, Twilight of the Idols and Other Writings*, ed. Aaron Ridley and Judith Norman (Cambridge, 2005), p. 50.

[4] See Taubes, 'The justification of ugliness', p. 76.

[5] Nietzsche, *The Antichrist*, pp. 44, 21. Badiou, *Saint Paul*, p. 71, states that '"the world" that Paul declares has been crucified with Jesus is the Greek cosmos, the reassuring totality that allots places and orders thought to consent to those places'.

I argue that Paul's subversive challenge to the wisdom of the ancient world informs Shakespeare's *A Midsummer Night's Dream* and *The Winter's Tale*. In these plays, I suggest, normative ideals of beauty and the hierarchical models of identity to which these ideals are tied are subjected to a specifically Pauline interrogation.[6]

In the ancient world, the reign of beauty was supreme, and not simply for aesthetic reasons: Greco-Roman society used the body as an expression of status, with beauty playing a key role in the maintenance of hierarchy. As Dale Martin points out, the body in this 'status-obsessed' world was 'usually pictured as a vertical spectrum stretching from inhuman or barbaric ugliness to divine beauty'.[7] Greco-Roman culture interwove beauty with high status, moral purity and physical health, as beauty took its place as a central pillar of imperial order, reinforcing an ostensibly natural hierarchical social structure. Within such a system, where deformity was equated with low class criminality and weakness, ugliness was an object of derision, associated with intellectual and moral as well as physical defectiveness. Such 'defectiveness', however, becomes Paul's badge of honour. 'I speak foolishly', and 'I speak as a fool', he declares, deploying the term used to denote 'the lower class moron'.[8] Originally named Saul, a 'regal name' reminiscent of a king who 'surpassed all Israelites, not only in beauty, but also in stature', Paul signifies his messianic vocation by re-naming himself – *paulus*, in Latin, means 'small, of little significance'.[9] He goes on to describe himself and his fellow workers as 'the refuse of the world, the offscouring of all things' (1 Corinthians 4:13), noting that he preaches 'in weakness of flesh' (Galatians 4:13–15) and drawing attention to his 'thorn in the flesh' (2 Corinthians 12:7), an unidentified source of weakness. The notes to the Geneva Bible emphasize the point, stating that 'Paul is called weak, in that he seemeth to the Corinthians a vile and abject man, a beggarly artificer, a most wretched and miserable idiot'.[10] Paul is 'not an imposing figure', comments Luther, 'but is small and skinny'.[11] The content of Paul's message, moreover, is as abject as is his own status. He states that he 'know[s] nothing ... but Jesus Christ and Him crucified' (1 Corinthians 2:2), thus linking the Messiah with the shameful and 'utterly offensive' form of execution reserved largely for slaves, the taboo status of which meant that it was barely referred to by ancient writers outside of the Gospels.[12] Paul's declaration of 'Messiah crucified' thus represents a violent and obscene dislocation of the divine into the criminally abject.

The grotesquely foolish nature of Paul's 'word of the cross' was not lost on the ancient world, as one of the earliest known visual representations of Jesus's crucifixion illustrates. Dating to the third century CE, a graffito from Palatine Hill in Rome depicts a man raising his hand to the crucified figure of a man with the head of a donkey, with the inscription 'Alexamenos worships [his] god'.[13] Illustrating the pervasiveness of such imagery in the mockery of the early Christians, Tertullian describes the anti-Christian image of a 'Donkey Priest', a man wearing a toga with the ears of a donkey, and also refers to the accusation that the Christian 'god is an ass's head'.[14]

On Paul's critique of ancient cosmos see also Gideon Baker, 'Paul and political theology: Nihilism, empire and the messianic vocation', *Philosophy and Social Criticism* 41 (2015), 293–315.

[6] Recent work on *The Winter's Tale* in relation to Paul includes Ken Jackson, '"Grace to boot": St. Paul, messianic time, and Shakespeare's *The Winter's Tale*', in *The Return of Theory in Early Modern Studies: Tarrying with the Subjunctive*, ed. Paul Cefalu and Bryan Reynolds (Basingstoke, 2011), pp. 192–210, and James Kuzner, '*The Winter's Tale*: Faith in law and the law of faith', *Exemplaria* 24 (2012), 260–81.

[7] Dale B. Martin, *The Corinthian Body* (New Haven, 1995), p. 34.

[8] 2 Corinthians 11:21, 23; L. L. Welborn, *Paul, the Fool of Christ* (London, 2005), p. 1.

[9] Agamben, *Time That Remains*, p. 9.

[10] Note to 2 Corinthians 11:21, 1599 Geneva Bible.

[11] Martin Luther, *Commentary on 1 Corinthians*, in *Luther's Works*, vol. 28, ed. Hilton C. Oswald (Saint Louis, 1973), p. 85.

[12] Martin Hengel, *Crucifixion in the Ancient World and the Folly of the Message of the Cross* (London, 1977), p. 22.

[13] See Welborn, *Paul*, pp. 141–2.

[14] Tertullian, Apology XVI, in *The Ante-Nicene Fathers*, ed. James Donaldson, Alexander Roberts and A. Cleveland Coxe, vol. 3 (Grand Rapids, 1968), pp. 30–1.

As L. L. Welborn points out, the 'ass-man' is a fixture in ancient mime, representing lower-class figures who are the objects of abuse and mockery. Drawing on despicable derided figures from the mime, the graffito draws attention to the monstrosity of the Christian gospel, signalling the collision of values between ancient culture and Paul's teachings. Paul's 'word of the cross', rhetorically shaped perhaps in relation to the discourse of the fool in the ancient mime, is thus one of grotesque, even obscene, foolishness.[15] To Paul, however, God has chosen the 'foolish things of the world to confound the wise': it is in the earthen vessels that the messianic treasure is to be found (2 Corinthians 4:7). This subversive perspective, I suggest, informs the representation of ugliness in Shakespeare's plays, where beauty does not always operate as a straightforward good and where the ugly body has the perhaps surprising potential to become the site where messianic possibilities are made manifest.

The presence of Pauline thought in Shakespeare's plays does not necessarily indicate Reformed sympathies in the playwright but it is nevertheless difficult to overstate the significance of Paul for the Reformation, one plausible definition of which is 'people reading Paul'.[16] For Martin Luther, who positioned himself as the true heir of Paul, Christianity had become polluted since the time of the apostle by a toxic infusion of Greek metaphysics.[17] The Hellenization of Christianity had generated a system of belief referred to scornfully by Luther as the *theologia gloriae*, in which God functions as the being of beings, a radiant object of aesthetic contemplation, able to be intuited by human reason.[18] Where Paul states that he knows nothing but Jesus Christ 'and him crucified' (1 Corinthians 2:2), insisting on the earthly Jesus as the focus of his faith, Hellenistic influences from the earliest days of Christianity encouraged the celebration of Christ as a glorified, divine being, offering a means to transcend earthly existence.[19] Paul's first letter to the Corinthians goes to war with such Gnostic tendencies in the Corinthian community, yet tensions remained in early Christianity between Greek metaphysics and Paul's 'word of the cross'. These tensions are apparent in early Christian debates about Christ's physical appearance.[20] As Jacob Taubes establishes, ancient opponents of Christianity mocked the faith for its suggestion that a divine being could be anything other than radiantly beautiful. The Church Father Origen counters such criticisms yet nevertheless remains influenced by the metaphysical philosophy they articulate, as he claims that Christ's humble appearance was merely the form in which he presented himself to those unable to comprehend the 'glorious', 'majestic' and 'marvellous' nature of his 'surpassing loveliness'.[21] Other early Christians nevertheless follow messianic imagery drawn from Isaiah, as they insist that Christ was, in fact, ugly. Justin Martyr, for instance, comments that Christ was of 'uncomely and dishonoured appearance, and inglorious', while Tertullian states that men 'despised his outward appearance, so far was his body from being of human comeliness'.[22]

---

[15] See Welborn, *Paul*, p. 2.

[16] David Daniell defines the Reformation in these terms in 'Shakespeare and the Protestant Mind', in *Shakespeare Survey 54* (Cambridge, 2001), p. 9. On the importance of Paul for the English Reformation, see John S. Coolidge, *The Pauline Renaissance in England* (Oxford, 1970); on the importance of Reformed thinking to the early modern theatre, see Jennifer Waldron, *Reformations of the Body: Idolatry, Sacrifice, and Early Modern Theater* (Basingstoke, 2013). Waldron notes 'trends in Reformation thinking that had shifted the location of the sacred toward the horizontal plane of everyday life', implicitly picking up on the Pauline messianism at the heart of Reformation thinking (p. 2).

[17] See John van Buren, *The Young Heidegger: Rumor of the Hidden King* (Bloomington, 1994), p. 160; S. J. McGrath, *The Early Heidegger and Medieval Philosophy: Phenomenology for the Godforsaken* (Washington, 2006), pp. 152–3.

[18] Van Buren, *Young Heidegger*, p. 161.

[19] See Ulrich Wilckens, *God's Revelation: A Way through the New Testament*, trans. William Glen-Doepel (London, 1967), pp. 90–1.

[20] See Taubes, 'The justification of ugliness', pp. 90–3. For a brief historical summary of depictions of an ugly, suffering Christ, see Umberto Eco, *On Ugliness*, trans. Alastair McEwen (London, 2007), pp. 49–53.

[21] Origen, *Contra Celsum*, VI, p. 77; cited in Taubes, 'Justification of ugliness', p. 92.

[22] Justin Martyr, *Dialogue with Trypho*, ch. 36; cited in Taubes, 'Justification of ugliness', p. 90; Tertullian, *On the Flesh of Christ*, p. 9; cited in Taubes, 'Justification of ugliness', p. 93.

To Luther, there can be no doubt about the matter. Pauline messianism, he insists, finds God not in transcendent beauty but in the violence and deformity of historical particularity: God can be 'found only in suffering and the cross'.[23] Paul thus necessarily confronts us with a shockingly ugly Christ: 'Paul preaches Christ alone as misshapen and as crucified. And so He must always be preached.'[24]

As well as identifying Christ with the historical rather than with the otherworldly, the ugliness of the messianic revelation, for Luther, embodies its resistance to rational categorization. Christ does not exist as a beautiful object to be contemplated and understood from a safe distance but as an abject figure, generating a visceral response: 'His appearance will be so vile that many will be sick and offended. *At Him.*'[25] Rather than offering us a glimpse of a divine realm, and thereby confirming our ability to know or in a sense to 'possess' God, Paul's misshapen Messiah, for Luther, forces us to confront our own inadequacy and ugliness.[26] Contrary to the Aristotelian models of self-realization on which the 'theology of glory' is premised, Luther insists that salvation is premised on an experience of self-shattering.[27] It is in this context that he makes the startling claim that 'God's works always appear deformed': the messianic life is one in which we accept that 'there is neither [radiant] form or beauty in us, but our life is hidden in God'.[28] The ugliness of Protestant subjectivity, alienated from the 'radiant form' and 'beauty' of metaphysical models of the divine, is interpreted in most critical readings as a pathological form of abjection and despair.[29] For Luther, however, as for Paul, this self-acknowledged ugliness is a form of emancipation. We are 'called in ugliness', and are thus liberated from the shackles of 'radiant form' and 'beauty', so that our life can be 'hidden in God'.[30] It is only from the starting point of ugly not-being that we can enter into the perpetual becoming definitive of Paul's model of messianic living. In a characteristically Pauline gesture, beauty and ugliness, for Luther, are thus radically transvalued: '[w]hosoever is most beautiful in the sight of God is the most ugly, and, vice versa, whoever is ugliest is the most beautiful'.[31]

Rather than nihilistically celebrating the abject for its own sake, Luther's inversion of the value of beauty and ugliness builds on Paul's subversive critique of normative models of identity. Paul interrogates identity as one aspect of his interrogation of law, defined not simply as the Torah or any other specific legal system, but as the generalized 'apotheosis of nomos' characteristic of the ancient world.[32] He exposes the link between law and identity: the law defines, it divides, it particularizes, it places and it names, all of which, for Paul, amounts to saying that it kills.[33] Yet Paul announces that the messianic revelation cuts across the identities upon which the law depends for its operations:

---

[23] Martin Luther, *Heidelberg Disputation*, in *Luther's Works*, vol. 31, ed. Harold J. Grimm (Philadelphia, 1957), p. 53.

[24] Martin Luther, *Lectures on Isaiah*, in *Luther's Works*, vol. 17, ed. Hilton C. Oswald (Saint Louis, 1972), p. 217.

[25] Luther, *Lectures on Isaiah*, p. 216.

[26] On Luther's critique of our ability to 'possess' God, see Benjamin D. Crowe, *Heidegger's Religious Origins: Destruction and Authenticity* (Bloomington, 2006), pp. 46–7. See also, McGrath, *Early Heidegger*, p. 154. Lisa Freinkel, *Reading Shakespeare's Will* (New York, 2002), p. 156, states that Luther 'brings the Word close in all of its strangeness, in all its unreasonable and alienating demand'.

[27] See Crowe, *Heidegger's Religious Origins*, pp. 46–54.

[28] Luther, *Heidelberg Disputation*, pp. 43–4.

[29] Adrian Streete, for instance, describes the 'failure to achieve a unified feeling of fixity within the self' as a source of terror for the Protestant subject, arguing that 'Calvinism wants divine transcendence on the one hand and total human abjection on the other' (*Protestantism and Drama in Early Modern England* (Cambridge, 2009), pp. 98, 108). On the alienation of the Protestant subject, see also Freinkel, *Reading Shakespeare's Will*, pp. 118–40, and John Stachniewski, *The Persecutory Imagination: English Puritanism and the Literature of Religious Despair* (Oxford, 1991).

[30] Luther, *1 Corinthians*, pp. 43–4.

[31] Martin Luther, *First Lectures on the Psalms*, in *Luther's Works*, vol. 10, ed. Hilton C. Oswald (Saint Louis, 1974), p. 239.

[32] Giorgio Agamben, *Potentialities: Collected Essays in Philosophy* (Stanford, 1999), p. 162; Agamben, *Time That Remains*, p. 3; Taubes, *Political Theology*, p. 23.

[33] Badiou, *Saint Paul*, p. 76, discusses the manner in which 'the law always designates a particularity' and is that which 'enumerates, names, and controls the parts of a situation'.

But before faith came, we were kept under the Law, shut up unto the faith, which should afterwards be revealed... But after that faith is come, we are no longer under a schoolmaster... There is neither Jew, nor Greek, there is neither bond nor free, there is neither male nor female, for ye are all one in Christ Jesus.

(Galatians 3:23–8)

This statement, as Alain Badiou comments, is 'genuinely stupefying... when one knows the rules of the ancient world'. Badiou consequently celebrates Paul as a 'militant figure' who is able to break the hold of the identities definitive of the ancient world in order to declare 'a subject devoid of all identity, and suspended to an event'.[34] Released from the (deadly) grip of a socially defined identity, the messianic subject is able to engage in the emancipatory and ongoing process of 'work[ing] out' his or her salvation (Philippians 2:12).

Paul's 'word of the cross' is therefore premised on a radically temporal experience of becoming. Instead of possessing an identity, the subject of grace is a work-in-progress: 'one cannot stand still', says Luther, 'on the road of God'.[35] In emphasizing the perpetual development of the believer, Luther draws on Paul's insistence that apocalyptic transformation is not something we are awaiting in the future but is an experience that is already underway, generating what Stanislas Breton describes as a 'permanent metamorphosis' that 'prevents [beings] from being shut up within the borders of a defined nature'.[36] As Luther emphasizes, Paul presents the messianic life as one that is relentlessly orientated to the future: we must 'learn from the apostle to consider creation as it waits, groans and travails, that is, as it turns away in disgust from what now is and desires that which is still in the future'.[37] Located in the messianic time established by the already experienced arrival of the Messiah in tension with his promised final revelation, those living 'under grace' are always moving towards the fulfilment of that which they have already become:

Rom 12:1 *But be transformed*... he is speaking of those people who already have begun to be Christians. Their life is not a static thing, but in movement from good to better, just as a sick man proceeds from sickness to health... through his new birth he moves from sin to righteousness, and thus from nonbeing through becoming to being... But from this new being, which is really a nonbeing, man proceeds and passes to another new... he proceeds to become better, and from this again into something new. Thus it is most correct to say that man is always in privation, always in becoming or in potentiality, in matter, and always in action... Man is always in nonbeing, in becoming.[38]

'Always in nonbeing, in becoming', the subject of the messianic call, in Luther's reading of Paul, rejects static, closed models of identity and being in the name of ugly, fluid and endlessly transformative not-being.

Paul's politically charged transvaluation of (beautiful) being and (ugly) not-being, I suggest, informs Shakespeare's representation of beauty and of identity in *A Midsummer Night's Dream* and *The Winter's Tale*. Undermining fixed or 'natural' models of identity in the name of 'permanent metamorphosis', the plays draw on aspects of Luther's Paul, one for whom metaphysical illusions of static and glorious being are brought 'to naught' by the abject ugliness of the cross.[39] While the post-Lutheran theological tradition has been associated with the construction of an introspective Paul, one used to create the 'guilty conscience' of the Western individual, the Pauline messianism informing these plays does not shore up a discrete, individualistic model of the self, but instead exposes the pathological nature of such forms of identity.[40] In both plays, as in Paul's

---

[34] Badiou, *Saint Paul*, pp. 49, 9, 5.

[35] Martin Luther, *Lectures on Romans*, in *Luther's Works*, vol. 25, ed. Hilton C. Oswald (Saint Louis, 1972), p. 225.

[36] Stanislas Breton, *A Radical Philosophy of Saint Paul*, trans. Joseph N. Ballan (New York, 2011), pp. 117, 120.

[37] Luther, *Romans*, p. 225. See McGrath, *Early Heidegger*, p. 165.

[38] Luther, *Romans*, pp. 433–4.

[39] Freinkel describes Shakespeare as 'a Lutheran author', stating that 'we cannot properly understand his poetry without recognizing it as a response to Luther' (*Reading Shakespeare's Will*, pp. xxvi, xxi).

[40] For a critique of the tradition of reading Paul 'as a hero of the introspective conscience', see Krister Stendahl, 'The Apostle Paul and the introspective conscience of the West',

writings, rigid models of identity are shown to be inseparable from violent hierarchies and ultimately from death. Following Paul, then, the plays celebrate not the beauty of static, individualized forms of being but the ugliness of not-being, that which is open to the radical possibilities of becoming.

II

Given Paul's insistence on his own vulgar foolishness, it should come as no surprise that his mouthpiece in *A Midsummer Night's Dream* is the buffoonish Bottom, one of the 'rude mechanicals' (3.2.9) whose memory of Scripture is as befuddled as is his diction:

I have had a most rare vision. I have had a dream past the wit of man to say what dream it was. Man is but an ass if he go about t'expound this dream. Methought I was – there is no man can tell what. Methought I was, and methought I had – but man is but a patched fool if he will offer to say what methought I had. The eye of man hath not heard, the ear of man hath not seen, man's hand is not able to taste, his tongue to conceive, nor his heart to report what my dream was. (4.1.202–11)[41]

This speech has divided critics, who struggle to reconcile the low comedy of the words and the crude weaver speaking them with the visionary allusiveness of the Corinthians references.[42] If Bottom's declaration is understood within the wider context of the experience of 'translation' to which it refers, however, the biblical allusions draw attention to the Pauline messianism informing the play. This is not to underplay the complex allusiveness of this work: evidently the extraordinary richness of Shakespeare's comedy derives from its hybrid mingling of classical and popular as well as biblical themes. Ovidian metamorphosis merges almost seamlessly with Pauline transformation in the play; yet it remains the case that critics have underplayed the messianic elements with which Shakespeare's fantastical drama is shot through. Whether or not Bottom's name alludes to the early English Bible translations which mention the 'Bottom of Goddes secretes', the weaver who foolishly garbles Scripture while echoing Paul's status as a 'beggarly artificer' disrupts the imperial cosmic hierarchy represented by both Athens and the fairy kingdom.[43] A 'base' entity by name and by nature, he embodies the Pauline principle that the 'vile things of the world, and things which are despised . . . and things which are not' will 'bring to nought [the] things that are' (1 Corinthians 1:28). Bottom's physical and social metamorphoses, together with his confused and incomplete statements of self-definition ('Methought I was – . . . methought I had —') and his openness to a 'translation' that operates beyond the limits of 'cool reason' stand in stark contrast to the rigid boundaries of law and identity in force elsewhere in the play, showing such structures to be 'airy nothing[s]' (5.1.16).[44]

The 'sharp Athenian law' (1.1.162) from which both the lovers and the lower-class actors seek refuge in the woods is explicitly identified with

---

The Harvard Theological Review 56 (1963), 199–215. Kuzner also argues that *The Winter's Tale* mounts a Pauline critique of 'defined subjects', noting that the play adopts a 'skeptical attitude toward positive law that locates subjects', asking instead 'that we embrace a law of faith that leaves us divided and undefined' ('Faith in law', pp. 260–81).

[41] All Shakespeare quotations taken from *William Shakespeare: The Complete Works*, ed. Stanley Wells, *et. al.* (Oxford, 1988).

[42] Bottom misquotes 1 Corinthians 2:9–10: 'The things which eye hath not seen, neither ear hath heard, neither came into man's heart, are, which God hath prepared for them that love him' (1599 Geneva Bible). The passage also alludes to 2 Corinthians 12:1–4, where Paul describes a vision in which he 'was taken up into the third heaven': 'I cannot tell: God knoweth, how that he was taken up into Paradise, and heard words which cannot be spoken which are not possible for man to utter' (1599 Geneva Bible).

[43] On Bottom's name, see Thomas B. Stroup, 'Bottom's name and his epiphany', *Shakespeare Quarterly* 29 (1978), 79–82, and Robert F. Willson, Jr., 'God's secrets and Bottom's name: A reply', *Shakespeare Quarterly* 30 (1979), 407–8. Paul is described as a 'beggarly artificer' in the Geneva Bible's note to 2 Corinthians 11:21. On Bottom as a subversive figure, see David Laird, '"If we offend, it is with our good will": Staging dissent in *A Midsummer Night's Dream*', *Connotations* 12 (2002/03), 35–51.

[44] On the significance of translation in the play, see David Lucking 'Translation and metamorphosis in *A Midsummer Night's Dream*,' *Essays in Criticism* 61 (2011), 137–54; p. 149.

violence in the play. 'I wooed thee with my sword / And won thy love doing thee injuries' (1.1. 16–17), gloats Theseus to his conquered bride, while Egeus 'beg[s] the ancient privilege of Athens' to 'dispose' of his daughter to death, rather than see her cross his command (1.1.41–2). Athens is also a world locked within the oppressive operations of time, as Theseus establishes in the first speech of the play, depicting himself at the mercy of the 'stepdame' or 'dowager' moon (1.1.5) by whom he is tortured as she makes her unrelentingly slow progress towards the moment of his marriage. The restrictive structures of law and time in the classical world of the play are matched by a brutally hierarchical discourse of beauty, which is explicitly linked to patriarchal control. 'To you your father should be as a god', Theseus instructs the rebellious Hermia,

> One that composed your beauties, yea, and one
> To whom you are but as a form in wax,
> By him imprinted, and within his power
> To leave the figure or disfigure it. (1.1.47–51)

Beauty, equated here with form, is in the gift of the father and in his power to remove, its codification one of the pillars of patriarchal law. Transgressive women in the play are those who refuse to see through male eyes: 'your eyes must with his judgement look' (1.1.57), Hermia is instructed. They are tamed when they accept male aesthetic judgements: Titania's final acquiescence to Oberon's perspective – 'O, how mine eyes do loathe his visage now!' (4.1.78), she declares of Bottom, after the spell is reversed – marks the moment she is brought into line with the fairy king's will. The pivotal role of beauty in the hierarchies of both Athens and the fairy kingdom in the play is further evident in Oberon's final speech, where the authorized union of the couples is sanctioned by his insistence that

> ... the blots of nature's hand
> Shall not in their issue stand.
> Never mole, harelip, nor scar,
> Nor mark prodigious such as are
> Despisèd in nativity
> Shall upon their children be. (5.2.39–44)

A crucial aspect of the imposition of order at the end of the play, then, is the Neoplatonic insistence on beauty as a marker of aristocratic purity and health, qualities set against the lower-class monstrosity and chaos witnessed in the middle section.[45] Deformity is coded here as a form of political and moral as well as physical disruption which must be expelled if sovereign power is to remain in force.

The fairy kingdom echoes the patriarchal order of Athens in its mystification of cosmic order, similarly suggesting that the orderly operations of time and the establishment of beauty and regularity are linked to hierarchical rule. Titania laments the chaos generated by her discord with Oberon, suggesting that the natural order has been thrown into tumult by their arguments:

> The spring, the summer,
> The childing autumn, angry winter change
> Their wonted liveries, and the mazèd world
> By their increase now knows not which is which;
> And this same progeny of evils comes
> From our debate, from our dissension.
> We are their parents and original. (2.1.111–17)

Sovereign figures thus set the tone for the natural order, mystifying the maintenance of hierarchy as the means by which the workings of time and the seasons are preserved.

The terms in which Titania laments the confusion of the seasons recalls the lexicon of late sixteenth-century moralists who decried the confusion of gender and class markers in those who brazenly 'change[d] / Their wonted liveries', thus undermining a key register for the maintenance of an ostensibly natural, divinely ordained hierarchical order. 'There is such a confuse[d] mingle mangle of apparel', laments the moralist Phillip Stubbes,

---

[45] Sarah Carter discusses the extent to which Neoplatonism is undercut by Ovidian motifs in the play in 'From the ridiculous to the sublime: Ovidian and neoplatonic registers in *A Midsummer Night's Dream*', *Early Modern Literary Studies*, 12.1 (2006), http://purl.oclc.org/emls/12-1/cartmnd.htm.

as everyone is permitted to flaunt it out, in what apparel he lust himselfe, or can get by anie meanes. So that it is very hard to knowe, who is noble, who is worshipfull, who is a gentleman, who is not.

The 'great confusion' caused by this breakdown in sartorial signification results, according to Stubbes, in monstrosity: 'our novell Inventions and new fangled fashions rather deforme us than adorne us ... making us rather to resemble savage Beastes and stearne Monsters, then continent, sober and chaste Christians'.[46]

Such accusations were, of course, similarly levelled at the theatre, where the 'confuse[d] mingle mangle' of both dress and identity reached its apotheosis.[47] The very concept of acting a role, to William Prynne, is an affront to God, 'in whom there is no variablenesse, no shadow of change, no fei[g]ning, no hypocrisie'. God 'hath given a uniform distinct and proper being to every creature, the bounds of which may not be exceeded': men must 'be such in shew, as they are in truth'. They must 'act themselves, not others'.[48] While impersonating others by definition transgresses our divinely appointed identity (an identity which is nevertheless itself performative, it seems), the social and gender transvestism involved in acting on the early modern stage took such transgressions to an extreme. Actors, to Prynne, are 'Man-women monsters' or 'beastly male-monsters', whose bodies, souls and minds are rendered effeminate by their transvestite roles. Displaying the manner in which Paul is invoked in support of a variety of theological and political positions in the early modern period, both conservative and radical, the anti-theatricalists cite Paul in support of their insistence on a natural hierarchical order obscenely undermined by the transformations of the stage. Prynne, for instance, cites ancient commentaries on Paul's writings to make his case for a natural gender difference breached by theatrical cross-dressing:

it is an unnaturall and disorderly thing to see flowers in winter, or women clothed in mans, or men attired in womens apparel. For (as Elias comments) the first of these disturbes the times; the other yeelds an inconvenient forme to nature, the ornament both of the man and woman being changed, and the order which nature hath prescribed to them, being confounded.[49]

Prynne thus echoes Titania's allusions to the orderly progression of clearly demarcated seasons as a model for a natural, hierarchical order, claiming Pauline and Church authority to make the case that this order is divinely appointed. Shakespeare is nevertheless able to draw on Paul to precisely the opposite effect, perhaps deliberately rejecting the deployment of the apostle in defence of fixed, 'natural', imperial order in his celebration of a specifically Pauline, as well as theatrical, monstrosity.[50] (Contrary to his deployment by the anti-theatricalists, this is an apostle, after all, who may have been a stage carpenter and who described himself as 'a theatre-act to the world' (1 Corinthians 4:9–10).)[51]

The language of 'riot' and 'disorder' running through the anti-theatrical tracts is suggestive of the political implications of these debates: the hierarchical order of 'uniform, distinct and proper being' is explicitly set against a socially disruptive 'general disorder' concomitant upon a 'riotous excesse in apparell'. The fact that men are transgressing their 'degree, estate and condition of life' in their role-playing bespeaks not only moral and physical monstrosity but also a dangerous

---

[46] Philip Stubbes, *The Anatomie of Abuses* (1583), n.p.

[47] On cross-dressing in early modern theatre see Jean E. Howard, 'Cross dressing, the theatre, and gender struggle in early modern England', *Shakespeare Quarterly* 39 (1988), 418–40.

[48] William Prynne, *Histrio-mastix: the players scourge, or actors tragedie* (1633), n.p.

[49] Prynne, n.p. Paul discusses apparel and hairstyles in 1 Corinthians 11:14–15.

[50] Huston Diehl argues that 'Shakespeare recognized in the historical Paul a rich source of material with which to defend the stage against antitheatricalist attacks denouncing it as idolatrous' ('"Does not the stone rebuke me?": The Pauline rebuke and Paulina's lawful magic in The Winter's Tale', in *Shakespeare and the Cultures of Performance*, ed. Paul Yachin and Patricia Badir (Aldershot, 2008), pp. 69–82, 74).

[51] Welborn suggests that the term usually taken to identify Paul as a tent-maker could potentially refer to a stage carpenter. He also translates 1 Corinthians 4:9–10 as 'we have become a theatre-act to the world, both to angels and to human beings', *Paul*, pp. 249, 3.

unruliness. The chief crime entailed in monstrous 'translation', as Bottom finds out, is that of rising above one's appointed station: 'Shall the clay say unto the potter, why hast thou made me thus?' (Romans 9:20). The lower-class status of most actors makes their presumptive role-playing all the more threatening. The vulgar are 'spit[ting] against heaven', upending not only a social but also a cosmic hierarchy: 'these riche ornaments and sumptuous vestments' do not merely display 'the rich estate and glory of the owner' but 'shew forth the power, wealth, dignity, riches and glory of the Lord'.[52] Any undermining of 'distinct and proper being', by implication, entails an anarchic unravelling of the closely intertwined social, gendered and religious structures of cosmic order. Titania's speech identifying the natural order with the constitution of sovereigns thus illuminates the threat posed to naturalized systems of governance by the 'shaping fantasies' of imaginative transformation. Theseus has good political reason to decry the 'fine frenzy' of the poet, able to '[body] forth / The forms of things unknown' (5.1.12, 14–15). Through the creation of radical, metamorphosed forms, the ostensibly natural beings upon which sovereign rule depends are anarchically called into question.

Into the fantastical structure of cosmic sovereign order depicted in *A Midsummer Night's Dream* stumbles Bottom, a crude weaver and a 'mimic' actor, whose transformation into an 'ass-man' involves him becoming the lover of a Queen. Neoplatonic hierarchy is thus thrown into collision with a figure of Ovidian metamorphosis and Pauline foolishness. Classed as a 'rude' mechanical, Bottom's rudeness, as Patricia Parker observes, is suggestive of shapeless matter.[53] Unlike the aristocratic women whose 'wax' forms have been fixed and defined as 'beautiful' by patriarchal law, Bottom is un-formed, abject, ugly. Monstrously fusing the human and the animal together, Bottom's profanity extends beyond physical hybridity: intruding into the court of a Queen, he is entertained in her bower in a manner suggestive of bestiality, while his recitation of Paul's letter to the Corinthians entails an almost blasphemous garbling of Scripture in which the mystical transports of the apostle are deployed to evoke the perverse sexual adventures of a weaver with the head of an ass.

As the Palatine graffito indicates, the foolishness of the ass and its deployment as a figure of mockery has an ancient heritage, one which remains visible in the medieval Asses' Feast, linked to the Feast of Fools.[54] The stupidity of the ass nevertheless also has a long tradition of working to confound the wisdom of the wise. In the biblical account of Balaam and his ass, for instance, the 'wise' Balaam sets off on a journey to place a curse on Israel, only to be confronted by an angel who is initially only visible to the ass on which he is riding.[55] Refusing to proceed, the ass is beaten until she unexpectedly begins to talk, informing Balaam about the angel. Balaam may be a seer, then, but he is blind in comparison with his ass, who turns out not to be such a dumb beast after all. Balaam's talking ass made frequent appearances in medieval drama. From the twelfth-century Laon *Ordo Prophetarum*, in which the confrontation between Balaam, his ass and the angel appears as a 'miniature drama', to the recreation of the episode in the early sixteenth-century Chester mystery play *Moses and the Law: Balaack and Balaam*, the comic sight of an ass talking back to her master evidently captured the imaginations of playwrights and audiences alike.[56] As Kurt Schreyer argues, Balaam's ass is in fact a more obvious theatrical ancestor to Shakespeare's Bottom than are the classical sources more commonly cited in relation to the play.[57]

---

[52] Stubbes, *Anatomie of Abuses*, n.p.
[53] Patricia Parker, *Shakespeare from the Margins: Language, Culture, Context* (Chicago, 1996), p. 84. Laird, '"If we offend, it is with our good will"', p.39, also discusses Bottom's 'linguistic transgression'.
[54] See Deborah Baker Wyrick, 'The ass motif in *The Comedy of Errors* and *A Midsummer Night's Dream*', *Shakespeare Quarterly* 33 (1982), p. 433.
[55] Balaam's encounter with the angel is described in Numbers 22:21–38.
[56] See E. K. Chambers, *The Mediaeval Stage*, vol. 2 (Oxford, 1903), p. 55; Kurt Schreyer, 'Balaam to Bottom: Artifact and theatrical translation in the sixteenth century', *Journal of Medieval and Early Modern Studies* 42 (2012), 422–5.
[57] See Schreyer, 'Balaam to Bottom', p. 422.

As well as illustrating the Pauline principle that God uses foolish things to confound the wise, Balaam and his ass carry specifically messianic overtones. The Laon *Ordo Prophetarum*, in which the Balaam episode was first staged, was performed during the Christmas season as a typological exercise, displaying Old Testament foretellings of the birth of Christ. Balaam's prophecy that 'there shall come a Star of Jacob' (Numbers 24:17) was interpreted in both rabbinic and Christian traditions in messianic terms. In Christian traditions, the 'Star of Jacob' is linked to the star seen by the Magi at the birth of Christ. Not only does Balaam foretell the arrival of the Messiah, then, but his prophecy anticipates Paul's quest to widen the messianic call beyond the Jews to the gentile order represented by the Magi.[58] The Pauline framework through which the Balaam episode was interpreted in Christian traditions thus establishes a link between Bottom's allusions to Paul's writings and his transformation into an 'ass-man'. Bottom's evocation of Balaam and his ass also illuminates the extent to which Bottom's idiocy does not run counter to his ability to represent or articulate moments of messianic wisdom. Like Balaam, regarded in Christian traditions as a profane figure, and his ass, Bottom never achieves any kind of fully fledged wisdom: his moments of inspiration, like theirs, are transitory and ephemeral, mysterious and elusive.[59] Through his comic and profane intrusion into the cosmic order of Athens and the fairies, however, Bottom evokes an alternative order, one in which the foolish and the ugly may hold the key to an emancipation from the violently rigid and hierarchical identities available elsewhere in the play.

Although Bottom's transformation into an 'ass man' is imposed upon him, it accords with his desire for change throughout the play. His comic eagerness to play every part in 'Pyramus and Thisbe' is matched by his enthusiasm to modify his body through prosthetic additions. Open to the seemingly endless possibilities offered by 'your straw-colour beard, your orange-tawny beard, your purple-in-grain beard, or your French-crown-colour beard' (1.2.86–8), his later adoption of the ass's head and abrupt transportation from the role of weaver to that of the fairy queen's favourite is the culmination of his openness to transformation, throwing into relief the painful rigidity entailed in the reign of 'wisdom' and 'beauty' elsewhere in the play. 'Bless thee, Bottom, bless thee. Thou art translated' (3.1.113), cries Quince, echoing the letter to the Colossians attributed to Paul, where the Messiah is said to have 'translated' his followers from the 'power of darkness' into an alternative kingdom.[60] Bottom is thus framed by allusions to the monstrous inversions through which Paul undermines the static categories of the classical cosmos. 'Thou art as wise as thou art beautiful' (3.1.140), states Titania to the 'translated' Bottom, evoking the transvaluations at the heart of Paul's declaration of the messianic. Bottom's comic foolishness does not undermine his status as Pauline visionary, then, but is crucial to it.[61] Blundering in his crude and senseless way through the enchanted world of the fairies and the aristocratic Athenian court, he illuminates the oppressive imperial structures in which the possibility of transformation is necessarily pathologized as the product of 'seething

---

[58] See Robert C. Lagueux, 'Sermons, exegesis, and performance: The Laon *Ordo Prophetarum* and the meaning of advent', *Comparative Drama* 43 (2009), 215.

[59] On the moral ambiguity of Balaam, see J. R. Baskin, 'Origen on Balaam: The dilemma of the unworthy prophet', *Vigiliae Christianae* 37 (1983), 22–35.

[60] Colossians 1:13. Luther comments on Paul's claim in Galatians 1:4 that we have been delivered from 'this present evil world' with reference to the statement in Colossians that 'we are translated' by Christ from a kingdom of darkness into one of light, *Commentary on Galatians*, ed. E. Middleton (London, 1864), p. 26.

[61] Anthony B. Dawson, by contrast, argues that Bottom's allusions to Paul are 'a clear example of the theatre cannibalizing and carnivalizing religious discourse and the authority that goes with it'. See his 'The secular theater', in *Shakespeare and Religious Change*, ed. Kenneth J. E. Graham and Philip D. Collington (Basingstoke, 2009), p. 248. For a recent reading of Bottom as 'not mangling the Gospel so much as he is seriocomically extending Paul's arguments', see Jennifer Waldron, '"The eye of man hath not heard": Shakespeare, synaesthesia and post-Reformation phenomenology', *Criticism* 54 (2012), 403–17. R. Chris Hassel Jr. also argues for the 'central position' of Paul in the 'comic vision' of the play in his *Faith and Folly in Shakespeare's Romantic Comedies* (Athens, GA, 1980), pp. 52–76.

brains' (5.1.4). While the law of the father relies on the fixing of a static beauty created in its own image, Bottom's 'translation' introduces an alternative, messianic ugliness, one articulated in distinctly Pauline terms, where 'Things base and vile, holding no quantity, / Love can transpose to form and dignity' (1.1.232–3).

III

If *A Midsummer Night's Dream* explores the radical implications of being 'translated', *The Winter's Tale* stages the emancipatory potential of 'mingling'. After an opening act in which we witness the violence attendant upon a sovereign insistence on clearly defined identity, the play leads us into an alternative order, one in which 'gallimaufry' (4.4.326) or the rag-bag, becomes the reigning principle.[62] Leontes is possessed by dread at the thought of being confused with another: 'You have mistook, my lady – / Polixenes for Leontes' (2.1.83–4), he cries, betraying the reliance upon identity at the heart of his despotic rule. Opening his home to another has resulted in a loss of his sense of self.[63] 'To mingle friendship farre is mingling bloods' (1.2.111), he observes, articulating a sense of personal invasion at the forcing of his 'gates' (1.2.198), which he projects onto his wife's body.[64] Hospitality, as Derrida points out, requires absolute openness to the other, to the extent that 'I give place to them.'[65] This radical displacement of the host by the guest is not one easily countenanced by Leontes, however, who is perhaps a man of his times as he focuses more upon the risks to the host than upon the ethical requirement to give way to the guest. Hospitality is closely aligned with grace: 'it is gracious', as Derrida states, and cannot be reduced to the economy of reciprocal exchange.[66] As a result, it is at heart an ethic which threatens to undermine rather than to shore up identity. Unable to embrace the threat to his 'gates', or to the borders of his subjectivity, necessarily entailed in the hospitable encounter, Leontes resorts to a violent expulsion of that which he interprets as an infection (1.2.307), one which may 'hiss [him] to [his] grave' (1.2.190).

Instead of opening himself to the other, he insists on self-definition to the point of psychosis.[67] The need to define the terms of his own world overrides all other considerations, including those of reason: 'what need we / Commune with you of this, but rather follow / Our forceful instigation?' (2.1.163–5), he declares to his court, relieved to be able to 'appoint [himself]' (1.2.328) in opposition to all forms of community, including those based upon shared principles of evidence-based justice.

Appointing herself a 'medicinal' figure, able to speak truth to (psychotic) power, Paulina, as many critics have noted, is associated in the play with the apostle from whom she derives her name.[68] Fearlessly speaking truth to a sovereign figure without regard for personal safety, she embodies the quality of *parrhesia* identified by Foucault in ancient culture, one he describes as the 'apostolic virtue *par excellence*'.[69] Yet it is perhaps Florizel who represents the clearest alternative in the play to the rigid self-definition exposed as the bedfellow of despotic power. A figure of militant conviction, who, to James Kuzner, sounds 'Pauline from the outset', Florizel insists that imperial patriarchal structures spell death.[70] The counter to these

---

[62] Diehl, '"Does not the stone rebuke me?"', p. 69, comments that the play is a 'mongrel drama, one that delights in mingling high and low', and one that 'promiscuously mingles the myths, beliefs, and historical details of various epochs and cultures, creating a curiously hybrid world'.

[63] Julia Reinhard Lupton discusses hospitality in the play but focuses on Hermione rather than Leontes. See her *Thinking with Shakespeare* (Chicago, 2011), pp. 161–85.

[64] Diehl comments that a 'fear of mingling, and of the impurity that result from it, pervades [the play]' ('"Does not the stone rebuke me?"', p. 69).

[65] Jacques Derrida, *Of Hospitality*, trans. Rachel Bowlby (Stanford, 2000), p. 77.

[66] Derrida, *Hospitality*, p. 83.

[67] Lupton uses the term 'psychotic' of Leontes in *Thinking with Shakespeare*, pp. 168–9.

[68] See, for instance, Diehl, '"Does not the stone rebuke me?"', pp. 69–82.

[69] Michel Foucault, *The Courage of Truth: Government of the Self and Others II*, ed. Frederic Gros, trans. Graham Burchell (Basingstoke, 2011), p. 330.

[70] Kuzner, 'Faith in law', p. 270.

structures is love, for which Florizel rejects the rank and place given to him by the law of his father:

[W]ere I crowned the most imperial monarch,
Thereof most worthy, were I the fairest youth
That ever made eye swerve, had force and knowledge
More than was ever man's, I would not prize them
Without her love.   (4.4.370–4)

As Kuzner notes, Florizel's renunciation of power, beauty, strength and wisdom in the name of love echoes Paul's famous declaration to the Corinthians that love must take priority over 'all secrets and all knowledge', as well as faith or acts of charity: without love, they all 'profiteth ... nothing' (1 Corinthians 13:1–3).[71] Instead of seeking to preserve a sense of fixed being, Florizel embraces the 'continual transit' and the fidelity to the call characteristic of Pauline messianism.[72] 'From my succession wipe me, father', he declares: 'I / Am heir to my affection' (4.4.480–1). 'More [for] straining on' than 'for plucking back' (4.4.465), he echoes Paul's relentlessly forward movement. Identifying himself only as one of the 'heirs by promise' (Galatians 3:29), Paul likewise 'forget[s] that which is behind, and endeavour[s] [himself] unto that which is before' (Philippians 3:14).

Where 'mingling', to Leontes, is a principle of terror, bespeaking a horrifying dissolution of self, the play therefore deploys Pauline principles to demonstrate the alternative possibilities inaugurated by those who abandon rigid models of being in order to 'mingle faith'. Perdita has to be educated in such principles: her initial insistence that artificially generated flowers ('nature's bastards' (4.4.83)) must be rejected in the name of an apparently pure nature prioritizes static being over dynamic processes of transformation in a manner shown by the play to be inseparable from injustice and oppression. Polixenes attempts to teach her the benefits of 'marry[ing] / A gentler scion to the wildest stock' (4.4.92–4), recalling Paul's discussion of 'grafting', where he likewise celebrates the grafting of the 'wild' gentile olive tree, 'contrary to nature', onto the 'right' Jewish root (Romans 11:17–24). Pauline models of grace, then, are articulated in terms of intermingling, grafting and hybridity, principles Perdita, at this point in the play, has yet to embrace. By the time she counters Polixenes's assertion of 'natural' hierarchical order with the statement that 'The selfsame sun that shines upon his court / Hides not his visage from our cottage' (4.4.444–5), however, she is echoing the description of grace from Matthew 5:44–5, which undermines categories of friend or enemy. The 'gallimaufry' of elements characteristic of the festival scenes, and of the hybrid nature of the play itself, likewise celebrates a grotesque fluidity, one which undermines the violent imposition of sovereign power in the name of monstrous mingling.[73]

The Pauline discourses shaping the play are most apparent, however, in its final scene, where the binary division between life and death itself is breached in the mysterious staging of Hermione's resurrection. *The Winter's Tale* frames Hermione's resurrection in explicitly Pauline terms, most notably through the pivotal role of Paulina. Having invested significant effort in creating the statue, Paulina, as Huston Diehl notes, echoes the labours of her namesake, an apostle who, according to Luther, 'with great travel and diligence set forth Christ plainly' to the Galatians,

even as if a painter had portrayed Christ Jesus before their eyes ... as if he said: There is no painter that with his colours can so lively set out Christ unto you, as I have painted him out by my preaching.[74]

Paulina's role as the patron of the statue is thus a crucial aspect of her representation of Paul in the play. She is the one ultimately responsible for creating an image of resurrection truth; she 'plainly shew[s] and paint[s] [it] out before your eyes, that ye may see it, and touch it with your hands', as

---

[71] Kuzner, 'Faith in law', p. 270, cites the Corinthians' passage alongside Florizel's speech.
[72] Breton, *A Radical Philosophy*, p. 120.
[73] Diehl describes the 'mongrel' nature of the play in '"Does not the stone rebuke me?"', p. 69.
[74] Luther, *Galatians*, p. 148. Diehl cites this allusion in '"Does not the stone rebuke me?"', p. 71.

Luther said of Paul.[75] Paul's 'bitter' denunciation of the Galatians nevertheless points to his fears of the futility of his creative effort. Despite having the image of the resurrected Christ before them through his words, the Galatians fail to understand its significance and consequently threaten to 'crucify [Christ] again'.[76] Paulina evidently fears a similarly inappropriate response, warning Leontes not to 'shun her', or else 'You kill her double' (5.3.105–7).

'Every wink of an eye some new grace will be born' (5.2.109–10), we are told in the run up to Hermione's re-animation, echoing Paul's description of resurrection, when '[i]n a moment, in the twinkling of an eye ... the trumpet shall blow, and the dead shall be raised up incorruptible, and we shall be changed' (1 Corinthians 15:52). The resurrected or 'glorified' body depicted by Paul is characterized by hybridity. Rejecting the view of some of his contemporaries that only the spirit can be raised, Paul insists that physical bodies are resurrected, albeit in altered form.[77] The resurrected body, consequently, fuses together the material and the spiritual, as attested by his description of this entity as a 'spiritual body' (1 Corinthians 15:44). His terminology, in fact, suggests that resurrection involves the prosthetic addition of the immortal to the mortal, resulting in a curiously hybrid form: 'for this corruptible must put on incorruption, and this mortal must put on immortality' (1 Corinthians 15:53). Paul's language, as Calvin points out, suggests that we adopt immortality as 'a garment'.[78] The prosthetic addition nevertheless becomes constitutive of the glorified body: 'this blessed garment of incorruption', notes Martin Day in an early seventeenth-century sermon on the apocalypse, 'shall run through all the veynes of man; it shall possess him every where; it shall be as the life is in all the parts of the body'.[79]

Paul's model of the resurrected form as a hybrid, prosthetic body was nevertheless fused uneasily from the time of the Church fathers onwards with Neoplatonic ideals of perfect being, so that the resurrected body in Christian traditions, both visual and textual, is often depicted as static, whole and, crucially, beautiful.[80] The resurrected body, imagined in wholly future terms, shall be of 'exquisite feature and stature, beautified by God's own blessed almighty hand, with the utmost of created comeliness, and matchlesse proportion', claims Robert Bolton, insisting that the glorified will be free 'from all defects and imperfections, diseases and distempers, infirmities and deformities, maimednesse and monstrous shapes, infancy or decrepitnesse of stature'.[81] For Paul, however, resurrected life is not confined to the future but is an experience of living 'in Christ' that begins now and continues as a dynamic process in which the righteous are progressively 'changed ... from glory to glory' (2 Corinthians 3:18). This process, moreover, is resolutely communal, resisting models of individual identity: it is 'quite impossible', notes John A. T. Robinson in relation to Pauline theology, 'to think of the resurrection hope in terms of the individual unit'.[82] Pauline models of the resurrection instead insist that the self is displaced as the subject is increasingly incorporated into the 'body of Christ' (1 Corinthians 1:9; 10:16).

The resurrected body, in its Pauline formulation, thus radically undercuts notions of individual and discrete being. Following this model, it is

---

[75] Luther, *Galatians*, p. 151. On Paulina as patron of the statue, see Chloe Porter, *Making and Unmaking in Early Modern English Drama: Spectators, Aesthetics and Incompletion* (Manchester, 2013), pp. 71–9.

[76] Luther, *Galatians*, p. 150.

[77] See Martin, *The Corinthian Body*, p. 136.

[78] John Calvin, *Commentary on the Epistles of Paul the Apostle to the Corinthian*, vol. 2 (Edinburgh, 1849), p. 61.

[79] Martin Day, *Doomes-Day: or, A Treatise of the Resurrection of the Body* (1636), p. 177.

[80] Candida R. Moss, 'Heavenly healing: Eschatological cleansing and the resurrection of the dead in the early Church', *Journal of the American Academy of Religion* 79 (2011), 991–1017, discusses the Christian tradition of depicting resurrected bodies as 'perfect' and 'complete'.

[81] Robert Bolton, *Mr. Bolton's Last and Learned Work of the Foure Last Things: Death, Judgment, Hell and Heaven* (1633), pp. 137, 129–31.

[82] 'The carrier of the glory ... is not the individual but the Church', he continues. John A. T. Robinson, *The Body: A Study in Pauline Theology* (London, 1952), pp. 81–2.

precisely as a hybrid, unstable, prosthetic entity, rather than as a fixed, natural being, that the resurrected Hermione operates as a figure of messianic hope. Created as the image of Hermione, by the co-operation of patron and sculptor, and awakened partly through interaction with those observing her, the animated statue on multiple levels undercuts the violent individualism of the play's opening act. Living and dead, artificial and natural, illicitly magical and lawful, touchable and untouchable, Hermione and not Hermione, the statue defies logical categorization.[83] The monstrosity of Hermione's resurrected form is anticipated earlier in the play when Paulina comments that Perdita's return would be 'as monstrous to our human reason / As my Antigonus to break his grave / And come again to me' (5.1.41–3). Resisting fixity in categorization, the statue is also materially unstable, threatening, in abject terms, to leak beyond its own borders.[84] '[T]he colour's / Not dry', Hermione warns Perdita, while refusing to let Leontes kiss the statue: 'The ruddiness upon her lip is wet. / You'll mar it if you kiss it, stain your own / With oily painting' (5.3.47–8, 81–3). Far from 'stony', the statue of Hermione is 'but newly fixed' or, more accurately, not fixed at all: permeable and vulnerable to being 'mar[red]' by the touch of others, it also threatens to 'stain' those in its vicinity. Where Leontes's actions in the first act were driven by a need to expel that which may infect him, he is now forced to confront the contamination attendant upon openness to the other.

As an abject entity threateningly transgressing the borders of self and other, Hermione's statue undercuts the coherent unity of form central to Neoplatonic models of beauty. Crucially, then, and in a manner that is often overlooked in criticism of the play, she is described as ugly: her wrinkles, as well as her leaky body, mark a striking departure from the classical beauty her statuesque form otherwise suggests.[85] Her lined features also set her apart from most early modern accounts of the resurrected body, in which the absence of wrinkles tends to feature prominently. When 'old age begins to rivle the face, and to draw the complexion into furrows ... then there is a wofull spectacle of weaknesse', states Day, insisting that the resurrected are, on the contrary, characterized by (wrinkle-free) strength. For Paul, however, such insistence on beauty, defined by stable, unmarked being, represents the aesthetic and political aspirations of 'the wise', against which he posits the 'foolishness' and physical brokenness of the cross. Following Pauline models, *The Winter's Tale* aligns the stony fixity of beauty with the 'numbness' of death, whereas the wrinkled, seeping mutability of the resurrected Hermione signifies the hope of living, and loving, community.[86]

'If this be magic, let it be an art / Lawful as eating' (5.3.110–11), states Leontes, displaying a promising new openness to the possibility of transformation. His words recall Paul's subversive statements discarding the prohibition on eating food that has been sacrificed to idols. Such customary laws, states the apostle, are irrelevant to those who are now defined solely in relation to the Messiah: 'What say I then? That the idol is anything? Or that which is sacrificed to idols, is anything? Nay' (1 Corinthians 10:19–20). It is a matter of indifference: 'all things are lawful for me' (1 Corinthians 10:23). The opening up of the previously sacred or taboo for everyday use is an act of profanation, and the apostle to the Gentiles, he who declares that the previously exclusive is now universally available, instigates a principle of profanation that is perpetuated in *The Winter's Tale*.[87]

---

[83] Kuzner discusses the 'unclassifiable' nature of Hermione in the final scene in 'Faith in law', p. 274.

[84] On the unstable nature of Hermione's statue, see Porter, *Making and Unmaking*, pp. 77–8.

[85] On ugliness as that which transgresses borders, see Mark Cousins 'The ugly', *AA Files* 28 (1994), 61–4 and 29; (1995), 3–6.

[86] Renuka Gusain discusses the violence underlying male attempts to fix female beauty into statuesque form in '"With what's unreal thou coactive art": The problem and possibilities of beauty in *The Winter's Tale*', *Shakespeare* 9 (2013), 52–75.

[87] Kuzner, 'Faith in law', p. 278, refers to the play as 'Pauline, but secular', yet the play, in my reading, comes closer to the profane than to the secular. Julia Reinhard Lupton refers to 'a

Paulina's chapel doubles as an art gallery and, equally disturbingly, as a theatre. 'Plaies' are listed alongside 'feasts, banquets, Church ales [and] drinkinges' as 'prophane usages' of churches in Archbishop Bancroft's visitation articles of 1605, indicating the contemporary sensitivities of this issue.[88] Hermione's resurrection, moreover, is witnessed by a socially mixed audience, increasing the impression that this is a profane scene, one in which the sacred is being opened up for general use.[89] In its profanity, its critique of identity and its deployment of resurrection in ugly, hybrid terms, *The Winter's Tale* thus draws on a specifically Pauline messianism. That which 'should be hooted at' (5.3.117), once again, encodes a higher form of wisdom.

'We were disseverd' (5.3.156), admits Leontes in the final line of the play, recognizing the violent individuality that instigated its tragic beginnings. Yet hierarchical separation has given way to a topsy-turvy world operating under a new principle, which, as Kuzner states, 'explodes the notion of individual integrity', inaugurating the potential for overhauled relationships.[90] The Clown breathlessly relates that

[T]he King's son took me by the hand and called me brother; and then the two kings called my father brother; and then the Prince my brother and the Princess my sister called my father father; and so we wept.
(5.2.138–42)

Apocalypse, in the play, as largely in Paul, is the unearthing of a new order hidden in the midst of the old. Its terminology, then, is deployed not primarily in relation to the future or to the otherworldly but in the forging of new connections in the here-and-now: in the reunion of Leontes and Camillo, for instance, the men, overcome by a 'passion of wonder', 'looked as they had heard of a world ransomed, or one destroyed' (5.2.14–16). The staging of resurrection life in the play similarly issues a call for reconfigured forms of community. Unafraid to disavow the sacred and aesthetic tenets upholding the imperial order of the ancient world, Paul thus inspires Shakespeare not to shore up the borders of any particular identity, confessional or otherwise, but to embrace a politically charged messianism which exposes the pathological nature of normative identities. Elevating the profane and the monstrous over the well-formed and the beautiful, Shakespeare thus displays the radical potential of Pauline discourses to be deployed on the early modern stage as a challenge to the violent reign of beauty and identity in the name of an ugly non-being that will '[t]ug for the time to come' (4.4.497).

---

profane Paulinism' in 'Renaissance profanations: Religion and literature in the age of Agamben', *Religion and Literature* 41 (2009), 246–57; p. 249.

[88] James Stokes, ed., *Records of Early English Drama: Somerset*, vol. 1 (Toronto, 1996), p. 424, cited in Phebe Jensen, *Religion and Revelry in Shakespeare's Festive World* (Cambridge, 2008), p. 31.

[89] On the social mix of the audience in the final scene of *The Winter's Tale*, see Chloe Porter, 'Interactions between English Drama and Visual Culture, 1576–1642' (unpublished PhD diss., University of Manchester, 2007), p. 216.

[90] Kuzner, 'Faith in law', p. 275.

SHAKESPEARE PERFORMANCES IN ENGLAND, 2016

STEPHEN PURCELL

As the 400th anniversary of Shakespeare's death, 2016 was quite a year. It was so packed with Shakespearean productions that I had to limit myself to those making their UK premieres, and even then I was unable to review as many as I would have liked. In the UK, it was the year of the EU referendum, in which 51.9 per cent of voters opted to make Britain a more isolated nation and following which the country remained bitterly divided; the three *Cymbelines* and four *King Lears* I watched this year felt more topical than ever. Further afield, it was the year of Donald Trump, a figure whose presence haunted numerous productions. Culture wars were fought in the theatrical community, too: the artistic direction of Shakespeare's Globe became a matter of debate in the national media, and Shakespearean theatre made remarkable strides towards gender equality with an unprecedented number of high-profile cross-gender performances. Productions seemed especially concerned with nationhood, gender, sexuality, power and violence; some addressed Shakespeare's own cultural authority and inheritance through parody or adaptation. At the same time, a number of productions seemed to want to retreat from modernity into a world of fairy tale or myth.

DROMGOOLE DEPARTS

Dominic Dromgoole marked the end of his eleven-year artistic directorship of Shakespeare's Globe with a season of Shakespeare's late plays in the Sam Wanamaker Playhouse – the first Shakespearean productions to be directed specifically for the indoor theatre since its opening in 2014. Dromgoole bookended the season with his own productions of *Pericles* and *The Tempest*, which opened either side of Sam Yates's *Cymbeline* and Michael Longhurst's *The Winter's Tale*. All four made different uses of the candlelit auditorium but certain themes resurfaced: a co-opting of the audience through moments of direct address; a sense of fairy-tale magic or of religious ritual, often invoked through the act of lighting candles; and a hushed, furtive or confidential tone, weighting these tragicomic plays more heavily towards tragedy than might usually be the case. Appropriately, given the valedictory nature of the season, the candlelight frequently gave an impression of sunset.

Dromgoole's *Pericles* was a much more illusionistic, pared-down and serious affair than might have been expected from this director. The candles were completely extinguished as the show started, plunging the auditorium into the kind of darkness that tends to open a play in any conventional modern theatre space. Sheila Reid's Gower emerged from the trapdoor, carrying a candle, while the three players in the opening scene – Pericles, Antiochus and Antiochus's daughter – each lit themselves with handheld candelabra. This opening sequence was dark in tone, too: contrary to Gower's narration, Antiochus's incestuous relationship with his daughter was clearly not consensual. His daughter (Tia Bannon) flinched as he touched her and was clearly looking to Pericles to rescue her; when James Garnon's

Pericles responded with horror rather than sympathy, she was quietly distraught.

The first few scenes of the play were low energy, almost static. This forced a close attention to the language of the play but it also established a register of low-key realism from which the production struggled to escape in its later, more fantastical episodes. By the end of the Pentapolis sequence, the performance had entered a more festive and game-like register; this is perhaps inevitable, given the theatricality of the knights' contest, the playful nature of the scene in which Simonedes feigns disapproval of Pericles and Thaisa's match, and the subsequent scene on shipboard which, though tragic in tone, requires the imaginative complicity of the audience to transform a solid stage into a rocking boat. Here, a huge white sail descended from the roof, while a plank was attached perpendicularly to the front edge of the stage. Pericles stood in the auditorium on the tip of this plank, grasping two ropes either side of him for support, while members of the cast swung the sail behind him. The wafts of air produced by the billowing of the sail had the pleasing effect of gently rocking the Wanamaker's chandeliers, creating a disorienting combination of light, movement and sensation that evoked the stormy sea.

The production thus seemed caught between two contradictory impulses. On the one hand, it was played as a fantastical yarn – literally an 'old wives' tale', since Reid's Gower was a tiny elderly woman in the garb of an early modern peasant, friendly and wide-eyed, enjoying the far-fetched absurdity of her tale. Dromgoole's doubling emphasized the play's folk-tale symmetry: Simon Armstrong as the two father-kings, one good (Simonides), one bad (Antiochus); Dorothea Myer-Bennet as the two mother-queens, one good (Thaisa), one bad (Dionyza); Kirsty Woodward as Marina's two female guardians, one good (Lychorida), one bad (the Bawd). Tia Bannon was the deliverer of two fateful riddles, one propelling Pericles into danger at the start of his story (Antiochus's daughter spoke the lines of her own riddle in this production) and the other returning him to happiness at the end (her Diana descended from the heavens on a wire).

On the other hand, the production returned repeatedly to an emotional realist mode. This was at its most jarring in Act 5, when the play moves into its most obviously mythical register. Garnon, now wearing a long wig and fake beard, played the king as a man who had barely moved or spoken for sixteen years. As Jessica Baglow's Marina roused him from his catatonia, he seemed utterly unpractised at both speech and movement, stuttering, gasping and speaking haltingly: 'Well, um ... s-s-speak on. Uh ... Where – where were you born?' (21.143). This may have evoked an element of verisimilitude but it disrupted the verse and slowed down the scene, and Garnon's valiant attempts at naturalistically portraying the behaviour of a man broken by grief who finds out that his long-dead daughter is alive and well paradoxically had the effect (for me, at least) of foregrounding the implausibility of the plot.

Cymbeline, the second production in the season, was more consistent in its register. Brendan O'Hea's first gentleman set the tone in the opening scene by taking a kind of gossipy relish in his news, delivering it not just to the second gentleman but to the whole audience. This was a production that gained its effects largely from its direct address to spectators, and its speed. Emily Barber's Innogen was direct and engaging, listing her griefs matter-of-factly rather than with any sense of melodrama. She was also frequently very funny, silencing the chatting audience at end of the interval by striding onto the stage in her masculine attire and then immediately provoking a laugh with her observation, 'I see a man's life is a tedious one' (3.6.1). Her speech in which she reacted to the presence of Cloten's headless corpse (here a horribly realistic dummy complete with lashings of stage blood) trod a precarious line between tragic and comic, as I think it probably needs to.

Eugene O'Hare's Iachimo was evidently someone who got by on blind luck and self-belief rather than any real intelligence. He launched into a hammy set-piece on 'What, are men mad?'

(1.6.33), and returned to this self-consciously stagey mode of delivery as he backed out of his ill-advised attempt at seduction to declare that the whole episode had been a test of her virtue; that Innogen fell for this transparently false story was not much to her credit. The scene in her bedchamber was genuinely creepy, the small space and candlelight of the Wanamaker adding a sense of voyeurism and emphasizing the violation of Iachimo's trespass. He kissed Innogen lingeringly, and when he lifted her top to peer at her breast, the fact that he wanted to share his delight with the audience seemed almost as indecent as the act itself.

The production was at its most unsettling during such moments of direct address. Jonjo O'Neill's Posthumus was straightforward and sympathetic at first, sincere in his love for Innogen and entering the bet with Iachimo because of his righteous anger on her behalf; in their second scene together, he shouted 'This is her *honour*!' (2.4.91), outraged that Iachimo could be so careless with it. But when Iachimo produced her bracelet and proceeded to describe her body, Posthumus shared his reaction with the audience as if he were asking us to check his reasoning: 'I am sure / She would not lose it. Her attendants are / All sworn and honourable. They induced to steal it? / And by a stranger?' (2.4.123–6). As he left the stage promising 'to tear her limb-meal' (2.4.147), there was a sense that in our silent acquiescence we had somehow enabled his shift into violent misogyny. Seconds later, he returned to the stage, directing his questions angrily at us: 'This yellow Iachimo, in an hour – wast not? – / Or less? At *first*?' (2.5.14–15). We had been there for that scene too, he seemed to suggest – we *must* know. His anguished repentance at the end just about made his reunion with Innogen palatable; his injunction to Iachimo to 'live, / And deal with others better' (5.6.420–1) seemed just as much a reminder to himself.

Unlike Dromgoole's *Pericles*, the climax to Yate's *Cymbeline* was played fast, so that the twists and turns of its narrative came almost too quickly – a nice effect, since the audience seemed to be surprised by events they might otherwise have been expected to anticipate. *Cymbeline*'s final scene often suffers from pacing problems – after all, spectators already know all twenty-odd pieces of plot information that are revealed over the course of the scene. But Yates's production paced the scene perfectly, exploiting the relentless pulse of the metre to drive it forward, and thus avoided the temptation to wallow in emotional realism to which *Pericles*'s final act had succumbed. Each revelation was accompanied by appreciative audience laughter, suggesting that each fact was being revealed *just* at the moment the spectators themselves remembered it, almost in the manner of a farce.

Direct address was also exploited to unsettling effects in Michael Longhurst's *The Winter's Tale*. The marriage between John Light's Leontes and Rachael Stirling's Hermione was clearly dysfunctional from the start: when she convinced Polixenes to stay, Leontes's response, 'At my request he would not', was an unmistakeable challenge, as was his sullen reference to the 'Three crabbed months' it took to persuade her to marry him (1.2.89, 104). His numerous asides and soliloquies in this scene were delivered at first lightly, almost conversationally, his eyes skittering across the Wanamaker's auditorium as if in search of support for his suspicions. Whereas most actors tend to make a clear distinction between Leontes's asides and his lines to the other characters onstage, Light's Leontes seemed always to be aware of the presence of the audience, desperately attempting to demonstrate how reasonable his suspicions were.

As the play progressed, it became clear that this Leontes was distrustful not just of Hermione and Polixenes, but also of everybody. His mouth opened into a snarling smile as Niamh Cusack's Paulina resolved not to call him 'tyrant' (2.3.116), as if it simply confirmed what he had suspected all along: that Paulina's defence of Hermione was a cynical and politically motivated attack on his legitimacy as ruler. At the end of the scene, as he insisted to his attendant Lord that Hermione would have 'A just and open trial' (2.3.205), he stared at his subordinate as if daring him to contradict him. When the Oracle proclaimed Leontes 'a jealous tyrant' (3.2.133), he stared furiously at Hermione

19. *The Winter's Tale*, 2.2, Sam Wanamaker Playhouse, directed by Michael Longhurst. Niamh Cusack as Paulina. Photograph by Marc Brenner.

and Paulina, once again seeing confirmation of a political plot against him. This Leontes *knew* he was not a tyrant, but he knew too that everyone secretly thought he was. He even tried to goad the audience into giving themselves away, eyeballing us combatively as he asked, 'Shall I live on, to see this bastard kneel / And call me father? *Huh?* Better burn it now / Than curse it then. *Huh?*' (2.3.155–6).

Storytelling seemed to be the theme of the Wanamaker's winter season, and Longhurst's contribution was heavily inflected by fairy tales. At the start of 2.2, Cusack's Paulina entered like a folk-tale witch or a fairy godmother, a cloaked, hooded figure carrying a single candle (Illustration 19). There was something impish in her second appearance, too, as she smuggled the infant Perdita into Leontes's chamber under her cloak, revealing the baby with a flourish. Leontes's immediate reply – 'A mankind witch!' (2.3.68) – seemed to confirm the magical impression of the moment. Cusack's Paulina was hard-edged and sarcastic – she spoke the line 'Good queen, my lord, good queen, I say good queen' (2.3.60) as if she were pretending Leontes was hard of hearing – but at the core of her performance was an understanding of the character as deeply passionate and empathetic. Cusack doubled as Time, emphasizing Paulina's role as a semi-magical and benevolent agent.

The reunions of the final scene were played as an unambiguously happy ending. Hermione's statue was revealed in the discovery space, surrounded by flickering candles like a religious shrine. Leontes and Hermione shared a long kiss as her statue came to life; this maintained the momentum of her miraculous resurrection over Polixenes, Camillo and Paulina's lines, so that the moment achieved its emotional gut-punch not on the usual 'O, she's warm' (5.3.109), but on Hermione's first line to her daughter ('You gods, look down / And from your sacred vials pour your graces / Upon my daughter's head'; 5.3.122–4), which Stirling played as the eruption of sixteen years of maternal yearning. Leontes's hasty arrangement of a marriage between Paulina and Camillo was played without irony or awkwardness: Camillo did reach out to Paulina as if asking her consent but she just smiled and took his hands obligingly. Leontes and Hermione shared a kiss again as the stage emptied, the culmination of what read to me as a parable about forgiveness.

The final production of the season, and of Dromgoole's artistic directorship, was *The Tempest*. Whereas the Globe's most recent Prospero – Roger Allam's in 2013 – had been appealingly vulnerable, Tim McMullan's was director-like, powerful and coolly in control, summoning storms, spirits and visions almost as if he were cuing entrances and exits. The opening scene was deeply metatheatrical: as Prospero conjured the storm, the doors to the discovery space were flung open and a piece of scenery was thrust out – a set of flat, painted wooden cut-outs being manipulated by visible stagehands to give the illusion of rocking waves. On a thrust stage, of course, the mechanism behind the illusion was exposed: the magic, here, was that of the showman. McMullan's Prospero was also director-like in his dealings with the other characters. He clicked his fingers at Phoebe Pryce's Miranda to silence her, had no qualms about sending her to sleep when he had other business to attend to and, later, shooed her away as he took Dharmesh Patel's Ferdinand aside to discuss her forthcoming marriage. He summoned Pippa Nixon's Ariel with a trembling hand and commanded Fisayo Akinade's Caliban with calm authority. McMullan's sonorous baritone was easy on the ear but gave little sense of a character whose view of himself was ever under any serious threat.

Nixon's Ariel was also emotionally detached. She moved gracefully, with a slow fluidity, always leaning slightly forwards and staring at the figures around her with an open-faced expression. Her steady gaze was almost that of a puppeteer; indeed, she was invisible to all but Prospero and frequently touched the unseeing humans in order to provoke an emotional change in them, usually from distress to calmness, such as when she hugged the grief-stricken Ferdinand from behind or stroked Caliban's head as he became agitated by his memory of the island's mysterious noises. But her fixed stare also seemed to signify a curiosity about human emotion. 'Do you love me, master? No?' (4.1.48) was spoken not as if she had any need to be loved but as if she were trying to accurately identify the emotion. Her disarmingly emotionless 'Mine would, sir, were I human' (5.1.20) pointed up the fact that Ariel was not especially moved by the humans' plight but understood that Prospero ought to be. Tellingly, it was when she touched his chest during this exchange that he decided to take the part of his 'nobler reason' against his 'fury' (5.1.26).

Dromgoole was alert to the post-colonial politics of Shakespeare's play but I am not sure he had any particularly progressive solutions to its problems. The production's two black actors, Joseph Marcell and Fisayo Akinade, were cast race-consciously (especially striking, since the other minority ethnic cast members seemed to have been cast colour-blind). Marcell's Gonzalo was evidently the character who had recommended the marriage between Claribel and the King of Tunis; the other courtiers all flinched slightly when he brought it up and Sebastian's anger at Alonso's decision to 'loose her to an African' (2.1.131) seemed directed at Gonzalo just as much as it was at the King. Akinade's fur-clad Caliban, meanwhile, was clearly a victim of European colonialism, speaking softly with an African-inflected accent and scuttling around with a limp that suggested over-work and physical abuse at the hands of his master (or his supernatural agents). If this low-status, sympathetic Caliban implied a progressive reading of the play, however, it was rather undermined by a tendency on the part of the other characters to treat him as if he were an unruly-but-loveable pet – Stephano, Ariel and Prospero all stroked his hair at various points. His shamefaced apology to the magnanimous Prospero at the play's end showed that he had learned to be a good colonial subject, and nothing about the production's handling of the scene implied that this was anything other than a good thing.

RICE ROCKS THE GROUND

Shortly after Dromgoole's *Tempest* closed, Emma Rice's tenure as the new Artistic Director of the Globe opened with her *A Midsummer Night's Dream* in the main house. The production certainly served to advertise Rice's departure from the aesthetic style of her predecessor. Controversially, she had installed sound and lighting rigs: actors wearing radio mics thus had no need to strain their voices as they sang over amplified music or entered through the yard and, for the first time in my experience at the theatre, the audience faded into darkness as the sun set. Dramaturg Tanika Gupta had rewritten parts of the play's dialogue (mostly that of the mechanicals), and she and Rice had made space at several moments for characters to burst into short renditions of modern pop songs. Original songs were interspersed throughout, and near-constant underscoring dictated the emotional tone of each scene. Rice had titled her inaugural season the 'Wonder Season', and the physical environment that she and designer Börkur Jónsson had created was clearly meant to inspire spectators to experience the 'magic' of Shakespeare's forest in an immersive way. The pavement and piazza outside the Globe had been festooned with fake silver trees, while inside the theatre, over thirty inflatable white orbs of various sizes bobbed in the sky above groundlings' heads. Hanging garlands of colourful flowers were draped over the tiring house's multiple entrances and, over the stage, a huge red neon sign invited spectators to 'Rock the ground' (4.1.85).

It became clear as the performance started that Rice wanted both to celebrate and to parody the history of the building she had inherited. The show opened with Lucy Thackeray's clownish Rita Quince welcoming the audience to the theatre, introducing her team (all of whom wore the distinctive T-shirts of Globe stewards) and making a few 'Health and Safety' announcements. Despite the Globe's interest in 'Original Practices', we were told, we should refrain from 'public urination and spreading syphilis'. Bottom (Ewan Wardrop) informed us that we should watch out for symptoms of dehydration such as tiredness and confusion, though he conceded that these might be difficult to distinguish from the usual experience of watching a Shakespeare play. Rice's rude mechanicals were, she insisted in the programme, a celebration of the theatre's stewards, 'the most magnificent band of volunteers in the country' – but they were also a parodic portrait of Globe enthusiasts. 'This tambourine was given to me by Mark Rylance', claimed Quince proudly at one point; later, upon being cast as Pyramus, Bottom immediately changed into the kind of doublet-and-hose outfit typical of previous Globe productions. Rice's *Dream* thus positioned itself, like her 2006 *Cymbeline* for the RSC, as both a popular reclamation of Shakespeare and a playful subversion of its historical and high-culture trappings.

Shakespeare's cultural authority was addressed in a different way in the production's presentation of the supernatural world. The fairies' costumes combined Elizabethan elements such as ruffs and bumrolls with anachronistic intrusions such as nipple tassels and hotpants. Katy Owen's mischievous Puck was dressed in a green doublet and fishnet stockings, and she carried a plastic water pistol with which she squirted actors and groundlings alike. Zubin Varla's Oberon wore an ornately patterned doublet and hose that contrasted with his rolled-down socks and smudged make-up, while his beard and hairline made him look like a dishevelled cartoon version of Shakespeare himself. But if this Oberon was an author-figure, he was a frustrated and impotent one: he made his first appearance swigging angrily from a bottle of cheap cider, and he ran his hands longingly over the unseeing faces of the mortal lovers. He engineered the play's amorous encounters, it seemed, because he was lonely himself, and his desire for Titania's changeling boy – represented here by a life-size puppet – appeared to be motivated by his jealousy of Titania's easy intimacy with her followers. When he finally managed to steal the boy from them, the puppet, wrenched from the hands of its puppeteers, died in his arms, only to be revived after Oberon and Titania were reconciled.

In an inspired piece of casting, Titania was played by the cabaret performance artist Meow Meow. She made a spectacular first entrance, lowered down from the heavens trap on wires, to applause and cheering from the audience. This Titania was glamorous and goofy, sensual and clumsy, projecting a sense of both sexual power and emotional warmth – a stark contrast with Varla's lonely, begrudging Oberon. In a hilarious sequence of physical comedy, she became tangled up in her tights whilst trying to remove them during an overblown love duet with Bottom. But this was not a performance that ignored the play's dark undertones. When Oberon invaded her bower to apply the love juice, it was evidently a sexual violation (Illustration 20). Meow Meow's simultaneous dancer-like precision and clown-like klutziness helped to suggest a character who was not in control of herself, and who was on some level aware of, and troubled by, that lack of control.

20. *A Midsummer Night's Dream*, 2.2, Shakespeare's Globe, directed by Emma Rice. Zubin Varla as Oberon and Meow Meow as Titania. Photograph by Steve Tanner.

The contrast between the repressed, backward-looking Oberon and the progressive, pansexual Titania was emphasized in the production's concluding song: as Oberon promised, 'Jack will have Jill / Jill will have Jack / Nought shall go ill / No turning back', Titania replied, 'Jill will have Jill / Jack will have Jack / No one will need / An aphrodisiac.'

This theme was echoed in the lovers' plot, too. Like the clowns, the lovers were meant to hail from the world of the audience, references to 'Athens' being universally replaced with 'London' or 'Bankside'. The production's most superficially radical innovation was to turn Helena into Helenus (Ankur Bahl), a young man. This brought out some interesting new meanings: when Theseus (Varla again) heard that Demetrius (Ncuti Gatwa) had 'made love' to Helenus (1.1.107), the Duke slapped Demetrius, clearly intent on enforcing heterosexuality. Demetrius's 'I am sick when I do look on thee' (2.1.212) had the ring of a closeted gay man in denial about his sexuality and, at the end, his admission of his 'natural taste' for Helenus seemed to be a belated acceptance of it (4.1.173). There were one or two unfortunate side-effects of the change, however. Helenus sometimes threatened to lapse into gay stereotype, and it did not entirely ring true that Hermia's first assumption on discovering that Lysander had fallen for another man was that the latter had 'urged his height' (3.2.292). Perhaps more troublingly, the change gave one of the play's best roles for women (and arguably the most sympathetic of the four lovers) to a man, leaving Anjana Vasan's Hermia as the play's sole representative of younger women.

The climactic performance of *Pyramus and Thisbe* seemed to mock not the old regime but the new. Quince added an intrusive layer of underscoring from her electronic keyboard, and her actors extended the text with sequences of self-indulgent physical theatre and bursts of song. When Nandi Bhebhe's Starveling emerged 'with silver suit and latex orb' as Moonshine (her white balloon a smaller copy of the larger spheres suspended above spectators' heads), Theseus objected that she should be the man *on* the moon, not the man in the moon; she snapped back, 'It's a visual concept! Why is that so hard to understand? Why is everyone so obsessed with text?' The outburst got a big laugh when I saw it, including from me, but as I reflected upon it afterwards, I found myself unsure as to the target of the joke. Theseus, the stickler for textual precision in a new era of visual and physical theatre? Starveling, whose pretentious visual conceit at this moment was, after all, fairly ludicrous? Or maybe both?

The next production in Rice's inaugural season was Caroline Byrne's *The Taming of the Shrew*, in which Shakespeare's play was relocated to the Ireland of the 1916 Easter Rising (2016 was, of course, an anniversary year not only for Shakespeareans). The show opened with a stage strewn with empty pairs of shoes, and Katherine (Aoife Duffin) singing a lament in a hoarse, strident voice. She vowed to 'trouble the living stream' – a quotation from Yeats's poem 'Easter 1916', but also an anticipation, perhaps, of Katherine's own observation at the end of the play that 'A woman moved is like a fountain troubled' (5.2.147). According to the programme, the lyrics to this ballad, titled 'Numbered in the Song', had been written by dramaturg Morna Regan as a direct response to Yeats, whose poem had understated the role of women in the Easter Rising. Thus, Byrne's production framed the shrew-taming narrative not with Christopher Sly but with a woman singing full-throatedly about her own literary circumscription. Katherine sang with a defiant hope: 'You can act a different part / From the one already writ.'

The song returned three times in the production. Just before the wedding, Katherine was fastened into a corset and bound by several other women, while she sang, 'Neither of us is free / If one of us is bound' (Illustration 21). The song returned again at the end of the first half, as the newly married Katherine descended halfway into an onstage pool, drenching her dress – a costume that had, by this point, become a potent symbol of her oppression. Her speech of submission at the end of the show was vehement and seemingly sincere, but when she referred to her husband as 'one that cares for thee, / And for thy maintenance commits his body / To painful labour' (5.2.152–4), her sad gesture at her now-ragged dress on the word 'maintenance' got a big, ironic laugh. As she referred to her 'soft and weak and smooth' body (5.2.170), she unfastened the corset. Kneeling, she offered her hand for Petruchio's foot, but when he took it, she pulled him down to a kneeling position too. The rest of his triumphant dialogue was cut, indicating, perhaps, that he too had learned that 'Neither of us is free / If one of us is bound.' The production ended with a final reprise of the song, as Katherine resolved to 'make the end a better start, / Be reimagined new'. The rest of the company joined in, removing their shoes as they invited the audience to 'Rise up and walk along with me, / Walk in these shoes.'

The production could be characterized as one of two halves. The first was played as knockabout farce, the full stage and monochrome design giving it the look of an old Keystone Cops movie. Aaron Heffernan was a cartoonishly clumsy Lucentio, sharing a number of physical set-pieces with Imogen Doel's Tranio. This half of the play also featured a great deal of audience interaction, not least from Edward MacLiam's Petruchio, who whipped up applause upon his first entrance and shared his excitement at the prospect of meeting Katherine directly with spectators ('O, how I long to have some chat with her!', 2.1.162). 'He that knows better how to tame a shrew, / Now let him speak' was a genuine question, asked sincerely of

21. *The Taming of the Shrew*, 3.2, Shakespeare's Globe, directed by Caroline Byrne. Amy Conroy and Imogen Doel as servants, Aoife Duffin as Katherine and Genevieve Hulme-Beaman as Bianca. Photograph by Marc Brenner.

the audience (4.1.196–7). The second half, however, veered suddenly into tragicomedy. After the busy ensemble sequences of the first half, the stage now seemed stark and empty. As the sun set and spectators disappeared into darkness, audience interaction started to dwindle, and the play too took a darker turn: both Petruchio's treatment of Katherine and Vincentio's revenge on Tranio and Biondello were ugly and violent. As Petruchio forced Katherine to kiss him 'in the midst of the street' (5.1.135), the kiss they shared was long, limp and unloving; Katherine was clearly broken and he was mercilessly demonstrating his domination of her. I got the feeling that Byrne wanted her audience to be shocked into uncomfortable silence at this moment, confronted with their earlier complicity in the shrew-taming plot – but when I saw it, the kiss was met with wolf-whistles and giggles as spectators seemed to be attempting to re-trivialize the play. I wonder whether this was an unconscious response to the absence of shared light: attempts to shut down the audience's volubility at the Globe can result in its returning with a vengeance.

Next up was Iqbal Khan's *Macbeth*. For this production, the Globe stage was done up like a nightclub, with crimson curtains, wrought metal grilles and multicoloured lighting. Costumes were an anachronistic mix of modern overcoats and Elizabethan doublets and armour. As with the other productions, amplified music underscored much of the action. Puppetry was employed once again for some of the play's supernatural elements: the witches were created by four women manipulating detached limbs, heads and bones in order to form and re-form a number of nightmarish, insect-like creatures. Like the other directors, Khan had evidently encouraged his cast to ad lib and to whip up audience participation. Some of this worked well – Nadia Albina's Porter, for example, interacted with the groundlings to humorous effect and made topical jokes, seeming momentarily to forget 'th' other devil's name' before remembering, 'Oh, I've got it ... Trump!' (2.3.7). But elsewhere, audience interaction seemed to be incorporated for its own sake. When Macduff (Jacob Fortune-Lloyd) promised Malcolm (Freddie Stewart) that 'We have willing dames enough', he turned to the crowd and shouted, 'Eh, ladies?', getting a huge cheer (4.3.74). Interactions of this sort framed the action of the play as non-serious, fostering an ironic, detached mode of spectatorship. This would not have been a problem if they were not also sometimes narratively incoherent. Lloyd Thomas, the actor listed in the programme as Seyton, opened the second half with a solo, direct-address version of 3.6, in which he encouraged spectators to cheer for Macbeth's murder of Duncan's grooms ('Was not that nobly done?') and asked a nearby groundling if he could tell where Macduff had bestowed himself (3.6.23–4). When the groundling admitted he had 'no idea', Seyton/Thomas mocked him for not having followed the play closely enough – a tad unreasonably, since the play had not yet revealed this information. This treatment lost the irony of the equivalent scene in Shakespeare's play, muddled its exposition and made it unclear who was speaking (a defecting thane? Macbeth's spin doctor?).

This kind of acting was conspicuous by its absence from the two central performances. Ray Fearon performed Macbeth with the disciplined attention to verse that might be expected of an RSC stalwart, communicating clearly with spectators without any need for interpolations. He delivered 'This supernatural soliciting / Cannot be ill' with great confidence, before being suddenly shaken by a new thought: 'cannot be good' (1.3.129–30). He banished the thought, only for it to return again and gnaw at him. We were watching a character think, and using *us* to help him think.

Later, when he described life as a 'tale / Told by an idiot, full of sound and fury', he paused for a moment after 'signifying', searching for an answer, before concluding, his full-bodied voice suddenly becoming weak, 'nothing' (5.5.25–7).

Tara Fitzgerald's Lady Macbeth was the warmest and most audience-friendly portrayal of the character I have seen, striking a balance between the silly interactivity on display elsewhere and Fearon's more serious direct address. She entered 1.5 reading Macbeth's letter to the audience, sharing her excitement – upon reading the words 'my dearest partner of greatness' (1.5.10), her voice broke slightly and she proudly tapped her chest, making the audience laugh. When she returned to the stage after Duncan's murder, she delivered 'That which hath made them drunk hath made me bold' (2.2.1) as a kind of gossipy boast – I have never heard this line get a laugh before but here it got a big one, and what was even more surprising was that this playing of it worked. This Lady Macbeth was not evil but childishly amoral. Her breakdown was well foreshadowed: she wept slightly as she welcomed Duncan to Dunsinane, hastily brushing away her tears as she thanked him for 'those honours deep and broad wherewith / Your majesty loads our house' (1.6.17–18), repressing her stirring feelings of guilt. We saw her repeat the gesture of wiping away a tear several times; upon ''Tis safer to be that which we destroy / Than by destruction dwell in doubtful joy', she lost control for a moment as repressed emotions bubbled to the surface (3.2.8–9). She finally broke down into uncontrollable sobbing at the end of the banquet scene, as her husband told her, 'We are yet but young in deed' (3.4.143). In her sleepwalking scene, the tear-wiping gesture returned as a kind of hollow ritual.

The Globe's touring production of *The Two Gentlemen of Verona*, directed by Nick Bagnall, visited the Wanamaker in September. The production had been designed for touring nationally and internationally, both indoors and outdoors. I suspect that the Wanamaker was its most intimate venue, so if it felt a little overblown and strenuous at times, it may have been because of the incongruity with the venue, rather than a fault of the production in itself. Its central concept was to use the pop music and culture wars of the 1960s as a metaphor for the play's various attitudes towards youth, sex and love. It was performed by a mostly young cast of actor-musicians on a psychedelic red, yellow and orange set, at the centre of which sat the drum kit, keyboard, microphones and electric guitars with which they would accompany much of the play's action. As the play opened, most of them were mooning over a record by an old-fashioned crooner. Valentine (Guy Hughes) sat away from the others, uninterested in the record; before long, he had embarked for Milan with his guitar strung on his back, seeking a different musical scene. It soon transpired that Milan was represented by cool sixties pop and Carnaby Street-style fashions; its Duke was a capricious, drug-addled old rocker, played cartoonishly by Gary Cooper. The outlaws were hippies with electric guitars, literally a band called The Outlaws. Valentine squared off against them with his acoustic guitar, and was presented with an electric one upon being accepted as one of their number.

There was a strongly homoerotic dimension to Valentine's friendship with Proteus (Dharmesh Patel). This was played for laughs in 2.4, when the two became entwined in an enthusiastically sexual embrace as Valentine rapturously described his love for Sylvia. But this dimension took on a darker tone in the final scene: when Valentine interrupted Proteus's attempted rape of Sylvia (Aruhan Galieva), he was more concerned with his own feelings of betrayal by Proteus than he was with the sufferings of his supposed lover, whom he left lying on the floor without a second thought. In this context, 'All that was mine in Silvia I give thee' (5.4.83) became a desperate attempt to patch up the friendship that evidently meant more to him than anything else. In the closing moments, as the Duke pardoned Valentine and promised him Sylvia's hand in marriage, the three men stood aloft on the platform above the band, all but ignoring the young women on the main stage beneath them. The Duke remained vain and impulsive, Proteus as shifty and cunning as ever; Valentine was gazing at his friend in lovestruck oblivion. Left alone, Julia (Leah Brotherhead) helped Sylvia up and the two women stepped up to the microphones to sing a loudly defiant song about loneliness. I found myself undecided as to whether or not this ending, coming as it did out of an otherwise frothy and untroubling production, was an effective and provocative twist, or simply jarring and unearned.

Rice's summer season concluded with Matthew Dunster's *Imogen*, a 'renamed and reclaimed' version of *Cymbeline*. Like the rest of the season, *Imogen* updated the setting of its source play, rewrote several lines and added a soundtrack of amplified music. Its late September opening meant that the sun had set before it even started, which gave me another experience familiar from other theatres but as yet unknown at the Globe: that of the house lights going down at the start of the show. It was, in its own way, rather brilliant; the sort of thing that physical theatre company Frantic Assembly might do with a big budget in an open-air venue. The show opened with a long sequence of choreographed movement, illustrating the industrial-scale drug manufacturing outfit of which Jonathan McGuinness's Cymbeline was 'king'; in a further dance sequence we witnessed Imogen (Maddy Hill) and Posthumus's (Ira Mandela Siobhan) childhood friendship turn into an erotic physical relationship, which was quickly and violently disrupted by Cymbeline's guards.

In a programme note that seemed to be taking aim at Yates's recent Wanamaker production – and perhaps at Rice's own 2006 version with Kneehigh – Dunster complained that some directors place too much emphasis on *Cymbeline*'s 'fairy tale' qualities at the expense of its 'really aggressive and violent' elements. In *Imogen*, then, we had a Cymbeline who regularly threatened sympathetic characters with immediate torture. His mostly silent guards lurked around (mimed) doorways and often erupted into realistic violence. Joshua Lacey's football hooligan Cloten was a pumped-up psychopath who picked fights at the least provocation. Belarius's cave was on the outer edges of

Cymbeline's drug empire, a remote greenhouse in which Belarius and his adopted sons grew cannabis. Though it was part of the violent world of the play, it was also something of an oasis: Arviragus was played by a deaf actor, William Grint, so Belarius (Martin Marquez) and Guiderius (Scott Karim) tended to sign their lines as well as speaking, and the care and consideration that this involved characterized this family of characters strongly. Perhaps the final scene's most moving moment was when Cymbeline was reunited with his sons and began haltingly to sign to Arviragus, as if he were remembering a skill he had thought he would never have to use again whilst reviving a father–son intimacy he had long given up as lost.

This was a deeply patriarchal world, all the more uncomfortable for its modernity. The modern setting and urban accents hammered home that, even now, it is not unusual to hear men discussing a woman's value in terms of her sexuality, to sneeringly refer to her as 'easy' or to condemn her as a 'whore'. Some new lines were added to the final scene to make Imogen and Posthumus's reconciliation more acceptable to a modern audience. As Cymbeline observed that 'Posthumus anchors upon Imogen, / And she, like harmless lightning, throws her eye / On him' (5.6.394–6), Imogen interrupted her father's speech with an angry outburst:

IMOGEN.   You made this wager? I'm your wife.
POSTHUMUS.   Is it enough that I am sorry?
IMOGEN.   No!

In fourteen lines of newly written blank verse (based on fragments from elsewhere in the play), Imogen berated her husband for his willingness to allow Giacomo to taint his 'nobler heart / And brain with needless jealousy'.[1] As Giacomo (Matthew Needham) knelt to Posthumus for forgiveness, Imogen shouted 'Kneel not to him', and insisted that the power to forgive him was *hers*. Just as Posthumus does in Shakespeare, she then exercised this power, telling him to 'Live, / And deal with others better' (5.6.420–1), before forgiving her husband, too, with a hug. The performance finished with the entire company returning to the stage in a wild and energetic urban jig, a fusion of the Globe's established tradition with grime music and street dance styles. It functioned more effectively than any other jig I can remember in joining together cast and audience in a shared celebration of the performance: the applause was wild and groundlings were dancing along.

Shortly after the summer season closed, the Globe announced that Rice would be stepping down as Artistic Director after the 2017/18 Winter Season. The theatre's CEO Neil Constable explained that while Rice's first season had been a commercial and critical success, it had prompted a 'productive debate concerning the purpose and theatrical practice of the Globe', following which the board had concluded the theatre should return to a programme 'structured around "shared light" productions without designed sound and light rigging'.[2] The implication was that Rice and the board had reached an impasse over the role of these technologies in future work at the Globe, and that either she or the board would not be renewing her contract as a result. This news was not well received in the press and on social media, where it was widely interpreted as a backwards step both aesthetically and ideologically (David Grieg wrote a piece for the *New Statesman* arguing that it felt 'a bit Brexity').[3] Rice had, after all, succeeded in attracting a diverse popular audience and had come close to achieving her goal of onstage gender parity.[4] One of the real victories of Rice's 50/50 rule was that it made

---

[1] Matthew Dunster, *Imogen: William Shakespeare's Cymbeline Renamed and Reclaimed* (London, 2016), p. 78, adapted from *Cymbeline*, 5.5.159–60.
[2] Shakespeare's Globe, 'Statement regarding the Globe's future Artistic Direction', 25 October 2016, http://blog.shakespearesglobe.com/post/152286922818/statement-regarding-the-globes-future-artistic.
[3] David Grieg, 'Emma Rice's exit from Shakespeare's Globe feels a bit Brexity', *New Statesman*, 26 October 2016.
[4] Mark Brown, 'The Globe's Emma Rice: "If anybody bended gender it was Shakespeare"', *The Guardian*, 5 January 2016.

gender-blind casting almost unremarkable but at certain moments it achieved some striking effects: in *Two Gentlemen*, for example, it was productively alienating to hear some of Lance's more misogynistic jokes from the mouth of a female performer (Charlotte Mills), while the re-gendered Philaria in *Imogen* (Erica Kouassi) added a nicely cynical presence to Posthumus and Giacomo's deeply sexist arguments about Imogen's fidelity. In a pointed comment on gender roles, all the servants in *Shrew* were played by women.

I was saddened to read the news of Rice's departure and, though I was largely unconvinced by the season's use of artificial sound and rigged lighting, I had been planning to write a defence of Rice's right to experiment. I had hoped that she and her team would learn from the season's successes and failures, and find ways of using lighting and sound technologies that did not replicate the conventions of indoor theatres but rather adapt to the particularities of the Globe space. On the positive side, the spectacular lighting effects and the loud and frequent bursts of amplified music were often thrilling, and gave the theatre the feel of an open-air pop concert or festival. On the other hand, the Globe has always been a theatre in which audiences have tremendous power, and Rice's technological interventions seemed to me an attempt to limit that power, even to dominate it: the use of microphones put the actors at a privileged remove from the audience and the musical underscoring could be intrusive and coercive. The lighting rig, meanwhile, tended to focus entirely on the stage; this meant that the visible audience, so important to the collaborative construction of theatrical meaning at the Globe, disappeared after sunset (though they still asserted their presence vocally, and occasionally disruptively, as in *Shrew*). The rigged lighting also meant that audiences at matinees were seeing a different kind of show, in which lighting effects would inevitably be diminished. It seems rather wasteful that Rice and the Globe board were so irreconcilably polarized over an issue that could really have affected only 50 per cent of performances.

PLAYS FOR THE NATION AT THE RSC

In the year of the EU referendum, national identity was a hot topic. The Royal Shakespeare Company's programming this year seemed particularly concerned with the problem of representing the nation and of nationhood in general. This was at its most evident in *A Midsummer Night's Dream: A Play for the Nation*, which I caught halfway through its national tour at the Marlowe Theatre in Canterbury. At each of its venues, the RSC's professional company was joined by six local amateur actors in the roles of Bottom and the mechanicals and a company of local schoolchildren as the chorus of fairies. Tom Piper's set suggested a bombed-out theatre and the costumes evoked the 1940s. While the mortal world seemed to be a space of post-war trauma and austerity, the fairy realm was constructed out of items that looked as though they had been left over from an abandoned pre-war theatrical extravaganza – a rotating staircase, two stand-alone doors on casters and, as Titania's bower, a grand piano. Visually, at least, the implication was that the scenes in the fairy world were a celebration of the restorative powers of theatre.

I chose to see Erica Whyman's production in Canterbury because it offered something of a landmark: Lisa Nightingale of The Canterbury Players would be the RSC's first ever female Bottom and, in a year of high-profile cross-gender performances, the opportunity was too tempting to miss. As it turned out, Nightingale's Bottom seemed so integral to the performance in Canterbury that I found it hard to imagine how the production could be nearly as interesting without her. She was as glamorous a Bottom as I have seen, her red donkey ears and woolly hair perfectly matching her bright red lipstick and high-heeled shoes. She burst into song not because she was afraid of being abandoned in the forest but because her solitude gave her space to give the kind of unrestrained performance for which Quince and company kept telling her off. When Ayesha Dharker's gentle Titania awoke from her slumber, her exclamation 'What angel wakes me from my

22. *A Midsummer Night's Dream: A Play for the Nation*, 2.1, RSC, touring, directed by Erica Whyman. Lucy Ellinson as Puck and Chu Omambala as Oberon. Photograph by Topher McGrillis.

flow'ry bed?' (3.1.122) was met not with audience laughter but an electric silence. That silence seemed to register the possibility that Titania's attraction to Bottom was no parodic inversion of romantic love but a touching moment of sexual liberation. Bottom responded to Titania's advances with a bashfulness we had not yet seen from the character but she seemed more than willing to let herself be seduced.

The production's gently radical gay politics did not end there. Lucy Ellinson's Puck – a small, cartoonishly androgynous figure in an oversized top hat and a scruffy black suit – channelled all the enthusiasm and sweetness of Charlie Chaplin (Illustration 22). When Chu Omambala's Oberon indicated the sleeping couple and asked, 'Seest thou this sweet sight?' (4.1.45), Puck smiled and nodded, enormously proud of the results of his/her handiwork. When Oberon continued, making it clear that he saw Titania's love as 'dotage' and Bottom as a 'hateful fool' (4.1.46–8), Puck's face dropped with disappointment. Ellinson's Puck, who earlier in the evening had blown fervent, childish kisses at Mercy Ojelade's Hermia, was charmed and fascinated by love in all its forms, and Oberon's heartless attempt to condemn some kinds of attraction as taboo visibly filled this warm-hearted figure with sadness. Oberon and Titania's reconciliation was played relatively unproblematically – Dharker's Titania had clearly forgotten all about both the Indian boy and Bottom, and was more than willing to forgive Oberon for their quarrel. Only Puck remembered and looked on from the sidelines mournfully.

The gay subtext continued into the final act. When she woke up, Bottom could not articulate her 'rare vision', because she was only just starting to become conscious of its implications (4.1.202). When she returned to the mechanicals, she likewise found herself unable to 'discourse wonders' because those wonders had profoundly unsettled her sense of identity (4.2.26). At the end of this scene, she and Sarah Gooch's female Quince shared a moment of eye contact and handholding that subtly suggested an unspoken dimension to their friendship that, for Bottom, had found expression in the dreamworld of the forest. This was a refreshing, quietly radical production which asked its audience to celebrate a variety of homoerotic relationships between women, and it is striking that these meanings can surely have emerged for the first time only in this performance, two months into the production's run. It is a vindication of the experiment that the production allowed space for such contingency.

That there were three major productions of *Cymbeline* in 2016 is perhaps an indication that, as Ros King's programme notes for Melly Still's RSC production put it, 'this is a play whose time has come'. All three articles in this programme framed this explicitly in light of the EU referendum, which was just over a month away when Still's production opened: *Cymbeline* does, after all, tell the story of a Britain that goes to war over the influence of a larger continental European power. Still's *Cymbeline* was set in a dystopian future version of Britain following some kind of environmental disaster, in which the country had become a cut-off, impoverished cousin to its wealthier European neighbours. In Anna Fleischle's set, huge walls of concrete blocks and flaking paint were scrawled with nostalgic graffiti: 'There was peace', 'Remember how it was', 'When I was younger this was trees'. To emphasize the point, the centrepiece of the set was a tree-trunk encased in a glass display box, as if it were a sacred relic of Britain before the collapse. The costumes were made from reclaimed items: a pair of jeans repurposed into a top, a cloak stitched together from grain sacks, fragments of two mismatching waistcoats sewn together to make a new one.

Several characters had been re-gendered: Gillian Bevan's Cymbeline was a Queen, married to James Clyde's scheming Duke. Innogen remained female, but Guiderius became Guideria, meaning that Still's imaginary future Britain was a matriarchy in which the leader, the current heir to her throne, and the long-lost true heir were all female. But paradoxically, Bethan Cullinane's Innogen seemed to be more a victim of patriarchy than ever. She started the show literally trapped on a pedestal: wearing the frayed white tutu that seemed to have been her wedding dress, she stood on top of the glass box as if she were trapped by the four wires that extended from its corners up to the heavens. Her status as an objectified possession was even more emphatic in this production where the agency of other female characters was less delimited. When Kelly Williams's androgynous, punk-haired Pisania insisted that Innogen should 'forget to be a woman' and pass herself off as a boy (3.4.155), the implication was that Pisania herself could traverse the country in safety as a woman only because she was streetwise and tough, having shed traditionally feminine modes of behaviour, and that Innogen was altogether more sheltered and vulnerable.

The re-gendering left some verbal oddities in places, often in ways that exposed the original play's use of gender stereotypes. When the Duke defended himself against 'the slander of most stepfathers' (1.1.72), it made no sense unless we were meant to assume that this futuristic world had developed a new set of folk tales about wicked stepfathers. Clyde played the Duke as a middle-aged, absent-minded-professor type who controlled his wife not by dominating or sexually manipulating her but through a kind of Machiavellian humbleness that masked his murderous desires. It seemed odd, then, that Cymbeline's first thought on explaining his ability to deceive her was his 'beauty' (5.6.63), but perhaps this made its own point. Elsewhere, the production's re-gendering worked more positively: Natalie Simpson's athletic Guideria was the most proficient hunter and therefore 'master of the feast' (3.6.29), and her instinctive protectiveness over

Fidele/Innogen no longer reinforced the stereotype of man-as-protector. Similarly, her admiration for Fidele's 'neat cookery' (4.2.50) was less wince-inducing than it can be in the mouth of a male actor.

At moments, the production was almost an essay on male entitlement. Hiran Abeysekera's Posthumus was small and spry, almost childlike, succumbing to Iachimo's deception because he was at heart deeply insecure about his own masculinity. Oliver Johnstone's Iachimo, by contrast, was suave and cocksure, building up to his seduction of Innogen gradually before crucially misjudging his own irresistibility. Like O'Hare's Iachimo at the Wanamaker, he made use of the presence of the audience during the scene in Innogen's bedchamber, noticing our judgemental gaze as he fantasized about stealing a kiss from her before adding, as if he were justifying it to us, '*one* kiss', and taking our silence for assent (2.2.17). Marcus Griffith's high-status, good-looking Cloten seemed genuinely baffled by Innogen's refusal to submit to him and repeatedly shared his frustration with the audience as if he expected us to agree; he raised a sympathetic laugh as he shared his hurt at being held in less respect than Posthumus's garment, before silencing us with the sudden brutality of his plan to 'ravish her' (3.5.138).

The production was oddly reliant on stereotypes for its presentation of continental Europe. For the segue to Rome, the stage filled with dancers, some of them cross-dressed, writhing in sync to generic Europop. The guests at Philario's house were all deliberate caricatures: the Italian Iachimo in an immaculate white suit, the Frenchman in blue and white stripes, the Spaniard in a matador outfit. They spoke the languages of their respective nations as English translations were projected onto the back wall, their multiple languages serving to alienate the nervous, monoglot Posthumus. I wondered whether this was an attempt to stage an Englishman's nightmare vision of Europe, all strange languages, funny clothes and threatening sexuality: I found it hard to understand why a production so evidently sensitive to the upcoming EU referendum would otherwise engage in such blatant stereotyping.

Simon Godwin's *Hamlet* explored nationhood in a different way. Like Gregory Doran's 2012 *Julius Caesar*, it was set in an unspecific modern African state, though unlike that production it largely eschewed African accents in favour of received pronunciation. This African 'Denmark' was contrasted in various ways with the European location of Hamlet's education at Wittenberg University. All of the characters of Claudius's court were played by black actors but the figures associated with Hamlet's education were not: Horatio was played by Sri Lankan actor Hiran Abeysekera in his natural accent, while Rosencrantz (James Cooney) and Guildenstern (Bethan Cullinane) were both white and clearly British, bringing Clarence Smith's Claudius gifts of Scottish shortbread and a teapot in the shape of a red telephone box. At the start of the show we saw Paapa Essiedu's Hamlet collecting his degree certificate from Wittenberg's Chancellor (white actor Byron Mondahl), pausing for a photograph before a noise like a gunshot prompted a nightmarish segue into Claudius's Denmark: Claudius and Gertrude appeared on a balcony, Gertrude with a fixed smile on her face, as the Old King's glass coffin was carried across the stage below them. Later, the appearance of the Ghost was heralded by the frenetic playing of African drums, the stage filling with dry ice before it cleared to reveal Old Hamlet (Ewart James Walters) standing in the same traditional robes in which he had been buried – a striking contrast to the modern European-style outfits worn by the rest of the cast so far. Clearly this sequence was asking us to associate the Ghost's call to revenge with the eruption of a more traditional mode of 'Africanness'. While the moment was thrillingly effective, I was uncomfortable that once again, as in Doran's *Julius Caesar*, 'Africa' was being used to signify the mythic, the violent and the vengeful, and set in contrast with the rational, the intellectual and the 'civilized' as represented by the European Wittenberg.

Godwin's production was especially concerned with the symbolism and performance of power. Much of it was set in Claudius's throne room, in artist: he changed into a multi-coloured suit decorated all over with hand-painted crowns and other symbols (Illustration 23) and, in full view of Polonius, he spray-painted a bright pink crown and an 'H' onto the portrait of Claudius and Gertrude, and added male and female toilet signs to their twin thrones. The setting for 3.1 was Hamlet's art studio, which was hung with huge, colourful, Basquiat-style paintings of skulls, crowns and snippets of text ('REMEMBER ME' and 'SERPENT KING'). 'The Mousetrap' was a flagrantly subversive piece of political theatre which the affronted Gertrude saw straight through.

The highlight of the production was its central performance. Essiedu was a dynamic, mercurial Hamlet, combining high energy and introspection, mockery and seriousness, flirtation and hostility. Wide-eyed, open-faced and unusually smiley, he was childlike in his vulnerability and his petulant defiance of authority figures. He was both open and defensive in his soliloquies: when he wished that 'the Everlasting had not fixed / His canon 'gainst self-slaughter' (1.2.131), he paused to stare confrontationally around the audience as if to say, 'so deal with *that*', but then, finding his assertion met with impassivity, it was he, not us, who crumpled with emotion. He used a similar technique at various moments throughout the show, defying the audience to judge him for his decision to kill his uncle, for example, before realizing that he was his own sternest critic.

Essiedu returned to the Royal Shakespeare Theatre as Edmund in Gregory Doran's *King Lear*. His performance in the play's first scene drew attention to the similarities between the roles: his Edmund was wearing black, listening in sullen silence as David Troughton's Gloucester, the father figure for whom he harboured a murderous hatred, patronized him in the third person. Indeed, Essiedu continued in the Hamlet vein for much of this performance, skulking at the side of the stage, observing the characters of the court. He delivered his soliloquies with the same combination of bitter sarcasm and genuine hurt, playing mockingly with the word 'legitimate' moments after seeming tortured by the word 'base' (1.2.6–21). This was an

23. *Hamlet*, 3.1, RSC, Royal Shakespeare Theatre, directed by Simon Godwin. Paapa Essiedu as Hamlet. Photograph by Manuel Harlan.

which a painting of Claudius and Gertrude hung above their twin thrones, a single piece of furniture that represented the inextricable link between Claudius's own claim to power and Gertrude's. 'One may smile and smile and be a villain' (1.5.109) applied more to Gertrude than it did to Claudius in this production: Tanya Moodie spent much of the play projecting a broad but joyless smile, Gertrude's political front. Cyril Nri's Polonius was a nervous master of ceremonies, keen to ensure that all subjects were behaving appropriately. He seemed worried throughout 1.2 about what Hamlet was going to say and do, watching him anxiously. Essiedu's Hamlet, meanwhile, understood the centrality of symbolism to his uncle's grip on power and, when he adopted his 'antic disposition', it was as a subversive visual

Edmund deeply scarred by his father's disdain for his illegitimacy. When Gloucester finally hugged him in 3.3, he looked for a moment as though he did not know what to do: here, too late, was the intimacy he had been denied, and now he had betrayed the man he thought would never give it to him.

Antony Sher's Lear was strongly characterized by his first entrance, atop a kind of sedan-chair-cum-throne inside a glass cube. This cube looked partly like a hermetically sealed box and partly like a glass hearse: this was a Lear sealed off from the world outside, a volatile substance, artificially preserved. He sprung the love-test on his daughters without warning, seeming to enjoy their confusion and distress. He was utterly convinced of his god-like powers, holding one arm to the sky as he invoked 'the sacred radiance of the sun' and moving his hands slowly over the incantation that followed (1.1.109). He adopted the same pattern of movement later in the play, first when he banished Kent and then later as he cursed Goneril with infertility. He tried to repeat the invocation as he threatened both Goneril and Regan in 2.2, his diatribe breaking down into senseless fragments as he promised 'such revenges on you both / That all the world shall – I will do such things – / What they are, yet I know not' (2.2.453–5). Finally, all connection between this ritual and meaningful action severed, it reappeared during his mad scene at Dover: dressed in long johns and crowned with leaves, he held up his hand to demonstrate, 'Ay, every inch a king' (4.5.107). In fact his supposedly divine authority had been undercut much earlier in the production: Doran had filled the stage in 1.4 with a large group of around sixteen knights, a mob of raucous, aggressive, highly sexed young men for whose company Lear was evidently paying. Next to this group, Lear seemed a rather pathetic figure.

One of the central motifs in Doran's production was the presence of the 'Poor naked wretches' of Lear's kingdom (3.4.28). The show opened with Gloucester shooing away a group of beggars in ragged shawls and cloaks; these figures returned to the stage at the start of 1.3, when they were given bread by Goneril (Nia Gwynne) before being dispersed once again. We saw them again in Act 3, suffering in the storm. In a strangely sculptural moment, Lear delivered 'Blow, winds, and crack your cheeks' (3.2.1) on top of a pedestal in the middle of a huge golden cloth, the Fool (Graham Turner) crouching at his feet. I was uncertain whether to read this as a heroic image or as one of a Lear utterly disconnected from the world around him. He and the Fool descended to stage-level to enter the hovel, encountering the beggars on the way; the beggars processed down the sides of the stage, two by two, as Lear stared at them in fear and declaimed 'O, I have ta'en / Too little care of this' (3.4.32–3). I was not convinced that this was a moment of awakening social conscience on Lear's part – he still seemed aloof, making no effort to speak to them. Perhaps they were spectral figures, tormenting him with his own loss of status. Significantly, the Fool left Lear at the end of the first half to join the traipsing beggars, leaving his ukulele and his coxcomb behind and disappearing from the play.

Blanche McIntyre's *Two Noble Kinsmen* at the Swan Theatre did a great deal to emphasize the homoerotic undertones of Shakespeare and Fletcher's play. The show opened with Chris Jack's despondent Pirithous and Gyuri Sarossy's militaristic Theseus snatching a kiss before the latter's marriage to Hippolyta (Allison McKenzie), and suggested an unspoken rivalry between Pirithous and Hippolyta for Theseus's affections throughout. For his part, Theseus took a full-bodied, almost sexual delight as he devised and then anticipated the violent contest between Arcite and Palamon; in 4.2, he engaged in frenetic push-ups as he listened to the heroic descriptions of the warriors who were to fight alongside them. There was a strong sense of the physical intimacy and mutual affection between Jamie Wilkes's Arcite and James Corrigan's Palamon, too: as they armed each other in 3.6, they repeatedly squared off against one another before finding yet another excuse to break off – an exchange of weapons, a final embrace. Their fight, which started in a mannered, formal style, quickly descended into a physical scrap and then an almost erotic clinch.

Frances McNamee's Emilia was also consumed with same-sex desire, recalling her love for Flavina with her whole body, breathlessly and enthusiastically (1.3.49–82). In 2.2, it became clear that Emilia was also powerfully attracted to her waiting woman (Eloise Secker), their conversation reinvented as Emilia's awkward and only semi-deliberate attempt to chat her up.

McNamee's Emilia was in many ways the centre of the production. She was a plausible Amazon, going off to hunt alongside her chainsaw-wielding sister in 1.3 carrying a bow and quiver of arrows (the production used a combination of modern dress and postmodern, semi-fantastical costume). But, as the performance continued, it demonstrated her ensnarement into Theseus's patriarchy. The prison of 2.2 was evoked by two walls of metal grilles descending either side of the stage, the imprisoned Arcite and Palamon positioned outside the bars on the outer edges of the thrust; thus, when Emilia and her attendant entered the middle of stage, they were the ones who looked as though they were in prison. The staging was a potent metaphor for the way in which Emilia becomes imprisoned by the kinsmen's gaze, trapped in the role of love object against her will and powerless to prevent the destruction carried out in her name. In 3.6, when Palamon revealed to Theseus and his party that Emilia was the subject of their quarrel, she seemed bewildered; her appeal to Theseus to spare their lives was underpinned by her sense of the absurdity of the situation. When Theseus asked, 'If one of them were dead – as one must – are you / Content to take the other to your husband?' (3.6.272–3), she looked shocked and angry – the question suddenly made her responsible for a fight to the death to which she had never consented. Over the last part of the play, her costume changed from the practical hunting outfits of the first few acts to an elaborate and restrictive wedding gown, tight around her waist and legs and ballooning ostentatiously around her shoulders. Around her neck she wore a large ornate metal necklace that looked almost like a shackle.

The production's take on its male protagonists might be summed up by Arcite's line 'You play the child extremely' (2.2.208). Arcite and Palamon were both boyish and impulsive, climbing the grilles of their prison as though they were in an adventure playground, self-congratulatory in their assurances of their love for one another and childish in their competition. Corrigan's Palamon recalled Hugh Laurie's Bertie Wooster in his combination of outlandish overstatement, naïve enthusiasm and aristocratic privilege. His thoughtless exploitation of the Jailer's Daughter (Danusia Samal) prompted her descent into madness, which was played here as a case study in early modern ideas about 'green sickness': she caressed and slowly undressed herself as the play went on until she finally exited the stage with her fake 'Palamon', resting her head on his shoulder. Palamon's casual enquiry after her in 5.6 was indicative of a man oblivious to the effects of his actions on others, and his collection of a few notes from his comrades as a token of his gratitude seemed almost offensive in its careless privilege. In the final moments, he cradled his cousin's dead body without really looking at Emilia, realizing that he had lost the true love of his life in pursuing an idealized fiction that had been destructive for all involved. He, Emilia and Hippolyta left the stage individually during Theseus's final speech, which was cut so that the play finished on the observation that they had all been 'children in some kind' (5.6.134).

The RSC's Christmas show was Doran's *Tempest*, a production that was both highly modern and deeply traditional. Its modernity was in its collaboration with Intel and performance capture specialists The Imaginarium Studios. Mark Quartley's Ariel was a combination of live action and motion capture, digitally projected onto a number of onstage surfaces. Most of Ariel's appearances were in the flesh, but his more spectacular moments – his first appearance, fresh from the tempest, and his later transformation into a harpy, for example – were performed in tandem, the actor at the side or back of the stage and his computer-generated avatar projected into the middle of the set. I often found myself more inclined to watch the live actor than his animated counterpart, perhaps because his immediate physical form seemed

24. *The Tempest*, 1.2, RSC, Royal Shakespeare Theatre, directed by Gregory Doran. Mark Quartley as Ariel and Simon Russell Beale as Prospero. Photograph by Topher McGrillis.

more responsive to the stimulus of his fellow actors – the fractional delay between the actor's movements and his avatar's made the latter feel a little dislocated from the drama. But the digital elements allowed for some truly impressive moments, an early standout being the illustration of Ariel's confinement in the 'cloven pine' (1.2.278), in which Ariel's avatar, projected onto a central cylindrical spiral, was encased in a web of wooden tendrils that suddenly covered all the stage's open surfaces (Illustration 24). The production's best use of its resources, though, was in the masque sequence, in which computer-animated backgrounds of starry skies, rolling hills, psychedelic flowers and fanning peacock feathers filled the floor and cyclorama while Iris, Ceres and Juno offered their blessings in three-part harmony. The sequence overwhelmed the senses as it rarely does in modern productions, rendering Prospero's interruption of it all the more effective. For all of its up-to-the-moment technological sophistication, though, the production was strangely old-fashioned. The costume design was clearly drawing on a nineteenth-century inheritance: Simon Trinder's Trinculo was a Grimaldi-like clown in whiteface, sporting three coloured spikes of hair from his bald head, while Joe Dixon's Caliban was a hunched, lumpy monster with a protruding belly and a crooked spine. In some ways, the digital animation was a modern inheritor of Victorian visual spectacle.

The production had a strong human core. Simon Russell Beale's Prospero was a rather sad and lonely figure. Barefoot and plainly dressed, he seemed to be clinging to his magic because it provided a substitute for the loss of his dukedom and a bulwark against the imminent loss of his newly adult daughter (Jenny Rainsford). He was evidently torn over whether or not he wanted

Miranda to marry Ferdinand (Daniel Easton), keen to advance his plan for reconciliation but deeply reluctant to lose his exclusive hold on her affections. As they watched the masque, he held her in a tight embrace, forcing Ferdinand to sit on his own. When Miranda and Ferdinand joined in with the dance of the nymphs and reapers, Prospero interrupted the dance with a sudden shout just as the young lovers were about to embrace one another. He justified his impulsive response retrospectively, and unconvincingly, as having been prompted by his recollection of Caliban's conspiracy: the true reason was painfully visible. His suppressed rage became clearer as the play neared its climax: after Ariel suggested that the effects of Prospero's charm on its victims would make his affections 'tender', were he 'human', Prospero made two short, sharp cries of pure rage straight into the spirit's face before falling silent and resolving, 'And mine shall' (5.1.17–20).

When Prospero observed of Caliban that 'as with age his body uglier grows, / So his mind cankers' (4.1.191–2), there was a sense that the magus was displacing his own sense of guilt onto a convenient scapegoat. Indeed, Caliban was a pitiable figure in Dixon's portrayal. Caliban's face registered shock at Prospero's accusation that he had attempted to rape Miranda, and his response, 'O ho, O ho! Would't had been done!' (1.2.351), was an expression of anger at what he evidently saw as a mischaracterization of his actions. As he entered carrying wood in 2.2, Prospero's spirits were cruelly tormenting him: a butterfly, invisibly manipulated by one of them, caught his attention, and he stared at it in fascination before the spirit flattened it with a blow of her hand. Prospero made good on his promise to break his staff immediately after his soliloquy in 5.1, and he showed the broken pieces to the repentant Caliban later in the scene as if to illustrate the end of his hold over him. Caliban immediately straightened up for the first time in the play, suddenly a figure of power and dignity, and looked for a moment as if he were squaring up to his former master, ready to kill him. But then he softened slightly, resolving of his own free will to 'be wise hereafter, / And seek for grace' (5.1.298–9). He took the broken pieces of Prospero's staff and threw them into the pile of firewood.

CROSS-GENDER SHAKESPEARES

With the RSC's cross-cast *Cymbeline* and Emma Rice's 50/50 casting rule at the Globe, 2016 was an especially good year for cross-gender casting. Several other prominent productions pushed the experiment further. Robert Hastie's *Henry V* at Regent's Park had Michelle Terry in the title role, with other female actors playing Fluellen, Jamy, Macmorris, Gower, Ely and Montjoy, and a male actor as Katherine (Illustration 25). This was a downbeat, intelligent, anti-war production that used its cross-casting to Brechtian effect. As it opened, the entire company wandered onstage in rehearsal clothes; during her first speech, Charlotte Cornwell's Chorus moved through the assembled crowd with the crown in her hands, looking for a likely Henry, shaking her head amusedly at the keen young alpha male of the company (Alex Bhat, who would go on to play the Dauphin) before settling on the seemingly reluctant Terry. The production retained the masculine pronouns in reference to the character but Terry made no attempt at male impersonation and remained in her feminine rehearsal clothes (a waistcoat and matching shorts) for the first act, during which the stage was bare and only token props and costume items were used. As the play went on, however, elements of verisimilitude begin to creep in and, by 'Once more unto the breach' (3.1.1), everyone onstage was in full camouflage military uniform and carrying guns, while smoke and explosions filled both the stage and the auditorium. Perhaps the idea was that the audience would initially be alienated by the self-conscious theatricality, including the cross-casting, before being pulled slowly into theatrical illusion. Certainly as the costumes became more detailed, the cross-casting became harder to spot: Catrin Aaron's Fluellen could have been a small, wiry man upon his first appearance in military fatigues, while Ben Wiggins's Katherine likewise

25. *Henry V*, 3.6, Regent's Park Open Air Theatre, directed by Robert Hastie. Jessica Regan as Montjoy and Michelle Terry as Henry V. Photograph by Johan Persson.

could have been a muscular woman, appearing for the first time in fencing gear with her visor down.

The production framed Henry's French campaign as a sophisticated piece of political manipulation. Henry IV's deathbed advice that his son should 'busy giddy minds / With foreign quarrels' (4.3.342–3) was incorporated into Canterbury's opening conversation with Ely, making this a more overtly cynical scene; in the following scene, Henry was handed Canterbury's rationale for the invasion of France in what was clearly a 'dodgy dossier' (an especially resonant prop in the same week that the Chilcot Inquiry into Britain's involvement in the Iraq war finally published its report). Terry's performance emphasized the role of Henry's oratory in motivating his troops: Henry delivered 'Once more unto the breach' directly to Bedford (Syrus Lowe), who had run downstage to vomit as the scene began, the apparent inattention of the other soldiers onstage undercutting the speech's usual crowd-stirring effect. This got a payoff later, as it was Bedford (not York) who begged the 'leading of the vaward' in 4.3 and was subsequently killed in action. The latter half of the St Crispin's Day speech was similarly aimed at a sole addressee, in this case Jack McMullen's mutinous Williams. In 4.1, Williams had been openly contemptuous of the ideology that led working men like him to risk their lives for a dubious cause; when Henry granted permission for 'he which hath no stomach to this fight' to depart (4.3.35–6), Williams lost no time in relinquishing his rifle and walking offstage into the auditorium. Henry, sensing that Williams's departure could risk further desertions, used the rest of his speech to persuade the sceptical soldier to return, even adding 'Williams' to his list of names that would become as familiar 'as household words' (4.3.52–4). Once, again, Henry's rhetoric achieved its goal, persuading the soldier to stay and fight. This was a Henry who knew how to use words to political effect: Terry did not soften the ugliness and misogyny of Henry's threats to the Governor of Harfleur, which were all the more chilling in a female voice, and his instruction to 'Use mercy to them all' (3.3.137) was *sotto voce*, clearly not for the Governor to hear.

Hastie's production showed the ugliness of war, depicting much of the violence that usually happens offstage. Bardolph was led onto the stage and tied to a post in 3.6, and Henry, avoiding the horrified gaze of Pistol and Nym, ordered his erstwhile friend's execution on the spot. Moments after hearing the news of Bedford's death, Henry vented his rage by ordering the execution of the prisoners, shouting the command into the face of the terrified Monsieur Le Fer; Fluellen took the hesitating Pistol's dagger and slit the Frenchman's throat there and then. Following the battle, however, the production returned to the pared-down, metatheatrical aesthetic with which it had opened, showing the two kings speaking into tabletop microphones as they negotiated their peace deal, their bulging ring binders indicating the complexity of their settlement. The wooing scene, of course, was completely gender-reversed, lending it a layer of Brechtian alienation: Terry played it in a businesslike manner, colder than many Henrys, making the sexual politics of the scene, in which a young woman's hand in marriage is used as a political bargaining chip, impossible to overlook.

The autumn saw the opening of Phyllida Lloyd's *The Tempest*, the third in her trilogy of all-female Shakespeares for the Donmar Warehouse. The previous two productions, *Julius Caesar* and *Henry IV*, were revived to form a season at the King's Cross Theatre: like them, *The Tempest* was cut down to around two hours, played in-the-round without an interval, and presented as if it were being performed by the inmates of a women's prison. Harriet Walter began the performance by introducing herself as 'Hannah', a woman who had been serving a life sentence since 1981 for a 'politically-motivated bank robbery' that had resulted in the deaths of three people. 'Hannah's' story of confinement and atonement was central to the production, blurring ambiguously in and out of Prospero's own. At the start, Hannah watched impassively as the rest of the company banged noisily on the metal gates around the edges of the auditorium, calmly observing the distress of newer prisoners with shorter sentences who had not, like her, made peace with their confinement; the moment also functioned as Prospero overseeing the chaos of the tempest he had conjured. After Leah Harvey's Miranda shed her cardigan in order to pledge herself to Ferdinand (Sheila Atim) in 3.1, Prospero/Hannah picked it up and hugged it lovingly, a symbol both of Prospero's sadness at Miranda's imminent departure and of Hannah's regret at losing a younger inmate with whom she had developed a close friendship (Illustration 26). Walter's tearful delivery of 'Our revels now are ended' (4.1.146–63), a meditation on the ephemerality not only of theatrical illusion but also of life itself, was lent additional poignancy by the frame: Hannah's brief excursion into theatrical performance would soon be over, and she would return to a confinement in the prison that would be relieved only by her death. Just prior to 'Ye elves of hills, brooks, standing lakes and groves' (5.1.33), Jade Anouka's Ariel asked spectators to turn on the small LED torch they would find beneath their seats, so that Prospero's incantation was accompanied by hundreds of tiny lights, dancing in the darkness of the auditorium – a moment of theatrical magic into which spectators were directly co-opted. But as the speech ended, and Prospero relinquished his power over the spirits he commanded, so we were asked to turn off our torches, abjuring 'this rough magic' just as he did (5.1.50).

26. *The Tempest*, 3.1, Donmar at King's Cross, King's Cross Theatre, directed by Phyllida Lloyd. Harriet Walter as Prospero. Photograph by Helen Maybanks.

If Hannah/Prospero's calm control was one way of dealing with a life sentence, Sophie Stanton's Caliban suggested another – unfocused, impotent rage. The two characters were in competition for ownership of their space, and once again this functioned doubly: Caliban was furious at Prospero's seizure of his island but the two prisoners playing these characters seemed also to be in some kind of power tussle. This was also class-coded – Walter's Hannah/Prospero was middle-class and clearly educated, while Stanton's Caliban spoke with a strong working-class Suffolk accent. 'You taught me language, and my profit on't / Is I know how to curse' (1.2.365–6) became readable as resistance to Hannah's class privilege. It was striking that in a cast where the majority of actors were from ethnic minorities and a number of global accents could be heard, Caliban, Stefano and Trinculo were all played by white actors and spoke with regional working-class British accents (Suffolk, London and Glasgow respectively). At one point, in what was on one level simply a throwaway visual gag, Karen Dunbar's Scottish Trinculo and Jackie Clune's cockney Stefano emerged in Saltire and Union Jack boxer shorts respectively. The production seemed to be linking the Caliban subplot not with the now-familiar theme of British colonialism but with a dispossessed class much closer to home. In the weeks following the EU referendum, many commentators attributed the result to a feeling of anger and disempowerment amongst the white British working class. In this context, 'This island's mine' took on a potent new meaning (1.2.333).

The cross-gender casting moved in and out of focus over the performance. The cast's prison overalls tended to obscure their gender, and they had obviously worked on male physicality, taking up space, making wide, emphatic gestures, and often attempting to dominate each other with body language. Sometimes it was possible to forget the gender of the performer: Sheila Atim's Ferdinand, for example, functioned as a classic male romantic lead, while Dunbar's Trinculo was a comic example of a low status man who over-performed his masculinity, strutting pugnaciously. But these performances were also punctured by moments that brought the performance of gender into sharp relief, Ferdinand impersonating Miranda's stereotypically 'girly' behaviour, Trinculo and Stefano bursting into the first few lines of the all-female duet 'I Know Him So Well' from the musical *Chess* and donning the white dressing gowns and hairnets of a luxury spa. At the end of the play, most of the cast returned to the stage in civilian clothes, ready to leave the prison. What had been a mostly gender-neutral cast (and often a convincingly masculine one) was suddenly re-figured into a more conventional depiction of femininity, in skirts, jewellery and bright colours. This made the performance of femininity itself seem suddenly strange.

Opening at the Old Vic in November, Deborah Warner's *King Lear* followed Hastie's *Henry V* and

Lloyd's *Shakespeare Trilogy* in staging a cross-gender central performance within a metatheatrical frame. Glenda Jackson's performance as Lear was a much-anticipated event, marking the actress's return to the stage following twenty-three years as a Member of Parliament. Hers was the only cross-gender role in the production. During a pre-show sequence and then again during the interval, actors and stagehands milled around the large, bare stage, the actors wearing casual modern clothes that made them almost indistinguishable from their backstage colleagues. Sargon Yelda's Kent started the play by flicking though what appeared to be a script and casually observing, 'I thought the King had more affected the Duke of Albany than Cornwall' (1.1.1–2), as if he were commenting on his interpretation of the text. The production was thus framed as highly self-aware: once again, we were being primed to meet the actors halfway in the game of theatrical make-believe.

Jackson was an androgynous Lear, maintaining a dual sense both of the male character and of the well-known female politician playing him. Her hair was cropped short and, on her first entrance, she wore trousers and a shirt beneath a long, androgynous red cardigan. Her commanding, husky voice had a masculine quality to it, its extraordinary force all the more striking issuing as it did from her tiny physical form. Jackson's Lear was a man who enjoyed his power, his lines dripping with irony. He seemed almost to relish his banishment of Cordelia (Morfydd Clark), grinning maliciously as he disowned her. He was deeply sarcastic with Goneril and Regan; Celia Imrie's Goneril was past child-bearing age, making his preoccupation with her infertility simultaneously more vindictive and more impotent than usual. In 1.4, the King, now wearing a red baseball cap, was accompanied by a plausibly riotous group of lager-swigging followers who jeered and catcalled in his defence throughout the scene, and gave nods of macho approval when the disguised Kent recognized the 'Authority' inherent in Lear's face (1.4.30). In November 2016, there were unavoidable echoes here of the newly elected Donald Trump and his army of noisy enablers. Jackson herself tended to come in and out of focus: Lear's misogyny brought her gender to the fore, as did his obsession with his own masculinity, and of course the line about the 'scurvy politician' got a knowing laugh (4.5.167). Lear became more feminine, perhaps more maternal, as the play went on, appearing in a pair of orange culottes for his mad scene at Dover.

Rhys Ifans's Fool seemed sincerely to believe that Lear was on the verge of seeing the error of his ways. In 1.5, as Lear started to become upset at the thought of Cordelia, the Gentleman made as if to comfort him but the Fool held out a delaying hand: Lear needed to complete this line of thought, however painful. His foolery was not an attempt to distract his master but an ongoing project to nudge him towards clearer understanding. As the play continued, though, the Fool lost faith in his ability to make a difference, speaking his apocalyptic storm scene prophecy alone as the rainclouds on the video screen behind him suddenly changed to more closely resemble dust clouds in the aftermath of an explosion. Having been viciously attacked by his master in 3.6, the Fool wept bitterly on the ground before gathering himself up into Poor Tom's abandoned shopping trolley and going to sleep, where he remained into the interval.

PAIRED PRODUCTIONS

Kenneth Branagh staged two Shakespearean productions as part of his year-long season at London's Garrick Theatre. The first of these was *The Winter's Tale*, co-directed by Branagh and Rob Ashford and starring Branagh as Leontes. It opened with a scene of Christmas in times gone by, Jessie Buckley's Perdita singing ethereally as Paulina and Mamillius sat beneath a candlelit Christmas tree. Judi Dench's Paulina, borrowing a line from 2.1, asked the boy to tell her a tale. Determining that 'A sad tale's best for winter' (2.1.27), he began his tale as Christmas carollers flooded the stage, gathering to watch projected grainy film footage of the young Leontes and Polixenes playing and training together. This framing emphasized many of the production's key motifs: a sense of festivity, of childish wonder at being spun a yarn and of nostalgia for a better time in the not-too-distant but irrecoverable past. Act 4 moved to a timelessly pastoral setting, a sort of no-when Mummerset untouched by technology and yet also somehow of the late nineteenth or early twentieth century; the narrative slide of sixteen years did not seem to have taken us any further forward in historical time. Act 5, meanwhile, moved inexplicably from the 'middle summer' of the previous act to a midwinter setting, Leontes's home having become something resembling the Snow Queen's palace, all glittery blues and greys. To complain that this paid too little attention to chronology, however, would be to miss the point: fairy tales operate outside of time and history, and so, of course, did this production.

The production's male protagonists were vulnerable and psychologically volatile. Branagh's Leontes descended from mellifluous verse-speaking into stuttering and barking as the character lost control of his thoughts, but even at his darkest moment there was a hint that on some level Leontes knew his actions were wrong: as he threatened his infant daughter with death by fire, he was clutching the child almost tenderly. Hadley Fraser's Polixenes, suave and assured in the first act, began to echo some of Leontes's verbal tics during his fury in Act 4; even Tom Bateman's Florizel succumbed to the disease, albeit briefly, as he shouted in defiance of his father. In true fairy-tale style, however, the female leads and the supporting characters were entirely without blemish. Miranda Raison's Hermione, costumed in white for both the trial and the statue scenes, was faithful and loyal to the point of self-abnegation: her first thought upon hearing of Mamillius's death was to reach out to her husband, a gesture that was interrupted as she lost consciousness and finally concluded as she returned from the seemingly dead in the play's final scene. Michael Pennington's Antigonus was selfless too, deliberately distracting the offstage bear from the baby Perdita by roaring back at it and gesturing to himself on 'this is the chase' (3.3.56). Judi Dench's Paulina was a figure of understated moral strength, sincere in her apology for having spoken too sternly to Leontes (3.2.217–19) and grief-stricken at the loss of Mamillius – she broke down, movingly, as she described the child's 'honourable thoughts' (3.2.194). For this Paulina, keeping Hermione hidden until Perdita was found was the act primarily of a storyteller: she was prolonging Leontes's grief not in order to impose any kind of punishment or penance but simply because the moment needed to be accompanied by as complete a family reunion as possible in order to achieve its full force as a fable of reconciliation and forgiveness.

Branagh continued the fairy tale theme in his *Romeo and Juliet* by casting the stars of his recent *Cinderella* in the title roles. Lily James gave a highly physical performance as Juliet, youthful and gushing with emotion, while Richard Madden made a ruggedly handsome and surprisingly mature Romeo. The production was given a stylish 1950s Italian setting. Branagh made the protagonists' love at first sight part of a musical sequence: Juliet sang a ballad as part of the Capulet masque and she caught Romeo's gaze halfway through. But if this moment seemed to encourage the audience to view Juliet through Romeo's eyes, the production reversed this tendency over the scenes that followed. In the balcony scene, James's Juliet comically undercut Romeo's praise of her, swigging from a bottle she had smuggled from the party. She was fidgety, physically tense with excitement, plausibly experiencing sexual desire for the first time; Madden's Romeo, on the other hand, was noticeably more collected as he made his commentary from the side of the stage, too assured and unconfused to evoke adolescence. Later, when Meera Syal's Nurse returned with hastily arranged plans for her charge's marriage, Juliet was so overwhelmed by the news that she started to hiccup. James's kinaesthetic, empathetic performance meant that, as in *Cinderella*, her character provided the audience's main subject position, transforming Madden's character into the object of the gaze and of desire.

Branagh's casting made counter-intuitive use of age in several roles. Derek Jacobi was a jaded, world-weary Mercutio, a man in his seventies who acted as a kind of badly behaved mentor to the much-younger Romeo and Benvolio. He was a man who had known grief, who wanted the younger generation to learn from his experience: his Queen Mab speech turned from a witty digression into an angry rant, and he seemed to want to teach the young upstart Tybalt a lesson rather than actually to fight him. Conversely, the Friar was played by Samuel Valentine as a young man of around Romeo's age. The Friar thus became a sort of alternative Romeo, perhaps a childhood friend who had chosen a different path in life. When this Friar noted that 'Young men's love then lies / Not truly in their hearts, but in their eyes' (2.2.67–8), he seemed to be articulating something he felt he ought to have known himself but had only been able to conclude by observation. His naivety certainly helped to explain the impracticality of the Friar's plans.

There was another pair of Shakespearean productions on offer this year in the form of the Tobacco Factory's annual Shakespeare season in Bristol. First to open was Andrew Hilton's *Hamlet*, with Alan Mahon in the title role. Mahon's youthful looks and lanky frame made Hamlet something of an awkward adolescent, and his default setting in the performance was one of earnest indignation. In some ways, this worked well as a reading of the character: he was earnestly indignant as he mused upon his mother's remarriage, earnestly indignant as he learned of his father's murder, earnestly indignant as he hurled a barrage of abuse at Ophelia, and earnestly indignant as he confronted his mother and killed Polonius. The persistent return to this one note, however, rendered this Hamlet rather hard to like. In the final scene, as he pinched a cloak from a relatively inoffensive Osric and used it to goad Callum McIntyre's grief-stricken Laertes as if he were a bull-fighter, I am afraid I found myself actively wishing for his imminent demise.

Earnestness was the keynote of the production in general. Polonius's advice to his children, often played as the hackneyed ramblings of an overbearing old pedant, was played in earnest by Ian Barritt. Isabella Marshall's Ophelia was earnest in her madness, fixing each of her addressees with a firm stare and shouting her lines as if she were making a series of angry, coded accusations. Julia Hills's Gertrude was tense and watchful from her first appearance, stiffening as Claudius clasped her hand, her eyes flitting from one courtier to the next as though she were uncomfortably aware that she was being observed herself. Alan Coveney's Horatio was clearly Hamlet's tutor rather than a fellow student, older than him by far and something of a mentor. 'So Guildenstern and Rosencrantz go to't' (5.2.57) was spoken with disappointment bordering on disgust; he turned away sadly, making as if to leave, as Hamlet followed him desperately trying to justify his actions. 'Why, what a king is this!' (5.2.63) was a condemnation of Hamlet, not Claudius – and Hamlet, earnestly indignant as ever, failed to notice.

Hilton's *All's Well That Ends Well* was a more unusual production. Shakespeare's text had been heavily adapted by Dominic Power. Power cleared up the plot, foregrounding the ring so crucial to the play's denouement, and rendered the play's sexual politics more palatable to a modern audience. Hilton and Power set the production in nineteenth-century continental Europe, and both the setting and the rewrites seemed to be aimed at giving the piece a Chekhovian feel. For Helena, Lavatch and perhaps Bertram too, 'Paris' was a mythical site of desire, an escape from the unfulfilled desires represented by the Countess's rural retreat – but unlike the characters of Chekhov's *Three Sisters*, who become increasingly frustrated by their thwarted ambitions to get to Moscow, *All's Well*'s characters all got to Paris sooner or later, and most of them actually got what they wanted there. Power's major intervention was to reinvent Lavatch as a melancholy dancing tutor, somewhat reminiscent of *As You Like It*'s Jaques. His clowning was cut almost entirely. Far from the 'foul-mouth'd and calumnious knave' suggested by Shakespeare, Marc Geoffrey's Lavatch was actually rather prissy, unable to bring himself to say the word 'fistula' (''tis a vile word, it has no savour of regality') and making pedantic points in Latin about the validity of Helena's marriage to Bertram.[5] He was eaten up by an unexpressed love for Bertram and cattily jealous of Helena. In Act 4, he went briefly mad with lovesickness, and in the final scene he appeared as a mirror image of the now-humbled Parolles (Paul Currier), both of them now wearing simple peasant clothing.

Bertram (Craig Fuller) was given an arc that made more of his repentance. He had the look of a Dickensian rake, dark-haired and handsome but slightly greasy. There was a sense that he was jealous of the strong maternal bond between the Countess and Helena: 'Madam, I desire your holy wishes' was an impatient demand for attention (1.1.56). He was clearly fond of Helena (Eleanor Yates), sharing long physical embraces with her both times they parted; the implication was that he refused her hand in marriage not because he did not love her but because he resented the imposition of the King's will. The production was constantly hinting that Bertram did not really mean what he said, but that he spoke out of angry self-defence and unwillingness to confront emotional pain. In this sense he was the production's most Chekhovian character, and the fact that his thoughts were generally unavailable to the audience except though naturalistic subtext made it surprising that Power added in a new scene in which Bertram heard of Helena's apparent death and started to soliloquise:

> Helena dead? The playmate of my youth
> Turn'd to dust by my indifference?...
> Appetite and pride have at a stroke
> Murder'd the lady and my immortal soul.[6]

Act 5 scene 1 was extended slightly so that Helena heard about Bertram's contrition, which meant that her actions in the final scene were more obviously a test of his repentance. The ending was much augmented: after a rewritten reconciliation between the penitent Bertram and a forgiving, happy Helena, Lavatch led the assembled company in one last dance. He concluded that 'In graceful execution may we learn / To know ourselves', and in the final line, Helena insisted that 'In this eternal instant, all is well.'[7]

A WORLD ELSEWHERE

The National Theatre's Shakespearean contribution to 2016 was Polly Findlay's *As You Like It*, the first major Shakespearean production at the theatre under Rufus Norris's artistic directorship. As the audience entered the Olivier auditorium, we were faced with a brightly coloured postmodern office complex in which various workers in colour-coded teams were beavering away at arcane bureaucratic tasks. Lizzie Clachan's gaudy set evoked the sort of corporate space in which all activity is tightly regulated and monitored but where empty gestures are made towards creativity: each desk was topped with a tiny bonsai tree. In Findlay's dystopia, the wrestling scene, all spangly costumes, rock music and trash-talking into microphones, became a 'bread and circuses' exercise in keeping the Duke's workforce superficially entertained rather than recognizing the reality of their exploitation.

The production's *coup de theatre* was its transition from the world of the court to the Forest of Arden. As the metal grid representing the office ceiling began to rise, it became clear that all the desks, lamps and chairs were attached to one another by invisible wires: within seconds, twisted chains of office furniture were suspended across the full vertical length of the Olivier stage to represent trees (Illustration 27). Findlay's Arden was a literal dismantling of the corporate confinement of Duke Frederick's court, a wild space free from its fastidious management of human behaviour. But it was a dangerous space, too: Findlay chose to set the first few forest scenes in midwinter, and the 'churlish chiding of the winter's wind' (2.1.7) was a continuous presence as ensemble members, perched among the 'trees', provided a soundtrack of moaning winds, hooting owls, dripping branches and flapping wings. Duke Senior and his

---

[5] Dominic Power, *All's Well That Ends Well: Revised Text*, Shakespeare at the Tobacco Factory, pp. 9, 30, http://stf-theatre.org.uk/wp-content/uploads/2016/06/Alls-Well-That-Ends-Well.pdf.
[6] Power, *All's Well*, p. 48. [7] Power, *All's Well*, p. 64.

with the eruption of spring, which was cleverly signified by the addition to the set of 'leaves' of green notepaper, simultaneously representing both Orlando's poems and the leaves of spring.

The forest provided an environment in which Rosalie Craig's Rosalind could throw off the shackles of the court and its gender roles. Appearing in her first scene in a tight-fitted dress and high-heeled shoes, Craig's Rosalind became convincingly androgynous upon her transition into the forest, shearing off her hair and donning a lumberjack shirt and gilet. She started to adopt the confident strides of her masculine alter-ego even when she was alone or accompanied only by her fellow outcast, Patsy Ferran's Celia. Joe Bannister's Orlando was twitchy and nervous, a likeable and hapless underdog who was painfully aware of his attraction to the (as he supposed) male Ganymede. Towards the end of the play, he seemed on the verge of coming out to Ganymede as he tugged nervously at his own sleeves on the line 'I can live no longer by thinking' (5.2.48); his 'If this be so, why blame you me to love you?' (5.2.100) was clearly an impulsive admission of love for the boy, from which he immediately tried to row back. The production's playful dismantling of gender binaries was rather undermined by the conclusion, however, which saw the female protagonists return to a more conventional kind of femininity: Rosalind and Celia returned to the stage wearing 1950s-style circle dresses and the same shoes they had worn at the start of the play, and Rosalind's long hair had miraculously regrown. There was no sense of gender ambiguity in her epilogue, either, the line 'If I were a woman' amended to 'As I am a woman' (17–18).

27. *As You Like It*, 2.4, National Theatre, Olivier Theatre, directed by Polly Findlay. Rosalie Craig as Rosalind. Photograph by Johan Persson.

followers were wrapped up in shabby overcoats, one of them afflicted with a hacking cough; it was not hard to understand Orlando's desperation in a place where death from starvation or exposure seemed a likely prospect. Act Two, in fact, might have been subtitled *A Midwinter Night's Dream*: Findlay interpolated a number of short scenes in which young lovers chased each other through the dark and inhospitable forest, William wooing Audrey with a ham-fisted enquiry after her goats, and Phebe fleeing Silvius with a line borrowed from Demetrius ('I love thee not, therefore pursue me not'). Silvius was even pranked by the supernatural creatures that lived in the trees, being repeatedly drenched with dripping water. The mood of the forest scenes changed, of course,

Carrie Cracknell and Lucy Guerin's *Macbeth*, a co-production between the Young Vic and Birmingham Repertory Theatre, was a taut, physical adaptation of the play. It played at two hours without an interval, and was built around a feeling of claustrophobia and impending doom. Lizzie Clachan's set gave the audience the illusion of looking down a long corridor lined with doors, though in fact it consisted of a sloping floor and tapering walls leading towards a small central aperture at the back. Sometimes this was a lit corridor, leading back towards an ominous black nothingness; at other times the aperture was flooded with light while the corridor was in darkness (the elusive 'light at the end of the tunnel', perhaps). The illusion of depth was often subverted by the blocking: actors used the central aperture as an entrance, and taller actors were often positioned towards the back of the set, strategies that made the performers look disproportionately large. In a particularly disorienting effect that recalled Alfred Hitchcock's famous shot from *Vertigo*, the ensemble sometimes rushed down the length of the set from the back and then suddenly backwards towards its vanishing point. Much of the text was replaced by Guerin's choreography, Banquo's murder, for example, becoming a dance sequence with almost no dialogue. The witches were played by dancers in surgical-looking flesh-coloured leotards; they moved jerkily, like pop-culture zombies, making eerie percussive noises as they pulled their fingers suddenly from their mouths. The text was edited to make them seem almost like puppets, speaking their prophecies in unison as if possessed by demonic forces.

The production's human world was a contemporary and violent one. In a short opening montage lit by flashes, we saw the gruesome murder of Macdonald, John Heffernan's Macbeth suffocating him with a polythene bag; after a snap blackout, we saw a head in the bag and a decapitated corpse, Macbeth and Banquo slumped exhaustedly against the wall downstage. As Duncan conversed with the wounded sergeant in 1.2, soldiers in the background dragged on corpse-like bundles in plastic bags, including a number of child-sized sacks. At the beginning of 1.4 we glimpsed a figure, presumably the Thane of Cawdor, being electrocuted with a bag over his head; in the next scene, Malcolm's report of the Thane's noble demise thus seemed disingenuous. But, as the play went on, this viscerally realistic register gave way to a more nightmarish one. Prasanna Puwanarajah's murdered Banquo returned to the slumped downstage position in which he had begun the play and spoke fragments of Shakespearean text into a microphone, narrating Lady Macbeth's madness, the advance of the English army and the demoralization of Macbeth's troops, and speaking the lines of many of Act 5's messengers and servants. Macbeth's death at Macduff's hands was played to recall the opening, flashes of light showing snapshots of Macbeth being suffocated in a plastic bag before having his throat cut.

For all its expressionistic elements, this was ultimately a psychological production, focused on the minds of its two protagonists. John Heffernan's Macbeth was softly spoken and conscience-stricken, an oddly innocent figure in this violent world. He seemed horrified by the violence in which he was complicit, as if he were somehow not responsible for it: as Banquo prepared to depart, Macbeth noticed Fleance's games console, and spoke 'Goes Fleance with you?' (3.1.37) as the sad realization that Fleance must die too. Anna Maxwell Martin's Lady Macbeth seemed both psychologically and physically trapped, frequently leaning against the walls of the set. She was nervous and tense, calling upon the evil spirits as if uncertain of their existence and unsure whether or not she really wanted to invoke them at all. Later, when Macbeth summoned 'seeling night' to aid his own diabolical endeavours, she muttered and shook her head, backing away and collapsing against the wall, now utterly convinced of the terrifying power of supernatural forces (3.2.47–54). He began to shout his invocation and she screamed; he stood over her quivering body, a dominating arm against the wall, for the rest of the speech. But his confidence was short-lived. By the end of the play, he was hiding beneath a trapdoor, paying lip service to the thought of his infallibility as his actions betrayed his unconscious acknowledgement of the truth.

Ivo van Hove's *Kings of War*, which visited the Barbican in April, was in some ways a follow-up to his 2007 production *Roman Tragedies*, a six-hour modern-dress epic that had combined *Coriolanus*, *Julius Caesar* and *Antony and Cleopatra*. *Kings of War*, adapted in Dutch by Bart van den Eynde and Peter van Kraaij from six different Shakespearean History plays, built on this foundation, though it seemed less interested than its predecessor in the politics of spectatorship and more in the tactics and psychologies of political leaders. Thus, where *Roman Tragedies* had invited its spectators to move around during its many intervals and watch its events from the stage, becoming part of the spectacle of power themselves, over the four-and-three-quarter hours of *Kings of War* we were confined to our seats and consigned to watch the narrative from a remote and powerless distance. This not only made *Kings of War* a more arduous experience physically but also reflected an altogether bleaker conception of the relationship between power and the people in these plays.

Jan Versweyveld's set evoked the kind of large bunker in which leaders might find themselves during times of war: a cavernous space without windows upon whose walls were hung various campaign maps and screens displaying radar and drone footage. The stage was surrounded by an offstage, white-walled corridor that was visible only in glimpses through the doors at the back and sides, though it soon became evident that the events taking place in this corridor would often be relayed via live film on the huge video screen that dominated the middle of the set. In the first scene (adapted from *2 Henry IV*) we witnessed the young Henry V (Ramsey Nasr) playfully tossing the crown and being instructed by his dying father to 'busy giddy minds / With foreign quarrels' (4.3.342–3).[8] Henry immediately set about implementing his father's advice. Before long, he had donned a military uniform in order to exhort his unseen troops, via camera, to return to the breach. This was no war hero, leading from the front; Nasr's Henry was an amoral strategist, manipulating his mediatized public image in order to gain political advantage. He spoke a version of the Prologue to Act 4 himself, clearly attempting to impose his own mythologization on the camera footage of demoralized English soldiers. His St Crispin's Day oration was delivered offstage to an unseen audience of soldiers, audible only through its increasingly echoing electronic relay. Its prosaic translation rendered the chilling effect of its rhetoric all the more clear, as Henry began to sound inescapably like a militaristic despot.

The next segment focused on Eelco Smits's nervous and bespectacled Henry VI. Once again, the battles and uprisings of Shakespeare's plays were entirely absent from the onstage action, either elided completely or simply reported as offstage action. Where during Henry V's reign the set had been a war room, under his son it seemed to be a fully functioning residential bunker in which this reluctant and inexperienced young man was hiding from the world semi-permanently. This segment drew much of its material from the first half of Shakespeare's *2 Henry VI*, focused as it is on the deals and deceptions that go on backstage in the corridors of power (here, of course, this metaphor was literalized). Unlike *Henry V*, the onstage characters in this segment were generally unaware of the presence of the camera, which was now recording their private conversations in close-up.

The final section of the performance was based on *Richard III*. Hans Kesting's Richard was a dangerous narcissist, delivering his first soliloquy not to the audience but to himself, via a large mirror. He was concerned with his image not for political reasons, as Henry V had been, but vanity; he kept turning to one side and admiring his reflection in profile. At one point, he tried on the crown and pulled a rug over his shoulders, play-acting at being king; he picked up each of the three telephones in the bunker and pretended, in English, German and Russian respectively, to be on the telephone to Obama, Merkel and Putin in turn. High on power, his descent into full-blown insanity followed hard upon his coronation. Ramsey Nasr's Richmond was no redeemer but a chilling echo of the same actor's Henry V: like Henry, he was convinced that 'God and our good cause fight upon our side' (5.5.194) and inspired his troops with the cry 'God and Saint George!' (5.5.224). The parallel implied, darkly, that the cycle was simply starting all over again. The power vacuum

---

[8] The surtitles were largely prosaic paraphrases of Shakespeare's lines; all quotations here are based on the Oxford Shakespeare and not on the particular translation used for the surtitles at the Barbican.

28. *King Lear*, 1.1, Talawa Theatre Company, Royal Exchange Theatre, Manchester, directed by Michael Buffong. Don Warrington as Lear. Photograph by Jonathan Keenan.

left behind by Henry V, a leader who had based his rule on righteous rhetoric and displays of might, had created precisely the kind of environment in which an opportunistic narcissist such as Richard III could flourish: in this year in particular, that was a terrifying thought.

This year was one of *Lear*s. The productions starring Antony Sher and Glenda Jackson have already been discussed; I was unable to get to the concurrent Lears of Michael Pennington or Timothy West but I was able to see Don Warrington's at the Royal Exchange Theatre in Manchester. In addition, 2016 marked the 30th anniversary of Talawa Theatre Company, which was founded in 1986 in order to create more opportunities for black theatre artists. Since Shakespeare remains such a potent symbol of Britishness, productions of his plays are an important site for the cultural visibility of modern black Britons. This was reason enough for Talawa to produce *King Lear* with a majority black cast. The politics of this casting, in fact, lay in the fact that it rapidly became irrelevant: this was not a production that wanted to say anything in particular about race other than making an implicit case that black actors deserve the same opportunities as their white counterparts in classical roles. In this, it made a refreshing contrast to the RSC's pseudo-African *Hamlet*.[9]

Michael Buffong's production was a straightforward and compelling one, opting for stark simplicity and playing for the most part in a naturalistic register. Warrington's Lear started the play as a rather terrifying authority figure, visually impressive in his crown, fur collar and large black cloak, his voice assaulting the ear with its loud, unrelenting rasp (Illustration 28). But as soon as he had parted his kingdom between his sons-in-law, his authority evaporated. He entered his next scene, 1.4, wearing a simple blue jerkin and accompanied by three nonchalant attendants who were already exhibiting signs that they no longer saw him as a king. They lounged around on the floor and the wooden benches, oblivious to his inquiries about the whereabouts of his Fool; when the disguised Kent asserted that Lear had 'authority' in his countenance (1.4.30), they simply laughed. When Miltos Yerolemou's Fool entered, his black eye make-up was already streaked with tears, as if he had foreseen the violent results of the King's decision to give up his crown. The Fool understood, as nobody else yet did, that power is about the control of soldiers and resources, not the niceties of titles and social status; as Goneril and Regan verbally reduced Lear's train from fifty followers to none, the Fool slowly sank to his knees in despair. Warrington's Lear was furious, cursing Rakie Ayola's Goneril with such force and vehemence that she fell to

---

[9] Later in the year, Black Theatre Live toured a mid-scale production of *Hamlet* with an all-black cast, set in 'a Black Empire of modern England'. Again, my full schedule meant I was unable to see it.

the floor; later, he pushed Debbie Korley's Regan to the ground. But there was a clear sense that, for all his rage, he was ultimately powerless: he had a trademark move of lunging impotently towards the subjects of his wrath with a fist raised, a gesture that returned as a parody of itself during his mad scene.

Fraser Ayres was an earnest and methodical Edmund, whose slight stoop made him look rather hungry. While Edmund is often played as a charismatic trickster, Ayres portrayed him as the sort of person who might easily disappear into the background (and might, perhaps, be all the more dangerous as a result). There was something almost Uriah Heepish about his carefully performed humility; when Kent promised to 'love you, and sue to know you better', Edmund's delighted reply, 'Sir, I shall study deserving', was just a little too eager to please (1.1.29–30). In soliloquy he rarely smiled and, when he did, it was without warmth or humour; he told us of his duplicitous plans with the chilling calmness of a psychopath. Interestingly, the production cut virtually all the asides and soliloquies that were not Edmund's. This meant that Cordelia's first line was not her aside to the audience but her reply to Lear, 'Nothing, my Lord' (1.1.87) – we were given no insight into her thoughts leading up to this decision other than her subsequent explanation to her father. The biggest loss was to the role of Edgar (Alfred Enoch), who was stripped of all of his soliloquies and most of his asides. There was thus no break in his Poor Tom persona from the moment he adopted it until he finally dropped it. This had the effect of rendering Edgar a completely naturalistic character who could be judged and understood only by his actions; it also made him unusually mysterious.

The production's climax was nuanced and moving. Lear's grief over Cordelia was stark and inescapable, played simply on a virtually empty stage. Albany, Edgar and Kent moved to the periphery of the playing area as Mark Springer's Albany delivered what sounded, in this context, like a final speech, promising to 'resign / During the life of this old majesty / To him our absolute power' (5.3.274–6). The lights began to fade on these three as a spotlight narrowed on Lear and the body of Cordelia. Lear's 'Why should a dog, a horse, a rat have life, / And thou no breath at all?' took on the quality of an epilogue, and his slow, soft delivery of 'Never, never, never, never, never' sounded for a moment like its conclusion (5.3.282–4). For a few thrilling seconds I wondered whether this production was going to leave us with an image of a heartbroken, still-living Lear, frozen in an eternal moment of grief; it was almost a relief when the production allowed him to die after all.

I saw one other *Lear* this year, this one a more self-conscious act of cultural appropriation. Michael Kantor's adaptation *The Shadow King* relocated the play to an indigenous community in Australia. Shakespeare's text was truncated and paraphrased, combining English with Kriol and indigenous languages; much of it was recognizable as line-for-line paraphrase, though there were a few direct quotations. At the back of a large stage filled with red sand, a video screen played film footage of Australian landscapes, both natural and urban. The Fool (Kamahi Djordon King) opened the show as a narrator, explaining to the Barbican audience that the company would be performing 'one of your dreamtime stories – but tonight it's ours'. The production was thus framed as both an act of intercultural appropriation and the retelling of a myth. As the Fool told the story in Kriol of trucks sweeping into the landscape, the set surged forward, a huge truck-like construction fronted with two pairs of dazzling headlights; the suddenness and violence of this set-change mirrored that of Australia's own cultural transformation. The motif of trucks driving through the landscape returned several times, both on the screen and in the movement of the set; the truck and its blinding headlights were thrust forward again at the end as Lear and Cordelia were defeated.

This was a story about generational tensions in the indigenous community. Goneril, Regan and Edmund were keen to gain possession of their parents' mining royalties. Tom E. Lewis's Lear was a playful and impulsive local patriarch who frequently entered the stage singing pop songs,

29. *The Shadow King*, Malthouse Theatre, Barbican Theatre, directed by Michael Kantor. Kamahi Djordon King as the Fool and Damion Hunter as Edgar. Photograph by Jeff Busby.

dancing to the accompaniment of the onstage band. He clearly saw the land as his to bestow, though in an early aside, Rarriwuy Hick's Cordelia complained that the land could not be owned in this manner. Gloucester (Frances Djulibing) was re-invented as a matriarch, the most traditional of all the characters onstage; she spoke the highest proportion of lines in indigenous languages and carried around a dilly bag. Jimi Bani's Edmund was atheistic and cynical, unbelieving in the spiritual presence of the ancestors or the land, and he saw the religious older generation as 'traitors' to his own. He spurred on Goneril (Jada Alberts) and Regan (Natasha Wanganeen) to attack Lear and Gloucester on this basis, and his own murder of the Fool, and Goneril and Regan's simultaneous blinding of Gloucester, were conflated into a single scene. Subsequently, Goneril seemed more distressed by her destruction of Gloucester's dilly bag, the symbol of her cultural heritage, than she was by her participation in the old woman's blinding.

Damion Hunter's Edgar, by contrast, adopted a headdress and costume of grass and feathers for his Poor Tom persona, daubing himself with white clay (Illustration 29). This persona was interpreted by the Fool as a ghost from the past. Lear's encounter with him thus changed in meaning: 'Is man no more than this?' (3.4.96–7) was not a confrontation with the human being as an animal, but rather with an older way of being; in Lear's words, this was a figure 'unburdened by modernity'. It was striking that the line 'a dog's obeyed in office' (4.5.154–5) was rephrased as 'These days, a dog's obeyed more than a King'. Making this an observation about degenerate modernity rather than about authority in general rather changed its politics: the production, or at least Lear, seemed nostalgic for an older, now-marginalized cultural order rather than disillusioned about the workings of power and ideology in general. The performance concluded with the Fool's ghost musing on the folly of thinking you own the land when in fact the land owns you; he concluded that Lear, a 'stubborn' old man, had finally learned 'from the land'. Clearly, the production wanted us to agree that Lear had been foolish to think that he could claim ownership of the land; I wondered whether it also wanted us to agree, on some level, that the old ways are the best.

Rupert Goold's *Richard III* at the Almeida also played with ideas about power and the past. The production opened by staging a version of the recent excavation at Leicester, as modern archaeologists in protective suits and hard hats lifted Richard's sword and crooked spine from his grave. As the production flashed back to a past that was somehow still of the present – the actors were all in modern dress – the open grave was covered with glass. It re-opened intermittently throughout the show to double as the graves of other characters, such as Rivers and Buckingham, before serving as the site of Richard's death in the play's closing moments. As the play neared its climax, medieval elements started to creep back in: slowly the stage started to fill with men in armour, carrying swords. At the end, after Richard was killed in the open grave, an archaeologist reappeared, setting up a pair of floodlights to illuminate it. The moment recontextualized the story – somewhat dubiously – as history.

Ralph Fiennes's Richard had a nice air in mock humility at first. After hearing news of the King's poor health, he said 'He cannot live!' as if mortified, before adding, 'I hope' (1.1.145). In 1.3, as the characters filed offstage concerned about the King, he began to recite a 'Hail Mary', trailing off and shrugging as soon as they were out of earshot. He was also power-hungry and deeply misogynistic. In his dialogue with Joanna Vanderham's Lady Anne, he seemed to be testing her to see what she would let him get away with, removing his ring from his finger with his mouth. When he grabbed her crotch, she slapped him; he paused for a moment and slapped her back. Afterwards, he assumed our approval, asking 'Was ever woman in this humour wooed?' and pausing for an answer – 'Mm?' – to laughter (1.2.215). He was given an extra soliloquy at the end of 1.3, building further on his close, gloating relationship with the audience: 'Can I do this, and cannot get a crown?' (imported from *3 Henry VI*, 3.2.124–95). Immediately following his coronation, he shed his gown, orb, sceptre and even his crown, leaving a figure dressed in plain black sat amidst the discarded iconography of royal power, an emblem of naked ambition. Finbar Lynch's practical and unemotional Buckingham was Richard's PR man, repeatedly interrupting him in order to avoid any revealing slips. It was his undervaluing of Buckingham's understated pragmatism that was Richard's ruin: while he was still in league with Buckingham, he tended to hide his desires from the world, operating by stealth and using people's fear rather than simply taking what he wanted. Once Buckingham was gone, Richard started more and more to do the latter.

The production was edited and directed so that virtually every supporting character had a complete arc. Vanderham's Lady Anne was given much of the dialogue of 2.3's anonymous citizens, so that her story became a sustained portrait of a woman slowly realizing she is caught in a political machine over which she has no control. Hastings (James Garnon) was a professional politician, constantly checking the news on his mobile phone; the first part of 3.2 was ingeniously adapted into a soliloquy, in which Hastings, working late into the night, shared a series of text messages with Stanley, reading them aloud and sharing his thoughts with the audience. Following Richard's sudden *volte face* in 3.4, Hastings was deeply in shock, regarding his own trembling hands almost as if he were puzzled by his physical reaction to his death sentence. The Bishop of Ely (Simon Coates) became a more substantial role, conflating several characters: it was Ely who objected to the violation of the Prince's sanctuary in 3.1, before realizing how the political landscape had shifted and rapidly acquiescing; it was he who, ashamed of his own silence in the face of Richard's abuse of power, delivered the scrivener's speech in 3.6; it was also Ely whom Richard co-opted as an unwilling visual prop at Baynard's castle in the following scene. The production's conflation of several minor characters in this way ensured that few cast members had to double: this meant that every death was permanent, leaving that actor out of the show until he or she returned as a ghost. Skulls were illuminated in turn in a number of alcoves on the back wall as the number of Richard's victims grew.

Margaret and Elizabeth were key figures in the production. For almost the duration of the show, Vanessa Redgrave's Margaret carried a grubby, broken doll, a symbol of the immeasurable pain she carried as a result of the death of her son, and of the grudge she nursed against those who had bereft her in this way. She wore a boiler suit, visually linking her with the archaeologists from the opening. Redgrave delivered her curses calmly, as if she were expressing not a personal vendetta but simply some sort of universal law of karma. She finally passed the doll to Aislín McGuckin's Elizabeth in 4.4, gently informing her erstwhile rival that she must now take on the mantle of the wronged, vengeful queen. Richard's subsequent dialogue with Elizabeth was a high point of the evening in many ways, dynamic and urgent, McGuckin playing the Queen's anger with a fiery clarity. But in what was, for me, a directorial flourish too far, the scene concluded with Richard's onstage rape of Elizabeth. On one level, this made sense as the culmination of Richard's deep-seated misogyny and his tendency to take whatever he wanted, regardless of the consequences. But I have serious reservations about the ethics of using a graphic rape scene as an emblem of the perpetrator's depravity when the production seems uninterested in its effect upon the victim (Elizabeth had no further lines after this scene, and only a handful after the rape itself). To read 4.4 as Elizabeth's defeat is also, I think, a misreading that takes Richard's own conclusion ('Relenting fool, and shallow, changing woman', 4.4.362) at face value.

COMPLETE WORKS

As an anniversary year, it was perhaps inevitable that there would be some attempts at staging Shakespeare's 'complete works'. The first of these was Forced Entertainment's *Complete Works: Table Top Shakespeare*, which was hosted at the Barbican over a week in March. This was a series of hour-long retellings of Shakespearean plays, using everyday household items to represent the characters. A team of six narrators divided thirty-six plays between them (no *Two Noble Kinsmen*, *Henry VIII* or indeed *Arden of Faversham* here). Like the same company's *Five Day Lear* (1999), it was about narrative, imagination and the possibilities and the limits of human memory, filtered through the prism of attempts to recall the plot of a Shakespearean play. Director Tim Etchells had also staged an early development of the idea in *Be Stone No More*, a 2012 collaboration with the RSC; *Complete Works* was itself staged in Berlin in 2015. I went to see three of the thirty-six Barbican performances: Terry O'Connor's retelling of *The Merry Wives of Windsor*, Jerry Killick's *Troilus and Cressida* and Richard Lowden's *Much Ado About Nothing*.

The 'stage' was a rectangular wooden table, flanked on each side by shelves on which the tabletop items for all the plays were stacked. This gave the impression not only of some sort of apothecary's shop or alchemist's laboratory (a metaphor, maybe, for the transformative power of narrative fiction) but also of two galleries full of spectators watching a stage. With the actual audience making up a third, the stage was thus an approximation of an Elizabethan galleried playhouse with a bare wooden stage in the centre. The human performer sat behind the table for each show, the inanimate players for their narratives placed on plastic crates either side of them. These objects were often well-chosen symbols for the characters they represented: Falstaff, for example, was a bulbous, ornate bottle of liqueur, while Mistresses Ford and Page were plastic bottles of honey (a visual pun, presumably, on the 'honey pot' trap the women set). Some casting choices emphasized contrasts and parallels:

Beatrice was an orange-and-white bottle of sun cream (a reference, perhaps, to her line 'Thus goes every one to the world but I, and I am sun-burnt', 2.1.298–9), while Hero was a similarly shaped translucent pink bottle of Johnson's baby oil; Benedick was a can of ale while Claudio was a bottle of lager. In *Troilus and Cressida*, all the Greek characters were played by bathroom products (Nestor was a mostly used-up tube of toothpaste) while the Trojans were represented by boxes, tins and bottles of food.

Etchells encouraged the performers to think 'diagrammatically' about their storytelling. Scenes were sketched out visually so as to emphasize groupings of characters, regroupings, parallels and oppositions. Page's conversation with Nym and Ford's with Pistol in 2.1 of *Merry Wives*, for example, were staged by placing the cans of food representing the husbands and the energy drinks representing Falstaff's sidekicks literally parallel to each other. The technique often imposed a kind of folk-tale symmetry where Shakespeare is less clear-cut. Lowden made *Much Ado*'s gulling scenes more similar than they are in Shakespeare, staging them as mirror images of each other: he added Margaret to the second, so that both had three tricksters onstage gulling a lone dupe, and narrated both conversations identically, stressing the lines which suggested that Benedick or Beatrice would die if their love were not requited by the other. Both characters opined at the end of each scene that the other was 'not so bad after all'.

The objects were certainly actors. The performers I saw combined narrative storytelling – in which they addressed the audience directly while pointing at the 'characters' to which they were referring – with something closer to puppetry, in which they focused their gaze on the objects to which they were currently giving voice and action, taking on aspects of the characters' physicalities in their own bodies. All three were careful to include telltale performative details in their narration: Shallow and Sir Hugh 'rolled their eyes at each other' whenever Slender said something stupid; Falstaff stood too close to Mistress Ford and 'breathed on her'; Cressida 'curled up in Diomedes's lap' after being kissed by the Greek commanders. But in fact, the objects 'performed' even without explicit narration. After Ann Page and Fenton 'looked at each other' during their love scene, the bar of soap playing Ann silently broke away and moved downstage, an action that told its own story. Diomedes left Cressida alone after having extracted a promise of sex from her, pausing to turn round at the entrance to the tent; when Killick made a clicking sound with his mouth, it was all we needed to let us know that Diomedes had winked at her. Beatrice and Benedick stood very close to each other as they confessed their love, but when she told him to kill Claudio – a development met with a gasp from some in the audience when I saw it – the can of beer playing Benedick wordlessly backed away from her. The performances were enormously effective, encouraging spectators to project their own imaginations onto the objects; I was reminded of the Shakespearean work of Tim Crouch, whose *I, Caliban* (2003) made similar use of inanimate objects to represent the characters of *The Tempest*.

Later in the year, I was able to see Crouch's own take on the 'complete works', his collaboration with the clown company Spymonkey. *The Complete Deaths* promised to stage all seventy-five onstage deaths from the works of Shakespeare. The collaboration exploited the strengths of both parties. An opening monologue by Toby Park played on his long-established Spymonkey persona as the pretentious and ambitious member of the clown troupe, who longs to create radical and challenging art; it also carried echoes of Crouch's *I, Malvolio* (2010) in its comically patronizing contempt for what Park projected as a complacent and conservative audience. We were told that this was a performance by 'the performance collective formerly known as Spymonkey' and that, if we were expecting easy laughs and pratfalls, we were to be disappointed: this was a show about death, both literally and figuratively (among the deaths Park promised to explore was 'the death of the grand narrative'). Of course, Park's hubris was instantly undermined by the rest of the troupe: Petra Massey, who thought they should be doing

30. *The Complete Deaths*, Spymonkey, touring, directed by Tim Crouch. Aitor Basauri as himself/Shakespeare. Photograph by Ludovic des Cognets, courtesy of Spymonkey (www.spymonkey.co.uk).

something more fun; Stephan Kreiss, who was wrestling with a microphone for much of the opening monologue; and Aitor Basauri, who entered in full Elizabethan costume, proudly displaying his physical likeness to Shakespeare (Illustration 30).

A loose frame narrative held the show together. The artistic tensions among the quartet were threatening to tear Spymonkey apart: as they started to perform the first of the performance's seventy-five deaths, Park was told that he, like Coriolanus, would not listen to 'what the people want'. In a series of Pythonesque interludes, a vision of Shakespeare appeared on the video screen at the back of the stage, telling Basauri that he was a great Shakespearean actor and that he must shun Spymonkey and learn to do proper classical acting (which, he was told, involved standing with one's feet wide apart, pointing at things, rolling one's 'R's and spitting a lot). Massey was desperate to do Ophelia's death scene despite the fact that it happens offstage, which Park insisted made it ineligible under the concept structuring the show, but Massey repeatedly tried to smuggle it into the performance. By the end of the show, the frame narrative and the enactment of the deaths had fused, and Park was metaphorically 'stabbed in the back' by the other three as they performed the assassination of Julius Caesar. Telling him they wanted him out of Spymonkey after eighteen years together, they forced him out of the show so that they could get back to being funny. 'Et tu, Andy?' said Park to the stage manager, who entered with a box of his belongings ready packed. He left the stage, heartbroken, reciting a few lines of Enobarbus's death speech.

Most of the show was, of course, very silly. The deaths from *Titus Andronicus* were presented with the use of a cartoonish mincing machine; those from *Macbeth* as part of a dance sequence in overly revealing kilts. Romeo and Juliet got into a suggestive tangle with one another's corpses and, when Basauri and Kreiss performed Polonius's murder, it became clear that they had misheard 'stabbed through the arras'. This was, in part, a parody of the fundamental hubris of attempting to represent death on stage: Basauri called an audience member up onto the stage to play Strato for Brutus's death scene, asking the spectator to hold the prop sword on which he would impale himself, to turn away and to 'look a bit sad'. He pretended to be deeply impressed as the audience member mimed wiping away a tear, re-performing the same gesture as Brutus died. It was also a satire on artistic pretension in general, Basauri gravely announcing that though Pyramus's death was normally performed in a comic style, Park would attempt to bring out 'anti-establishment', 'anti-capitalist' and 'Brexit' themes. At another point, Park insisted that the audience should use the time that would otherwise have been spent on the 110 lines of Antony's death sequence discussing solutions to political conflict in the Middle East.

But despite, or perhaps because of the silliness, there were moments which became genuinely affecting. The murder of Cinna the Poet – a death that Crouch has used elsewhere as the basis for his one-man play *I, Cinna the Poet* (2012) – was presented using puppets made of newspaper and sellotape. The cast voiced the Shakespearean dialogue, while the video screen showed close-up footage of the puppets they were manipulating, and the scene was oddly disturbing in its slow pace and sense of menace. In an echo of the 2012 RSC production with which Crouch's play was paired, the Cinna puppet was doused in lighter fuel and set on fire. Like much of Crouch's work, the sequence was marked by the conviction that a simple, pared-down, non-illusionistic representation can engage an audience's imagination more effectively than any straightforward attempt at naturalistic re-creation.

At the end of the show, the four clowns reunited to perform the four climactic deaths in *Hamlet*, leaving a single death on the countdown display board. This turned out to be the fly from *Titus Andronicus*. The fly had been a recurring presence from the show's opening moments, when the video screen had shown Massey and Kreiss taking turns to film one of the puppet flies landing on the other's 'dead' body. These puppets had returned at intervals throughout the show. Now, at the end, the video screen showed footage of the dying throes of a real fly. The fly became still, and the fact of death was presented simply and inescapably. The company immediately undercut it, of course, staging a spectacular funeral for the fly, and the show ended on a note of pleasure rather than disturbance. But I was left with some resonant thoughts as I exited the theatre, about laughter as a means of making the unbearable bearable and about the ethics of attempting to represent something as profound and as real as death on the stage at all, in any production, ever.

PROFESSIONAL SHAKESPEARE PRODUCTIONS IN THE BRITISH ISLES, JANUARY–DECEMBER 2015

JAMES SHAW

Most of the productions listed are by professional companies, but some amateur productions are included. The information is taken from *Touchstone* (www.touchstone.bham.ac.uk), a Shakespeare resource maintained by the Shakespeare Institute Library. Touchstone includes a monthly list of current and forthcoming UK Shakespeare productions from listings information. The websites provided for theatre companies were accurate at the time of going to press.

ANTONY AND CLEOPATRA

Theatre Royal, York, 22 February. Rehearsed reading.
www.yorktheatreroyal.co.uk
Director: George Costigan
Cleopatra: Niamh Cusack
Antony: Paterson Joseph
In aid of the York Theatre Royal redevelopment fund.

Madder Market Theatre Company. Madder Market Theatre, Norwich, 23 April–2 May.
www.maddermarket.co.uk
Director: Peter Beck

AS YOU LIKE IT

Shakespeare's Globe. Globe Theatre, London, 20 May–5 September.
www.shakespearesglobe.com
Director: Blanche McIntyre
Rosalind: Michelle Terry

Festival Players Theatre Company. Manor House Museum, Hall Green Road, 30 May and UK tour to 4 September.
www.thefestivalplayers.co.uk

BMH Productions. Oxford Castle, 22 June–4 July; Dorchester Abbey Cloister Gardens, 2 August.
www.bmhproductions.co.uk

Creation Theatre. Lady Margaret Hall, Norham Gardens, Oxford, 28 July–12 September.
www.creationtheatre.co.uk
Director: Tom Littler

National Theatre. Olivier Theatre, London, 26 October–5 March 2016.
www.nationaltheatre.org.uk
Director: Polly Findlay
Rosalind: Rosalie Craig

THE COMEDY OF ERRORS

Adaptation

National Theatre. Temporary Theatre, London, 22 October–6 November; and on tour.
www.nationaltheatre.org.uk
Director: Bijan Sheibani
One-hour version aimed at audiences aged between six and twelve.

CYMBELINE

Albatross Theatre. Waterloo East Theatre, London, 24–9 March.
www.waterlooeast.co.uk

Shakespeare's Globe. Globe Theatre, London, 2 December–21 April 2016.
www.shakespearesglobe.com
Director: Sam Yates
Innogen: Emily Barber

PRODUCTIONS IN THE BRITISH ISLES, JANUARY–DECEMBER 2015

Adaptation

The Injur'd Princess, or The Fatal Wager
Shakespeare's Globe Theatre. Sam Wanamaker Playhouse, 22 November.
www.shakespearesglobe.com
Playwright: Thomas D'Urfey
Part of the Read not Dead season of script-in-hand performances.

HAMLET

New Venture Theatre, Brighton, 16–24 January.
www.newventure.org.uk
Director: Steven O'Shea
Abridged version.

Clwyd Theatr Cymru. Anthony Hopkins Theatre, Mold, 10 February–7 March; and on tour.
www.clwyd-theatr-cymru.co.uk
Director: Terry Hands
Hamlet: Lee Haven-Jones
Terry Hands's final production as Artistic Director.

English Repertory Theatre. Cockpit, London, 10 February–15 March; and on tour.
www.englishrep.com
Director: Gavin Davis
Hamlet: Rachel Waring
Gender-blind casting of *Hamlet*.

Barbican Theatre in association with Thelma Holt Ltd. Barbican Theatre, London, 21–4 May; and on tour.
www.barbican.org.uk
Director: Yukio Ninagawa
In Japanese with English surtitles. The eighth time Yukio Ninagawa has directed *Hamlet*.

Folksy Theatre Company. Bristol Shakespeare Festival, Boiling Wells Amphitheatre, 24–5 July and on tour to 23 August.
www.folksytheatre.co.uk

Barbican Theatre, London, 5 August–31 October. Broadcast to cinemas worldwide by National Theatre Live, 15 October.
www.barbican.org.uk
Director: Lyndsey Turner
Hamlet: Benedict Cumberbatch
Gertrude: Anastasia Hille
"To be or not to be" opened the show during previews but was later reinstated in Act 3.

Adaptation

Hamlets
Birmingham Repertory Theatre's Young REP. Birmingham Library, Birmingham, 17–21 March.
www.birmingham-rep.co.uk
Director: Daniel Tyler
Ten interpretations of *Hamlet* played over the ten floors of the Library of Birmingham.

H(2)O. Teatr Strefa Otwarta of Wroclaw. De Grey Rooms, York, 9–11 May.
www.yorktheatreroyal.co.uk
Adaptors and Performers: Anna Rakowska and Piotr Misztela
Two-hander exploring the relationship between Hamlet and Ophelia.

Prince H. Universe
Parrabbola in association with Hamletscenen from Helsingoer Denmark. Friargate Theatre, York, 9–10 May.
www.yorktheatreroyal.co.uk
Writer and Director: Lars Romann Engel
Prince H. tells autobiographical stories from a fictional radio studio.

Hamlet Diagnosis
Companyia Pelmànec. St Peter's School, York, 11–12 May.
Performer: Miquel Gallardo
www.yorktheatreroyal.co.uk
A puppet version in Spanish with English subtitles.

Hamlet: Who's There?
Flute Theatre. Festiwal Szekspirowski, Gdanski Teatr Szekspirowski, Gdansk, 4 August; Mercury Theatre, Colchester, 15–16 April 2016; at Elsinore Castle, Denmark, 8–9 August 2016; and on tour.
www.flutetheatre.co.uk
Director and Gertrude: Kelly Hunter
Hamlet: Mark Quartley
90-minute version without interval.

Roll Over Beethoven
Queen's Theatre, Hornchurch, 24 August–12 September.
Director: Matt Devitt
Playwright: Bob Eaton
Rock'n'Roll reworking opening in Denmark Street, London's Tin Pan Alley.

JAMES SHAW

Hamlet is Dead. No Gravity
Red Tape Theatre. Arcola Theatre, London, 2–12 September.
http://redtapetheatre.org
Playwright: Ewald Palmetshofer
Director: Seth Bockley
Tragicomedy. English language world premiere.

HENRY IV PART 1

Royal Shakespeare Company. Barbican Centre, London, 29 November–24 January 2016.
www.rsc.org.uk
Director: Gregory Doran
Falstaff: Antony Sher
Henry IV: Jasper Britton
Prince Hal: Alex Hassell

Adaptation

Festival Players Theatre Company. Kington and Dormston Village Hall, Dormston, Worcs, 15 May; and on tour to 5 September.
www.thefestivalplayers.co.uk
Conflation of Parts 1 and 2.

The Famous Victories of Henry V
Royal Shakespeare Company. Swan Theatre, Stratford-upon-Avon, 5 June; Hull Truck Theatre, 18–20 June; Theatre Royal, Newcastle-upon-Tyne, 30 June.
www.rsc.org.uk
Director: Owen Horsley
Adaptation of extracts from *Henry IV Parts I* and *II* and *Henry V*. Part of First Encounters, Shakespeare for Younger Audiences.

HENRY IV PART 2

Royal Shakespeare Company. Barbican Centre, London, 29 November–24 January 2016.
www.rsc.org.uk
Director: Gregory Doran
Falstaff: Antony Sher
Henry IV: Jasper Britton
Prince Hal: Alex Hassell
Mistress Quickly: Paola Dionisotti

Adaptation

Festival Players Theatre Company. Kington and Dormston Village Hall, Dormston, Worcs, 15 May; and on tour to 5 September.
www.thefestivalplayers.co.uk
Conflation of Parts 1 and 2.

The Famous Victories of Henry V
Royal Shakespeare Company. Swan Theatre, Stratford-upon-Avon, 5 June; Hull Truck Theatre, 18–20 June; Theatre Royal, Newcastle-upon-Tyne, 30 June.
www.rsc.org.uk
Director: Owen Horsley
Adaptation of extracts from *Henry IV Parts I* and *II* and *Henry V*. Part of First Encounters, Shakespeare for Younger Audiences.

HENRY V

Passion in Practice Shakespeare Ensemble. Sam Wanamaker Playhouse, Shakespeare's Globe, London, 26 July; Loft at Tanner Street, London, 4–5 August.
www.passioninpractice.com
Director: Ben Crystal
In Original Pronunciation.

Antic Disposition. Temple Church, London, 24 August–5 September; at Middle Temple Hall, London, 26 March–6 April 2016; and on tour.
www.anticdisposition.co.uk
Directors: Ben Horslen and John Risebero

Royal Shakespeare Company. Royal Shakespeare Theatre, Stratford-upon-Avon, 12 September–25 October; Barbican, London, 11 November–30 December; at the BAM Harvey Theater, Brooklyn, New York, 31 March–1 May 2016; and on tour.
www.rsc.org.uk
Director: Gregory Doran
Henry V: Alex Hassell

York Shakespeare Project. Upstage Theatre, York, 21–31 October.
www.yorkshakespeareproject.org

PRODUCTIONS IN THE BRITISH ISLES, JANUARY–DECEMBER 2015

Director: Maggie Smales
All-female cast. Munitions workers stage *Henry V* during the First World War.

Adaptation

Henry V – Lion of England
Maverick Theatre. The Wheatsheaf Pub, Rathbone Place, Fitzrovia, London. 24 April–14 June.
One-man show. Production aimed at young people.

The Famous Victories of Henry V
Royal Shakespeare Company. Swan Theatre, Stratford-upon-Avon, 5 June; Hull Truck Theatre, 18–20 June; Theatre Royal, Newcastle-upon-Tyne, 30 June.
www.rsc.org.uk
Director: Owen Horsley
Adaptation of extracts from *Henry IV Parts I* and *II* and *Henry V*. Part of First Encounters, Shakespeare for Younger Audiences.

HENRY VI, PARTS 1–3

Adaptation

H VI: Play of Thrones
Union Theatre, London, 8–24 January.
www.uniontheatre.biz
Director: Phil Willmott
Richard III: Michael Keane
Adapted from *Henry VI Parts 1–3*.

KING JOHN

Shakespeare's Globe and Royal and Derngate Northampton. Temple Church, London, 16–19 April; Church of the Holy Sepulchre, Northampton, 24 April–16 May; Globe Theatre, London, 5–28 June.
www.shakespearesglobe.com
Director: James Dacre
King John: Jo Stone-Fewings

Adaptation

Hammerpuzzle. The Egg, Bath, 4–5 March, and small-scale tour to 14 March.
www.hammerpuzzle.co.uk
Director: Bryn Holding

KING LEAR

Guildford Shakespeare Company. Holy Trinity Church, Guildford, 20 January–14 February.
www.guildford-shakespeare-company.co.uk
Director: Caroline Devlin
King Lear: Brian Blessed

Northern Broadsides. Viaduct Theatre, Halifax, 27 February–7 March; York International Shakespeare Festival, TFTV Mainstage, University of York, York, 12–16 May; Rose Theatre, Kingston, 19–23 May; and on tour to 13 June.
www.northern-broadsides.co.uk
Director: Jonathan Miller
King Lear: Barrie Rutter
The eighth time Jonathan Miller has directed *King Lear*.

The Malachites. Peckham Asylum, London, February; The Rose Playhouse, London, 7–30 April.
www.themalachites.co.uk
Director: Benjamin Blyth
King Lear: John McEnery

Adaptation

Songs of Lear
Song of the Goat Theatre. Battersea Arts Centre, London, 19–22 February. First UK performance at 2012 Edinburgh Fringe.
http://piesnkozla.pl/en
Director: Grzegorz Bral
Song cycle with choral songs performed in Latin, Polish and English.

King Lear with Sheep
Courtyard Theatre, London, 12–16 August.
www.thecourtyard.org.uk
King Lear: Suffolk Cross Sheep 1
Cordelia: Suffolk Cross Sheep 2
A stubborn director attempts to direct *King Lear* with live sheep.

LOVE'S LABOUR'S LOST

Bowler Crab Productions. Half House Farm, Three Oaks, Sussex, 20 June–4 July.
www.bowler-crab.com
Director: Stephen John

Bard in the Botanics. Botanic Gardens, Glasgow, 26 June–11 July.
http://bardinthebotanics.co.uk
Director: Gordon Barr
Promenade production.

Cease and Desist Theatre Company. Rosemary Branch Theatre, London, 19 July–31 July.
Director: Diana Vucane and Luke Jasztal

Royal Shakespeare Company. Royal Shakespeare Theatre, Stratford-upon-Avon, 23 September 2014–14 March.
www.rsc.org.uk
Director: Christopher Luscombe
Rosaline: Michelle Terry
Berowne: Edward Bennett
Paired with *Much Ado About Nothing* which was billed as *Love's Labour's Won*.

MACBETH

Filter Theatre and Tobacco Factory Theatres. Citizens Theatre, Glasgow, 20–31 January; VAULT Festival, London, 4–15 February; and on tour. www.filtertheatre.com
Director: Tom Haines
75-minute version with a cast of six.

Tara Arts (in association with Queen's Hall Arts and Black Theatre Live). Queen's Hall Arts Centre, Hexham, 25–7 February; and on tour to 9 May.
http://tara-arts.com
Director: Jatinder Verma

Orange Tree Theatre, Richmond, 16–23 March.
www.orangetreetheatre.co.uk
Director: Imogen Bond

The Malachites. The Rose Playhouse, London, 5–30 May.
www.themalachites.co.uk
Director: Benjamin Blyth

Insane Root Theatre. Bristol Shakespeare Festival, Redcliffe Caves, Bristol, 11–27 July.
www.insaneroot.co.uk
Director: Hannah Drake

Tang Shu-wing Theatre Studio. Shakespeare's Globe Theatre, 17–23 August. www.shakespearesglobe.com
Director: Tang Shu Wing
Performed in Cantonese with scene synopses in English. First played at the Globe during the 2012 Globe to Globe festival.

Cordial Productions. Lion and Unicorn Theatre, London, 15 September–10 October.
www.cordialproductions.co.uk
Director: Anthony Cord

The Pantaloons Theatre Company. Blackfriars Arts Centre, Boston, Lincolnshire, 7 October and UK tour to 26 November.
www.thepantaloons.co.uk

The Watermill Theatre, Newbury, 2–7 November.
www.watermill.org.uk
Director: Cressida Brown
75-minute version.

Young Vic and Birmingham Repertory Theatre. Young Vic Main House, London, 26 November–23 January 2016; and on tour.
www.youngvic.org
Directors: Carrie Cracknell and Lucy Guerin
Macbeth: John Heffernan
Lady Macbeth: Anna Maxwell Martin

Adaptation

Macbeth – A Two Man Macbeth
Out of Chaos. Midlands Arts Centre (MAC) Theatre, Birmingham, 11–13 February.
Director: Mike Tweddle
80-minute version.

The Devil Speaks True
Goat and Monkey. The Vaults, London, 17–27 February; and on tour to 19 March.
www.goatandmonkey.co.uk
Director: Joel Scott
Adaptation from Banquo's perspective. Set in total darkness with audience members given headphones.

Macbeth in Silence
Ludens Ensemble. Hidden Door Festival, Old Lighting Depot, Kings Stable Road, Edinburgh, 22–9 May; and on tour.
www.ludensensemble.co.uk
Director: Philippos Philippou
Wordless performance with three performers, film projections and subtitles.

PRODUCTIONS IN THE BRITISH ISLES, JANUARY–DECEMBER 2015

Macbeth – Blood will have Blood
Contender Charlie, China Plate and Warwick Arts Centre. New Wolsey Theatre, Ipswich, 29 September–2 October.
www.contendercharlie.com
Aimed at 9–13 year olds.

Opera
Royal Opera House, London, 9 September.
www.roh.org.uk
Composer: Luke Styles
A one-act chamber opera.

Lady Macbeth of Mtsensk
English National Opera. London Coliseum, London, 26 September–20 October.
www.eno.org
Composer: Dmitri Shostakovich

MEASURE FOR MEASURE

Cheek by Jowl and Moscow's Pushkin Theatre. Barbican Theatre, London, 15–25 April; Playhouse, Oxford 28 April–2 May.
www.barbican.org.uk
Director: Declan Donnellan
In Russian with English surtitles.

Shakespeare's Globe. Globe Theatre, London, 1 July–17 October.
www.shakespearesglobe.com
Director: Dominic Dromgoole
Dromgoole's farewell production as Artistic Director.

Factory Theatre Company. Willow Globe, Powys, 25 July.
www.factorytheatre.co.uk

Young Vic. Main House, London, 1 October–14 November.
www.youngvic.org
Director: Joe Hill-Gibbins

Adaptation

Desperate Measures
Banter Productions in association with Jermyn Street Theatre. Jermyn Street Theatre, London, 27 November–20 December.
www.jermynstreettheatre.co.uk
Director: Chris Barton

Composer: Chris Barton and Robin Kingsland
Musical adaptation.

THE MERCHANT OF VENICE

Almeida Theatre, London, 5 December 2014–14 February. Revival of a 2011 Royal Shakespeare Company production.
www.almeida.co.uk
Director: Rupert Goold
Shylock: Ian McDiarmid
Portia: Susannah Fielding
Set in Las Vegas.

Shakespeare's Globe. Globe Theatre, London, 23 April–7 June; at Shakespeare 400 Chicago, Chicago Shakespeare Theater on Navy Pier, 4–14 August 2016; and on tour.
www.shakespearesglobe.com
Director: Jonathan Munby
Shylock: Jonathan Pryce

Royal Shakespeare Company. Royal Shakespeare Theatre, Stratford-upon-Avon, 14 May–2 September.
www.rsc.org.uk
Director: Polly Findlay
Shylock: Makram J. Khoury
Portia: Patsy Ferran

Bard in the Botanics. Botanic Gardens, Glasgow, 18 July–1 August. http://bardinthebotanics.co.uk
Director: Gordon Barr

Shit-Faced Shakespeare. Magnificent Bastards Productions. Underbelly, Edinburgh, 7–31 August; and on tour.
www.shit-facedshakespeare.com
Improvisational performance that includes one genuinely drunk actor during each performance.

Adaptation

The Folger Consort with Derek Jacobi. Shakespeare's Globe Theatre, London, 7–8 March.
www.shakespearesglobe.com
Selection of music with passages from *The Merchant of Venice*.

National Youth Theatre. The Ambassador's Theatre, London, 29 September–2 December.

JAMES SHAW

Director: Anna Nilaand

Pocket Merchant
Propeller Theatre Company. Playhouse Theatre, Norwich, 30 September–1 October; and on tour to 22 October.
http://propeller.org.uk/productions/pocket-merchant
Director: Edward Hall
A condensed version of their 2009 production.

The Merchant of Vembly
Cockpit Theatre, London, 6–25 October.
http://thecockpit.org.uk
Playwright: Shishir Kurup
Set in contemporary Wembley.

THE MERRY WIVES OF WINDSOR

Shakespeare at the George, 23 June–4 July.
www.satg.org.uk
Director: Steph Hamert

The Cambridge Shakespeare Festival. King's College Gardens, Cambridge; 13 July–1 August.
www.cambridgeshakespeare.com

Grosvenor Park Theatre Company. Grosvenor Park Open Theatre, Chester, 24 July–23 August.
www.chesterperforms.com
Director: Rebecca Gatwood

Opera
Royal Opera House, La Scala Milan, and Canadian Opera Company. Royal Opera House, London, 6–18 July.
www.roh.org.uk
Composer: Giuseppe Verdi

Tobacco Factory Theatre, Bristol, 14–24 October
www.tobaccofactorytheatres.com
Composer: Giuseppe Verdi

A MIDSUMMER NIGHT'S DREAM

Liverpool Everyman and Playhouse. Everyman Theatre, Liverpool, 21 March–18 April.
www.everymanplayhouse.com
Director: Nick Bagnall

Lakeside and Nottingham New Theatre. Djanogly Theatre, Lakeside Arts Centre, University of Nottingham, 27 April–2 May.
www.lakesidearts.org.uk
Director: Martin Berry

Chapterhouse Theatre Company. Moorland Garden Hotel, Yelverton, Devon, 11 June; and UK tour to 28 August.
www.chapterhouse.org

The HandleBards. River Hill Gardens, Sevenoaks, 24 June; and on tour to 8 September.
www.peculius.com/handlebards.html
A company that cycles between venues.

Watch Your Head. Savill Garden, Windsor Great Park, Windsor, Berkshire, 26 June–19 July.
http://watch-your-head.co.uk
Director: Sasha McMurray
Promenade production.

Bard in the Botanics. Botanic Gardens, Glasgow, 2–11 July.
http://bardinthebotanics.co.uk
Director: Emily Reutlinger
95-minute version with cast of six.

MadCap Theatre Productions. St Andrew's Church, Droitwich Spa, 4 July and on tour to August.

Garsington Opera and the Royal Shakespeare Company. Gasingston Opera, Stonechurch, Wormsley, 16–19 July; Royal Shakespeare Theatre, Stratford-upon-Avon, 26 July.
www.garsingtonopera.org
Director: Owen Horsley
Bottom: Forbes Masson
Abridged version with Mendelssohn's entire score.

Gin and Tonic Productions at Edinburgh Festival Fringe, August; and on tour.
Director: Elske Waite

Adaptation
Arcola Queer Collective. Arcola Theatre, London, 20–4 January.
www.arcolatheatre.com
Director: Nick Connaughton
Blending cabaret, drag, spoken word and music.

PRODUCTIONS IN THE BRITISH ISLES, JANUARY–DECEMBER 2015

Titania – A Solo Cabaret
Moon Fool. Demonstration Room, Summerhall, Edinburgh, 5–30 August.
Performer: Anna-Helena McLean
Stern Alarum. The Tea House Theatre, Vauxhall, London, 10–12 September.
www.sternalarum.co.uk
Set in Athens College with Professor Theseus publishing his new book *Bottom's Up!*.

Opera

Pyramus and Thisbe
Opera Restor'd in association with Hand Made Opera. National Centre for Early Music, York, 10 May.
Director: Colin Baldy
Composer: John Fredrick Lampe

MUCH ADO ABOUT NOTHING

Wyrd Sisters Theatre Company. New Wimbledon Theatre Studio, London, 29 April–2 May; Drayton Arms Theatre, London, 18 August–5 September.
www.wyrdsisterstheatre.com
Director: Joanna Freeman

Oddsocks. Thoresby Riding Hall, Newark, 20 June; and on tour to 25 August.
www.oddsocks.co.uk

Stafford Gatehouse Theatre. Stafford Castle, 25 June–11 July.
www.staffordgatehousetheatre.co.uk

Professional Help Productions. Camden People's Theatre, 30 June–19 July.
www.cptheatre.co.uk
Director: Linda Miller

GB Theatre Company. Appleby Castle Shakespeare Festival, Appleby-in-Westmorland, Cumbria, 2–6 July, Bristol Shakespeare Festival, Brandon Hill Old Bowling Green, Bristol, 11–12 July; and on tour to 29 August.
www.gbtheatrecompany.com
Director: Ed Viney

Shakespeare's Globe Theatre. Fulham Palace, Bishops Avenue, Fulham, 17–19 July and UK tour to 26 September.
www.shakespearesglobe.com
Director: Max Webster

Rainbow Shakespeare. Highdown Gardens, Worthing, 21–6 July.
www.rainbow-theatre.com

Shit-Faced Shakespeare. Magnificent Bastards Productions, at Edinburgh Festival Fringe, Edinburgh, 3–25 August; and on tour.
Improvisational performance that includes one genuinely drunk actor during each performance.

Royal Shakespeare Company. Royal Shakespeare Theatre, Stratford-upon-Avon, 3 October 2014–14 March.
www.rsc.org.uk
Director: Christopher Luscombe
Beatrice: Michelle Terry
Benedick: Edward Bennett
Billed as *Love's Labour's Won* to pair with *Love's Labour's Lost*.

OTHELLO

Frantic Assembly. Lyric Hammersmith, London, 13 January–7 February. Revival of a 2008 production.
www.franticassembly.co.uk
Director: Scott Graham
Othello: Mark Ebulue
Iago: Steven Miller
Climaxes with a 10-minute dance sequence.

Shakespeare's Globe. Globe Theatre, London, March–April.
www.shakespearesglobe.com
Director: Bill Buckhurst
Othello: Lloyd Everitt
Iago: Jamie Beamish

Royal Shakespeare Company. Royal Shakespeare Theatre, Stratford-upon-Avon, 11 June–28 August.
www.rsc.org.uk
Director: Iqbal Khan
Othello: Hugh Quarshie
Iago: Lucian Msamati
First Stratford production to cast a black actor as Iago.

PERICLES

Shakespeare's Globe. Sam Wanamaker Playhouse, London, 19 November–21 April 2016.
www.shakespearesglobe.com

Director: Dominic Dromgoole
Pericles: James Garnon
Gower: Sheila Reid

RICHARD II

Scena Mundi Theatre Company. St Bartholomew-the-Great, West Smithfield, London, 4 June–3 July.
Director: Cecilia Dorland

Bronzehead Theatre. The Stained Glass Centre, St Martin cum Gregory, York, 8–12 July; Poppleton Tithe Barn, York, 17 July.
www.yorktheatreroyal.co.uk
Director: Tom Straszewski

Bard in the Botanics. Botanic Gardens, Glasgow, 22 July–1 August.
http://bardinthebotanics.co.uk
Director: Jennifer Dick
Cast of four with Bolingbroke played as a woman.

Shakespeare's Globe. Globe Theatre, London, 22 July–18 October.
www.shakespearesglobe.com
Director: Simon Godwin
Richard II: Charles Edwards
Begins with the coronation of 10-year-old Richard.

RICHARD III

National Theatre of China. Shakespeare's Globe Theatre, 20–5 July.
www.shakespearesglobe.com
Director: Wang Ziaoying
Performed in Mandarin.

West Yorkshire Playhouse. The Quarry, Leeds, 25 September–17 October.
www.wyp.org.uk
Director: Mark Rosenblatt
Richard III: Reece Dinsdale

ROMEO AND JULIET

The Faction. New Diorama Theatre, 15–16 Triton Street, London, 6 January–28 February.
www.newdiorama.com

Bard in the Botanics. Eastwood Park, Glasgow, 12 February; and on tour. Revival of a 2012 production.
http://bardinthebotanics.co.uk
Director: Gordon Barr
Company of five.

Shakespeare at the Tobacco Factory. Tobacco Factory, Bristol, 24 February–4 April.
www.tobaccofactorytheatres.com
Director: Polina Kalinina

The Watermill Theatre, Newbury, 25 February–2 April.
www.watermill.org.uk
Director: Paul Hart

Romeo + Juliet

Rose Theatre, Kingston, 4–21 March.
www.rosetheatrekingston.org
Director: Sally Cookson
Sets Juliet's age at 16 and Lady Capulet plays both Capulets in one role.

Flanagan Collective. York International Shakespeare Festival, St Olave's Church, York, 7–23 May.
http://theflanagancollective.blogspot.com
Director: Alexander Wright

Grosvenor Park Theatre Company. Grosvenor Park Open Theatre, Chester, 2 July–22 August.
www.chesterperforms.com
Director: Alex Clifton

Shakespeare's Globe. Dundee Repertory Theatre, Dundee, Scotland, 14–17 July; and on tour to 8 August.
www.shakespearesglobe.com
Directors: Dominic Dromgoole and Tim Hoare

Oxford University Dramatic Society and Thelma Holt Ltd Southwark Playhouse, London, 5–8 August; and on tour to 2–5 September.
www.ouds.org
Director: Thomas Bailey

Sheffield Theatres. Crucible, Sheffield, 23 September–17 October.
www.sheffieldtheatres.co.uk

PRODUCTIONS IN THE BRITISH ISLES, JANUARY–DECEMBER 2015

Director: Jonathan Humphreys

Immersion Theatre. Harrow Arts Centre, London, 1 October; and on tour to 17 November.
www.immersiontheatre.co.uk

Fred Theatre Company. AE Harris, Jewellery Quarter, Birmingham, 3–14 November.
www.fred-theatre.co.uk
Director: Robert F. Ball

KDC Theatre. Rosemary Branch Theatre, London, 17–21 November.
www.kdctheatre.com
Director: Duncan Moore

Ballet

Moscow City Ballet. Corn Exchange, Cambridge, 4 January.
Composer: Sergei Prokofiev

Ballet West Company. Corran Halls, Oban, 23–4 January; and on tour to 14 February.
www.balletwest.co.uk

Bad Boys of Dance. Sadler's Wells, Peacock Theatre, London, 3–29 March.
Choreographer: Adrienne Canterna
Director: Rasta Thomas

The Monte Carlo Ballet. London Coliseum, London. 23–5 April.
www.eno.org
Choreographer: Jean-Christophe Maillot

The Royal Ballet. Royal Opera House, London, 19 September–2 December.
www.roh.org.uk
Choreographer: Kenneth MacMillan

English National Ballet. Bristol Hippodrome, 14–17 October and on tour to 28 November.
www.ballet.org.uk
Choreographer: Rudolf Nureyev

Adaptation

Box Clever Theatre Company. Drill Hall, London, 12 January.
www.boxclevertheatre.co.uk
Director: Iqbal Khan

Blends the original text with contemporary language.

Romeo and Rosaline
Bread and Roses Theatre, Clapham, London, 27 January–14 February.
www.breadandrosestheatre.co.uk
Playwright: Sharon Jennings
Prequel featuring the story of Rosaline.

The Flanagan Collective in association with York Theatre Royal. St Olave's Church, York, 7–23 May.
All-female adaptation with Paris the only male character.

Shakespeare's R&J
Chapel Lane Theatre Company. The Tabard Theatre, London, 30 June–8 August.
www.chapellane.co.uk
Playwright: Joe Calarco
Directed: Christopher Harvey

THE TAMING OF THE SHREW

Two Gents Productions. York International Shakespeare Festival, Friargate Theatre, York, 15–16 May.
www.twogentsproductions.co.uk
Director: Arne Pohlmeier
Two hander.

Illyria Theatre Company. Brahan, Dingwall, Inverness, 24 June; and on tour though 6 September.
www.illyria.uk.com

Guildford Shakespeare Company. Guildford College of Law, Guildford, 11–25 July.
www.guildford-shakespeare-company.co.uk
Director: Caroline Devlin

Adaptation

Arrows and Traps. New Wimbledon Theatre Studio, Wimbledon, 26 May–20 June.
www.arrowsandtraps.com
Adaptor and Director: Ross McGregor
Full cast gender reversal with Petruchia wooing Kajetano.

Shrew
Camden People's Theatre, London, 23–8 June.
Performer: Ami Jay
Solo piece exploring the character of Katharina.

JAMES SHAW

Kiss Me Kate
Opera North and Welsh National Opera. Grand Theatre and Opera House, Leeds, 24 September–31 October; and on tour to 21 November.
www.operanorth.co.uk
Composer: Cole Porter
Director: Jo Davies

THE TEMPEST

The Apollo Theatre, Newport, Isle of Wight, 15–23 May.

New Wimbledon Theatre, London, 20–3 May.

Rain or Shine Theatre Company. Bryngarw House Lawn, Bryngarw Country Park, Brynmenyn, 29 May; and UK tour to 30 August.
www.rainorshine.co.uk
Director: James Reynard

Butterfly. Bristol Shakespeare Festival, Leigh Woods National Nature Reserve, Bristol, 11–17 July.
http://wearebutterfly.com
Director: Aileen Gonsalves

Improbably Theatre. Northern Stage (previously known as Newcastle Haymarket Playhouse), Oxford Playhouse and Improbable Theatre Company. Northern Stage, Newcastle-upon-Tyne, 25 September–10 October; Oxford Playhouse, Oxford, 14–24 October.
www.northernstage.co.uk
Director: Phelim McDermott
Prospero: Tyrone Huggins

London Theatre Workshop. Eel Brook Pub, Fulham, London 7–24 October. http://londontheatreworkshop.co.uk
Director: Brandon Force

Adaptation

Amaluna
Cirque du Soleil. Royal Albert Hall, London, 16 January–6 March.
www.cirquedusoleil.com
Set on an island where Prospera directs her daughter's coming-of-age ceremony.

Return to the Forbidden Planet
Cut to the Chase Theatre Company. Queen's Theatre, Hornchurch. Theatre Royal, Brighton, 20–4 January; and on tour to 9 May.
www.queens-theatre.co.uk
Director: Bob Carlton

Mirando the Gay Tempest
Theatre North. Theatre North, Brighton, 1–10 May.
Solo version with Prospero's daughter transformed into his son Mirando.

This Last Tempest
Uninvited Guests and Fuel. Brighton Dome, Brighton, 20–1 March; and on tour to 16 May.
www.uninvited-guests.net
Sequel following Caliban and Ariel after the courtiers have left the island.

TIMON OF ATHENS

York Shakespeare Project. York International Shakespeare Festival, De Grey Ballroom, York, 14–17 May.
www.yorkshakespeareproject.org
Director: Ruby Clarke

The Cambridge Shakespeare Festival. Robinson College Gardens, Cambridge, 3–29 August.
www.cambridgeshakespeare.com

TITUS ANDRONICUS

Royal Conservatoire of Scotland and the Dundee Rep Ensemble. Dundee Rep, 8–24 April.
www.dundeerep.co.uk
Director: Steward Laing

Smooth Faced Gentlemen. Greenwich Theatre, London, 28 April–2 May.
www.greenwichtheatre.org.uk
Director: Yaz Al-Shaater
All-female production.

The Cambridge Shakespeare Festival. Robinson College Gardens, Cambridge, 13 July–1 August.
www.cambridgeshakespeare.com

Arrows and Traps. New Wimbledon Theatre, London, 20 October–14 November.
www.arrowsandtraps.com
Director: Ross McGregor

PRODUCTIONS IN THE BRITISH ISLES, JANUARY–DECEMBER 2015

TROILUS AND CRESSIDA

Rainbow Shakespeare. Highdown Gardens, Worthing, 14–19 July.
www.rainbow-theatre.com
Director: Daniel Sullivan

TWELFTH NIGHT

Dionysia Productions. Moors Theatre, Crouch End, London, 5–11 January.
http://moorstheatre.webs.com
Director: Bryonny Ruddock

Lord Chamberlain's Men. King's Ely, Cambridge, 9 June; and on tour to 6 September.
www.tlcm.co.uk
Director: Andrew Normington

Oddsocks. Oakengates Theatre, Telford, 18 June; and on tour to 22 August.
www.oddsocks.co.uk

Iris Theatre. St Paul's Church, Covent Garden, London, 29 June–24 July.
http://iristheatre.com
Director: Vik Sivalingam
Promenade production.

Oxford Shakespeare Company. Wadham College Gardens, Oxford, 29 June–15 August.
www.oxfordshakespearecompany.co.uk
Director: Nicholas Green

GB Theatre Company. Appleby Castle Shakespeare Festival, Appleby-in-Westmoreland, Cumbria, 2–6 July; and on tour to 29 August.
www.gbtheatrecompany.com
Director: Ed Viney

Pocket Theatre. Hangar Farm Arts Centre, Totton, 21–4 July; Swan Theatre, Yeovil, 14–19 September.
http://swan-theatre.co.uk
Director: Ian White

Rose Playhouse. Bankside, London, 6–30 October.
www.rosetheatre.org.uk
Director: Natasha Rickman
Rotating performances of four 90-minute versions: all-male, all-female, cast play own gender, cast play opposite gender.

THE TWO NOBLE KINSMEN

Instant Classics. White Bear Theatre, London, 9–27 June.
http://instantclassics.co.uk
Director: David Cottis

THE WINTER'S TALE

Lion and Unicorn Theatre, London, 9 December–3 January 2015.
www.giantolive.com

Taking Flight Theatre. Thompson's Park, Canton, Cardiff, 11–18 June; Bristol Shakespeare Festival, Blaise Castle, Bristol, 25–6 July; and on tour.
www.takingflighttheatre.co.uk
Translated into British Sign Language by Daryl Jackson, Sami Thorpe and Stephen Collins.

Northern Broadsides. Harrogate Theatre, Harrogate, 18–26 September; and on tour to 28 November.
www.northern-broadsides.co.uk
Director and Leontes: Conrad Nelson

Kenneth Branagh Theatre Company. Garrick Theatre, London, 17 October–16 January 2016.
www.branaghtheatre.com
Directors: Kenneth Branagh and Rob Ashford
Leontes: Kenneth Branagh
Paulina: Judi Dench

POEMS AND APOCRYPHA

Venus and Adonis

Holdfast Theatre. The Tea House Theatre, London, 5 April.
www.teahousetheatre.co.uk
Director: Gareth Armstrong
A dramatic reading.

The Rape of Lucretia

Glyndebourne Opera. Glyndebourne, Lewes. 5 July–19 August.
Composer: Benjamin Britten
Director: Fiona Shaw

JAMES SHAW

MISCELLANEOUS

The Complete Deaths

Spymonkey. Royal & Derngate Theatre, Northampton, 5–7 May, then at the Brighton Festival.
www.spymonkey.co.uk
Director: Tim Crouch
All Shakespeare's death scenes.

Faustaff

Cockpit Theatre, London, 17 November–6 December.
http://thecockpit.org.uk
Playwright: Diego Sosa
Modern retelling of the Faust story. Inspired by Falstaff but without obvious reference to Shakespeare's character.

The Herbal Bed

Clwyd Theatr Cymru, Mold, 5–28 March.
www.clwyd-theatr-cymru.co.uk
Playwright: Peter Whelan
Director: Emma Lucia

Mrs. Shakespeare

Wild Productions. Bristol Shakespeare Festival, Alma Tavern and Theatre, Bristol, 30 June–2 July.
http://wildproductions.wix.com
Director: Ian Wild
William Shakespeare, reincarnated as a woman, rewrites *Hamlet* as *Ophelia*.

Red Velvet

Garrick Theatre, London, 23 January–27 February. Revival of 2012 Tricycle Theatre production.
Playwright: Lolita Chakrabarti
Director: Rob Ashford
Ira Aldridge: Adrian Lester

Shakespeare and the Alchemy of Gender

Rose Playhouse, 14–26 July.
Performer: Lisa Wolpe
Autobiographical piece illustrated by excerpts from Shakespeare.

Shakespeare in his Cups

Gillygate Pub, York, 11–12 May.
Performers: Martin Barrass, Jonathan Race and Robin Simpson.
Three actors tell drunken anecdotes at the end of a tour.

Shakespeare in Love

Disney Theatrical Productions. Noel Coward Theatre, London, 2 July – ongoing.
http://shakespeareinlove.com
Director: Declan Donnellan
Adaptor: Lee Hall
Shakespeare: Tom Bateman
Viola: Lucy Briggs-Owen
Stage adaptation of *Shakespeare in Love*.

Shakespeare in Shoreditch

New Diorama Theatre. Rose Lipman Building, London, 30 September–10 October.
www.shakespeareinshoreditch.in
Four new plays written and developed in Shoreditch: *Grey Man* by Lulu Raczka; *The H-Word* by David Watson; *Pelican Daughters* by Amy Rosenthal; *This is Art* by Charlene James.

Shakespeare's Sister

Theatre Royal Haymarket, Masterclass Trust's Pitch Your Play, London, September.
Director: Asia Osborne
Playwright: Emma Whipday
Staged reading to celebrate publication by Samuel French Ltd. Prompted by Virginia Woolf, the play imagines Judith Shakespeare as a talented playwright.

The Stories of Shakey P

Charlie Dupré. York International Shakespeare Festival, De Grey Rooms, York, 9 May.
www.charliedupre.com
Director and Playwright: Charlie Dupré
Hip-hop inspired selections from Shakespeare.

PRODUCTIONS IN THE BRITISH ISLES, JANUARY–DECEMBER 2015

To Build a Wooden O

Malvern Theatres, Malvern, 9–12 September.
Playwright: Nick Wilkes
The story of the construction of the Globe Theatre.

Two Shakespeare Heroines: Lady Macbeth and Visions of Ophelia

York International Shakespeare Festival. De Grey Rooms, York, 8–10 May.
www.yorktheatreroyal.co.uk
Director: Aki Isoda
Solo performance.

The Wars of the Roses

Rose Theatre Company. Rose Theatre, Kingston, 3–31 October.
www.rosetheatrekingston.org
Director: Trevor Nunn
Adaptor: John Barton in collaboration with Peter Hall
Adapted from *Henry VI Pts. 1–3* and *Richard III*. First performed by the Royal Shakespeare Company in 1963.

THE YEAR'S CONTRIBUTION TO SHAKESPEARE STUDIES

1. CRITICAL STUDIES
reviewed by CHARLOTTE SCOTT

I began writing this review a week before Shakespeare's birth/death day, and the Shakespeare 400 machine is in magnificent motion. Every day I read something different about Shakespeare in the press, from the excavation, or rather not, of a missing skull, to a London Underground Tube map depicting the characters from his plays, to renewed questions of authorship and the discovery of a Folio in a house in a remote Scottish island, there seems no end to the ways in which Shakespeare can be reinvented and re-discovered. Unsurprisingly, there are books galore this year that have radiated beyond the remit of 'critical studies' into an amblongus pie of Shakespeare-related topics. Many of these books have already made their way into the mainstream press: some of them are wonderful – Emma Smith's compassionate biography of the First Folio; John Kerrigan's dazzlingly learned and brilliant *Shakespeare's Oaths*; James Shapiro's urbane and compelling *1606, the Year of Lear*. There have also been various creative endeavours that have taken Shakespeare as a prompt, reworking stories and sentiments through a different, if not necessarily modern, idiom. Howard Jacobson's *The Merchant of Venice* and Jeanette Winterson's *The Gap of Time* are perhaps a testimony of the enduring dynamic between human relationships and stories, while Hannah Crawforth and Elizabeth Scott-Baumann's edited collection, *On Shakespeare's Sonnets: A Poet's Celebration*, allows celebrated poets to write their own version of a Shakespearean sonnet. Many of these are wonderful – Wendy Cope's take on sonnet 22; Andrew Motion on sonnet 12; and a powerfully lyrical collection of responses to the themes of Time, the natural world, secrets and losses. Only a very few seem to miss the point entirely, including Simon Armitage, whose take on Morse code and iambic pentameter, which produces fourteen lines of 'di-di-di-dahs', is a travesty of sonnet 20.

REMEMBERING SHAKESPEARE

Turning more specifically to literary criticism, however, I start with Edmondson and Wells's edited collection, *The Shakespeare Circle*, which offers a range of essays on the people, places and things that gave Shakespeare his context. The essays focus in the main on Shakespeare's family, from his parents to his wife, in-laws and children. Some chapters extend to the less immediate connections and explore the family of Shakespeare's sister, the Harts, or his 'cousin' Thomas Greene. René

Weis's essay on Shakespeare's granddaughter Elizabeth Hall offers very poignant insights into the last surviving member of the Shakespeares. The second section of the book extends its analysis to friends and neighbours, including Richard Field and Ben Jonson, and the final section deals with 'colleagues and patrons'. Here we are largely among theatre practitioners, including actors, playwrights and patrons. Essays on Middleton, Wilkins and Fletcher extend the Warwickshire context into questions of collaboration and working practice. As an 'alternative biography', *Shakespeare's Circle* embraces the wider networks that inform not only who Shakespeare was but how we understand and read him now; the voices of the contributors give reign to a vigorous impulse to know but also to think beyond the documentary evidence and into the many fascinating strands of implication. David Fallow, for example, in writing about Shakespeare's father, speculates that it may well have been John's wool business, and not the theatre, that took his son to the capital. The book is a delightful celebration of the importance and intricacies of social context and rightly establishes Shakespeare as one part of a matrix of personal, professional and historic heritage.

Thinking of Shakespeare in this way enables the shift in perspective necessary to appreciate Peter Kirwan's *Shakespeare and the Idea of Apocrypha*. Kirwan's book is primarily invested in how the question of authorial identity has mapped the rise and fall of some of the eighty plays once variously attributed to Shakespeare. Concentrating on some of the more widely read texts, including *Sir Thomas More*, *Edward III*, *Arden of Faversham* and *Double Falsehood*, Kirwan examines the fate of plays that might be Shakespeare's. Central to Kirwan's thesis is what 'Shakespeare' means as a structure of value. This is perhaps the most prescient and timely question of the year since it engages with the forces that determine marketability, quality and style; in other words, 'the models of identity for which attribution scholars are searching'. What makes Shakespeare Shakespeare is a fascinating subject in itself and very revealing in terms of cultural tastes and ideological expectations. Kirwan's book is less invested in why, for example, centuries of scholarship was so reluctant to attribute *Titus* to Shakespeare and apparently happy to adopt *Pericles* but more keenly concentrated on what drives editorial decisions and repertory writing. The book works through the various premises on which the idea of apocrypha has been established, including the 'might be but not' Shakespeare. Perhaps the most compelling element of the book is the relationship between authorial identity and literary criticism that 'offer[s] a means by which authorship inquiries can open up new, productive questions about a text rather than serving as a final means of categorisation and isolation'. Kirwan demonstrates that Shakespeare's unique position as an 'embedded' dramatist for the Chamberlain–King's Men allows him to work across a range of plays in the repertory system so that we can experience 'Shakespeare' as both 'individual and plural, a human author and a shorthand for the company's output'. With this in mind we can appreciate the relationship between Shakespeare and apocrypha not as privileged, in that the plays occasionally attributed to Shakespeare have special status, but as indicative of a wider interconnectedness between repertory and writers. There are two central tenets of Kirwan's book: one is to loosen the focus on 'Shakespeare' as a mechanistic framework through which we determine value and quality; and the other is to release the plays once designated as 'Apocrypha' from their faulty associations with Shakespeare so that they can be appreciated, and understood, as valuable and fascinating examples of their own kind. Kirwan's thesis raises numerous questions, not least of all 'how helpful is the attribution of Shakespeare's authorship' to the study of early modern plays? That in turn begs its own question as to what we mean by Shakespeare and what he has variously represented over the last four hundred years. Kirwan does not resolve these questions – how could he, the answers being many and various? But he does offer up a gentle and rewarding scepticism in the way canonical drama has been traditionally read. His forensic approach leads him to how editors and critics read their Shakespeare and how critical attitudes have shaped, at times defined, the plays in question. Bringing neglected plays into conversation with Shakespeare throws up some intriguing dynamics, not least of all the possible relationship between *Locrine* (1595) and *Titus*. Here Kirwan suggests that the 'compelling links' between the two plays impose upon the narrative action. Referring to *Locrine*'s use of an allegorical figure of Revenge who presides over each act with a dumb show, Shakespeare incorporates this figure as a recognizable trope so that 'Titus sees directly through the allegorical figures to the "pair of cursed hell hounds and their dam" beneath'. Reading the drama in this way demonstrates the inter-legibility of early modern drama and allows for a much more capacious, generous relationship between plays in performance. *Shakespeare and the Idea of Apocrypha* has no specific agenda in terms of assigning or relinquishing Shakespeare as author of any of these plays; in fact, to quote Nicholas Brooke, 'The text is decidedly more important than the identity of the author(s)' and Kirwan makes that the focus of his book. What emerges is a celebration of Shakespeare, not as an ever-fixed mark against which certain elusive and exclusive standards can be measured but as an idea of playwriting in which the boundaries between the exceptional and the early modern can be dissolved. In the process we appreciate a much more nuanced and inclusive sense of the development of early modern English drama, as well as its reception and the often very revealing decisions that critical history has made to shape its 'Shakespeare'. One of the most thoughtful elements of this study is the devastating impact of the terms through which the Shakespearean cannon has often been negotiated: seemingly descriptive labels like 'apocrypha' and 'anonymous', for example, are actually valued judgements that relegate certain works to certain piles, some of which will never see the light of day again. To decide that a play is 'apocrypha' Shakespeare is very different in terms of both impact and understanding to designating it as anonymous: the former denotes a lacking, a failure somehow to be Shakespeare; while the latter records its descent into oblivion, written, as it were, by 'no one'. The danger with all such terms, Kirwan notes, is that they bind diverse texts into an apparently homogenous bundle of failure or obliquity and that the critical drive towards cohesion and collation has denuded our collective ability to discern and appreciate the importance of diversity. There is, he suggests, a commercial imperative here which attempts to fulfil a nebulous consumer desire for works that 'belong' both to each other and to the period in which they were written. Kirwan is occasionally a little cynical about the consumer-driven choices of textual editors but this does not seem out of place: what resonates, however, is that much of what this book celebrates is also at the forefront of recent studies in textual scholarship and a growing awareness for the importance of plurality as well as transparency. To this end, *Shakespeare and the Idea of Apocrypha* celebrates the road less travelled and that, as Robert Frost once said, makes all the difference.

From the whimsical road of destiny to the great globe itself and a series of essays subtitled 'Worldmaking in Early Modern Literature'. *This Distracted Globe*, edited by Marcie Frank, Jonathan Goldberg and Karen Newman, sets out to reconsider the materiality of early modern drama and the multiplicity of 'matter' in an array of texts. The title of this collection deliberately references the instability of the sign and the various ways in which objects and ideas intersect and interact, mutating from one to the other in a single moment. Hamlet's globe stands at the forefront of this collection precisely because it defines a single instance of infinite plurality. The essays are grouped according to their shared reflections on the meaning of the term 'world'. The three categories that structure the book are defined as 'Materiality', 'Sociality' and 'Universality' but even within these terms the critical approaches, methodologies and interpretations differ widely. The idea of the world ranges over objects, stuff and matter to relationships, travels, the cosmos and the hereafter and attempts to provide a critical framework through which the term *world* can be understood to contain many contradictions as well as suggestions.

The most resonant, and perhaps most consistent, concern is one of boundaries and binaries and how and where they exist in worldmaking and self-reflection, identity and subject formation. The pleasure of this book lies in the range of texts through which the contributors pursue their worlds, and this includes Spenser, Marlowe, Shakespeare, Donne and the Rajasthan folk tale of Chouboli's *Dastan*. The metaphysical and philosophical interests offer a light touch on Marvell, Browne and Milton. Finally, however, the book offers a celebration of Jonathan Goldberg's work by returning the focus to the importance of 'queer' and re-evaluating the limiting and impossible categories of absolute difference. Aaron Kunin provides a great essay on Marlowe (and Shakespeare and chairs, for that matter) which examines the human footstool and the implications this has for the human/object relation: 'Tamburlaine's footstool is an unnecessarily graphic representation of what people want from furniture' as it is also a powerful image of enactment and subjugation, where the footstool, Bajazeth, both wants and is wanted. As Kunin muses, 'Why does he [Marlowe/Tamburlaine] make so many allowances for the eccentricities of his furniture?'

In *Anecdotal Shakespeare*, however, eccentricity extends way beyond the furniture and into Paul Menzer's often funny and delightfully random excursion into the performance history of Shakespeare's plays. That is not to say that Hamlet's skull, 'Olivier's Dick' (you'll have to read the book for an explanation of that one) or indeed Othello's [smudged] make-up embody the existential drama of Marlowe's footstools: Menzer's accounts of the stories behind the curtain offer a very different perspective on performance but in the process they reveal an absorbing delve into the culture of theatre and the changing appetites for illusion. Many of the most amusing and illuminating stories centre on Kean and Kemble and the accidents and intentions behind their Shakespeares. As Menzer observes, 'Anecdotes often make a comedy of catastrophe and play the comic sidekick to thuggish tragedy' but they also serve as a vital, if alternative, history to the reception of Shakespeare. Menzer's book returns repeatedly to the complex shadows of Shakespeare's plays, the expectations and challenges that each culture attempts to reinvent or supress and the deep magic of fantasy that keeps the history of 'Shakespeare' in perpetual motion. Many of the anecdotes in Menzer's book will be edited out of history for their embarrassing traces of crass cultures gone by (blacked-up actors playing Othello, dangling air-drawn daggers that do not make it on to the props list or mock weapons substituted by real ones, with fatal results) but this lovely book is a great testimony to the power of imperfection and accident, to failure and ambition, and ends with a timely reminder that Dulwich College still stands in London because Edward Alleyn got spooked in *Faustus* (or maybe *Macbeth* . . .) 'by an Apparition of the Devil, which so worked on his Fancy, that he made a Vow, which he performed at this Place'. At the heart of this book is a celebration of stories both within and about the drama which animates the shared life of Shakespeare's plays.

If Menzer's focus is on making individual memories history, Isabel Karreman shifts our attention to *The Drama of Memory in Shakespeare's History Plays*. Central to Karreman's thesis is the relationship between memory and oblivion, or forgetting. These are not exclusive terms; quite the contrary, her methodological approach understands memory as a predominantly collective, social and cultural act in which events, pasts, perceptions and histories are sorted and evaluated in the collective mind's eye. Within this model, which she identifies as owing much to the work of Raymond Williams, Benedict Anderson and Maurice Halbwachs, Karreman explores the processes through which memory may be understood to select or discard and how these processes are actively reinforced by media (understood in its early modern sense to mean the transmission of information over print, orality, theatre and visual arts). Unsurprisingly, the theatre is a significant area of concern because it rehearses many of the dominant ways in which memories are formed and adopted. Thinking about narrative structure in the history plays allows

Karreman to show how the history play partakes in, as well as extends, a 'mnemonic economy of signs'. Attending to what is being remembered as well as forgotten, her discussion ranges over stage craft, including properties and effects, as well as structure, sound, formal arrangement and discourse. Rather than observe distinctions between forgetting and remembering, the past and the present, perception and event, Karreman's book is more assiduously interested in the interplay and crossover between these terms and their products. Within this model, Karreman perceives Shakespeare's theatre as profoundly self-reflective in its dependence on the dramatic potential of the contingency of history. Focusing on the second tetralogy, the book considers how history is represented on stage and the various means through which the drama produces interactions between, as well as representations of, transmission and event. Moving the discussion into concerns with stagecraft and state craft, Karreman examines ceremony, embodiment, iconography and the complex codes of reformation politics. The final chapter deals with *Henry VIII, or All is True*, and is keenly attuned to questions of 'nostalgia' and how historical moments create emotional effects in order to rewrite their recent history as well as invoke specific responses to the present. Thoughtful and diligent, the book opens up many important questions, not least of all the ethics of memory and our collective responsibility to the past as well as the present.

FEELING SHAKESPEARE

The title of Brian Walsh's book, *Unsettled Toleration*, seems especially resonant in the context of contemporary anxieties about religious difference. Focusing on an 'intra-Christian conflict' between dominant and minority believers, Walsh's thesis re-engages with the relationships between faiths in early modern drama. The theatre itself is of central concern here and the ways in which the developing forms of representation and discourse supported the playing out of certain scenarios and sympathies. Attending to 'the confusing proliferation of religious identities' in the sixteenth century and the role of the English stage as a 'social barometer' in the seventeenth century, Walsh analyses the instrumental role that the theatre played to 'create, enlarge, and sustain an open-ended public conversation on the vicissitudes of getting along in a sectarian world'. Walsh's argument is not that Shakespeare's theatre produced liberal versions of religious pluralism but rather that the stage 'hatched imagined scenarios of confessional conflict'. The book explores the status of religious identities in a range of authors, including Marlowe, Middleton, Chapman, Rowley and Shakespeare. Despite, or because of, the many and various attitudes to religious difference here, Walsh identifies two central strands: one adheres to the relationships between Puritans and non-Puritans, and the other reflects negotiations with the past, specifically the Reformation. The sections on Shakespeare deal with *Twelfth Night*, *Measure for Measure* and *Pericles*. The chapter on *Measure* and *Twelfth Night* examines the figure of the Puritan, how Shakespeare represents the faith and how the characters define or negotiate their religious affiliations. In the different representations of Puritanism in Malvolio and Angelo, for example, Walsh perceives Shakespeare's 'depiction of Puritan issues in contrast to other trends on the contemporary stage'. In *Pericles*, the concern is the medieval past and the 'benevolent and motivating presence of a Catholic figure', John Gower. Over the course of the book, Walsh examines the roles of rites, ceremonies, words, images, ideas and objects for the diverse and multiple ways in which they can represent faiths. Most interesting is the plurality of religious identities and rites and the various ways in which the drama reproduces the putative affiliation in different ways. Set on the 'secularising' stage this produces some key arguments about transmission and the continual power of faiths 'to move people' if not necessarily convert them.

Like Walsh, a number of other writers have been moved this year by what has become known as an 'affective turn', not just in the ways in which we understand the impacts of religious beliefs and dissents but also in an increasingly broad interest in the history of emotions. R. S. White, in his introduction to a collection co-edited with Mark Houlahan and Katrina O'Loughlin, *Shakespeare and Emotions*, observes that attitudes to literature, or, more broadly, art, have always, in some ways, been driven by the debate between reason and emotion, judgement and empathy. Tracing the foundations of this debate from Plato to New Historicism, White identifies the critical role that emotions have played in determining and driving literary criticism. Reflecting on the cynical and cyclical turns in theory which became increasingly hostile to Shakespeare in the 1990s, he observes that 'Shakespeare was rescued by a saviour from the most unexpected direction – popular culture itself, and film specifically'. Identifying both Branagh and Luhrmann as instrumental in hauling Shakespeare to dry ground, White notes that such a rescue was mounted almost exclusively on the value of emotions, 'stirred by the plays in new audiences which re-established Shakespeare's popularity'. That is not to say, however, that we have returned to the heartlands of the new critics: White is right to point out, and the book bears this out, that the best of 'New Emotionalism' (White's phrase) takes in a long legacy of complex and competing revisionisms, including gender studies, reader response, performance studies and historicism. *Shakespeare and Emotions* produces over twenty essays, which, in assorted ways, navigate the paradoxes in 'see[ing] it feelingly'. The essays cover a wide range of approaches and methodologies as well as Shakespeare's plays and poems. Beginning with classical tradition, Danijela Kambaskovic explores love as a deep-seated form of spirituality and creativity that sits comfortably within a Platonic paradigm of 'love madness', while Brid Phillips looks at Ovid and the emotion of place. There are essays on fairy tale and myth, metaphysics and the after-life, humours, bodies, sex, gender and regionalism. Peter Groves provides a fine analysis of poetic metre in his exploration of how rhythm generates feeling. This intricate essay details the subtle metrical shifts, reversals and 'shunts', as Groves calls them, which perform emphasis and produce emotional arousal, whereas Ruth Lumney's chapter discusses audience experience and Alison V. Scott explores 'giddiness', a surprisingly wide-ranging term in Shakespeare. One of the virtues of this book is the range of plays that the collection considers and the wonderful variety of 'feelings' under consideration, including those produced by sound, objects, images, memories and the imagination. Heather Kerr's essay on 'sociable tears' in *The Tempest* pursues an argument for shared feeling and the production of communal, and inherently empathetic, signs of response.

Most of the essays in *Shakespeare and Emotions* acknowledge the problematic discourse of moral virtue that underpins so much of the debate between reason and emotion. In Erin Sullivan's *Beyond Melancholy*, however, the emphasis is less on the collective production of social emotion and more on the place of sadness in early modern subjectivity. Like many of the books reviewed in this and recent years, Sullivan begins with an emphasis on the Reformation and the ways in which the devotional schism precipitated ' a widespread cultural ambiguity about the meaning and value of sadness, and a corresponding need to clarify its significance through active and wilful interpretation'. The book is most concerned with the different forms that such 'active and wilful interpretation' could take and how these processes reflected and formed notions of selfhood. Sullivan goes on to assert that her major intervention in the history of this condition is to distinguish between melancholy and sadness and thereby unpack some of the aesthetic, ontological and cultural requisites that have come to define early modern emotional identity. Central to this argument is an interest in the intellectual, emotional and spiritual environments that shape human passions. Moving away from the now conventional narratives of humourology, Sullivan focuses on some of the early modern impulses that create an 'affective environment', including various products of print culture (from doctor's records and mortality records to printed texts). Her insistence on the range and 'strikingly different manifestations' of sadness does not seem especially surprising. More interesting is the renewed interest in many of this year's books on the processes by which any given culture and moment records and evaluates its emotional categories and the more diverse these records are the more rich they become. It is a very intelligent and thoughtful book which produces a fascinating range of examples, including the number of deaths recorded from grief, the proportion of men who suffered from melancholy as opposed to women, and the various symptoms associated with melancholy, including light-headedness, heart problems and urinary problems. Even among these gripping testimonies to feeling, however, the construction of sadness remains somewhat illusive: Sullivan gestures towards the complexities inherent in evaluating or even defining such a subjective, yet social, emotion but we never really get any closer to what sadness might mean and how it is identified as such across the literature. Or rather, there is a great deal of identification of and with sadness but the emotion manifests very broadly through grief, melancholy, anger, tummy troubles, religious despair, broken heart, affliction and ecstasy. If there is a common thread, however, it is that these multiple forms of sadness operate most powerfully as regulators of social values and to that end they provide very revealing instances of the relationship between personal and social codes. In *King Lear*, for example, Sullivan equates sorrow, grief and misery with self-knowledge and enlightenment, and observes how the experience of sorrow can lead some characters to identify themselves as distinct in 'asserting [their] ... own sense of self-experience' whilst also rehearsing the failure of social values to protect them. Sullivan's book is predominantly interested in the cognitive rather than performative manifestations of sadness, and so she is less concerned with how characters might make their sadness visible or readable on stage and more with how such sorrow functions within a range of intellectual, social and spiritual traditions.

The same cannot be said, however, of Farah Karim-Cooper's *The Hand on the Shakespearean Stage* which is especially, if not exclusively, invested in exploring the multiple and multifaceted implications of the body in performance. Her particular attention to gesture, and the discourses of the hand, belongs to a growing study of the discursive body in early modern performance. Focusing on John Bulwer's fascinating *Chirologia*, Karim-Cooper begins to explore how and why the hand could be perceived as 'the most important agent of communication on the human body'. Central to this thesis is the multiple meanings the hand could both convey and symbolize: on the one hand (forgive for the pun), it could offer a fixed, and very specific, array of meanings according to how it was held, used, waved, positioned, etc; on the other, it became an almost infinite site of meaning in its relationship to handwriting, to character, to palmistry, to individuality and also to conformity – unique and yet infinitely copy-able. Opening up the deep textures of this layered term and body part, Karim-Cooper begins to identify and explore some of the ways in which early modern playwrights utilized but also created a culture of the hand. Moving through the various rhetorical precepts that depend on gesture and the subtle but significant movements of the speaking hand, Karim-Cooper traces how these are redeployed in Shakespeare's plays. From the fretting fingers, paddling palms, embracing arms, severed hands and soft gloves of (mostly) women, the book examines the erotic and performative potential of the hand. Whilst most rhetorical manuals observe the male hand as a mode of amplification and communication, a site of power and a demonstrative vehicle of persuasion, in women the hand is altogether less stable, charged with the potential for eroticism or intimacy: it is rarely a member of authority and frequently a site of vulnerability. Over the course of the book, Karim-Cooper considers the implications of this and how touch, the fingers or the glove reproduced and embedded the performance on sexuality on stage. Most revealing, here, is amputation or dismemberment and the different cultural codes it represents in the bodies of male and female characters, as well as at different moments in history. Moving through discourses of amputation and the political frameworks they establish, either allegiance or aggression, Karim-Cooper investigates that most obsessive of hand plays, *Titus*

Andronicus. Offering fascinating accounts of the 2014 Globe production, she navigates the 'emotional encounter with amputation' and the powerful impacts that it continues to produce (Karim-Cooper reports that some audience members fainted and vomited in this production). What resonates, however, is the vast and spectacular place that the hand occupies in Shakespeare's drama as well as its enduring and infinite role in our interpretation of character, emotion, expression, sincerity, persuasion and spirituality. The list of things that the hand can do or symbolize is very long indeed and constantly in a process of redefinition; from the Hand of God to the finger of accusation, the touch of compassion or the gesture of forgiveness, reconciliation or indeed approval, the hand remains, as Bulwer observed, the single most expressive part of the human body.

MOVING SHAKESPEARE

In *Privacy in the Age of Shakespeare*, Ronald Hubert sets out to revise the long held assumption that privacy was not available or even understood at the dawn of the early modern period. Drawing on an eclectic range of material, Hubert supports his argument that 'the line between public and private was not drawn in precisely the same place by early modern writers as it would be today but it was drawn and it did matter. Furthermore, while privacy was by no means equally available to everyone, it was a highly desirable objective'. Hubert gets a little tangled in his attempts to define privacy, which he does through a series of assumptions about how the subject may or may not control access to the self. The idea of privacy remains most powerful when it is understood in opposition to the public, not just because this sits easily with our assumptions about the early modern period, as well as retaining an Aristotelian focus on difference and similitude, but because it acknowledges the multiple ways in which privacy can function in a single space (including a public one). Hubert works on the basis of a four-fold definition of the term: a form of lacking or absence, refuge, concealment, interiority. He examines the changing values and terms through which the idea of privacy develops into something much more consistent with both individuality and social stability. Beginning with More's *Utopia*, the book sets out to establish how privacy functions ideologically – what does it mean to More's social vision – and how it effects individual notions of happiness, pleasure or security. Attending to questions of interiority, spiritual as well as subjective, Hubert explores the value of privacy in *Hamlet* and *Twelfth Night*. The middle sections of the book address questions of secrecy, including titillation and voyeurism, especially in *Much Ado* and *The Duchess of Malfi*, as well as the poetry of Herrick. The final sections of the book are concerned with notions of private property, propriety and gender, including Milton's *Paradise Lost* and the poetry of Marvell. The book takes in a much wider range of material than this brief summary suggests, including diaries, manuscripts, 'life writings', commonplace books as well as scientific and humanists texts, drama and poetry. The concern with privacy produces some fascinating networks of interpretation, especially across genre and historical moment, and tends towards a range of instances rather than linear narratives. Central to these networks is the paradox of privacy and how we recover or lay claim to anything beyond the representational, as Hubert concludes, 'privacy is an emerging expectation within early modern culture, and therefore will always be a moving target'. The fact that it is moving, then as now, perhaps, makes it all the more fascinating.

In *Celebrating Shakespeare, Commemoration and Cultural Memory*, edited by Clara Calvo and Coppélia Kahn, the volume's contributors explore, establish even, how Shakespeare has defined and shaped cultural legacies beyond those of his own dramas. Considering the 'dense social contexts' through which Shakespeare is celebrated and invoked, this collection of essays ranges through specific historical moments (Garrick Jubilee, the Easter Rising and numerous anniversary festivities) to a range of diverse 'commemorations' and the forms and festivities they have produced. Central to this focus is an engagement with how commemoration shapes cultural memories and what practices it takes in determining and celebrating notions of value as well as legacy. Particularly interesting in this respect is the development of the Shakespeare myth and how, in hindsight, it seems so precarious, so whimsical and removed from the drama. Beginning with Garrick's 'Jubilee', and the performance of his idolatry, played out through various images, objects and occasions, Peter Holland establishes how 'the new Shakespeare religion, the cult of Shakespeare' was perceived as both a triumph of secularization as well as a dangerous rehearsal of residual Catholicism. Either way, what stands out is the deeply conflicted responses to worship, and what that means for the idol as well as the practice itself. Observing how Shakespeare, the man, and Shakespeare, the plays and poems, are modulated over the past four hundred years, the essays here travel a variety of avenues. Richard Schoch determines the extent to which Betterton and Irving's performances attempted to recreate an authentic Shakespeare and what implications this may have had for the text in production. The collection follows a loosely chronological narrative in which we can discern how anniversaries become markers of change, crisis, reflection or fantasy. Most powerfully, perhaps, are the moments in which they coincide or collaborate with imperial and national imperatives, from the Battle of Waterloo, colonial, and post-colonial, India and the Easter Rising. Reflecting on the celebration of Shakespeare's quatercentenary in India, Supriya Chaudhuri examines the effects of a specially commissioned 'Shakespeare Commemoration Volume'. The volume produced a history of translation, adaptation and pedagogy, which, despite its uncritical reproduction of a colonial legacy, came to represent an archive which 'gave textual substance to cultural memory, unquestionably demonstrating more than a century's work with Shakespeare in the languages of the subcontinent, work that, in its many angles of deployment, its gaps and silences, its transformations and distortions, could serve as a memory site for the future'. Such observations underpin many of the essays here which produce a vital narrative of how cultural memory is created and sustained and the often random, strategic, accidental or ideological ways in which Shakespeare – the man as much as the works – has charted the rise and fall of the languages of belonging. Beyond the wonderful anecdotes and evidences, one of the great contributions of this book is to the study of cultural memory and the often unthinking ways in which cultures and moments adopt and erase their Shakespeares. Quoting Pierre Nora, Clara Calvo notes, 'We speak so much of memory ... because there is so little of it left.' Such pointed observations are deeply revealing and the collection offers a very vivid and poignant insight into the losses of memories, as well as their constructions.

WORDY SHAKESPEARE

The idea of celebration and commemoration runs throughout many of this year's books, even when not explicitly stated as such. Paul Yachnin's edited collection, *Shakespeare's World of Words*, offers another celebration: not in fact of Florio but of the infinite variety of Shakespeare's language arts. Each of the ten short essays analyse the behaviour of certain words, image clusters or gestures in a specific play: Michael Bristol and Sara Coodin assess the language of religious identity in the speeches of Shylock; David Schalkwyk follows the implications and instabilities of proper names in *Troilus and Cressida*; Lucy Munro considers the homonym 'antic/antique' and its interpretative implications in *Love's Labour's* and *2 Henry IV*. Other chapters include investigations of colour in *Hamlet* (specifically in relation to Ophelia's 'loneliness'); fishing and stealing in *The Winter's Tale*; a fine chapter on grammar moods in *1 Henry VI* by Lynne Magnusson; and the slippery referents in *Othello*, as well as Helena's 'heart-sieve' in *All's Well* and timing in *The Comedy of Errors*. Each essay offers a slightly different methodological and linguistic approach but takes inspiration from Bakhtin's concept of heteroglossia which, as

Yachnin argues, provides the basis for the book's scope which makes 'an argument for the artistically and socially creative pre-eminence of Shakespeare's world of worlds'. In the process, many of the contributors reveal a rich tapestry of meaning in which words and signs are continually unfolding, making their mark and then morphing, like mercury, into another sign, word or gesture.

In *Circumstantial Shakespeare*, Lorna Hutson revitalizes some of these semantic questions through her attention not to the multiplicity of meaning but to Shakespeare's investment in sixteenth-century rhetorical pedagogy. Here the terms 'circumstance' and 'circumstantial' refer not only to legal models of evidence but also to the conditions and environments in which the dramatic worlds take shape. Drawing on classical and contemporary texts, Hutson shows that the dramatic action takes shape across a range of modes, which all require, in one form or another, active engagement of the critical imagination. The word 'circumstance', 'was powerfully associated with narrative, with the forensic invention of so-called artificial or technical proof (*probationes artificiales*), and with descriptions so vivid that they conjure up visual and auditory illusion (*enargeia*) and evoke strong emotions'. Within this model, Hutson examines the subtle ways in which the language of the drama inflects sensory experience to produce vivid notions of happening. Arguing against the largely accepted critical commonplace that Shakespeare was disinterested in neo-classical expectations of time and place, Hutson shows how 'circumstances' produced often very dense narratives of experience in which both time and place are clearly and carefully defined:

Shakespeare exploited a rhetorical tradition in which the circumstances of time, place, manner, and so forth were both shaped as arguments in disputes about motive and intention, and were, at the same time, metonymic details, or 'accidents' through which whole scenarios could be vividly and economically depicted in order to arouse emotion.

In *Romeo and Juliet*, for example, Hutson argues that Shakespeare's characters rehearse arguments 'of possible motives or purposes as a means of enabling us to imagine the transitions of time and place proper to narrative as if experiencing them subjectively in the "now" of the stage'. Building on this she demonstrates how effectively and 'pervasively references to *circumstantiae* were in Renaissance compositional theory' and how significant they were in determining not only Time and Place but also intention, motive and cause. Pursuing temporality in *Lear* and *Lucrece*, Hutson tracks the term 'opportunity' and its rhetorical adherents to foresight, as a way 'of perceiving the present moment from the vantage of foresight'. Addressing the temporal problems of *Lear* – letters arriving before they have been sent, things referred to before they have happened – Hutson examines the dramatic opportunities of occurrence and the circumstances of opportunity and how 'these all contribute to a sense of the canny and uncanny shaping of time and place as opportunity'. A chapter on *The Two Gentlemen of Verona* and *The Maid's Tragedy* explores the 'circumstance-creating vocabularies' of the plays, while the final chapter on *Macbeth* turns to an analysis of 'tragic feeling and the politics of nationhood'. Here she considers the forensic rhetoric of circumstance and the 'arousal of more complex emotions that implicitly identify monarchical charisma with English *constitutionality*, or with English *popular custom* as a source of law and justice'. Thus, the Scottish play, according to Hutson, 'powerfully distorts and eclipses the constitutional foundations of Scottish national consciousness'. This, Shakespeare does, she argues, through the presentation of sleep: according to Cicero in *Pro Roscio Amerino*, sleep is a proof of innocence but it is also an argument for motive in the context of parricide. In this way, the 'topic of sleep-as-innocence was displaced from its expected role as part of the rhetoric of forensic enquiry and became, rather, the expression of Macbeth's tormented recognition of his deed's dehumanizing effects'. Macbeth's expulsion from the circumstances of domestic nourishment, alongside the weird sisters and his curse of Scottish tyranny produce 'something which seems real to us [so] that it has become more powerful than history'.

Nathalie Vienne-Guerrin's marvellous *A Pragmatic Dictionary of Shakespeare's Insults* does not include an entry on the weird sisters but it does include one on 'woman', 'a common insult'. The wonderful elements of this book are not simply the often amusing, horrifying, intriguing, surprising and delightful definitions that Vienne-Guerrin provides but the approach she takes to the insult itself. Derogatory terms come in all forms it seems and the book includes the colloquial (losel, minnow, punk, pantler and shrimp, for example) but also the contextually powerful instances of 'dirt', 'humidity', 'footballer', 'Remnant' and 'Puppet'. Some of these terms perform an insulting function at specific moments – 'Richard', Senator, Moor and Natural, for example – whereas others are perennially denigrating – sponger, slave, milksop, nag, scum, Hungarian and hedgehog. The entries are very well thought through and established according to both usage and contemporary hard word dictionaries. Vienne-Guerrin frequently observes how the terms can differ across plays as well as speeches but how each instance of its usage determines a particular set of characteristics and associations that tarnish or incriminate. She draws on many contemporary writers, not least Florio, Rabelais, Erasmus and Wilson but also other dramatists and there are often fascinating divergences of use across plays and playwrights. Where dirt, for Mary Douglas, may be 'matter out of place', for Shakespeare it is distinctly grubby. Many of the words retain their early modern identity (e.g. slut), while others have only lightly transitioned (e.g. sheep, as emblematic of stupidity – my grandmother would call me a 'silly sheep' if I did something careless). Other terms are historically very revealing, such as Turk and Moor, and the ways in which the words can be used to define models of allegiance, in both satire and earnest. There are some very subtle terms: a wittol, who is 'A cuckold who knows he is a cuckold and does nothing about it'; or a 'football player', indicating someone of 'lower class' who takes part in what Elyot refers to as a 'devilish pastime'. As a dictionary format, Vienne-Guerrin is less concerned with a specific methodology of interpretations but there are resonant parallels with Kay Stanton's *Shakespeare's Whores* (reviewed 2015) in which we witnessed the movements of the term 'whore' across a range of women and instances, where it could function as a mode of exclusion, but also, paradoxically, of celebration. Within this context, the gendered insult is especially fascinating. Similarly, we can observe the mobility of certain words, such as face, for example, and their relative performances of defacing or disfiguring; in this, and with a great many of the terms listed here, the focus is on usage and implication and the rich variety that one word can offer over a vast range of utterances.

According to John Kerrigan's *Shakespeare's Binding Language*, 'casual, everyday profanity gave shape and texture to life', and this is certainly borne out by the hypermobility of the insults in Vienne-Guerrin's dictionary. For Kerrigan, however, such shape and texture is informed by the networks of meaning – social, legal, historical, parochial and professional – that bind the subject to the word. Setting out to establish how oaths are used in Shakespeare's work, to what language codes they belong and the valued histories they import, Kerrigan asserts that 'across the Shakespeare canon, oaths are sworn and bonds dissolved at points of decision and uncertainty that produce what we now call "character"'. On the one hand, then, oaths are speech acts that determine narrative events or 'precipitate action'; they bind characters to circumstances, people, institutions or faiths; but they are also casual, conversational, even utterances that slide between the violent and the vacuous, or, frequently, both. The book is structured according to groups of oaths, social and professional, depending on their purpose and usage; for example, revenge, profanity, legal, institutional, religious or professional. Frequently, although not unproblematically, these groups collide – marriage oaths function as legal, institutional and religious; bonds that are broken or severed may begin as legal and become social, or vice versa. 'But', as Kerrigan notes, 'the drive to qualification goes deeper. Because of psychological and communicative ambiguities, the binding word generates verbiage.'

More often than not, it is the rich tapestry of that interpretation that generates meaning here; the oath is at its most precarious when it is subjected to performance. Tone and gesture modulate the oath so that they become 'an acutely sensitive resource for judgements of intention by audiences, and a subtle opportunity for the actor, who can qualify the absoluteness of asseveration or promise enshrined in the speech act'. Such performative aspects of the oath make it radically unstable and, as Kerrigan puts it so elegantly, we find ourselves

… in a nest of paradoxes congenial to a dramatist who was drawn to plurality and interpenetrating ambiguities. The word that cannot be fixed is subverted by its performance and needs massive supplements to explicate. It is a forceful commitment of the self couched in markedly derivative language. Oaths and vows can reinforce the very doubt they are means to allay.

Drawing on the bonds, and asseverations, of love, loyalty, debt, faith, promises and all sorts of other things that characters vow to keep or maintain, the book explores the many ways in which Shakespeare's plays exploit the potential of the oath to bind as well as break the ties of kinship. Within this Kerrigan offers some compelling and intricate readings of oaths and their roles within the plays (and sometimes Sonnets) discussed. At almost every instance a fracture occurs at the moment the oath is uttered, either in the act of surety itself or in the effects it produces; indeed, at the end of *The Merchant of Venice*, Kerrigan notes: 'The usurer takes, the charitable man gives; that is the orthodoxy travestied by the outcome of the trial.' One of the great pleasures of this book is the layered readings between and across the plays: Kerrigan moves through a huge range of material, Shakespearean as well as other early modern writings and dramatists, and in the process reveals the incredibly dense life of the oath and its reverberations throughout, not only the terms that surround it (that which the oath refers to) but also the social, religious and political assumptions that it confronts. The subtexts or undersides to the oath, lies and denials are equally absorbing and often very subtle as they disclose an electric atmosphere of deceit choreographed by a playwright who is wilfully exploiting the power of cultural blind spots to oppress and condemn. As Kerrigan asserts, 'Shakespeare was not just drawn to oaths, vows, sealed bonds, and the like because of what they brought into performance, but was more substantially and deeply preoccupied with what they tell us about the make up of truth.'

GREEN SHAKESPEARE

Gabriel Egan's *Shakespeare and Ecocritical Theory* offers an accessible and thoughtful introduction to the movements and concerns of ecocriticism, which begins from the standpoint of speculative regret: 'If we value a particular state of affairs then it is better to conserve it than destroy it in the hope of restoring it later.' This view, fundamental to environmentalism, is at the heart of many of Shakespeare's plays and one that is held up to scrutiny in terms of both historical determinacy and individual responsibility. Central to Egan's approach is a focus on time and how many of Shakespeare's dramas address the question of the future, as one of progress but also reckoning. The book is structured according to the key questions which govern our understanding of ecology: Elizabethan and Jacobean attitudes to the nature of life; contemporary relevance and significance of those conceptions of nature; how the key debates of the Renaissance can or should be reinterpreted through a clarified conception of the natural world; and the heuristic value of theories of interconnectedness for both the past and the present understanding of the natural worlds. Only in the first chapter does Egan engage directly with the critical field of eco-studies, which emerges as a very uneven school of thought predicated on how 'word choices and forms of expression can reveal implicit assumptions about an ecological topic'. The following three sections engage with some of the theories and implications of evolutionary perspectives, including current shifts in our apprehension as well as their implications for our knowledge of the past. Understanding recent questions on the 'nature of life', or even the 'meaning of life', presents fresh challenges for our conceptions of nature in Shakespeare's plays, not least of all genetics and biology. The section on the animal/human dynamic is more obviously linked to ecocritism in its attention to Cartesian questions of distinction but is also acutely aware of the critical inadequacies of such distinctions since they remain steadfastly anthropocentric. Egan's philosophical approach to many of the questions raised by attention to life, matter and art is at its most rewarding when he engages directly with the plays: the section on the nature of Crab in *The Two Gentlemen of Verona* is especially good. The final section deals with crowd sourcing and social networks, an infinitely modern phenomenon, but also a strangely resonant one within the context of a non-digitized early modern era. Here Egan demonstrates the power of the crowd, both in the plays and in the audience, as they become complex motifs for questions of economics and opinion. Structures – biological, social, political, linguistic, global and material – are central to the thesis of this book, which is less engaged with eco-criticism per se and more engaged with the cross-currents of certain scientific and philosophical narratives. 'Time and tide wait for no man', and Egan is concerned with the environmental implications of both, as a resource and as an index of human authorities.

In *Shakespeare and Ecology*, Randall Martin offers a more exclusively eco-critical approach to some of Shakespeare's plays. Concentrating on questions of environmental change, natural disasters, the depletion of fossil fuels, population growth and biodiversity, he suggests that Shakespeare contributed 'to the formation of a public ecological consciousness', as well as 'opening up creative pathways for re-imagining future human relationships with the natural world and non-human life'. Beginning with deforestation, Martin traces an environmental narrative which shows Shakespeare's remarkable sensitivity to the changing consumer practices in early modern England. Examining the symbolic resonance of Herne's oak in *The Merry Wives of Windsor*, Martin explores the play's emblematic discourses on sustainability. In chapter two, Martin focuses on husbandry and 'man-made diversity', and Shakespeare's apparent understanding of environmental historicity and the impact of the human footprint. Chapter three attends to the controversies that surrounded, and even drove, the manufacture and use of gunpowder, while chapters four and five focus on particular ecologies, or the produced landscapes of the plays and their inhabitants (*Hamlet*'s relationships to the worm is of particular note here).

One of the most rewarding aspects of this book is not the eco-critical insights, since many have been well documented, but the highly intelligent and perspicacious way in which Martin observes and explores the dynamic between a pre- and post-environmentally articulate period. Looking at 'ecological optics', or the ways in which human and non-human species adapt to and interact with their environments, the diversification of land use and mixed farming and the development of 'biodynamic cultivation', the book presents a highly articulate exploration of Shakespeare's imprints of early modern ecology. Within this discussion, and even within the broad range of modern environmental discourses, Martin retains his attention on historicity, including enclosures, changing resources, sea-coal, saltpetre and wood, as well as shifting practices in land management, food production, exploitation and regeneration of the English landscape. The natural world is relentlessly animated and articulated through human responses to it, and Martin's book engages with these discourses at a conceptual as well as practical level. Some of the most convincing readings emerge when this conflict reaches a crisis point, especially in *Macbeth*, where Martin observes how 'Gleaning and recycling the global reflux of competitive state violence, the Weird Sisters perform dark invoices of bio accountability.' In this way, the witches become implicated in a war-ravaged, devastated Scotland in which the theatre is exposed as 'complicit [in] the presentation of the natural world as a back-drop for gunpowder-enhanced heroism, marketed as urban entertainment'. Although I am not entirely convinced by the play as a kind of Michael Moore exposé of imperial investment in military industrialization, the point is powerfully made.

In *Shakespeare and the Natural World*, Tom MacFaul takes a different critical approach in that he is less concerned with ecocriticism and more concerned with the history of ideas and how early modern perceptions of nature belonged to a philosophical, social, ethical, Christian and material network of theories about the human and its environment: 'The natural world, in all its complexity, is used to channel and compromise human motives, challenging the vain notion of what Macbeth calls the "single state of man" (1.3.140) – whether that notion is driven by ideas of religious transcendence, political power, or scientific knowledge.' For MacFaul it is the unbounded complexities of these relationships that define the interests of this book: 'that sense of excess, of the irreducible untidiness and slipperiness of the natural world'. Underneath this slipperiness is an understanding of the natural world as both creative and, at least potentially, redemptive. The book proceeds through an appreciation of nature, not in contrast to the human or its worldviews but in conversation, so that 'nature was not a way of escaping from a religious perspective but rather enabled a broadening of religious questions, and perhaps offered ways of solving them'. Structured according to some of the key questions attendant on changing conceptions of both human and nature, MacFaul demonstrates the powerful ways in which the idea of nature produces a multitude of conflicting arguments about love, sympathy, landscape, boundaries and binaries. Exploring a range of plays and poems, including a wonderful section on *Venus and Adonis*, MacFaul sustains complex arguments and conflicting sympathies across Shakespeare's works. The idea of Nature, as Shakespeare employs the concept, is a capacious one and the book's attention to the weight of its emotional pulls is rewarding, especially through the sections that deal with the esoteric – *Antony and Cleopatra, King Lear, The Tempest* – as well as the earthy – *Titus Andronicus, Richard III, A Midsummer Night's Dream, Comedy of Errors*. MacFaul also considers a number of non-Shakespearean texts including *The Witch of Edmonton* and Donne's *Metempsychosis*. One of the great pleasures of this book is MacFaul's synthesis of the metaphysical, philosophical and philological natures of Shakespeare's imagination which present us with dizzying moments of insight into the experiences of the play-world: Scipio-like we hover above the worlds of Shakespeare's dramatic imaginations and glimpse the apple-island in Gonzalo's pocket, 'I think he will carry this island home in his pocket and give it his son for an apple.' The fruit of temptation, the symbol, the shape, the world, the school boy's treat – the humble apple is also the island, the dream and Gombrich's duck-rabbit of interpretation.

Moving from ecology to economy, we discover David Hawkes's *Shakespeare and Economic Theory*. Divided into two parts, the first half of the book deals with the history of economic theory and the various traditions through which it has developed, including the distinctions between exchange and use value, as well as the more holistic Aristotelian sense, which included ethics and aesthetics. Hawkes defines these approaches as 'restricted' ('chrematistics') and 'general' (social and political). The second part of the book deals with Shakespeare's works, and examines key words as well as key ideas. Central to Hawkes's thesis is the transitional moment in which Shakespeare was writing when many of these terms and ideas were under scrutiny. According to Hawkes, 'The vocabulary and concepts of modern "economics" were first developed in early modern England and ... Shakespeare was an active and influential participant in that process.' Hawkes moves fluently between complex economic theories and dense language networks of meaning at work in and across the plays: in the process he produces, and sometimes rehabilitates, some fascinating readings including those on capitalism in *Lear*, consumerism in *Titus* and trade in *Troilus* Hawkes often talks about the same play across different contexts and so produces some very multivalent and compelling cross-readings.

On an entirely different note but of interest this year is *Locating the Queen's Men, 1583–1603*, edited by Helen Ostovich, Holger Schott Syme and Andrew Griffin, which offers a series of essays dedicated to the material practices of the repertory company. The essays provide a range of perspectives on the movements, economies, dramaturgical practices, performances and preoccupations of the playing company, and in the process record and develop some pertinent insights into the conditions of early modern theatre, which, as the editors suggest, allow the 'company to emerge not as a relic in its own lifetime, but as a less brash participant in the complicated and multiple self-contradictory ideological and dramaturgical negotiations that shaped the canon usually defined by Marlowe, Shakespeare, and Jonson'. Of particular interest are Lloyd Kermode on Wilson's *Three Ladies of London* and the shifting place of usury in the moral and financial economies of early modern England, Tiffany Stern on the Curtain, Richard Dutton on the Folio text of *Henry V*, and William N. West on the jig.

SHAKESPEARE IN PRINT

Finally, however, I'd like to end where it all begins, with the First Folio and Emma Smith's biography of the book that, second only to the Bible, provides the most supporting evidence for word use and meaning in the Oxford English Dictionary and, in George Steevens's words, 'the most expensive single book in our language'. Beginning with Sir Edward Dering's purchase of the book on 5 December 1623, Smith follows the records of four centuries of such purchases, observing the 'sociable networks of interpersonal relations' that this book-buying reveals, including the theatre and the book trade, patrons, stationers, writers and readers: recording the tastes of the ambitious, the aesthetic, the aspirational and the admiring, buying Shakespeare's First Folio was a serious business. Tracing this business, Smith observes that the book is not especially rare but that 'the value of individual First Folio copies, and of the edition itself, derives from this complex historical process of accrual'. In order to understand this historical process, Smith divides the book into sections on owning, reading, decoding, performing and perfecting, which loosely amounts to the book's history of canonicalization, interpretation, attribution, production and editing. The story takes in the fascinating acquisitions of Thomas Bodley and Henry Clay Folger, among others, whose stealthy and steady collections have redefined the scope of academic scholarship. Bodley, famous for his dismissal of 'plays' and 'baggage books' accepted a copy of the Folio on the basis that its size seemed to matter more than its content. On its return from binding 'the First Folio was given the shelf mark S.2.17 Art, and was chained, with its fore-edge out from the shelf, in the Arts end of the Library'. There is something slightly ignominious about being consigned to the 'Arts end of the library', but it is in these lovely details that we appreciate Smith's capacity for biography and her compassionate eye for the material object. Exploring how the book was read, Smith reveals a counter-narrative to the traditional conception of women readers: contrary to contemporary accounts of the dangerous scope of the female imagination (upheld in many of the marginal comments of male readers), women 'were active agents of Shakespearean meanings: attested female readers of Shakespeare's First Folio seem more numerous than for many other early modern books'. The book's sections on performing are especially revealing in terms of cultural taste and capital as the great actors and critics of the eighteenth and nineteenth centuries use their Folios discretely – 'a talisman rather than a work of professional reference'. The talismanic quality of the work eventually gives way to facsimiles (and forgeries). Smith is, I think, circumspect about the value of such projects: 'Facsimile Folios have served to substitute for, to supplement, to perfect, and to validate the original: they have contributed to its increasing reification even as they threaten to undermine that singularity.' The story of the First Folio is not one of singularity, though: it is a glorious, captivating, irreverent and loving story of a 'magic encyclopaedia'. I spent my first portion of disposable income on the cheapest facsimile of the First Folio I could find: years later my husband bought me a beautiful, elegant facsimile. Both tell a story and Smith's biography is a wonderful testimony to the 'world's most expensive' book and the readers who keep it that way.

THE YEAR'S CONTRIBUTIONS TO SHAKESPEARE STUDIES

WORKS REVIEWED

Calvo, Clara and Coppelia Kahn, eds., *Celebrating Shakespeare, Commemoration and Cultural Memory* (Cambridge, 2015)

Crawforth, Hannah and Elizabeth Scott-Baumann, *On Shakespeare's Sonnets, A Poet's Celebration* (London, 2016)

Edmondson, Paul and Stanley Wells, *The Shakespeare Circle* (Cambridge, 2015)

Egan, Gabriel, *Shakespeare and EcoCritical Theory* (London, 2015)

Frank, Marcie, Jonathan Goldberg and Karen Newman, eds., *This Distracted Globe: Worldmaking in Early Modern Literature* (New York, 2016)

Hawkes, David, *Shakespeare and Economic Theory* (London, 2015)

Hubert, Ronald, *Privacy in the Age of Shakespeare* (Toronto, 2016)

Hutson, Lorna, *Circumstantial Shakespeare* (Oxford, 2015)

Karim-Cooper, Farah, *The Hand on the Shakespeare Stage* (London, 2016)

Karreman, Isabel, *The Drama of Memory in Shakespeare's History Plays* (Cambridge, 2015)

Kerrigan, John, *Shakespeare's Binding Language* (Oxford, 2016)

Kirwan, Peter, *Shakespeare and the Idea of Apocrypha: Negotiating the Boundaries of the Dramatic Canon* (Cambridge, 2015)

MacFaul, Tom, *Shakespeare and the Natural World* (Cambridge, 2015)

Martin, Randall, *Shakespeare and Ecology* (Oxford, 2015)

Menzer, Paul, *Anecdotal Shakespeare: A New Performance History* (London, 2015)

Ostovich, Helen, Holger Schott Syme and Andre Griffin, eds., *Locating the Queen's Men, 1583–1603* (Ashgate, 2016)

Smith, Emma, *Shakespeare's First Folio: Four Centuries of an Iconic Book* (Oxford, 2016)

Sullivan, Erin, *Beyond Melancholy, Sadness and Selfhood in Renaissance England* (Oxford, 2016)

Vienne-Guerrin, Nathalie, *Shakespeare's Insults: A Pragmatic Dictionary* (London, 2016)

Walsh, Brian, *Unsettled Toleration, Religious Difference on the Shakespearean Stage* (Oxford, 2016)

White, R. S., Mark Houlahan and Katrina O'Loughlin, eds., *Shakespeare and Emotions, Inheritances, Enactments, Legacies* (Palgrave, 2015)

Yachnin, Paul, ed., *Shakespeare's World of Words* (London, 2015)

2. THE CAMBRIDGE GUIDE TO THE WORLDS OF SHAKESPEARE

reviewed by RUSSELL JACKSON

The print edition of *The Cambridge Guide to the Worlds of Shakespeare* consists of two double-columned volumes (11¼ by 9 ins. / 28.5 by 22.5 cm.), with 277 articles by 285 contributors, 1,974 main-text pages, 332 illustrations and (by the estimate of the editor, Bruce R. Smith) 1,700,000 words. It is both welcoming and challenging. Welcoming, because, as Smith suggests, 'the word "guide" invites you to notice the landmarks but leaves you free to make your way through the worlds on offer here' (Preface, xxii); challenging, because once the reader has started the journey, it is difficult to stop. In fact, the structure of the work facilitates a plurality of journeys through a multiplicity of worlds. One article leads to another, within and between the two volumes, whose subtitles indicate a radical dimension of this extraordinary undertaking: Volume One, 'Shakespeare's World, 1500–1660', has the Chandos portrait on its cover, while Volume Two, 'The World's Shakespeare, 1660–Present', confronts the reader with the striking head-shot of a white-faced actor with a red blindfold (Kazunori Akitaya in the Tokyo Globe Company's production of *King Lear*).

Faced with this plenitude and variety, what is the reviewer to do? I lived with the books for a few weeks, taking the editor at his word, allowing breaks for rest and refreshment and – I frankly admit – not expecting to read every one of those 1,700,000 words. Leaving sticky yellow notes as I went, like breadcrumbs allowing me to retrace my steps, I adopted the strategy of beginning with articles on topics I know little or nothing about, proceeding to those of which I have at least some knowledge, and then homing in on the fields in which I have some claim to expertise. Because the articles achieve a consistently high level of clarity in exposition as well as scholarly and critical insight, those in the first and second of my classifications left me surprised and (I hope) enlightened while those in the third reminded me of work I need to be better acquainted with and perspectives new to me. This use of the *Guide* accords with my preference when visiting art exhibitions: not to follow the path prescribed by the audio guides but to wander freely and then move back to a previously sampled room. Then, perhaps having purchased and read through the catalogue, I hope to come back later and see the show with an altered, more informed gaze. Consequently my path through the Guide sometimes zigzags across the 'Parts', sometimes follows the numbered order.[1]

The Introduction to Part I, 'Mapping Shakespeare's World' by Peter Whitfield, prepares the ground for what is to follow through both volumes with the suggestion that the 'powerful maps that claimed to display the structure of the cosmos and man's place in it' were affirmations that the universe was 'not infinite, not empty, not hostile, but self-contained, hierarchical, purposeful and, in a sense, *living*' (4, italics in original). The paradoxical possibility is that 'the Elizabethans were more at home in their mysterious but interpreted world than we are in ours' (4). Subsequent articles on climate (4, Mike Hulme) and Botany (38, Leah Knight) show that the element of interpretation is common to the Elizabethan conception of other topics of this kind. Early modern herbalists reveal a 'turn to similitude ... in the absence of later descriptive techniques' (281), a factor that connects their work directly with that of poets and playwrights:

---

[1] Individual articles have been identified by the number followed after a comma by the title and/or the name(s) of the author(s).

'Both poet and herbalist engaged in a highly intertextual mode of composition' (282). The employment of herbs by such non-professional healers as 'wise women' and other dispensers of traditional remedies – Friar Laurence in *Romeo and Juliet* being a case in point – made them 'key figures in delivering early modern health care'. At this point the reader is alerted to 'Healing and Healers' (99, Richelle Minkhoff), where 'simples' and the 'compound medicinal recipes' figure among the other *materia medica*. The tendency of all the articles in this section is to illustrate how both direct experience and theories of the physical world infused imaginative writing, notably in shared modes of expression. Julian Yates, in 'Agriculture, Food Distribution, Cooking' (41), 'assume[s] some continuity between the kitchen and the stage as places of performance, places whose textual remains – cookbooks and dietaries, published play texts and promptbooks – express a desire on the part of cook and player, recipe and play text, to become something else' (293). This correspondence may be stretched an ounce too far in the suggestion that in *The Tempest* 'the whole island is Prospero's kitchen, even if no one has thus far suggested that his fabled books were cookbooks' – you heard it here first – 'but his kitchening of Alonso and his courtiers carries with it the power to remove hunger, induce sleep, and to make them feel passion, weep and pray' (301). Nevertheless, Yates's article is an example of the manner in which the *Guide* opens up new perspectives of interpretation and emotional response.

Three articles in Part IX, 'England, 1560–1650' – 'Trade and Commerce: Mercantilism' (80, Michael Tratner), 'Sorts, Classes, Hierarchies' (79, David Schalkwyk) and 'Shakespeare's Money' (81, David J. Baker) – include notably clear definitions of concepts and distinctions, such as Tratner's lucid account of usury (625), and demonstrate their presence in the fabric of Shakespeare's writing. By moving to 'Gender Relations and the Position of Women' (83, Adelaide Meira Serras) and 'Race and Nation' (86, Margo Hendricks), the reader will already have assembled essential elements of the material world and the world of the imagination in (for example) *The Merchant of Venice*.

The division of the volumes between 'Shakespeare's World' and 'The World's Shakespeare' asserts implicitly that the poet's works do not constitute a fixed and fully achieved entity, available to be modified by subsequent interpretative and performance. Rather, the relationship between reader/audience and the plays and poems is one of mutual and varied exchange across years and continents. A sign of this is the distribution of aspects of the theatre of Shakespeare's time among articles in sections devoted to 'Changing Technologies of Performance' (Part XX), 'Audiences' (XXI), 'Making the Scene' (XVI) and 'Production History' (XXII). Thus, 'Physical Structures' in Part XX (196, Ronnie Mulryne) moves from the earliest theatres to the present century, and can be complemented by a later article on 'Globe Theatre Replicas' (144, Yu Jin Koo). The latter is included in Part XV, 'International Encounters', which opens the second volume, and might have found a home elsewhere, but this is another example not merely of the inter-relationships between articles but also of their multivalency, by which connections made by the reader as well as the editorial team contribute to the effectiveness of the *Guide*. Past and present encounter each other in the account of 'Audiences at the Old Globe and the New' (211, Penelope Woods), which complements 'Original Practices' (203, Don Weingust) in the 'Changing Technologies' section and Koo's article on the 'Replicas'. 'Audiences' also encompasses not only strictly historical accounts of expectations and behaviour in different periods, but also 'Shakespeare for Soldiers and Seniors' (208, Amy Scott-Douglass) and 'Diversely Abled Audiences' (210, Maura Michelle Tarnoff). These might lead to the use of American Sign Language in performance for deaf or partially hearing audiences, as described in 'Signing Shakespeare (ASL)' (186, Peter Novak) in Part XIX ('Translation'), and 'Shakespeare Behind Bars' (160, Niels Herold) which follows 'Shakespeare Festivals and Jubilees' and precedes 'The Folger Shakespeare Library' in Part XVII, 'Shakespeare as a Cultural Icon'. A case can be made for the inclusion of prison Shakespeare in this grouping, and this is one of a handful of instances where a topic seems to have missed its 'natural' home without contributing to the collective discourse between the articles within the Part where it is lodged.

Articles in 'Making the Scene' (XVI), which discuss selected scenes and their afterlife, are effective in demonstrating the varied life of the plays. For example, Mariacristina Cavecchi's account of the 'balcony scene' in *Romeo and Juliet* (149) traces its pilgrimage through 'various genres and cultural contexts' (1135). 'Production History' (XXII) includes twelve articles drawing on the previously published work, from introductions in volumes in the New Cambridge Shakespeare and the same publisher's 'Shakespeare in production' series. Taken together, these substantial extracts cover general aspects of the history of Shakespearean performance as well as illuminating individual plays, but some readers may be frustrated by having to zig-zag a little too much in order to achieve the synthesis of an overview. It is at this point that, for all the pleasure of being incited to take the initiative by the *Guide*, a reader might seek the aid of more conventional summaries such as those in the *Oxford Companion to Shakespeare*.[2] Moreover, this suggests that an interesting test for the Guide could be the response of a reader new to the field of Shakespeare Studies, to whom its stimulating revisionism might not be apparent.

The reader frequently turns a corner – to return to the art gallery metaphor – and encounters perspectives that may be unfamiliar, such as Nicolas Sanchez's observation in 'Translation for the Screen' (188) that the subtitlers of films are frequently guilty of 'sacrificing Shakespeare's exuberance on the altar of conciseness' (1370), and Dominique Goy-Blanquet's reflections in 'Shakespeare Quotations in French' (237) on the significance of the remark '*C'est du Shakespeare*' (1701). Some topics illuminate aspects of the wider field that may be unfamiliar to many readers.

A case in point is Jeffrey Todd Knight's 'Collecting and Reading Shakespeare's Quartos' (232), which focuses on the material life of these well-known 'Shakespeare' artefacts rather than simply treating them as witnesses in the textual debate. Goy-Blanquet's and Knight's articles both appear in Part XXIV, 'Shakespeare and the Book', which follows on effectively from the articles on the textual history of the plays in 'Printing and Reception History' (Part XXIII), although the contents of both parts might easily have been classified as dealing with 'reception', and the sequence on quotation consists of six two-page articles (234–9) sandwiched between necessarily longer accounts of broader topics.

But here as elsewhere the grouping of articles has for the most part a cumulative and coherent effect, in which the familiar is spiced with the surprising, both in information and in strategy of approach. In Volume One David Kathman's concise and forthright account of the vagaries of the authorship controversy (110) sits well with Erin Blake's 'Likeness and Paintings' (111) and Macdonald P. Jackson's analysis of the Stratford 'Memorial Bust' (112), which applies the principles of textual scholarship to the evidence for the monument's earlier states. The three articles are united by the understanding, voiced by Blake, that 'a satisfying portrait depicts the person we want to see or expect to see; otherwise it is not credible. Shakespeare's works and cultural influences are too wide ranging ever to be pinned down to a single image once and for all' (861).

The treatment of literary criticism is refreshing and original. Rather than present a chronological account of a progression from one century to another, Lars Engle introduces in Part XXV a series of articles that examine tendencies and strategies from a synchronic viewpoint. Despite this, the first in the section, 'Rhetoric, Form, Aesthetics' (245, Mark David Rasmussen) espouses

---

[2] Michael Dobson, Stanley Wells, Will Sharpe and Erin Sullivan, eds., *Oxford Companion to Shakespeare*, 2nd edn (Oxford, 2016).

chronology to trace 'some of the main lines of critical response over a period of nearly four centuries', thus allowing us 'to discover, in other words, how we have arrived where we find ourselves today' (1739). Rasmussen's succinct account of 'New Criticism' and its relationship with the rhetorically oriented work of Kenneth Burke and others places this and other movements in their wider cultural and political context. Julia Reinhard Lupton, writing on 'Character and Psychoanalytic Criticism' (248), does not simply describe the varied manifestations of Freudian and post-Freudian approaches but revaluates their status, noting (for example) that 'in literary studies, psychoanalytic theory has melded with other approaches ... in order to address character as a deeply layered and transactional phenomenon at the heart of drama as a medium' (1761).

The introductions to each Part are themselves illuminating, contributing not simply an overview but a choice of critical approaches for what is to follow. Generally, the articles achieve an impressive clarity of exposition as well as engaging and convincing critical analysis. There is a growing market in academic publishing of compendious collaborative 'Handbooks', 'Companions' and so on, frequently priced beyond the reach of almost all individual readers but devised for a productive existence in libraries and online. Editing and writing for these calls for a skilful negotiation between the needs of the publication itself and the temptation to offer what is effectively a stand-alone critical and scholarly article of the kind that wins kudos with institutional and national assessment regimes. For the most part the articles in the *Guide* achieve a remarkable twofold feat as 'contributions to knowledge' while remaining accessible to that lucky individual the 'intelligent general reader'. Here, the analyses of Shakespeare in popular culture – from caricatures to Manga, and from the movies to self-help books – is sophisticated without condescension, while topics more conventionally regarded as 'canonical' are addressed with the highest level of *haute vulgarisation*: there is nothing here to make the judicious grieve. Very occasionally an article may leave the general reader behind, as in the technical account of sonata form in 'Symphonic Music' (257), but more typical is the clear and effective account of reception theories in 'Performance, Perception, Reception' (252, James Keanrye) and of two new buzz-words of performance studies in 'Cognition and Affect' (253, Kristine Steenbergh). Michael Ingham's 'Jazz' (260) not only defines its titular term with brilliant concision, but proceeds to what might be ideal liner notes for CDs of the performances in question. In 'Ballet' (255), Nancy Isenberg addresses the major critical, cultural and aesthetic issues of the medium, while commenting in enlightening detail on major examples of the choreographers' work. I would have welcomed her responses on Kenneth Macmillan's as well as John Cranko's *Romeo and Juliet*, not simply because of its long stage life and continuing currency on film and video, but because Macmillan's treatment of the erotic would have chimed with other aspects of her article. But this is in itself a reflection of the overall tendency of the *Guide*'s contributors to prompt further thinking, reading and viewing. It is difficult to imagine Cranko's *Taming of the Shrew* being more effectively analysed. Sometimes, too the *mot juste* is achieved simply, as in the final subheading of Tetsuo Kishi's 'Musical Comedy' (256): 'Masterpieces: *Kiss me, Kate*'.

In conclusion, another aspect of the *Guide* must be acknowledged: it constitutes a valuable summation of the state of Shakespeare studies in the first decades of the new millennium. There are very few gaps in the topic-by-topic coverage, and the involvement of an impressively international range of scholars makes this the equivalent of a virtual conference (or World Congress) where none of the papers could be missed with impunity, even for the sake of commingling in the social spaces. The high quality, as well as extraordinary quantity, achieved by the *Guide* is a tribute to the perspicacity and, no doubt, persistence of Bruce R. Smith, his associate general editor Katherine Rowe and their associate editors and assistants. This 'interdisciplinary, cross-cultural guidebook' (Preface, xxi) is a handsome, generous-spirited work in every respect, and its thirty-six-page index and the guidance offered by the introductions to the parts facilitate movement from one section and article to another. Online it will be enhanced by the ability to search electronically and to cross-refer from the main text to editions in the *New Cambridge Shakespeare*. Appropriately, the final article, by Luke McKernan, is 'Shakespeare and Online Video', looking with qualified optimism towards the future of what may be an ephemeral medium but for the time being is yet another of the transformations that have marked the four hundred years of Shakespeare's afterlife: 'a creative revolution is taking place and we should value it – while we can experience it at all' (1973). Implicitly, the *Guide* exhibits comprehensively and invitingly the evidence of the playwright's role in such revolutions as well as their impact on the perception of him and his works.

3. SHAKESPEARE IN PERFORMANCE
reviewed by RUSSELL JACKSON

With the exception of *Shakespeare in Ten Acts*, the 'book of' the exhibition at the British Library, none of the works reviewed this year is related directly to the Shakspeare quatercentenary. There have been notable accounts of the experience of working on, in and with the plays in performance, offering valuable insights into the processes of production or potential models for exploration.

Both Anthony Sher's *The Year of the Fat Knight* and Michael Pennington's *King Lear in Brooklyn* are in the form of a diary, the former more a chronicle of day by day than the latter. Like *The Year of the King* (1986), an account of his work in the title role of Bill Alexander's RSC production of *Richard III*, the new book is illustrated with the drawings and paintings of himself and others in the role which are an important part of the actor's preparation, as well as sketches of his fellow-actors and members of the creative team. Greg Doran, Sher's husband, is not only the production's director but also the company's artistic director – a position referred to wryly as 'the job' – so that the domestic and institutional complexities of their shared situation lend added value to the description of the production's progress towards public performance, with Sher's search for the perfect 'fat suit', the painstaking process of learning the part, and the unfolding sense of the sophistication of the character and the play. Although the notion of a modern-dress production is soon dismissed, the actor's ambition to find other ways of avoiding the 'traditional' image is at the centre of the exploration of the physicality of Falstaff so that 'he doesn't have to look like some Toby jug from the souvenir shops' (31). This early stage in the search is described in a chapter on 'Character Acting', a shrewd discussion of the concept itself and its relation to Sher's own acting. As for learning the lines, Sher reminds the reader how sophisticated this can be, a matter not merely of a feat of trained memory (and its anxieties) but savouring the 'taste of the words' and discovering the personality through them, even as a physical sensation. This transfers itself to finding the lexical meaning of the words: 'There is the most delicious sensation – a taste in the mouth again – when you make sense of a difficult Shakespeare line, when you can speak it with the gist held inside it, but speak it effortlessly, not spelling it out but making it sound second nature' (59).

Sher's book, informative in its descriptions of the workings of the company, also affords insight into the Falstaff phenomenon, its influence and significance in the two plays and the ramifications of such issues as the sense of sickness that seems to permeate Part Two. Drawing on his own experience of overcoming addiction, Sher considers playing Falstaff as an alcoholic – far enough from the jolly toper of the Toby jug image – which will inform the 'hangover scene' at the beginning of the second scene of Part One and also, paradoxically, the great encomium to 'sherry sack' (*2 Henry IV*, 4.2.83–121). Ideas come and go in rehearsal, leaving more or less residue in performance, and at times the actor seems to hit a brick wall of frustration. William Charles Macready, the 'eminent tragedian' much given to venting his anger in the safe space of his diary (and sometimes in less secure places) would have appreciated the sentiment if not the language of Sher's outburst to himself as he approaches the read-through for Part One after two weeks of 'table work': 'A bad attack of nerves tonight ... With two weeks' work already done, there's more need to deliver than normal. Yet why am I frightened – after forty fucking years in the job?! It pisses me off. Well, good, I'll get through it as I got through all pressurized situations – on *anger*' (102).

Michael Pennington's account of work on *King Lear* encompasses the processes of preparation, rehearsal, the gradual coming together of a company and a production, and the intersections between private and communal life. This *King*

Lear originated in Brooklyn, at Theatre for a New Audience's new theatre, the Polonsky Shakespeare Centre, where it was directed by Arin Arbus; subsequently Pennington has toured in a production directed by Max Webster. The actor's thinking about the role had evolved over a long period, notably in conversations with another accomplished and perceptive actor, Philip Franks. Setting aside differences of temperament and circumstances, Pennington's writing differs from Sher's in the nature of its attention to the play as a whole. As well as writing out his own thoughts, in the persona of the king, about each stage of the play's journey, Pennington voices the imagined attitudes and anxieties of other characters. For example, in 2.4, when Lear arrives at the castle of Cornwall and Regan:

CORNWALL: I thought the first thing to do was to set the servant [i.e. Caius/Kent] free, just as a gesture to the old man.
REGAN: I thought the first thing to do was to be nice to the old man, tell him how pleased I am he's here.
KING LEAR: It's Cornwall who greets me first, I notice, but still she says she's pleased to see me. I believe her, I should think she is. Of course she's glad, or she'd be no daughter and my wife would have been no true wife, and I'd divorce her even though she's dead.
Regan straightens my collar, which has ridden up, to spruce me up a little. This also puts me at a disadvantage.
REGAN: Well, it didn't last. Immediately he complains about my sister. What a fool he is; does he think he can please me, denouncing her? (131)

Passages of this kind lend the book the effect of Pennington's 'User's Guides' to *Hamlet* and other plays, master classes from an actor who always has an eye for the overall picture as well as on individual roles. His alertness to the formal qualities of the writing is exemplified in the analysis of the play's final scene – Lear's eleventh. 'Sorry to labour the point to myself', he writes after counting out the syllables, 'but that's two hundred and thirty-two monosyllables, only thirty disyllables, four trisyllables and two words of four syllables each for Lear in the final scene, and that's the end of him. Even in Edgar's final speech, there are only three non-monosyllabic words. Did Shakespeare plan this, or was it all instinct?' (225). Appropriately, the question remains rhetorical: the paragraph reflects the author's respect for the playwright's craft without any hint of mystification: like the moments when an idea emerges in the company's own work, the right attitude is that of accepting the perceived technique as a gift without enquiring too curiously.

Theatre for a New Audience is one of many North American companies for whose programmes Shakespeare is a staple, not simply – though in truth partly – because the better-known plays are reliable at the box office but because the challenges and opportunities are vital in their artistic well-being. In *Directing Shakespeare in America: Current Practices*, Charles Ney brings together the voices of more than sixty experienced directors. The organization into a series of sections according to the stages of the production process allows for a diversity of techniques to be documented and opinions to be aired. The cumulative evidence for a distinctively American approach to the task is less persuasive than one might think. Occasionally preconceptions about British Shakespeare are aired. Kathleen Conlin, associate artistic director of the Utah Shakespeare Festival, identifies 'having strong speech and a highly physical production' as markers of national identity, 'because American culture is more athletic than anything else. We respond to movement, whether it's our own or another's' (75). Her Utah colleague David Ivers describes himself as asking 'Are we classical enough and colloquial enough and clear enough that we're reaching across just in terms of pure meaning?' At the same time as 'honouring Shakespeare's verse' and 'the structure of the language', he insists that 'we're not overly round. We're not overly British. We're not overly polite about it. It's extraordinarily muscular, language that needs to move and have vibrancy' (61). It's hard to square this notion of 'British' Shakespeare speaking with the actual practice of actors and teachers in the twenty-first century: it seems to reflect a received idea, based on memories of an earlier generation rather than anything to be heard on stages this side of the Atlantic or advocated by such 'voice and text' experts as Cicely Berry, Giles Block and Patsy Rodenburg. With a few exceptions the assembled directors describe rehearsal room methods very like those of their cisatlantic counterparts, with varying degrees of emphasis on 'table work', the prioritizing of individual and collective attention to character and scene construction, and so on. Thus the widely experienced freelance director Mark Lamos regards verse speaking as 'the muscular core of the production', so that 'everything else about the production flows out of its rhythmic certainty. Speech evolves and then action follows' (59). Tina Packer describes a process she calls 'dropping in': this is defined as 'going word-by-word through the text, sitting eyeball to eyeball with your fellow actor'. It is, she suggests, 'almost the opposite of table work – it asks the actor to be in touch with his/her body, breathe, let the sound of the word have an effect, see what's in the unconscious mind and then notice what comes up' (206). The word 'unconscious' here may set alarm bells ringing about the alleged curse of the 'Method', but Packer is referring to an engagement with the play's language rather than any delving into the emotional memory as such. One valuable aspect of Ney's book is its dispelling of any lingering preconception that all American acting is to be identified in terms of the Actor's Studio. Although the case for a distinctive American approach is not as conclusive as might have been expected, *Directing Shakespeare in America* documents a wide range of insights and practice from expert practitioners. There is a strong sense of where we as actors and audiences are now, not so much geographically, as in relation to another dimension: 'Time', reflects Brian Kulick of New York's Classic Stage Company, 'has become a very serious co-author of these works and keeps insidiously reshaping them' (39).

Then there is cutting. Barbara Gaines has no qualms about cutting for clarity and relative brevity to accommodate the needs of her Chicago audience – 'I believe it's our responsibility to tell a great story and help them make their trains too' (136). She cites the example of a *King Lear* in which she 'wanted the script to be totally focused on Lear's journey' so that 'the back stories about Oswald and Kent didn't make the final cut, leaving 'a laser like focus on [Lear's] descent' (140). This may seem to have been a cut too far, but the consensus among these directors is that 'You don't necessarily honour a play by doing every single line' (134, Darko Tresnjak). There is, after all, a heightened intimacy with the text that can be achieved only by reshaping it, a process that reveals the specific function of the components that are cut, and sometimes when cuts are made in or before rehearsal there is a lurking anxiety of the kind that comes from having taken a well-crafted mechanism to pieces and not being sure one will be able to put it back together again so that it will not seize up or fall apart when the electric current is turned back on. Anthony Sher describes this exhilarating but somewhat tentative aspect of his work with Doran on the preparation of the script for Falstaff's scenes as 'a very enjoyable learning process', because 'before you can cut a scene ... you have to really understand it' (37). Then of course you may realize why you cannot remove it after all.

Cutting, approached from a different but complementary angle, is the theme of Bruce R. Smith's *Shakespeare | Cut, Rethinking Cutwork in an Age of Distraction*. Smith often pursues an idea or a word with brio, sometimes swerving into metaphor but then returning with aplomb into an enriched version of its literal meaning. The ability is given free rein in this engaging and acutely argued book. By 'paying particular attention to a curiosity that sets cuts apart from other manipulations of flesh, paper, words, cloth, vinyl, celluloid film, and video', he demonstrates that 'a "cut" can be the space opened up between the things being cut apart, or it can be either of the resulting pieces, or it can be what is left when one of the resulting pieces has been discarded' (20). Smith transitions without any sense of a jump-cut from what neuroscience tells us about blinking to the editing of a performance text (90), and from 'the technologies that have produced the cutting edge between life and figure' to the effect of sound recording on perceptions of 'Shakespeare' (102). Although most readers/viewers/listeners may not be aware of the effect of digital cameras splitting everything into 'an array of 1 | 0 digital cuts' (120), or convinced for that matter of the significance of the process, from this the argument segues persuasively into a discussion of the figures at the back of the stage in the frontispiece to Nathaniel Richardson's *Messalina* (1640) and the discovery scenes in *The Tempest* and *The Winter's Tale* – and thence to a Yoruba-language performance of the latter at Shakespeare's globe in 2012 (126–7). By his final chapter, 'The New Cut: Shuffling Cuts Since 1900' – a title oddly suggestive of a butcher's claim to being an old established business – Smith has moved to the recutting of plays on Internet platforms such as YouTube, where (he claims) guidance to understanding the predominance of parodies can be found in the words of Michel Foucault: 'Knowledge is not made for understanding, it is made for cutting' (175). Then there's Tom Stoppard and William Burroughs – and, well, here comes everybody. The special value of this entertaining and at times dizzying book, originating in the 2011 Oxford Wells Shakespeare Lectures, lies in the validity of its overarching contention: that the cut is 'a phenomenon fundamental not only to perception but to artistic creation' (185).

Although the title may suggest more about cutting, the papers collected in *Shaping Shakespeare for Performance. The Bear Stage* edited by Catherine Loomis and Sid Ray cover a range of topics related to the task of putting the plays on stage. The subtitle, in a play on words embraced enthusiastically by the editors, refers to the device used at the Blackfriars Conference held at the theatre of that name in Staunton, Virginia: if a speaker goes beyond her or his allotted time, a bear enters and seizes the paper. (An actor in a bear skin, suitably adjusted according the conference's honoree: in this case George Walton Williams, whose characteristic bow-tie and spectacles were adopted by the ursine intervener.) The beast from *The Winter's Tale* might profitably be encouraged to appear elsewhere: overlong discourses, however irksome, rarely if ever engender a desire in the auditors to see the speaker eaten alive, but this decisive but benign intervention seems an entirely acceptable alternative. In the first section of the volume, three essays address the specific topic of 'editing Shakespeare for the Stage and the Page', with Cass Morris's '"Why do you thus exclaim": Emotionally inflected punctuation in editorial practice and in performance' raising important questions that affect the work of editors and performer alike. Thus in *The Two Gentlemen of Verona* Proteus's reflections on his conflicts of conscience takes on a different quality in the Folio, where the first and second of the following lines, quoted here as they appear in 'many modern editions', each end with a question mark:

> To leave my Julia, shall I be forsworn;
> To love fair Silvia, shall I be forsworn;
> To wrong my friend, I shall be much forsworn.
> (2.6.1–3)

Morris points out that the Folio's 'transition from interrogatives, regarding the women, to a declarative, regarding Valentine, illustrates a key point in Proteus's character'. Unsure about the consequences of his behaviour in a heterosexual relationship, he is more confident about what it will mean in a homosocial one (31). Like much else in the collection, the point at issue brings to bear the intimately conjoined practicalities of editing and theatre. Sybille Bruun, in '"You that way, we this way": Letters and possibilities in *Love's Labour's Lost*', engages with the circulation of letters that provides a mainspring for much of the play's comedy and at the same time perplexes stage managers who have to provide the props in question. Sid Ray's '"To make the unskillful laugh": A rhetoric of belches in *Twelfth Night*' carries out the promise of its subtitle, and among the other papers are considerations of the problematics of well-known scenes (such as the 'glove' business in *Henry V*), unfamiliar passages and their performance (the epilogue to 2 *Henry IV*) and such significant details as the absence or presence of what has come to be labelled tweely as a 'baby bump' in the denouement of *All's Well That Ends Well*. The variety and acuteness of the essays and the skilful organization achieved by the editors make this a companionable volume. Loomis's own contribution reflects on the evidence for and against a live animal being deployed in *The Winter's Tale*, relating this well-covered topic to the notion (raised by Thomas Cooper in 1615) that 'an appreciation for bear-baiting can lead to a tolerance for tyranny' and the suggestion that this 'tightens the link' between bear-baiting and the play (179).

The volume is bookended by contributions from Ann Thompson, combining discussion of stage directions and the editor's task with a tribute to George Walton Williams's contributions as associate general editor of the Arden Shakespeare, and Russ McDonald's 'Shakespeare and the history of the bookish'. McDonald's stylish wit and impressive but lightly worn learning are deployed in a 'critique of various kinds of reduction – textual, theatrical and, implicitly, pedagogical', countering 'instances of diminution' on the part of critics and directors with 'a defense of the unnecessary' (259). Here the focus is very much on the kind of 'shaping' that caused McDonald's disappointment with the BBC's 2012 series *The Hollow Crown*, which he looked forward to with something of the excited anticipation he experienced during his childhood in the 1950s when the live television broadcast of *Peter Pan* with Mary Martin was announced. For him, *2 Henry IV* was 'the text most brutally treated by the editorial scissors':

At some 3,000 lines, this hefty history, which ought to run at least three hours, this formidable drama in which the experience of leisure and waiting, of frustration and expectation are all part of its meaning, this masterpiece came in at one hour and fifty-two minutes. (266)

As examples of scenes that regularly fall prey to the shears, McDonald examines the scene between two spies, 'a Roman and a Volscian' (Adrian and Nicanor), in *Coriolanus* (4.3) and that in *The Winter's Tale* (3.1) between Cleomenes and Dion, on their way back from consulting the Oracle. Any director inclined to discard these as 'unnecessary' would, one hopes, be shamed by McDonald's lucid exposition of the contribution they make to their respective plays to 'furnish depth, layers, complexity – the main word is *texture*' (274, italics in original).

The books discussed so far reflect an open-minded approach on the part of scholars and theatre practitioners, a variety of working methods grounded in the text but free to range widely in interpretation. In some quarters, though, the very title of the collection *Designer's Shakespeare*, edited by the late John Russell Brown and Stephen Di Benedetto, may evoke controversies from the mid-1980s, when some actors in the subsidized theatres of Britain protested against the overpowering of plays by 'concept' at the expense of the work of actors on and with the script, in what seemed an unholy alliance between dictatorial directors and self-willed visual artists. *Designers' Shakespeare* originated in plans for a *Routledge Companion*, to figure alongside the same publisher's *Directors' Shakespeare* (edited by Brown, 2008) and *Actors' Shakespeare* (edited by Brown and Kevin Ewert, 2011). As Di Benedetto explains, this project 'transformed in time to a collection showcasing tactics of design and tools of design as seen through contemporary Shakespearean practice' (Preface, xviii). The result is a good deal shorter than the *Companions* and less comprehensive in its treatment of its topic: ten chapters as against the thirty-one of *Directors' Shakespeare* and the twenty of the volume on actors. Consequently it does not claim to offer an historical overview. Christian M. Billing's essay on Josef Svoboda gives some sense of his significant precursors, so that Craig and other early twentieth-century designers receive some attention, and Liam Doona, writing on 'Scenography at the Royal Shakespeare Company, 1963–1968', conveys the wider significance of his specific topic. Billings's account of Svoboda is especially informative and persuasive in outlining the political contexts of the designer's work in the theatres of the former Czechoslovakia. As well as Billings's study of Svoboda, three essays deal with major figures with comparable sophistication and scholarship: Arnold Aronson writes on Ming Cho Lee, notable for his work in New York and in North American regional theatres; Klaus van den Berg describes the 'unfolding of Shakespeare's space' by Karl-Ernst Herrmann, whose credits include Peter Stein's *Shakespeare's Memory* (1976) and *As You Like It* (1977) for the Berlin Schaubühne, and George Tabori's *Othello* at the Vienna Burgtheater (1990); and Maria Shevtsova traces Robert Wilson's pursuit of his aim to 'by-pass realistic acting and the psycho-emotional characterization that goes with it in favour of clear and accurate exposition' (123). Wilson is both director and designer. His best work has exceptional power and visual beauty but his treatment of actors may be reflected in the remarks of the octogenarian Marianne Hoppe, chosen for the title role in his *King Lear* (Schauspielhaus, Frankfurt, 1990): 'This Wilson can't fool me. I started out at the Deutsches Theater with Max Reinhardt. I know what a director is. Wilson is not a director. He's a lighting designer. A Wilson actor runs here and there only because there's a change of lights on the Wilson stage. Light pushes the actors around. Light is important, but in Shakespeare, the language is also important. I can speak the lines the way he wants, but I don't believe Shakespeare wrote the part of Lear to be recited by an autistic child' (124). *Hamlet* (Berliner Ensemble, 1995) consisted of fifteen scenes in which Wilson – now a triple-threat as actor/designer/director – not only played the title role but also spoke what remained of the speeches of all the other characters in the 'extremely compact' one-and-half hour performance (120–1). (Comparison might be made with Robert LePage's *Elsinore*, also first performed in 1995, in which the actor-director achieved a similar feat, albeit with the support of a designer.)

Two contributors address more general topics in comparable depth: Adrian Curtin writes on the often overlooked subject of 'Designing sound for Shakespeare'; and Dorita Hannah, in 'Beyond Language: Performing "true meant design"', concludes the book with a position paper on 'designing Shakespearean performance beyond the bard's initial language' (171) that encompasses the variations on postmodernist aesthetics of such companies as Punchdrunk and Toneelgroep Amsterdam. Less theoretically oriented essays by practitioners describe the working practices of two notable designers: Alison Chitty and Catherine Zuber. Light is shed on important aspects of the designers' approach. Hilary Baxter describes Chitty's use of storyboards as a means of envisaging movement within a production's spaces, and notes her insistence that a designer should think of 'clothes' rather than 'costumes'. Brandin Barón-Nusbaum illustrates Zuber's responsiveness to the emotional arc of a play and its characters with her own colour sketches as well as renderings by the artist. By situating their respective subjects in the context of their predecessors and the prevailing production aesthetic of the mid-century, both contributors suggest something of the wider – and longer – perspective that the book fails to achieve and that the *Companion* as originally envisaged would undoubtedly have provided.

Actors, directors, designers and editors can be said to 'do' Shakespeare, but what of the commentators, academic and otherwise, who observe the performances? What can – or should – they be doing? Rob Conkie's *Writing Performative Shakespeares. New Forms for Performance Criticism* challenges preconceptions in its very title by using a plural for the dramatist's name and indicating by 'performative' that the writing in question will be interventionist rather than passive. By bringing together 'the various spheres, materials, practices and discourses that are constitutive of Shakespearean theatrical meaning-making' Conkie (with a little help from his friends) seeks to demonstrate that 'such meanings are relative and constructive' (21). In some chapters this involves facilitating an enhanced form of dialogue among critics. Chapter 4, 'Graphic Shakespeare', convenes a round table discussion of the Toneelgroep *Roman Tragedies* and represents it in the form of a strip cartoon. In 'Engaging Shakespeare' Conkie's responses to a production are commented on by a group of fellow-Shakespeareans whose thoughts are registered in extensive marginalia. In this chapter the aim is to achieve an analysis of the ways 'an affective force of a Shakespearean performance – the way that Shakespearean production engages its audiences – is created by the confluence of a number of affective spheres'. These 'affects' are identified as those of the actor, the character, the narrative, the audience member's 'personal affect', and the 'performative affect' generated by 'the atmosphere specific to a production and other factors'. Taken together, these create 'the cumulative performative affect' (112). Conkie's 'attempts at creating a heteroglot criticism' (18), achieved by variations from the standard format and expository modes of academic writing as well as by engaging with other critics, are complemented by (and contribute to) challenges to conventional pedagogical and dramaturgical practice. 'Sudoku Shakespeare' (chapter 2) may not be an engaging prospect for everyone, but 'Red Button Shakespeare' (chapter 3) invokes to good effect the techniques offered by another spectatorial medium to examine the experience of viewing a Shakespeare's Globe production of *King Lear* from different positions and noting the responses of other audience members as well as his own. Chapters 5, 'Engaging Shakespeare', and 6, 'Ghosting Shakespeare', focus on two of the author's own productions: an 'original practices' *1 Henry IV* and an 'Indigeneity-focused reading of *Hamlet*' (134). Conkie's conclusion suggests that 'the writing of performative Shakespeares . . . generates performances in excess of the re-performance of the chosen productions' (155). Such excess is surely welcome.

Performances provide the armature of *Shakespeare in Ten Acts*, edited by Gordon McMullan and Zoë Wilcox, a lavishly illustrated accompaniment (rather than catalogue) for the British Library's 2016 exhibition of the same name Vivien Leigh, as Titania in Tyrone Guthrie's 1937 Old Vic production of *A Midsummer Night's Dream*, points with commanding and sexy glamour on the book's cover as she did in the exhibition's posters: an imperious and inviting alignment of 'Shakespeare' with magic. This is not a work of bland or nostalgic celebration. The contributors all achieve notable feats of expertly informed and accessible exposition, connecting the chosen performance events with wider contexts in the history of 'Shakespeare' – works, historical or imagined person, icon – in world culture. When Ian De Jong asserts that the performance of *Hamlet* at the Globe in 1600 'lit the fuse of a cultural bombshell whose shock waves still reverberate today' (25), the hyperbole seems appropriate to the occasion, and the cumulative effect of the ten chapters is to illustrate the myriad contradictions as well as the undoubted achievements of the Shakespeare phenomenon. After Eric Rasmussen's opening survey of the playwright's 'beginnings of a life in performance', the strategy is to focus on specific productions, such as Peter Brook's *Dream* in Peter Holland's chapter, or a related series of events, as in Kathryn Johnson and Greg Buzwell's account of the Ireland forgeries and the *Vortigern* fiasco (Chapter 5) and Judith Buchanan's '"Look here upon this picture": Theatrofilm, the Wooster group and the Film Industry' (Chapter 10). Gordon MacMullan takes *The Tempest* from the Blackfriars in 1611 to the ceremonies attending the London Olympics and Paralympics in 2012, concluding that 'For all the renegotiations of the play over the last century – political, sexual, colonial – the spectacular *Tempest* would seem to be alive and well' (61). The phenomenon of 'global' Shakespeare is aptly characterized by Sonia Massai in her description of a production of *The Merry Wives of Windsor* by the Theatre Company of Kenya in collaboration with Bitter Pill in the 2012 Globe to Globe Festival as 'a thoroughly intercultural, collaborative production within which Shakespeare became a globally recognisable, mobile and versatile resource or meeting point' (79). *Shakespeare in Ten Acts*, like the exhibition itself, displays both the plays and 'Shakespeare' as a transhistorical as well as transnational asset, from Shakespeare's own Globe Theatre to Shakespeare's Globe as it now stands on the south bank of the Thames. What is documented is effectively a centuries-long process of innovation, variously defined and not invariably welcomed but always stimulating and responsive to the pressure of the times. The white-box *Dream* in 1970 and *Twelfth Night* at the Middle Temple and the reconstructed Globe in 2002 share the quality that Farah

Karim-Cooper identifies in her account of the latter as experiments that were 'bold – in some ways, outrageously so' (189). The message is that Shakespeare is open for business, and that his status as a world dramatist is secure as an enabler rather than a monument.

The ways in which the performance media have helped to establish and at the same time co-opted this figure and, effectively, the Shakespeare brand are included in Paul Franssen's lively survey *Shakespeare's Literary Lives. The Author as Character in Fiction and Film*. Arguably the most influential fictional variation on the dramatist's career of recent years has been the film *Shakespeare in Love* (1999), and Franssen argues convincingly for the American emphasis in its orientation towards money as a signifier of success and acumen, a fanfare for the common playwright on the make in which 'social class is defined not in terms of birth but of money' (141). Most of Franssen's examples are drawn from literary and biographical sources, but treatments of the subject in cinema and television drama have predominated in creating the Shakespeare at the centre of the phenomenon dubbed 'Shakespop' by Douglas Lanier in *Shakespeare and Modern Popular Culture* (Oxford, 2002) and other publications. Franssen cites Lanier's diagnosis of a 'tension between reverence and resistance' in attitudes, which he identifies specifically in 'time travel' fictions, including the special episode of *Blackadder*, shown at the inauguration of London's 'Millenium Dome' (an expensive folly that was not for an age but for a limited time) in which the eponymous hero boards a time machine and is able to give Shakespeare a dressing down and a sound cuffing in revenge for the pain inflicted on him by the plays at school and even kicks him as recompense 'for Ken Branagh's four-hour endless uncut version of *Hamlet*' (232). Franssen's conclusion is that the varied conceptions of Shakespeare, are 'mostly rooted in deep convictions about life or art', and 'an index to the ways in which we use cultural icons to make sense of our lives, our ideals and fears, as individuals or collectively' (247). His assertion that 'Shakespeare may be disagreed with or debunked, but it is hard to ignore him' shows no anxiety regarding 'Shakespeare' as an instrument of an oppressive cultural and, by extension, social and political hegemony.

In *Shakespeare, Cinema, Counter-Culture*, Ailsa Grant Ferguson, far less sanguine about the uses to which the playwright is put, 'presents non-hegemonic and in any sense countercultural appropriation of Shakespeare's monolithic works as carnivalesque', while insisting that the 'monolithic' attribute is not so much inherent in the Shakespearean works themselves as constituted by the 'Western cultural hegemony'. On the contrary, 'the carnivalesque, the marginal, the oppositional and the counter-cultural' are 'fundamental' to Shakespeare's works as well as the appropriations studied (1–2). Mikhail Bakhtin's theory of carnival underpins her project, and the undertaking to 'uncrown dominant ideologies' is conducted through detailed and effective analysis of a series of productions, most of them self-evidently Shakespearean in their adoption of whole plays or elements of them, others less directly so. The films are not 'wisps of Shakespeare' from 'the depths of the film archives' (1), but with the possible exception of *The Filth and the Fury* (shades of *Richard III* in a 2000 documentary on the Sex Pistols) might be said to constitute a mainstream of the counter-cultural. This is certainly the case with *My Own Private Idaho* (dir. Gus Van Sant, 1991), *The King is Alive* (Kristian Levring, 2000), Michael Almereyda's *Hamlet* (2000) and the Finnish director Aki Kaurismaki's *Hamlet Liikemaailmassa* (*Hamlet Goes Business*, 1987). Chapter 4, 'Festivity and Sedition', begins with a discussion of *Festen* (*The Celebration*, dir. Thomas Vinterberg, 1998). This was the first production under the Danish group Dogme 95's 'charter', which itself counters the cult of the auteur and other manifestations of 'mainstream' film-making, including production and post-production techniques. *Festen*'s central character, Christian, is 'presented as a returning son, horrified by both his parents' behaviour, vengeful, grieving, haunted (both literally it would seem, and metaphysically) and ambiguously presenting "an antic disposition"' (108). Christian certainly has more than a smack of Hamlet in him, though beyond that the film's structure – the prolonged sixtieth birthday party of the patriarch of an extended family, assembled in a hotel he owns – does not reflect *Hamlet* beyond sharing the somewhat strained festive spirit of the opening of the play's second scene. In some respects the film resembles an Alan Ayckbourn play of family betrayals and frustrations, but with added incest and minimized comedy. (The hapless toastmaster who has to call the guests to order for the speech-making and the pianist who has to keep playing for dancing despite the mayhem seem distinctly Ayckbournian.) The punctuation of the meal by accumulating accusations of incestuous rape on the part of the father and complicity on the part of the mother give the film its momentum, and the suicide of one of Christian's sisters is the principal Ophelia-like dimension in a film that the director (according to an interview with the publicist in a DVD extra) thought of calling *The Blood of the Bourgeoisie*, a title rejected as too reminiscent of Luis Buñuel – presumably the title of *The Discreet Charm of the Bourgeoisie* (1972), though the dinner party in *The Exterminating Angel* (1962) offers a parallel for the plot.[1] *Festen*'s Hamlet-ish protagonist is a sympathetic avenger, whereas *Hamlet Goes Business* transforms Shakespeare's 'vengeful, contemplative prince' into 'a patricidal megalomaniac, who appears to have neither a discernible conscience nor any particular anxiety around his own mortality' (102). Kaurismaki's louche Hamlet seeks to govern the industrial concern his uncle has 'usurped' by taking advantage of the poisoning that (it transpires) he himself has carried out, and his own death is at the hands of the forces of social revolution represented by his chauffeur and a maid on behalf of the worker's union. Almereyda's film, closer to the play in many respects, shares with it the oppositional stance of a 'prince' towards a usurper, but here Hamlet's own counter-cultural lifestyle makes it unlikely that he wants to be CEO of the 'Denmark Corporation'. These variations on *Hamlet* are representative of the variety and force of the counter-cultural approaches examined in the other chapters.

Whilst *Shakespeare, Cinema, Counter-Culture* addresses itself to films outside the mainstream, *Queering the Shakespeare Film* by Anthony Guy Patricia deals with mainstream films. These are examined from the perspective of queer theory, not in the spirit of 'outing' directors who may or may not be themselves homosexual, but rather of identifying the ways, not always explicit, in which important dimensions of the plays are represented in films that, at least on the surface, accept heterosexual union as the 'gold standard'. This is a generous, provocative study that enriches rather than limits the reader's subsequent re-viewings. Patricia does not pull his punches but the assertiveness is always earned and the provocation enriches the effect of the films. 'Under the pressure of critical interpretation' he claims in the Conclusion, 'queerness reveals itself' in the 1935 *Midsummer Night's Dream*, directed by Max Reinhardt and William Dieterle, 'through misogyny, gender trouble, bigamy, implied incest and bestiality and male effeminacy' (213). In the chapter discussing the film in detail he makes an important distinction regarding the film's engagement with 'four signifying registers' of queerness, 'gender, sodomy, marriage and masculinity, all of which, in this instance at least, have nothing to do with genital homosexuality *per se* in any form' (3).

The credentials of MGM's 1936 *Romeo and Juliet* are, he points out, attested by the known homosexuality of George Cukor and the designer Oliver Messel and reinforced by the gay playwright and composer – though arguments for the influence of Tchaikovsky's love-life are somewhat tenuous. In the case of *Romeo and Juliet* much is made of the influence of the mature male principals cast alongside Leslie Howard's Romeo and the effect of the form-fitting tights they wear. One might note that beyond the immediate circle of Romeo and Benvolio, Cukor is able to festoon the background with plenty of attractive younger men in similar outfits. The 'latent queer spirit' in these

---

[1] *Festen*, 10th anniversary edn, DVD (Metrodome Distribution Ltd, 2008).

Hollywood films (Patricia suggests) 'only wanted for the kind of sensitive, informed and enlightening reading done by Richard Burt nearly two decades ago' (213). There is a lot to be said for this kind of reading against the grain, and Patricia's queer eye for the ostensibly straight film offers insights into the sheer oddity of much in the 1935 *Dream* and the incongruously effeminate behaviour of John Barrymore's Mercutio in Cukor's film, where he does indeed come across as 'a gay man with a large coterie of devoted female followers – a bevy of "fag hags" to put it more colloquially – rather than a randy, red-blooded, heterosexual playboy eager to conquer the opposite sex with his amorous prowess' (52). The analyses of Zeffirelli's 1968 *Romeo and Juliet* and Luhrmann's 1996 version are acute and persuasive, and Patricia argues convincingly that the latter steers away from the potential for a homosexual interpretation of the Romeo–Mercutio relationship. Throughout the governing approach is that of a queer spectator, itself a persuasive correction to assumptions of a hegemonic heterosexuality in the viewing as well as making of the films. Patricia's response to the ending of Trevor Nunn's *Twelfth Night* is a case in point: 'when Nunn shows Antonio stalking away – alone – from Olivia's estate into the cold gray twilight, queer viewers of the movie and their allies have every right to feel betrayed and with a similar longing [to Antonio's] for what could have – indeed should have, been' (176). It should be noted that many stage productions have inflected the Orsino/Cesario and Antonio/Sebastian relationships in a decisively queer fashion. One outstanding example was Cheek by Jowl's *Twelfth Night* (1987) in which Orsino's attraction to the disguised Cesario was unequivocal. As for Sebastian, Antonio's 'In the south suburbs at the Elephant / Is best to lodge . . . There you shall have me' (3.1.39–40; 42) was an unambiguous invitation, and in the concluding scene he was paired off with Feste for their own happy ending. But such comparisons, which would have lengthened Patricia's book unmanageably, might be useful in this context simply as a reminder of the limitations of 'mainstream' cinema as against the freedoms of the stage. *Queering the Shakespeare Film* is a telling account of the ways in which, like the enterprising inhabitants of Kansas City as reported in *Oklahoma!*, filmmakers have gone just about as far as they can go.

WORKS REVIEWED

Brown, John Russell and Stephen Di Benedetto, eds., *Designers' Shakespeare* (Abingdon and New York, 2016)

Conkie, Rob, *Writing Performative Shakespeares. New Forms for Performance Criticism* (Cambridge, 2016)

Franssen, Paul, *Shakespeare's Literary Lives. The Author as Character in Fiction and Film* (Cambridge, 2016)

Grant Ferguson, Ailsa, *Shakespeare, Cinema, Counter-Culture. Appropriation and Inversion* (New York and Abingdon, 2016)

Loomis, Catherine and Sid Ray, eds., *Shaping Shakespeare for Performance. The Bear Stage* (Madison and Teaneck, NJ, 2016)

McMullan, Gordon and Zoë Wilcox, eds., *Shakespeare in Ten Acts* (London, 2016)

Ney, Charles, ed., *Directing Shakespeare in America. Current Practices* (London and New York, 2016)

Patricia, Anthony Guy, *Queering the Shakespeare Film. Gender Trouble, Gay Spectatorship and Male Homoeroticism* (London and New York, 2017)

Pennington, Michael, *King Lear in Brooklyn* (London, 2016)

Sher, Anthony, *Year of the Fat Knight. The Falstaff Diaries* (London, 2015)

Smith, Bruce R., *Shakespeare | Cut, Rethinking Cutwork in an Age of Distraction* (Oxford, 2016)

4. EDITIONS AND TEXTUAL STUDIES
reviewed by PETER KIRWAN

COMPLETE WORKS

The most telling difference between the print versions of the second and third editions of *The Norton Shakespeare* is the disappearance of the legend 'Based on the Oxford Edition' from its privileged place between 'Norton' and 'Shakespeare' on both front cover and spine. The parting of the ways was marked in 2016 by the appearance of the third edition of *The Norton Shakespeare* and of *The New Oxford Shakespeare* (NOS), both 'born digital' but with an accompanying, traditionally presented print volume of the 'complete works'. The NOS will be reviewed in the next volume once all of its constituent parts have been released, and it will be fascinating to see how the two projects diverge as both investigate the possibilities of simultaneous electronic and print publication.

Norton 3 is an odd combination of new and old, and indeed the casual purchaser of the print volume may be surprised at the similarities. The general introduction and individual play introductions by Walter Cohen, Stephen Greenblatt, Jean E. Howard and Katharine Eisaman Maus remain in place with relatively light revision (though helpfully updated bibliographies), and the presentation and organization of the texts and appendices is substantially unchanged. The major new features of the print edition – a general textual introduction by Gordon McMullan and Suzanne Gossett, Holger Schott Syme's new introduction to Shakespeare's theatre, and the individual textual introductions to each play – are in many respects additions to rather than revisions of the older work.

In the most substantially revised section of his general introduction, Greenblatt reassures the reader that '[a]bandoning the dream of direct access to Shakespeare's final and definitive intentions is not a cause for despair, nor should it lead us to throw our hands up and declare that one text is as good as another. What it does is to encourage us to be actively interested in the editorial principles that underlie the particular edition that we are using' (73). While the edition's retention of the basic layout of the second edition does not intuitively help with this aim, the new General Textual Introduction that follows is a highlight, offering a cogent practical and theoretical defence of the edition's practice of 'single-text editing', and Greenblatt's evocation and acceptance of the anxiety of a lack of a definitive text acts as an effective passing of the baton to the waiting hands of McMullan and Gossett.

Where Greenblatt still wants to meet Shakespeare (74), McMullan and Gossett offer a Derridean displacement of the author in a student-friendly introduction to the basic theory of single-text editing. Throughout, they argue '[o]ur underlying editorial principle has been, at its simplest, to edit the *text*, not the *work*' (85). This edition marks the logical culmination of recent interest in multitext editing by offering the largest number of edited variant texts yet to appear in a Complete Works volume, including four *Hamlet*s, three *King Lear*s and neglected quarto versions of several other plays. While the edition still implies a hierarchy of texts (in most cases, only one text is included in the print version), it provides an extraordinary resource for classroom use by delivering clean, edited variant versions that will make basic questions of textual difference accessible to less experienced users. Further, despite the emphasis on materiality in the textual introduction, the editors are not editing the *book*; for those interested in original orthography and layout, full facsimiles are incorporated into the digital edition. The general principle is to emend the base text only where sense or clarity is at stake, and McMullan and Gossett illustrate this with well-chosen examples of instances where early variant texts provide equally viable alternatives (88–91);

these pages alone will be a fine resource for instructors introducing students to the basics of this conversation.

Of course, even such an impressive display of variety cannot be complete. Line Cottegnies offers an efficient summary of the complexity of the early texts of *2 Henry IV*, for instance, but nowhere does the volume explore the possibility that it could theoretically have included another text representing the first issue of the quarto, so that readers could encounter a version of the play that lacks 3.1. The point is pedantic, but makes McMullan and Gossett's assertions of productive uncertainty (variants of the phrase 'we cannot know' permeate their introduction) all the more important. The edition curates modern editorial interpretations of specific iterations of substantially variant texts, with an eye on student use; it does this effectively, but this should not be mistaken for completeness.

The biggest surprise is that, while the texts are freshly edited, the glosses and textual notes are essentially unchanged. To take a representative example, Matthew Dimmock's text of *2 Henry VI* 1.1 retains verbatim twenty of Jean Howard's footnotes from the second edition and sixty-seven of her marginal glosses. He deletes only three footnotes and a handful of glosses that no longer apply to his text, alters a final footnote to the opening stage direction and adds two glosses ('fully provided' for 'replete' and 'prostitutes' for 'courtesans'). While this was no doubt more efficient than beginning the work of commentary and glossing from scratch unnecessarily, it has the effect of rendering the work of the new editors largely invisible; the vast majority of visible signs of editorial work are made by Howard, not Dimmock. Given that the USP of this edition is its new approach to the edited text, it is a shame that the edition so rarely draws attention to the unusual or interesting readings this approach offers, or justifies those moments where editors depart from their copy text. For instance, Lois Potter follows the majority of modern editors of *Pericles* in rendering lines 5 and 6 of the Prologue thus: 'It hath been sung at festivals, / On ember eves and holy ales', and glosses 'holy ales' as 'country festivals'. Yet the quarto's 'Holydayes', while not fitting with the speech's rhyme scheme, is not an error of sense. I don't dispute Potter's choice of preferred reading here, but it is an important reminder that this edition is still an *edition*, its editors making choices of preference even when the copy-text offers a plausible reading. While the readings of the copy-text are preserved in the accompanying facsimiles in the electronic version, the paucity of new textual notes is disappointing.

While the lack of fuller justification for choices is a shame, the focus on a handful of textual issues for each play does provide focus. Clare McManus, for instance, includes ten textual comments for the Folio text of *Othello*, including discussion of the use of 'Moor' in stage directions, the implications of who speaks 2.1.112, 'Oh fie upon thee, slanderer!', and the Indian/Judean textual crux at 5.2.340. These appear as long notes in the digital edition. Here, and throughout, the editors are judicious in selecting textual moments with significant interpretative significance. The accompanying textual introductions (identical in both the print and the electronic versions of the edition) are uniformly efficient, using their brief space to summarize the print history of the play, significant variant versions, and idiosyncrasies of the copy text(s). McManus, for instance, continues the interest of the textual notes in Desdemona by using her introduction to focus on the differences caused in that character's presentation by both major changes (the presence or absence of the willow song) and minor differences (the Folio's 'world of kisses' versus the Quarto's 'world of sighs').

For an edition that is 'born digital' (84), the look and feel of the digital interface owes a lot to print. Each section (e.g. 'Textual Introduction', 'Act One', 'Performance Notes') exists as a separate page, and there is surprisingly little hyperlinking, although a left-hand bar allows for convenient navigation between the sections. The interface is sometimes deeply frustrating, however. Plays are presented with one act to a page, but textual comments appear at the top; so, when reading the Folio version of *Hamlet*, the reader who clicks on the textual note at 1.5.153–4 has to scroll back up to *Act One Scene One* to view the note, then find their own way back to their original place. Given the volume of marginal white space, there is no obvious reason why the note should not appear in place; as, indeed, is the case with the glosses. These are indicated with optional underlining, and the gloss/note appears in a small comment bubble immediately above the glossed text (and remains visible even if the reader clicks on another window). The longer textual and performance notes are also available as lists, and the reader wishing to consult them can at least have them open in a separate window.

The electronic version includes several other features, some better realized than others. As a pleasing nod to accessibility there is a 'read aloud' function, although the electronic voice annoyingly pauses at the end of each line regardless of continuity or sense. The 'Documents' section includes a large selection of early modern materials with helpful glossing (although it would have been even more helpful to, say, link directly from *The Return to Parnassus* to the relevant passages in *Venus and Adonis*). The maps and images are well rendered, and the genealogies, while not interactive, can at least be manipulated and zoomed in on. Much more successful are the in-text resources, such as recordings of songs, including 'Roses, their sharp spines' alongside the song's appearance at the start of *The Two Noble Kinsmen*. A lot of thought has gone into presenting the quarto and folio facsimiles, which appear as individual pages at the appropriate location in the edited text (and again, with an easy-to-use zoom function). Making the facsimiles so easily accessible and navigable will be an enormous aid to increasing their use in the classroom. Another useful teaching resource is a selection of eight sets of comparative scenes between variant versions, allowing immediate visual access to, say, the effect of the omission of the willow song from the folio text of *Othello*, or comparison of Sonnets 138 and 144 with their equivalents in *The Passionate Pilgrim*. While the examples are limited – and hopefully, future editions will allow users to create their own comparative scenes – they stand as a fine example of the best of what the edition has to offer in privileging different versions of the text. Further basic interactive features allow students and teachers to annotate their texts.

The other substantial set of new contributions, by Syme and Brett Gamboa, relates to historical and contemporary theatre practice. Syme's 'The Theater of Shakespeare's Time' replaces Andrew Gurr's *Norton 2* essay entirely, and shares methodological ground with McMullan and Gossett's essay in acknowledging lack of certainty and disrupting older assumed narratives such as the existence of a duopoly (99). His emphasis on the importance of sharers, the uniqueness of Shakespeare's company's business model, and the role of the trade guild system, all contribute to a rich understanding of the material conditions of the theatre for which Shakespeare wrote, and the discussion of rehearsal and acting practices is refreshing. Syme navigates source material adroitly to articulate the complex (to modern sensibilities) notion that the early modern spectator can both acknowledge artificiality and yet be affected by the performance of boy players (111), and he is particularly strong in anticipating the assumptions of the contemporary student reader (e.g. about modern notions of character) and carefully addressing these with historical re-contextualization.

Gamboa contributes a two-to-three paragraph 'Performance Note' to each introduction. These notes are dramaturgical rather than historical, usually summarizing what 'some directors' rather than specific productions do. Instead, he sets up either/or binaries for how characters and plot elements might be played (the rhetorical strategy does not imply that these are the only options), which hammer home the point that meaning is never fixed. Gamboa handles these well, offering important points for directors such as the warning that 'Each of [*The Merchant of Venice*'s] first six scenes initiates a new subplot featuring a new character' (1338). In the digital edition Gamboa is able to get into much more detail, with highlights including an extended discussion of the implications for characterization of the modern tendency to cut 2.7.79 from *The Merchant of Venice* (Portia's 'Let all of his complexion choose me so') and discussion in the same play of the National Theatre's 1973 handling of 4.1.172, where Portia's question 'Which is the merchant here and which the Jew?' was played sincerely, underscoring a genuine likeness between the two enemies.

Norton 3 is an ambitious and largely successful project let down somewhat by the tentativeness with which it breaks from its predecessor. By leaving the introduction and notes of the *Norton 2* editors in their privileged place, the edition squanders its potential to demonstrate the distinctiveness of single-text editing and the new work done by the textual editors, and in some cases (such as the substantially revised chronology) there is no explanation of the new edition's reasoning (other than that it is 'based on current understanding of the evidence' ('Timeline'). It is also a shame that the electronic version does not take more advantage of the medium in relation to connectivity. But the wealth of resource available here, and in particular the navigability and presentation of variant texts and facsimiles, will make this an important intervention in the teaching of Shakespeare's texts.

SINGLE-TEXT EDITIONS

Internet Shakespeare Editions's commendable practice of posting material in stages can make it difficult to pick the best moment to review a new edition, but Jessica Slights's *Othello* has now been peer-reviewed and is functionally complete. Her lively introduction stresses the affective qualities of the play, its power deriving 'in part from its disconcerting insistence on both the participation and the impotence of its audience' (Introduction 2). The introduction is rather too insistent on homogeneous audience response and collective language ('Iago fascinates us', 'We are left to watch with increasing revulsion', Introduction 4), employing coercive tactics uncomfortably reminiscent of Iago's own. More effective are discussions of the dangers that Venice's martial ethos poses to women (10), the elasticity of the term 'Moor' (13–16) and the play's insistence that 'narrative control is always contingent' (25).

Her critical history gives a brief sketch of historical approaches to the play, particularly noting the prominence of character criticism. Slights's investment in critical approaches both to and by women prompts fascinating focus on early readings of Desdemona as the tragedy's central figure, a woman 'whose dominant features – her goodness and gentleness – are both beyond her control and adequate to ensure her survival' (A Survey of Criticism, 7). The survey is strongest in its sketch of the development of approaches influenced by the American civil rights movement and the ensuing conflict between historicized cultural approaches to race and the universalizing tendency that was the legacy of A. C. Bradley (13). A subsequent section on 'A History of Performance' bizarrely devotes almost half its length to the play on film while cramming all mentions of twentieth- and twenty-first-century productions into two short paragraphs; the survey here is too brief, though it is somewhat compensated for by the ongoing compilation of performances in the accompanying database. At the time of writing, the database for *Othello* is overwhelmingly dominated by North American productions, but this will hopefully develop further.

A very brief textual introduction outlines Slights's view that the Folio offers 'deliberate additions to an earlier, less complete text from which Q1 was derived', and she thus bases her text on F with certain readings incorporated from Q1 and occasionally Q2 (Textual Introduction 3). The edition presents several interesting variations on standard practice. Desdemona's statement that Barbary 'had a "Song of Willow"' (4.3.2998), for instance, creates a much more emphatic introduction to the song. The eclectic annotations cover a broad range of potential interests. The start of 5.2, for instance, includes a substantial description of Orson Welles's 'incantatory repetition' of 'Put out the light' to start his final scene (3256 n); discussion of entrances in/on beds as not unusual for the period (3239 n); and explanations of mythical and religious allusions as well as standard glossing. Her note on 3266 ('Have you prayed tonight, Desdemon?') is particularly interesting in its citation of the actorly tradition of emphasizing the 'trochaic rhythms of this line as a means of drawing attention to the demonic play on words within Desdemona's name' (3266 n).

Arden 3.5 has upped its pace of delivery, with four new updated editions. Three of these – Claire McEachern's *Much Ado about Nothing*, Ann Thompson and Neil Taylor's *Hamlet* and David Bevington's *Troilus and Cressida* – make only modest additions to the introduction, as well as offering attractive new cover art. McEachern concentrates on Joss Whedon's 2012 film and considers a selection of other recent productions (helpfully prioritizing those available on DVD). She notes that recent performances have tended towards the darker elements of the play, 'particularly the sinister sides of militarism and male bonding' (154). The remainder of the new material is a short essay on Elizabethan understandings of cuckolds, particularly the visual tradition of Moses as a horned man, which she suggests may help editors gloss the reference to the Priests of Bel at 3.3.129–31 (179).

Thompson and Taylor provide a full survey of new criticism. The editors favour coverage, referencing debates while remaining themselves agnostic about their implications. Their most important section is an extended discussion of new developments in textual scholarship of *Hamlet*. The editors modestly acknowledge their own influence by cataloguing the various responses to it, and provide collegial space for the complaints of Paul Werstine and Gabriel Egan about their choices. Several of Egan's proposed new readings are listed, though not incorporated into the text (154). A final section on performance covers a range of global productions, though limited largely to what the authors were themselves able to see in London.

Bevington, like McEachern, concentrates on performance history, arguing that the play's 'existential bleakness and its candour now seemed admirably suited to a modern world of disillusionment about sexuality, about war, about human relationships' (125). The survey of recent productions is impressively international, and he notes that many have found an interest in 'the resistance of native and minority peoples to imperialist domination' (126). Unlike McEachern, Bevington attempts to summarize the trends in recent scholarship, offering a survey of approaches considering *Troilus and Cressida* in the context of the 'Poets' War', and perhaps most helpfully demonstrates how recent approaches have opened up the issue of the play's treatment of sexual identity and homosocial relations (139–40).

Owners of the original editions of the above volumes will decide for themselves whether the additional twenty pages in each are worth a second purchase, but Ayanna Thompson's revision of the late E. A. J. Honigmann's *Othello* is of another order. While the text, commentary, longer notes and appendices are all unchanged, Honigmann's introduction is entirely replaced with Thompson's new, 166-page introduction. Thompson avoids tampering with Honigmann's text even when she disagrees with his choices; as she notes, there is 'no textual evidence' to support Honigmann's re-assignment of 'This Lodovico is a proper man' from Desdemona to Emilia (47). Instead, she provides a new set of framing contexts for *Othello* that engage in productive conversation with Honigmann's textual choices. She foregrounds her own agency in framing the play: 'inviting you to imagine if, when and how different readers and audience members were affected by these histories, contexts and performances' (5).

Thompson is particularly attuned to the play's treatment of sex and race, and the ways in which these topics are addressed by the play's interpreters. Much of the introduction is devoted to stage histories and new writing but, rather than merely recounting histories, she navigates the thorny issues raised in performance. Her important section on 'Black Actors, White Actresses' (84–96) confronts the very different attitudes that black actors have held towards the title role – from the opportunity that James Hewlett and Ira Aldridge took to present 'a powerful, proud and strong black man' (85) to Hugh Quarshie's belief that the play Shakespeare wrote is irredeemably racist (87–9) to the millennial tendency to argue that the play is not about race at all (90) – and places these alongside the shifts in representations of Desdemona from a virtuous but passive romantic victim to a resistant woman in the mid-twentieth century, and then recently to treatments that emphasize her youth and inexperience.

Thompson's approach reinvigorates the introduction as neither survey nor history but as an engaged, conflicting set of responses to a play itself in conflict. Where she offers a more linear history of reception, she offers counterpoints (Antony Sher's anger with Coleridge's influential claims for Iago's 'motiveless malignity' (58), for instance). This multifaceted view is most important in the repeated turn to the question of race, which recurs as she unpacks new work on cosmetics and prostheses (28), the transatlantic differences in critical responses to Olivier's blackface Othello (82) and the rewriting of Othello as everything from minstrel show to indictment of intercultural murder, and her interest in bodies and sex also delves into areas underexplored by Honigmann, such as the pornographic loadings of the handkerchief and its symbolic function standing in for Othello and Desdemona's blood-soaked sheets (51).

James C. Bulman's new Arden edition of *King Henry IV, Part 2* trails David Scott Kastan's edition of *Part One* by some fourteen years, but this is to the advantage of an edition whose agenda is to consider *Part Two* as an independent play. For Bulman, this is 'Shakespeare's most radical experiment in dramatizing English history', offering 'a panorama of an England unrecorded by chroniclers' (2). Bulman confronts head-on the play's difficulties in being 'second-born' and makes a case instead for the play's unique features, making this a consistently surprising and refreshing edition.

Bulman's comprehensive textual appendix summarizes the difficulties of establishing a text 'that might reasonably accord with what was performed by Shakespeare's company in 1597' (432) given the lack of a 'fully authoritative' text. Bulman begins by countering the long-standing assumption that the quarto (Qa) was based on an uncorrected authorial draft. Influenced by the work of Paul Werstine and William B. Long, he argues persuasively that the idiosyncratic features of the quarto (ghost characters, variant spellings and speech prefixes, permissive stage directions etc.) are not untypical of early playbooks that have undergone theatrical annotation, and as such he treats Qa as a text prepared for performance. The narrative is complicated by the second issue (Qb) of the quarto, the first to include 3.1 (the King's first appearance). Bulman offers the common-sense argument that the scene had been misplaced rather than censored, perhaps halfway through the original printing (442), and analyses the errors introduced by the compositor when undertaking the re-setting necessary to accommodate it. Given that the compositor was almost certainly responsible for Qa as well as Qb, Bulman notes the need to be wary of his work (448).

Bulman incorporates the eight additional passages from the Folio and other small changes into the body of his text, marking Folio-only material with superscript 'F'. The visual markers of interpolated material are a helpful reminder throughout of the extent of conflation, although Bulman chooses to follow and gloss Q wherever possible rather than emend. He is unpersuaded by arguments that the additional passages in the Folio are later additions with an eye on the larger cycle, and he prefers the counter-argument that the sense and metre of Q requires at least seven of the eight (449–51). Bulman thus views the Folio's passages as cut scenes, suggesting that they might have been part of an early attempt to make the play (one of the longest in the canon) a suitable length for performance. In this, he casts the Folio text of *2 Henry IV* as a 'literary' version in the sense championed by Lukas Erne, arguing that the standardization of speech prefixes and stage directions, the fuller entrance and exit directions and the clarification of 'permissive' directions are typical of a text prepared for readership, as opposed to the playhouse (460).

Yet despite the care taken in the preparation of the Folio text, Bulman offers two compelling reasons for not adopting it as his own copy-text. The first is the effect of standardization on the regional and colloquial language of the play (458).

A substantial part of the introduction (54–99) is devoted to 'Falstaff and his Friends', and much of this considers the effect of the diverse and contrarian voices that *Part Two* privileges: for instance, the 'riotously original' malapropisms and double entendres of the Hostess that associate her social aspirations and current employment with the wider social upheaval of England (77). Bulman argues that the oral memories of Shallow and Silence 'resist incorporation into the play's dramatization of dynastic struggle in England's Plantagenet past' (83), and that the tragic irony building up to Falstaff's rejection by Henry V brings a tonal harshness that emphasizes the silencing of yet another dissident voice. Bulman concludes that 'if the play ends with a repressive assertion of hegemonic order, nevertheless those voices have been heard, and heard memorably' (99). These critical observations justify Bulman's choice to retain the idiosyncrasies of Q. The Folio text is also compromised by misjudgements in the casting off of the text, and Bulman provides an excellent set of illustrated examples from sig. G2^r that show the compositor's radical cutting and editing in order to compress the text into the available space (472–4).

The introduction wrestles throughout with the spectre of *Part One*, and Bulman advances his own theory 'that the original *Henry IV* play was always planned to end with the Battle of Shrewsbury, and that its sequel – perhaps to be called *Henry V* – was to have begun with events now dramatized in the last act and one-half of *Part Two* and continued through the reign of Henry V' (15). Yet rather than consider this opportunism, Bulman feels that this means Shakespeare 'was liberated to write a more original play' (16). The villain in Bulman's story is E. M. W. Tillyard. *Part Two* was performed for centuries as either a stand-alone chronicle history on its own merits or (in a cut version) as a comedy star vehicle for Falstaff (24). It was in the early twentieth century, following Tillyard's foregrounding of *bildungsroman* as the central tissue of the *Henry* plays, that it began to be performed 'only to justify the political imperatives of what had come to be known as the second tetralogy' (34). For Bulman, this is a betrayal of the play's 'subversive intent' (5) in which its parallels with *Part One* undermine chivalric and heroic values. As part of a cycle, productions of *Part Two* have – both consciously and unwittingly – allowed individuals to be overpowered by the mechanics of history, and Falstaff has been moved to the margins, his unbalancing carnivalesque potential restrained in favour of a 'disturbing pathology' (45). The performance history is supplemented by a substantial appendix (478–504) that shows how little of *Part Two* has historically survived in performances of conflated versions of *Henry IV*, always retaining scenes from the end of the play and thus contributing to the suppression of the alternative, subversive voices that Bulman feels constitute the primary value of *Part Two*.

The annotations are dense, owing to Bulman's preference for glossing over emendation. A long footnote to 3.2.312, for instance, justifies the retention of 'invincible' rather than emending to 'invisible' by arguing that 'invincible' can indeed mean 'invisible', and the note on punctuation at 1.1.83 records Bulman's preference for an emendation by Capell while retaining the justifiable arrangement of Q and F; yet both notes are mistakenly asterisked as emendations. The footnotes largely ignore performance history, concentrating instead on explicating the complex prose of the comic scenes and analysing the political subtexts of the chronicle history plot. One of the more interesting decisions is Bulman's retention of prose for Pistol's comic rehashing of Marlovian verse in 2.4; while many editions reset this as verse, Bulman justifies the prose as 'theatrical imposture ... misremembered scraps of unfashionable plays' (2.4.157–200 n). The prose visually preserves Pistol's confused blustering and the 'absurdly eclectic hodgepodge', and is in keeping with Bulman's strategy of preserving idiosyncrasies of the quarto where they offer insight into the distinctive voice of characters.

The interpolations from the Folio are accompanied by helpful explication of Bulman's rationale for their incorporation, and Bulman also does helpful work in clarifying entrances and exits, although I am less persuaded than he that a mass entry for the recruits in Gloucestershire (3.2), as specified in

F, would be less effective than entering individually as they are called, as he prefers; this seems to me to mute the comic potential of the silent community of waiting recruits. But here, as elsewhere, Bulman shows himself sensitive to the political, theatrical and subversive qualities of a play recast here as Shakespeare's most experimental engagement with history.

THE SHAKESPEAREAN BOOK TRADE AFTER SHAKESPEARE

A distinctive highlight of the last year has been the wealth of new work on Shakespeare's posthumous book trade. In particular, this has been a vintage year for those invested in the niche but expanding subgenre of 'Books about the First Folio by Emma Smith', with no fewer than three appearing, all with different audiences in mind.

The purpose of the first, *The Making of Shakespeare's First Folio*, is to introduce the processes that created the First Folio to a broader non-specialist audience, and in doing so it serves as a useful introduction to early modern book production. Smith's interest is in juxtaposing the role of the book in stressing the 'singularity' of Shakespeare (85) with a material history that renders it 'the product of a number of very specific social, cultural and commercial contexts, and of numerous individuals with different skills and different agendas' (2). The monograph thus serves both as a beginner's introduction to the circumstances and contingencies that resulted in the creation of the book and as a critical analysis of the effect of the Folio's choices on the presentation of the works and their author, and it covers a great deal of ground in a relatively small space.

Shakespeare's First Folio: Four Centuries of an Iconic Book picks up precisely where the previous book finishes, covering the afterlife of the Folio(s); or 'where traditional biography starts – with the emergence of its subject into the world' (18). Her first chapter traces the Folio's history from practical reading matter to secular relic. Smith uses a series of case studies of the movements of individual copies of the Folio to illustrate 'some of the ways that Folios follow money' (87), from stories of the public crowdfunding needed to buy back the Bodleian's stolen copy in the early twentieth century, to the pathologizing of Henry and Emily Folger's habits of collection. The history inevitably tends towards the elite but this is countered somewhat in Chapter Two in Smith's account of marginalia in extant copies as an index to early reading practices, and she again recognizes the value of the idiosyncratic example here (including diligently noting which two copies retain the pawprints of cats, and what plays they have walked across, 122).

Smith conducted her work independently of that undertaken by Eric Rasmussen and Anthony James West in their 2012 *The Shakespeare First Folios: A Descriptive Catalogue* (although conveniently uses their cataloguing system) but her project is indicative rather than comprehensive. Smith shows great empathy for individual reader response rather than overarching critical claims, and converges with the work of Sonia Massai as she moves on to manuscript corrections of errors in Folio copies, although even here is keen to stress that these show 'intermittent engagement' (154) rather than systematic practice. The third chapter takes this further by showing that, even for the earliest professional editors, having a copy of the First Folio 'seems to have been more an editorial talisman than a research resource' (194), and Smith shows how the Folio only gradually accrued its value for editors. Her juxtaposition of two key uses of the Folio – Charlton Hinman's 1963 *The Printing and Proof-Reading of the First Folio of Shakespeare* and Ignatius Donnelly's 1888 *The Great Cryptogram* – is particularly instructive as both, despite their radically different agendas, 'identify the main interest of the First Folio in its apparently accidental, even chaotic, features of type and layout, and for both, these random-seeming elements rearrange themselves into meaningful, human patterns' (215).

The talismanic use of the Folio recurs in Chapter Four in the tendency of early actors and theatre-managers to own for symbolic value, rather than use, copies of the First Folio. Smith notes that the tendency to treat the orthography, punctuation and layout of the Folio as a code to speaking the lines is a very recent trend, emerging from 1877 onwards (267) but exploding in the 1990s. The arguments for the Folio preserving actorly orthography are in direct competition with the work of analytical bibliographers, and Smith astutely pairs the theatrical associations of the Folio with the investment in it as an object that holds secrets (274). The final chapter draws on the more recent emphasis on individual copies of the Folio as unique to raise the spectre of a 'perfect' First Folio. Smith argues that the rhetoric of 'perfect' and 'pure' has pervaded the Folio's commercial history, and the elite history re-emerges here as assumptions about the 'best' copy residing in particular libraries or belonging to aristocratic owners clash with the claims of dealers for the superiority of their own copies.

The book concludes with warnings of overvaluing the Folio and over-determining its history, sober conclusions shared in Adam Hooks's afterword to Smith's *The Cambridge Companion to Shakespeare's First Folio*. Hooks identifies 'foliolatry' as a tendency that 'does violence' to the memory of Shakespeare (195) by occluding the work of so many others and mistaking a flawed but fetishized object for the real object of study. Hooks's sceptical but sensitive attitude towards the confusion of book and man underpins his excellent monograph *Selling Shakespeare*, of which more below.

As a contributor to *The Cambridge Companion* myself, I glance only briefly at it here. As the third pillar of Smith's re-envisioning of the Folio, it addresses the question 'what can we *do* with the Folio?' Smith's own contribution is a fine complement to the first chapter of her *Making Of*, giving a brief overview of some of the ways in which a readerly engagement with the Folio itself – confronting such unfamiliar instances as Juliet's 'What? in a names that which we call a Rose' – can provoke productive fresh engagements with the plays. Elsewhere, the volume offers short, accessible essays on individual aspects of the Folio's production (Eric Rasmussen, B. D. R. Higgins and Gabriel Egan on the publishing, printing and provenance of the Folio) and reception (Jean-Christophe Mayer, Edmund King and Steven Galbraith respectively on early buyers and readers, editors and collectors), and Sarah Werner's introduction to digital editions of the Folio is a particularly useful guide to the importance of metadata and the practical opportunities and constraints of digitization.

The cumulative effect of Smith's three First Folio publications is to foreground the role of books in determining legacy. Hooks, in *Selling Shakespeare*, offers a 'bio-bibliography' (1) in place of Smith's 'biblio-biography', a life through books, rather than the life of a book, but is invested in a similar project of aligning and separating out the idea of an author from the physical circulation of books. He attends to 'the reputation and authorial personae created, bought, and sold by the early modern book trade' (3), and ambitiously offers this as a new kind of biographical investigation and historicist criticism that reveals 'how our ideas of Shakespearean authorship ... came into being as commercial, conceptual, and critical categories' (4).

Hooks's book is refreshing for its carefully contextualized appreciation of the unsung and derided efforts of early biographers and bibliographers who do not fit conveniently into the patterns expected by modern biographers. Figures such as Thomas Fuller, Francis Kirkman and Gerard Langbaine are key to Hooks's narrative as the pioneers of models of collating lives of both books and people, and he argues that booksellers were 'the first bibliographers *and* the first biographers of Shakespeare' (15). As he states, the study of Shakespeare's life is a form of posthumous criticism dependent upon his printed books, which has led to a critical confusion between bibliography and biography. Hooks has several stated aims: 'to demonstrate the ways in which the evidentiary methods and disciplinary authority of bibliography have been used to make a fundamentally biographical argument about Shakespeare's attitude toward authorship' (22), and to give space to the 'alternative systems of value that cannot be reduced to – and in fact helped to constitute what we now consider to be – "literary"' (29). Hooks contends that 'Shakespeare's value was determined by his vendibility' (28) and his project is to use case studies of the emergence of the Shakespeare persona in print as an alternative to standard biographical approaches.

Hooks's case studies are well chosen. He begins with *Venus and Adonis* (1593), showing how the biographical fascination with the printer of that book, Shakespeare's fellow Stratfordian Richard Field, has come at the expense of the more significant roles of Field's partner, John Harrison, and Harrison's successor as the book's vendor, William Leake (38). The use of Field as 'a guarantor of Shakespeare's authorial status' relies on speculative narratives about connections between the two (42) but Hooks points out that Field's association with Shakespeare was brief. Harrison, on the other hand, was closely associated with the Ovidian milieu of the 1590s as a seller of both Shakespeare's poems and of Ovid's collected love poetry at the White Greyhound (52), and his presentation of *Venus and Adonis* and *The Rape of Lucrece* as companion pieces was influential in ensuring they were read and praised as part of the fashion for epyllia (58). Hooks argues that the role of stationers at the Greyhound provides the crucial interpretive framework for understanding the continuing popularity and profile of the poems (65).

Chapter Two continues this work by looking at Andrew Wise's publication of Shakespeare's history plays in the context of his other work, especially his publication of Thomas Playfere's sermons. The particular significance of Wise, for Hooks, is in his decision to add Shakespeare's name to subsequent editions of plays that he initially published anonymously (67). Hooks contends that Wise specialized in 'a brand of eloquence' (70) that led to Shakespeare being characterized as 'sweet' and, more tenuously, *Richard II* being interpreted as a lyrical rather than political work, an observation based on a poem by John Weever associating Romeo with 'Richard' (80–1). Hooks is more persuasive in tracing the appearance of *Richard II* in contemporary commonplace books alongside the similar use of Playfere's sermons, creating the potential for readers to engage with them in similar ways (85).

Hooks extends his contribution to Smith's project in his third chapter's argument that 'the Folio's current critical and cultural value has encouraged critics to overstate what it accomplished' (31). Hooks is at pains to point out that the main claims that the Folio makes are not to literary status but to *consumption*; it is the vendibility, not the cultural status, of the plays that makes the project a legitimate endeavour (102–3). Hooks's bold move, also taken by Zachary Lesser and Peter Stallybrass in an essay I discuss below, is to rechristen the Pavier quartos 'The Jaggard quartos' in recognition of Jaggard's unique connection to all of the 1619 quartos (112–24). Hooks argues that the Folio's most important innovations are its simultaneous rhetorical casting of the volume as a continuously organized corpus of works (as opposed to individual printings bound together) and its genre-based organization and marketing, building on the successful work of serialization undertaken in the Jaggard quartos, which perhaps served as the first indicator of the vendibility of a collection of commercial playbooks (123).

The final chapter skips to the 1650s and to the booksellers' catalogues that began to make a categorical distinction between plays and other types of book, anticipating what would become the English dramatic canon. The classification of plays as a discrete category indicated their emergence as a viable conceptual category as well as commercial product (139), and Hooks notes the remarkable lack of other comparable lists based on subject or genre. Francis Kirkman's list, comparing favourably with W. W. Greg's a quarter of a millennium later, was also the first to use authors as an organizational principle (149–50). Hooks argues that these lists mark the beginnings of bio-bibliography, as evidenced in the early annotations of the collector Anthony à Wood of his own booksellers' catalogue, and his expressed desire for more biographical information about the authors behind them (170).

Hooks's book concludes rather suddenly and a more substantial conclusion tying the rich threads of his multifaceted explorations together would have been welcome. In some ways his rather broad conclusion – that not only Shakespeare's reputation but also the very idea and value of dramatic authorship were still being constructed and defined by the often-forgotten print agents of the seventeenth century – seems perhaps too simplistic after such a dense and rewarding book. But part of the point is that these narratives do not create easy teleological or biographical narratives but instead expose a complex set of commercial, textual and economic networks that repay further study.

Such further study will be enabled by Judith Milhous and Robert D. Hume's magisterial new volume *The Publication of Plays in London 1660–1800*. This book is a major asset for historians of the early modern playbook trade pushing beyond the arbitrary end-point set by the English Civil War and Restoration. As their preface notes,

[T]here is no 'bibliography' of the plays [of the late seventeenth and eighteenth centuries] comparable to W. W. Greg's magisterial account of earlier English drama . . . the cartography of this field remains crude at best, while analytic consideration of the writing and publishing of plays remains a fragmentary enterprise barely out of its infancy . . . our hope is that the present book will lay the groundwork on which the next generation of scholars can build.   (xi–xiii)

With sixty pages of appendices tabulating the copyright payments for plays, the plays sold in anthologies and copyright transfer agreements, their hopes will doubtless be realized. Much of the foundational data for grasping the movements of plays (and the reverse movement of payments) is contained herein and clearly presented.

The book's introduction is unnecessarily aggressive, especially given the relative brevity of their engagement with the wealth of scholarship on the earlier Shakespearean book trade. Their fair concern is that there is a tendency for scholars to build on limited and idiosyncratic examples in their pursuit of wishful narratives (a concern shared and countered more effectively by Hooks), and the authors instead work here with large data and trends. Much of the book is concerned with new plays but the primary value for Shakespeare scholars comes in Part II, with an overview of the economics of the early Tonson editions, and Part III, which includes sections on collected editions of Shakespeare from 1709 and on John Bell's editions (discussed also by Peter Holland and Keir Elam in *Shakespeare and Textual Studies*).

Milhous and Hume correct several misunderstandings in the history of Shakespeare's print reception through appropriate historical contextualization. For instance, the 1714 duodecimo reprint of Rowe's 1709 works, often assumed to be a 'cheap popular reprint', in fact seems to have been only 3s cheaper than the 1709 editions, or '35% more than the average cost of a folio' (154–5), and there is no evidence for the oft-assumed claim that Tonson simultaneously issued the plays in individual editions. Conversely, Milhous and Hume argue that Pope's 1725 edition was a relative commercial success for the Tonson cartel (159), as opposed to the ill-conceived business venture of Theobald's 1733 edition (162).

To provide context for the business plan for Rowe's venture, Milhous and Hume collect tables of the availability of Shakespeare 'singleton' editions, concluding that by 1709 only four of Shakespeare's plays 'could easily be purchased and read in fundamentally faithful texts' (234). The subsequent publication of fifty collected editions in London during the eighteenth century points to what the authors call 'an astonishingly strong market for luxury collected editions at premium prices' (235) even before the making of Shakespeare as 'national poet' c. 1769. The book thus highlights the importance of the 1734–5 price wars between Jacob Tonson and Robert Walker as the key moment in forming Shakespeare's reputation, with the author benefitting from public exposure and the sudden availability of cheap editions, many in individual copies for the first time (240). In their interest in John Bell's 'first serious attempt to make and keep Shakespeare available to the general public at a non-human price' (255), finally, they demonstrate the importance of attending to work too often dismissed as 'popular', but essential in shaping Shakespeare's reception.

TEXTUAL STUDIES

The most substantial contribution to textual studies this year has been Margaret Jane Kidnie and Sonia Massai's *Shakespeare and Textual Studies*. Its impressive range and contributor list across twenty-five short essays position it as a 'state of play' document from those at the forefront of the New Textualism (1), and the combination of case studies and broad overviews responds to challenges and technologies both new and old. Disappointingly, the introduction does little beyond summarize the contents but the ensuing polyvocal effect is in tune with the calls of many of the contributors for approaches that highlight neglected areas of study and decentre authority within the discipline.

Part One, 'Scripts and Manuscripts', is largely concerned with deconstructing received narratives. Heather Hirschfeld's opening chapter offers a bold critique of approaches to collaborative authorship and attribution studies. She models the author as 'dramatist-as-pen' (17) to stress the moment of inscribing rather than the ultimate destination of publication (whether page or stage) in order to accommodate the complexity of other agents in the collaborative documents of performance and publication. Hirschfeld warns that attribution study cannot be an end in itself but is a productive stimulus to further conversation. James Purkis picks up on the role of individual authors in his incisive dissection of the *Thomas More* manuscript. His case attacks the idea of character consistency as the marker of individual authorial agency, arguing brilliantly that what Hand D exemplifies is 'a sense of openness [that] pertains to all dramatic writing' (51), identifying the individual author leaving the space for collaborative revision (the implications of Purkis's argument are pursued further in his recent monograph, *Shakespeare and Manuscript Drama*, through further study of *More* and other early playbooks). Paul Werstine also focuses on manuscripts, showing how a scholarly tendency to generalize about 'scribal manuscripts' problematically overlooks the diversity of practice within and between the work of professionals such as Ralph Crane and Edward Knight. Noting wryly that 'Crane-spotting is hard to do' (34), Werstine makes a characteristically incisive case for attending to actual practice, warnings taken seriously by Emma Smith as she writes on character lists in (naturally) the First Folio, arguing that the idiosyncratic appearance and design of these lists is an indicator of collection rather than editing, typical of a volume that 'makes few concessions to its readers' (146).

Part Two, 'Making Books; Building Reputations' continues critiquing standard narratives in its attention to overlooked aspects of print. Sonia Massai investigates the decline of new Shakespeare books in the early seventeenth century, which she attributes to the rise in popularity of new plays by the children's companies. Alan Farmer bolsters established arguments about Shakespeare's print popularity with the evidence of 'editorial pledges', particularly showing how Shakespeare's name was unusually associated with assertions of 'correction' or 'revision' (91). I would have been interested to see him consider *Locrine* ('corrected by W. S.') as part of this, as his quantitative argument for the unusual association of Shakespeare with correction and revision has important implications for reading title pages. The two other chapters in this section both share coverage with Hooks in *Selling Shakespeare*: Helen Smith's analysis of the social communities of the booksellers and print agents within which Shakespeare's works circulated from 1593–8, and Zachary Lesser and Peter Stallybrass's work on the period 1608–19, dominated by their groundbreaking case (made on the evidence of stitch-holes) that the 'Jaggard quartos' were part of a bound stationers' collection, including *A Woman Killed with Kindness*, that actually marks the first bound collection of plays not based on a single author (132).

Part Three 'From Print to Manuscript', might be more simply titled 'Using'. The diverse essays here focus on the use of material texts, including the transcription of commonplaces (Laura Estill), annotation and transcription for performance (Jean-Christophe Mayer), and collection, the last in an essay by Jeffrey Todd Knight whose methodological introduction is particularly important. Discussing the 'curatorial' work of Garrick and Kemble, he argues that critical focus on marginal annotation, with its tendency towards case studies, is just 'one empirical subset of a larger enterprise of active response, one that includes theoretical constructs of organization and assemblage, each with the potential to create meaning beyond the confines of the individual text' (184). Also essential from a methodological standpoint is Alan Galey's exhilarating discussion of encoding as a form of slow reading that allows us to 'understand our materials anew through the act of making digital representations of them' (199), going closer than any other essay into the detail of text, including the precise size of white space and the problems of representing non-linear stage directions. W. B. Worthen's timely appraisal of Shakespeare- and acting-focused apps closes this section by pointing to the double-edged nature of 'interactive' texts that resist the more lasting interventions that inform the other chapters; apps offer 'a text that can finally be freed from our corrupting use of it' (229) by allowing erasable annotation while preserving the clean underlying text.

Part Four, 'Editorial Legacies', takes the long historical view of less-explored textual manifestations. Peter Holland traces theatre editions from the 1676 *Hamlet* to the Donmar's 2009 souvenir play-text of the same play, pointing to the work done by such texts that separates them from both early texts and from the performances they evoke. Andrew Murphy begins his account of 'the intimate relationships between formats and readerships' (271) with miniature editions, before tracing the fortunes of the overlooked mass-produced editions of the eighteenth, nineteenth and twentieth centuries. Keir Elam considers illustrated editions, and Leah Marcus discusses the role played by the 'Introduction' through examples of *Tempest* editions from 1773 to 2011. Her particular discovery is the indebtedness of the format and agenda of Arden 1 to the colonial editions prepared by English scholars for Indian schools, betraying the editor's attempts to control meaning and access. The section concludes with Lukas Erne's account of the ongoing battle between 'uneditors' and 'interventionist editors'. Provocatively, Erne recasts the debate in religious terms: the 'Catholic' tradition that allows the editor to, priest-like, mediate the text to the faithful, and the 'Protestant' approach which feels that 'the textual clergy has all too often led the community of readers into error' (312). The analogy is rich, and Erne's ecumenical understanding that different communities value different approaches draws critical attention to what is at stake.

Part Five is dedicated to a series of editorial minefields as editors and critics discuss some of the finer problems of realizing a text. John Jowett provides a technically complex critique of practices towards 'textual ephemera', his term for 'accidentals', and Matthew Dimmock discusses the dangers of standardizing voices coded as 'strange' in Shakespeare's plays, from representations of different dialects and languages to the standardization of punctuation such as the Prince of Morocco's that may deliberately indicate a collapse of linguistic confidence. Alan Dessen and Tiffany Stern, meanwhile, both attend to the textual representation of the performance event. Dessen asks 'to what extent do post-Elizabethan notions of scene division and "place" blur or eliminate potentially meaningful images available to the original playgoers?' (338), in an essay that shares important intellectual work with Alan Galey in considering how the processes of editorial standardization can elide moments of theatre's productive ambiguity. Stern, more provocatively, queries the (lack of) textual representation in modern editions of the performance event at the start and end of plays, from trumpet blasts to jigs and prayers, noting the intellectual problems of deferring to only the lexical content of plays.

The book's final section trails into miscellanea. Jill Levenson's essay would be better paired with Marcus's, tracing as it does (in necessarily broad strokes) four centuries of the development of scholarly introductions and apparatus. Eric Rasmussen's pithy piece makes a defence of the editorial collation in the digital age, arguing that the presentation of collation needs the optionality afforded by electronic editions. But the closing essay by the technologist and cultural commentator David Weinberger is a stunning climax to a collection invested in the state of (the text of) the play. He argues that, in moving from a paper-based to a network-based (Internet) culture, so too do models of scholarship need to change:

[W]e have acted as if disagreement and argument were temporary phases as we work toward settled knowledge. That is an understandable assumption when the medium of knowledge was paper, for that assumption essentially repeats the publishing metaphor: ideas go through a period of development, and when they are ready and finalized they are committed to paper and put into the public sphere. (414)

Weinberger's rallying cry, at the end of an often iconoclastic and always thought-provoking collection, is to embrace open access, to post as well as publish, to put notes and metadata into the public sphere, and to always link, 'not just a scholarly responsibility but a social duty' (405). As with so many of the contributors to this volume, Weinberger roots the value of the editor (whether as curator, compiler, guide or creative interventionist) in enabling new forms of creative response and discovery. As a call for reconsideration of what scholars are actually *for* in an age of networked texts, it allows the book to close on a necessary challenge with ramifications beyond editing.

WORKS REVIEWED

Bevington, David, ed., *Troilus and Cressida*, rev. edn (London, 2015)

Bulman, James C., ed., *King Henry IV Part 2* (London, 2016)

Greenblatt, Stephen, Walter Cohen, Suzanne Gossett, Jean E. Howard, Katharine Eisaman Maus and Gordon McMullan, eds., *The Norton Shakespeare*, 3rd edn, International Student edition (New York, 2016)

Honigmann, E. A. J., ed., *Othello*, rev. edn with a new introduction by Ayanna Thompson (London, 2016)

Hooks, Adam G., *Selling Shakespeare: Biography, Bibliography, and the Book Trade* (Cambridge, 2016)

Kidnie, Margaret Jane, and Sonia Massai, eds., *Shakespeare and Textual Studies* (Cambridge, 2015)

McEachern, Claire, ed., *Much Ado about Nothing*, rev. edn (London, 2016)

Milhous, Judith and Robert D. Hume, *The Publication of Plays in London 1660–1800: Playwrights, Publishers and the Market* (London, 2015)

Slights, Jessica, ed., *Othello*, Internet Shakespeare Editions (accessed 2 January 2017)

Smith, Emma, *Shakespeare's First Folio: Four Centuries of an Iconic Book* (Oxford, 2016)

Smith, Emma, *The Making of Shakespeare's First Folio* (Oxford, 2015)

Smith, Emma, ed., *The Cambridge Companion to Shakespeare's First Folio* (Cambridge, 2016)

Thompson, Ann and Neil Taylor, eds., *Hamlet*, rev. edn (London, 2016)

ABSTRACTS OF ARTICLES IN *SHAKESPEARE SURVEY 70*

GREGORY DORAN
'**Think when we talk of horses . . .**'
Gregory Doran, Artistic Director of the Royal Shakespeare Company, gave the opening paper at the World Shakespeare Congress. He explored the immediacy of Shakespeare's writing and the ways in which his descriptions are filmic before tracing the surprisingly long history of filmed Shakespeare in the theatres of Stratford-upon-Avon.

ADRIAN LESTER
In Dialogue with Ayanna Thompson
This chapter provides an edited transcript of the conversation between the acclaimed, black-British actor Adrian Lester and the performance scholar Ayanna Thompson at the 2016 World Shakespeare Congress. Lester gives rich details about the way he approaches Shakespearean characters, with information about his linguistic and physical work.

HOWARD JACOBSON AND ADRIAN POOLE
Shakespeare and the Novel: A Conversation
Prize-winning novelist Howard Jacobson and literary critic Adrian Poole discuss *My Name is Shylock*, one of the first of a Hogarth Press series in which leading contemporary writers re-imagine a Shakespeare play, in this case *The Merchant of Venice*. Together they address the provocations and opportunities afforded by the challenge of re-writing a drama from more than 400 years ago and turning it into a novel set in the here-and-now.

CLAIRE VAN KAMPEN
'Music Still': Understanding and Reconstructing Shakespeare's Use of Musical Underscore
Claire van Kampen, Director of Theatre Music at Shakespeare's Globe from its opening in 1997, considers the careful ways in which Shakespeare texts prescribe music as underscoring for particular moments, noting the choice of instruments to ensure they do not drown out the actors and the effects the music creates.

GORDON MCMULLAN
Remembering and Forgetting in 1916: Israel Gollancz, the Shakespeare Tercentenary and the National Theatre
The largely forgotten cultural entrepreneurship of Israel Gollancz in relation to the 1916 Shakespeare tercentenary contributed to the creation of the National Theatre and also to the Royal Shakespeare Company and Shakespeare's Globe, serving as a case study in the selective rememberings and forgettings that constitute the processes of memorialization.

ABSTRACTS OF ARTICLES IN *SHAKESPEARE SURVEY 70*

MICHAEL DOBSON

Four Centuries of Centenaries: Stratford-upon-Avon
This chapter reviews the development of Shakespearean commemorations in Stratford from 1616 to 2016, looking especially at the centenaries of the playwright's birth and death marked in 1764 (albeit belatedly, at the 1769 Jubilee), 1864, 1916 and 1964. It closes by discussing various Stratford-based quatercentenary events organized in 2016.

PAUL EDMONDSON

Writing and Re-writing Shakespeare's Life: A Roundtable Discussion with Margreta de Grazia, Katherine Scheil, James Shapiro and Stanley Wells
An edited roundtable discussion from the World Shakespeare Congress 2016 about biography and history, the nature of speculation, relating the works to the life, the craft of biography, recent trends, a subject's afterlife and whether we even need Shakespearian biography.

SHAUL BASSI

The Merchant *in* Venice: Re-creating Shakespeare in the Ghetto
The chapter illustrates the premises and history of the first performance of Shakespeare's *Merchant of Venice* in the Ghetto of Venice in 2016, a Ca'Foscari/Colombari production staged 400 years after the death of Shakespeare and 500 since the institution of the paradigmatic Jewish quarter where the play is ideally set.

CAROL CHILLINGTON RUTTER

Shakespeare's *The Merchant of Venice* in and beyond the Ghetto
This review documents a historic production of *The Merchant of Venice* staged in 2016 to mark the 400th anniversary of Shakespeare's death and the 500th anniversary of the institution of the Jewish Ghetto in Venice, and staged on location, in the very ghetto that has bequeathed to every subsequent ghetto its name. It brought home the most famous Venetian Jew who never lived.

JOSÉ A. PÉREZ DÍEZ

What the Quills Can Tell: The Case of John Fletcher and Philip Massinger's *Love's Cure*
Fletcher and Massinger's *Love's Cure, or The Martial Maid* (c. 1615) was based on Guillén de Castro's *La fuerza de la costumbre* (c. 1610), only printed in 1625. This chapter examines how the extant manuscripts of Castro's play enable the theory that this Spanish *comedia* was imported into England in pre-printed form.

JESÚS TRONCH

What if Greg and Werstine Had Examined Early Modern Spanish Dramatic Manuscripts?
This chapter in comparative textual criticism applies Werstine's analysis of early modern play-texts annotated to guide performance (2013) to sixteen analogous manuscripts from seventeenth-century Spanish drama. It concludes that the Spanish evidence generally supports Werstine's invalidation of Greg's notions of 'foul papers' and 'promptbooks' as categories to identify printer's copy.

JOHN JOWETT

Exit Manuscripts: The Archive of Theatre and the Archive of Print
Surviving early modern playhouse manuscripts were usually based on a transcript and were modified through time. Such documents became superfluous when copied. Only the superfluous manuscript could be sold for printing. Accordingly, this chapter distinguishes between the theatre archive and the overlapping but distinct 'archive' of printed plays.

ABSTRACTS OF ARTICLES IN *SHAKESPEARE SURVEY 70*

LUCY MUNRO
''Sblood!': Hamlet's Oaths and the Editing of Shakespeare's Plays
This chapter analyses the often inconsistent and inadequate treatment of blasphemous oaths in critical editions of Shakespeare's plays. Arguing that swearing provides a crucial point of access into character, genre and debates about the status of extreme language, it explores new approaches to glossing and annotating these unruly words.

ADAM ZUCKER
Antihonorificabilitudinitatibus: *Love's Labour's Lost* and Unteachable Words
This chapter uses difficult and nonsensical words in *Love's Labour's Lost* to explore the limits of explanation in pedagogical contexts. Jacques Rancière's *Ignorant Schoolmaster* and early nonsense poetry help identify the place of the inexplicable in our own experience of the play, and in its early printings as well.

GARY TAYLOR, JOHN V. NANCE, AND KEEGAN COOPER
Shakespeare and Who? Aeschylus, *Edward III* and Thomas Kyd
A new stylometric test demonstrates that Kyd did not write the Mariner's long speech (Scene 4), which was influenced by Ubaldini's account of the defeat of the Spanish Armada and the messenger speech in *The Persians*. Marlowe probably wrote it, but we lack reliable tests for Lodge, Nashe and Watson.

HUGH CRAIG
Authorial Attribution and Shakespearean Variety: Genre, Form and Chronology
Authorial contrasts in the language of the plays of Shakespeare and his contemporaries comfortably transcend cross-cutting contrasts from other sources, such as genre, era, character and prose versus verse. This aspect of the patterning of the style of dialogue in the plays confirms the feasibility of authorial attribution using quantitative measures.

HESTER LEES-JEFFRIES
'My mother's maids, when they did sew and spin': Staging Sewing, Telling Tales
Sewing is often evoked or staged in Shakespeare's plays. Such moments can occasion reflection on the status of story-telling, the processes of literary and dramatic making, and performance (especially of gender). This chapter suggests that there were more sewing scenes on the early modern stage than surviving stage directions indicate.

HELEN COOPER
Why Prospero Drowned his Books, and Other Catholic Folklore
This chapter surveys the evidence for Shakespeare's knowledge of Caxton's *Golden Legend*, last printed in 1527 but surviving in numerous copies in Elizabethan England. In particular, it considers the rare instance of a magician's drowning of his magic books in the Life of St James the Greater as a possible source for *The Tempest*.

PAMELA ALLEN BROWN
Why Did the English Stage Take Boys for Actresses?
In 1989 Stephen Orgel asked 'Why did the English stage take boys for women?' The question should be reworded to reflect the impact of the first actresses. The English knew about this innovation from diplomats, travellers and returning players and from visits by mixed-gender Italian troupes to Elizabeth's court. Writers emulated them by creating crowd-pleasing roles: self-aware, charismatic, histrionic. Simulating the *innamorata* as played by the divas, the English diversified their repertory and staved off 'the specter of female performance'.

ABSTRACTS OF ARTICLES IN *SHAKESPEARE SURVEY 70*

SIMON SMITH

Acting Amiss: Towards a History of Actorly Craft and Playhouse Judgement
This chapter argues that early modern playgoers habitually judged actorly craft, a mode of engagement often associated exclusively with play-makers. It also traces a wider culture of Shakespearean playgoing in which pleasure and judgement were not separate responses, but rather two components of an individual playgoer's engagements with drama.

ELISABETH LUTTEMAN

'What imports this song?': Spontaneous Singers and Spaces of Meaning in Shakespeare
Engaging with moments of song in *Hamlet* and *King Lear*, this chapters traces ways in which the songs create spaces of commentary and experience that resonate with central themes in the plays, and open up spaces of multiple, ambiguous meaning for listeners both onstage and off.

RUTH MORSE

Shakespeare's Depriving Particles
Shakespeare often used prefixes to convey the simultaneous absence or negation of an evaluative-descriptive noun to create unease about the characters who speak them. This chapter focuses on Anglo-Saxon derived 'un-', glancing also at the Latin/French 'diss-', which does slightly different work. These 'depriving particles', or 'privatives', embed and emphasize the values they lack or negate, for example, 'unthought' and 'dishonour'. They suggest ethical judgement.

LAURIE SHANNON

Shakespeare's Comedy of Upright Status: Standing Bears and Fallen Humans
Asking how Shakespeare and Darwin might converse, this chapter pursues the question of upright status central to evolutionary theory and Renaissance ideas of humanity alike. It suggests a human *negative* exceptionalism of weakness and prostration, comparing standing bears and staggering men in *The Winter's Tale* and *Taming of the Shrew*.

MARGARET TUDEAU-CLAYTON

'Worth the Name of a Christian'?: The Parabolic Economy of *The Two Gentlemen of Verona*
Viewed from the scene of the one instance in the Shakespearean canon of the word 'parable', *Two Gentlemen of Verona* may be seen as exemplifying a parabolic economy even as it evokes the 'charity' that is the just Christian response to the unlimited debt-gift economy of the plot of redemption.

MEGAN ELIZABETH ALLEN

'Titus, unkind': Shakespeare's Revision of Virgil's Aeneas in *Titus Andronicus*
Shakespeare's *Titus Andronicus* (1594) responds to burgeoning nervousness over the Elizabethan succession via appropriation of Virgil's portrayal of *pietas* in structuring republic versus monarchic political states. This appropriation suggests the reciprocal impact of political structures on kinship by figuring inheritance as resemblance to reveal the violence inherent in primogeniture ideals.

JULIA REINHARD LUPTON

'Cut him out in little stars': Juliet's Cute Classicism
Developing the concept of cuteness from Sianne Ngai's *Our Aesthetic Categories*, this chapter argues that Juliet repurposes heroic stellification into a soft topography that promotes tenderness as both an erotic comportment and a hermeneutic attitude. Juliet is the poet of a 'minor' classicism characterized by extreme youth, a handheld, part-object eroticism, and the galloping apace of anticipation.

ABSTRACTS OF ARTICLES IN *SHAKESPEARE SURVEY 70*

KATHARINE EISAMAN MAUS
The Will of Caesar: Choice-making, the Death of the Roman Republic and the Development of Shakespearean Character
This chapter looks at the way Shakespeare's techniques of dramatic characterization change as he moves, in 1599, from the English to Roman history in *Julius Caesar*. In *Julius Caesar*, Mark Antony's reading of Caesar's will incites the Roman populace to turn decisively against Brutus, Cassius and the other conspirators. This momentous piece of political theatre could not have occurred in history plays because English medieval (and early modern) land law would have precluded the making of such a will. In *Julius Caesar* Shakespeare focuses on the 'liberty' of the Roman citizen to choose both heirs and ancestors. More generally, I argue, the ancient Roman setting encourages Shakespeare to give a new attention to processes of choice-making, and to find innovative ways to represent those processes onstage.

NATÁLIA PIKLI
'As for that light hobby-horse, my sister': Shakespearean Influences and Popular Discourses in *Blurt Master Constable*
This chapter addresses the complexity of reciprocal relations and possible influences among canonical and non-canonical authors and texts, considering theatrical contexts and shared cultural discourses around 1600, with a focus on the 'hobby-horse' image in Thomas Dekker's *Blurt Master Constable* (1601), Shakespearean comedies and Nicholas Breton's *Pasquils Mistresse* (1600).

NAOMI BAKER
Messianic Ugliness in *A Midsummer Night's Dream* and *The Winter's Tale*
This chapter argues that *A Midsummer Night's Dream* and *The Winter's Tale* follow Paul in their questioning of normative ideals of beauty. Drawing on Pauline discourses, the plays reject static, individualized and thus beautiful forms of being, celebrating instead the ugliness that is open to possibilities of becoming.

SHAKESPEARE SURVEY 70 INDEX

Aaron, Catrin 307
Abeysekera, Hiran 302
Aboab, Rabbi Samuel ben Abraham 74–5
Abraham, F. Murray 77
Ackroyd, Peter 64
Adorno, Theodor 241, 247
Aebischer, Pascal 13, 14
Aeschylus 150–3, 387
Aesop 165
Agamben, Giorgio 213, 272n1, 273n9, 275n32
Ahmed, Sara 231n15
Akinade, Fisayo 291
Akitaya, Kazunori 356
Alberts, Jada 320
Albina, Nadia 296
Aldridge, Ira 375–6
Alexander, Bill 5, 361
Alexandra, Princess, the Hon. Lady Ogilvy 56
Allam, Roger 290
Allen, Megan 228–39n53, 388
Alleyn, Edward 89, 343
Almereyda, Michael 368, 369
Al-Shaater, Yaz 336
Anderson, Anthony 129n35
Anderson, Benedict 343
Andreini, Isabella 183, 184
Anouka, Jade 309
Antas, Delmiro 107n57
Aquinas, Thomas 178n18
Arbus, Arin 362
Archer, William 42, 45, 46–7
Arellano, Ignacio 108n61, 108n60, 111n67
Arendt, Hannah 241, 246
Aristotle 215n12
Armani, Virginia 183
Armin, Robert 35, 159n17, 161–2n18
Armitage, Simon 340
Armstrong, Edward 207
Armstrong, Gareth 337
Armstrong, N. 268n37
Armstrong, Simon 288
Arne, Thomas 51, 56
Arnold, Matthew 154

Aronson, Arnold 365–6
Ashford, Rob 311–12, 337, 338
Assmann, Jan 259n2
Astington, John 189, 192–3, 194, 196
Atim, Sheila 309, 310
Aubrey, John 59
Auden, W. H. 200, 204n29
Augustine of Hippo 222
Ayckbourn, Alan 369
Ayola, Rakie 318–19
Ayres, Fraser 319

Baddeley, Angela 3
Badger, Richard 42
Badiou, Alain 272–3n1–5, 275n33, 276
Badir, Patricia 137n4, 279n50
Baglow, Jessica 288
Bagnall, Nick 296–7, 332
Bahl, Ankur 293–4
Bailey, Thomas 334
Baker, David J. 357
Baker, Gideon 272–3n5
Baker, Naomi 272–86, 389
Baker, Sir Richard 195, 196
Bakewell, Michael 3
Bakhtin, Mikhail 268n37, 348–9, 368
Baldwin, T. W. 136n3, 194n25
Baldy, Colin 333
Ball, Robert F. 335
Bancroft, Richard, Archbishop of Canterbury 286
Bani, Jimi 320
Bannister, Joe 315
Bannon, Cynthia J. 237n48, 237n46
Bannon, Tia 287–8
Barber, Charles 207
Barber, Emily 288, 326
Bardsley, Sandy 126n24
Bargagli, Girolamo 184n8
Barker, Harley Granville 42, 45, 46
Baron, Salo 70–1
Barón-Nusbaum, Brandin 366
Barr, Gordon 330, 331, 334
Barrass, Martin 338

Barret, J. K. 230n7
Barrett, James 150n14, 152n21
Barritt, Ian 313
Barrow, Isaac 127
Barrymore, John 370
Barstow, Josephine 7
Bartels, Emily C. 153n23
Bartholomeus Anglicus 207–8
Bartolomé Benito, Fernando 97n38
Barton, Chris 331
Barton, John 3, 55n18, 339
Basauri, Aitor 324Illus.30, 324
Baskin, J. R. 281n59
Bassett, Lytta 224–5n31
Bassi, Gino 70
Bassi, Shaul 67–78, 79, 80, 82n5, 241–2, 246n29, 386
Bate, Jonathan 46n19, 129n38, 146n1, 154, 167n9, 238n50, 239n52
Bateman, Tom 312, 338
Baxter, Hilary 366
Baynes, Thomas Spencer 136n3
Beal, Peter 116n7
Beale, Simon Russell 306Illus.24, 306–7
Beamish, Jamie 333
Beamish, Sally 56,
Bearman, Robert 61, 63
Beauman, Sally 46
Beaumont, Francis 100, 159n17, 349
Beaurline, L. A. 126
Beck, Peter 326
Becket, Thomas 176
Beckwith, Sarah 224, 225–6
Bell, John 381
Benjamin, Walter 241
Bennett, Edward 330, 333
Benson, Frank 1–3
Beolco, Angelo 82
Berger, Peter 219–20, 220n7, 223, 225–6
Berger, Thomas Leland 261n13, 261n9, 261–8n9–36, 262n13, 266n27, 269n39
Bergmann, Fredrick Louis 51n2
Berkeley, Sir Thomas 36

SHAKESPEARE SURVEY 70 INDEX

Berry, Cicely 362–3
Berry, Martin 332
Bertani, Bruna 77n27
Berthoud, Jacques 229n5, 230n8, 230, 237n45
Bess of Hardwick (Elizabeth Talbot, Countess of Shrewsbury) 173, 244
Betterton, Thomas Patrick 348
Betty, Henry 53
Bevan, Gillian 301
Bevington, David M. 125n15, 375, 384
Bhat, Alex 307
Bhebhe, Nandi 294
Biberman, Matthew 72n18
Biesta, Gert J. J. 135n1
Billing, Christian M. 365
Bishop, Tom 194n22
Blake, Erin 358
Blake, Norman 223n18
Blayney, Peter W. M. 119
Blessed, Brian 329
Block, Giles 362–3
Blyth, Benjamin 329, 330
Boas, F. S. 120n22
Boccaccio, Giovanni 214, 269n39
Bockley, Seth 328
Bodley, Thomas 354
Boehrer, Bruce 260n6
Bolens, Guillemette 195
Bolton, Robert 284
Bond, Imogen 330
Booth, Mark W. 203
Booth, Stephen 142n22
Bosley, Vivien 132n51, 132
Bourdieu, Pierre 144n30
Bourne, Claire 139n11
Bourus, Terri 150n12, 159
Bowers, Fredson 100, 119, 261n10
Boyd, Brian 149n9
Boyd, Michael 8–9
Bradley, A. C. 374
Bral, Grzegorz 329
Branagh, Kenneth 4, 13, 311–13, 337, 345, 368
Brandl, Alois 118n13
Braunmuller, A. R. 152n21
Brennan, Joseph Xavier 221n10
Breton, Nicholas 260–1, 269–70, 389
Breton, Stanislas 276n36, 276
Bridges-Adams, William 46
Bright, Timothy 168
Brimson-Lewis, Stephen 57
Brissenden, Alan 267n32
Bristol, Michael 216, 348
Britten, Benjamin 7, 337
Britton, Jasper 328,
Broadhead, H. D. 150n15
Brock, Susan 37n5, 52n10
Brook, Peter 5–6, 10, 13, 15, 367–8
Brooke, Arthur 241, 244

Brooke, Nicholas 342
Brooks, Harold F. 36n3
Brotherhead, Leah 297
Brower, Reuben Arthur 238n50
Brown, Arthur 116n8
Brown, Cressida 330
Brown, J. Ross 53, 54, 54Illus.1
Brown, John Russell 55, 84n9, 365–6, 370
Brown, Mark 298n4
Brown, Pamela Allen 182–7, 387
Browne, Thomas 215, 343
Bruerton, Courtney 96
Brugnera, Andrea 56Illus.6, 86
Bruun, Sybille 364
Buc, Sir George 115
Buchanan, Judith 367
Buckhurst, Bill 333
Buckle, Richard 55–6
Buckley, Jessie 311
Buffong, Michael 318–19, 318Illus.28
Bullough, Geoffrey 180n34, 259
Bulman, James C. 376–8, 384
Bulwer, John 193n17, 346, 347
Buñuel, Luis 369
Burbage, Richard 32, 59, 120n22
Burgess, Anthony 60–1
Burke, Peter 269
Burns, Edward 191–2
Burroughs, William 364
Burt, Richard 369–70
Burton, Robert 266n30
Butler, Martin 240n3
Buzwell, Greg 367
Byrne, Caroline 294–5, 295Illus.21

Cahill, Patricia 153n23
Calabi, Donatella 71
Calarco, Joe 335
Calderón de la Barca, Pedro 91, 105n40, 107, 108n61, 109Illus.8, 111, 112
Caldwell, John 202n11
Calimani, Dario 71n17
Calimani, Riccardo 67n2, 70
Callaghan, Dympna 185
Calvin, John 224, 225, 284
Calvo, Clara 41n2, 51n3, 55n18, 55n18, 347–8, 355
Campbell, Wilfred 43
Caneda Cabrera, Javier M. Teresa 223n18
Canterna, Adriene 336
Cantor, P. A. 228n1
Capell, Edward 377
Cappa, Felice 77n27
Cardanus, Fascitus (Fascizo Cardano) 178
Carey, Elizabeth, Lady Berkeley (d.635) 36
Carey, Sir George 36
Carlton, Bob 336
Carney, Jo Eldridge 230n10
Carrier, Roch 132

Carroll, William C. 137n4, 219n4, 221n11, 223n21, 223n18, 224
Carson, Christie 48n30
Carter, Sarah 278n45
Cartwright, Kent 72
Cartwright, William 120
Castillo Solórzano, Alonso del 108n60, 108, 110, 111
Castro, Guillén de 90–8, 386
Cathey, Reginald E. 73
Cavecchi, Mariacristina 358
Caxton, William 174, 176, 177
Cefalu, Paul 273
Céline, Louis-Ferdinand 24
Cerasano, S. P. 227n40
Cervantes, Miguel de 98n40
Chakrabarti, Lolita 13, 18, 338
Chamberlain, John 193–4
Chambers, David 69n8, 69n7
Chambers, E. K. 59–60, 280n56
Chambers, Robert 213n2
Chapman, George 155, 157n13, 158n14, 159n17, 161–2n18, 162n18, 163n20, 164, 184n8, 344
Charles I, King of Great Britain 240
Charnes, Linda 71–2
Charney, Maurice 228n1
Chaucer, Geoffrey 176, 267
Chaudhuri, Supriya 348
Chazelle, Damien 247
Chernaik, Warren 228
Chettle, Henry 101–4, 158n14
Chitty, Alison 366
Cicero 193, 194, 196, 254, 349
Clachan, Lizzie 314, 315–16
Claramonte, Andrés de 106, 107Illus.7, 108, 109, 110Illus.9, 111, 112
Clare, Janet 43n11
Clark, Morfydd 311
Clarke, Mary Cowden 25
Clarke, Ruby 336
Clavell, John 101–4
Clercq, René de 43
Clifford, Anne, Countess of Dorset, Pembroke and Montgomery 168
Clifton, Alex 334
Clubb, Louise George 184n8
Clune, Jackie 310
Clyde, James 301
Coates, Simon 321–2
Cochran, William G. 155n10
Coffman, Elizabeth 77n27
Cohen, Walter 371, 384
Coldiron, A. E. B. 207n3
Coleridge, Samuel Taylor 376
Collier, J. P. 59
Collington, Philip D. 281n61
Collins, Stephen 337
Colls, Kevin 63, 65n6

391

Comensoli, Viviana 182n1
Conkie, Rob 366–7, 370
Conlin, Kathleen 362
Connaughton, Nick 332
Conroy, Amy 295Illus.21
Constable, Neil 298
Coodin, Sara 348
Cook, Deborah 241n9
Cooke, Dominic 172n35
Cooke, John 158n14, 159n17, 161–2n18
Cookson, Sally 334
Coolidge, John S. 274n16
Cooney, James 302
Coonrod, Karin 67–78, 80, 82n6, 82n6, 83, 84n8, 85, 87
Cooper, Gary 297
Cooper, Helen 167n10, 174–81, 387
Cooper, Keegan 146–53, 387
Cooper, Thomas 365
Cope, Sir Walter 198
Cope, Wendy 340
Cord, Anthony 330
Cormack, Bradin 241n6, 249n3
Cornwell, Charlotte 307
Corrigan, James 304–5
Coryat(e), Thomas 67, 73–4, 142, 143, 183–4
Costigan, George 326
Cottegnies, Line 372
Cottis, David 337
Cousins, Mark 285n85
Coveney, Alan 313
Cox, John D. 119n21
Cracknell, Carrie 315–16, 330
Craig, Edward Gordon 365
Craig, Hugh 148n7, 153n25, 154–64, 387
Craig, Rosalie 315Illus.27, 326
Craik, Katharine 142–3
Crane, Ralph 382
Cranko, John 359
Crawforth, Hannah 340, 355
Cress, Donald 213n2
Crooke, Helkiah 215
Crouch, Tim 323–5, 338Illus.30
Crowe, Benjamin D. 275n27, 275n26
Crystal, Ben 328
Ctesias 151
Cukor, George 369, 370
Cullinane, Bethan 301, 302
Cumber, John 101–4
Cumberbatch, Benedict 327
Cummings, Brian 64, 128, 129n36, 221n9, 223
Cunca, Paloma 107n56
Cunningham, John 53n12
Currier, Paul 314
Curtin, Adrian 366
Curtis, Richard 123, 134
Cusack, Niamh 289, 290Illus.19, 326

Daborne, Robert 158n14

Dacre, James 329
Dahlgren, Marta 223n18
Daniell, David 274n16
Danson, Lawrence 202, 204n27
Darwin, Charles 213–15, 218
databases, selected
   DICAT (Diccionario biográfico de actores del teatro clásico español, University of Valencia) 90
   Henslowe-Alleyn Digitisation Project 89
   Manos (formerly Manos teatrales, of Biblioteca Nacional de España) 90, 91, 96, 99n5, 105n41
   Touchstone 326
Davenant, Sir William 36
Dávidházi, Péter 52n7
Davies, Douglas Brooks 244n26
Davies, Jo 336
Davies, Oliver Ford 1–2
Davis, Gavin 327
Davis, Robert C. 67n2
Dawson, Anthony B. 281n61
Day, John 158n14, 159n17, 161–2n18
Day, Martin 284, 285
de Grazia, Margreta 58–66n9, 100n7, 386
De Jong, Ian 367
Deelman, Christian 51n2
Dekker, Thomas 147, 158n14, 159n17, 161n18, 161–2n18, 162n18, 167, 180, 261–2, 262n14, 262n14, 389
del Lungo, Isidore 43
Dench, Judi 4, 311, 312, 337
Dent, Arthur 128
Dering, Sir Edward 354
Derrida, Jacques 282
Descartes, René 213
Dessen, Alan 383
Detmer-Goebel, Emily 232n20, 232
Devitt, Matt 327
Devlin, Caroline 329, 335
Dharker, Ayesha 299–300, 301
Di Benedetto, Stephen 365–6, 370
di Lenardo, Isabella 69n11, 79n1
Diamante, Juan Bautista 106, 108, 111, 112
Díaz, Pedro 105n43
Dibdin, Charles 51n4
Dick, Jennifer 334
Dickens, Charles 61
Dickson, Andrew 53n12
Dickson, Vernon Guy 233n28, 233, 238n50
Diehl, Huston 279n50, 282n64, 282n62, 283n73, 283
Dieterle, William 369, 370
Dillon, Janette 201
Dimmock, Matthew 372, 383
Dinsdale, Reece 334

Dionisotti, Paola 328
DiPietro, Cary 100n9
Distiller, Natasha 43n11
Dixon, Joe 306, 307
Djulibing, Frances 320
Dobson, Michael 50–7, 358, 386
Doel, Imogen 294, 295Illus.21
Donadio, Rachel 77n26
Donne, John 343, 353
Donnellan, Declan 331, 338
Donnelly, Ignatius 378
Doona, Liam 365
Doran, Gregory 2–9, 302, 303–4, 305–7, 306Illus.24, 328, 361, 363, 385
Doran, Susan 231n14
Dorland, Celia 334
Douglas, Gavin 231n12
Douglas, Mary 350
Dowd, Michelle M. 170n30
Downame, John 126n26
Drake, Hannah 330
Dromgoole, Dominic 63, 287–8, 290, 331, 333–4
Duffin, Aoife 202n8, 203n20, 204n32, 205n37, 205n37, 205, 294, 295Illus.21
Duffin, Ross 200n2, 201
Duffy, Carol Ann 56, 66
Duffy, Eamon 174n1
Dunbar, Karen 310
Duncan-Jones, Katherine 62
Duneier, Mitchell 69n10
Dunn, Leslie C. 204n29, 204, 206
Dunster, Matthew 297–8
Dupré, Charlie 338
Durán, Agustín 94, 95
Durán-Loriga, Juan 97n38
D'Urfey, Thomas 327
Durning-Lawrence, Sir Edward 138–9, 139Illus.10
Dutton, Richard 181n40, 354

Easton, Daniel 306–7
Eaton, Bob 327
Ebulue, Mark 333
Eco, Umberto 274n20
Edinburgh, Prince Philip, Duke of 56
Edmondson, Paul 57n23, 58–66n9, 65n6, 82n6, 340–1, 386
Edward VI, King of England 176
Edward, Richard 205
Edwards, Charles 334
Edwards, Philip 125n18, 125
Egan, Gabriel 100n9, 101n17, 118n13, 147n3, 148n7, 150n11, 159, 198n40, 351–2, 355, 375, 379
Eisen, Mark 148n7
Eisenberg, Ned 74Illus.4, 86Illus.6
Elam, Keir 137n4, 381, 383
Elder, Elinor 2–3

Eliot, George 25
Elizabeth I, Queen of England 130–1, 170, 183, 184, 185, 198
Ellinson, Lucy 300, 300Illus.22
Elliot, Michael 4
Elliott, Gertrude 44
Elliott, Ward E. Y. 163n19
Elton, W. R. 101n17
Elyot, Thomas 350
Emmerichs, Sharon 228n1, 229n3, 230n9
Engel, Amir 272n2
Engel, Lars Romann 327, 358
England, Martha W. 51n2
Engler, Balz 42–3n8
Enoch, Alfred 319
Enterline, Lynn 194n24
Erasmus, Desiderius 138, 221n9, 222, 227n39, 350
Erickson, Amy Louise 169
Erne, Lukas 376, 383
Essiedu, Paapa 9, 302, 303Illus.23
Estill, Laura 382
Etchells, Tim 322–3
Eusebius 175
Evans, Malcolm 137n4
Everitt, Lloyd 333
Ewert, Kevin 365
Eynde, Bart van der 316–18

Fagles, Robert 233n21
Fall, Rebecca 142n22
Fallow, David 341
Farmer, Alan 382
Farr, David 172n35
Farrah, Abdel 4
Farré, Judith 106n49
Fearon, Ray 296
Fei, Alberto Toso 68n6
Fellows, Jennifer 179n26
Ferguson, Ailsa Grant 40, 44n12, 45n15, 45, 368–9, 370
Fernández, Laura 106n49
Fernandez Colmeiro, Teresa 223n18
Fernández de Béthencourt, Francisco 93n19
Fernie, Ewan 57n23
Ferran, Patsy 315, 331
Ferrer Valls, Teresa 106n46
Field, Nathan 101–4, 120n22, 158n14, 161–2n18
Field, Richard 159n17, 177, 341, 380
Fielding, Susannah 331
Fiennes, Ralph 321
Findlay, Alison 181n40
Findlay, Polly 314, 315, 315Illus.27, 326, 331
Fiorentino, Ser Giovanni 67
Fisher, Thomas 270
Fitzgerald, Tara 296
Flaherty, Kate 40, 45n15
Flaminia, Barbara 183
Fleischle, Anna 301

Fletcher, John 64, 89–98, 100, 101–4, 117, 155, 157n13, 158n14, 159n17, 159, 161–2n18, 164, 171, 304–5, 341, 386
Florio, John 167n11, 350
Flower, Archibald 46
Foakes, R. A. 204n26
Folger, Emily 378
Folger, Henry Clay 354, 378
Fonrobert, Charlotte Elisheva 272n2
Forbes-Robertson, Johnston 44
Force, Brandon 336
Ford, John 158n14, 170
Forest-Hill, Lynn 126n24
Forman, Simon 189
Forrest, John 267n32
Fortune-Lloyd, Jacob 296
Foucault, Michel 213, 282, 364
Foulkes, Richard 43n9, 53n12
Fox, Adam 166, 167n11
Fox, Cora 234n30
Fox-Good, Jacquelyn Ann 200n2
Foxe, John 168
Francis, Clive 57n23
Frank, Marcie 342–3, 355
Franks, Philip 362
Franssen, Paul 368, 370
Fraser, Hadley 312
Freedman, Barbara 223n20
Freeman, Joanna 333
Freinkel, Lisa 275n29, 275n26, 276n39
Freire López, Ana 104n35
Freud, Sigmund 222n16
Frijlink, Wilhelmina P. 115
Fripp, Edgar I. 61
Frye, Susan 165, 168n18, 168–9n23
Fuller, Craig 314
Fuller, Thomas 379
Fumerton, Patricia 166n4
Furness, Horace Howard 140n14
Furnivall, F. J. 41
Fuseli, Henry 57n24

Gager, William 152
Gaines, Barbara 363
Gair, Reavley 261n13, 261–2n13, 262n14, 265n26, 266n27
Galbraith, Steven 379
Galey, Alan 383
Galieva, Aruhan 297
Gallardo, Miquel 327
Galsworthy, John 43
Galván, Luis 108n61, 111n67
Gamboa, Brett 373–4
Garavello, Monica 83
García, Anton 105n43
García Oro, José 97n38
García Reidy, Alejandro 90, 99n5, 105n41, 107n54
Gardiner, Samuel 224–5n31
Gardner, Helen 100n9

Garnier, Robert 147
Garnon, James 287–8, 321, 333–4
Garrick, David 51–2, 56, 348, 383
Gatwa, Ncuti 293
Gatwood, Rebecca 332
Gazzard, Hugh 123–4
Geoffrey, Marc 313–14
George V, King of Great Britain 42–3
Gerritsen, Johan 99, 100
Ghose, Indira 135
Gibbons, Orlando 191–2
Gibson, Abraham 126–7
Gilborne, Samuel 37
Gill, Roma 125n22, 125n13, 126n23
Ginsburg, Ruth Bader 77
Glapthorne, Henry 101–4
Godwin, Simon 204n25, 302–3, 303Illus.23, 334
Goethe, Johann Wolfgang von 52, 62
Goldberg, Jonathan 342–3, 355
Goldin-Meadow, Susan 193n17
Golding, Arthur 242n13
Gollancz, Israel 40–9, 55, 385
Gollob, Herman 63
Gombrich, Ernst 353
Gómez, Jesús 107n56
Gondomar, Diego Sarmiento de Acuña, Count of 193
Gonsalves, Aileen 336
Gooch, Sarah 301
Goodale, Thomas 115
Goodbody, Buzz 4
Goold, Rupert 167n12, 321–2, 331
Gosse, Edmund 43
Gossett, Suzanne 371–2, 373, 384
Gosson, Stephen 197
Gouwens, Kenneth 215
Gower, John 176, 179
Goy-Blanquet, Dominique 358
Grady, Hugh 246, 247
Graham, Kenneth J. E. 281n61
Graham, Scott 333
Grantley, Daryll 262n18, 262n17
Gray, Jonathan 129
Gray, Thomas 52
Grazzini, Anton Francesco 184n8
Greatley-Hirsch, Brett 163n20
Green, Jonathon 128n34
Green, Nicholas 337
Greenblatt, Stephen 77, 255, 371, 384
Greene, Robert 101–4, 119, 150, 152–3, 158n14, 196n36
Greene, Thomas 340–1
Greer, Margaret Rich 90, 91, 99n5, 105n41, 106n47, 106n44
Greg, W. W. 99–112, 113, 114n4, 116, 118n16, 118n16, 118n13, 121, 141, 380, 381, 386
Gregg, Melissa 231n15
Gregory, Patrick 190n7
Greig, David 298n3

SHAKESPEARE SURVEY 70 INDEX

Griffin, Andrew 353–4, 355
Griffith, Jane 143n28
Griffith, Marcus 302
Grint, William 298
Groves, Beatrice 129n36
Groves, Peter 345
Gruber, Elizabeth D. 239n53
Grundy, Bill 127
Guarini, Giovanni Battista 184n8
Guerin, Lucy 315–16, 330
Guidi, Michele Athos 83
Gupta, Tanika 291
Gurr, Andrew 59, 112, 120n22, 189, 190n6, 191n10, 194n23, 195n31, 199, 373
Gusain, Renuka 285n86
Guthrie, Tyrone 367
Gwynne, Nia 304

Hadfield, Andrew 230n11, 249
Haines, Tom 330
Halbwachs, Maurice 343
Hall, Arthur 152
Hall, Edward 172n35, 332
Hall, Elizabeth 341
Hall, Lee 338
Hall, Peter 3–4, 55n18, 339
Hall, Susanna 65
Halliwell-Phillipps, James Orchard 53, 62
Hamert, Steph 332
Hamilton-Dyer, Peter 35
Hands, Terry 4–5, 327
Hannah, Dorita 366
Harbage, Alfred 155n7, 190n6
Hardie, Sean 123n1
Harding, Ted 77n27
Harmon, A. G. 176n13
Harran, Don 74n23
Harris, Jonathan Gil 165
Harrison, John 380
Harsnett, Samuel 174–5, 180
Hart, Paul 334
Harvey, Christopher 335
Harvey, Gabriel 152
Harvey, Leah 309
Hassel, R. Chris Jr. 220, 281n61
Hassell, Alex 328
Hastie, Robert 307–9, 308Illus.25
Hathaway, Anne 59, 65–6
Haughton, William 158n14, 159n17, 161–2n18
Haven-Jones, Lee 327
Hawes, Stephen 126
Hawkes, David 353, 355
Hawkes, Sophie 243n16
Heffernan, Aaron 294
Heffernan, John 316, 330
Heffernan, Julian Jiménez 241–2
Helgerson, Richard 223
Henderson, Diana 77n27
Hendricks, Margo 357

Hengel, Martin 273n12
Henke, Robert 183n7
Henrietta Maria, Queen of England 182
Henslowe, Philip 89, 172, 216
Herford, C. H. 44
Herington, C. J. 150n15
Herodotus 151
Herold, Niels 358
Herrick, Robert 241n5, 347
Herrmann, Karl Ernst 366
Hewlett, James 375–6
Heywood, Thomas 101–4, 114, 115, 116, 117, 118, 147, 158n14, 159n17, 161–2n18, 182–3, 189, 192, 193, 196
Hibbard, G. R. 125, 126, 137n6
Hick, Rarriwuy 320
Higgins, B. D. R. 379
Hildy, Franklin J. 48n30
Hill, Maddy 297
Hille, Anastasia 327
Hill-Gibbins, Joe 331
Hills, Julia 313
Hilton, Andrew 313–14
Hinman, Charlton 378
Hirsch, James 256
Hirschfeld, Heather 382
Hoare, Tim 334
Hoby, Elizabeth 168
Hodgdon, Barbara 213n4, 217n21, 218n23
Hoenselaars, Ton 262n17
Hofele, Andreas 216
Hoffman, Dustin 70
Holborn, H. and A. 221n9
Holderness, Graham 62, 63–4, 68n6
Holding, Bryn 329
Holinshed, Raphael 151, 171, 176
Holland, Henry 128
Holland, Peter 47n22, 51n3, 186n14, 261n7, 348, 367, 381, 383
Holland, Philemon 214n7
Holles, John 196
Holm, Ian 4
Holmes, James 127
Holroyd, Michael 58
Homer 152
Honan, Park 50n1, 62, 64, 219n4, 222
Honig, Bonnie 246n32, 246n30
Honigmann, E. A. J. 37n5, 124n8, 124n7, 125n12, 125, 375–6, 384
Hooks, Adam G. 66, 379–81, 384
Hoole, Charles 195
Hope, Jonathan 182n2, 208–9
Hopkins, 235n35
Hoppe, Marianne 366
Horace 165
Horslen, Ben 328
Horsley, Owen 328, 329, 332
Hoskins, John 143
Houlahan, Mark 40, 45n15, 345, 355
Hove, Ivo van 316–18

Howard, Alan 4, 5
Howard, Henry, Earl of Surrey 205, 230–1n12
Howard, Jean E. 42n6, 279n47, 371, 372, 384
Howard, Leslie 369
Howard-Hill, Thomas 193n19
Hoy, Cyrus 261n10
Huebert, Ronald 347, 355
Huffman, Clifford Chalmers 238n51
Huggins, Tyrone 336
Hughes, Guy 297
Hulme, Mike 356
Hulme-Beaman, Genevieve 295Illus.21
Hume, Robert D. 381, 384
Humphreys, Jonathan 335
Hunsdon, Henry Carey, 1st Baron 36
Hunt, Arnold 224–6n27–n34
Hunt, Simon 166n4
Hunter, Damion 320Illus.29
Hunter, G. K. 229
Hunter, Kelly 327
Hutson, Lorna 349–50, 355
Hyde, Douglas 43, 44
Hytner, Nicholas 16, 17

Ifans, Rhys 311
Iglesias, Noelia 107n53, 109n64
Imrie, Celia 311
Ingham, Michael 359
Ioppolo, Grace 89, 99n3
Ireland, Samuel 65–6, 367
Irving, Henry 58, 348
Isenberg, Nancy 359
Isoda, Aki 339
Iurissevich, Adriano 83, 85, 86Illus.6
Ivers, David 362

Jack, Chris 304
Jackson, Daryl 337
Jackson, Glenda 311
Jackson, Henry 190, 192, 193, 198
Jackson, Ken 273
Jackson, MacDonald P. 115n6, 147n3, 153n24, 261, 358
Jackson, Michael 7
Jackson, Russell 356–60, 361–70
Jacobi, Derek 5, 312–13, 331
Jacobson, Howard 19–29, 340, 385
Jacobus de Voragine 174, 175
Jacotot, Joseph 136n2
Jaffe-Berg, Erith 75n24
Jaggard, William 380, 382
James, Charlene 338
James, Heather 230–1n12, 240–1
James, Henry 26
James, Lily 312
Jankélévitch, Vladimir 75
Jansohn, Christa 53n12, 54n16
Jasztal, Luke 330
Jay, Ami 335

394

SHAKESPEARE SURVEY 70 INDEX

Jeffere, John 184n8
Jeffries, Hester Lees 173
Jenkins, Harold 55, 121, 262n14, 268n38
Jennings, Sharon 335
Jensen, Phebe 181n40, 286n88
Jerome, Stephen 128–9
Jiménez Heffernan, Julian 241–2
John, Stephen 329
Johnson, Kathryn 367
Johnson, Richard 4
Johnson, Samuel 26, 154
Johnstone, Oliver 302
Jones, Ann Rosalind 165n3, 165, 166n6, 169, 172, 173
Jones, Nancy A. 204n29
Jones, Thomas 52
Jonson, Ben 147, 155, 157n13, 158n14, 159n17, 159, 161–2n18, 164, 190, 229, 240, 241, 244n26, 259, 262n19, 262n14, 267n35, 341
Jónsson, Börkur 292
Joseph, B. L. 189, 193n16
Joseph, Paterson 326
Jowett, John 100n14, 100n12, 113–22, 141, 159, 210, 211n9, 383, 386
Joyce, James 154
Juliá Martínez, Eduardo 94
Justin Martyr 274

Kahane, Henry 79n2
Kahn, Coppélia 41n2, 43n11, 43, 51n3, 55n18, 55n18, 230n11, 232, 236, 347–8, 355
Kalinina, Polina 334
Kambaskovic, Danijela 345
Kane, John 5
Kantor, Michael 319–21, 320Illus.29
Karim, Scott 298
Karim-Cooper, Farah 48n30, 346–7, 355, 367–8
Karremann, Isabel 343–4, 355
Kastan, David Scott 72, 101n17, 119n21, 126, 228n1
Kathman, David 97n37, 358
Kaurismaki, Aki 368, 369
Kean, Edmund 343
Keane, Michael 329
Keanrye, James 359
Keilen, Sean 240, 242
Kelley, Shannon 243n20
Kelly, Philippa 178n24
Kemble, John Philip 52, 343, 383
Kemble, Roger 52
Kemp, Brian 50n1
Kendon, Adam 193n17
Kermode, Lloyd 354
Kerr, Heather 345
Kerrigan, John 129n36, 340, 350–1, 355
Kesting, Hans 317
Kestleman, Sarah 5

Kewes, Pauline 228n1, 230n7, 237n47
Khan, Iqbal 295–6, 333, 335
Khoury, Makram J. 331
Kidnie, Margaret Jane 191n10, 382–4
Kieckhefer, Richard 177n16, 178n17, 178n17
Killick, Jerry 322–3
King, Edmund 379
King, Kamahi Djordon 319, 320Illus.29
King, Ros 301
Kingsland, Robin 331
Kingsley, Ben 4
Kinnear, Rory 17
Kinney, Arthur 148n7, 153n25
Kirkman, Francis 261, 379, 380
Kirwan, Peter 341–2, 355, 371–84
Kishi Tetsuo 359
Kitzinger, Celia 223n19
Knapp, Jeffrey 219, 227
Knight, Edward 117, 382
Knight, Jeffrey Todd 383
Knight, Leah 356–7
Knowles, James 188n2
Koo Yu Jin 357
Korda, Natasha 165, 170n30, 186n13
Korley, Debbie 319
Kosky, Barry 247
Kottman, Paul 237, 246n31, 248
Kouassi, Erica 299
Kraaij, Peter van 316–18
Kreiss, Stephan 324, 325
Ksander, Peter 82n6
Kulick, Brian 363
Kunin, Aaron 343
Kurup, Shishir 332
Kuzner, James 273, 276–7n40, 282–3, 285n87, 285n83, 286n87
Kyd, Thomas 146–53, 158n14, 182–3, 184, 262, 263, 387

La Cecla, Franco 75
Lacey, Joshua 297
Ladouceur, Louise 132n51
Lafont, Agnès 243n18
Lagueux, Robert C. 281n58
Laing, Steward 336
Laird, David 277n42, 280n53
Lake, Peter 235n33
Lamb, Mary Ellen 269
Lamos, Mark 363
Lampe, John Frederick **333**
Langbaine, Gerard 379
Langhans, Edward 112n69
Langis, Unhae 244n22
Lanier, Douglas 368
Lanier, Emilia 61
Lanini, Pedro Francisco de 109
Laroque, François 221n14
Latimer, Hugh, Bishop of Worcester 168
Laughton, Charles 3
Laula, Lerothodi 43n11

Lavagnino, James 193n20, 196n34
Lea-Jones, Jenni 85–6, 86Illus.6
Leake, William 380
Lee, Brian S. 229n4
Lee, M. Owen 234n32, 235n36, 236n41
Lee, Sir Sidney 55
Lees-Jeffries, Hester 387
Leigh, Vivien 367
Lembke, Janet 150n15
Lenardo, Isabella di 69n11, 79n1
LePage, Robert 366
Lesser, Zachary 380, 382
Lester, Adrian 10–18, 338, 385
Levenson, Jill 383
Leveridge, Richard 51
Levring, Krtistian 368
Levy, Santina M. 244n24
Lewis, B. Roland 59
Lewis, Tom E. 319–20
Light, John 289–90
Lindley, David 33, 200n1, 202n14, 202, 203n18, 204n30, 205
Lindsay, Hugh 253
Ling, Nicholas 120
Littler, Tom 326
Littlewood, S. R. 48n27
Livingstone, Rodney 259n2
Lloyd, Janet 221n14
Lloyd, John 123n1
Lloyd, Phyllida 7, 309–10, 310Illus.26
Lodge, Thomas 101–4, 148, 150, 151, 152, 153
London, Frank 76, 82n6
Long, John H. 200n1, 202n16, 202, 203n22
Long, William B. 99, 100–1, 115, 376
Longhurst, Michael 287, 289–90, 290Illus.19
Loomis, C. Grant 175n8
Loomis, Catherine 364–5, 370
Lopez, Jeremy 189
Lorente Medina, Antonio 104n35
Lotman, Maria Kristiina 114n3
Lotman, Mikhail 114n3
Loughnane, Rory 118n13, 150n11
Loughrey, Brian 132, 133
Lowden, Richard 322–3
Lowe, Syrus 308
Lucia, Emma 338
Lucking, David 277n44
Luhrmann, Baz 345, 370
Lumney, Ruth 345
Lupton, Julia Reinhard 72n18, 240–8n38, 282n67, 282n63, 285–6n87, 359, 388
Luscombe, Christopher 330, 333
Luther, Martin 272, 273, 274, 275, 276, 281n60, 283–4, 284n76
Lutteman, Elizabeth 200–6,
Lyly, John 159n17, 161–2n18, 184, 262n19
Lynch, Finbar 321

395

Lyttelton, Oliver 46–7

Mabbe, James 97
McCafferty, S. 133n53
MacCallum, Mungo 228n1
McDermott, Phelim 336
McDiarmid, Ian 331
McDonald, Russ 365
McEachern, Claire 248n37, 263n21, 264n24, 375, 384
McEnery, John 329
MacFaul, Tom 353, 355
McGrath, S. J. 274n17, 275n26, 276n37
McGregor, Ross 335, 336
McGuckin, Aislin 322
McGuinness, Jonathan 297
McGuire, Kristy and David 57n24
Machin, Gervase 161–2n18
Machit, Melissa Renee 92, 93, 94, 95, 96n34
McIntyre, Blanche 304–5, 326
McIntyre, Callum 313
MacIntyre, Jean 172n36
McKellen, Ian 4
McKenzie, Allison 304
McKernan, Luke 360
Mackintosh, Iain 57n23
McLean, Anna Helena 333
MacLiam, Edward 294–5
McLuskie, Kathleen E. 261–2n13
McManus, Clare 186n13, 372
MacMillan, Kenneth 335, 359
McMillin, Scott 186n14
McMullan, Gordon 40–9, 50, 55n18, 55, 132n49, 182n2, 367–8, 370, 371–2, 373, 384, 385
McMullan, Tim 290–1
McMullen, Jack 308–9
McMurray, Sasha 332
McNamee, Frances 305
MacNeil, Anne 183n6
McNeill, David 193n17
McNeill, Fiona 166
McPherson, David C. 68n6
Macready, William Charles 361
Madden, Richard 312
Madsen, Carsten 143
Magnusson, Lynne 137n4, 140, 348
Maguire, Laurie 194n23
Mahon, Alan 313
Maillot, Jean-Christophe 335
Maisano, Scott 215
Malcolm, Noel 137–8n7, 142
Malone, Edmond 60, 62, 150
Mann, David 182n4, 185n12
Manningham, John 59, 198
Manovich, Lev 248n38
Manso Porto, Carmen 97n38
Manson, William R. 107n59, 107n58
Mantel, Hilary 171
Marcell, Joseph 291

Marcello, Elena E. 104n35
Marcus, Leah 383
Markham, Lewis 161–2n18
Marlowe, Christopher 146, 147, 148–9, 150, 151, 152–3, 158n14, 182–3, 210, 256, 343, 344, 387
Marquez, Martin 298
Marrapodi, Michele 233n27
Marsh, Christopher 196n35, 205n36
Marshall, Isabella 313
Marston, John (d.1599, father of poet) 188
Marston, John (d.1634, poet) 138, 158n14, 159n17, 161–2n18, 188n1, 188, 189, 192, 194, 262, 263–4, 265n26, 266
Martellini, Drusiano 183
Martin, Anna Maxwell 316, 330
Martin, Dale B. 273, 284n77
Martin, David 223n20
Martin, John Jeffries 215n14
Martin, Randall 352, 355
Martindale, Charles 229, 230–1n12
Martínez del Barrio, Javier Ignacio 93
Marvell, Andrew 343, 347
Mary I, Queen of England 176
Mary, Queen of Great Britain (consort of George V) 42–3
Mary, Queen of Scots 173
Maslen, R.W. 221n9
Mason, James 177n16
Massai, Sonia 101n19, 141n18, 191n10, 367, 378, 382–4
Massey, Petra 323–4, 325
Massinger, Philip 89–98, 98n40, 101–4, 117n12, 159n17, 180, 386
Masson, Forbes 332
Maus, Katharine Eisaman 249–58, 371, 384, 389
May, James M. 194n26
Mayer, Jean-Christophe 231n14, 379, 382–3
Mazzio, Carla 142n22, 241n6
Mead, Philip 40, 45n15
Meale, Carol 179n26
Mehl, Dieter 53n12, 54n16
Meira Serras, Adelaide 357
Melchiori, Giorgio 130n41, 152n21
Mendelssohn, Félix 332
Mendoza, Bernardino de 130–1n46
Menzer, Paul 343, 355
Meow Meow 292–3, 293Illus.20
Meres, Francis 270
Meriam, Thomas 114n3
Merrix, Robert P. 242n14
Messel, Oliver 369
Michaud, Philippe-Alain 243n16
Middleton, Thomas 64, 115, 132, 133, 146, 147, 155, 157n13, 158n14, 158–9n14, 159n17, 159n17, 161–2n18, 164, 193–4, 196, 261, 341, 344

Milhous, Judith 381, 384
Mill, James 208, 209
Miller, Jonathan 329
Miller, Linda 333
Miller, Steven 333
Mills, Charlotte 299
Mills, Maldwyn 179n26
Mills, Perry 172n39
Milton, John 343, 347
Ming Cho Lee 365–6
Minkhoff, Richelle 357
Minton, Gretchen 129n39
Miola, Robert S. 228n1, 235
Mirk, John 174n1
Mirren, Helen 4, 5, 8
Misztela, Piotr 327
Mitchell, William 63, 65n6
Mohr, Melissa 124n3, 126n24
Mond, Frida 47n23
Mondahl, Byron 302
Montaigne, Michel Eyquem de 168, 215
Montgomery, William 100n14, 121n27
Moodie, Tanya 303
Moore, Duncan 335
Moore, J. K. 119
Mora, George 177n16, 178n18, 178n18
More, Thomas 143, 347
Morgan, Jude 64
Morley, Thomas 38
Morris, Cass 364
Morris, Sylvia 52n10
Morse, Ruth 207–12, 388
Moryson, Fynes 183–4
Moschovakis, Nicholas R. 233n22, 233, 238n50, 240n1
Moss, Candida R. 284n80
Motion, Andrew 340
Mountfort, Walter 101–4
Mowat, Barbara A. 100n7, 125n11, 125n11
Msamati, Lucian 333
Mueller, Sara 170n30
Muir, Kenneth 125n9
Mulryne, Ronnie 357
Munby, Jonathan 331
Munday, Anthony 101–4, 114, 115, 118, 153, 168–9, 184n8
Munro, Lucy 123–34, 135, 186n13, 348, 387
Murphy, Andrew 43, 100n9, 383
Myer-Bennet, Dorothea 288

Nance, John V. 146–53, 163n19, 387
Nashe, Thomas 130, 146, 149, 150, 152, 153, 182–3, 196–7, 270
Nasr, Ramsey 317
Needham, Matthew 298
Neill, Michael 125n14, 125
Nelson, Conrad 337
Neville, Oliver 15
Newcomb, James 152

Newman, Karen 342–3, 355
Ney, Charles 362
Ngai, Sianne 241–2, 244n23, 246n32, 246
Nicholl, Charles 61, 62, 63
Nicholls, Mark 191n8
Nicolao, Stefano 76, 82n6
Nietzsche, Friedrich 272–3
Nightingale, Lisa 299–300
Nilaand, Anna 332
Nims, Jonathan Frederick 242n15, 242n13
Ninagawa Yukio 327
Nixon, Pippa 291
Noble, Adrian 4, 6
Noble, Richmond 200n1, 201, 220, 223n22, 224
Nora, Pierre 348
Normington, Andrew 337
Norris, Rufus 314
Northbrooke, John 219n2
Novak, Peter 357
Nri, Cyril 303
Nunn, Trevor 4, 339, 370
Nureyev, Rudolf 335

O'Brien, Tim 57
O'Callaghan, Michelle 142–3
O'Connor, Marion F. 42n6, 47n24, 48n31
O'Connor, Terry 322–3
O'Hare, Eugene 288–9
O'Hea, Brendan 288
Ojelade, Mercy 301
Olivier, Laurence 3, 376
Olleson, Edward 202n11
O'Loughlin, Katrina 345, 355
Omambala, Chu 300Illus.22, 301
O'Neill, Jonjo 289
O'Neill, Stephen 43n11
Orgel, Stephen 141, 185n11, 185, 186n14, 200n2, 261n7
Origen 274
Orlando, Silvio 76
Orlin, Lena Cowen 44n12, 66, 165–6, 166n4, 168n22, 168, 170n31, 170
Orrell, John 31
Osborne, Asia 338
O'Shea, Steven 327
Ostovich, Helen 353–4, 355
Osuna, Dukes of 92–3
Otes, Samuel 128
Overbury, Sir Thomas 266n30
Ovid 167, 168, 171, 173, 176, 230–1n12, 240–1, 242–3, 277, 278n45, 280, 345, 380
Owen, Katy 292
Owen, Lucy Briggs 338

Packer, Tina 363
Palfrey, Simon 89, 188n3
Palmetshofer, Ewald 328
Park, Tim 324–5

Park, Toby 323
Parker, Matthew, Archbishop of Canterbury 175
Parker, Patricia 137n4, 138, 140, 280
Parker, Rozsika 165
Parolin, Peter 185n10
Parr, Anthony 142–3
Pasqualigo, Luigi 184n8
Pastore, Matthieu 83
Patel, Dharmesh 291, 297
Patricia, Anthony Guy 369–70,
Patrides, C. A. 215
Paul, St 222, 272–7, 277n42, 279, 280, 281–6, 389
Paul IV, Pope 69, 71
Paz y Meliá, A. 99n5, 106n44, 106n47, 108n62
Peacham, Henry 142, 143
Peale, C. George 107n59, 107n58
Pedicord, Harry William 51n2
Pedraza Jiménez, Felipe B. 104n35
Peele, George 146, 147, 148, 149, 150, 152–3, 158n14, 237
Pellone, Elena 79n2, 83n7, 83, 85n11
Pennington, Michael 63, 312, 318, 361–2, 370
Pérez Díez, José A. 89–98, 386
Pérez Guerra, Javier 223n18
Perkins, Richard 120n22
Perske, Hunter 83
Persons, Robert 231n14
Philip, Prince, Duke of Edinburgh 56
Philippou, Philippos 330
Philips, James Emerson 228n1
Phillimore, John Francis 79n1
Phillips, Augustine 37
Phillips, Bríd 345
Piccolomini, Alessandro 184n8
Piissimi, Vittoria 183
Pikli, Natália 259–71, 389
Piper, Tom 299
Plaatje, Solomon 43, 44
Plato 151
Platt, Isaac Hull 138–9
Platt, Michael 228n1
Platter, Thomas 197–8
Plautus 176, 262n19
Playfere, Thomas 380
Pliny the Elder 214, 218
Plutarch 151, 176, 254, 258
Poel, William 42, 47–8, 48n31, 49
Pohlmeier, Arne 335
Pollard, Alfred W. 100
Pontón, Gonzalo 106n49
Poole, Adrian 19–29, 55n18, 385
Porter, Chloe 165, 169n28, 173, 284n75, 285n84, 286n89
Porter, Cole 336
Porter, Henry 158n14
Potter, Lois 167–8, 196, 372

Powell, Anton 233, 234n29, 236n43, 237n49, 238n50
Powell, Linda 83n7, 83n7, 83, 84
Powell, Walter 129n35
Power, Dominic 313
Preiss, Richard 194n22
Prescott, Anne 137–8n7
Prescott, Paul 47–8, 195n31
Presotto, Marco 104n35, 105n39, 105n38, 106n45, 108n63
Prokofiev, Sergei 335
Pryce, Jonathan 331
Pryce, Phoebe 291
Prynne, William 279
Pudsey, Edward 261
Pugh, Sytithe 240n3, 241n5
Pullan, Brian 69n8, 69n7
Purcell, Stephen 287–325
Purchas, Samuel 224–5
Purdie, Susan 222n16
Purkis, James 116n8, 118n15, 118n13, 382
Puttenham, George 220, 270
Puwanarajah, Prasanna 316

Quarles, Francis 191
Quarshie, Hugh 16, 333, 375–6
Quartley, Mark 305–6, 306Illus.24, 327
Quayle, Anthony 3
Quintilian 193, 194, 221n10, 229

Raab, Felix 96
Rabelais, François 350
Race, Jonathan 338
Racine, Jean 8
Rackham, Horace 214n7
Raczka, Lulu 338
Rainsford, Jenny 306
Raison, Miranda 312
Rakowska, Anna 327
Ralegh, Sir Walter 191–2
Rameau, Philippe 247
Rancière, Jacques 135, 136, 144n31, 387
Randolph, Thomas 142
Rankins, William 219, 220, 227
Rasmussen, Eric 367, 378, 379, 383–4
Rasmussen, Mark David 358–9
Ravelhofer, Barbara 216
Ravid, Benjamin 67n2
Ray, Sid 364–5, 370
Rebhorn, Wayne 255
Redgrave, Vanessa 4, 322
Redman, Joyce 3
Rees, Roger 4
Reeves, William Pember 43
Refskou, Anne Sophie 228n1
Regan, Jessica 308Illus.25
Regan, Morna 294
Reid, Sheila 287, 288, 333–4
Reinhardt, Max 71, 79–80, 366, 369, 370
Renwick, W. L. 102n26
Reutlinger, Emily 332

Reynard, James 336
Reynolds, Brian 273
Ribeiro, Alejandro 148n7
Rice, Emma 291–4, 293Illus.20, 297, 298–9, 307
Richardson, Catherine 148n5, 165
Richardson, Ian 4, 5
Richardson, Nathaniel 364
Rickman, Natasha 337
Rijswijck, Dirck van 245Illus.18
Risebero, John 328
Roach, Joseph R. 189, 193n16
Robertson, Jean 269, 270n49
Robeson, Paul 3
Robinson, John A. T. 284
Rochester, Joanne M. 179n30
Rodenburg, Patsy 362–3
Rodríguez Cáceres, Milagros 104n35
Rodríguez Gallego, Fernando 107n55
Rodríguez López-Vázquez, Alfredo 106n47, 106n50, 109n65
Rodríguez Rodríguez, Beatriz 266n28
Romera Castillo, José Nicolás 104n35
Romney, Sir George 57n24
Rosenblatt, Mark 334
Rosenthal, Amy 338
Rosenthal, Daniel 45
Ross, Kristin 135
Ross, Sir Ronald 43
Rostand, Edmond 5
Roulon, Nathalie 202n17, 203–4
Rouse, William Henry Denham 246n28
Rowe, Katherine 359
Rowe, Nicholas 60
Rowland, David 266n28
Rowlands, Avril 65
Rowley, Samuel 158n14
Rowley, William 147, 158n14, 161–2n18, 263–4, 344
Rubright, Marjorie 139n11
Ruddock, Bryonny 337
Rudick, Michael 191n11
Rudman, Joseph 155, 156, 161
Rush, Christopher 64
Russell, Anne 182n1
Russell, Donald A. 194n27, 221n10
Russell, Isabella 170
Russell, Sibylla 170
Rutter, Barrie 329
Rutter, Carol Chillington 79–86, 386
Ryan, Kiernan 219, 222n16, 226, 227
Rylance, Mark 5, 32, 292

St. Hilaire, Danielle 231, 231n16, 234n31, 235, 239n53
Sale, Carolyn 230n11, 230n9
Saller, Richard 252
Samal, Danusia 305
Sanchez, Nicholas 358
Sánchez Mariana, Manuel 104n35
Sanders, Norman 125n10, 130n41

Sanders, Wilbur 28
Sands, James 37
Sandys, George 183–4
Santner, Eric 213
Sarmiento de Acuña, Don Diego, Count of Gondomar 97
Sarossy, Gyuri 304
Saunders, Corinne 177n16
Schalkwyk, David 43, 207–8n2 5, 348, 357
Schama, Simon 179n29
Schanzer, Ernest 197n39, 198n40
Scheil, Katherine 58–66n9, 386
Scherini, Stefano 83, 85
Schiermeister, Jessica 185n10
Schoch, Richard 348
Schoenbaum, Samuel 50n1, 59, 62, 155n7
Schreyer, Kurt 280n56, 280
Schwartz, Leo W. 71n14
Scot, Reginald 174–5, 178
Scott, Alison V. 345
Scott, Charlotte 340–55
Scott, Joel 330
Scott, Lindsey 230n8
Scott-Baumann, Elizabeth 340, 355
Scott-Douglas, Amy 357
Secker, Eloise 305
Seddon, Deborah 43n11
Segarra, Santiago 148n7
Seigworth, Gregory J. 231n15
Semenza, Greg M. Colón 243n19
Semler, Liam 178n24
Seneca the Younger 150, 152, 230–1n12
Seng, Peter J. 200n1, 203
Seron, Diego 105n43
Sex Pistols 127
al-Shaater, Yaz 336
Shaheen, Naseeb 220, 220n7
Shakespeare, Hamnet 61
Shakespeare, John 66, 176, 341
Shakespeare, William
  editions
    Arden 375–8, 384
    Bell 381
    Folger 126
    Folio
      First (1623) 31, 35–7, 38, 50–1, 114n2, 120, 121–2, 124, 125–6, 129, 141, 243, 262n14, 263n21, 340, 354, 372, 373, 374, 376–7, 378–9, 380, 382, 384
      Third (1664) 51
    Internet Shakespeare 374–5, 384
    MIT 210
    New Cambridge 360
    New Oxford (2016) 159, 371
    Norton 3 371–4, 384
    Oxford 210
    Oxford Complete Works 59n2, 166n5, 209n7, 213n4, 251n6, 251, 260n5

    Oxford Schools 126
    Pope 381
    quarto 36–7, 113–22, 124, 129, 139, 140–1, 243, 262n14, 263n21, 270, 371, 372, 373, 374, 376, 380, 382
    Riverside 210
    Rowe 381
    Theobald 140, 263n21, 381
    Tonson 381
  plays
    All's Well That Ends Well 34, 155n8, 157n13, 159n17, 161–2n18, 263–4, 313–14, 348, 364–5
    Antony and Cleopatra 18, 31, 34, 155n8, 157n13, 171, 185, 186, 199, 324–5, 326, 353
    As You Like It 9, 10, 13, 18, 155n8, 157n13, 159n17, 184, 185, 191, 262, 266n30, 269, 314–15, 315Illus.27, 326, 366
    The Comedy of Errors 155n8, 158n14, 159n17, 161–2n18, 176, 179, 348, 353
    Coriolanus 3, 5, 34, 35–6, 64, 155n8, 157n13, 171, 172, 324, 365
    Cymbeline 159n17, 228n1, 287, 288–9, 297, 301–2, 307, 326, 327
    Hamlet 1, 4, 5, 8, 10, 11, 12–13, 15, 19, 20, 26–7, 33, 62, 120–1, 123–4, 125–6, 129, 130–4, 155n8, 157n13, 168, 170, 199, 200–6, 208–10, 211–12, 221n11, 235, 258, 262, 268, 270n51, 302–3, 303Illus.23, 313, 324, 325, 327–8, 343, 347, 348, 366, 367, 368, 371, 375, 383, 384
    1 Henry IV 121, 124, 125, 126, 133, 158n14, 251, 262n19, 328, 361, 363, 367
    2 Henry IV 5, 251, 308, 328, 348, 361, 363, 364, 372, 376–8, 384
    Henry V 1–2, 4, 11, 13, 25, 172n40, 173, 249, 251, 307–9, 308Illus.25, 328–9, 354, 364
    Henry VI 5, 146, 148, 251
    1 Henry VI 34, 146, 148, 149, 348
    2 Henry VI 148, 208–9, 372
    3 Henry VI 149, 321
    Henry VIII 34, 171–2, 180, 344
    Julius Caesar 8, 9, 25, 31, 155n8, 157n13, 197, 249–58, 302, 324, 325, 389
    King John 61, 126, 329
    King Lear 1–2, 4, 9, 18, 36, 64, 155n8, 157n13, 180, 199, 200, 201–3, 206, 269, 287, 303–4, 310, 318–21, 329, 346, 349, 353, 361–2, 363, 366, 367, 371

Love's Labour's Lost 13, 34, 135–45, 155n8, 157n13, 159n17, 198, 221n11, 262, 264, 266–7, 268, 329–30, 348, 364, 387
Macbeth 1, 4, 6–7, 9, 12, 29, 64, 167n12, 208, 295–6, 315–16, 324, 330–1, 343, 349–50, 352, 353
Measure For Measure 10–11, 64, 157n13, 172n38, 263–4, 331, 344
The Merchant of Venice 34, 39, 67–78, 79–86, 155n8, 157n13, 159n17, 184, 255–6, 331–2, 348, 351, 357, 373–4, 385, 386
The Merry Wives of Windsor 5, 155n8, 157n13, 159n17, 262n19, 332, 352, 367
A Midsummer Night's Dream 1, 5, 35, 36, 38, 57, 82, 155n8, 159n17, 169, 176, 184, 208–9, 270, 277–82, 288–301, 293Illus.20, 324, 332–3, 353, 367–8, 369, 370, 389
Much Ado About Nothing 54, 155n8, 157n13, 159n17, 262, 263n21, 263n21, 263, 264–5, 266n30, 266, 267–8, 271, 333, 347, 375, 384
Othello 1, 3, 4, 5, 9, 11, 13, 16–17, 54, 124–5, 126, 129–30, 133, 155n8, 157n13, 178–9, 190, 203–4, 210, 212, 267n34, 333, 343, 348, 366, 372, 373, 374–6, 384
Pericles 170, 176, 179–80, 287–8, 333–4, 341, 344, 372
Richard II 11, 31, 121, 149, 176n13, 210, 243, 251, 255, 334, 380
Richard III 1, 5, 18, 25, 33, 126, 129, 149, 150, 158n14, 208–9, 210–11, 251, 321–2, 334, 353, 361
Romeo and Juliet 9, 22, 25, 26, 36–8, 121, 126, 133, 155n8, 157n13, 158n14, 184–5, 240–8n38, 262, 263, 269, 312–13, 324, 334–5, 349, 357, 358, 359, 369, 370, 379, 380, 388
Sir Thomas More 101–4, 114–15, 117–19, 222, 341, 382
The Taming of the Shrew 155n8, 159n17, 161–2n18, 184, 213, 217–18, 294–5, 299, 335–6, 359, 388
The Tempest 1, 19, 31, 38, 61, 64, 71–2, 80, 155n8, 159n17, 161–2n18, 177–8, 217n22, 287, 290, 305–7, 306Illus.24, 309–10, 310Illus.26, 336, 345, 353, 357, 364, 367, 383, 387
Timon of Athens 336

Titus Andronicus 6, 125, 126, 129, 146, 166, 228–39n53, 324, 325, 336, 341, 342, 346–7, 353, 388
Troilus and Cressida 121–2, 155n8, 157n13, 337, 348, 353, 375, 384
Twelfth Night 21, 34–5, 143n27, 155n8, 159n17, 161n18–2n18, 166–7, 184, 186, 197, 198, 199, 337, 344, 347, 364, 367–8, 370
The Two Gentlemen of Verona 82, 155n8, 157n13, 159n17, 184, 219–27n40, 296–7, 299, 349, 352, 364, 388
The Two Noble Kinsmen 304–5, 337, 373
The Winter's Tale 6, 38, 64, 141, 159n17, 172–3, 179, 213, 216–17, 224, 260, 267n34, 273, 276–7, 282–6, 287, 289–90, 290Illus.19, 311–12, 337, 348, 364, 365, 388, 389
plays, apocryphal
  Arden of Faversham 341
  Double Falsehood 341
  Edward III 146–53, 158n14, 341
  Locrine 342, 382
poems 337
  The Passionate Pilgrim 373
  The Rape of Lucrece 170, 228n1, 256, 257, 337, 349, 380
  Sonnets 61, 269n39, 340
    12 340
    20 340
    22 340
    138 373
    144 373
    145 59
  Venus and Adonis 59, 337, 353, 380
adaptations
  of *Antony and Cleopatra*
    Antony and Cleopatra (film, Nunn) 4
  of *All's Well That Ends Well*
    All's Well That Ends Well (Power, dir. Hilton) 313 14
  of *As You Like It*
    As You Like It (film, Elliot) 4
  of *The Comedy of Errors*
    The Comedy of Errors (abridged, for children) 326
    The Comedy of Errors (film, Williams) 4
    The Comedy of Errors (musical, Woolfenden) 4
  of *Cymbeline*
    Imogen (Dunster) 297–8, 299
    The Injur'd Princess, or The Fatal Wager (D'Urfey) 327
  of *Hamlet*
    Elsinore (LePage) 366

Festen (Danish film, Vinterberg) 368–9
Gertrude and Claudius (novel, Updike) 25
H(2)O (two-hander, Hamlet and Ophelia) 327
Hamlet (film, Almereyda) 368, 369
Hamlet (film, Brook) 13, 15
Hamlet (live streaming to cinemas, Doran) 8, 9
Hamlet: Who's There? (90-minute version) 327
Hamlet Diagnosis (puppet version) 327
Hamlet is dead. no gravity (tragicomedy, Palmetshofer) 328
Hamlet Liikemaailmassa (Finnish film, Kaurismaki) 368, 369
Hamlets (10 interpretations over 10 floors of Library of Birmingham) 327
Prince H. Universe (one-man talk show, Engel) 327
Roll Over Beethoven (Rock 'n' Roll re-working, Eaton) 327
The Skinhead Hamlet (parody, Curtis) 123–4, 134
Two Shakespeare Heroines: Lady Macbeth and Visions of Ophelia (Isoda) 339
of *Henry IV*, Parts 1 and 2
  The Famous Victories of Henry V (extracts in adaptation for younger audiences) 328
  Henry IV (Festival Players) 328
  Henry IV (Lloyd, all-female abridged version) 309
  Kings of War (van der Eynde and van Kraaij, in Dutch) 317
  My Own Private Idaho (film, Van Sant) 369
  The Wars of the Roses (Barton and Hall) 339
of *Henry V*
  The Famous Victories of Henry V (for younger audiences) 329
  Henry V (film, Branagh) 4
  Henry V – Lion of England (one-man show, for young people) 329
  Kings of War (van der Eynde and van Kraaij, in Dutch) 317
of *Henry VI*
  H VI: Play of Thrones (adapted from Parts 1–3) 329
  The Hollow Crown (BBC TV series) 365
  Kings of War (van der Eynde and van Kraaij, in Dutch) 317
of *Julius Caesar*

Shakespeare, William (cont.)
  Julius Caesar (film, Benson) 1–3
  Julius Caesar (film, Doran) 8
  Julius Caesar (Lloyd, all-female abridged version) 309
  of *King John*
    King John (Hammerpuzzle) 329
  of *King Lear*
    The King Is Alive (film, Levring) 368
    King Lear (film, Brook) 5
    King Lear (TV film, RSC) 4
    King Lear with Sheep (with live sheep) 329
    The Shadow King (Australian indigenous adaptation, Kantor) 319–21, 320Illus.29
    Songs of Lear (song cycle) 329
    A Thousand Acres (novel, Smiley) 25
  of *Love's Labour's Lost*
    Love's Labour's Lost (film, Branagh) 13
  of *Macbeth*
    The Devil Speaks True (from Banquo's perspective, in darkness) 330
    Lady Macbeth of Mtsensk (opera, Shostakovich) 331
    Macbeth (film, Benson) 2
    Macbeth (film, Doran) 6–7
    Macbeth (film, Goold) 167n12
    Macbeth (film, Nunn) 4
    Macbeth (film, Welles) 7
    Macbeth (one-act opera, Styles) 331
    Macbeth (physical adaptation, Cracknell and Guerin) 315–16
    Macbeth – Blood Will Have Blood (for 9–13 year olds) 331
    Macbeth – A Two Man Macbeth (dir. Tweddle) 330
    Macbeth in Silence (wordless performance) 330
    Two Shakespeare Heroines: Lady Macbeth and Visions of Ophelia (Isoda) 339
  of *Much Ado About Nothing*
    Much Ado About Nothing (film, Whedon) 375
    Much Ado About Nothing: Table Top Shakespeare (retelling using household items) 322–3
  of *A Midsummer Night's Dream*
    A Midsummer Night's Dream (cabaret and drag adaptation) 332
    A Midsummer Night's Dream (film, Hall) 4
    A Midsummer Night's Dream (film, Noble) 6

A Midsummer Night's Dream (film, Reinhardt and Dieterle) 369, 370
A Midsummer Night's Dream (TV film, RSC, 1959) 3
Pyramus and Thisbe (opera, Lampe) 333
Titania – a solo cabaret (McLean) 333
of *The Merchant of Venice*
  The Folger Consort with Derek Jacobi (music and readings) 331
  The Merchant of Vembly (Kurup) 332
  The Merchant of Venice (dir. Nilaand) 331–2
  Pocket Merchant (abridged, dir. Hall) 332
  Shylock is My Name (novel, Jacobson) 19–29, 340, 385
  Shylock's Ghost (BBC TV documentary) 76
of *Measure For Measure*
  Desperate Measures (musical adaptation) 331
of *The Merry Wives of Windsor*
  The Merry Wives of Windsor (film, Shaw) 3
  The Merry Wives of Windsor (opera, Verdi) 332
  The Merry Wives of Windsor: Table Top Shakespeare (retelling using household items) 322–3
of *Othello*
  Othello (film, National Theatre Live) 14–15
of *The Rape of Lucrece*
  The Rape of Lucretia (opera, Britten) 337
of *Richard II*
  Richard II (film, Warner) 7
  Richard II (live streaming to cinemas, Doran) 1, 8
of *Richard III*:
  The Filth and the Fury (overtones in documentary on Sex Pistols) 368
  Kings of War (van der Eynde and van Kraaij, in Dutch) 317–18
  Richard III (film, Benson: 1.19, 1911) 3
  Richard III (film, McKellen) 4
  The Wars of the Roses (stage production, Barton and Hall) 339
  The Wars of the Roses (film, Barton and Hall) 4
of *Romeo and Juliet*
  Romeo + Juliet (film, Luhrmann) 370

Romeo and Juliet (ballet, Prokofiev) 335
Romeo and Juliet (blending original and contemporary language, Khan) 335
Romeo and Juliet (film, Cukor) 369, 370
Romeo and Juliet (film, Zeffirelli) 370
Romeo and Rosaline (prequel, Jennings) 335
Shakespeare's R&J (Calarco) 335
of the Sonnets: *On Shakespeare's Sonnets: A Poet's Celebration* (ed. Crawforth and Scott-Baumann): 340
of *The Tempest*
  Amaluna (Cirque du Soleil) 336
  I, Caliban (solo performance, Crouch) 323
  Mirando the Gay Tempest (solo version) 336
  Return to the Forbidden Planet (dir. Carlton) 336
  The Tempest (film, Doran with Intel and Imaginarium Studios) 9
  The Tempest (Lloyd, all-female abridged version) 309–10, 310Illus.26
  This Last Tempest (sequel) 336
of *Titus Andronicus*
  Titus Andronicus (film for South African TV, Doran) 6
of *Troilus and Cressida*
  Troilus and Cressida: Table Top Shakespeare (retelling using household items) 322–3
of *Twelfth Night*
  Twelfth Night (film, Nunn) 370
of *The Taming of the Shrew*
  Kiss Me Kate (musical) 336, 359
  Shrew (solo piece, Jay) 335
  The Taming of the Shrew (film, Benson) 2
  The Taming of the Shrew (gender-reversal, McGregor) 335
  Vinegar Girl (novel, Tyler) 25
of *The Winter's Tale*
  The Gap of Time (novel, Winterson) 25, 340
  The Winter's Tale (BSL translation) 337
  The Winter's Tale (film, Doran) 6
general
  An Age of Kings (BBC TV films) 3
  Blackadder (BBC TV, special episode for opening of Millennium Dome) 368

British Library Essential
    Shakespeare CD set (archived
    RSC recordings) 3
The Complete Deaths (all
    Shakespeare's death scenes,
    Crouch and Spymonkey)
    323–5, 324Illus.30, 338
*Complete Works: Table Top
    Shakespeare* (retellings using
    household items) 322–3
Faustaff (Sosa) 338
The Herbal Bed (Whelan) 338
Kings of War (van der Eynde and
    van Kraaij, in Dutch) 316–18
Live From Stratford-upon-Avon;
    streaming to cinemas 9
Mrs Shakespeare (one-woman
    comedy, Wild) 338
Mrs Shakespeare . . . the Poet's Wife
    (Rolands) 65
National Theatre Live; streaming
    to cinemas 14–15
Red Velvet (Chakrabarti) 338
RSC films 1–2
*Shakespeare and the Alchemy of
    Gender* (Wolpe) 338
Shakespeare in his Cups 338
Shakespeare in Love (film) 368
Shakespeare in Love (stage
    adaptation) 338
Shakespeare in Shoreditch (four new
    plays) 338
Shakespeare's Sister (Whipday) 338
The Stories of Shakey P (hip-hop
    inspired selections) 338
To Build a Wooden O (Wilkes) 339
Tug of War: Foreign Quarrels
    (Chicago Shakespeare Theatre)
    152
*Two Shakespeare Heroines: Lady
    Macbeth and Visions of Ophelia*
    (Isoda) 339
The Wars of the Roses (RSC stage
    production, Barton and Hall)
    3–4, 55n18,
    (revival) 339
Shannon, Laurie 213–18n25, 388
Shapiro, James 23, 24, 28, 58–66n9,
    67n4, 72, 73, 77, 249, 340,
    386
Shapiro, Michael 182n1
Sharpe, Will 146n1, 358
Sharpham, Edward 101–4, 159n17,
    161–2n18
Shaughnessy, Robert 53n14
Shaw, Fiona 7, 337
Shaw, George Bernard 47
Shaw, Glenn Byam 3
Shaw, James 326–39,
Sheibani, Bijan 326
Shell, Alison 175n8, 175n5

Sher, Antony 5, 6, 304, 328, 361, 363, 370,
    376
Sherlock, Peter 50n1
Shevtsova, Maria 366
Shirley, Frances A. 125, 130n41, 130n41,
    130–1
Shirley, James 98n40, 142, 158
Shostakovich, Dmitri 331
Siddons, Sarah 52
Sidnell, Jack 223n19
Sidney, Philip 183–4, 221n9, 223, 240–1,
    244, 270
Siemon, James R. 129n37
Simmons, J. L. 228n1
Simpson, Natalie 301–2
Simpson, Robin 338
Sims, James 220
Siobhan, Ira Mandela 297
Sivalingam, Vik 337
Skeat, Walter William 41
Skidmore, Jeffrey 56
Skinner, Quentin 194n25, 254
Slights, Jessica 374–5, 384
Smales, Maggie 329
Smiley, Jane 25
Smith, Bruce R 32, 204n28, 244n23, 356,
    359, 363–4, 370
Smith, Chris 7
Smith, Clarence 302
Smith, Emma 153n23, 340, 354, 355,
    378–9, 382, 384
Smith, Helen 382
Smith, Herbert Weir 151n17
Smith, Simon 188–99, 388
Smits, Eelco 317
Smuts, Malcolm 240n3
Snedecor, George W. 155n10
Sokolova, Boika 83n7
Sommerville, John 232
Sosa, Diego 338
Southampton, Henry Wriothesley, 3rd
    Earl of 61
Speed, John 130n46–1n46
Spencer, T. J. B. 125n17
Spenser, Edmund 168, 343
Spera, Paul 84
Spiller, Elizabeth 169–70
Springer, Mark 319
Spurgeon, Caroline 207, 208
Stachniewski, John 275n29
Stallybrass, Peter 165, 166n6, 169, 172,
    173, 228n1, 268n37, 380, 382
Stanley, William, Earl of Derby 36
Stanton, Barry 5
Stanton, Kay 350
Stanton, Sophie 310
Stauffer, Donald A. 175n7
Steenbergh, Kristine 359
Steevens, George 354
Stefánsson, Jón 43
Stein, Gertrude 242

Stein, Peter 366
Stendahl, Krister 276–7n40
Stephen, Leslie 213
Stern, Tiffany 89, 173n42, 188n3, 189,
    191n10, 192, 261n8, 261,
    265n25, 354, 383
Sternfeld, F. W. 200n1, 202n17, 202
Stewart, Freddie 296
Stewart, Patrick 5, 167n12
St. Hilaire, Danielle 231, 231n16, 234n31,
    235, 239n53
Still, Melly 301–2
Stirling, Rachael 289, 290
Stivers, Tanya 223n19
Stokes, James 286n88
Stone-Fewings, Jo 329
Stoppard, Tom 338, 364
Straszewski, Tom 334
Streete, Adrian 275n29
Stroup, Thomas B. 277n42
Stubbes, Philip 127–8, 278–9, 279n46
Styles, Luke 331
Styles, Philip 52n9
Suchet, David 5
Suetonius 253
Sullam, Sarra Copia 74
Sullivan, Daniel 337
Sullivan, Erin 345–6, 355, 358
Surrey, Henry Howard, Earl of 205,
    230–1n12
Susenbrotus, Joannes 221n10
Suzman, Janet 4
Svoboda, Josef 365
Syal, Meera 312
Syme, Holger Schott 353–4, 355, 371,
    373

Tabori, George 366
Tacitus 257
Tagore, Rabindranath 43
Talbot, Elizabeth, Countess of
    Shrewsbury (Bess of Hardwick)
    173, 244
Tang Shu Wing 330
Tarlinskaja, Marina 114n3
Tarnhoff, Maura Michelle 357
Tasso, Torquato 184n8
Taubes, Jacob 272n2, 272n1–4, 274n20
Tawyer, William 35
Taylor, Albert Booth 229n6
Taylor, Gary 100n14, 118n13, 121n27,
    122n30, 124, 146–53, 147n4,
    159, 193n20, 196n34, 261, 387
Taylor, John 142–3,
Taylor, Neil 124n7, 125n16, 131, 132, 133,
    375, 384
Téllez, Gabriel 105n40
Téllez-Girón, Juan, Duke of Osuna 92–3
Tellez-Girón, Mariano, Duke of Osuna 96
Tellez-Girón, Pedro, Duke of Osuna 92–3
Tempera, Mariangela 233n27

401

Tennenhouse, Leonard 228n1, 268n37
Tennyson, Alfred, 1st Baron Tennyson 213n2
Terry, Ellen 44, 58
Terry, Michelle 307, 308Illus.25, 326, 330, 333
Tertullian 273–5,
Thackeray, Lucy 292
Thomas, Lloyd 296
Thomas, Rasta 335
Thompson, Ann 124n7, 125n16, 131, 132n49, 133n53, 365, 375, 384
Thompson, Ayanna 10–18, 375–6, 384, 385
Thomson, Patricia 165n1
Thorpe, Sami 337
Tiffany, Grace 64
Tillyard, E. M. W. 377
Tilney, Edmund 114, 115
Timm, Viola 245n27, 246
Tiramani, Jenny 32n1
Tirso de Molina 98n40
Todd Knight, Jeffrey 358
Toich, Francesca Sarah 81–2, 81Illus.5
Tomlinson, Sophie 182
Tonson, Jacob 60, 381
Topsell, Edward 214n5, 215–16
Tourneur, Cyril 158n14
Tratner, Michael 357
Traversi, Derek Antona 228n1
Tremblay, Michel 132
Tresnjak, Darko 363
Trettien, Whitney 168n21
Trevisa, John 207–8
Tribble, Evelyn B. 186n14, 189, 192–3, 196
Trinder, Simon 306
Tronch, Jesús 99–112, 386
Troughton, David 303
Trump, Donald, US President 77, 287, 296, 311
Trundle, Thomas 120
Tudeau-Clayton, Margaret 219–27n40, 388
Turner, Graham 304
Turner, Lyndsey 327
Tweddle, Mike 330
Tyler, Anne 25
Tyler, Daniel 327
Tyndale, William 222

Ubaldini, Petruccio 150, 151, 387
Udall, Nicholas 167, 221n13
Updike, John 25
Uranowitz, Michelle 83n7, 84
Usmiani, Renate 132n51

Valentine, Samuel 313
Valenza, Robert J. 163n19
Valeri, Walter 76

Valls, Teresa Ferrer 90
Valls-Russell, Janice 243n18
van Buren, John 274n18, 274n17
van der Berg, Klaus 366
van der Eynde, Bart 316–18
Vanderham, Joanna 321
van Es, Bart 261–2n13
van Hove, Ivo 316–18
van Kampen, Claire 30–9, 385
van Kraaij, Peter 316–18
Van Sant, Gus 368
Varela, Edouardo J. 223n18
Varla, Zubin 292–93, 293Illus.20
Vasan, Anjana 293–4
Vaughan, Virginia Mason 44n12
Vaux, Thomas, 2nd Baron Vaux 201
Vega Carpio, Lope de 91, 98n40, 102–9, 105n38, 111
Vélez de Guevara, Luis 107, 108, 111
Verdi, Giuseppe 332
Vere, Elizabeth, Countess of Derby 36
Vermal, Jatinder 330
Versweyveld, Jan 317
Vickers, Brian 146–53
passim, 156n12, 237n47
Vienne-Guerrin, Nathalie 350, 355
Villeneuve, Denis 247
Vinckenboom (painter) 260n4
Vincze, Ernie 7
Viney, Ed 333, 337
Vinterberg, Thomas 368–9
Virgil 152, 179, 228–39n53, 240–1, 388
Voghera, Gadi Luzzatto 71n16
Vucane, Diana 330

Wadia, Sorab 74Illus.4, 79, 85, 86Illus.6
Waite, Elske 332
Waith, Eugene M. 125n15
Waldron, Jennifer 274n16, 281n61
Walker, D. P. 244n22
Walker, Greg 165n1
Walker, Robert 381
Wall, Wendy 168–9
Walsh, Brian 129n36, 344, 355
Walsingham, Sir Francis 203
Walter, Harriet 7, 309, 310Illus.26
Walters, Ewart James 302
Wanamaker, Sam 32, 47–8
Wang Ziaoying 334
Wanganeen, Natasha 320
Warburg, Aby 243, 247
Wardrop, Ewan 292
Waring, Rachel 327
Warner, Deborah 7, 310
Warner, Lawrence 178–9
Warrington, Don 318–19,
Watson, David 338
Watson, Nicola J. 53n14
Watson, Robert 208
Watson, Thomas 152, 153
Watt, Timothy Irish 153n25

Webb, John 169n25
Weber, William W. 228n1, 233n27, 237n47
Webster, John 147, 158n14, 182–3, 347
Webster, Max 333, 362
Weever, John 380
Weinberger, David 384
Weingust, Don 357
Weis, René 61, 243n21, 243, 341
Weiss, Judith 179n26
Welborn, L. L. 273n13, 273n8, 274n15, 274, 279n51
Welles, Orson 7, 374
Wells, Stanley 55, 58–66n9, 59n2, 71, 82n6, 100n14, 100n7, 121n27, 132n49, 141n18, 196n33, 340–1, 358, 386
Wentersdorf, Karl P. 150
Werner, Sarah 379
Werstine, Paul 89, 99–112, 113, 116, 117, 118n13, 120, 121, 122n32, 122n32, 122, 125n11, 125n11, 141, 375, 376, 382, 386
West, Anthony James 378
West, Grace Starry 230n11, 238n50
West, Samuel 56Illus.2,
West, Timothy 318
West, William N. 248n38, 354
Westbrook, Raymond 232
Weyer, Johann 178
Whedon, Joss 375
Whelan, Peter 338
Whetstone, George 183–4
Whipday, Emma 338
White, Helen C. 175n6
White, Ian 337
White, R. S. 345, 355
White, Willard 4
White, William 141n16
Whitebrook, Peter 46n20
Whitefield, Agnes 132n51
Whitfield, Peter 356
Whitney, Charley 189
Whittaker, David 74n22
Whitworth, Geoffrey 45–6
Whyman, Erica 57, 288–301, 300Illus.22
Wiesel, Elie 70
Wiggins, Ben 307–8
Wiggins, Martin 90n6, 91, 148n5, 150, 260n4, 261
Wilbourne, Emily 183n6
Wilckens, Ulrich 274n19
Wilcox, Helen 132n49
Wilcox, Zoë 367–8, 370
Wild, Ian 338
Wilkes, Jamie 304–5
Wilkes, Nick 339
Wilkins, George 64, 147, 341
Williams, Clifford 4
Williams, George Walton 91, 97, 364, 365

SHAKESPEARE SURVEY 70 INDEX

Williams, Kelly 301
Williams, Laurence 56
Williams, Michael 4
Williams, Penry 191n8
Williams, Raymond 343
Williams, William Proctor 99n4
Willmott, Phil 329
Willson, Robert F., Jr. 277n42
Wilson, Edward M. 93n15,
Wilson, Effingham 53
Wilson, F. W. 100n9
Wilson, John Dover 120–1
Wilson, Richard 181n40
Wilson, Robert 350, 354, 366
Wilson, Thomas 195
Wilson, Woodrow, US President 42–3
Winkler, Amanda Eubanks 203n18, 204n29, 204n30
Winnicott, D. W. 242, 246
Winterson, Jeanette 25, 340
Wise, Andrew 380

Wiseman, Susan 196n35
Wisse, Jakob 194n26
Wither, George 261n8
Wolfe, Heather 66
Wollenberg, Susan 202n11
Wolpe, Lisa 338
Womack, Peter 180n32
Wood, Anthony à 380
Woodhead, Linda 223n20
Woods, Penelope 357
Woodward, Kirsty 288
Woolfenden, Guy 4
Worthen, W. B. 383
Wotton, Sir Henry 74, 79n1
Woudhuysen, H. R. 137n5, 266n29, 268
Wright, Alexander 334
Wright, Charles 135n1
Wriothesley, Henry, 3rd Earl of Southampton 61
Wroth, Lady Mary 197
Wyatt, Thomas 165, 166, 167

Wynkyn de Worde 174n3
Wyrick, Deborah Baker 280n54
Wyver, John 4, 7, 8

Yachnin, Paul 137n4, 279n50, 348–9, 355
Yates, Eleanor 314
Yates, Frances A. 238n50
Yates, Julian 357
Yates, Sam 287, 288–9, 297, 326
Yeats, W. B. 154, 294
Yeaxlee, Basil 45
Yelda, Sargon 311
Yerolemou, Miltos 318
Young, Alan R. 54n16, 55n20, 223, 224n31–5n31

Zagni, Enrico 83
Zamora Vicente, Alonso 95n32
Zeffirelli, Franco 370
Zuber, Catherine 366
Zucker, Adam 135–45, 387

403

DATE DUE

FEB 0 6 2018